Finished November 14, 2003

A Diplomatic Revolution

A Diplomatic Revolution

Algeria's Fight for Independence and the
Origins of the Post–Cold War Era

Matthew Connelly

OXFORD

UNIVERSITY PRESS

2002

OXFORD
UNIVERSITY PRESS

Oxford   New York
Auckland   Bangkok   Buenos Aires   Cape Town   Chennai
Dar es Salaam   Delhi   Hong Kong   Istanbul   Karachi   Kolkata
Kuala Lumpur   Madrid   Melbourne   Mexico City   Mumbai   Nairobi
São Paulo   Shanghai   Singapore   Taipei   Tokyo   Toronto

and an associated company in Berlin

Copyright © 2002 by Matthew Connelly

Published by Oxford University Press, Inc.
198 Madison Avenue, New York, New York 10016

www.oup.com

Oxford is a registered trademark of Oxford University Press

Library of Congress Cataloging-in-Publication Data
Connelly, Matthew James.
A diplomatic revolution: Algeria's fight for independence and the
origins of the post-cold war era / Matthew Connelly.
p. cm.
Includes bibliographical references and index.
ISBN 0-19-514513-5
1. Algeria—History—Revolution, 1954–1962. I. Title: Algeria's fight
for independence and the origins of the post-cold war era. II. Title.
DT295 .C6115 2002
965'.0462—dc21   2002001234

1 3 5 7 9 8 6 4 2

Printed in the United States of America
on acid-free paper

For my brother Stephen,
and a night in Tunisia . . .

Preface

The historian is "a witness to what has been found on a voyage of discovery," as Peter Novick once put it. Readers will never know—even if they wished to—all that was seen. All they can expect is a good story, one that speaks to their concerns or, still better, says something new about timeless themes. But at some point in the narrative, with impatience or real interest, they may wonder what impelled the voyage in the first place—especially one that ranged from Kansas to Cairo, London to Tunis, at no small expense to two universities and several foundations.[1]

The answer to that question begins with a road not taken and a scholarly debate without end. Originally this was to be a diplomatic history of America's involvement in the Algerian War. If it were still, I might never have ventured beyond American shores. Leading scholars have argued that since U.S. foreign policy emerges from the perceptions and motives of its practitioners, U.S. archives can account for their actions. Given America's exceptional power in the Cold War period, what critics deride as "the world according to Washington" warrants special attention. Nevertheless, even proponents of this view concede that one cannot assess the effects or effectiveness of U.S. policies without doing research abroad.[2]

While there is doubtless interesting work to be done on American officials' perceptions of the Algerian War, I wanted to know about the impact of their actions. Moreover, I did not understand how I could invoke U.S. power to validate my work even while admitting that my sources could only reveal how Americans *reacted* to external events and influences. I therefore resolved to conduct archival research and, when the archives were unavailing, interviews in Europe and North Africa.

I soon discovered that the United States did indeed have great influence in France and Algeria, and much of this study concerns the triangular relationship between these countries. Yet that influence was not always what American officials intended and assumed it to be. Even states the size of Tunisia—indeed, even a stateless people like the Algerians—could manipulate U.S. power for their own purposes. The meaning of American power, and thus the meaningfulness of the studies it is said to justify, is determined by how it was mediated abroad.[3]

What some U.S. diplomatic historians took to be axiomatic—America's exceptional power—began to appear more like an assumption, one that their methodology is incapable of testing. This is not to suggest that America was weak but rather that we only know what power is by determining what power does in particular cases. In a sense, a state's archives reveal nothing so much as its self-perceptions and conceits—what Ronald Robinson and John Gallagher once called the "official mind."[4] Foreign contemporaries provide the fairest measure of its mental limitations, knowing as they did neither more nor less than how the world appeared from different vantage points. Of course, one misses some of the detail in the interminable fights between State Department bureaucrats by assuming distance from them, but one also begins to lose interest. What then seems more compelling is how they interacted with others to affect the fate of nations in ways they sometimes did not intend, or even imagine.

I therefore began to redefine my study as a more general international history not only of how the United States and other states influenced the Algerian War but also how these countries were themselves influenced by it. Indeed, I came to see these two lines of inquiry as practically inseparable, linked by feedback loops that made diplomatic history's conventional distinction between *Innenpolitik* and *Aussenpolitik* appear increasingly artificial. For instance, in their attempts to alter U.S. policy on North Africa, French officials hired Madison Avenue public relations firms, took members of Congress and journalists on junkets to Algeria, and at one time considered denouncing unsympathetic foreign service officers to Joe McCarthy. The North Africans, for their part, fought to win over many of the same reporters, politicians, and citizen's groups. Was American opinion on Algeria American in origin? The question is akin to asking the nationality of a Japanese-designed car assembled in Tennessee with Mexican parts. Even if one could devise an answer, is this really the most interesting line of inquiry?

Some diplomatic historians insist that we "more rigorously distinguish between the domestic and foreign sources of America's international behavior."[5] But while this might guarantee work for some, it would limit them to a shrinking subfield of U.S. history at the very moment when their colleagues in social, cultural, labor, and other fields of inquiry are pressing for internationalization.[6] This is not just a matter of academic fashion but rather reflects one of the defining features of our age: the increasing *interpenetration* of domestic and foreign affairs. I therefore came to agree with the other aspect of the internationalist critique, which pictures official U.S. policy and public opinion as parts of a complex network of relations linking American society to the rest of the world—an evolving international and even transnational system that also includes the media, multinational corporations, and diasporas. Would-be international historians must therefore examine "structures," the nongovernmental phenomena that have changed the basis of interstate relations.[7]

The main criticism of these proposals for reconceptualizing diplomatic history as international history is that together they are too much for any one historian or even an entire field to handle in more than a superficial fashion. In terms of both geographical areas and areas of inquiry, ranging too far afield can result in a work without real insight into any particular one. Alternatively, in using research from several states and nonstate organizations to reconstruct the web of relations between them, one can lose control of the material and become lost in the complexity.[8] Some historians have held out the hope that "the *next* generation of graduate students, or the one after that, will readily traverse this international terrain."[9] But graduate students of my generation could not afford to be so complacent, especially considering that scholars as different as Gabriel Kolko and Ernest May had been calling for greater attention to foreign archives and structural approaches a quarter of a century ago. It seemed that what they wanted—and what is increasingly required—is readily commendable but impossible to achieve.[10]

Faced with this daunting prospect, I delved into the origins of the debate by examining the life and work of the man who first made it possible to imagine history that would be truly international in its sources and scope: Fernand Braudel and his magnum opus, *The Mediterranean and the Mediterranean World in the Age of Philip II*. I was surprised to discover that he had originally planned to write a traditional diplomatic history to account for Habsburg Spain's shift of strategic priorities to the Atlantic after 1580. He became dissatisfied with the idea that this sea change was merely a matter of personalities and high politics. Instead, he looked to centuries-old *structures* and *conjonctures* that were decades in duration, such as agricultural practices and trading patterns. In Braudel's telling, leaders like Philip II and the events they shaped were themselves shaped by these more profound forces—so profound, in fact, that statesmen remained oblivious to them. To uncover these causal links, he strove for a "total history" that was both international in range and interdisciplinary in method. This was an overly ambitious goal, but in attempting it Braudel helped to redefine the discipline. His successors scaled back his bold design and many began to ignore interstate relations, asserting that, since most early modern peoples lived out their lives in a confined area, each village was a "small world" unto itself and has to be studied as such.[11]

Diplomatic historians, on the other hand, have been on the defensive ever since, as reflected in their repeated admission that they have not given sufficient attention to "structures."

Interestingly enough, Braudel made his great discovery in Algeria, where he spent the years 1923–1932 thinking through the main ideas of his dissertation while teaching at a *lycée*. He later wrote that "this spectacle, the Mediterranean as seen from the opposite shore, upside down, had considerable impact on my vision of history." From his perspective, the different communities along its littoral formed a unity, of which *Algérie française* might have seemed its fullest expression. Braudel admitted he "did not personally feel any twinges of conscience" about the ways in which France maintained this unity; indeed he did not even see "the social, political, and colonial drama which was, nevertheless, right before my eyes."[12]

Yet, in the course of my research, I discovered that the forces that were transforming Algeria were not invisible to French administrators. Indeed, they were alarmed by the rapid growth and migrations of the Muslim population and changes in agriculture, communications technology, and the environment—the very factors that filled Braudelian history. Before and during the war, they drew on the expertise of demographers, anthropologists, and sociologists—including such luminaries as Alfred Sauvy, Jacques Berque, and Pierre Bourdieu—to trace the socioeconomic trends that were contributing to political instability. Braudel's contemporaries were therefore well aware that the *structures* and *conjonctures* underlying French rule had begun to shift, and with unsettling speed. Moreover, French authorities in Algiers recognized that many of these changes were partly the result of their own policies, whether intended or not, and sought to reverse what they had wrought with all the power of a technocratic state—such power as Philip II would have attributed only to God.

I finally concluded that the Mediterranean world of Fernand Braudel resembled our own age much more than Philip II's, and to distinguish between the history of events and the history of "structures" was more misleading than illuminating. Indeed, the words "small world" already signified *global* village, as intercontinental labor markets and new means of communications linked the remotest regions. Historians cannot, therefore, dismiss high politics as ephemeral since policymakers could effect the most fundamental changes in how people lived and worked. On the other hand, they must address nonstate actors and structural factors, just as policymakers of the period had come to recognize the power of the international media and accept population and environment as affairs of state. Their papers, along with the works of social scientists from the period, are invaluable primary sources—not only for international historians, but for anyone trying to discover the roots of our present predicament. The "self-consciousness" that characterizes contemporary history has therefore made it necessary *and possible* for diplomatic historians to do what has for so long been demanded of them.

But if we are to command the attention of other fields and disciplines—rather than merely draw on their insights—we must do even more, since they have not been standing still in the meantime. Indeed, a number have taken what has been called a "historic turn." In sociology and political science, this has meant a renewed interest in the role of human agency and the explanatory power of narrative, interests that have long distinguished diplomatic history. But in others, like anthropology and the expanding field of "cultural studies," the turn is against disciplinary traditions that have reflected power relations if they have not actually served imperial projects.[13]

The history of the Algerian War provides compelling examples of how these approaches can be put to practical use. They alert us to the ways in which the significance assigned to what Braudel considered structural factors could change depending on the political needs of the moment. For example, while Algerians endured gross economic and political inequality, French social scientists insisted that *demographic* disparities explained the war and that only French-led development could address them.[14] This same factor later helped convince de Gaulle to withdraw, as he asked incredulously how "the French body could absorb ten million Muslims, who tomorrow will be twenty million and the day after that forty?" Population growth and the apparent threat of reverse colonization were finally invoked in arguments for aid to newly independent countries.[15]

More "structural" than the political agitation that appeared to flow from population growth were the images with which it was represented. Time and again, it was depicted as a "rising tide" or a river overflowing its banks—even by anticolonialists like the director Gillo Pontecorvo. His *Battle of Algiers*, the most famous film about the war, deliberately pictured Algerians as a flooding river sweeping the French before them.[16]

But while analyzing these discourses can often illuminate an unexpected connection, research in colonial archives can also demonstrate their impact in particular contexts. For instance, depicting anticolonial nationalism as a force of nature demeaned the individuality and conscious agency of colonized peoples, as "subaltern" scholars argue, but it also made resistance to their demands appear irrational. In other cases, "discourses of power" based on dichotomies between "the West" and "the rest" befuddled and enfeebled colonialists and their allies. Indeed, research in *anti*colonial archives reveals that nationalists consciously exploited them to empower themselves.[17]

Thus, international, multi-archival research on how power works in particular cases can yield rather surprising results, demonstrating that seemingly "hegemonic" discourses can have the most varied and paradoxical consequences. But as part of a larger program—one that brings agent and structure, text and context, cultural practices and political economy into the same analytic field—the most unexpected result of all would be to make the study of international politics a key entrepot of intellectual exchange. Arguments for international history have been called "conceptual imperialism" and the field of imperial history itself is said to be undergoing "colonization" by "literary invaders."[18] But in fact, the way forward is not to create some new breed that can seize and hold this contested terrain, nor—as Michael Hunt suggests—to divide it into different "realms" that coexist only because scholars keep off each other's "turf."[19] It is instead for international historians to become *diplomatic* historians, not in the sense that they should limit their interests to the affairs of ambassadors, but rather that they themselves will be ambassadors of different fields and disciplines that attack or ignore one another.

If I can contribute to this endeavor, it is only because many people and institutions have helped along the way. It is a great pleasure finally to acknowledge at least a few of them. My notes will quickly make clear my debt to other historians of the Algerian War, but I am especially grateful to Daniel Byrne, Daho Djerbal, Martin Thomas, and Irwin Wall for providing advance copies of their work, and to Charles Shrader for sharing research and insights that made possible the graphs in the appendix. Moreover, I could not hope to make an original contribution of my own were it not for the archivists who have worked to make new sources accessible. Annie-France Renaudin at the Quai d'Orsay, Odile Gaultier-Voituriez at the Fondation Nationale des Sciences Politiques, Patrick Facon at the Service historique de l'Armée de l'Air, Jeanne Mrad at the Center for Maghreb Studies in Tunis, and Fadila Takour at the Centre National des Archives Algériennes were particularly patient and helpful. And while I list some of those who were kind enough to grant interviews in the bibliography, many, many more French and North Africans have opened their homes and extended their hospitality to help me understand the human dimension of a history that is only dimly reflected in the documentary record—especially Jallel Boussedra, Daho Djerbal, Samer Emalhayene, and, not least, Maurice Lagrange and the other members of the *Association des Anciens Combattants Parachutistes* of Aix-en-Provence. Of course, I would not have met any of them were it not for the generosity of Yale University, the University of Michigan, the Council on European Studies, the Institute for the Study of World Politics, and the MacArthur, Olin, and Smith Richardson foundations. And in the end I might have had little to show for all of this support were if not for the initial enthusiasm and enduring faith of Susan Ferber and Oxford University Press.

The support of family and friends has been no less important and is even harder to acknowledge adequately. First and most obviously, there is my father, who has never stopped encouraging me to expand my horizons, and my mother, to whom I am still but a poor apprentice in the craft of storytelling. It is also hard to miss my many siblings, in whose company I am always filled with humility and pride. Laura Altinger, Will Hitchcock, David Javdan, Firoozeh Kashani-Sabet, Martin Keady, Thomas LeBien, Darrin McMahon, and Kasra Paydavousi are also *anciens combattants* of my long struggle, having endured Algerian War stories without end. But no one has been more patient than my wife, Nathalie James, about whom I would write much more if I did not have to obey certain conventions of academic propriety.

In bringing this project to completion, I was fortunate to find good fellowship and great intellectual excitement among colleagues in and around the University of Michigan, particularly Bob Axelrod, Michael Bonner, Jane Burbank, Geoff Eley, Gabrielle Hecht, Ann Lin, Bradford Perkins, Ron Suny, David Thacher, and Maris Vinovskis. For their close reading and copious notes on earlier versions of the manuscript, Isaac Campos, Fred Cooper, and Jonathan Marwil merit special mention. All in all, I cannot imagine a more congenial place to learn and teach, which is due to their continuing efforts to make Michigan a community as well as a university.

But I will always have a special fondness for my first role models and mentors: Doron Ben-Atar, John Lewis Gaddis, Paul Kennedy, Geoffrey Parker, William Quandt, and Gaddis Smith. I would attempt to thank them individually if I did not think that it would exhaust a reader's patience. There is one appreciation, however, that applies to all. While writing this account, I often recalled the times in graduate school when I and my classmates pulled on the loose ends and poked at the weak points of books by our elders and betters. I will always be grateful—and amazed— that the aforementioned professors suffered our precocity with nothing more reproving than wry smiles. In that way I was encouraged to test my own limits during my "voyage of discovery," though now I cannot help but wonder—and worry—how my work will fare under similar scrutiny.

I have not covered all this ground to cover myself—my treatment of some areas is clearly thinner than others—but rather because an approach that encompassed the wider context and traced the myriad connections between seemingly unrelated elements appeared best suited to a war that was itself something of an epic. After as many as half a million deaths and the exile of another million, the last and perhaps least forgivable tragedy of this war would be for historians to miss the enduring significance of such a sacrifice. While great events need not have great causes, or even "great men," the Algerian War was replete with both. If this account does not adequately convey both the overwhelming magnitude and the underlying meaning of what transpired, that fault, with all the others, is assuredly my own.

I wish to acknowledge the following for permission to reprint passages from my essays that appeared in them.

"Rethinking the Cold War and Decolonization: The Grand Strategy of the Algerian War for Independence," *The International Journal of Middle East Studies* 33 (May 2001): 221–245.

"Taking off the Cold War Lens: Visions of North-South Conflict

During the Algerian War for Independence," *The American Historical Review* 105 (June 2000): 739–769.

"America, France, and the Algerian War: The Forgotten Conflict over a 'Clash of Civilizations,'" *Naval Strategy and Policy in the Mediterranean: Past, Present, and Future,* ed. John B. Hattendorf (Portland, OR: Frank Cass, 1999), 329–343.

"The French-American Conflict in North Africa and the Fall of the Fourth Republic," *Revue française d'Histoire d'Outre-mer* 84 (June 1997): 9–27.

Contents

Acronyms and Abbreviations

AFL American Federation of Labor
AL Arab League Documentation and Information Center
ALN *Armée de Libération Nationale*
AN *Archives Nationales*
AOM *Archives d'Outre-Mer*
AWF Ann Whitman File
CAB *Fonds du Cabinet Civil du Gouverneur Général de l'Algérie*
CCE *Comité de coordination et d'exécution*
CNAA *Centre National des Archives Algériennes*
CNRA *Conseil National de la Révolution Algérienne*
CRUA *Comité Révolutionnaire d'Unité et d'Action*
DDEL Dwight D. Eisenhower Library
DDF *Documents Diplomatiques Français*
DE-CE *Direction des Affaires Economiques/Service de Coopération Economique*
EDC European Defense Community
EEC European Economic Community
EMGDN *Etat-Major Général de la Défense Nationale*
EOF Eisenhower Office Files
EPU European Payments Union
FIS *Front Islamique du Salut*
FLN *Front de Libération Nationale*
FNSP *Fondation Nationale des Sciences Politiques*
FRUS Foreign Relations of the United States

GGA	*Gouvernement Général de l'Algérie*
GPRA	*Gouvernement Provisoire de la République Algérienne*
GS	*Groupe Socialiste Parlementaire*
IMF	International Monetary Fund
JFKL	John F. Kennedy Library
MA	*Série MA, Affaires Algériennes*
MAE	*Ministère des Affaires Etrangères*
Memcon	Memorandum of conversation
MLA	*Mission de liaison algérien*
MNA	*Mouvement National Algérien*
MRP	*Mouvement Républicain Populaire*
MTC	Minutes of Telephone Conversations
MTLD	*Mouvement pour le Triomphe des Libertés Démocratiques*
NIE	National Intelligence Estimate
NSC	National Security Council
OAS	*Organisation armée secrète*
OEEC	Organisation for European Economic Co-operation
ONU	*Organisation des Nations Unies*
OS	*Organisation Spéciale*
PPA	*Parti du Peuple Algérien*
PPS	Policy Planning Staff
PRO	Public Record Office
SAC	Strategic Air Command
SAS	*Sections Administratives Specialisées*
SDECE	*Service de Documentation Extérieure et de Contre-Espionnage*
SEAA	*Secrétariat d'Etat aux Affaires algériennes*
SHAA	*Service historique de l'Armée de l'Air*
SHAT	*Service historique de l'Armée de Terre*
UDMA	*Union Démocratique du Manifeste Algérien*
UGCA	*Union Générale des Commerçants Algériens*
UGTA	*Union Générale des Travailleurs Algériens*
UPA	University Publications of America
USNA	U.S. National Archives
USRAF	*Union pour le Salut et le Renouveau de l'Algérie Française*
UT	*Unités territoriales*

A Diplomatic Revolution

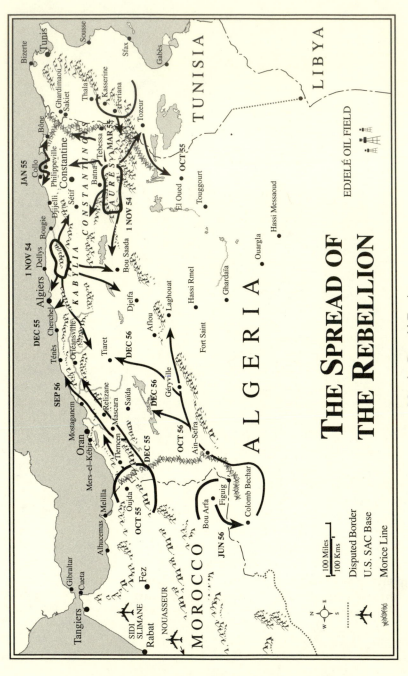

THE SPREAD OF
THE REBELLION

Map by Donald Frazier.

Introduction

At ten o'clock one May morning in 1961, three Swiss Army helicopters skimmed across the waters of Lake Geneva toward the French resort town of Evian. One after the other, each landed by the water's edge, disgorged three passengers, and then lifted off to make room for the next. Stooped under the swooping blades, the assembled men smoothed their suits before making their way to a group of French officials awaiting them. Just out of sight, anti-aircraft guns were positioned along a defensive perimeter, while armed patrols and road blocks covered the countryside beyond. Even the lake, the only thing that seemed pacific about the place, concealed frogmen swimming beneath the surface.[1]

The arriving delegation represented the "Provisional Government of the Algerian Republic"—or GPRA, its French acronym—though it could not truthfully claim to govern any territory in Algeria. All of their ministers were exiled in Tunis and Cairo or imprisoned on a fortified island off the Breton coast. Their forces in Algeria had dwindled to less than 15,000 operating in groups of no more than ten or twenty men. With nothing heavier than mortars and machine guns, the *mujahadeen* faced an occupying army of half a million men that was then testing its first nuclear weapons in the Sahara. The Algerians' most effective actions were bombings and assassinations in Algeria and France, which would claim 133 lives during this first round of formal negotiations. The leader of the delegation, Belkacem Krim, had himself twice been sentenced to the guillotine.

Yet those whom French authorities feared most—and the reason for the extraordinary security at Evian—were their own military commanders and settlers in Algeria, who bitterly opposed these negotiations. A month earlier, a military junta had briefly seized power in Algiers and threatened to land paratroops in Paris, while the Secret Army Organization (OAS)—a terrorist militia made up of the most diehard settlers—had already murdered the mayor of Evian because of his chance association with what would happen there. Renegade army officers and remnants of the OAS would persist in attempts to assassinate President Charles de Gaulle long after the Evian accords sealed the fate of French Algeria almost a year later.

Why, then, was de Gaulle ready to risk his life and the Republic itself to hand over a part of the *patrie* and a million citizens of European descent to men considered criminals under French common law? After all, there had never been an Algerian equivalent of Dien Bien Phu, or even of the Tet Offensive. Instead, the French won the Battle of Algiers in 1957, effectively sealed off the borders in 1958, and had reduced the *mujahadeen* remaining in Algeria to scattered and increasingly desperate bands by 1960. Yet all along they gave ground on the question of Algeria's future status and finally accepted the inevitability of its secession when the insurgency was at its weakest. The inverse relationship between France's preponderant military strength in Algeria and the progressive deterioration of its bargaining position vis-à-vis the nationalists was—as de Gaulle's biographer, Jean Lacouture, put it—"the supreme paradox" of the Algerian War.[2]

To understand this paradox, one must recognize the tenacity and bravery of the rebels, from the back alleys of Algiers to the border villages of the Constantinois, who fought and organized for more than seven years against atrocious repression. But the principal part of the answer—and of this history—must range far beyond the borders of Algeria. Based on archival research and interviews in Europe, North Africa, and the United States, this book argues that what the Algerians called "the Revolution" was distinctively *diplomatic* in nature, and that its most decisive struggles occurred in the international arena. For weapons the Algerians employed human rights reports, press conferences, and youth congresses, fighting over world opinion and international law more than conventional military objectives. By the end, when they hardly attempted to breach the border fortifications erected around Algeria, the GPRA had rallied majorities against France at the United Nations, won the accolades of international conferences, and gained 21-gun salutes in capitals across the globe. These accomplishments, in turn, inspired the hard-pressed *mujahadeen* to endure in their struggle. Together with the rebel armies and administrators sheltered by Morocco and Tunisia and supported by countries as diverse as Saudi Arabia and Communist China, they outlasted a government that had become obsessed with the war's impact on its reputation abroad. Essentially, the Algerians won by outflanking French forces and border fortifications and surmounting the *invisible* barriers of censorship and sovereignty around Algeria. Once impregnable, these physical and intellectual defenses proved as obsolete as a crusader's castle before the batteries of the international media and the U.N. General Assembly—though the siege took over seven years and as many as 500,000 lives.[3]

Algeria's fight for independence was also a diplomatic revolution, according to the conventional meaning of the term, in that it helped to reorder international relations. Here, too, is a paradox: France's repeated attempts to contain the conflict only ensured that it would have the most far-reaching repercussions. It was the immediate cause of Paris's concession of independence to the protectorates of Morocco and Tunisia and it accelerated the decolonization of sub-Saharan Africa. A determination to confront the rebels' foreign backers contributed to the Suez crisis and triggered the events leading to the fall of the Fourth Republic and the return of de Gaulle. *Le général* began to withdraw French forces from NATO commands partly to retaliate against America's unwillingness to support the war. And all along Algeria was a rallying point for the non-aligned movement and Arab nationalism. Indeed, this was the first time a subject people who lacked the means to control any of the territory they claimed declared their independence and won the recognition that finally made independence possible. Their example inspired the African National Congress, the Palestine Liberation Organization, and many other such movements.

Algeria's progress toward independence did not affect state sovereignty so much as it reflected emerging challenges to this institution, which had for centuries served as the organizing principle of international politics. After all, waves of economic and technological change were already eroding the borders that separate states from one another and from the world community as a whole. To gauge the importance of the international aspect of the war and, conversely, the war's effects abroad, it should therefore be viewed within that wider context. But to describe that scene in more than a superficial fashion, one must also sketch its underlying structures. This will reveal the third great paradox of the Algerian War—and the third dimension of this diplomatic revolution: it shows how "globalization" through integrating markets, migrations, and new means of mass communications exacerbated cultural conflicts and caused increasing political fragmentation. The Algerian War thus serves as a laboratory for observing the velocity of trends that were sweeping the Cold War world and shaped the contemporary era.

This introduction sketches each of these three arguments in turn, beginning with the international struggle, proceeding to its effects on the international system, and concluding with perspectives on how it can help us to understand the ongoing transformation of international politics. The chapters to follow will sustain and substantiate these arguments through a narrative history of the war's origins, course, and consequences.

The Algerian War in the International Arena

After long neglect, the international history of the Algerian War has inspired a new wave of scholarship. The opening of French, American, and British archives has shown that Washington and London were deeply involved and influential in what had long been depicted as a national

drama in French scholarship and popular culture.[4] But it is only by consulting the Algerians' own archives that one can assess the importance to
both protagonists of *all* their allies and adversaries and thus write an international history centered on the war itself rather than its effects on the
Atlantic Alliance. Even more important, the GPRA records reveal the
Algerians as full participants in their own history, which is indispensable
if we are to understand how they finally prevailed.[5]

Algerians had learned through long and bitter experience that they
could not defeat France through force of arms alone. Years before they
formed the *Front de Libération Nationale* in 1954, future FLN leaders
began to craft a political strategy aimed at bringing the pressure of international opinion to bear on Paris. When hostilities commenced, French
authorities claimed not to care what others thought about what they considered to be a purely internal problem, but they had to dispel the Algerians' hopes if they were ever to bring them to terms. Both sides well
remembered from Indochina that outsiders could have a decisive role in
colonial conflicts. Indeed, the 1958 crisis that ended with the return of
de Gaulle—the pivotal event of the war—began as a reaction against an
American attempt to force France to conclude peace. The Algerians, for
their part, had to contend with pressure from their allies to accept a compromise settlement—by 1960 the bulk of their effective fighting strength
was sheltered in Tunisia and Morocco at the sufferance of their two rulers.
More generally, it made sense for both sides to strive for the support of
even the smallest states in such a protracted, hard-fought struggle.

Yet the war's international aspect often loomed even larger in people's
imaginations—and actions—than the real dimensions of outside aid
would appear to have justified. While the rebels immediately announced
their intent to "internationalize the Algerian question" and made critical
decisions based on the hoped-for effect abroad, outside support often fell
short of expectations. In fact, the failure of the nationalists' external leadership to secure more aid for the insurgents was a key issue in the internecine wrangling within the rebel camp.

Nevertheless, the French exaggerated the extent of foreign aid and
influence in the rebellion. They therefore timed and tailored their peace
proposals to influence world opinion, usually coinciding with the annual
debates in the U.N. General Assembly. Even de Gaulle—who denied too
often the influence of foreign opinion on his decisions—greatly expanded
efforts to influence it. Until the final negotiations, top French officials
continued to believe that, if only their allies supported them and their
adversaries stayed out, they could conclude the war on their own terms.
Even if it were possible to disprove this contention, its demonstrable
influence on French decision-making would in no way be diminished.

The international aspect of the war was therefore significant in part
because so many people *believed* it was important and acted on the assumption that the fighting in Algeria had begun and would one day end
because of events elsewhere. Moreover, many in France reached this con-

clusion in the first days of the war, when the identity of the rebels—much less their strategy—was still obscure. This suggests that preexisting attitudes helped produce and sustain the extraordinary interest in the role of outsiders. One must therefore analyze French images and ideas about others and themselves that led them to believe that the fighting in Algeria had external causes and global consequences.

Much of the French diplomatic effort to win over foreign governments and their publics was organized around the idea that "Algeria is France"—that the Algerian *départements*, constitutionally a part of France since 1848, were a French creation. For the FLN, on the other hand, the war was an attempt to *restore* Algeria's existence as an independent nation. With the formation of the GPRA in 1958, the FLN began to demand recognition as its legitimate government. For this purpose, nongovernmental organizations could also make a contribution. Although the attendance of GPRA delegates at an international labor conference or their accession to the Geneva Conventions might not seem like matters of great import, they appeared to give substance to the Algerians' claims and so became tests of strength between the two antagonists.

In the fight for world opinion, both sides employed propagandists and cultivated foreign news media and intellectuals. Since they were waging what was sometimes the only shooting war in the world, they were assured of an attentive audience, especially as the issues involved—Arab nationalism, African decolonization, and strains in the Atlantic Alliance—were all at the top of the international agenda. From the beginning Paris recognized that the media could keep Algeria on that agenda even if the army drove the FLN underground. Battle was joined in radio and television studios, the corridors of the United Nations, and campus debates, and the echoes could be heard in the councils of decision makers. If unmoved by the occasional rally or the innumerable petitions of Paris intellectuals, policymakers' approach to the Algerian problem was shaped by a climate of opinion that insisted on racial equality, secularism, and cooperative "development." Both sides had an interest in adapting to that climate, and the peace they made at Evian reflected the expectations of the age, even if it did not fulfill them.

Reversals of Fortune

Just as the outside world acted on Algeria's history, the war provoked an equal if not opposite reaction abroad—what Elie Kedourie called "prodigious peripeties," borrowing the French word for reversals of fortune.[6] One of the most important was the Algerians' challenge to the principle that had protected states from foreign scrutiny of their domestic affairs. The crux of the problem for French officials could be seen in the contradictions of their arguments: in insisting that Algeria was their own affair, they claimed that the war would have been quickly won were it not for external interference—either actual, as in aid by Egypt and Tunisia, or potential, as in their belief that the rebels would hold out as long as it appeared that international pressure might force Paris to sue for peace. But to counteract this effect, the French had to act outside Algeria, whether by asking for material aid and full diplomatic backing from their allies—which forced them to consider their preferences in formulating policy—or by direct action against the FLN's allies, which belied the idea that Algeria was a domestic difficulty concerning France alone. Indeed, nothing "internationalized" the war so much as France's increasingly desperate attempts to isolate it.

France's first major effort to isolate Algeria was the concession of "independence within interdependence" to the two protectorates on its eastern and western flanks. French officials calculated that they could use residual economic leverage and military bases to prevent Tunisia and Morocco from aiding the rebels and perhaps enlist their support in negotiations to end the war. Such a strategy would have required considerable discipline and some flexibility about the future of Algeria, but the French were too divided to make it effective. Instead, military commanders seized arms shipments off the coasts of Morocco and captured the rebels' external leadership in midflight to Tunisia, thus expanding the conflict to international waters and airspace. While they succeeded in stopping peace negotiations, they made adversaries of Algeria's two neighbors and provided ammunition for FLN arguments that France's conduct could no longer be considered its own affair.

The November 1956 assault on Egypt proved to be an even more grievous self-inflicted wound, because it not only destroyed Paris' remaining prestige in the Arab world but transformed its relations with Washington. Until the Suez crisis, the Americans had followed a "middle of the road" policy between the French and the North African nationalists, hoping to avoid either a split in the Atlantic Alliance or criticism from Arab allies. But they would not allow the French (or the British) to escalate their fight with Arab nationalism and perhaps engulf all of North Africa in conflict. France's humiliation at American hands had other causes and consequences that will be discussed in due course, especially in terms of Franco-Israeli relations and their respective nuclear programs. But the most important consequence for Algeria was to exacerbate the financial deficits that made France vulnerable to U.S. coercion.

Through 1957, the French tried to resist American pressure for a compromise peace while pursuing more direct means of isolating Algeria, such as constructing a line of electrified barbed wire, mine fields, and radar-directed artillery along its borders with Tunisia and Morocco. Refugees streamed out of Algeria, while the rebels began to strike back across the frontiers. Consequently, the French military claimed the right of hot pursuit and in 1958 bombed a Tunisian border village in retaliation for local FLN attacks. Once again the Americans used economic diplomacy to protect an FLN ally and increased pressure on Paris to accept a political settlement with the Algerians. But a defiant National Assembly repudiated U.S. mediation and with it the penultimate government of the Fourth

Republic. The interregnum ended with a settler uprising in Algiers, which returned de Gaulle to power.

While de Gaulle's original intentions in Algeria remain obscure, he demanded unreserved support for the war as a condition for cooperation in the Atlantic Alliance. When Washington refused, de Gaulle began the process that would end in 1966 with the withdrawal of all French forces from integrated commands. At the same time the Algerian War helped to divide France and the United States it also exemplified one of the main policy differences between the two Communist powers, with Beijing pushing for full support of this and other national liberation movements and Moscow remaining more interested in profiting from the U.S.-French conflict.

At that time, the nonaligned movement posed the most direct challenge to the East-West structure of international politics, and here, too, the Algerians were at the forefront. For those who had recently won their independence, or still aspired to it, the Algerian struggle was a rallying point and an inspiration. People across the Arab world followed events in the press, listened to reports on Egypt's *Voice of the Arabs*, and watched FLN propaganda films. In addition to Nasser, a heroic figure for many, charismatic leaders like Sukarno, Kwame Nkrumah, and Fidel Castro all embraced the cause. The Algerians were "present at the creation" of the movement at the Bandung conference and helped it to become an effective force by coordinating bloc voting at the United Nations and collective lobbying of the superpowers. Thus, if the idea of a free Algeria eventually triumphed over *Algérie française* partly because of the power of the nonaligned movement, the war itself was both a cause and a consequence of that movement's emergence.

In his recent book, Robert Malley described how this history gave Algerians a privileged place in the "pantheon" of Third World powers. But he cautions that they and their French counterparts too often credited their every action with world-shaking significance. Immersed in the papers they left behind, scholars can forget the difference between words and deeds and exaggerate the war's importance as an agent for change. One could argue that Algeria's was just one of many anticolonial movements that resulted from broader, deeper economic, social, and cultural developments interacting with political events far more momentous than anything isolated to North Africa—like World War II and the ensuing Soviet-American rivalry. From this perspective, Algeria is prominent due to its position at the crest of a wave of anticolonialism that began to swell in South and East Asia in the 1930s and finally rolled into the southernmost parts of Africa forty years later. Indeed, Algeria's formal status as French *départements* and the bitterness with which Paris fought to keep it made it something of an anomaly—or at least a problematic candidate for a case study.

This account anticipates that argument by taking it further still: Algeria was extreme in almost every way. It was extreme in the intensity of its colonial experience and in the destructiveness of its decolonization. It was extreme even in what made it typical: rapid population growth, over-exploitation of lands, a rural exodus, emigration, and cultural conflicts between secular nationalist and religious reform influences—the main engines of revolutionary change throughout the colonial world. Moreover, from the Moroccan crises before World War I until Algerian independence, North Africa was continually buffeted by great power conflicts.

In all of these ways, Algeria was an extreme example of a common problem: the simultaneous fragmentation and integration of the world community. The socioeconomic fault line dividing North from South was deepest and narrowest here, running right through Algeria's cities and countryside. On the other hand, nowhere was the pressure for economic, political, and cultural integration—and the clash that resulted—so powerful, sending tremors around the Cold War world. By focusing on this epicenter of nascent North-South conflict, we can see how and why the ground began to shift beneath the surface of the superpower competition.

The North-South Frontier

The term fault line conveys a sense of the wider implications of what was happening in Algeria, the slow buildup of countervailing forces, and their sudden eruption. Yet the different sides were not so well delineated. Rather than facing each other across a chasm, leaders ranged along a continuum: from the first president of the GPRA, Ferhat Abbas, who spoke little Arabic and once wrote that there was no such thing as an Algerian nation, to those settlers—often of Spanish and Italian origin—who called themselves Algerians and threatened secession from Paris when it suited them. In a sense, the war was about redrawing the borders between the different territories and communities that overlapped in Algeria, at the intersection of the Atlantic, European, Arab, and African worlds. While this study will continue to emphasize the salience of the North-South division, the word frontier best describes Algeria's intermediate—and indeterminate—position between them.

Algeria's more populated northern areas are just 100 miles south of Spain and 400 miles from France, which began to extend control over them in 1830. In 1848—when Haute-Savoie and Nice were not yet French—they were designated *départements*, in theory no different from the French *départements* of continental Europe, which were called the *metropole*. A century later, French Algeria was explicitly included in the North Atlantic Treaty and then the Treaty of Rome and thus became part of the new European strategic and economic community. The discovery in 1956 of immense oil and natural gas reserves made the Algerian *départements* seem all the more integral to the industrial economies. France accounted for more than three-quarters of their exports and even more of their imports. Algeria had almost no industry of its own. Instead, one in seven Muslim men worked in the metropole, where they already numbered 300,000 on the eve of war.

French people of the metropole called Muslim immigrants stoking coal on cargo-boats *pieds noirs* because of their black feet. The term became a way to insult settlers, but by the 1950s Algeria's nearly one million citizens of European descent had made this epithet their own. Though they studied in French-language schools, fought in French wars, and elected deputies to the National Assembly, the *pieds noirs* cultivated a hybrid Mediterranean culture. Visitors to Algiers could easily imagine themselves in Marseilles, while Oran seemed to many a Spanish city. Their broad avenues were lined with cafes, their parks were populated with old men playing *pétanque*, their beaches were filled with young people in shorts and swimsuits. From where they stood, Algeria seemed like a reflection of the opposite shore.

But if one turned south and traveled inland to the rural villages where 70 percent of Muslims lived, the scene would have been quite different, the prospects more ominous. From here Algeria appeared more a reflection of the Middle East and Africa beyond the Sahara. For every pied noir sipping pastis in Algiers and Oran, there were nine Muslims, more than half under 20, typically subsisting on whatever could be scratched out of small plots of marginal land without irrigation or farm machinery. Deforestation and soil erosion contributed to stagnant or declining agricultural production. Paradoxically, this situation resulted from one of the few genuine contributions by colonial authorities to the lives of ordinary Muslims: public health measures that had dramatically reduced mortality rates. Since birthrates remained high, the Muslim population had more than doubled in less than fifty years and was growing at one of the fastest rates in the world.

For most French observers, the only solution was to accelerate and complete the process of "development," making Muslims economically, culturally, and, above all, demographically "modern."[7] But from Indonesia to Indochina to North Africa, colonial authorities were finding that efforts to increase production of foodstuffs for local consumption and export upset the patron-client relationships through which they maintained control. The expansion of large-scale, mechanized agriculture caused them to lose contact with the local population while increasing migration to the cities and emigration to Europe. Like black African and Asian immigrants, Algerian Muslims maintained contact with their families and often returned to their communities, sometimes with unsettling results. Indeed, the first Algerian nationalist movement of the twentieth century emerged among these emigrants in France.

Development theorists anticipated that a period of instability would accompany the transition from tradition to modernity in areas like Algeria, so the beginning of the insurgency in 1954 made modernization appear even more urgent. But closer inspection revealed that the events here and around the Third World represented a significant departure from the development model. Rather than creating consumer societies in the colonies, new means of mass communications were mobilizing Third

World peoples against the West. Instead of fostering industry and a disciplined workforce, integration in global markets was allowing migrant laborers to sustain subsistence economies. Contrary to expectations that urbanization would reduce birthrates, population growth in Algeria and a host of other countries was continuing to accelerate. And rather than being mere objects of Westernization, North Africans were themselves reshaping the cities and the metropole. In 1947, a study of Algerian demography was already warning of "a real invasion and a berberisation of whole neighborhoods in Marseilles and Paris."[8]

The war came because French Algeria reflected North *and* South—their attraction *and* polarization. Here as elsewhere, the main ingredients of integration—new communications technologies, global markets, migration flows—also exacerbated communal conflicts. Contacts between the French and the Algerians, whether in the form of temporary residence or exposure to cultural influences, were as likely to elicit armed resistance as mutual identification. Indeed, the FLN itself embraced both Western and Islamic influences and rejected the bipolarities that were supposed to exist between them. As the FLN's official newspaper, *El Moudjahid*, declared:

> The Algerian people are at the same time the most nationalist and the most cosmopolitan, the most loyal to Islam and the most receptive to non-Islamic values. Among Muslim peoples it is perhaps one of the most attached to the Muslim faith and the most penetrated by the spirit of the modern West.[9]

In time the spirit of Algerian independence penetrated France itself, as youths and intellectuals idealized the cause and aligned with immigrants against the state, which resulted in pitched battles in the streets of Paris with hundreds of casualties. Thus, instead of denoting the extent of the imperial sway, the old colonial slogan of a France extending "from Dunkirk to Tamanrasset"—one of the southernmost towns of the Sahara—came to delineate a zone of insecurity, both physical and mental, as France's deepening engagement with Algeria and Algerians became as disturbing as it was dangerous. Rather than a struggle to bring Algeria into the "modern world," the war became a fight over the very meaning and purpose of modernity.

Under these circumstances, some turned to an older view of the future of North and South, one that portrayed international relations as race relations. Rather than assuming the inevitability of progress, it depicted the Algerian revolt as a harbinger of a "clash of civilizations." In this way, Algeria's fight for independence also reflected both past and future—seeming to recall older conflicts between Islam and Christendom while foreshadowing "culture wars" and racial and religious violence, including racist attacks on immigrants and Islamist assaults on westerners.

In the aftermath of the Cold War, the simultaneous integration and fragmentation of the world community have inspired a vast literature investigating their various aspects: from the consolidation of global markets to the increasing pluralism of international politics, from the proliferation of cross-cultural interactions to the growing inequality within and between societies. This book will instead examine how some of those trends characteristic of the post–Cold War era operated in an earlier time — indeed, at the very height of the superpower confrontation. In this way, we will see how, for instance, population growth, environmental scarcities, international institutions, new media, and, not least, the conscious agency of colonized peoples were already combining to cause radical change — of a recognizably new kind — when some might assume the international system was frozen into an ideological contest between East and West, one in which the South only provided stakes in the game or a place for proxy wars. We will also witness how, even then, people realized that these processes of integration and fragmentation were transforming their world. Thus, Algeria not only affords a privileged perspective on the wider process of decolonization, it also provides a preview of how the postcolonial world would grapple with what may be "the supreme paradox" of our age.[10]

When the last of the Swiss Army helicopters lifted off and the French and the Algerians were left alone across a table in the Hôtel du Parc, they started debating a question that remains unanswered to this day: How could diverse but interconnected cultures coexist without clashing within each country and across the Mediterranean? These negotiations will be described at the close of this narrative. But it will be suggested that they did not end, perhaps cannot end as long as the global processes of integration and fragmentation continue to transform Algerian, French, and international society. Even when the different sides prefer fighting to talking — when, as François Mitterrand declared, "the only negotiation is war" — their conflicts as much as their conversations determine how these historical forces will be expressed in diverse societies through their different languages. As Pierre Bourdieu once observed, "[W]ar remains a dialogue when all is said and done."[11]

I

Algeria and the International System

1

The Failure of Progress

Algeria and the Crisis of the Colonial World

It is true that most of our people are still illiterate. But politically that counts far less than it did twenty years ago. . . . Radio has changed everything. . . . Today people in the most remote villages hear of what is happening everywhere and form their opinions. Leaders cannot govern as they once did. We live in a new world.

Gamal Abdel Nasser [1]

Asia and Africa could potentially form a union capable first of transforming the colonial problem—in countries which still submit to European allegiance—into a problem of European minorities in countries which have gained their autonomy and are capable, furthermore, of changing the face of the world.

These perspectives can only convince European nations to abandon their petty squabbles. Otherwise they will not even be left the choice of the sauce with which they will be eaten.

Maurice Papon, secrétaire général, French Protectorate of Morocco [2]

In 1952 the French government of Algeria commissioned a study of local conditions based on a questionnaire given to the heads of every commune—the smallest administrative unit. The responses came back over the following two years and covered a broad array of issues, ranging from Islamic reformism to immigration, from population growth to nationalist parties. As they compiled these answers, the authors of "Algeria at Mid-Century" were mainly concerned with the perennial question of political reform: whether it was possible to assimilate Muslims as citizens, in this case by abolishing the old system of "mixed communes," which subjected them to military administration. But this report leads one to question whether any reform could have kept Algeria French. Quite unconsciously, its authors had cataloged all the main causes of the coming revolt.[3]

From the perspective of colonial authorities, the greatest problem facing French Algeria was the increasing preponderance of its Muslim population. Aside from a temporary surge during the Spanish Civil War, relatively few Europeans settled in Algeria after the turn of the century. Their numbers rose from 833,000 in 1926 to 984,000 by 1954, a natural rate of increase of about one percent a year. The Muslim population, on the other hand, was growing twice as fast by the eve of war, rising from just over 5 million to 8,546,000 in the same period (not including the 300,000 working in France).[4] Between 1900 and 1954, average death rates in the Muslim population fell from 24–27 to 17.5 per thousand. At the same time, birth rates remained high, rising to 42–44 per thousand in 1954 — 2.5 times the rate for Europeans.[5]

French officials not only possessed precise data on the scale of this problem, they also understood its principal causes. As the chief of Tizi-Ouzou commune explained:

> We cannot rely upon "natural selection" which could operate when the country was abundantly "taxed" by illness, insecurity, and war. Today security is total, the average life expectancy has considerably risen, epidemics have disappeared, and families are growing with typical oriental abandon.[6]

Insecticides, vaccines, and antibiotics had indeed succeeded in stamping out plague and curbing cholera, typhus, and malaria, though public health programs were for the benefit of the colonists more than the Muslims. As the Scientific Congress of Algiers declared in honoring the French Army doctor, François Clément Maillot, who pioneered the use of quinine, "It is thanks to Maillot that Algeria has become a French land; it is he who closed and sealed forever this tomb of Christians" (a statement that reads altogether differently in the light of subsequent events).[7]

The improved health and subsequent growth of the Muslim population inspired a palpable sense of foreboding among French officials. The one in Phillippeville found himself "isolated among 41,000 still primitive Muslims whose reactions are often unpredictable and violent."[8] All but three hundred Europeans had sold their land and moved to the cities. His colleague in the Kellermann commune reported that its thirty European families "feel literally absorbed by the indigenous mass, and they do not hide their pessimism. Kellermann," he concluded, "is a dying center."[9]

For Europeans the distress was psychological. For Muslims, population growth in combination with a transformation of the rural economy produced physical suffering on an appalling scale. Since the passage in the nineteenth century of property laws intended to disorganize Muslim society — and resistance — and free up land for settlement, a system of joint control by tribes, families, and religious foundations had been replaced by individual ownership.[10] Over time, those lands not consolidated by the colonists or more prosperous Muslims were typically divided and subdivided until they could no longer support their owners. While a family needed an estimated 12 to 20 hectares to stave off malnutrition, by 1950 70 percent had less than 10. The top 2 percent of the rural population, on the other hand, controlled a quarter of the cultivable land. They typically benefited from credit and irrigation programs to produce crops for export.[11]

Poorer Muslims sometimes found seasonal work on the large estates, but the mechanization of agriculture reduced demand for their labor. From 1934 to 1954, the number of tractors increased fourfold, and combine harvesters multiplied by seven—each of the latter replacing a hundred hired hands. By 1954, half of the working-age population in the countryside was usually unemployed. Moreover, intensive cultivation—especially as it expanded into forests and the pastoral lands of the high plains and steppe—led to exhausted soil and ruinous erosion.[12] As one administrator concluded with Malthusian fatalism: "While humans multiply, the soil's yield is regressing. . . . This is the eternal problem of over-populated and poor countries."[13]

In fact, the problem was not "eternal," but man-made. Property transfers, population growth, and changing modes of production—each caused or conditioned by colonial policies—degraded the living standards of most Muslims along with the lands that had once supported them. This rural crisis also eroded the foundations of French rule. The exodus of small-scale European farmers from the countryside deprived the administration of eyes and ears. Moreover, replacing tenant farmers with wage laborers or even farm machinery broke traditional bonds of patronage between landowners and the local population.[14] "Today calm prevails everywhere," observed the head of Fedj M'zala. "But the barely evolved, very fanatic population is always susceptible to follow the least reasonable movement."[15]

Who then would lead the uprising that so many officials had come to see as inevitable? For most, "the least reasonable movement" was the Association of Muslim Algerian *'Ulama*, or religious scholars. Beginning at the turn of the century, they had sought to restore their moral authority by regaining control of training and appointments from the French and imposing orthodoxy on popular practices. The movement's leadership came from older, declining towns like Constantine, Tlemcen, and Nedroma and had their strongest support among the middling peasants.[16] The head of Akbou commune spoke for many of his colleagues when he asserted that the 'ulama "represent the stable base upon which nationalist and panislamist sentiments develop. . . . Their action is so insidious, flexible and rigorous at the same time. They are certainly our most dangerous enemies."[17]

The image of Islam as the basis of opposition to French rule was an old idea that served a continuing need: opposition to colonialism could in this way be made to appear as xenophobia, nationalism as fanaticism, revolution as *jihad*.[18] While the Islamic influence on the development of Algerian nationalism cannot be dismissed as a colonialist canard, it was far more complex than most of the French imagined. Some historians have suggested that the real roots of national resistance are to be found not among the 'ulama—politically cautious and socially conservative—but their doctrinal opponents, the Sufis, who were leading populist revolts even under the Turks. The 'ulama fully shared the administrators' disdain for the religious mysticism exemplified by the Sufis and their veneration of holy men, the marabouts.[19]

Yet, on a more basic level, if France's difficulty in Algeria was not the "irrationalism" of Algerian Muslims but rather their refusal to become French, then the 'ulama were undoubtedly part of the problem. Since the 1930s 'ulama schools, circles, and associations had taught a generation to proclaim, "Islam is my religion, Arabic is my language, Algeria is my fatherland." Though they distinguished between the cultural and political spheres and disavowed any ambition to overthrow the colonial regime, their successful defense of a distinct Algerian nation was sufficient to cast the most serious doubts on the future of French Algeria. As their leader, Abd al-Hamid Ben Badis, defiantly affirmed: "[T]his Algerian Muslim nation is not France; it is not possible that it be France; it does not want to become France; and even if it wished, it could not be France."[20]

If the 'ulama wanted to have nothing to do with the French, some administrators made clear the feeling was mutual: "This people, who has known different masters, has not modified its way of life," complained the chief of Clauzel commune. "Primitive morals and customs remain. Development is mediocre. No elite. Development manifests itself particularly in the (anti-French) political arena. Very easily influenced character: mistrustful, fatalistic, prone to lie, and above all, to steal."[21] Such sentiments could be expressed in this kind of shorthand because they were so widespread, but they spoke volumes about the attitude of many administrators toward their *mission civilisatrice*.

More enlightened officials bemoaned the mutual incomprehension and mistrust characterizing relations between Muslims and Europeans, blaming *colon* racism and the lack of contact between the two communities.[22] But would integration inevitably lead to mutual tolerance? The question was critical since an increasing number of Muslims were migrating to the cities, where four out of five pieds noirs lived in 1954. By then Muslims made up 60 percent of the population of the thirty largest cities and towns, with one-third living in *bidonvilles*, or shantytowns.[23]

The famed French anthropologist Jacques Berque later produced a vivid portrait of this growing population and the menace it appeared to pose to Algeria's cities: "Far from the elegant crowd, the well-stocked shops, the lit-up districts, some other crowds move about, infinitely larger, in districts infinitely less bright. Behind the hills, in the curves of the ravines . . . a powerful and miserable life has been gathering . . ."[24] Part of what made *les miserables* seem so powerful was that they did not integrate themselves into an urban way of life but instead appeared to settle and organize themselves as tribes with no regular source of income. In 1962, Berque's colleague Pierre Bourdieu found that it was impossible to categorize their lives as traditional or capitalist—indeed, they existed entirely outside this framework of analysis.[25] The administrators saw it as much more than an intellectual challenge. One warned that it was imperative to "slow the creation of an uncontrollable and miserable urban proletariat, easily drawn into turbulence."[26] In fact, the authorities periodically bulldozed *bidonvilles* and trucked their inhabitants out to the country. But their places were quickly taken by new arrivals, who set up their cardboard and tin-can constructions in the very heart of the city. Some of those lucky enough to find an apartment lived fifteen or sixteen to a room.[27]

If there was any hope of turning these peasants into Frenchmen, it rested in the schools. Yet due to the initial resistance of some Muslims and the continuing objections of the pieds noirs, only a small portion of non-Europeans ever received a French education—less than 9 percent in 1944. Most attended separate classes with high student-teacher ratios and low standards. In 1935, for instance, classes for Muslims averaged eighty-three students—hardly an ideal atmosphere for imparting an appreciation of French civilization. Though Muslim parents had begun to clamor for an improved and expanded school system in the interwar years, 80 percent of outlays for education continued to go to Europeans, who made up just 14 percent of the population.[28] Thus, if the *'ulama* were "the true school of North African nationalism," as the administrator in Bourd-Bou-Arreridj complained, the reason may have been that so few other schools were open.[29]

In 1944 de Gaulle's provisional government finally initiated a crash program to educate more Muslims. But even after ten years, only 13 percent of boys were enrolled in primary schools while 86 percent of the adult male population remained illiterate. Among women it was even worse: only one-fifth as many attended school and just one in twenty could read, further limiting the French influence on Muslim families.[30] Some administrators recognized this as both a problem and an opportunity. As the head of Cassaigne commune argued, "Women are more accessible to our civilization and our customs than men. They could constitute a remarkable channel for French action and propaganda." (In fact, Algerian women would come to see education as a "channel for action" against the French.)[31]

Some Muslims did manage to attend integrated schools and a few even pursued more advanced studies—6,260 in lycées and 589 at the University of Algiers in 1954, with another 200 going to universities in the metropole. But that year, there were still just 28 non-European engineers, 185 secondary school teachers, 354 lawyers and notaries, and 165 doctors, dentists, and pharmacists in all of Algeria. Altogether, this professional class accounted for less than one in ten thousand Muslims.[32] And even they could not all be counted as converts to the *mission civilisatrice*. The majority came from modest backgrounds and had received a traditional Muslim upbringing. Outnumbered 10 or 20 to 1 in their classes at the University of Algiers, they were the most likely to encounter European racism and official condescension. Even those who renounced their

separate legal status in order to acquire French citizenship typically returned to the *shariah*, or Islamic law, for marriage and inheritance.[33]

Nevertheless, while much of this elite was privately ambivalent about
their cultural identity, publicly most kept faith with France. The Young
Algerian movement, which emerged after the turn of the century among
these *évolués* — as the more "evolved" or "advanced" elements were called —
eventually divided between those who accepted full French citizenship and
those who wanted all Muslims to have that status without appearing to
renounce Islam. None questioned the goal of assimilation. The history of
their efforts to expand Muslim voting, educational, and employment opportunities is protracted and complex. But it never amounted to more
than halting, incremental progress because of the pieds noirs' powerful
lobby in the National Assembly. In 1936, they forced even the Popular
Front government of Léon Blum to withdraw support for a bill that
would have extended suffrage to a small minority of Muslim soldiers,
professionals, and public employees.[34]

French historians have long treated the defeat of the Blum-Viollette
bill as a turning point — the point at which pied noir intransigence completely discredited loyal Muslim opposition. But this interpretation draws
a false distinction between colonialism and the colonists, as if there was
some essential — and essentially good — idea of French Algeria that existed
apart from its historical reality. The prospect of a reformed society that
would afford equal opportunities to all was important to the self-image
of évolués and their supporter and was the centerpiece of French wartime
propaganda. But in retrospect — and from the perspective of the vast majority of Muslims and pieds noirs at the time — *Algérie française* would
then have lost its raison d'être.[35]

The North African Star

One group of Muslims opposed the Blum-Viollette bill from the beginning, Messali Hadj's North African Star (*Etoile Nord-Africaine*, or ENA),
which succeeded the 'ulama and the évolués in leading the opposition.
Messali had the most support not in the countryside nor the cities of
Algeria, where he was little known before 1936, but among North African
workers in France. Like their évolué counterparts in French classrooms,
Muslim émigrés came to a new consciousness of their second-class status
through direct exposure to France — beginning with restrictions on immigration imposed during economic downturns.[36] It was not until after
1944 — when Muslims became citizens and could circulate more freely to
the metropole — that emigration really started to increase. By 1949, there
were about two hundred thousand living in France and by the eve of war
nearly three hundred thousand — more than the entire Muslim workforce
in Algeria's own cities. Here, too, Algerians tended to settle according to
their place of origin, with a particular *quartier* in Paris populated by the
former inhabitants of a particular Berber village.[37]

The vast majority of these immigrants were men who were unmarried or had left their families behind, supporting them with their remittances before returning after a few years. In some cases, their earnings enabled them to purchase new properties, and in that way the area of land sold by colonists to Muslims after 1940 began to exceed that sold by Muslims to colonists.[38] But French administrators were most concerned about the cultural impact of crossing the Mediterranean. As one complained: "Few return satisfied or wealthy. On the other hand, they bring with them rather harmful social and political ideas."[39]

What were these ideas? Since the time of Toussaint L'Ouverture, colonialists had found that the most dangerous ideas were French ideals, which appeared radical when applied irrespective of race and religion.[40] Many of the items on the ENA's first list of demands—equal access to education, application of French social legislation to Algeria, abolition of the discriminatory *code d'indigénat*, universal suffrage, freedom of press and association—reflected the republican principles of equal rights and responsibilities. In this respect, they did not differ from the évolués. On the other hand, Messali also called for the creation of Arabic language schools like the 'ulama before him. And along with the Communists, who originally encouraged him to form the ENA before he repudiated the party over its complaisance toward colonialism, he favored confiscating the big estates and nationalizing banks and industry. The originality of Messali's ENA was to incorporate the desiderata of all the other opposition groups and, unlike any of them, demand independence from the beginning. For this reason, the authorities banned it in 1937 but it quickly regrouped as the Parti du Peuple Algérien (PPA). As Muslims traveled to and from France in growing numbers, the PPA became the dominant nationalist movement on both sides of the Mediterranean.[41]

In the course of World War II, France's loss of prestige, the sacrifices of Muslim soldiers, and economic hardships all raised expectations of reform. In March 1943, the new leader of the moderate opposition, Ferhat Abbas, drafted a "Manifesto of the Algerian People" which echoed many of the ENA's original demands. A year later, de Gaulle abolished the *code d'indigénat* and accorded Muslim men citizenship and universal suffrage, though they would still elect only half the National Assembly delegation.[42]

By now Muslims had come to expect much more. In March 1945, the PPA managed to take over a meeting of Abbas's *Amis du Manifeste et de la Liberté* and force through resolutions favoring an Algerian government and proclaiming Messali "the uncontested leader of the Algerian people." French authorities then deported him amid rumors that the United Nations conference, which was shortly to convene in San Francisco, would declare Algeria independent. The nationalists associated themselves with American anticolonialism and scheduled celebratory marches for V-E Day. These quickly turned into bloody clashes in the towns of Guelma and Sétif, and for the following week Muslims attacked European settlements in the surrounding areas. More than a hundred *pieds noirs* were killed as the authorities unleashed a ferocious repression, including aerial bombardment, naval gunfire, and summary executions. The PPA belatedly called for a general revolt, which succeeded only in increasing the casualties.[43] In the aftermath, one high official in Algiers, Commissaire Bergé, judged that "if instead of facing local and uncoordinated uprisings we had clashed with a general and well-organized insurrection . . . few French people would have made it back to the Metropole."[44]

No one knows exactly how many Muslims perished. French historians speak of six thousand to eight thousand, Algerians put the figure at forty-five thousand. At the time Bergé and the rest of the French administration in Algeria preferred not to know. He acknowledged that they could "dig up some bodies" and punish wrongdoers, but only the nationalists and France's British and American rivals would benefit: "[W]e should ask ourselves if the country is capable of withstanding this dose of truth," he concluded, "if the cure is not worse than the disease."[45]

Instead, local authorities resorted to a more traditional remedy. Ten days later, an Interior Ministry informant described how the militia and gendarmes of Guelma were using Italian POWs to disinter and burn some five hundred corpses of Muslims who had been summarily executed—more than three times the official death toll. And rather than acting in the heat of battle, as was claimed at the time, the militia had actually rounded up Muslim political activists using lists provided by the local Gendarmerie. They had hoped to ensure secrecy by shooting one of the truck drivers *pour encourager les autres*.[46] Perhaps emboldened by this evidence—and harried by the Communists in the Assembly—Interior Minister Adrien Tixier pressed for action on complaints filed by families of the slain. The administration in Algiers then put Commissaire Bergé—the very same Bergé who had ruled out any serious inquiry—in charge of monitoring the investigation. The Interior Ministry finally dropped the matter.[47]

PPA militants regrouped as the *Mouvement pour le Triomphe des Libertés Démocratiques* (MTLD) and won municipal elections across Algeria.[48] Indeed, by January 1948 the new interior minister, Jules Moch, was worried that the nationalists might be voted into power. The previous year the National Assembly had finally passed a new statute for Algeria that established a local assembly. Its powers were limited, however; the *pied noir* minority was guaranteed half the seats, and all measures required a two-thirds vote. Even so, Moch took no chances. In a letter to the prime minister, Robert Schuman, he advised against dissolving the MTLD outright since it "would have a bad effect abroad." Instead, he would back progovernment candidates wherever possible, favor Abbas's new *Union Démocratique du Manifeste Algérien* (UDMA) everywhere else, and block or arrest all MTLD candidates.[49] Along with blatant fraud, this succeeded in electing "Beni oui-ouis"—or Muslim yes-men—to forty-one of sixty seats. Subsequent elections were also spurious, and the assembly proved to be all but powerless. Similarly, five years after the statute mandated the abolition of "mixed communes"—which did not display even the semblance of democracy—French authorities were still debating the matter. By that point, even Abbas concluded that "there is no other solution but the machine-gun."[50]

Of course, Abbas and the UDMA would not be the ones to wield it. Only the MTLD had a force prepared for armed revolt, the *Organisation Spéciale* (OS), counting one thousand to fifteen hundred members by 1950. But that year a French crackdown completely dismantled it.[51] Moreover, the MTLD had already been weakened by the so-called Berberist crisis. Constituting some 25 percent of Algeria's population, the Berbers descend from the earliest inhabitants of North Africa—that is, predating the influx of Arabic-speaking peoples in the seventh and eleventh centuries. Concentrated in the densely populated, impoverished areas of Kabylia and the Aurès mountains, they were the first to emigrate to the metropole and many more settled in Algerian cities. French authorities favored them with the first schools, and a disproportionate number served as minor officials. Nevertheless, Berbers were also heavily represented among France's enemies, sustaining the only effective *maquis* after the dissolution of the OS, and producing many of the FLN's outstanding leaders—another example of how increasing integration through urbanization, education, and emigration undermined colonial control. On the other hand, they also suffered Messali's wrath for resisting his emphasis on Arabism and Islam, instead favoring a less exclusive, more secular Algerian identity.[52]

Though Berber-Arab tensions would resurface during the war for independence and afterward, this was not the most important issue among Algerians in the preceding years. Instead, members of the MTLD disagreed on the question of whether it was best to continue political opposition, cooperate with the colonial administration, or reconstitute a paramilitary organization—and whether Messali would make this decision by himself. After years of failure in both elections and armed resistance, the MTLD could no longer abide his autocratic style, epitomized by his election as president for life in July 1954. Most of the Central Committee broke away and began to plan a broad coalition with other parties.[53]

A third faction, led by former OS members, rejected both Messali's personality cult and the Centralists' politicking. They proclaimed their program with the very name of their group: the *Comité Révolutionnaire d'Unité et d'Action* (CRUA), which was rechristened the FLN after they launched the war for independence. But this was neither a clean break nor a radical departure. As Mohammed Harbi argues, the Front shared with their former comrades in the MTLD "the same preoccupations, the same political itinerary, the same social base" and were indebted to all of the pre-1954 nationalist movements for their ideas.[54] They eventually inherited many of the followers of Messali, the more upwardly mobile Centralists, the assimilationist UDMA, and the 'ulama, too.[55]

The CRUA militants always hoped that other nationalists would rally to their cause, though in 1954 they could not have counted on it. But as desperate as matters appeared to them, French officials were still more pessimistic. One of the most striking facts brought out in "Algeria at Mid-Century" is the failure, even before the war, of these officials to distinguish between the "extremist parties"—equating the UDMA and the *'ulama*, accusing the PPA of inciting religious intolerance, and so on. Many of the administrators assumed that Muslim society as a whole was merely awaiting the opportunity to throw off French rule. Thus, one could already foresee "the day when, in overwhelming masses, carefully prepared and hardened elements will unmask themselves . . . and seek to overthrow the tricolored flag in this territory, following the example of Indochina, whose evolution is observed here with great interest.[56]

Part of the administrators' pessimism was doubtless due to their experience in Vietnam—and Morocco, and Tunisia—where nationalists had constructed broad coalitions against French rule. But how were *Muslims* in Algeria able to follow events as far away as Indochina? Though the vast majority were still illiterate, by the 1950s they could hear radio broadcasts in cafes across Algeria, with battery-powered models reaching even the most remote villages. Ironically, French authorities had pioneered the use of radio in the 1920s as a cheaper, more reliable alternative to submarine cables for communicating with their colonies in Africa and Indochina.[57] Now this same technology guaranteed that their defeat at Dien Bien Phu would be announced instantaneously in every part of the empire. The news arrived on the same day the CRUA had its first full meeting and helped to persuade them to begin planning the November uprising.[58]

The ironies of the Algerian case exemplify the larger history of decolonization, in which the more advanced "tools of empire"—insecticides, combine harvesters, radio—became the mechanisms of its demise; "development" simultaneously weakened and sustained a subsistence economy while creating an intolerable burden for the metropole; and exposure to Western ideas inspired demands for both the realization of liberal rhetoric and a renewal and reassertion of indigenous cultures. In these conditions French administrators began to lose their sense of direction and a few even wanted to shift into reverse. One suggested that they reform traditional marabout schools, arguing that, "[a]fter having been our most bitter adversaries, the 'marabouts' have in general become our best auxiliaries." Another agreed that encouraging the particularism of the Sufi brotherhoods was their best defense against pan-Islamism. Others questioned whether improved standards of living would really lower fertility rates or whether additional social services in the cities might not simply encourage more Muslims to migrate. One even wondered whether they ought not to let "natural selection" among infants produce a hardier (and smaller) Muslim population. While the head of La Meskiana commune was still confident that a new influx of colonists could make Algeria truly French within ten years, others were actually considering the resettlement of Algerian Muslims in underpopulated parts of France.[59] With officials proposing the promotion of Sufism and local saints, the deliberate elevation of infant mortality, and reverse colonization, the *mission civilisatrice* had begun to seem a little mad.[60]

What ailed the colonial project were not just its "internal contradictions" and unintended consequences. It also suffered from the discrediting of the ideas that had long separated ruler and ruled and legitimated imperial power. In the aftermath of Nazi atrocities, explicitly racist justifications were no longer acceptable.[61] French authorities could—and would—continue to justify their rule based on seemingly objective technical and economic criteria, arguing that Algeria's development depended on its continued cooperation with France. During the war, the "civilizing mission" was recast as a "modernizing mission." Yet this position was also problematic, and not just because subscribing to a universalist model of modernization undermined their claim to a particular vocation in Algeria.[62] The underlying problem for French authorities and eventually the Algerians, too, was much deeper. To uncover it Algeria must be viewed in the wider context of the colonial world.

The Crisis of the Colonial World

The Algerian War came at the crest of a wave of anticolonial insurgencies that presented both challenges and opportunities to the two superpowers. Yet until Khrushchev, Stalinist dogma hobbled Soviet diplomacy, positing as it did that any nationalist movement not led by Communists was the tool of local bourgeoisie and foreign capital. As Anastas Mikoyan scathingly remarked to the members of the Soviet Institute of Oriental Studies in 1956, "[A]lthough in our day the whole East has awakened, this institute is still sleeping."[63] Similarly, George C. Marshall was awed by the unrest sweeping the colonial world:

> We are in the middle of a world revolution—and I don't mean Communism. The Communists are . . . just moving in on the crest of a wave. The revolution I'm talking about is that of the little people all over the world. They're beginning to learn what there is in life, and to learn what they are missing.[64]

American social scientists were quicker than their Soviet counterparts to respond to the demand for "development" or "modernization" theory, and their work became conventional wisdom in France as well as the United States.[65]

Like Marshall, most theorists were confident that what Third World peoples wanted was to grow up—that is, to become more modern, "more like us." It was therefore up to the West to steady them through their growing pains. Implicit in the "little people" imagery and modernization theory's more sophisticated schema of "stages of economic growth" was the conviction that they could not *interact* with outside influences but could only adhere to tradition or accept modernity through either its capitalist or communist variants—though most Western observers thought the latter would eventually be proved fraudulent. They were oblivious to the tautology inherent in arguing that "the Western model of modernization" was universally relevant since all modernizing societies were—by definition—becoming more Western.[66]

While modernization theory generated a vast literature, perhaps the quintessential work was Daniel Lerner's *The Passing of Traditional Society*, which studied the impact of new means of mass communications in six Middle Eastern countries.[67] Lerner believed that the ability to empathize, to imagine oneself in the place of another, was the mark of modernity. Like other development theorists, he stressed radio's role in teaching Third World peoples "what there is in life," which he defined as what the West had to offer. Dangers were inherent in the resulting "revolution in rising expectations," but at least the direction of progress was clear: the new media raised expectations, and economic and social development would meet them. It remained only to balance the demand and supply sides of development and measure with "empathy indexes" and statistical analyses the rate of advance along the road to modernity.

In 1951, Lerner's survey teams found that radio and film had begun to reach broad sections of Middle Eastern societies. In Egypt, for instance, 78 percent of workers reported listening to radios every day and 45 percent said that they attended movies weekly. Among farmers, 42 percent heard radio broadcasts daily, while more than half went to the movies once or twice a month. What they heard and saw, however, did not just come from the *Voice of America* and Hollywood. In this period, the Cairo-based *Voice of the Arabs* became the most popular service in the region, reaching listeners from Morocco to Iraq. Beginning in 1953, the service coordinated its broadcasts with North African nationalists, and it announced the rebels' "proclamation to the Algerian people" on the first day of the revolt.[68] By 1956, the FLN had its own *Voice of Algeria* broadcasting from clandestine transmitters just beyond its borders. Muslims responded by buying up every transistor radio in the markets. French authorities tried to control sales and then turned to jamming transmissions but with only intermittent success. As the famed FLN theorist and diplomat Frantz Fanon observed: "[T]he purchase of a radio in Algeria has meant, not the adoption of a modern technique for getting news, but the obtaining of access to the only means of entering into communication with the Revolution."[69]

Egypt's movie industry also radiated its influence throughout the region. In Algeria alone, over two hundred and fifty Egyptian films had been granted import licenses by 1956 for screening in the nearly one thousand movie houses across the country.[70] Though devoid of overt political content, authorities came to fear that they were one of the principal vehicles for the spread of Arab nationalism. However anodyne and inoffensive, they subverted French rule by representing a "supposedly free and modern" Arab society.[71]

After being refused any new import licenses, the Egyptians began producing pro-FLN films like *Djamila Bouhired*, which celebrated an urban guerrilla who hid bombs in her handbag before being captured and tortured by French soldiers. Instead of simply rejecting European influence, the film's hero is taught that French education "is a weapon we shall use against our enemies." Likewise, the film's protagonists mobilize the international media and arouse world opinion to save Bouhired from execution.[72] Paris tried to ban its foreign distribution but had little success.[73] The French responded by training Muslims to make Arabic language films following the official line. But almost all of those selected for an accelerated course defected and began producing FLN propaganda films instead, parts of which eventually appeared on American television.[74]

Of course, the French possessed powerful means of propagating their own message and waged "psychological warfare" with unprecedented intensity. They were particularly effective in controlling the print media within Algeria, seizing left and liberal newspapers from the metropole and banning over a hundred foreign publications. By 1957, no independent Arabic-language newspaper remained in the country.[75] But rumor, or the "Arab telephone," could reinterpret the official line and rally resistance. In 1954, one Muslim remembered hearing "that there was no longer any French army; that it had been destroyed in Indo-China." When the *Voice of the Arabs* broadcast assurances of Arab solidarity after the start of the war, some of their audience began to speak of a seventy thousand-man Egyptian army descending on Algeria. Nationalist leaders eventually found it necessary—but difficult—to discourage their compatriots from placing their hopes in an international intervention. Muslims were not, therefore, mere receptors of the propaganda of either side, but rather active participants in a creative process that reimagined Algeria and its people as a concern of the wider world. In this way, radio and rumor together formed a nervous system that connected colonized peoples and encouraged a new consciousness of their common condition and the possibilities of collective action.[76]

Arabs' use of new communications technologies posed a conceptual problem for modernization theory, especially given their message. Lerner complained that in Egypt the *Voice of the Arabs* "unleashed the violent xenophobia of fanatics while silencing the voices of modern rationality." In North Africa, it "became a major relay in the chain-reaction of assassination and mob violence through the area." Even in the languages of Pakistan and Indonesia, it preached Nasser's theme of "Islamic World Power," while in Swahili it called for a renewal of the Mau Mau revolt against white rule "not only in Kenya but in the entire continent . . . until Africa belongs to the Africans." Measured by radio listenership, film attendance, and rising expectations, Asians and Africans were becoming ever more modern, but not in the way modernization theorists had in mind.[77] As Irene Gendzier has shown, if these trends led to an anti-Western regime, as in Iran, Lerner associated them with alienation rather than modernity, while "those who exhibited an enthusiasm for social change, previously considered a sign of empathy, were now castigated as trouble-makers."[78]

If the demand side of the modernization model challenged Western expectations, the supply side was still more aberrant. Development theory anticipated that Third World peoples would endure deprivation and threaten unrest during a transition phase, though integration in the world economy through specialization and trade would eventually lead to greater prosperity. In this respect, Algeria exhibited all the key features of the erosion of traditional economies occurring across the Third World: In China, too, commercialization had led to the abolition of public granaries. In Mexico and Vietnam, as in Algeria, it threatened peasant control of communal land. In both these cases and Cuba as well, property seizures by colonists or private companies drove peasants onto marginal lands insufficient for their subsistence, just as in Algeria.[79] In all these countries, peasants challenged the new economic order. Development theorists and their critics would agree that the commercialization of agrarian society was a primary cause of political unrest, even while disagreeing about whether this painful process was unavoidable.[80] But neither group explained why development—or exploitation—did not pay.

In Algeria, for instance, integration with global markets was exemplified by the fact that, by 1954, wine accounted for more than half of all exports of this Muslim country. Yet the government paid wine growers 25 percent more than the market value of their product, much of which was considered unsaleable. Moreover, from 1952 on, the metropole had to make up for annual shortfalls in the Algerian budget as social services strained to accommodate the expanding, increasingly urban population. Just like their French counterparts across the Mediterranean, nonagricultural workers were entitled to family allowances and, beginning in 1950, school-enrollment bonuses for their children.[81]

But rather than forming a consumer society, many Muslims in the cities continued to live outside the cash economy. As Bourdieu observed, the real Algerian Muslim proletariat had emigrated to France only to send most of their earnings home, thus shoring up the rural economy. On the other hand—and despite massive development projects—private capital began to flow out of Algeria at an accelerating rate: 3.6 billion (old) francs in 1954, 19.5 billion in 1955; 121.1 billion in 1956.[82]

In this respect, Algeria was an extreme case of a problem confronting colonial authorities throughout the continent. After World War II, Britain and France began to devote considerable resources to developing their African colonies, but private capital did not follow public investment. Moreover, once the expense of imperialism had begun to pinch taxpayers, the press and publics in both countries began to subject it to cost-benefit analyses.[83] In the summer of 1956, Raymond Cartier argued in a series of influential articles for *Paris Match* that France ought to redirect investment to the metropole since it paid inflated prices for what little its African colonies had to offer.[84] Likewise, in 1959 John Strachey—former war minister under Clement Attlee—demonstrated that "imperialism has ceased to bring appreciable benefits to the advanced countries (without ceasing to be ruinous for the underdeveloped)."[85]

There *were* economic successes in Africa, but they did not fit the development model. Just as in Algeria, migrant laborers from other African states used their wages to strengthen the village economies, though British and French officials were little interested in the growth of exports from small farms. As Frederick Cooper has argued, they wanted to form a disciplined labor force but "Africans proved adept . . . at using mobility, kin networks, and the ability to move between alternative systems to avoid too much dependence on white employers"—in the same way that Algerian Muslims escaped the colonists and low wages by working in France despite official efforts to keep them on the farm.[86] This was a rational response to market incentives, but even the most liberal economists shudder at the thought of allowing labor to cross borders with the same freedom as capital, goods, and services.[87]

The issue of labor mobility was potentially explosive given the pattern of world population growth. According to the prevailing dogma on the "demographic transition"—demography's contribution to modernization theory—urbanization and industrialization reduced mortality rates and, after a lag period and rapid population growth, rates of natality. The population of developing countries was therefore expected to stabilize, just as in the West.[88] But by the late 1950s, demographers discovered that improved public health measures had rapidly reduced death rates in *non*-industrial economies not just in Algeria, but also in Ceylon, Malaya, the West Indies, and much of Latin America. Moreover, in Algeria (as well as India and Egypt), urbanization initially appeared to have no effect on birthrates.[89]

Indeed, the relative decline of Algeria's European population reflected a shift in the proportion of European and non-European peoples around the globe. Whereas Asians, Africans, and Latin Americans accounted for 55 percent of world population in the second half of the nineteenth century, by the 1950s they made up more than 77 percent, a trend that would accelerate in the following years.[90] From the perspective of Western policymakers, population growth made economic development more difficult but all the more imperative given the potential threat posed by impoverished Third World peoples. It threatened to overburden both the supply and demand sides of the development model and overturn the entire modernization project.

In this period, the focus of Western activity in the Third World began to shift from development to direct aid, from modernization to "basic needs." Some argued that aid should be given to developing areas as a moral imperative. But there was also a pragmatic argument for the alleviation of poverty in areas with rapidly growing populations—one based on Western self-interest, even survival. In 1959, a French National Assembly report asserted that advances in telecommunications were "making the misery that spans the globe each day less bearable. . . . And if, to-morrow, nothing is done, the demographic deadline of the year 2000 will see not only wealthy countries, above all North America, Europe and the USSR, unable to protect their wealth from others' misery, but misery and hunger will become the lot of all humanity."[91] New communications tech-nologies and the capacity of Third World peoples to empathize was not necessarily a formula for development. Western observers had begun to fear that, instead of *imagining* themselves in their place, impoverished masses might actually take possession of it.

Thus, the idea of modernization had become muddled in Algeria, which helps to explain its vulnerability to alternative views. New means of communications, market integration, and mass migration had so com-plicated ties between metropole and colony, city and countryside, mo-dernity and tradition as to make the relationships between these apparent dichotomies increasingly ambiguous. The question was not just who ruled in Algiers but whether it was still possible to constitute authority in a system that had become so decentered.

With their deepening engagement in Algeria, it became ever more difficult, even disturbing, for the French to go on defining themselves either against or through Algerian Muslims. When the Algerian—often living in their midst—might be both peasant and proletarian, neither lib-eral nor communist, French citizen, Algerian nationalist, and racial and religious separatist all at the same time, it became impossible to know the "other," or even to name him. Moreover, the fight against nascent Al-gerian nationalism led to violations of civil liberties integral to France's self image, which was still shaken by the Vichy experience. The ensuing domestic conflict ended with some aiding the rebels and others assaulting the state. But for all their partisan fervor, few were certain how French ideals that were supposedly universal could apply to the case of Algeria: liberty appeared to mean abandoning citizens to an Islamic state, equality required admitting a hundred Muslim deputies to the Assembly, and fra-ternity necessitated accepting—rather than assimilating—a culture that seemed alien even to the most cosmopolitan.[92]

This posed both a practical and an ideological challenge to the very identity of the nation and the integrity of the state. The question was not so much competing ideas of truth and justice but whether such concepts retained any real meaning. Fanon asserted that "truth is the property of the national cause. No absolute verity, no discourse on the purity of the soul, can shake this position. . . . Truth is that which hurries on the break-up of the colonialist regime." On the other side, Albert Camus declared that he would choose his pied noir mother over justice, indicating how ethnic violence could undermine faith in universal ideals even among the most committed humanists.[93]

Many of those who went on to pioneer poststructuralist and post-modernist theory were shaped by the Algerian experience. During Vichy, Jacques Derrida found himself excluded from his school in Algiers as Jews were rejected by both sides of a polarizing society. Marginality would be one of the main themes of an *oeuvre* distinguished by a profound distrust of all claims to authority.[94] Similarly, after Bourdieu's experience in Algeria—where social scientists served a repressive state—he espoused a more reflexive sociology and strove to transcend false antinomies.[95] "Something has changed now, radically," Philippe Sollers wrote after his best friend was killed in the war, "The world is less pure." He hoped to reclaim an autonomous space for texts and textual analysis by founding the journal *Tel Quel*, which became a hothouse for critical theory.[96] As Michael Fischer has observed, Algeria "focused attention on the need to find alternatives to the construction of totalizing ideologies, the need for theories and strategies of government that could accommodate multiple cultural perspectives and not insist that everyone see history or progress the same way."[97]

Of course, not everyone saw things this way. Most observers judged that modernization simply needed to be accelerated. Indeed, French propagandists moved beyond American development theory—which identified nationalism with modernity—to assert that, because of technological advances and economic integration, no nation was truly independent. Instead, they argued, France and Algeria were interdependent in an increasingly interdependent world. This made it impossible to be indifferent to the fate of human rights or the environment among other peoples. In films like *The Falling Veil*, they sought to convince American television audiences that only France could end "the Moslem tradition of female subjugation stretched back through the centuries of Arab rule"—an issue that was all the more important since, even then, educating women was recognized as a means of reducing birthrates.[98] In 1947, the *Manchester Guardian* offered an environmentalist argument against self-determination in North Africa that would often recur in French propaganda, albeit less explicitly:

> Which should come first: National independence or the development of a country and the conservation of its soil? To what extent has a nation the right to ruin its own land? . . . Is it really in the interests of the world to allow the desert to swallow up the last naturally green hills of Libya to satisfy their claims to self-government?[99]

In its latter phases, official propaganda tended to ignore the issue of self-determination altogether and instead trumpeted French aspirations and achievements in liberating Muslim women and developing Algeria, all the while implying that the war was over but for the shouting. But the international media proved to be more interested in reporting the anarchy and atrocities that were actually occurring. Moreover, officials undercut their claims to be opening Algeria to the world by constructing barbed wire fences around it, banning foreign films and newspapers, and jamming international radio transmissions. The Algerians, on the other hand, cultivated the media and presented themselves as a secular, nationalist movement in which men and women participated equally in building a modern nation.[100] Indeed, at this time — and partly because of the progress of such movements — the "end of history" was already in sight. "The fundamental political problems of the industrial revolution have been solved," Seymour Martin Lipset asserted, ". . . [T]his very triumph of democratic social revolution in the West ends domestic politics for those intellectuals who must have . . . utopias to motivate them to social action.[101] The FLN won over international opinion by portraying itself as part of that "democratic social revolution." But there were others, on both sides, who were motivated by *dystopias*, some indeed who felt that they were living in the shadow of a new dark age.

The Specter of Jihad

Despite the contradictions and contrary evidence, the idea of "development" could support these different political projects because of its deep roots in a powerful intellectual tradition that views progress as "inevitable and inevitably directional from lower to higher forms of society, knowledge, religion."[102] But another intellectual tradition, less respectable but no less influential, posits the inevitability of *decline*.[103] It emphasizes fragmentation rather than integration, racial and religious conflict instead of universal ideals. We will not find a body of "Medievalization theory" backed by empirical research and expressed in social science jargon, but this approach to international politics never depended on evidence. Long before demographic trends turned against them, Europeans and Americans found reason to fear that their own decadence might invite the overthrow of Western civilization. From Hermann Knackfuss's famous painting *Die Gelbe Gefahr* through American "Yellow Peril" novels, nonwhites were imagined as a nameless, faceless mob crowding about the periphery.[104] By the 1930s, demographers had begun to provide data supporting the idea that Europeans and their progeny were increasingly outnumbered. In 1932, Oswald Spengler warned that "the battle for the planet has begun" amid a wave of anticolonialist unrest in East Asia, Africa, and the West Indies. He castigated Europeans for having given way to pacifism and infertility in the face of "a colored world-revolution."[105] Similarly, Paul Valéry was only the best known of a number of French writers who foresaw the relative decline of Europe, wondering whether it would "become *what it is in reality* — that is, a little promontory on the continent of Asia?"[106]

Cold War–era policymakers grew up in this period, so it should be no surprise that fear of population decline and international race war influenced them through the 1950s. But it did not necessarily run contrary to the idea of "development." The two were usually presented as alternatives. As John Foster Dulles told Robert Schuman in 1949, when Schuman was serving as foreign minister:

There are in Africa vast resources which can be developed to the natural advantage of Africa and West Europe and more than make good the loss of access to the natural resources of Eastern Europe and the loss of Asiatic colonies. This North-South development, however, requires friendly collaboration between the native peoples and the peoples of Europe. . . . If the Italian colonies were dealt with in a manner which excited a Moslem Holy War or race war of black against white, then the foundation of North-South development would disappear.[107]

Once he had become secretary of state, Dulles often reiterated this same hope and fear. Thus, in 1958, he said that North Africa was "to be considered as a kind of pool of raw materials for Western Europe like the Western states were for the thirteen colonies during the formation of our republic." But he warned that a confrontational policy undermined moderate nationalists and strengthened the extremists, leading to "grave dissension between the West and Islam."[108]

Of course, there was another side to the frontier. That same year another American official, George Allen, shortly to become director of the U.S. Information Agency, advised a French colleague to arm the *pieds noirs*. He explained that, in view of the history of the American West, this "would evoke sympathy for a white community settled for many generations in a non-European country, exposed to the attacks of the natives, who organize themselves for the defense of their hearths and homes."[109]

French leaders also thought of Algeria as a potential frontier in the positive as well as the negative sense. Jacques Soustelle, the governor-general, described the Sahara as "a little like the Far West, the opening towards the future, a hope for a country which had begun to be without hope."[110] Alternatively, Michel Debré, de Gaulle's first prime minister, argued in his investiture speech that without the French Algeria would become "a frontier between two hostile worlds."[111] Over the years, official propaganda displayed both aspects of the frontier, with France promising development and cooperation while an FLN victory portended anarchy and holy war.

While this analysis could conflict with an East-West, Cold War approach to international politics, French spokesmen reconciled the two by arguing that the Communists would take advantage of any disorder to turn NATO's flank from the south. Even so, they gave inordinate attention to China years before there was any evidence of its providing aid to the rebels. For instance, when army officers gave a briefing at Oxford on the threat to North Africa, their maps displayed arrows emanating from the Eastern bloc. But by far, the biggest arrow swept from the heart of China through India and the Middle East to point directly at Casablanca.[112]

Sometimes French officials were so serious about the Chinese that they appeared ridiculous—as when strategists illustrated Chinese subversion by plotting the path of their acrobatic team as it toured Africa, or when their consul in Hong Kong warned that they would have to "pay particular attention to the exodus toward Europe of pseudo students and Chinese chefs."[113] But even ridiculous ideas can have an influence, especially when they are entertained at the highest levels. Thus, in 1956, Prime Minister Guy Mollet told Henry Cabot Lodge that "the world hero to whom the people look for leadership was not any Algerian leader; nor was it Colonel Nasser nor was it Khrushchev. The man they talked about was Mao Tse-tung." The recent defeat in Indochina helps to explain this obsession, but the racial dimension clearly colored such thinking. Mollet went on to assert that "they looked to Mao Tse-tung as the man who had thrown out the white man." Similarly, France's representative in Rabat judged that, "Much more than Russia, which seems white and Western to them, it is China, yellow and Asian, that seduces maghrebans longing for decolonization."[114] The vision of an international race war or jihad was so compelling that the Soviets sometimes were left out of the picture.[115] The Quai d'Orsay's briefing book on Algeria—what they called their "bible"—characterized the rebellion as "pan-Islamic" and "pan-Arabic," a "furious wave of fanaticism and xenophobia" that was "one part of the fight of the peoples of Africa and Asia . . . against the West."[116]

The question of whether the Algerian conflict can indeed be characterized as a religious or racial war is complex and controversial. During the war, the FLN used Islamic names and symbols, in some instances rallying supporters with explicit appeals to their religiosity and even to their pride as a "pure and superior race."[117] In 1956, rebel commanders in the Aurès region called on fellow Muslims fighting with the French to quit this "army of infidels" and "heretics." While they were subsequently relieved, such appeals indicate how the struggle could be represented in religious terms.[118]

One would never suspect that some participants in the Algerian War saw it as a defense of Islam from the far more famous writings of Frantz Fanon. In *The Wretched of the Earth*, he instead described decolonization as a winner-takes-all race war. While this vision seized the imagination of some European intellectuals, his FLN colleagues considered it a losing strategy in a world still dominated by white powers.[119] Indeed, the editor of their official newspaper, *El Moudjahid*, once had to stop the presses to prevent publication of one of his more inflammatory pieces. The party organ could not have been more emphatic in rejecting the idea that they were waging jihad, much less race war: "Ours is an organized revolution—it is not an anarchic revolt. Ours is a national struggle to destroy an anarchic colonial regime—it is NOT a religious war. It represents a march forward in the historical path of human progress."[120] But to the extent that westerners conceived of the conflict as a jihad or race war, the French were probably hurt more than the Algerians. Raising the specter of an anarchic and implacably antiwestern North Africa could only undermine their argument that Algeria could be pacified, prosperous, and retained as an integral part of France.[121]

Appeals to white solidarity certainly did not win favor with key U.S. policymakers, who were inclined to distance themselves from their ally in colonial confrontations. When ordering a review of North African policy in July 1955, Dulles argued that the United States had to avoid alienating "the great mass of mankind which is non-white and non-European." The Americans were made to pay for the "sins" of their colonial allies, he later complained, along with their own racial problems at home, and were lumped in with "the whites." Dulles felt that this was more than a moral concern, but rather ". . . a very grave problem, and it affects our whole military-political strategy."[122]

Dulles did not credit French claims that the Communists were the cause of their troubles in North Africa, but he agreed that Moscow would back or at least benefit from a wider conflict.[123] After the seizure of the Suez Canal, he began to see Arab or Islamist nationalism as a serious threat in its own right and feared that Nasser might manipulate oil shipments to reduce Europe to dependency.[124] When the Joint Chiefs urged the preparation of contingency plans for using force to free the canal, Eisenhower did not rule out the option but dreaded that it would "array the world from Dakar to the Philippines against us."[125] The State Department even entertained the idea of a regional entente with the Soviets.[126] Toward the end of his presidency, Eisenhower sometimes appeared ambivalent as to whether or not the Third World might ultimately pose the greatest threat to American security. "We have had a narrower view than we should have," he told his National Security Council. "The real menace here was the one and a half billion hungry people in the world."[127]

The evidence on French and American anxiety about the Third World relative to fear of the Soviets is ambiguous. For one thing, the two concerns were not mutually exclusive. In both countries, the worst-case scenario was always an international lineup pitting "the West against the rest," with Moscow in the lead. Moreover, as a 1959 congressional report on foreign aid noted, "[T]he simple assumption that communism flows from poverty is so widely accepted in America that it is almost an article of faith."[128] So concern about Third World poverty and population growth—even when it was given higher priority than the direct confrontation with the Soviets—could be reconciled with a conventional, zero-sum game approach to the Cold War. But others were convinced that the Cold War coalitions would break down along racial lines. In a 1958 meeting with Chancellor Konrad Adenauer that renewed the Franco-German entente, Charles de Gaulle explained that it had to be extended to include Russia: "We know that the true danger is Asia," he explained, which was "all the more reason to revive Europe."[129]

The Algerian War was part of this ongoing process by which "the West" is constructed, its members counted, its borders patrolled. Consider, for instance, how in 1956 the French ambassador described for the foreign minister of Spain, which was then seeking entry to NATO, the choice it faced at the United Nation between "the countries of the Near

East and the Maghreb [and] those of the Atlantic Alliance." The question, he said, "was whether a Christian, Western power would give its moral support to the independence movement in Algeria. She would then isolate herself completely from the Western nations."[130] Three years later, Francisco Franco finally pledged support for "the cause of Western civilization."[131]

Clearly, Africa no longer began at the Pyrenees, but it was becoming ever more doubtful that France extended to Algeria—or that Muslims would always have entrée to Europe. French officials had already begun to assist German border control officers in identifying Algerian Muslims to discourage them from entering, deny them asylum, and obtain their fingerprints and photographs.[132] De Gaulle himself could not imagine how they could be part of the *patrie*. "These people are different from us," he told a Gaullist deputy. "Do you see yourself marrying our daughters with Arabs?"[133] Before the war, one of the French administrators had actually suggested, "very shyly. . . . a policy of mixed marriages."[134] But in 1959, de Gaulle thought the question was too absurd to warrant an answer. Instead, France had to "marry her time," as he declared in a speech which called for an *Algérie algérienne*.[135] While this was hailed as a progressive statement at the time, few seemed to grasp its logical counterpart: *une France française*.

The contemporary relevance of these issues will be addressed in the conclusion to this book, but the intellectual dimensions of the war will continue to unfold through the narrative. Since the FLN could not physically control territory, the basis for their claim to sovereignty was abstract: it rested in peoples' estimations of their legitimacy as the rightful rulers—not just people in Algeria, but in France, the United States, and anywhere else influence could be brought to bear on the course of events. In a very real sense, one of the most important battles in the Algerian War was waged in the realm of ideas. Its ultimate outcome is still uncertain.

2

The Ambivalence of Power

North Africa in International Politics, 1942–1954

The isolation has lasted too long.
The party that has the heavy responsibility of liberating Algeria
must break this isolation . . . This is an imperative, essential at this deci-
sive stage of preparation, which will make our revolutionary strategy one
of expansion and of opening onto the world.

Hocine Aït Ahmed, 1948 [1]

It is no secret that there is a vast conspiracy joining the religious
fanaticism and xenophobia of the Middle East with the anti-colonialist
ideology of America which seeks to ruin our position in North Africa. . . .
To round this dangerous cape it will be necessary to have a government
in Paris fiercely resolved to defend our imperial possessions foot by foot.

Général Alphonse Juin, 1951 [2]

Before dawn on November 8, 1942, three convoys consisting of more than five hundred American and British warships and transports closed on the coasts of Algeria and Morocco. Two Royal Navy destroyers carrying a mixed force of British and American commandos separated from the easternmost group and headed for the Bay of Algiers. Just after midnight, President Roosevelt's personal representative, Robert Murphy, had warned the French commander, Alphonse Juin, that he faced overwhelming odds. The armada carried nearly 10,000 vehicles and 100,000 allied servicemen, with another 150,000 on the way. But Murphy and General Dwight Eisenhower, the Allied supreme commander, assured the French that America had no designs on their North African possessions. "We come among you solely to defeat and rout your enemies," Roosevelt had declared in a radio speech to the French people. "Have faith in our words. We do not want to cause you any harm."[3]

The planners of "Operation Torch" had reason to be cautious. In July 1940, the Royal Navy had attacked the French fleet at Mers el-Kebir, fearing that it would fall into the hands of the Axis. It was hoped that what was made to look like a purely American force would not encounter any resistance. But as the first two British destroyers flying extra-large U.S. flags neared Algiers's harbor, the city lights went out and intense fire opened up, eventually forcing both to withdraw. In Oran, 270 miles to the west, two Royal Navy cutters supplemented the Stars and Stripes with loudspeakers proclaiming their friendly intentions. But the French defenders greeted them with point-blank fire from destroyers and shore batteries; almost 90 percent of an American attack force crowding the decks were killed or wounded. In Morocco, the U.S. destroyer-transport *Bernadou* encountered everything from rifle shot to 155-mm. shells as it entered the port of Safi. "A flare with American flag attached was released above the harbor in the hope of moderating the hostile reception," according to the official history. "For a brief period it assisted the French gun pointers but had no other effect." French sympathizers vainly attempted to seize control and separate the opposing sides. But in the end Eisenhower felt compelled to make a deal with the Vichy authorities, allowing them to continue administering North Africa.

Further adding to the confusion was a factor that no one had anticipated. "Almost from the first," the same official history notes, "civilian natives became a problem to the attacking troops."

> They gathered in awed crowds to observe the naval shelling; they were disdainfully unafraid of small arms fire. A soldier would snake his way painfully through rocks and rubble to set up a light machine gun, raise his head cautiously to aim, and find a dozen natives clustered solemnly around him.

Thus, ordinary North Africans discovered that they inhabited one of the most strategically vital areas in the world, a crucible of conflict between the Allies and Axis and among the different factions fighting over France's future. From here, Allied forces outflanked Rommel's threat to the Middle East, launched air attacks against Europe, and eventually unleashed invasions of Italy and France. By that point, Charles de Gaulle had used the region as a base to establish his authority and regain French autonomy. But the first hours of the Torch landings foreshadowed years of continuing international contention over North Africa. In the postwar period, the region remained of strategic importance, though political and economic considerations gradually came to outweigh its military utility. In later interventions, the Americans and British continued to claim to be working for France's own best interests—often while hiding behind each other—and continued to confront division and hostility. As president, Eisenhower would still see a trade-off between American values and interests in the question of who would lead France, and the answer would once again emerge from North Africa. Though the North Africans themselves were at first spectators in these conflicts, "turning their heads like a tennis gallery in trying to watch the exchange of fire," they soon became active participants, exploiting the divisions between France and its allies to pursue their own agendas.[4]

Many of the people who crossed paths in Algeria during the war went on to wield power in its aftermath, including Eisenhower, de Gaulle, Juin, Murphy, and his British counterpart, Harold Macmillan. None of them forgot their earlier experiences, and some harbored grievances. Fifteen years after Torch, the French still remembered and distrusted Murphy for having favored Vichy over de Gaulle.[5] Nearly twenty years after Ferhat Abbas addressed a "Message to the Responsible Authorities"—that is, the Anglo-American High Command, bypassing the French government to demand a Muslim assembly—de Gaulle had still not forgiven him and preferred other FLN interlocutors, even though they were more intransigent.[6] And illiterate Algerian peasants, though unable to give a child's date of birth, could count the years "after the Americans," so impressed were they by the might and material wealth of the invaders—which made the colonial authorities seem impotent by comparison—even if they could not read the emancipatory declarations of the Atlantic Charter.[7]

Chapter 1 alluded to other international events that impinged on Algeria in the context of the global demographic, economic, cultural, and technological trends undermining imperialism as a whole. Some of them favored or foreshadowed its independence struggle, including Egyptian aid to North African nationalists and France's defeat in Indochina. Yet the international context was also a source of difficulties and disappointments. After all, the allies ignored Abbas's demands and relied on the French to maintain stability; the Egyptians promised much more than they delivered; and the French army was *not* destroyed in Indochina—indeed, it emerged as a far more capable and determined counterinsurgency force.[8]

Thus, the Algerians chose to do battle in an international arena that included both dangers and opportunities. This chapter will set the stage and introduce some of the other protagonists, which requires turning the spotlight on Algeria's "wings," as Morocco and Tunisia were sometimes called. Although everyone, even the Arab League, distinguished between France's Algerian *départements* and the protectorates, their independence came to be seen as a precedent, and the two states were important players throughout the conflict.[9] As for the British and the Soviets, before the outbreak of the Algerian War neither was inclined to interfere with France's control of North Africa.[10] But the United States possessed both the means and the motives to intervene in France's empire as well as its domestic affairs. As in the French-Algerian relationship—and as this chapter will explain—tighter integration caused influence to flow both ways. Some Americans also sought to empower an integrated Europe and a "strongman" in France, even if both would be more independent of the United States. Finally, nonstate and international actors exerted significant influence, including American businesses, international labor organizations, and the Afro-Asian bloc in the United Nations. This chapter describes North Africa in relation to the great powers, especially the United States, and "power politics," but its principal theme throughout will be the *ambivalence* of power, both in the sense of the conflicted attitudes of those who wielded it and the ramified ways in which it worked.

North Africa in the Early Cold War

As North Africans began to think of themselves as part of a global anticolonialist movement and attempted to coordinate their actions, they confronted a system of states, already in place, with its own interests, its own rules, and a still exclusive membership. After World War II, the region figured in great power diplomacy in three ways: for its importance to France, weakened by the war but still perceived as essential to the construction of a new European order; for raw materials—though initially less in the region itself than in Arab states to the East, where oil reserves guaranteed them a hearing in advocating the nationalist cause; and for its strategic position adjacent to Europe, which made it a base of operations and potential front line if the continent fell to the Soviets. But the nature and extent of North Africa's importance in international politics at any given time was determined by other considerations, simple in themselves but complex in combination, which complete this analytical framework.

First, the three aspects of North Africa's strategic importance were interrelated. From the perspective of American planners, compliance with Arab states' demands on Algeria might help ensure the availability of Middle Eastern oil for Europe but only at the cost of jeopardizing French cooperation on the continent. On the other hand, endorsing French policy not only exacerbated relations with the Arab states but also endangered U.S. bases in Morocco. Each was an important interest without which the others appeared insufficient to guarantee American security. Reconciling them, however, proved to be an insuperable task.

While the Soviets did not have vital interests in North Africa, after 1955 they faced a similar dilemma in attempting to balance support for French Communists and French independence from Washington on the one hand with their increasing solicitude for Arab nationalists on the other. The British, for their part, first conciliated the French out of concern for the future of their own African colonies and then came to rue the effect on relations with their Arab clients. But by the late 1950s, obtaining de Gaulle's cooperation in forging a new economic relationship with Europe overshadowed Britain's interests in Africa and the Middle East—indeed, it even began to trouble the "special relationship" with the United States. A country like West Germany, on the other hand, did not have global interests—except perhaps for the competition for recognition with their Communist rivals—and always used North African issues instrumentally to improve relations with France.[11]

As these cases indicate, North Africa's importance in great power diplomacy changed over time. The region's location ensured that it was always a factor in European defense planning, but the American interest alternated between exploiting it as both a fallback position and platform for air power to merely denying it to the Soviets. Similarly, the discovery of vast oil and natural gas reserves in Algeria in 1956 promised France energy self-sufficiency at the very time its dependency on foreign sources made it vulnerable to manipulation.[12] For American oil companies, on the other hand, new discoveries in Libya two years later had to be concealed to avoid further glutting the global energy market.[13] Thus, the great powers approached war in Algeria with an array of interrelated, conflicting, and shifting interests.

Determining the fate of Libya, formerly an Italian colony, was the first postwar problem in North Africa to attract their attention. At the Potsdam conference, the Soviets demanded a trusteeship, sparking American and British suspicions about their intentions in Africa and the Middle East.[14] But the Soviets raised the demand to acquire a bargaining chip for bases on the Dardanelles.[15] In this period, they were far more concerned with their position in Europe than with the Third World and eventually supported Italy's desire to regain control of its former colony. The British were also careful to appease Italian sentiment, but they sought a trusteeship in eastern Libya as a backup for their increasingly vulnerable base at Suez. The French, for their part, wished to continue their occupation of Fezzan, the southwestern third of the country, to interdict clandestine arms shipments to Algeria. They also feared that Libyan independence might set off a chain reaction across North Africa.[16]

But in May 1949, Libyans rioted against a plan that prescribed a partition between Italian, British, and French trusteeships, encouraging the U.N. General Assembly to defeat it by a single vote.[17] The British foreign secretary, Ernest Bevin, recognized the emergence of an "Arab-Moslem-Asiatic bloc," and Libya has since been called "the child of the United Nations." But London then worked with the U.N. commissioner and against the Arab League to make the new state a loose federation that would be amenable to their wishes and American aid (the United States operated a base, Wheelus Field, east of Tripoli). Thus, while Libya was the first country in Africa to emerge from formal colonial rule in the postwar period—with the United Nations and the Libyan people themselves active in the process—it was also the first of many to pass under more *informal* methods of imperial management that had been revived from an earlier era to suit anticolonial sensibilities.[18]

The French had their own tradition of indirect rule in North Africa exemplified by the legendary Maréchal Lyautey's administration of Morocco. Consistent with the spirit if not the letter of the maréchal's record, it was not the sultan in Rabat or the bey in Tunis who enjoyed the most autonomy but France's own *résidents généraux*. Yet unlike Lyautey, they tended after the war to serve short terms and often became captives of their own administrations, which were staffed largely by local settlers. The more than 325,000 Europeans in Morocco and 240,000 in Tunisia also had considerable influence in Paris. French policies in the two protectorates were therefore contradictory and inconsistent, resulting from perpetual conflict between the settlers, *résidents généraux*, and their nominal superiors at the Quai d'Orsay. Whereas from 1947 to 1951, relatively liberal *résidents généraux* in Tunisia attempted to come to terms with the nationalist Neo Destour (New Constitution) party, Général Juin in Morocco—himself a pied noir—moved toward a confrontation with the Istiqlal (Independence) party, Sultan Mohammed V, and the Quai itself. At the same time, administrators in Algeria undermined even the modest reforms passed in Paris by stuffing the ballots for their Muslim protégés. As the former foreign minister, Robert Schuman, wrote in 1953, beyond simply hanging on and muddling through, there *was* no overall French policy in North Africa. Politicians merely reacted to the pressures of domestic constituencies, North African nationalists and, not least, outside powers.[19]

Luckily for the French, for most of the intervening period the nationalists were themselves divided and did not receive effective aid from the Arab League, which might have seemed to be their most natural backer abroad. When representatives from the Neo Destour, Istiqlal, and PPA convened a congress in Cairo in February 1947, the league's secretary general, Abd al-Rahman Azzam, pledged solidarity with their struggle. But he refused to bring it before the United Nations out of deference to France and a desire to concentrate on Palestine. Moreover, the member states contributed little to the new Bureau of the Arab Maghreb, made up of representatives of each party, which struggled to maintain offices around the region and in the United States as well. The nationalist front broke down for lack of funds and differences in strategy—the Neo Destour was willing to pursue independence in stages rather than as a precondition for negotiations.[20] Yet in the years ahead, they were clever enough to exaggerate their unity and league support, leading the French to attribute more strength and purpose to pan-Arabism than it actually possessed.

North Africans sought support simultaneously from the West, as shown in the aftermath of a clash between Moroccans and French colonial troops in April 1947. The sultan traveled to Tangier and, in a defiant speech before a large crowd of Moroccans, reaffirmed his country's attachment to Islam and hailed the Arab League without rendering the customary tribute to the protectorate. In the same visit, Princess Aisha, speaking partly in English before a more international audience, called for closer contact with Western civilization. In succeeding years, she came to represent the emancipation of Moroccan women and continued to appeal to Western audiences.[21]

In fact, the French rightly viewed the Americans as the main threat.[22] Two months after the Tangier visit, Secretary of State George C. Marshall ordered the American ambassador, Jefferson Caffery, to urge evolution toward "[d]ominion status within [the] French Union" to avoid a "situation in North Africa comparable to . . . Indo-China."[23] Caffery was reluctant to carry out this démarche, and when he finally talked to the secretary-general of the Quai d'Orsay, Jean Chauvel, he first assured him that "the United States government has never been more favorably inclined towards you." Indeed, that same week sixteen European delegations were meeting in Paris in response to Marshall's plan for European recovery. Caffery declared that the United States could not take their place in North Africa and did not want to try. "We therefore wish that you hold on," he continued, "but we are worried. We fear that . . . through attachment to outmoded colonialist formulas you will get yourselves kicked out. We know well enough what to think of certain internal liberties and of 'self-government.' But you have to give people the feeling that they are included."[24]

Caffery concluded with a brusque and breathtaking warning:

> Indochina interests us greatly, and we do not have a good opinion of what you are doing there and how it will all end. But we are much more interested in North Africa. Understand me well. If the conference [in Paris on the Marshall Plan] fails, Europe will be lost and it will be a great pity. But in no case will we allow the adversary to cross the oil line, which runs through North Africa.

By signaling that American backing was contingent on improved relations with the nationalists—based on British-style informal imperialism and less than full independence—Marshall and Caffery laid down the main line of a "middle-of-the-road" policy that the first Eisenhower administration would also follow. They had also raised the specter that would haunt all of their successors: "another Indochina."[25]

This new line was a victory for the State Department's Office of African Affairs in its long and usually losing battle with the European Bureau. Yet the deliberations of American diplomatic and consular agents who were meeting in Paris at the time reveal that the policy did not arise solely from the need to conciliate Arab opinion. They also thought that self-government for the protectorates—at this point no one dared to suggest self-government for Algeria—would actually strengthen France since it would ensure continued access to their natural resources over the long term.[26] Indeed, Colonel Charles H. Bonesteel, one of the "apostles" of European unification, had been arguing that developing the potential wealth of North Africa could help forge European unity and form the basis for continental recovery.[27] The following year the State Department's Policy Planning Staff studied a proposal for the Western European countries to pool their capital and colonies in Africa in a vast development scheme. "It would lend to the idea of Western European union that tangible objective for which everyone has been rather unsuccessfully groping in recent months," George Kennan suggested.[28]

In pushing a more united Europe—united *against* Soviet aggression and *for* African development—the State Department was as concerned about a nationalist dictator coming to power in Paris as by a Communist takeover.[29] De Gaulle's record of independence and opposition to German autonomy indicated that either one might advance Moscow's interests. Alternatively, France was seen as the leader of an economically integrated Europe, including West Germany, that would be fueled by Persian Gulf oil, free of debilitating colonial conflicts, and willing and able to face up to the Soviets.

Yet some important French political leaders rejected the very idea of developing cooperative relations with North African nationalists. Foreign Minister Georges Bidault, for instance, responded to Caffery's démarche by demanding a dossier from the Interior Ministry to demonstrate "the true character of the resistance that we meet from the nationalist elements . . . who mask under demagogic claims their racist and confessional prejudices and their desire to return to the most archaic forms of oriental despotism."[30] Yet many French agreed with the Americans on the desirability of North African development and some measure of self-government. Officials like Jean Monnet at the *Commissariat au Plan* saw modernizing the Maghreb and more closely integrating it with the metropole as a means to reassert and make real France's putative status as a great power. But, for that reason, they were not initially interested in broader European participation and fought American efforts to open up the Moroccan market.[31] Similarly, some of Bidault's subordinates in the Quai d'Orsay favored self-government in the sense that they hoped to enlist Istiqlal and Neo Destour support for administrative reforms. While North Africans might have gained greater participation in local government, the price would have been tighter integration within the French Union, postponing independence indefinitely. The nationalists' awareness of U.S. interest encouraged them to hold out for more, which helped to make the amicable settlement demanded by Americans impossible for France to achieve.[32]

Though the documentary evidence available from the North African side in this period is too scarce to be anything but suggestive, it is consistent on two points: the nationalists indeed felt themselves to be part of a global struggle against Western rule, sometimes defined in racial and religious terms. Yet they also recognized that playing on the divisions among the Western allies was the most practical strategy, especially since they could not maintain solidarity among themselves, let alone with the entire Afro-Asian world. For instance, in a July 1946 letter, Habib Bourguiba, leader of the Neo Destour in Tunisia, all but called Ferhat Abbas a traitor for his willingness to accept mere autonomy. Bourguiba, like Abbas, was known for his affinity for France, but they were now facing a Hobson's choice: "to submit and dissolve into [*se fondre*] the French nation, or insurrection until crushed leading sooner or later to a forced and inescapable fusion." But "times have changed," Bourguiba continued, "peoples of all races and all colors are rising up in an irresistible movement against the domination of the whites." In particular, the movement toward Arab unity had reversed the progress of assimilation in North Africa: "Despite the iron barrier raised by France around the Maghreb, the influence of the Arab League—thanks to the radio and clandestine infiltrations—becomes more visible each day." But Bourguiba made clear that he did not have the "naïveté" to think the Arabs of the Middle East would enter the fight against the French. Instead, their attitude was most valuable for its importance to the British and the Americans, who were increasingly preoccupied by the possibility of war against the Soviets:

> North Africa is one of the best [assets] in the eyes of the Anglo-Saxon world: key to the central Mediterranean and an ideal base of operations against a Europe on its way to Bolshevization. It is not therefore for our beautiful eyes that the Anglo-Saxons interest themselves more and more in our fate.[33]

Abbas's rivals in the PPA were less interested in allying with the Americans and the British than playing them off against the Soviets and against each other. In August 1948, the head of the PPA's paramilitary wing, the *Organisation Spéciale*, wrote a report on the tactics and strategy of a war for independence following the fraudulent elections earlier that year. Hocine Aït Ahmed, only twenty-seven at the time, analyzed earlier rebellions and examples from abroad before concluding that no other people had confronted so many obstacles to their independence: proximity to the metropole, disparity in population, exposed terrain, and so on. Above all, none had had to deal with such a sizable and politically powerful settler population.[34]

Aït Ahmed therefore prescribed nothing less than *une grande stratégie* for the coming war, relating finances, logistics, morale, propaganda, and foreign policy, a strategy that was all the more impressive in that it was resolutely pragmatic. While he recognized that Islam would be "a mobilizing factor" and that Algerians should seek to unify the Afro-Asian world, he argued that their foreign policy should be independent and eminently flexible: "placing the good on one side and the bad on the other would be to ignore the complexity and ambiguity of elements that determine the interest of each country or group of countries." Aït Ahmed would have the nationalists seek a balance between East and West: "Our strategy will follow this guideline in diplomatic matters: When we intend to put on our side of the scale an act of support from a Socialist country we will think at the same time of removing from the colonial side of the scale the weight of Western support." They would do so, he specified, by exploiting the area's strategic importance, British-French imperial rivalries, and the U.S.-European commercial competition. In December the party's Central Committee approved the report with near unanimity.[35]

Under de Gaulle, France had also sought greater independence by striking a balance between the Soviets and the Americans. But in January 1948, Foreign Minister Georges Bidault and Minister of War Pierre-

Henri Teitgen declared to a U.S. delegation that Paris had made its "final choice" in favor of the West. Even so, they were concerned about a "fear complex" that might sap "the very strength of the Western European peoples." They feared that,

> [s]hould war break out, the United States will abandon Western Europe to the Soviets; that the Russian hordes will occupy the area, raping women and deporting the male population for slave labor in the Soviet Union; that France and Western Europe will be occupied and devastated by the Soviet hordes and atomized by the United States.

At this time, memories of how Eastern Europe had been occupied by rapacious "Soviet hordes," including soldiers from the Central Asian republics, were still fresh, so the racial subtext of this scenario was apparent even before Bidault and Teitgen went on to describe the postwar world.[36] Europe would be "completely devastated and depopulated," they continued. "There would be no Western European civilization or population to share with the United States the task of reconstruction. In other words the United States after its victory would have only Asiatics and African and colonial natives with whom to cooperate in the task of world reconstruction."[37] The fall of China the following year and the simultaneous wars in Indochina and Korea made it easier to conceive of the Western alliance in terms of white solidarity. But such statements show how the French were already seeking to define "the West" not only against the East, but against "Asiatics and African and colonial natives" as well.

The emotionalism of the French appeal might be dismissed as histrionics. "Nobody took little Bidault seriously," one high-ranking State Department official later recalled. Recurrent cabinet crises did not help French credibility. How, the Americans might have asked, could they be sure that France "had made its final choice. . . . even if," as Bidault and Teitgen put it, they "were not in the Government tomorrow"? In fact, they were gone by July. But in the meantime, the February 1948 Czech coup and the Berlin airlift four months later touched off a genuine war scare affecting French society as a whole.[38]

During this period, U.S. strategists indeed held out little hope of a forward defense of the continent. Instead, they imagined World War III much like the last war. Allied forces would be driven from the continent in a matter of months, if not weeks. The United States would then mobilize for total war, conduct a lengthy atomic and conventional bombing campaign, and finally invade and occupy what little remained.[39] According to the December 1949 "Offtackle" plan—and just as Bidault feared—North Africa, not France, would be "the initial assembly area for U.S. forces."[40]

On the face of it, the French were in a pitiable position, seemingly unable to defend themselves, let alone North Africa. The Americans did agree to military aid and eventually a full-fledged alliance, with NATO's earliest war plans calling for a last-ditch defense of the Rhine. But privately, some U.S. officials considered such plans to be "pump-primers for European effort" and "Strictly for Show Windows."[41] Moreover, in exchange the French had had to agree to the emergence of a centralized West German state. The Americans also conditioned economic assistance on an austerity program that provoked a backlash against perceived interference in France's domestic affairs.[42]

Yet the power relationship between France and the United States was more ambiguous than it would first appear. Officials like Jean Monnet and politicians such as René Mayer and Henri Queuille favored austerity as a means eventually to restore French power, even if they used the promise of American aid, and the threat to withhold it, to gain parliamentary approval.[43] And as the Bidault-Teitgen presentation suggests, the French could use the precariousness of their position vis-à-vis their own public to secure better conditions.[44] They could also hold up American initiatives, even ones that they had themselves invited, until they incorporated their desiderata. Thus, in 1949 they blocked Norway's inclusion in the North Atlantic Treaty until their Algerian *départements* were also covered.[45] And once Washington pledged to defend Europe, the "iron law of alliance politics" came into effect: The more America was committed, the less the European allies had to do for themselves—indeed, the more they could demand for the "privilege" of defending them.[46]

An Entangling Alliance

"Is war inevitable?" This was the question George Butler of the State Department Policy Planning Staff posed in June 1949. He was taken aback by a Joint Chiefs of Staff proposal to establish air and naval bases all along the Eurasian periphery, with the sites in North Africa being "especially urgent."[47] At the time, the U.S. deterrent consisted almost entirely of medium-range bombers with little aerial-refueling capability. But the State Department resisted the Pentagon's demands, realizing that the allies would demand aid in exchange for bases in bilateral negotiations.[48] "If war is not believed to be imminent, in the sense of the next two or three or four years," Butler wrote, "we are faced with an essentially political problem and political factors should receive primary emphasis."[49]

Later that month, the Soviets exploded their first atomic bomb. The Americans feared that bases in Britain might be "Pearl Harbored" at the outset of hostilities while the Suez complex would eventually be overrun.[50] The vulnerability of the U.S. deterrent became all the more troubling after the North Korean invasion in the summer of 1950. The subsequent Chinese intervention made general war indeed seem inevitable, perhaps imminent. Just as importantly, the ensuing summit between Harry Truman and Clement Attlee revealed the political risks of relying on Britain and its base at Suez as the main staging areas for strikes on the Soviets. The Americans realized that their hosts held a virtual right of veto over the actual or threatened use of the bomb. As the Chinese began to cross the Yalu River in force and a worried Attlee urged Truman to back off atomic diplomacy, the United States concluded an agreement with France for four Strategic Air Command (SAC) bases and a port and naval air station in Morocco.[51]

The British were not the only ones to see the political leverage conferred by America's "servitude to bases"—as a Quai memorandum had already described it.[52] If U.S. bases posed a threat to French control of North Africa and, in the event of war, France's own physical safety, they also presented an opportunity to secure U.S. support for the protectorates and a measure of control over the American deterrent.

In July 1950, Ambassador Henri Bonnet advised Paris of what he called "a change of spirit and a new understanding" among the Americans. A month before, the assistant secretary of state for the United Nations, John Hickerson, had distanced the U.S. from anticolonialism at the U.N., admitting that the Americans were themselves not blameless. Yet Bonnet well understood that this was hardly a change of heart. In a telegram to Foreign Minister Robert Schuman, he noted that anticolonialism was still anchored in the American psyche and explained the shift as due entirely to strategic considerations. These would surely change with time, he argued, and in the meantime France would have to work for "the economic and social development of Africa." Just as importantly, representatives would have to explain French policies to the Americans to win their genuine support.[53]

In writing these lines, Bonnet might have been thinking of a speech given the previous month by the Republican senator from Nevada, George Malone, who complained that the United States had "sunk into the filthy business of bolstering colonial slavery." Malone had been informed by a letter from the Committee for the Freedom of North Africa, the New York office of the Bureau of the Arab Maghreb, accusing the settlers of misusing Marshall Plan money. Nearly a tenth of the French allocation went to the Maghreb. "The French are operating a police state in North Africa," Malone thundered. Assistant Secretary of State George McGhee answered the charge by arguing that the United States had to work with its allies against the Soviet threat to Africa.[54]

Bonnet had high hopes for McGhee, but he thought that it would take a considerable effort to instruct Americans about France's role in Africa: "One must not forget . . . that American education in African affairs has long been neglected and one runs the risk, in discussing the problems at too elevated a level, of losing all but a very small part of the audience." Indeed, McGhee's very title, assistant secretary of state for Near Eastern, South Asian, and African affairs, indicates the amount of attention the State Department had until then devoted to these parts of the world.[55] But as the Americans became more involved, the French would continue to assert that only they *knew* the Africans, an argument that was already familiar to Americans from domestic debates over race relations. The French could also point out that America's own record on these matters was not beyond reproach. The hard-line French governor general of Algeria, Marcel-Edmond Naegelen, warned that if the French gave way "other races would come who have not [the] breadth of spirit of France so far as religion, race, color, skin or freedom of opinion are concerned." Speaking sarcastically of Algerian nationalists, Naegelen suggested that they might prefer a regime "under which classes in railway cars would be [a] function of skin pigment."[56]

Thus, French officials had a protective, even proprietary attitude toward their colonial charges which conceded nothing to American pretensions to be an emancipatory power. Their *hauteur*, and the Americans' temporary obeisance to it, comes out in a January 1951 Washington meeting between Juin and McGhee. Juin had just delivered an ultimatum demanding that the sultan dismiss the Istiqlal's nationalist ministers from his cabinet and allow direct French participation in his government. The *général* said that he planned to "go back and settle this matter . . . and if the Sultan does not like it he (the Sultan) must go," despite the fact that the French recognized him as sovereign.[57] McGhee, for his part, acknowledged French authority over the North Africans by expressing "how glad we are that the Moroccan situation is in such good hands." As for the nationalists, he assured Juin that "we try to be polite with them while at the same time having confidence that the French can control the situation."[58]

But McGhee was hardly confident, and he did not support the French because of the political and economic programs with which Ambassador Bonnet hoped to impress him. Indeed, he told his staff that the French protectorates and Algeria were "anachronisms." McGhee's instructions to them reveal the crux of America's North African policy at the outset of the Korean War:

> In light of the present world situation, we must have . . . stability in this area against the possibility of military operations. . . . Accordingly, we cannot adopt an independent policy with respect to North Africa, nor intervene between the French and the Arab peoples. . . . [This] is no time in which to experiment in this regard . . . [I]t is always possible that the situation in North Africa may blow up in time. It is our hope that it will not do so in this critical period.[59]

The new American policy on North Africa was part of a more general shift in American strategy to back the European empires and South Africa. Almost everywhere they confronted the same dilemma: resistance to change threatened to drive Third World nationalists toward the Soviets and to waste resources that might have strengthened European reconstruction. On the other hand, policymakers feared that either chaos or communism would result from "premature" independence and judged that the European economies depended on the colonies. While one can criticize their developmentalist assumptions, a pronationalist policy would have risked relations with their most important allies at a time when war with the Soviets appeared to be a near-term possibility. Instead, U.S. support shored up the French empire in Indochina and North Africa as well as the British sphere of influence in the Middle East.[60] But by virtue of their assistance, the Americans could claim a say in their ally's affairs. In the case of North Africa, McGhee warned Juin against any "arbitrary action," such as deposing the sultan, and the *général* agreed to inform ben Youssef of the base agreement.[61]

But could the Americans trust their allies to be loyal "subimperialists"? Two days after the McGhee-Juin conversation, the general manager of the Coca-Cola franchise in Casablanca, Kenneth Pendar, walked into the State Department to warn that they were "making a very grave mistake." He said that, "since our military program in Morocco would render the French Protectorate one of the prime military targets in the world, he believed that it was unthinkable that the Government of the United States . . . should not undertake to inform the Sovereign of Morocco of our plans." In the long run, it was crucial that the United States maintain good relations with the sultan. Told that the French were to inform him of the bases, Pendar warned that they "could not be trusted."[62]

And he was right, for the French did not inform the sultan. Nor would they ever inform him.[63] Consequently, he considered the base agreement to be illegitimate—a fact which the French did not hesitate to bring up to the Americans, pointedly comparing it to Egypt's efforts to evict the British from Suez.[64] By interposing themselves between the indigenous population and U.S. power, they gave the Americans a compelling reason to maintain their support: the base agreements were valid only as long as the French were willing and able to uphold them. This was part of a general policy of preventing direct contact between the Americans and colonial peoples, whether army advisors in Vietnam or Marshall Plan administrators in Tunisia, through which the French protected their position and empowered themselves.[65]

As the McGhee-Juin conversation indicates, the Americans preferred the role of silent partner in France's North African policy. By selling stock in their enterprise, the French ensured that the United States had a stake in continued stability. But with their new investment, the Americans had also acquired voting rights and, when it fell into jeopardy, they were prepared to exercise them. While still partners, they would not remain silent.[66] When Juin returned to Morocco and his final showdown with the sultan, the Americans warned officials at the Quai d'Orsay that they would deny reports of their backing his abdication and would disassociate themselves from such action at the United Nations. The cabinet of René Pleven took these warnings to heart and Schuman cautioned Juin against threatening the sultan.[67]

Yet Juin had other plans. On February 25, he encouraged Berber tribesmen loyal to the Pasha of Marrakech to ride down from the mountains and surround Rabat. With horsemen nearing the gates of the palace, the sultan capitulated to most of his demands. But at this point, Juin would be satisfied with nothing less than his abdication, and in this *le général* would be bitterly disappointed. That very day, an envoy arrived from Paris renewing the Pleven cabinet's opposition to Juin's plan. "Should one have let [the abdication] happen?. . . . I admit that for a moment I hesitated . . . ," Juin admitted to Schuman, "but I was not raised to disobey and the instinct of discipline prevailed." He consoled himself by observing that the crisis had, at least, "given certain foreign chancelleries who meddle too much in our affairs something to think about."[68]

Once considered "rabidly pro-American" on defense matters, Juin now set a strict limit to the number of U.S. personnel he would allow on the bases. He also backed an initiative to establish a North African strategic command in time of war and threatened to resign if any troops were withdrawn from the region to reinforce Indochina.[69] With these peacetime preparations, he intended to ensure that France would retain control of North Africa if the metropole was overrun. Though France lacked its own A-bombs, the French base commanders and security troops mandated by the agreement would afford a measure of control over America's and protect national interests. Thus, Juin's position was not simply the army's death grip on French *grandeur;* instead it was a sophisticated reading of France's strategic situation and a shrewd plan for improving it. More generally, he had demonstrated how even such seemingly straightforward instruments of "power projection" as strategic air bases could actually empower a weaker party.[70]

Yet Schuman was wary of pushing the Americans too far. He insisted that Juin "take into account the importance and the vulnerability of our international positions." "We have an interest in avoiding all that may legitimately trouble our friends abroad," he said, adding that only the government could judge the whole of France's global responsibilities and the place of Morocco among them. The French were then engaged in difficult negotiations with the United States over aid to meet a budget deficit and the costs of the Indochina conflict while at the same time coming under pressure to acquiesce in German membership in NATO.[71]

The Americans were increasingly insistent that Juin relinquish his post in Morocco to take command of NATO's central theater. He finally did so in August 1951 on the condition that he could name his successor.[72] Meanwhile, the June 1951 elections strengthened the Gaullists, making it all the more difficult for the foreign minister to pursue the conciliatory policy he would have preferred. He still had the thankless task of soliciting more forthright support from the Americans for actions that were increasingly at odds with their stated preferences.

In September 1951, Schuman asked Secretary of State Dean Acheson for an exchange of notes in which the United States would publicly endorse French policy in North Africa, something that the State Department feared would amount to a "blank check" for repression. From that day forward, the French continually demanded this blank check to cover

America's existing debt in Morocco as well as any increase in force levels or new bases in Algeria and Tunisia. Acheson resisted the French request and continued to urge a more liberal policy. But, as he later described it, "I made an understandable but possibly the worst decision—to push Schuman hard enough to annoy but not hard enough to succeed"—a fatal defect in the "middle-of-the-road" strategy that also bedeviled Eisenhower and Dulles.[73]

If the Americans refused to write a blank check, they were already highly exposed. Two of the SAC airfields had gone into operation that July.[74] As the NSC policy paper for Morocco concluded in November 1951, "the strategic importance of this area to this government has been greatly enhanced," but so had local nationalism, "in direct ratio." While the United States would continue to work toward a resolution of the Franco-Moroccan conflict, "should open revolt ensue, the United States would have to support France."[75] That month the Joint Chiefs asked President Truman to authorize the transfer of atomic bomb components to the Moroccan bases—the first foreign sites to receive them after Great Britain. In January 1952 he agreed, though the French were not told of the move—to say nothing of the Moroccans.[76]

As long as the U.S. strategic interest seemed assured, Acheson preferred to put off choosing between the French and the North Africans. But private groups, including labor leaders and American businessmen in Morocco, encouraged the nationalists to persist in their defiance. The role of the American Federation of Labor (AFL) will be discussed in the next section, when it began to supplement its rhetorical support with financial assistance. But while the AFL worked with the State Department, even when criticizing it, the U.S. business community in Morocco went to Congress to compel a change in American policy.[77]

Like Pendar with his Coca-Cola franchise, many of these men had served in Morocco during the war and stayed on in the import-export business. They accused the French of violating U.S.-Moroccan treaties predating the protectorate by denying them extraterritorial status and discriminating against imports from outside the franc zone. In 1951, they persuaded Congress to attach a rider to aid legislation for France which required that the funds be withheld if the president determined that Paris had violated existing treaties. State Department officials privately agreed that the French were wrong. But even before the establishment of the bases, they held the strategic interest as paramount, reserving the issue until "such a time when the United States might feel compelled to intervene directly and energetically in Moroccan affairs."[78]

The French forced their hand by taking the dispute to the International Court of Justice at the Hague. The sultan, for his part, stalled French efforts to obtain supporting documents from the Sherifian archives and assured U.S. officials of his sympathy.[79] In August 1952, the court ruled in France's favor on the extraterritorial issue but for the United States on economic non-discrimination. The dispute was never really resolved, but the nationalists were encouraged by the mere fact that the United States, however reluctantly, had challenged the French protectorate and that the court recognized Moroccan sovereignty. As one nationalist paper headlined: "The Highest Judicial Authority in the World Confirms the Continuity of Morocco's International Personality."[80]

As the Arab League began to give their support to the nationalists following the February crisis, the Americans were again forced to confront the North African issue in the United Nations. When Egypt called on the General Assembly to consider French conduct in Morocco, the Americans helped to postpone debate. But international attention simply shifted to a new crisis in Tunisia. After hard-liners within the French cabinet outvoted Schuman and insisted on the "definitive character" of the protectorate in December 1951, the Tunisian cabinet petitioned the Security Council, which led to the arrest of Bourguiba and three other Neo Destour leaders. Once again the Americans abstained and the council referred the complaint to France as Tunisia's representative in foreign affairs. But twelve Asian and African nations took it up again in the General Assembly. Acheson decided it could not be kept off the agenda and voted for its inscription.[81] The French retaliated by supporting an Indian resolution on Korea, signaling that they too could side with the neutralist bloc against the United States "The UN has put us in a terrible situation," Acheson complained; "any irresponsible person like Nehru can make us discuss and vote on any question at all. They have us over the barrel."[82]

This was the first of many debates on North Africa in the assembly. The French often feigned indifference and insisted that they would have no impact on their policies. As the Quai's top official for Africa and the Levant, Jean Binoche, told the bey of Tunisia: "This assembly [is] stricken with powerlessness and [does] nothing that could seriously displease a great power."[83] But as Binoche's own stridency suggests, French governments were indeed concerned about the international body's "interference" in North Africa, and they lobbied other countries at the highest levels to keep it off the agenda. Even those who favored a more liberal policy were loathe to see it come about through outside pressure. It hurt French pride—and prestige—to find their country accused of violating the very rights of man of which they claimed authorship.[84]

There was also a more immediate concern: international condemnation could start a campaign to drive them from North Africa. That was precisely the intention of the Neo Destour, which called a general strike and unleashed a wave of attacks on protectorate authorities to coincide with its complaint to the Security Council.[85] In 1948, local agitation, U.N. condemnation, and American economic coercion had combined to end Dutch rule in Indonesia. Even Juin could not ignore this precedent, though he argued that France should withdraw from the United Nations rather than answer criticism from the Arab states.[86] The Quai d'Orsay was not yet ready to take so radical a step, but officials shared his anxiety. One warned that if they did not negotiate a new relationship with Morocco, it could be "imposed and dictated by the United Nations." But the "central difficulty" with the sultan, according to this same official, was that "if he is convinced, as one can fear, that the solution will come from an international intervention, he will likely persist in the tactics of obstruction that have for so long paralyzed all reforms." Similarly, the *résident général* in Tunisia, Jean de Hauteclocque, warned that if Bourguiba's tactics provoked an intervention it would be the "omen of the total independence of the country."[87] The British never wavered from the pro-French line and Soviet support was insufficient. Only the Americans, with their influence in the United Nations and economic leverage over France, could lead such an intervention or leave the nationalists to face France alone.

Yet Acheson continued to refuse to pledge noninterference in North Africa. He explained that he could not support the French more openly because of domestic political sentiment.[88] *The Washington Post, Baltimore Sun*, and *Christian Science Monitor* were particularly critical, and liberal Democrats, with Eleanor Roosevelt in the lead, called for a more positive line at the United Nations.[89] After a tour that stopped in Tunis, Tangier, and Algiers, a congressional mission issued a report suggesting that future legislation might include a declaration of U.S. sympathy for nationalist aspirations.[90] Yet internal State Department and NSC memoranda show that it was not members of Congress but disaffected North Africans, and the threat they posed to U.S. strategic interests, that most concerned policymakers. Indeed, American journalists and legislators themselves based their criticisms of French conduct in terms of U.S. interests in the Middle East and the Moroccan bases, expressing in public the very things U.S. diplomats were saying in private—to reporters, to members of Congress, and to the French themselves.

Fed up with pronationalist American diplomats, Juin's successor, Général Augustin Guillaume, apparently proposed to Schuman in November 1951 that they denounce them to Senator Joe McCarthy.[91] While rejecting this initiative, that same month the Quai d'Orsay began to plan a propaganda campaign that would eventually include speaking tours, short films, television documentaries, and the mass distribution of brochures.[92] The next month Moroccan nationalists countered with an "Office of Information and Documentation" in New York while the Neo Destour opened one of their own four months later.[93] This further demonstrates why it is difficult and perhaps misleading to distinguish sharply between domestic and foreign policy motivations in the U.S. approach to North Africa, since even American public opinion was not entirely home-grown.

State Department officials were themselves conflicted over how to reconcile American aims. Even if one ignored Arab sentiment and concentrated on the one concrete U.S. interest, the bases in Morocco, the problem still defied solution. If the Americans failed to support the protectorates, the French could make it impossible to operate these installations. If they did lend support, the Moroccans might target the bases in the nationalist uprising expected in the event of general war, if not sooner.[94] Indeed, riots had already erupted in Casablanca in December 1952 following the assassination of Ferhat Hached, the leader of Tunisia's nationalist trade union.[95]

While the Americans could press for the removal of uncooperative French commanders like Juin in Morocco or Raoul Salan in Indochina, they could not change a military and colonial culture that scorned political control from Paris. The coups and attempted coups of the Algerian War are best remembered, but military commanders had engaged in fait accomplis and outright insubordination throughout the French Union from the start of the Fourth Republic.[96] In 1951 Juin did not inform Schuman until two days after delivering his ultimatum to the sultan and would have acted on his threat if the foreign minister had not twice intervened.[97] The following March, de Hauteclocque arrested the Tunisian prime minister and Neo Destour cabinet members without even consulting Schuman.[98] But the worst incident from the point of view of U.S. policymakers came in August 1953. Despite American warnings and Quai d'Orsay assurances, Guillaume engineered another Berber uprising that forced the sultan from the throne and into exile.[99] Whereas before Binoche boasted that the General Assembly was "stricken with powerlessness," now he privately admitted that Paris had been forced yet again to accept a fait accompli, seeing no advantage in advertising their impotence.[100] If the governments of the Fourth Republic could not control their proconsuls, how could the Americans influence French colonial policy?

French military commanders and colonial administrations were able to act independently in part because of the weakness at the center. A multiplicity of irreconcilable differences between the parties over key issues led to frequent cabinet reshuffles, making it difficult for ministers to direct the bureaucrats in Paris, much less Rabat.[101] Though Bidault and Schuman of the *Mouvement Républicain Populaire* (MRP) retained the foreign ministry portfolio throughout this period, the governments to which they belonged lacked the authority to make the concessions necessary for peace or marshal the resources to win wars, whether in Indochina or North Africa. Yet if the French could not agree on policy, they would unite against anyone who tried to make their choices for them. After the Americans voted for the inscription of Tunisia in the General Assembly agenda and delivered a note announcing the reduction of military aid—and their expectation that French military spending would continue as before—Prime Minister Antoine Pinay refused to receive it and provoked a storm of protest against American pretensions, leaving the United States with less influence than before.[102]

Eventually Washington relented, lobbied for the French at the United Nations, paid for more than 40 percent of the costs of Indochina, and even acquiesced in the North Atlantic Council's endorsement of the war.[103] The Fourth Republic's lack of authority and its willingness to pander to the public's anti-Americanism elicited the contempt of U.S. officials, which finally led Eisenhower to conclude that the Fourth Republic might be nothing but a "hopeless, helpless mass of protoplasm."[104] But this "protoplasm" covered vast areas of potentially vital strategic importance, from the Mekong Delta to Dakar and the Saar. While something so amorphous and permeable could be pushed around and penetrated, it could not be made an instrument of one's will. Moreover, in the process, the Americans became ever more dependent on their ally to protect U.S. interests in Asia, Africa, and Europe—and ever more deeply involved in French domestic politics.

The Double Game

In January 1953, three weeks before Eisenhower's inaugural, Ambassador Bonnet reported a marked improvement in the level of American support for the French position in North Africa. The State Department had helped to secure a resolution on Tunisia that merely expressed the assembly's hope that the two sides would resume negotiations. Washington had come to realize, according to Bonnet, "the close links of interdependence which unite the problems of North Africa to the rest of French foreign policy and its contribution to the defense of the Free World"—and, it went without saying, that that contribution was contingent on America's help in solving those problems. Moreover, Bonnet thought that Eisenhower and Dulles would be even more helpful than their predecessors. But he warned that they could not count on America's support unless they put forward a program of reforms and defined their final objectives in North Africa. As long as that work was neglected—and recall that Bonnet advocated the very same thing two and a half years before—some would be tempted to play a "double game," especially the CIA.[105]

In fact, that game had already begun. While officially favoring limited self-government and continued cooperation with France, the Americans were taking options on the eventuality of North African independence. The AFL lobbied for the release of imprisoned nationalists and for the return of the sultan from exile. The CIA subsidized its international activities, especially the International Confederation of Free Trade Unions (ICFTU) and the money and training it provided for nationalist labor unions in Tunisia and Morocco.[106] It is difficult to establish the extent of direct CIA involvement and AFL anticommunists like Jay Lovestone and Irving Brown needed little encouragement. But we know that the new director of Central Intelligence, Allen Dulles (John Foster's brother), took "a great personal interest" in its connections with the AFL, according to the agency's official history, and the responsible officers reported directly to him in consultation with the undersecretary of state for political affairs, Robert Murphy.[107] Moreover, Lovestone was in daily communication with James Jesus Angleton, head of CIA counterintelligence. The French were certainly aware of the AFL's earlier collaboration with the CIA in aiding anticommunist unions in France and perceived it as an unofficial voice for American interests.[108]

Whatever the CIA's role, the labor campaign no less than the business lobby were alike filaments in a web of American influence, as illustrated by a story Brown told after one of his trips to North Africa. While enjoying a traditional meal in a Moroccan home—sitting cross-legged, eating with his hands—he asked for a cold drink. "And there, in this Oriental atmosphere, they served Coca-Cola." "Well," responded his host, "Coca-Cola is truly international!"[109] The image doubtless charmed an American audience, but from the French perspective it would have appeared rather more sinister: Pendar, entrepreneur and former OSS agent, bottled the drinks with which Brown, union organizer and CIA bag man, toasted American support for an independent Morocco. While diffuse and occasionally dissonant, like that of France, American power was far more expansive and self-confident. Both cultural and commercial, overt and covert, it posed a continual challenge to an overextended empire.

Yet if the Eisenhower administration itself were actually to coordinate a campaign against the French position in North Africa, it would not be for commercial interests, much less labor rights. The economic question was only "one of the minor preoccupations bearing on United States policy in this area," Bonnet concluded. The principal interest was the security of the bases, and French control would be a safer bet than self-rule.[110]

It is natural that Bonnet expected Eisenhower to think of North Africa in terms of its military utility. But the new president had a broader strategic vision. Even in strictly military terms, North Africa's importance to the Americans was beginning to change. In October 1951, an NSC paper had already predicted that, with the use of increasingly numerous atomic weapons, "areas of major strategic importance in continental Europe can be held by mid-1953." With each succeeding war plan, the front line of a future conflict crept farther north from the Mediterranean—and North Africa began to be relegated to the rear.[111]

If NATO could defend Europe, it made sense to move SAC infrastructure to the continent—closer to Soviet targets and far from the danger of a local uprising. Rather than quelling nationalist resistance, the sultan's exile had begun a period of terror and counter-terror amidst relentless anti-French propaganda broadcast by the *Voice of the Arabs*. As Nasser took control in Cairo, he made North Africa a top priority and endeavored to supply arms to the insurgents in Morocco and Tunisia.[112] American officials worried about the security of the bases if this escalated into a civil war—especially after they deployed nuclear bombs there in May 1954, the first time complete nuclear warheads were ever moved outside U.S. territory. The bases had become a "logical target [of] sabotage [by] Moroccans irate [at] US passive acceptance [of the] French coup," the Air Force and State Department agreed.[113] In October 1953, as the Moroccan question again loomed at the United Nations with the

Arab League in the lead, Eisenhower ordered that construction of new bases there be halted in favor of facilities in Spain. There was a "grave question about the reliability of the Moroccans," he and Dulles agreed. "We had paid through the nose there already."[114] Considering that most of the money for the Moroccan bases was already spent and Eisenhower was willing to put up another $800 million for "buying" Spain—as Undersecretary of State Bedell Smith put it—it appears that money was not what had been "paid through the nose," but rather, the political price of supporting the French.[115]

The Defense Department delayed closing down the Moroccan bases for nearly a decade. But in the meantime the H-bomb and more capable Soviet delivery systems raised concerns over the vulnerability of all overseas bases. Under Eisenhower, war planners focused on a massive preemptive strike with aerial-refueling to enable even medium-range bombers to reach Soviet targets from the United States. While still important for the post-strike refueling and recovery missions, overseas bases were no longer the centerpiece of SAC war plans.[116]

The other aspect of the new administration's strategy was eventually to withdraw U.S. troops from Europe, with the allies picking up the slack.[117] It proved difficult, however, to persuade the allies to invest in conventional forces for a European Defense Community (EDC) at the same time the administration was arguing at home that nuclear forces provided "more bang for the buck"—especially after Stalin's death in March 1953 sparked hopes for a thaw in the Cold War. But Eisenhower and Dulles's desire for European integration was based in part on a fear that predated the superpower confrontation and continued after its conclusion: a revival of European rivalries. As Dulles explained to the North Atlantic Council in December 1953: "Even if the Soviet threat were totally to disappear, would we be blind to the danger that the West may destroy itself? Surely there is an urgent, positive duty on all of us to seek to end that danger which comes from within."[118]

Ironically, one of the means the Americans employed to pressure Paris to accept the EDC helped to bring about a confrontation between France and Spain. Dulles wanted a defense agreement with Madrid as bargaining leverage against the French, threatening an "agonizing reappraisal" and a return to the peripheral strategy as the only alternative to the EDC.[119] But the new alliance emboldened the Spanish to challenge the French position in Morocco. They had long administered their own protectorate in the north—indeed, this had been the launching pad for Franco's attack on the republic in 1936, and he still surrounded himself with a Moroccan guard. But for the Caudillo, this was more than a sentimental attachment. Since the end of World War II, he had been seeking Arab support to break out of his diplomatic isolation in Europe and perhaps even make Spain a bridge between the two worlds.[120]

So when France failed to consult or even forewarn Madrid before deposing Mohammed V, it refused to recognize the new sultan, encouraged Muslim notables to declare their independence at Tetouan, and permitted Egypt to arm Istiqlal raiders. France reinforced the frontier and ordered warships to Agadir, but the Americans rebuffed requests to restrain Madrid. Coincidentally, or perhaps not, the Pentagon chose this moment to announce that is was sending arms to Spain. Bidault, who had taken over from Schuman at the Quai d'Orsay, was told that the Americans themselves were behind the Tetouan manifesto. While publicly supporting the French position at the United Nations, the United States had conveyed its displeasure with French policy in Morocco—and displayed another dimension of the double game.[121]

Straddling the straits of Gibraltar, Spain and Spanish Morocco exemplified the interrelationship of American interests in Europe and the European empires. Years later, after Morocco and Tunisia had won their independence amid mounting accusations of "dollar diplomacy" and CIA duplicity, Prime Minister Guy Mollet offered a nuanced assessment of Eisenhower's policy that acknowledged its basic sympathy for Europe in Africa:

> The United States doesn't play a double game in North Africa but a game with two aspects: on the one hand, they give France its chance to maintain its territories in the camp of liberty; on the other hand, if unfortunately we lose hold, the Americans would want to avoid that the entire African continent "turns" toward the Soviet side.[122]

Indeed, whatever the tactics of the moment, American strategy under Eisenhower favored continued, if reformed, French and British influence in their present and former colonies. Like the great majority of their contemporaries, the new president and his secretary of state assumed that decolonization would take a long time—Eisenhower spoke of a twenty-five-year timetable, Dulles believed it might last fifty years or more. They also thought that the Cold War would continue for at least as long.[123] The Soviets would therefore always threaten to take advantage of instability if decolonization were either too hasty or too slow. As Dulles testified to Congress in 1953:

> [T]here are plenty of social problems and unrest which would exist if there were no such thing as Soviet communism in the world, but what makes it a very dangerous problem for us is the fact that wherever those things exist, whether it is in Indo-China or Siam or Morocco, or Egypt or Arabia or Iran, for that matter, even in South America, the forces of unrest are captured by the Soviet communists . . . [W]e cannot make a transition without losing control of the whole situation.[124]

While Eisenhower thought that "[i]n some instances immediate independence would result in suffering for people and even anarchy," in the same breath he suggested that attempting to defend the status quo would lead to the same result. Shortly before his inauguration, he rejected Churchill's idea of joining forces to preserve colonialism: "In the present international complexities, any hope of establishing such [a] relationship is completely fatuous. Nationalism is on the march."[125]

One of the factors that drove Eisenhower and Dulles to overcome their initial caution and press the Europeans to adopt more informal means of influence began to emerge later that year. After Stalin's death, Moscow adopted a new Third World strategy, beginning with a campaign to repair relations with noncommunist nationalists. Whereas in 1949, Soviet commentators had called Nehru "a bloody strangler of the progressive forces" and neutralism a "rotten idea," now Georgi Malenkov, the new Soviet premier, complimented Indian foreign policy while flattering Pakistan, Afghanistan, Turkey, Burma, and Iran as well.[126] By 1955, following the famed "Czech arms deal" with Egypt, competition with the Soviets for the Arab states' favor was a major influence on U.S. policy toward French North Africa. But the administration's increasing impatience with France was not a matter of the Third World competition superceding European priorities. Instead, Eisenhower and Dulles perceived themselves as acting on behalf of Europe to further the interests of both the allies and dependent areas. Like Bonesteel and Kennan before them, their ultimate goal was the old dream of "Eurafrica." But they were concerned that the West might "commit suicide," as Eisenhower put it, by alienating the people who would one day control their supply of raw materials.[127]

If one can speak of a French policy toward the future of the colonies, it shared many of the Americans' assumptions and aims. Based on their experiences in Indochina and North Africa, even colonial officers came to acknowledge that there were dangers inherent in any developing country, though only the Communists were thought capable of manipulating genuine grievances to make a revolution.[128] On the other hand, neither soldiers nor civilians could imagine a clean break between Europe and the colonies. Many shared the American vision of Eurafrica—which, after all, was originally a French idea—not least the chance it offered for an "intercontinental equilibrium," and thus greater autonomy from the two superpowers.[129] As insurgencies escalated in Tunisia and Morocco, a consensus would coalesce around the idea that France would have to "leave in order to stay," with Pierre Mendès France, François Mitterrand, and Alain Savary emerging as the leading political spokesmen of the kind of informal imperium long favored in Washington.[130] Again, their differences with the Americans arose over the terms and pace of self-determination and economic development, not the desirability of these goals.

Yet others among the French concluded that North-South relations were *inherently* conflictual and came to think of themselves in North Africa not as agents of modernization but as defenders of Western civilization. This attitude was especially prevalent in the military and among colonial administrators, who were well placed to sabotage attempts at reform. Thus de Hauteclocque, the *résident général* in Tunisia, called for a clear statement that "France will always remain in Tunisia"—"the key to our Algerian house," as Jules Ferry had described it in 1883. This was all the more true seventy years later, he continued,

> while it is necessary to protect not only Algeria but North Africa and maybe even Africa as a whole against the very grave danger of an Arab nationalism of which no one can yet say whether it will not finally support itself on either Muscovite communism or on the expansionism of hundreds of millions of Asiatics.[131]

De Hauteclocque was not an isolated crank in his repeated warnings of "a new surge of Islam." Bidault himself had spoken of the danger of holy war in a discussion with Dulles, predicting that the French position south of the Sahara would be threatened "in the longer run by the development of this movement on the Islamic plane."[132]

In the same conversation, Bidault made a more credible observation about the future of relations between Europe and Africa, one that pointed to a critical flaw in the whole American conception of "Eurafrica." Why, he asked, did they encourage nationalism in Africa and elsewhere at the same time they urged its abandonment in Europe?[133] Whether contested or cooperative, decolonization doubtless harmed French self-esteem, making it all the more difficult for the nation to dissolve into a larger European entity. More generally, many in Britain and France felt that they remained great powers through their control of strategic territories, if only because they afforded leverage vis-à-vis the United States. A "United States of Europe," on the other hand, was a distant prospect. While in strategic terms it might have been unrealistic to try to retain both an empire and a preeminent position in Europe, to pose the old dilemma of French strategy, it was still thought politically impracticable to sacrifice one for the other.

The impact of France's defeat in Indochina on this debate was profound. Eisenhower took from it the idea that the French were doomed by their failure to promise eventual independence. He concluded that only a pro-active and progressive policy could win the confidence of Third World peoples and prevent anticolonialism from becoming a force for Communist expansion.[134] For many in the French military, on the other hand, such insurgencies were already instruments of Communist aggression, now allied with racial or religious "fanaticism," and could never be appeased.

Yet on one point Eisenhower and colonialist hard-liners appeared to agree: France's civilian leadership was proving incapable of handling colonial affairs and might have to turn over the reins. This was perhaps the most astonishing gambit in the "double game." If the politicians of the Fourth Republic would not lead, follow, or get out of the way, Washington would allow and even encourage their overthrow.

In June 1954, following the fall of Dien Bien Phu, U.N. Ambassador Henry Cabot Lodge traveled to France and described a government in total disarray. Even within the Quai d'Orsay, Bidault was undermined by disgruntled bureaucrats. Consequently, Lodge recommended that "a project be started immediately for revision of the French Constitution. Naturally," he said, "our hand should never show, but we should get the papers ready and get our friends set up in France so that when some further break comes, we can really move in." More specifically, Lodge reported that Juin, who was at the center of speculation over the possibility of a coup, had eagerly sought him out for a secret meeting to say that, despite his earlier opposition, he was "not really against EDC." Lodge judged that the move was "not without significance" and felt Juin was capable of seizing power.[135]

A year earlier, amid rumors of a military coup led by Juin, Eisenhower confessed that "he himself was beginning to feel that only a strong man could save France."[136] Now he had Lodge write to Juin as follows: "[The president] was most interested to hear a report of everything which you had said and asked me to write you this note to extend to you his very kind regards as well as his continued confidence in your fine qualities as a soldier and as a man. He particularly wished me to write this to you immediately."[137] When informing Dulles of the move, Lodge noted that "[n]o one knows about this besides you and the President and me."[138] But Juin did not stop Pierre Mendès France from becoming prime minister four days later. Within three months, the new premier had signed an armistice for Indochina, announced autonomy for Tunisia, and sent the EDC to the assembly without his endorsement—and without a chance.

Eisenhower and Dulles suspected that Mendès France had made a "global bargain" with Moscow and exerted economic and diplomatic pressure to undermine him. As Dulles asked the National Security Council in September 1954, "The Soviets successfully used Mendès-France to kill, or at least to maim, EDC. Will they now try to use him to destroy NATO?"[139] In fact, it was Bidault, not Mendès France, who had pursued a "global bargain." Moreover, by proposing that West Germany simply join NATO without the EDC—and by allowing the British to take credit for the idea—Mendès may have done "more than any other single individual to save the NATO system," as Marc Trachtenberg has argued. But for years afterward, the secretary continued to fear "another Indochina," linking the fate of French North Africa with that of the Atlantic Alliance.[140]

If Dulles was misguided about Mendès's basic loyalty to NATO, he did initiate the process that eventually shifted the bulk of French forces from Europe to North Africa, beginning with two divisions sent to Tunisia in September 1954. This dashed hopes that France might finally concentrate its military effort on the continent. And like so many issues in North Africa, this had an impact on U.S. interests in the Third World as well as Europe. As one State Department official remarked at the time: "I can think of few things that would be more damaging to the American position, not only in North Africa but in all of the Middle East and South Asia, than the use of American military equipment against North African nationalists."[141]

While Dulles still thought France was the indispensable leader of a united Europe—a "third great power bloc" to oppose the Soviets and reduce reliance on the United States—in the fall of 1954 that goal seemed very distant indeed.[142] Instead, France was thought to be in danger of collapse, opening up "power vacuums" into which communism could spread. Consequently, Eisenhower concluded that it might be time to "get rough." He offered direct aid to Ngo Dinh Diem despite French objections—the beginning of an American intervention that eventually squeezed France out of South Vietnam.[143] That same month a new NSC policy proposed that the United States might have to coerce France into conceding self-government in Morocco and Tunisia. Whereas earlier policy papers had stressed that the protectorates were unready for independence, now Washington was prepared, "[i]f circumstances so require, [to] press for French recognition of the eventual full freedom of Morocco and Tunisia."[144]

While Algerian militants could not have known about all of these developments as they prepared to launch an insurrection two weeks later, their prospects were not nearly as bleak as they might have appeared. Though they numbered less than twenty-five hundred, the *Voice of the Arabs* would broadcast their proclamation from Morocco to Iraq. And while they possessed fewer than four hundred rifles, Egypt had pledged its support and Libya was open to infiltration. With the Americans pressing in and France backing out, neither Tunisia nor Morocco could long be denied independence, completing the future supply routes to Algeria.[145]

More generally, the Libyan, Tunisian, and Moroccan cases had shown how even a small amount of violence could go a long way with the help of the international media and the Afro-Asian states at the United Nations, especially now that Moscow was starting to compete for their favor. And even if the Algerians were shut out of the State Department, they could seek covert support from the CIA, appeal directly to the U.S. public, and receive recognition in international forums like the International Court of Justice and the ICFTU.

But most important, the Algerians would be operating in an international arena where the "big battalions" did *not* always win. Like de Gaulle and Bidault before them, they could play off the Soviets against the Americans—in this case to compel Washington to exert pressure on the French. Following the example of so many Fourth Republic cabinets, the Tunisian government could claim it was impossible to defy the sentiments of its people, though now this "tyranny of the weak" would protect the FLN bases on the border. And whereas before the French used the U.S. bases to ensure support for the protectorate, with independence they gave Morocco leverage in demanding American aid for the Algerian cause. Finally, after having been subject to such machinations for so many years, the Americans approached the outbreak of fighting in Algeria with much less sympathy for the French than they might otherwise have mustered. Though Eisenhower recognized that Algeria was not just another colony, likening it to Texas rather than Tunisia or Morocco, North Africa as a whole now appeared to be "another Indochina." And if American policy toward Algeria could be summed up in a slogan, it was "no more Indochinas."[146]

In Paris too—and still more in the colonial outposts—Frenchmen were adamant that there would be "no more Indochinas," which brought to mind their ally's perfidiousness fully as much as Communist aggression. Yet if the French were weakened internationally that is precisely why they were determined not to lose their most valued possessions. And even if outside pressure compelled a French government to make concessions, the politicians were increasingly powerless to control events in the empire. Thus, while international politics and the ambivalence of power gave the Algerians a fighting chance, it also ensured that they would be fighting for a very long time.

North Africa's close proximity to Europe and commanding position alongside key Mediterranean chokepoints gave it great strategic value during both World War II—when this map was produced—and the early Cold War. (The Illustrated London News Picture Library)

When the rebels incited a mass uprising in the Constantinois in August 1955, French officers ordered their men "to shoot down every Arab we met." City officials in Philippeville corralled all the young men that they could find into the local stadium and killed every one of them. French authorities seized copies of *l'Humanité* when it printed this photo of the aftermath. (Keystone)

In October 1956, the French captured the FLN's first external delegation and presented them handcuffed before the international media, consistent with the French claim that they were part of a criminal conspiracy of foreign origin. From left: Ahmed Ben Bella, Mohammed Boudiaf, Hocine Aït Ahmed, Mostepha Lacheraf—a sympathizer traveling with them—and Mohammed Khider. (AFP Photo)

With the knife still in his hand and blood on his trousers, a French soldier stands over an Algerian he has just killed during the battle of Algiers. The shocked expressions suggest that he and his comrades were not expecting the Agence France Presse photographer to snap their picture for publication in newspapers around the world. (AFP Photo)

The "Morice line," 300 kilometers of electrified barbed wire fences and mine fields along the Tunisian frontier, took a terrible toll on the ALN as it struggled to resupply and reinforce the beleaguered *mujahadeen* inside Algeria. But their persistence together with a growing refugee population contributed to the international-ization of the conflict. (Keystone)

In January 1958, the United States arranged $655 million in credits for France to avert an economic crisis, but only after Paris promised to demobilize 150,000 troops and slash expenditures in Algeria. Resident Minister Robert Lacoste refused to make any statement to reporters three months later after the cabinet instead cut France's contribution to NATO. (Keystone)

The perception that Washington secretly favored North African nationalists incited European colonists to repeatedly attack U.S. diplomatic posts. The American Cultural Center in Algiers is shown here following the May 13, 1958, settler uprising. (Keystone)

Ferhat Abbas, first president of the Provisional Government of the Algerian Republic (GPRA), on September 19, 1958, the day it was first proclaimed. Walking to his right is Minister of the Interior Lakhdar Bentobbal and following behind and to his left is Ben Youssef Ben Khedda, who succeeded to the presidency in August 1961. (Keystone)

Jacques Soustelle, governor general from 1955 to 1956, became the leading advocate for integrating Algeria more closely with France. He appears here at a July 1959 press conference as the first minister of the Sahara. The heavy line separating it from the coastal *départements* and the pipeline running north through Tunisia indicate how de Gaulle would later try to retain control of its petroleum wealth even after Algeria became independent. (Keystone)

As GPRA foreign minister and lead negotiator at Evian, Belkacem Krim pursued a strategy of brinkmanship. By threatening France and its allies with actual and increasing communist support—including the use of Chinese "volunteers"—he would compel them to concede independence. He is pictured here with Mao Tse-tung. (Keystone)

BAFOUÉE PAR KROUCHTCHEV
RIDICULISÉE PAR NASSER
L'O.N.U. VEUT SE VENGER SUR LA FRANCE
LA FRANCE DIT NON

A propaganda poster suggests how the FLN's international campaign appeared to *Algérie française* activists. The French acronym for the United Nations—ONU—is written across the two hands ripping France from Algeria. (Union pour le salut et le renouveau de l'Algérie française)

The French delegation at the secret negotiations at Rousses is shown here at the final round in Evian, from left to right: Minister of Public Works Robert Buron, Secretary of State for Algerian Affairs Louis Joxe, and Secretary of State for Saharan Affairs Jean de Broglie. (Keystone)

The end of the line: a few of the approximately 800,000 *pieds noirs* who fled Algeria in the year following the Evian agreement. (Keystone)

Nelson Mandela came to North Africa to learn from the Algerian experience.
Shown here speaking with an ALN officer, he later wrote that the Algerians
appeared like an apparition of the future forces of the African National Congress.
(UWC Robben Island Mayibuye Archive)

II

The Internationalization of the Algerian Question, 1954–1956

3

From Conspiracy to Total War

[T]he National Liberation Front will have two essential tasks to pursue from the beginning and simultaneously: an interior action as much on the political level as on the level of action itself, and an exterior action with the support of our natural allies to make the Algerian problem a reality for the entire world.

This is a crushing task which requires the mobilization of all national energies and resources. It is true, the fight will be long, but the outcome is certain.

Proclamation, *Front de Libération Nationale*, November 1, 1954 [1]

[I]t could be even worse than Indochina, particularly for US and French relations. [Dulles] said he had been worried about [the] North African situation developing like it had in Indochina. This was close to home. He said he did not think it was unimportant but that perhaps it was the most serious problem that we faced. He said it might get NATO, it might break NATO apart.

John Foster Dulles to Pierre Mendès France, November 1954 [2]

On the morning of All Saints Day, November 1, 1954, French officials awoke to reports of assaults and ambushes across Algeria. The actual losses were slight, as inexperienced and ill-armed rebels bungled or aborted many of their operations. Altogether, thirty attacks left seven dead and a dozen wounded. The FLN had been less concerned with thorough planning and preparation than with the danger of detection and further delay. Even so, authorities immediately recognized that this was a coordinated operation with international implications. They worried that it was connected to the nascent insurgencies in Morocco and Tunisia and noted Egypt's role in broadcasting the FLN's first proclamation over the *Voice of the Arabs*, which declared among its aims the "Internationalization of the Algerian problem."[3]

The French had good reason to be concerned about the international dimension of the rebellion, if only because of its importance in the FLN's own plans. But this preoccupation predated the advent of effective foreign aid. For instance, Governor General Roger Léonard concluded that "the rioters obeyed foreign instructions" based on the *Voice of the Arabs* broadcast. Once Egypt began to supply significant quantities of arms, the French would offer even more exaggerated estimates of Cairo's influence.[4]

How can one explain how this legitimate concern grew into an obsession? It is hard to overstate the shadow cast by France's recent defeat in Indochina. It had been aided by the Chinese, abetted by American nonintervention, and ratified by an international conference. But while this factor is an essential part of any explanation, it hardly suffices, since in Indochina, too, the French blamed outsiders from the very start of the conflict. In one opinion poll in France, more than 60 percent of respondents listed Japan, Britain, China, and the United States as responsible for unrest in Indochina; just 5 percent felt that France bore responsibility. Similarly, 65 percent in another poll blamed Britain for the 1945 crisis that forced withdrawal from Syria—3 percent blamed themselves. "Since principled opposition to the universal values of French civilization was, by definition, impossible," Christopher Andrew explains, "vast conspiracy theories were required to explain nationalist opposition to French rule."[5]

Conspiracy theories had long been a forte of the extreme right, but they can also be found in the rhetoric of Gaullists, Socialists, and Communists. These theories could involve the Soviets, the Americans, or both at the same time. The right—especially the army—and the Socialists saw the sinister hand of Moscow lurking behind the rebellion. In a February 1955 conference at All Souls College, Oxford, former resident general of Morocco Augustin Guillaume described "a vast, brimming movement encompassing all from Peking to Casablanca" aiming at "the southern flank of Western Europe." The British in Malaysia and Kenya and the French in North Africa were therefore engaged in the same struggle. "All countries of Western Civilization," Guillaume concluded,

> are facing the gravest threat to have ever weighed on the life and liberty of their peoples. . . . [W]here should we find our salvation? To begin with, certainly in remaining faithful to our ideals, our civilization, all that gives meaning to life. But this won't be enough. The one and unique solution rests in our unity. Divided we are weak, united we are strong.[6]

Why, one might ask, did these countries need Guillaume to summon them to unity and self-defense in the face of such a threat? In fact, his portrait of a coalition of Communists and anticolonial movements, however fanciful, was precisely what was needed to make "Western civilization" seem like a valid geopolitical concept.[7]

For Communists and Gaullists, on the other hand, it was the CIA and, beginning in 1956, U.S. oil companies that were sabotaging French efforts in order to gain access to Algeria's resources. Some French officers imagined that the Soviets considered the Americans to be useful fools in plotting revolutionary war. But after years of accusing the Americans of secretly favoring the rebels, many French credited rumors that they had colluded in the generals' 1961 putsch aimed at preventing independence, rumors that were taken seriously by de Gaulle's government.[8]

However contradictory, these notions were nonetheless influential because they played on and perpetuated the anger and anxiety French people of all political persuasions felt about their diminished role in international affairs. At the same time they were reassuring, making sense of a bewildering series of setbacks while leaving France at the very center of international politics, if only as a target. As in Indochina, they also allowed people to think that the uprising was inspired and sustained by external forces rather than accept responsibility for decades of French repression and dispossession. As ever, conspiracy theories grew out of a sense of weakness and insecurity.

But to explain the particular forms these conspiracy theories assumed, one must also take into account preexisting attitudes toward Arabs and Islam. With little knowledge of Algerian society, observers in the metropole plunged into naturalistic explanations for apparently senseless acts of violence: "[O]ne has killed solely to kill, shot solely to shoot, burned only to burn . . . ," opined the Socialist Party paper, *Le Populaire*.[9] The recurring claim that the rebels killed without reason implied that this was intrinsic to their nature. Thus, when an article on facial mutilations committed by the FLN appeared in a French medical journal, subsequently reprinted by the Interior Ministry for distribution abroad, it included an engraving depicting "Tortures practiced in Algeria" from the 1637 *Histoire de Barbarie et de ses corsaires*. Another reprint, with five hundred copies sent to the French delegation to the United Nations, was accompanied by an article on "Aspects particular to Algerian criminality," which specified that "eight centuries of blood-stained anarchy have created reflexes that appear unthinkable to civilized people. The centurylong French presence has not been sufficient to extinguish them."[10] The Defense Ministry's official review went back still farther, explaining that the revolt was strongest in the Aurès because the people there "have kept most of the psychological and social traits that they had two thousand years ago."[11]

While relieving French consciences, this invocation of the image of North Africans as innately violent conjured up the specter of a pan-Arab race war or international jihad. Nasser, the Soviets, or the Americans had merely to channel this reservoir of bile to their own ends. Thus, less than two weeks after the start of the rebellion, a deputy from the Constantine region warned that "foreign forces"—not further specified—"have the desire and the will to restore this crescent of Islam for the benefit of a new Mediterranean policy by passing through Cairo and annexing all of North Africa."[12]

By blaming "foreign forces"—whether they operated from Cairo, Moscow, Washington, or all three—the French made the war appear as a particularly savage and pointless Punch and Judy show. As one of the leading French theorists of revolutionary warfare, Colonel Charles Lacheroy, would have it, "In the beginning there is nothing." That is, seeking the origins of unrest was beside the point if it did not actually serve the rebels' purposes.[13] The only important question was, "who is pulling the strings?"

The poverty and inequality existing in French Algeria could not forever escape the attention of the growing number of officials, correspondents, and conscripts traveling there. From their reports, the French public learned that Muslims had real grievances. Liberals like Mendès France and his choice for governor general, Jacques Soustelle, were critical of the *grands colons* and sensitive to the plight of Algerian Muslims. They argued that the only way to make the war just and winnable was to draw the Algerian *départements* closer to the metropole through political reforms and economic development. As long as that work remained unfinished, outsiders could exploit the cleavages that characterized a society in transition. With greater economic and political opportunity, individuals— rather than communities—would be emancipated and the state made more prosperous and secure. By combining repression and reform, liberal-minded leaders would make the war a defense of the republic and its ideals, keeping the enemy literally and figuratively outside—whether that enemy was Soviet communism, U.S. materialism, or "Islamic fanaticism."[14]

Yet if everyone could agree that the only threat to a developing Algeria came from outside, was that not where France would have to meet and defeat it? And if Algeria was part of a much larger conflict, how could France win it alone? French strategy therefore developed both an internal and an external dimension—like that of their nationalist adversaries—and talks like Guillaume's would be given at college campuses, chambers of commerce, and countless other venues in Western Europe, the United States, and Latin America. Internal reforms were important not only to advance integration but also to maintain the support of allies and answer the arguments of the emerging nonaligned movement. At the same time, exposing and—if need be—striking at the FLN's external backers would delegitimize their claims to speak for the Muslim population in Algeria and abroad.

But whereas for the FLN internal and external actions were mutually reinforcing and alike aimed at internationalizing the Algerian question, any connection the French drew between the Algerian conflict and the wider world, even by implication, undermined their position that it was an internal affair. As the French ambassador to London, Jean Chauvel, pointed out as early as March 1955: "Our associates will not blindly support any position or action we take. We risk seeing them arrogate the right of inspection."[15]

While seeking support abroad gradually undermined French authority in Algeria, situating this struggle in an international context made it all the more difficult for them to accept a compromise peace. If the adversary came from outside and Algeria was an integral part of the *patrie*—indeed, a symbol of its highest aspirations—any concession appeared to endanger the safety and identity of France. As Mendès France declared, "Algeria is France, not a foreign country. One does not compromise when it is a matter of defending the domestic peace of the union, the unity and integrity of the Republic."[16] Moreover, if the Algerian rebels were truly the vanguard of a larger threat with unlimited ambitions, then any direct dialogue with them amounted to appeasement, if not the beginning of the end of Western civilization. "The fellagha's actions do not allow us to conceive of any possible negotiation," Interior Minister François Mitterrand declared. "It can lead to only this result: war."[17]

Mitterrand's declaration of war is well remembered in France partly because it was so rare. As Benjamin Stora has observed, "[T]o say 'war' would be for France to admit a possible severance, a disembodiment of the 'One and Indivisible Republic.' " Practically no one, aside from Trotskyites and anarchists, seriously considered this in the first year of the struggle. Instead, Mitterrand himself emphasized that "we will avoid all which could appear as a state of war; we do not want that."[18]

In truth, from the very beginning the French imagined Algeria as an international, even civilizational conflict and waged it with astonishing ferocity. But officially the government referred to it with a succession of increasingly convoluted euphemisms: "events" in November 1954, "police operations" until the mass uprising in the Northern Constantine region in August 1955, "actions for the maintenance of order" after the vote of special powers in March 1956, and "operations for the reestablishment of the civil peace" with the advent of the Battle of Algiers in 1957. But this remained a "war without a name" not simply because of an oversupply of bureaucratic usage. To name something is to know it, to control or at least confront it, and it would be a long time before the French began to come to terms with the Algerian War.[19]

Repression and Reform

If Léonard was mistaken in asserting that the insurrection was commanded from abroad, the FLN indeed thought that the international context called for action. While the fight for North African independence was well under way in Tunisia and Morocco, the authors of the November 1 proclamation complained that they were "relegated to the rear." With the end of the Indochina war, France could concentrate its forces in North Africa. For that reason the Algerians judged that the moment had come "to take the national movement out of the dead-end where political infighting has driven it in order to launch it alongside [those of our] Moroccan and Tunisian brothers in the true revolutionary struggle."[20]

Thus, the founders of the FLN located its raison d'être at the juncture of international and domestic politics, animated by a sense that the gathering force of decolonization would leave their dithering leaders behind. If their demand to "restore" Algeria's independence was no different from that of many other anticolonial movements, the unique juridical status of

France's Algerian départements would require that they challenge the whole notion of distinct "domestic" and "foreign" affairs, and thus the foundation of state sovereignty—or at least France's sovereignty.

Mohammed Khider, Ahmed Ben Bella, and Hocine Aït Ahmed comprised the FLN's first external delegation. Aït Ahmed was the author of the PPA's plan for a general uprising, which was discussed in chapter 2. The scion of a distinguished Marabout family in Kabylia, he was the youngest and best educated of the three, having attained his baccalaureate. Khider, the most senior, was the self-educated son of a poor laborer. Passing in and out of prison during World War II, he won election in 1946 as a deputy for the MTLD in Algiers and began to speak out against the war in Indochina the following year. By then Ben Bella, a twice-decorated veteran of the Italian campaign, was a municipal councilor in his native Oranie. But after the fraudulent 1948 elections, he went underground and succeeded Aït Ahmed as head of the MTLD's *Organisation Spéciale* (OS) in 1949. That year, all three were involved in a holdup of the Oran post office intended to bankroll the OS. They escaped and had been working together in Cairo since 1952.[21]

The November 1 proclamation declared three "external objectives," according them the same emphasis as the "internal objectives":

1. Internationalization of the Algerian question.
2. Realization of North African unity in its natural Arab-Muslim framework.
3. In the framework of the United Nations charter, affirmation of our sympathy with regard to all nations that support our liberating actions.

Aït Ahmed would represent them in New York and at international conferences, while in Cairo Khider was responsible for the overall direction of FLN diplomacy. Meanwhile, Ben Bella traveled throughout the Middle East and North Africa arranging arms shipments and working with Mohammed Boudiaf—another veteran of both the French Army and the OS—to deliver them to the *Armée de Libération Nationale* (ALN).

The FLN's achievements in the international arena were initially no more impressive than its military campaigns. In April 1954, its representatives had signed a pact with their Moroccan and Tunisian counterparts in Cairo pledging to persist in their common struggle until each country attained its independence.[22] But just three weeks after the start of the Algerian insurrection, twenty-seven hundred Tunisian rebels began to hand over their arms to French authorities as part of the peace process Mendès France had initiated the previous July.[23] Nasser, for his part, had promised "unconditional support," but this amounted to just 5,000 Egyptian pounds, 28 rifles, and 11 machine guns that may not have even reached Algeria in time for the uprising.[24]

On the diplomatic front, an FLN delegation petitioned a December 1954 meeting of the Colombo group of neutral Asian countries—Burma, Ceylon, India, Indonesia, and Pakistan—to mention Algeria in their final communiqué. After long discussions, they finally refused, explaining that it was up to the Arab states to take the lead.[25] On Khider's urging, Saudi Arabia did petition the U.N. Security Council. But most Arab League members were unwilling to challenge French claims that Algeria was juridically part of the *patrie*. The Iranian representative, who held the council's rotating presidency, declared the whole affair to be "perfectly absurd."[26]

Nevertheless, that same day a Quai d'Orsay memorandum noted that the Saudi petition had "revealed the supposed existence of an Algerian question to American public opinion, which had been totally unaware of it before the recent events in the Aurès." The Quai therefore requested that the Interior Ministry provide them with information on the number of rebels and the scale of their operations to help "reduce the present events to their exact proportion."[27] The French were already concerned that military and diplomatic actions, however ineffectual in isolation, could together amplify Algerian demands through international organizations and the media, redounding to their disadvantage in world and especially American opinion.

While the French were initially oblivious to them, the contradictions in their response to the uprising were immediately apparent to their allies, as revealed by a discussion between Mendès and Dulles in Washington three weeks after the outbreak of hostilities. Franco-American relations were still embittered by the defeat of the EDC and the Americans' apparent intention to take France's place in Indochina. The National Assembly had specifically directed the prime minister to discuss the applicability of the North Atlantic Treaty to Algeria. His concessions to Tunisian nationalists and recognition that Algeria required reforms left him vulnerable to attacks by the colonial lobby while he was away. "The dogs are on the loose and . . . the big bloodhounds are leading the attack," his minister of Moroccan and Tunisian affairs, Christian Fouchet, had warned a few days earlier. "I swear to you that they're barking in the corridors, the party offices, and the newspapers."[28]

Mendès therefore "insisted long and stubbornly" in a three-hour meeting that the final communiqué address "external influences bearing on the North African situation." But Dulles would not budge: "he did not see how France could expect to derive strength and support from other nations, yet tell the other nations to keep out."[29] To the prime minister's repeated insistence that French Algeria was covered by the Atlantic Treaty, the secretary of state gave a reply worthy of Palmerston: "[I]t was unwise to quote treaty language," he said, since "the experience of mankind showed that nations act in accord with what they consider their basic interests and not by the letter of treaties." In other words,

Dulles would not render aid out of a sense of obligation—not after the Indochina defeat and Mendès's abandonment of the EDC. If Paris went to the North Atlantic Council, it "would feel a need for a greater voice . . . and he was not sure that France desired this."[30]

Dulles could not be sure because, in spite of Mendès's repeated insistence that Algeria was a domestic affair, the prime minister went on to say that "he needed US advice," twice asking, "What can France do."[31] Mendès himself had no plan for North Africa beyond conceding Tunisia internal autonomy and attempting to institute fully the 1947 statute for Algeria, though even this would prove too much for the assembly to swallow. More than a rhetorical strategy, his request for advice reflected another ambiguity that would continue to arise from the idea that Algeria was an internal affair with external causes: if the war was the work of outsiders, then perhaps only outsiders knew what would end it.

The secretary's statement that U.S.-French differences in North Africa could ultimately "get NATO" or "break NATO apart" might appear exaggerated, but the next session of the NSC showed that he was not the only one worrying about Algeria, nor was he the most critical of French actions. This meeting featured another attempt by the chairman of the joint chiefs, Arthur Radford, to press for a more "dynamic" policy against the Soviets, a code word for one that would risk war. When Eisenhower pressed him to be specific, Admiral Radford continually returned to North Africa, even on the subject of the Soviet nuclear threat.[32]

The troubles there indeed posed a problem for U.S. war plans. The NSC judged that the region "might be required as a new base of Allied operations in the event of World War III"—or if France vetoed German rearmament and neutralism swept the continent, another nightmare scenario. But Radford's concern was more complex. After repeatedly drawing an analogy to Indochina, he twice pointed to the central dilemma facing American policy: "the possibility of either losing our whole position in the Middle East by offending the Arabs, or else risking the rupture of our NATO position by offending the French." He advocated "outright support of the Arabs against the French." Dulles twice had to tell Radford, "with asperity," that it was "basically a political problem," and warned that going against France would prevent German rearmament. Eisenhower for his part warned that "the French were about to repeat in North Africa the serious mistakes they had made in Indochina. Military force alone would not hold these colonies."[33]

Indeed, at first Mendès had nothing but military force to offer Algeria. He dispatched ten battalions of infantry and riot police on the second day of the revolt and redeployed whole regiments returning from Indochina.[34] Nevertheless, the Americans supported the French position at the United Nations, voting against even the most innocuous resolutions on Morocco and urging Saudi Arabia to abandon its petition on behalf of the Algerians. They also pressed the Egyptians to moderate the *Voice of the Arabs*.[35] Dulles's priority remained German rearmament, though he was soon complaining that backing France had "cost us heavily in Arab relations."[36]

On December 30, Mendès finally persuaded the assembly to accept German entry into NATO. But the prime minister gained little credit in Washington, for by this point Eisenhower had said that he was prepared to rearm Germany whatever the assembly said or did. Mendès realized that France also had no choice but to accept some loss of control in North Africa and would be better off accepting it with good grace. Without an agreement with the Tunisian nationalists, violence would spread across the region, as the Quai's director for Africa and the Levant argued:

> Perhaps we are capable, as some seem to believe these days, of putting down a Tunisian insurrection. We do not have the means, however, to squelch a rebellion that extends to the whole of North Africa. And even if we disposed of such means, we would not have the moral option of using them without ruining our international position.

France's international position made a liberal policy imperative; its domestic politics, however, made it impossible. It is significant that this memorandum, though officially secret and addressed to the minister of Moroccan and Tunisian affairs, can be found among the papers of René Mayer—a wealthy *colon* who was Mendès's main opponent within his own Radical Party.[37] Two weeks later Mayer withdrew his support and so struck the death blow to Mendès's government: "I have no idea where you are going," Mayer declared before the assembly. "I cannot believe that a policy of action can find no middle course between passivity and wild experiment." In fact, the leaked memorandum indicates that Mayer did know where Mendès was going—or at least where some officials wished to take him in North Africa—and that may be what prompted him to act.[38]

With no settlement in Tunisia or Morocco and the Algerian rebellion spreading beyond the mountains of the Aurès and the Grande Kabylie, what were the alternatives facing his successor, Edgar Faure? In January, a new and better armed group appeared in the North Constantinois region, threatening communications between Mayer's constituency in Constantine and the coastal town of Philippeville. In March, the FLN struck within Philippeville itself as well as Bône and the Nementchas Mountains, both lying along the Tunisian border. French armored columns were ill suited to the mountainous terrain and the top commanders had little experience with guerrilla warfare.[39]

Moreover, enforcing "collective responsibility" through forced labor, destruction of villages, and indiscriminate use of torture yielded ready recruits for the FLN. "The Moslems in the countryside now know what electricity is" exclaimed the other deputy from Constantine, Mostefa Benbahmed, during the debate that brought down Mendès's government.[40] Indeed, in March 1955, a French official reported that forty of the sixty-one detainees he had interviewed complained of being tortured, many still showing the scars. Rather than condemning the practice, he argued that it should be regulated and officially sanctioned.[41] French military commanders would later argue that torturing suspects for information saved innocent lives. But, aside from the unplanned deaths of two school teachers on the first day of the revolt, the FLN—in contrast to the French—did not target civilians until May 1955.[42]

The rebels did attack Muslims who disobeyed their directives. In the first two and a half years of the war, they killed more than six times as many of their compatriots as Europeans, which led some to claim that only terror deterred Muslims from remaining loyal to their traditional leadership.[43] But it is hardly unusual for revolutions to consume their children and "collaborators" in greater numbers than the purported enemy, France's own Terror being only the best known example. The Muslim population's support for either side was undoubtedly elicited by a mix of political appeals and intimidation, though determining their inward feelings is even more difficult now than it was then. But if the army killed two hundred thousand rebels in the first five years, as de Gaulle later asserted,[44] then either the FLN had indeed mobilized a large part of the population or the French repression was every bit as indiscriminate as its critics claimed.

Yet the particular pattern of the insurgency's growth along the Tunisian border was linked to another factor that had not yet been publicized: the beginning of sizable Egyptian arms shipments to the FLN. Concerned that the hard-pressed insurgents could not wait for purchases from arms brokers, Ben Bella asked Mohamad Fathi Al Dib, Nasser's point man for North African affairs, to supply them from Egypt's own stocks. Nasser agreed while insisting on the utmost secrecy.[45]

On the night of December 7, Egyptian sailors in Tripoli harbor unloaded 200 rifles, 35 machine guns, 5 bazookas, and over 100,000 rounds of ammunition from the yacht *Intissar*. The Libyan prime minister concealed the crates until they were ready for overland transport through Tunisia. Though 50 of the rifles were given to disaffected Tunisians who were fighting the French under Bourguiba's rival, Salah Ben Youssef, the shipment still represented a substantial addition to the ALN arsenal. The rebels possessed fewer than 400 rifles at the start of the revolt, many of them hunting rifles.[46]

Nasser's decision to increase aid to the FLN may have been linked to France's recent shipment of *Ouragans* to Israel, the new state's first jet fighters. Egypt's support for the FLN would increase as its relations with the Western allies deteriorated. The downward spiral began in December 1954, when Dulles decided to deny military aid to Egypt absent an improvement in relations with Israel, and continued in February, when Turkey and Iraq announced the Baghdad Pact. The Americans realized that this alliance of "northern tier" states and Britain would be a "psychological shock" to Nasser, but they hoped that, together with the incentive of future aid, it would lead him to cooperate with U.S. efforts to broker a comprehensive settlement with Israel.[47] Instead, Nasser complained that the United States had "violated a gentleman's agreement" that Egypt would lead in constructing a purely Arab defense alliance.[48] Ironically, the French and the Israelis also opposed the pact. This created another shared interest for their nascent alliance—an alliance that would incite Nasser against *all* the Western allies.

In January, the Egyptians began to help the FLN prepare to open a western front in Algeria. Dib sponsored a meeting between Ben Bella, Aït Ahmed, Boudiaf, and Larbi Ben M'Hidi with Mohammed Allal al-Fassi, a leader of the Moroccan Istiqlal. Boudiaf had been unable to procure arms for the forces Ben M'Hidi commanded in Oranie, the western part of the country, which had seen little action since the start of the uprising. Al-Fassi, for his part, needed arms to transform the Istiqlal's sporadic attacks into a coordinated rebellion. Dib agreed, while once again reserving the larger part of the shipment for the Algerians.[49]

It was not until April 2 that a yacht belonging to the ex-queen of Egypt beached on a desolate shore of Spanish Morocco. The crew of the *Dinah* and waiting mujahadeen waded ashore with 300 rifles, 50 mortars, 130 machine guns, and 500 kilos of gelignite. Along with the weapons, ammunition, and explosives, the *Dinah* also transported seven Algerians trained in Egypt. Among them was Houari Boumedienne, who would one day become the ALN's chief of staff (and later president of the republic). With the agreement of the Spanish governor general, Rafael García-Valino, the Moroccans and Algerians set up a training base to stock arms and prepare a coordinated offensive under a joint "Supreme Military Command of North Africa."[50]

Thus, French fears of Egyptian aid to a generalized revolt across the region were not unfounded—that was precisely the intention of the FLN, Ben Youssef's faction of the Neo Destour, and al-Fassi's wing of the Istiqlal. France's eighty thousand soldiers and police were hardly adequate to patrol the more heavily populated coastal departments, which were half the size of the metropole. Even with the help of French forces in the protectorates and the garrison in Fezzan, sealing off the eastern and western borders was out of the question.[51] While the Oranie would remain quiet until the fall, by the end of March the French director general of security in Algeria, Jean Vaujour, reported that the area between the Tunisian border, Bône, and Constantine was "infested" with rebel bands.[52]

As so often occurred under the Fourth Republic, Faure therefore implemented the policy that had precipitated the removal of his predecessor: simultaneous repression and reform in Algeria and a settlement with Bourguiba. Units continued to pour into Algeria as the army implemented a strategy that combined a network of garrisons with mobile battalions. At the same time, the National Assembly declared a state of emergency in the Aurès and Kabylia and expanded police powers of curfew and detention as well as the army's authority to deal directly with "criminal activities." Perhaps anticipating the likely results, it also permitted censorship of the press, radio, and film.[53]

But as French forces pursued rebels deep into the heart of Algeria, they could see with their own eyes the causes of the incipient rebellion: overgrazed and exhausted land, goats dying of starvation, farmers eating their last seed grain. Though most Aurèsians had never been visited by a French doctor or teacher, " 'France's contribution' was everywhere," as Germaine Tillion would later write, "invisible but omnipresent." New roads and DDT had opened the way to the market and population growth, but these forces of national integration had disintegrated traditional society.[54]

Among those who toured the Aurès was the new governor general, Jacques Soustelle, a brilliant ethnologist who led de Gaulle's wartime secret service and then the ministries of information and colonies. Though he would end the war as an apologist for the OAS, when it started Soustelle was still a left-leaning Gaullist, Mendès's man, and thus doubly suspect to the pieds noirs. He asked Tillion to join his office, and together they led calls for a policy of integration, arguing that the only way to end the war was to "modernize" Algeria—and that only France could do it. Algerian peasants were promised new investments in infrastructure, irrigation, housing, and education while évolués would have an easier time entering the pied noir-dominated administration. But political equality was still a distant and unlikely prospect. Though the French sympathized with the Aurèsians, they were not about to give them proportional representation in the assembly.[55]

Altogether, French policy in North Africa remained a hash of high-minded ideals and harsh realities. By the time Soustelle managed to release some members of the MTLD—whom the French had arrested on the mistaken assumption that Messali's group was behind the rebellion—the army had already set up its first internment camp.[56] And while the governor general initially forbade indiscriminate reprisals, as Mitterrand had before him, by May General Paul Cherrière, commander of the Algeria military district, delegated to his subordinate in the Constantine "powers to decide, depending [on] circumstances, employment [of] machine-guns, rockets, and bombs, on bands in [the] new zone of the rebellion. Collective responsibility [is] to be vigorously applied," Cherrière emphasized, adding that "there will be no written instructions given to me by the Governor." In this way Soustelle avoided personal culpability while giving the army carte blanche in carrying out the repression. Later that month, he personally ordered that "all rebels captured with their weapons ought to be shot."[57] Many of the MTLD cadres that Soustelle released from detention naturally rallied to the FLN. One of them, Ben Youssef Ben Khedda, would one day become president of its provisional government.

Faure's cabinet also failed to confront the contradictions in its Tunisian policy. After nine months of negotiations and a last-minute meeting between the prime minister and Bourguiba on April 21, 1955, it finally agreed to accords on internal autonomy. While France retained responsibility for defense and foreign affairs, the Tunisians rejected any "permanent link." Indeed, they viewed the agreement as just another phase in the fight for full independence.[58] For Resident General Pierre Boyer de la Tour, on the other hand, it signaled the beginning of "a sort of new style 'colonial' adventure," as he told his officials three months later.[59] Thus, each side viewed the accords as a means to an end, though their ends were entirely different. And rather than complementing each other, policies of reform and repression were each the enemy of the other.

Resonance and Reciprocity

On the same day that Faure and Bourguiba agreed to paper over their differences, Ben Youssef, Aït Ahmed, and al-Fassi were at the Afro-Asian conference in Bandung, Indonesia, forging the wedge that would eventually drive them apart. Learning the lessons of the earlier conference, the Algerians prepared the ground by sending propaganda missions to the Colombo countries and joining a united North African delegation. They finally obtained recognition that Algeria, Morocco, and Tunisia all had a right to independence. In his closing remarks, Nehru summed up the "spirit of Bandung": "Asia wants to help Africa."[60] For one French intelligence officer, this signaled "the beginning of the end of the supremacy of the white race."[61]

Almost immediately there was a sharp increase in the number of FLN incidents in Algeria—from 158 in April to 432 in May—leading Faure to call up 8,000 reservists and delay the release of 100,000 draftees. This would be the first time French citizen soldiers would fight abroad while the metropole was at peace.[62] "We are moving," Juin warned, "toward a generalized insurrection under the sign of holy war."[63]

Philippe Tripier argues that this marked the start of a pattern that would continue through 1957: "[E]very important international event affecting the allies or sympathizers of the Algerian uprising would immediately have an effect on Algerian opinion and on the morale of the rebels themselves: commanders first of all, and then their troops." Amplified by FLN propaganda, "each one would draw from it a renewal of hope and aggressiveness." Conversely, every reported exploit of the rebels within Algeria aided the FLN's allies and irritated the friends of France. "One noticed a phenomenon of resonance and reciprocity," Tripier concluded, "a natural interaction between the Algerian event and its global context." Indeed, in September 1958 the French delegation to the United Nations ordered up a chart showing the relationship between General Assembly debates on Algeria and the incidence of FLN attacks in Kabylia.[64]

Many factors determined the rebels' military effectiveness. Yet Tripier's account does reflect the *perception* of French security forces that it depended essentially on external events—not surprisingly, since he served in an intelligence section of the wartime *Secrétariat Général de la Défense Nationale*. There is also ample contemporary evidence. In July 1955, the dossier prepared for the U.N. delegation from French intelligence reports went so far as to assert that the FLN leadership received its orders from Cairo and "is therefore nothing but an extension of Egyptian special services."[65] Two months later, Vaujour's successor as director general of security told the American consul in Algiers, Lewis Clark, that if the United States announced that it would not give any more money to Egypt and Spain "terrorist incidents" would end within two weeks. Indeed, without full support at the United Nations, "he would be fearful for [American diplomats'] safety."[66] After another year, Robert Lacoste, who had replaced Soustelle, was still claiming that order could be reestablished were it not for outside aid from Egypt, Morocco, and Tunisia. The lineup would change but the idea never did.[67]

Thus, while the French had not chosen the ground, they concluded that they could not avoid doing battle with the FLN in the international arena. The two sides therefore joined in waging the Algerian War as a kind of world war, a war for world opinion. America's clout at the United Nations and with the FLN's suppliers made it the most fiercely contested terrain. The French believed that Washington could easily command a majority in the General Assembly and virtually control the votes of many Latin American states. The French Ambassador to the United Nations, Hervé Alphand, joked with Henry Cabot Lodge that he could use "powerful arguments of a very practical character with both Guatemala and Bolivia." Lodge pretended he "did not know what they were," ignoring the fact that the CIA had installed Castillo Armas in power while Bolivia received massive U.S. economic aid.[68]

The French, based on their own relationship with Washington, might have realized that aid did not confer control. The Americans could not even prevent Paris from transferring U.S.-supplied equipment from Indochina to Algeria. Of course, the Quai preferred to have their permission and the endorsement it would imply. In particular, French forces needed helicopters to fight in the mountainous terrain of Kabylia, the Aurès, and Constantinois. Mitterrand's successor at the Interior Ministry, Maurice Bourgès-Maunoury, told a U.S. official that twenty would be worth more than a division.[69]

Yet the request for helicopters and more public U.S. support reignited the debate within the State Department over French—and American— policy on North Africa. Just as Chauvel had warned, soliciting aid invited criticism: "We cannot possibly express support for present French policies such as we understand them," Dulles wrote Ambassador Douglas Dillon, since it would "likely destroy our remaining influence [to] restrain Arab-Asians on [the] North African issue and jeopardize our own relations with [the] Arab-Asian world." Throughout 1955, Arab states appealed to Washington to bring pressure on the French in North Africa or at least reduce its support.[70] While the French had hoped that the Tunisian accords would prove their good intentions, Dulles cited them as a precedent and pushed for a similar approach to Algeria and Morocco.[71]

Faure and his foreign minister, Antoine Pinay, insisted that they intended to settle the conflict in Morocco and implement reforms in Algeria. But revelations about the nature of the repression undercut the official line. Vaujour confided to Clark that "the reforms reportedly proposed . . . may well be intended to cover up the harsh repressive measures now being ordered." He confirmed that the military had "already received instructions to bomb and shell native villages suspected of helping the rebels."[72]

Soustelle sacked Vaujour and kept U.S. diplomats under close surveillance.[73] But there was no concealing the fact that the insurgency was spreading. In June, it touched the outskirts of the capital itself for the first time since the start of the war. That same month, there were over eight hundred attacks in Morocco.[74] After Dillon appealed personally to Dulles, warning that the perception of American indifference or worse created "potentially by far the most serious [situation] I have faced here in France," the secretary agreed to allow the French to use the helicopters in Algeria.[75] Initially fearing a loss of face, Faure eventually made the decision public as proof of U.S. support. Whereas Clark had previously judged Soustelle to be a "cold fish," now he was "friendship itself." [76]

In fact, while temporarily veering toward the French, the State Department was still swerving back and forth across the "middle of the road." Dillon based his appeal not on Faure's reform program in North Africa but on the potential damage to overall U.S.-French relations, likening North Africa to "a festering sore hidden under the surface that could break open with devastating effects for our policies in Europe."[77] Faure had to portray the helicopters as an indication of the Americans' backing because they would not make an acceptable statement of support. After Walter Reuther of the AFL-CIO publicized and protested the decision, the Pentagon claimed that the helicopters were for "strictly humanitarian use." Ambassador Maurice Couve de Murville then told the State Department that "the less said by Americans on North Africa, the better."[78]

It was all depressingly familiar, as a State Department official concluded when preparing for a July heads-of-state conference in Geneva: the U.S. and French positions were virtually the same as they were when Acheson had sparred with his French counterparts three years before. Then as now, Washington refused to pledge its full support until Paris presented a liberal program that would gain the support of moderate North Africans, while Paris maintained that the North Africans rejected "reforms" precisely because Washington's equivocal position encouraged them to hold out for more. Rather than reassuring the French, Assistant Secretary of State for European Affairs Livingston Merchant now recommended that they "galvanize them into dramatic political action in North Africa." While raising the Indochina analogy, he emphasized that the stakes were "far bigger."[79]

The failure of reforms and the turn to war did change some features in the Franco-American dialogue, beginning with the bureaucratic politics of America's North African policy. This was no longer an unequal struggle between Europeanists and Africanists: the war was beginning to undermine U.S. interests on both continents. "The defense of Europe requires the presence of strong French forces in the line in Europe," Merchant argued. "They are being drained away to the South."[80] Indeed, by the end of the summer the number of French troops in Algeria topped one hundred and fifty thousand. Instead of guarding the Fulda gap against a Soviet invasion, motorized divisions were quite literally exchanging their tanks for mules to chase the mujahadeen up and down the Atlas Mountains.[81]

Ironically, now it was the French who were pursuing a peripheral strategy, trumpeting the strategic importance of North Africa and arguing that in fighting the Algerian nationalists they were defending NATO's southern flank. As veterans of the Indochina war began to arrive in Algeria, they would develop the doctrine of *Guerre Révolutionnaire*, according to which the FLN represented a new, more insidious kind of Soviet expansionism: an anti-Western insurgency that, if not Communist, *objectively* served the interests of Moscow.[82] This doctrine led the French to insist on pride of place in the alliance. As Soustelle argued in a 1956 *Foreign Affairs* article, France was not fighting a rearguard defense of colonialism but was instead "the vanguard of the Western world." As such, he bitterly observed, "she has received the hardest blows, and sometimes she feels that her sacrifices are not duly appreciated by her partners."[83]

State Department officials, on the other hand, judged that the French had little hope of winning a military victory and their pugnacity only discredited potential negotiating partners like Ferhat Abbas. To offer public support was therefore "politically inept," as another European desk officer put it.[84] George Allen, assistant secretary of state for Near Eastern, South Asian, and African affairs, was only too happy to endorse this position, adding that there was a danger of the communists taking over what were still "almost entirely nationalistic" movements in North Africa, just as they had in Indochina. Turning the French argument on its head, he claimed that they "might even welcome communist infiltration of Arab nationalists, to enable France to claim before American public opinion that France is fighting communism in North Africa."[85] Some officials felt so strongly about the subject that they voiced their concerns to *New York Times* columnist C. L. Sulzberger. "The time is coming when we will have to adopt a decisive attitude," he concluded, risking "a serious crisis in Franco-American relationships."[86]

Dulles himself had little sympathy left for the French in North Africa, but it appears that he did not want a confrontation before or during the

Geneva summit conference between the allies and the USSR. The secretary was concerned that "the French are so uncertain, so unhappy, and in such a mess all over everywhere that they may fall for some Soviet trick"—perhaps referring to his longstanding fear of a "global bargain" with the Soviets.[87] Nevertheless, he decided to have Julius Holmes, consul general in Tangier, review U.S. policy and come up with a plan of action, perhaps including an American mediator and "a long and protracted series of negotiations."[88] The secretary complained that the U.S. approach to North Africa had for too long been dominated by a concern for France. He thought that "the issues at stake for the United States in North Africa are much broader," and that it was "a danger to us—not only in North Africa, but also in other similar areas of the world—to consider such an area solely, or even primarily, from the standpoint of the effect of our policies upon the European powers." The United States thereby risked alienating "the great mass of mankind which is non-white and non-European."[89]

Yet Dulles was still undecided as to whether the greater danger lay in supporting independence movements or the status quo. In this same memo, he wrote in his own hand that "premature independence may be snatched away by extremists—usually Communist inspired." Even so, this represented a shift from two years before, when he told the Senate Foreign Relations Committee that a "somewhat backward position" was "the best of two evils."[90] By 1957, his conversion to the cause of accelerating decolonization—at least for North Africa—would be complete.

One reason for this conversion was the secretary's tendency to view decolonization as race relations between separate and increasingly unequal populations, a view that was also reflected in the "eyes only" dispatches he received from Holmes. Twenty-five million North Africans united—according to Holmes—by a common language, culture, and religion were increasing by five hundred thousand each year. The French, on the other hand, continued to base their policies "on juridical distinctions of their own making." They could not, Holmes argued,

> ignore the march of history as expressed by the wave of nationalism that has swept the former colonial world since the end of the war, and which, through unity of action, as shown at the United Nations and at Bandung, has become a powerful force with which Europe and America must reckon to an ever increasing degree.[91]

But Dulles did not want to take on the French over North Africa without consulting and perhaps acting in concert with the British. They also tended to look at Algeria in terms of demographics and race relations. Sir Gladwyn Jebb, their ambassador to France, observed that its Muslim population "was increasing to an alarming degree and is already pressing against the modest resources of the country." He favored "education and local autonomy for the native populations but the country still to be run by the whites."[92] Harold Macmillan, then secretary of state for foreign affairs, took it upon himself to write a reply. While he was in "general agreement" with Jebb, based on his previous experience in the region, he felt that to say "Algeria is France" was "foolish." "Algeria is African and Arab with a relatively large French population living there." Nevertheless, he opposed immediate intervention.[93] On August 17, Dulles agreed to defer action while leaving his options open: "I do not believe we should close our minds to the possibility that some positive action may become necessary."[94]

Population Control and Counterinsurgency

Three days later, violence of unprecedented ferocity swept across Algeria and Morocco. Authorities had anticipated trouble on the second anniversary of Mohamed V's deposition, and the new resident general, Gilbert Grandval, had been urging Faure to allow the sultan to return and form a transitional government.[95] But the premier was still working to overcome opposition from Foreign Minister Pinay when the Istiqlal-FLN alliance, months in the making, burst onto the scene. While there had already been sporadic violence in Rabat and Casablanca, for the first time Berber tribesmen joined town-dwelling Arab Istiqlal sympathizers in attacks on Europeans, including women and children, shattering the illusion that their mutual antipathy could serve as the basis of continued French rule.[96]

Meanwhile, in the Constantinois, some 200 ALN troops encouraged the local population to take up axes, knives, and clubs and join them in attacks on military barracks, European civilians, and Muslim collaborators.[97] Altogether they killed 123 men, women, and children—including 52 Muslims—sometimes in the most grisly fashion. Even if the FLN did not actually incite murder from the minarets and announce that the Egyptians were landing, as Soustelle later claimed, there can be no doubt that the French were frightened by the specter of jihad and responded with equal fervor.[98]

In Philippeville, soldiers would later recall how company commanders ordered them "to shoot down every Arab we met." There were so many bodies they had to be buried with bulldozers. The mayor personally directed lynchings. In one case, city officials corralled all the young Muslim men that they could find into the local stadium and killed them to a man. According to French figures, 1,273 Muslims died, or ten for every one slain in the initial attack.[99] But Soustelle's representative in Paris, Guy Calvet, told an American diplomat the next month that pieds noirs and the army were still "on a rampage . . . when some incident happens against some French citizen, the army goes in and just cleans up, killing hundreds of Arabs right and left. Contrary to what the French papers have reported, Calvet says that up to date more than 20,000 Arabs have been killed in the past month by the French."[100]

As Faure recalled sixty thousand more reservists and extended the state of emergency throughout Algeria Muslims took refuge in the mountains, many joining the rebel bands. By the end of the year, the number of ALN regulars had risen to six thousand, supplemented by perhaps ten to fifteen thousand nonuniformed auxiliaries.[101] French authorities could not be any more precise, which was exactly the problem. With FLN cells proliferating in urban areas and the ALN intermingled with refugees in the countryside, it was becoming impossible to distinguish rebels from the general population.

Was this the ALN's intention in launching the Constantinois uprising? According to those who participated in the planning, including Lakhdar Bentobbal and Ali Kafi, they were concerned to relieve their hard-pressed comrades in other *wilayat* and fully intended to force the uncommitted to take sides.[102] A notable success came on September 26, when sixty-one Muslim deputies in the Algerian Assembly declared that "the great majority of the population is now won over to the Algerian national idea."[103] The declaration dashed Soustelle's hopes to co-opt moderate leaders by winning their approval for his long-delayed reforms.

But while the rebels must have known the risk of retaliation, it is difficult to see why they should take the blame for French war crimes as well as their own just because, in this instance, they benefited from them. Even Yves Courrière, who implies that they wanted to maximize the number of martyrs through this "bestial unleashing," acknowledges that it was also revenge for summary executions of Muslim suspects and "systematic" rapes.[104] While these had been characterized as "police operations," now that the *rebels* had begun large-scale and indiscriminate attacks on civilians Calvet declared that Algeria had "almost reached the point of holy war." Soustelle's former aide, Vincent Monteil, warned that "race war, war unaccountable and merciless, is at our doors." In fact, French forces under Soustelle had already been waging the Algerian War as a race war. And while there was fanaticism—religious and otherwise—on *both* sides, the French had far more firepower with which to act on their impulses.[105]

Still, one must ask at what point the scale of killing becomes so disproportionate that it can no longer be considered mere excess or even a means to an end—exemplary terror—but might actually be an end in itself? At the time, even a moderate like Mohammed Bendjelloul, deputy from Constantine, alleged that "some Europeans were thinking in terms of exterminating the Moslems."[106] In view of Clausewitz's classic dictum that "war is nothing but the continuation of policy with other means," French conduct should be placed within the context of their overall approach to Algeria. This was already a subject for scrutiny—and salesmanship—in the international arena and therefore merits a closer analysis.

By July 1955, even propagandists, while continuing to insist on "the undeniably foreign character of the whole terrorist organization," had come to admit that there were deep causes for the troubles in Algeria.[107] But their most widely circulated pamphlet argued that it was the *demographic* inequality between Muslims and Europeans—not gross political and economic inequities—that caused the conflict.[108] The Quai d'Orsay's briefing book on Algeria—what they called their "bible"—agreed that "the demographic situation, [the] fundamental problem of Algeria, conditions all economic and social policy."[109]

Is it possible that the "demographic problem" also conditioned military policy—if not in a conscious sense, as Bendjelloul suspected, then in the kind of reflex actions that Calvet described, in which "the army goes in and just cleans up, killing hundreds of Arabs right and left"? Military commanders and civil officials, especially those in Philippeville, were acutely aware of the "demographic problem." As we have seen, even before the war one French administrator suggested that they allow "natural selection" to reduce the Muslim population.[110] In 1957, the general who commanded the Constantine region during the repression, Jacques Allard, painted an optimistic portrait of French efforts before pointing to "one shadow in this picture . . . the considerable expansion of the population."[111]

By 1958, the editors of a study on "Overpopulated Algeria" commissioned by the Catholic Church's *Secrétariat Social* observed that the demographic problem "for many, has become an obsession, and this in a dangerous fashion." But even while admitting that the notion of "overpopulation" was relative—demographic growth in France was then being celebrated as a sign of a national revival—some of the assembled authors analyzed Algerian demographics in an equally dangerous fashion.[112]

Thus, Henri Sanson's study of the "Characteristics of Overpopulation" judged that it resulted from "simple socio-cultural lagging or a real human disintegration." Either way, he concluded that the Muslims "behave practically on the animal social model."[113] Locating and developing new resources would not, therefore, provide a long-term solution to "overpopulation." As co-author Pierre Boyer had pointed out, Muslims had "proven incapable, *for whatever reason*, of benefiting from them." Instead, the editors suggested that one focus on the Muslim population and "fight systematically against socio-cultural underdevelopment."[114]

Muslims seemed unable to adapt to their environment only because these authors ignored the fact that losing the best land had compelled them to cultivate poorer soil and forage their livestock in woodlands. The resulting water and wood shortages and ruinous erosion were not "givens" that Muslims ignored to their peril, but products of French policies.[115] In fact, it was the pieds noirs who were oblivious to environmental scarcities—their disproportionate power allowed them to be. For instance, 5.3 million Muslim peasants consumed less potable water than did 120,000 predominantly European city-dwellers. The massive dams that served as symbols of "modernization" provided electric power and irrigation water for industry and wealthy landowners, but precious little for Algerian peasants.[116] While propagandists preached universal ideals, in practice French development policies were shaped by the prejudice that "Arabs belong to a different race, one inferior to my own," as the pied noir Jules Roy recalls being taught: ". . . their happiness was elsewhere, rather, if you please, like the happiness of cattle . . . 'They don't have the same needs we do . . . ,' I was always being told. . . . Who suffers seeing oxen sleep on straw or eating grass?" — especially, one might add, if they are lying in beds of their own making.[117]

As the defenders of French Algeria recast their *mission civilisatrice* as a *mission modernisatrice*, legitimating their rule not by their cultural leadership but by their mastery of the environment, the results were often no better and sometimes much worse for Muslims. They were still considered *a part of that environment*, though now a maladapted and overpopulous part.[118] Nowhere was this more apparent than in the campaign to "regroup" Algerian peasants begun in 1957, ideally in "model villages" but usually in barbed-wire enclosed camps. Living in barracks lined up at ninety-degree angles, they were obliged to attend "civic re-education" classes led by psychological warfare officers. However far-fetched, FLN propaganda claiming that the camps sterilized or even castrated their inhabitants reflected perceptions of their coercive purpose. While ostensibly aimed at "modernizing" Muslims, one colonel put the matter bluntly: "Call me a fascist if you like," he told *Le Monde*, "but we must make the population docile and manageable; everybody's acts must be controlled."[119] Meanwhile, the military bombed and napalmed anything that moved outside. Despite periodic reports that the camps' inhabitants faced slow death through starvation and exposure, and accusations that they were engaged in genocide, French officials continued to "regroup" Muslims until their number exceeded two million, fully one quarter of the total non-European population. This resettlement was judged to be in violation of the United Nations' "Convention on the Prevention and Punishment of the Crime of Genocide" by no less an authority than Raphael Lemkin, who led the fight for its creation.[120]

Thus, a "war against the underdevelopment of their land," as a propaganda film dubbed it, was no less a threat to Muslims than a war on pan-Islamism and pan-Arabism.[121] But it at least offered some hope for peace, since it allowed for the possibility of their "evolving." But what was to be done if Muslims kept reproducing at the same rate, seemingly unwilling to raise themselves out of their "natural" state? By 1958, it appeared that urbanization was making little difference in Muslims' natality. Jacques Breil went so far as to chart their conceptions according to the lunar calendar to show how, "even in urban communities, where the conditions most propitious to an evolution in this area are present, the behavior of Muslim couples remains based on natural impulses."[122] This uncontrolled population growth appeared to pose a danger not only to French rule in Algeria but to the future of France itself. "If Algeria became integrated with France, it is France that would become an expansion zone for Algerians," warned Hubert Deschamps, former governor of Madagascar — and former advocate of assimilation. "Our 1830 conquest would have the paradoxical consequence of an Islamic invasion, a revenge on Charles Martel."[123]

Counterinsurgency campaigns always take a heavy toll on civilians while warriors have for eons likened their enemies to animals. But considering the nature of *this* conflict and *these* enemies—an undeclared but otherwise unlimited war against a racially defined class of citizens—might the settlers' "rat hunts," the soldiers' "systematic" rapes, the high command's bombing of civilians and summary executions, and the administration's starvation-inducing resettlement program not have represented, in part, different responses to the same "problem" of Muslim "overpopulation"?[124]

Colonial authorities would justify these policies as a defense of Western civilization and an attack on "underdevelopment," but they gave the appearance of genocide, and "western values and genocide are incompatible," as Stéphane Bernard would write with reference to Morocco: "those who threaten [genocide] risk being removed from their command posts before they have even been able to put their schemes into practice. This phenomenon applies on every level, from the combat unit to the Atlantic Alliance."[125]

The leader of the Atlantic Alliance did not actually have the power to remove French officials from their posts. But these same officials displayed an almost obsessive interest in obtaining a statement of U.S. support. The next chapter will examine how they continued to seek the consent of the Americans to wage total war in Algeria and even to attack the FLN's allies abroad. The Algerians, for their part, made genocide a key theme in a growing diplomatic campaign.[126] By waging the Algerian War as a civilizational conflict the French only completed the internationalization of the Algerian question.

4

Confronting the Empire of Islam

The present period will be decisive for the future of the world. After having contained the offensive of pan-Slavism, the West must now confront that of pan-Islamism, which conspires with Soviet pan-Slavism.

Colonel Nasser, in his writings, has made his objective known: to re-create the empire of Islam around Egypt. . . .

There is only one game which is being played out in the Near East as in North Africa: that of the expansion of pan-Islamism.

Guy Mollet to Anthony Eden, March 11, 1956 [1]

We are Muslims and have the right to be bigamists. We can therefore marry ourselves to the East and to the West and be loyal to our two wives.

Prince Moulay Hassan of Morocco, June 1956 [2]

Like George Bernard Shaw's quip about Anglo Saxons, the French and the Americans were two peoples separated by a common language: they came to share the same discourse concerning the danger of civilizational conflict and the development of "Eurafrica" while differing over the timing, means, and manner of achieving their aims. Thus, like their French counterparts, Eisenhower and Dulles approached decolonization in terms of demographics and pictured Third World peoples as a force of nature, but they did not believe this was a force to be fought or even confronted. Thus, in urging Churchill to make decolonization his crowning achievement, Eisenhower wrote that "there is abroad in the world a fierce and growing spirit of nationalism."

> Should we try to dam it up completely, it would, like a mighty river, burst through the barriers and could create havoc. But again, like a river, if we are intelligent enough to make constructive use of this force, then the result, far from being disastrous, could redound greatly to our advantage, particularly in our struggle against the Kremlin's power.[3]

While demeaning to anticolonial movements, this way of portraying decolonization as taming nature made it part of modernization and coded counterinsurgency as unenlightened, even primitive.

What was to be done if the French were unwilling or unable to develop a more "modern" relationship with Third World nationalism? In September 1955, Julius Holmes wrote to Dulles that North Africa should be federated with France, since only self-government could "counteract the attractions of Pan-Arabism and the 'Brotherhood' of Islam." But Holmes was scathing in his assessment of France's chance for success, citing

> . . . the lingering national psychosis of defeat in World War II expressed by hypersensitivity and often strident self-assertions; the clinging to a traditional concept of greatness and glory in the face of failure to meet a changing world, without the sharp logic with which this logical people are supposed to be endowed.

Just as some French suspected that Muslims were incapable of self-improvement, Holmes thought the French were themselves "allergic to change."[4]

Yet while Holmes preferred to stereotype the French, his own report showed that it was not their nature but their politics that made change difficult. Two weeks earlier, Pierre July, the minister of Moroccan and Tunisian affairs, explained to American diplomats that the prime minister was "fully aware that the Algerian situation must be met eventually in the same basic way as Tunisia and Morocco, but that for tactical reasons he would not do so immediately." Fashioning a more liberal policy for Morocco had already "strained the government coalition to the breaking point."[5] It was only on September 27, 1955, that Faure won Pinay's support for negotiating with Moroccan nationalists. The foreign minister was in New York for the opening of the new General Assembly and was impressed by the force of anti-French sentiment there. That year seventeen states, most Eastern bloc or Afro-Asian, were to gain membership. In a speech to the Assembly two days later, he uttered the word "independence" for the first time in connection with Morocco. But Pinay would make no concession on the much more delicate problem of Algeria.[6]

Some delegations took up Bendjelloul's condemnation of the French repression, which had been reported in the New York press, as a violation of the Universal Declaration of Human Rights.[7] Tangible proof came when a Fox-Movietone cameraman captured a French gendarme gunning down a prisoner in Algiers. The newsreel was screened across the United States, Latin America, and even at the General Assembly itself.[8] Hoping to influence the debate over inscribing the Algeria question on the General Assembly's agenda, Muslim shopkeepers staged their first general strike while the French deployed troops, tanks, and sandbag barricades at strategic points around Algiers.[9] Soustelle was all too aware of the "relationship of resonance and reciprocity" between the FLN's internal and external campaigns when he dissolved the Algerian Assembly rather than risk a walkout, "the potentially grave consequences of which cannot be foreseen either on the national or international level."[10]

Three days later, the General Assembly delegates voted in "an electrified atmosphere," as Aït Ahmed later recalled, with his two deputies "counting on their toes." He had prepared a statement in case of defeat, but instead they won by a single vote, provoking thunderous applause. Now it was Pinay who felt obliged to walk out, making France the first state to boycott the United Nations since the Soviets protested the exclusion of Communist China five years before. A grateful Aït Ahmed considered it "wonderful publicity."[11] The Afro-Asian delegations themselves appeared astonished by their ability to outvote a Security Council member in an ostensibly domestic affair.[12]

At a New York dinner party that evening, the British representative, Sir Pierson Dixon, found Pinay to be "in a state of considerable emotion." Obviously preoccupied, Pinay hardly said a word until Soviet Foreign Minister Vyacheslav Molotov prepared to leave. It was then that "his pent-up feelings erupted into a ferocious attack on the Russians." He bitterly contrasted their vote at the United Nations with Khrushchev's recent statement that Algeria was a French affair.[13]

Absent primary evidence, one can only surmise that the reversal was another move in Moscow's campaign to expand its influence in the Third World. Khrushchev had scored his first major success the previous month with the arms deal with Egypt, thereby breaking a Western monopoly in the Middle East. In comparison, offending France at the United Nations was small beer. Faure and Pinay canceled a planned visit to Moscow, but they could do little else. Paris had lost most of its leverage vis-à-vis the USSR by approving German rearmament the previous spring.[14]

Despite Alphand's accusations that Lodge had done little to support them in the General Assembly, the French would now have to put their faith in Washington.[15] As Chauvel observed from London with regard to a proposed boycott: "everything depends on what the United States will think. Short of their assent and intervention with the South Americans, we can hope for nothing concrete."[16] The military situation in North Africa made the French all the more desperate. The day after the General Assembly vote, the Istiqlal and the FLN used a new Egyptian arms shipment and their base in Spanish Morocco to launch a joint offensive, including the first attacks in western Algeria since the start of the uprising. On October 4, al-Fassi in Cairo actually declared war on France and vowed that the Moroccans and Algerians would fight together until both were independent. The previous night, Algerian rebels had attacked French settlers in Tunisia, apparently intending to create "a zone of insecurity" between Libya and the Algerian border through which to smuggle arms.[17]

That same day, Pinay appealed to Ambassador Dillon for support, pointing to the "fusion" of the Bandung and Soviet blocs as "the gravest threat to the stability of the world." Citing America's own civil rights problem, the foreign minister warned that if they were able to gain control of the General Assembly and interfere in domestic issues "no country would be safe."[18] But Pinay need not have worried. Even before hearing his appeal, Dulles had rejected Holmes's proposal for a more pronation-alist position, telling him that "this is a terrible thing to butt into when you are not invited." While the secretary agreed that the French "seem temperamentally unable to make changes peacefully before they are forced to do so," he himself had long been "allergic to change" in U.S. policy.[19] He may have been particularly averse to a new initiative in North Africa at this time because Eisenhower could not give his approval and support. The president had suffered a heart attack on September 23, and no one knew yet whether he would even finish his first term.[20]

More generally, there was little point in pushing as long as Faure himself appeared determined to press reform in the face of dogged par-liamentary opposition. Indeed, while Eisenhower was still lying in a hos-pital bed, the prime minister was arguing his thesis about the relentless nature of nationalism and the power represented by the Bandung confer-ence before the French assembly. "Such aspirations," he asserted, "in a country like Morocco, cannot be denied, nor broken, and we must divert it towards cooperation with France."[21] Faure's domestic position was ac-tually strengthened by the diplomatic setback at the United Nations, since the Assembly did not want to turn him out so soon afterward. Not for the last time, a U.N. vote influenced the French because they did not wish to *appear* to be influenced.[22] Few entertained any illusions about what would follow when Faure allowed Mohamed V to return from Mad-agascar. The sultan could not rein in the militants unless he spoke with the authority of the throne and the promise of independence. The Tu-nisians could not then be denied the same status, since the French con-sidered them the more évolué of the two peoples.

While continuing to condemn "scandalous interference from abroad," even hard-liners had begun to realize that they might lose control of Al-geria if they did not contain the nascent rebellion in Morocco, the mirror image of Faure's judgment that he would lose the Moroccan settlement if he also attempted a political solution in Algeria.[23] Soustelle's reforms had still not been put to a vote and the government was no closer to defining what "integration" would actually mean, much less implementing it. "What has a clear sense," Bourgès-Maunoury suggested, "is its oppo-site, disintegration. Let us all agree to avoid this in Algeria, which would certainly precede that of the nation."[24]

Though Faure did not remain in power long enough to oversee it, the assembly would acquiesce in this new policy toward the protectorates to save Algeria and, apparently, France itself. To "divert" Moroccan and Tunisian nationalism into cooperation with France meant dividing Mo-hamed V from al-Fassi, Bourguiba from Ben Youssef, and, above all, isolating the FLN. The policy both reflected and reinforced the idea of a dichotomy between East and West and the values they were supposed to represent. As Bourgès explained it to Ambassador Dillon in February 1956, this was "a struggle between Middle Eastern Islamic fanaticism and Western-oriented moderate nationalism." Similarly, Alain Savary, who as the new secretary of state for Moroccan and Tunisian affairs would conduct the negotiations, told him that the "basic problem in all of North Africa is [a] contest between eastern and western points of view." In Tunisia, Bourguiba represented the West: "liberal, anti-clerical and possibly even republican at heart." Ben Youssef, on the other hand, relied on "fanatical Islamic elements." Another official told Dillon that they hoped to create a "break" in the " 'religious front' of Moslem hostility" that might lead to a solution in Algeria.[25]

But the idea of an oriental-occidental dichotomy had long predated this policy and gradually overpowered it. Indeed, aside from a few like Savary, most French officials never put their faith in "Western-oriented moderate nationalists" or the agreements they signed. They calculated, however, that the very forces that had undermined French rule—demographic growth and "underdevelopment"—might leave the former protectorates with no alternative to remaining "interdependent" with France. Tunisia, which one official derided as a "country of carpet salesmen," could not therefore be allowed to start a bidding war for foreign aid between France and all comers. Similarly, Faure was advised that his "foremost concern must be to avoid at all cost the internationalization of the Moroccan question, which Spain desires openly and the United States secretly."[26] By monopolizing and manipulating foreign aid and trade and leaving behind troops and bases, the French hoped to deter or defeat any further Tunisian or Moroccan assistance to the Algerians. The FLN was keenly aware of the danger. Noting the progress of the Moroccan-French talks, Khider concluded that "we could find ourselves in hot water."[27]

On November 6, Pinay and Mohamed V signed a declaration that announced negotiations to make Morocco "an independent state united with France by permanent ties of interdependence freely consented and defined."[28] The FLN suffered another setback later that month when the Afro-Asian bloc with Nehru in the lead agreed to adjourn debate on Algeria, though only after the supposedly absent and indifferent French delegation had vigorously lobbied behind the scenes.[29] Another element of the French design fell into place when Bourguiba managed to have Ben Youssef, the FLN's ally in armed struggle, expelled from the Neo Destour. Yet, in doing so, he exposed a critical flaw: he won the party's support only by explaining how his use of "threats," "seduction," and exploitation of every concession was the best way to "escape from French colonialism."[30] Thus, what Resident General Boyer de la Tour had called the "new style 'colonial' adventure" was ultimately an illusion: moderate nationalists held a mandate only to the extent that they could deliver real independence, and no North African leader could claim to be independent while appearing to support France's war in Algeria.[31] "Try to understand," Bourguiba would tell *Figaro* in April 1956. "We consider the French as friends. But the Algerians are our brothers. If we are forced to choose, we shall be at the side of our brothers."[32]

Incompatible with local political conditions, French policy was also poorly adapted to the global strategic environment—and particularly the intensifying competition between the United States and the Soviets to win over the Third World. After Khrushchev made the arms deal with Egypt and announced visits to India, Burma, and Afghanistan—where he would promise additional aid—Dulles told a November 1955 NSC meeting that "[t]he scene of the battle between the free world and the communist world was shifting."[33] Khrushchev would sometimes threaten war on behalf of Third World allies and always exaggerated Soviet nuclear forces, but Eisenhower correctly discerned that "the Soviets have been turned away from the military form of international action," as he told Secretary of Defense Charles Wilson in March 1956.[34] Khrushchev shifted resources to technological research—particularly in high-visibility areas like the space program—and raising living standards.[35] Together, these helped him to compete with the United States for Third World opinion, especially when coupled with showcase aid projects, trade fairs, and more foreign-language broadcasting.[36] At the same time, the KGB worked undercover purveying disinformation and funding front organizations.[37] This was a low-cost program that promised handsome payoffs, even in terms of the military balance. Military aid was generally drawn from stocks of used equipment, and by offering it with "no strings attached" the Soviets encouraged countries to demand a high price for permitting American bases if they were not to demand withdrawal.[38]

"The Soviets have every opportunity to play us for suckers," Eisenhower complained. He had begun his administration intending to shift from direct aid to increased trade with Third World countries and was not opposed to neutralism per se. But he quickly realized that "it would not be possible to reduce the total level of U.S. economic assistance for a long time to come," not with the Soviets prepared to move on targets of opportunity, like Morocco and Tunisia.[39]

While Dulles spoke of the superpower competition "shifting" to the Third World, he understood all too well that the different theaters of the Cold War remained linked by complex and conflictual political and economic ties. "The loss of the oil of the Middle East would be almost catastrophic to the West," Dulles warned during the same NSC meeting. "If Europe were to lose Africa, little would be left of Europe."[40] The United States could not preserve its interests in any of these regions unless they were mutually reconciled. Indeed, Dulles pondered the possibility of a "reverse Bandung," a conference "aimed at a demonstration of a community of interest across racial lines and a slowing down of the racially conscious antipathy now developing in non-white areas."[41] While nothing came of this initiative, State Department officials were already preparing to act as intermediaries between the French and the FLN.

On November 29, Faure lost a vote of confidence and, hoping to catch his opponents off guard, decided to dissolve the assembly. As the French scrambled for the January 2 elections, State Department officials in Washington and Tripoli began a series of clandestine meetings with Aït Ahmed and Ben Bella. They were particularly impressed with Aït Ahmed, whom they described as "silken in tone and marble-hard in content."

He protested against the use of American arms by French troops while stressing that the nerve center of the rebellion was in Algeria—not Cairo, as the French claimed. Most important, he warned that "the attitudes of an independent North Africa toward the West would depend on the circumstances in which she won her independence."[42]

Ben Bella was equally adept at playing on American anxieties. He criticized U.S. military aid to the French war effort not only because it hurt America's image in North Africa but also since it "weakened the defenses of Western Europe against the Soviet Union."

> There was no thought, he said, that the United States should exert public pressure on France. Such a move would be bound to fail. He hoped however that the United States behind the scenes would continually urge the French in the direction of finding a peaceful solution through negotiations with the Algerian Nationalists.[43]

The Americans could hardly disagree with Ben Bella's analysis of the problem, nor his suggested policy. Indeed, even Faure's eventual successor as prime minister, the Socialist Guy Mollet, had already described the assembly election as a choice between a "future of reconciliation and peace . . . and a stupid war without end."[44]

In fact, the election settled nothing. The center left and the center right lost seats to two extremes: the Communists and a new protest party under Pierre Poujade, an antitax shopkeeper married to a pied noir.[45] Mollet and every succeeding Fourth Republic premier could not therefore dispense with the support of the colonial lobby. Hard-liners were never reconciled to losing the protectorates, delivering trenchant critiques of a strategy that had left Algeria a "bird with clipped wings," as Bidault put it.[46] But the colonial lobby could not explain where they would find the taxes and troops necessary to keep Morocco and Tunisia in captivity. Mollet would soon be piling up debt and hollowing out France's contribution to NATO just to hold Algeria. It is doubtful that France could ever have cajoled or coerced Rabat and Tunis into helping them fight the FLN. But Bidault and his ilk ensured that this strategy was hardly tested, since they never consented to even meager aid without carping about the nationalists' bad faith and bad manners, thereby weakening whatever francophile constituency still existed in the former protectorates.

The hard-liners could also sabotage a conciliatory policy in Algeria. They set a precedent in February 1956 when Mollet decided to visit Algiers, ignoring warnings that he would meet a hostile reception. He had just named General Georges Catroux, who had been involved in the negotiations leading to Moroccan independence, as "resident minister." The new title signaled that Catroux would answer to Paris rather than the settlers.[47] But when Mollet went to lay a wreath at the war memorial, he was quickly surrounded by a mob of pieds noirs howling death threats. For two hours, the prime minister had to stand under a rain of rocks, garbage, and rotten tomatoes before being rescued by the army. Besieged in the Government House, Mollet finally accepted the resignation of his first resident minister. After the mob let him out, he returned to Paris and appointed the intransigent Robert Lacoste instead.[48]

Out of this maelstrom, Mollet emerged with what at first appeared to be a coherent policy. He declared that France would fight the rebels until they agreed to lay down their arms. Free elections would follow and everyone could participate, even the leaders of the FLN. Finally, his government would negotiate with the people's chosen representatives to determine the nature of the "Algerian personality," as he put it. "We will maintain indissoluble bonds," Mollet said, "but they will be freely negotiated and accepted." He pretended not to notice the contradiction, even though the Moroccans and Tunisians brought it to his attention every day they "freely negotiated" *their* "indissoluble bonds."[49]

Mollet actually pursued all three steps simultaneously—or rather, his motley cabinet did. Little coordination could be expected of ministers who privately referred to each other as *ce con*, "that ass," as did Mitterrand, Bourgès-Maunoury, and Mollet himself. They extended conscription to twenty-seven months to send 200,000 more troops to Algeria and obtained "special powers" to repress and reform. They tinkered endlessly with schemes that would somehow abolish the separate electoral colleges without allowing one hundred Muslims to enter the Assembly. And in April, they began secret talks with the FLN on the basis of self-rule, though using go-betweens who could be, and were, disavowed. By managing to combine martial words and deeds, promises and plans for reform, and the postponement of all difficult decisions, Mollet became the longest serving prime minister of the Fourth Republic.[50]

Three weeks after the settler riot in Algiers, Bourgès-Maunoury, the defense minister in the new government, made a startling admission to Ambassador Dillon. He said he had "come to realize that there was no solution to this problem":

> Any solution acceptable to Moslems would have to be imposed on [the] local French population by armed force, he then expressed [a] view which is now commonplace here that if France should be driven from Algeria, the Fourth Republic would not survive the shock and a drastic change of regime would take place in France.[51]

Bourgès could be congratulated for his foresight. But why, one might ask, did he not share it with the French people or at least refuse to serve a government that was prosecuting "a stupid war without end," as Mollet himself described it? Why did he instead give his word to military officers that this government, in contrast to its predecessors, was committed to French Algeria, urging them to impress the same faith on their men?[52] Why did he order these men to dishonor themselves by engaging in torture, or tolerating it, not to speak of other crimes?[53] And why would he, more than any other minister, press for *another* war against Egypt, as if Algerians were too few to pay the price for this folly?[54] If it was to save the Fourth Republic, which he knew could neither surmount nor survive its most important challenge, then one begins to see why its ministers won so little respect from their foreign counterparts, their public, or even each other.

The Return of the Blank Check

Eisenhower was hardly committed to preserving the Fourth Republic, but he feared an outright collapse that might shift the diplomatic alignment of not only North Africa but of France itself. Beginning on March 3, 1956, he received a series of panicky appeals through diplomatic and military channels. The monthly total of FLN bombings, ambushes, and assassinations had more than quadrupled since September 1955, from 584 to 2,624.[55] But perhaps the most telling statistic was the state of French reserves in Algeria: out of an army now totaling 200,000, only a few hundred men remained uncommitted. Unless and until reinforcements arrived, the French were limited to the static defense of strategic points and population centers.[56]

Meanwhile, American support appeared halfhearted in comparison with other states. Even Nikolai Bulganin had addressed his "warmest greetings to Guy Mollet on the successful settlement of the Moroccan and Tunisian problems," and French Communists joined the overwhelming majority that gave him "special powers" in Algeria.[57] Issuing a veiled demand that Americans "cease their intrigues," respected former President Vincent Auriol announced in *France-Soir* that it "is now time to recall that the Atlantic Pact includes Algeria, today's center of Islamic aggression."[58] Exploratory drilling had recently revealed the existence of large oil fields in the Sahara, which made French authorities all the more suspicious of U.S. intentions. Indeed, the previous month they had dispatched a platoon of foreign legionnaires with orders to use force to repel Standard Oil prospectors based in Libya.[59] The day after Auriol's article was published, Ambassador Dillon reported a "dangerously sharp rise in anti-American sentiment." He warned that without a strong, public statement of U.S. support the danger of an "explosion" was "imminent."[60] A week later a crowd of French colonists attacked and seriously damaged the American consulate in Tunis.[61]

The army attaché in Paris, General Frank Moorman, reported that a tearful Lacoste had told fellow ministers that they were "on the brink of disaster. They see coming in Algeria a state of anarchy marked by bloodshed, riot, and pillage. They are aware that such a state of affairs [in] Algeria could result in revolution in France culminating in Fascism or Communism or some weird combination of both."[62] Lest this be thought an exaggeration, Moorman attached a memorandum by General Jean Etienne Valluy, French representative to the NATO Standing Group, which warned that any attempt to replace French with "allied" influence "would be resented by France so bitterly that her fidelity in the Alliance would be shaken." Moscow might then "use for its own ends the nationalism of a country unjustly humiliated and cast down. . . . To stay in North Africa," Valluy concluded, ". . . has become, to France in the 20th century, a matter of life or death. She has decided to fight for life."[63]

The next day, four and one-half years after the French first asked for it, Eisenhower finally answered their demand for a forthright statement of American support.[64] The president acted not only for the sake of Franco-American relations, but also because he had grown worried about the increasing unity and power of the Arab and Islamic world. After failing to convince Nasser to settle his differences with Israel, he complained that "the Arabs, absorbing major consignments of arms from the Soviets, are daily growing more arrogant and disregarding the interests of Western Europe and of the United States in the Middle East region."[65] Indeed, he confided to a British visitor that "he had been spending much time reading up [on] the history of Arab nationalism and the wars of the crusades." He claimed that "Europe had suffered for a thousand years from the last Islamic surge and that we (repeat we) could not afford another."[66]

But there could be no question of joining in a new crusade. The need for oil still made any out-and-out confrontation seem suicidal. On the same day Eisenhower read Valluy's vow "to fight for life," he wrote in his diary that "the economy of [the] European countries would collapse if those oil supplies were cut off. If the economy of Europe would collapse, the United States would be in a situation of which the difficulty could scarcely be exaggerated."[67] Instead, he called for "a high class machiavellian plan . . . which would split the Arabs. . . ." Henceforth, U.S. policy aimed at isolating Egypt and building up King Saud, who had also given diplomatic and financial support to the North African nationalists. Moreover, he continued to hope that Nasser would eventually yield to American interests.[68] While implicitly giving the French what amounted to a last chance to prevail by force, he publicly urged a compromise respecting the "legitimate rights" of Algerians.[69]

On March 20, the same day French and Tunisian representatives were signing the protocol that ended the protectorate, Ambassador Dillon delivered what appeared to be the long-awaited "blank check" at a luncheon of the Diplomatic Press Association. With over one hundred journalists and diplomats in attendance, Dillon announced "once and for all," "with the greatest clarity and force," that America had "no desire to interfere in any way with the close relationship between France [Morocco and Tunisia]," which he called "one of the bulwarks of the Free World." He declared further, "so that there can be no possible misunderstanding," that the "United States stands solidly behind France in her search for a liberal and equitable solution of the problems in Algeria."[70]

Despite Dillon's theatrics, this was not unqualified backing. It was as if he had delivered an outsized check that was indeed blank but for a small notation: "amount not to exceed support for a *liberal* and *equitable* solution." Even so, the speech was broadcast on French radio networks, re-

ceived banner headlines in the Paris papers, and was reprinted in full by
The New York Times and *The Herald Tribune*.[71] In the following weeks, it
was backed up by a series of actions that lent weight to his words. First,
the Americans rebuffed Moroccan requests for aid.[72] They also approved
a North Atlantic Council resolution acquiescing in the transfer of French
forces to Algeria. At the same time, they allowed the diversion of more
U.S.-supplied equipment, gave priority to French orders for helicopters,
and sold them four hundred light planes at a discount. Though the Americans could not arm them with machine guns, they referred the French
to someone who would.[73] When combined with sixty B-26 medium
bombers, the volume of purchases left the French air force attaché and
his staff in Washington "bordering on exhaustion."[74]

The American position was bluntly, and privately, put by Deputy
Under Secretary of State Robert Murphy. He told a Quai d'Orsay official
that he recognized the French were making a tremendous effort and were
determined to succeed, but they had made the same promises in Indochina only to be "submerged." He warned that the United States could
not allow another such debacle since it feared nothing more than disorder
in North Africa. "But," he added, "we agree to let you try. If you truly
believe that you can solve the problem by force, do it but do it quickly.
If you succeed, no one will begrudge you for having been too tough. But,
if you cannot reestablish calm quickly, then make all the necessary concessions."[75]

Undeterred by the apparent shift in the U.S. position, Aït Ahmed
redoubled his efforts, pressing the Afro-Asian caucus to convene a special
session of the General Assembly and petition the Security Council. "The
more we push the US to implicate itself with colonialism," he predicted,
"the closer will be the day when they will see themselves obliged to bail
out." At the same time, he met with Irving Brown to cement American
labor's support and urged all of his allies to make démarches to the NATO
capitals and especially Washington and London. In particular, he called
on Khider to obtain "the most extreme positions possible" from the Arab
League. These efforts were interconnected and mutually reinforcing: "extreme" positions by the league would lend urgency to the arguments of
groups like the AFL-CIO and the démarches of even "moderate" states
such as India. The collective weight of domestic and international opinion
would compel France's allies to press for a compromise peace.[76]

Most ministers in the new French government did not actually believe
they could solve the Algerian problem by force alone, but rather by a
combination of concessions and coercion intended to create and exploit
breaks in what they continued to believe was a racial or "religious front."
Whatever Murphy thought, Minister of Colonies Gaston Defferre did not
want "the whole world [to] believe that France carries out reforms only
when blood begins to flow." In March 1956, the new government
therefore passed a *loi cadre* or framework law, which ended a policy of
assimilation that by now had become a platform for the political and

economic demands of labor leaders like Sékou Touré of Guinea. Universal franchise, territorial assemblies, and ministerial councils would require them to assume budgetary responsibility and, it was hoped, nurture more Francophile leaders like the Ivory Coast's Félix Houphouët-Boigny, a minister of state who had helped draft the plan.[77]

Encouraging pro-French elements was obviously even more imperative in Algeria. Four days after the new cabinet's investiture, Foreign Minister Christian Pineau told Dillon that they were determined to conclude an agreement with the Algerian nationalists. "However if [the] problem became one of Islam versus the French, partaking the aspects of a holy war, it was clear that the French could never find a solution and [the] eventual results were impossible to foresee." Pineau stressed that they would "need all the understanding and help they could possibly get" in order "to prevent Egyptians from fanning the flames."[78]

Mollet displayed little determination two days later when he caved in to rioting settlers. But the incident in Algiers could be turned to their advantage in direct appeals to Nasser. When President René Coty had warned the Egyptian ambassador the night before that another power might help the settlers to secede, the ambassador assured him that Cairo "greatly preferred the French presence to the American one in Algeria."[79]

The Scrutable Orient

Could the "religious front" be outflanked through Cairo? Even without counting the arms shipments, Egypt's backing was vital to the FLN. Time and again, potential supporters in Asia told Algerian representatives that the Arab states had to take the lead, and Egypt was easily the most influential among them. While Ben Bella had the warmest relations with Nasser's government, even Khider considered the Egyptians to be friends "despite many variations on their part."[80]

Some among the French were now prepared to bargain for a decisive shift. In March, Pineau paid a surprise visit. Mollet was not forewarned, so three days after the prime minister urged Eden to join him in opposing Nasser's "empire of Islam" his foreign minister found that the colonel was hardly a fanatic. Nasser promised that he would approve of any solution that had the support of Muslims and agreed to arrange a meeting between a French representative and the FLN. He also gave his word as an officer that no Algerians were receiving military training in Egypt.[81]

Pineau publicized this assurance and was embarrassed when it was later proved to be untrue. On the other hand, in the next three weeks there was a significant decline in the size of Egyptian arms shipments to Algeria.[82] Larbi Ben M'Hidi was left waiting in Madrid for a planned shipment to Oranie that never arrived. He then went to Cairo and returned with the conclusion that Egyptian aid was "subordinated to its diplomacy," particularly the Pineau-Nasser meeting.[83] Aït Ahmed and Khider also noted a weakening of diplomatic support at the United Nations and the Arab League as well as a marked decline in Egyptian media interest.[84]

That same month Nasser ordered Dib to review Egyptian policy. Noting that Egypt could destabilize North Africa, he outlined the concessions that might be extracted from France:

> It was possible to arrive at an agreement with the French government which could serve the Egyptian liberation policy if it accepted:
> —to limit arms aid from France to Israel and prevent the mobilization of French Jews for its benefit;
> —to prevent North African Jews from emigrating to Israel;
> —to continue to oppose the Baghdad Pact and not to take a position in the Middle East contrary to Egyptian policy;
> —to contribute to the search for a solution to the Palestinians' cause which would correspond to their aspirations;
> —to do something to improve the trade balance between Egypt and France; equally, to stop the anti-Egyptian campaigns in the French press

Thus, at the same time a political solution in North Africa was beginning to seem possible, Cairo was contemplating a range of French concessions that had nothing whatever to do with Algerian independence—except to the extent that they served the larger cause of "Arab nationalism" (as defined by Egypt).[85] It is not clear whether the Egyptians actually offered this deal. But Mollet did publicly reaffirm his opposition to the Baghdad Pact upon returning from London. This betrayed an agreement with Eden, according to which he would mute criticism in exchange for British help in stopping Egyptian arms shipments through Libya.[86]

Meanwhile, Mollet sent an envoy to Cairo to convey the French terms for an Algerian settlement. Georges Gorse, a future ambassador to Tunisia, promised significant autonomy for Algeria, liberation for political detainees, guarantees for the ALN, free elections, and negotiations with the winners. The Algerians found this inadequate, but they agreed to let Dib arrange an April 12 meeting with Joseph Begarra, a personal friend of Mollet. Begarra specified that the elections would take place after a cease-fire and would produce a single assembly, thus abolishing the two-college system that gave equal representation to the European minority. While the resident designated by Paris would remain the head of the government, the assembly would be responsible for all internal Algerian affairs except those affecting the personal status of Europeans. Responding for the external delegation, Khider insisted that only those designated by the FLN could negotiate, and they would not agree to a cease-fire unless France accepted the principle of Algeria's sovereign independence. Only then could elections empower a new government to determine the future of French-Algerian relations. Even these terms were provisional until the leaders of the interior gave their assent.[87] Nevertheless, merely by talking, and agreeing to continue talking, the two sides had made concessions: the French because their interlocutors had never been elected, the FLN because Paris had not yet accepted Algeria's ultimate independence. But this was the first and last such discussion to take place under Nasser's auspices — French-Egyptian relations were about to take a sharp turn for the worse.[88]

Even if Pineau had wished to make a deal like the one Dib describes, he probably would not have been able to pull it off. Mollet and Bourgès-Maunoury had a deep, sentimental attachment to Israel and might have been repulsed rather than attracted to the offer. Moreover, since the summer of 1955, the Quai d'Orsay had been powerless to stop the Defense Ministry from supplying Israel with tanks and planes. On the very eve of the first Begarra-Khider meeting, Israel took delivery of its first twelve Mystère IVs, the latest generation of French jet fighters.[89]

The Israelis, for their part, were pushing hard from the other direction. As early as June 1955, Shimon Peres, then director general of the Israeli Defense Ministry, observed that "every Frenchman killed in North Africa, like every Egyptian killed in the Gaza Strip, takes us one step further towards strengthening the ties between France and Israel."[90] His ultimate goal was to obtain a nuclear reactor. To overcome French hesitations, he authorized Israeli military intelligence to help their French counterparts with information on Egyptian aid to the FLN. Subsequently, their reports became detailed and damning, making a French-Egyptian rapprochement even more unlikely.[91] To add insult to injury, ten days after Nasser brokered the first Begarra-Khider meeting, Israeli Premier David Ben-Gurion singled France out for praise as the only country to supply them with weaponry. Finally, on May 15, *Le Monde* reported that the Israelis had contracted for another dozen Mystère IVs.[92]

That same day, Nasser asked Dib to reevaluate relations with France and North Africa. Dib began his analysis vaguely but revealingly by noting that Egypt had "another dimension and other perspectives on the level of the fight for the liberation of the Arab world which were not limited to North Africa." He argued that their ability to foment unrest there increased their international clout. Moreover, it did not risk French reprisals since these "depended on the Zionist influence in France as well as the worry in official circles about the threat that [Egypt] could pose to French interests in general." Though Dib appears oblivious to it, this point vitiated the heroic portrait he then painted of Nasser as he "took his decisions of defiance." "Sitting erect in his chair with a special gleam in his eyes,"

> Nasser reminded me . . . that the liberty of Egypt is incomplete without that of other Arab countries and that this liberty, such as we understand it, must be made real by sacrifices. Each Arab country which frees itself must assume its share of them, this had to be the profession of faith of revolutionaries.

According to Dib, Nasser reaffirmed his determination to support the Algerians whatever sacrifices that entailed for Egypt. But what were these sacrifices, one might ask, if it was actually the "Zionist influence" which provoked French reprisals, not Egyptian aid to the FLN?[93]

The orders that followed are equally puzzling. While Nasser directed Dib to deliver as many arms to the FLN as possible, even using air drops, he was equally concerned to "respond to French propaganda insinuating that Egypt had abandoned the cause of the Algerian revolution" by divulging the "peaceful role of Egypt" in the Begarra-Khider meetings. This would hardly dispel doubts as to Egypt's commitment to nothing less than full Algerian independence, but it would certainly endanger further French-FLN negotiations. In fact, these leaks forced Khider to formally deny that any negotiations were taking place. [94]

All of this raises the question of who would make the sacrifices Nasser referred to, and for whom. In fact, it provides further evidence that he used the FLN as an instrument in his policy toward France and Israel. Having finally given up on trying to stop the alliance between them, he now threw his full support behind Algerian independence. The French, for their part, continued to increase aid to Israel until, in September 1956, they agreed to supply a research reactor. Eventually it grew into the plutonium production and processing complex of Dimona.[95]

"A Clash of Two Civilizations"

The Franco-Israeli alliance and Nasser's increasing aid to the FLN made it ever more tempting for the French to portray their war in Algeria as part of a crusade against "Pan-Arabism" and "Pan-Islamism." With hundreds of thousands of draftees boarding trains and ships to Algeria—some of them rioting and pulling emergency cords along the way—it became imperative to provide them and their families with compelling reasons to fight. This was especially the case once they started to come home in caskets, horribly mutilated, like the twenty young reservists ambushed in Palestro on May 18 in the single most costly attack to date.[96] Great sacrifices demanded a great cause, and "Algeria is France" would not persuade many who had actually been there.

The day after the Palestro attack, Resident Minister Lacoste issued his first "General Directive" to officers in Algeria. He assured them "with absolute clarity *that the indefeasible rights of France in Algeria are absolutely unequivocal.*"[97] This was not just official boilerplate. The language of *droits imprescriptibles*, so sacred in French political discourse, not only committed his government to victory, it legitimated disobedience of any government that violated those rights. Yet this document is worth an extended analysis in that it shows how a binary view of the war in terms of "development" versus "overpopulation," France versus "foreign interference," "the West" versus "fanatical Islam" now structured a whole worldview, one in which the struggle was not just about Algeria, but nothing less than the fate of civilization in the face of encroaching anarchy.

"We are today confronted with a brutal fact," Lacoste began:

> A mass of some 8,000,000 French-Muslims, a large portion of which is under-evolved, under-administrated, under-employed and under-fed, is increasing at a [rapid] rate and will be 25% greater in ten years. This mass is being showered with fanatic, foreign propaganda. This propaganda, unfortunately helped by countless errors or hesitations on our part, has begun to dig a deep trench between this mass and a community said to be of "French stock."

Lacoste's quotation marks were meant to indicate his misgivings about the term, and he followed them with seemingly liberal sentiments. But even in his telling, foreign propaganda was obviously not the only thing that separated a "dynamic" French "community" defending its rights and a "mass" of "French Muslims" distinguished only by what it was not—"under-evolved, under-administrated," and so on—as well as an astonishing ability to breed. Nevertheless, Lacoste plunged ahead. "Subjected to a propaganda controlled from the outside," he continued,

> and which tries to cloak itself with religious pretexts to stir xenophobic unrest, [Muslims] are looking upon the rapid—too rapid—evolution of young neighboring states and asking themselves if the fact of having the same faith does not also confer upon them a different nationality from our own. Terrorized by crimes of an atrocious nature, they let themselves slide into a state of total passivity, and come to doubt France's will and justice.

If the Muslim population is propagandized and terrorized, "let[ting] themselves slide into total passivity," one never learns who is actually committing these crimes. But one thing is clear, the trouble comes from outside: "What is going on in Algeria is but one aspect of a gigantic global conflict where a number of Muslim countries, before collapsing into anarchy, are trying through Hitlerian strategies to install an invasive dictatorship on a section of the African continent."

The army's role was capital: to restore order while resisting FLN provocations, which "aim at triggering spontaneous acts of reprisals that they will then pin up to create the appearance of a war of extermination and to set against us international opinion and the great powers whose diplomatic support they seek." In other words, French officers would have to think globally while acting locally, since the local, national, and international levels of the struggle were interconnected and interdependent. What was at stake was not just French Algeria, or even France, but civilization itself: "The war we are waging in this country is that of the Western world, of civilization against anarchy, democracy against dictatorship."

Lest this view be considered extreme or unrepresentative, one could also cite the publications of the *Union pour le Salut et le Renouveau de l'Algérie Française* (USRAF), which was founded the previous February and launched its first public relations campaign in June. It included the likes of Albert Bayet, Paul Rivet, and Robert Delavignette, distinguished names long associated with a deep knowledge of and respect for foreign cultures. Nevertheless, they all appear on a brochure that described the FLN as follows:

> merciless assassins and pitiable hostages of Terror, impatient souls blinded by propaganda . . . the instruments of a theocratic imperialism, fanatic and racist—that of pan-Arabism—which threatens our Moroccan and Tunisian friends as much as our Algerian brothers. In truth, it is Liberty that is being challenged.[98]

Again, the passive voice is significant. Liberty "is being challenged"—but by whom? Not the "merciless assassins," since even they are "pitiable hostages . . . blinded by propaganda," mere "instruments" of a "theocratic imperialism." Once again, the threat comes from outside—but where?

What is most surprising about such statements is that they did not once refer to, or even allude to, the Soviets. Of course, for many it went without saying that Communists backed or benefited from this challenge aimed against liberty. But in some cases the Cold War itself was repackaged as a civilizational conflict. Thus, in a dispatch to all embassies preparing for the next General Assembly debates, the Quai d'Orsay explained that "our troubles in Algeria inscribe themselves in a great conflict that, since the end of the war, has set the East against the West. It is about more than the clash of different political visions: it is a clash of two civilizations." Best represented by Egypt, "the East" was described as a place where "resurgences from all of Asia's past cultures are mixed together, and which is characterized by the preeminence given to the collectivity over the human individual."[99]

Some felt obliged to reconcile the apparent contradiction represented by "the fusion of the Bandung and Soviet blocs" in a world increasingly divided by race and religion. Thus, in explaining how this "anti-Western Asiatic tide" might be led by Moscow, André Siegfried, a renowned political scientist and member of the *Académie*, wrote that the Soviets were "an intermediate society, half-Western, half-Asiatic, doubtless white but having renounced white solidarity." In combination with "the crusade of Islam," "the mounting tide, coming from the East . . . threatens all Western civilization. . . . [T]he enemy is at the gates of Rome."[100]

Others began to see the Soviets as potential allies. Thus, in March 1956, Mollet reported that Ambassador Sergei Vinogradov had told him that, "[a]s regards this business of yours in Algeria, it would be bad if Islam were to sweep all over Africa."[101] During a May visit to Moscow, Mollet and Pineau obtained a sympathetic statement from Khrushchev. But the Soviets soon disabused Mollet of any illusions about their interests in North Africa. On July 1, armed groups formed by the Algerian Communist Party disbanded and announced their allegiance to the FLN.[102] A week later, *Pravda* attacked French policy and implicitly backed Algerian independence. Khrushchev explained that "conditions had changed" since Mollet's visit, perhaps referring to Foreign Minister Dimitri Shepilov's visit to Cairo two weeks earlier. In a joint communiqué,

Shepilov and Nasser announced "full unanimity of views" and he reportedly offered considerable aid.[103]

That same month, July 1956, the United States and United Kingdom abruptly withdrew support for the Aswan Dam project. When Nasser retaliated by nationalizing the Suez Canal, the "Eastern" and "Western" coalitions would appear to have been complete, lined up—appropriately enough—over the narrow canal that divided Asia from Africa. But Mollet still felt he could not trust the Americans not to break ranks in the coming "clash of two civilizations." Thus, he told Dillon that "the US was embarking on the same course of error by appeasement that had been followed toward Hitler in the 1930s." Mollet then showed how far he was willing to go to obtain their support, summoning the Americans' nightmare vision of a "global bargain" with the Soviets—this time for North Africa:

> He said that it was made clear to him by the Soviet leaders when he was in Moscow that they were prepared, in concert with Nasser, to agree to bring about peace in Algeria on a basis acceptable to his government provided he would agree to come part way to meet their views on European matters. . . . Mollet said I must realize the temptation that such an offer regarding Algeria offered to any French statesman.

Because of his "firm rejection," Mollet concluded, the Americans owed him a sympathetic hearing.[104]

In fact, Dulles had considerable sympathy for the French premier's basic fear. Speaking to congressional leaders two weeks later, he warned that Nasser wanted to "unite the Arab world and if possible the Moslem world, and to use Mid-East oil and the Suez canal as weapons against the West." The secretary asserted that he was "an extremely dangerous fanatic" and admitted that, "if Nasser gets by with this action, the British and French are probably right in their appraisal of the consequences." But Dulles and Eisenhower judged that attacking Cairo was precisely what would make it the capital of a new "empire of Islam." When Eisenhower met with his advisers to decide the American response, CIA director Allen Dulles warned that precipitous military action "would arouse the whole Arab world. The President enlarged this to the whole Moslem world." The "mighty river" of Arab and Islamic nationalism Eisenhower had long feared was now threatening to overflow its banks. This was no time for gunboat diplomacy.[105]

Dulles flew to London and on August 1 told Pineau and Selwyn Lloyd, the British foreign secretary, that the United States opposed taking military action against Nasser. But Pineau claimed that France was prepared to act unilaterally. He explained that Nasser's influence was so great that, "according to very reliable information, we have only several weeks left to save North Africa. Obviously, the loss of North Africa would be followed by that of Black Africa, and thus the European role and influence in Africa would disappear."[106]

Pineau found it unnecessary to explain how France could lose North Africa to Nasser in a matter of weeks when they had 400,000 troops in Algeria alone, nor why the rest of the continent would necessarily follow. Such assertions had become articles of faith in a binary worldview now shared by all of those ministers making policy on Algeria and Suez. The Algerian War represented the struggle of "civilization against anarchy," as Lacoste described it, "Middle Eastern Islamic fanaticism and Western-oriented moderate nationalism," as Bourgès put it, "Islam versus the French," as Pineau said, when he still hoped to avert such a conflict. It made sense to strike at Egypt to end the Algerian revolt only if one accepted that Cairo was the capital of a nascent "empire of Islam," as Mollet did, and believed that there was "only one game which is being played out in the Near East as in North Africa: that of the expansion of pan-islamism."[107]

In fact, many games were being played out in the Near East and North Africa, even if the available evidence affords only a tentative and incomplete picture. One thing seems clear, and it is one of the supreme ironies of this war: France was preparing to strike at Nasser and "pan-Islamism" at the very moment the FLN rejected Egyptian influence and the very idea of jihad.[108]

French Strategy in Disarray

On August 20, as the French began moving forces to bases in Cyprus, the FLN's leadership within Algeria met secretly in the Soummam valley to compose a common platform and create a new organizational structure. Initially, representatives of the external delegation were to attend, but the summons never came.[109] Scholars have interpreted this as part of a feud between the "interior" and the "exterior," pitting the brilliant and ambitious Ramdane Abbane against Ben Bella.[110] But interviews and newly accessible archives indicate that the situation was more complex. Abbane had indeed become the first among equals inside Algeria. But he used his influence to broaden the FLN, bolstering its external delegation with such luminaries as the newly militant Ferhat Abbas, 'Ulama leader Tewfik al-Madani, and Messali's former deputy, Doctor Mohammed-Lamine Debaghine. French authorities were mistaken in imagining that Ben Bella led this disparate group—indeed, he resented many of them as arrivistes. Abbane, for his part, sought to consolidate his authority by designating Debaghine as their chief, but he conceded that the majority should rule and his emissary was initially isolated.[111]

Even so, Khider took care to stay in contact with "the interior," so much so that Abbane relied on him to relay messages and help resolve a leadership struggle in the Aurès. Abbane also sought the external delegation's approval for the Soummam congress's decisions before publicizing them, and Khider conveyed them to his compatriots without a word of criticism. This does not accord with the conventional view that they were all shut out, and it provides further evidence that the idea of an FLN bifurcated between "the interior" and "the exterior" is overdrawn.[112]

Instead, the Soummam platform targeted Ben Bella personally, both because of his close association with Nasser and his inability to deliver more arms. Thus, it criticized "the Arab states in general and Egypt in particular" for allowing their diplomacy and French pressure to limit their support.[113] When it declared the principle that the interior should have primacy over the exterior—something that leaders like Aït Ahmed and Khider had never contested—it was not merely an internal power play but a declaration of independence, affirming as it did that the struggle was "directed neither from Cairo, nor from London, nor from Moscow, nor from Washington." Given the vast difference between their policies, this evenhandedness was a slap to Ben Bella and a signal that the rest of the delegation should continue cultivating France's allies, Washington most of all. It went on to deny any role to Algerian Communists and condemned the equivocal position of the French Communist Party. Conversely, there was little criticism of U.S. and NATO support for the French—it downplayed their "rather embarrassed declarations"—and some praise for American media coverage of the war.[114]

Indeed, the Soummam platform reaffirmed the international strategy first outlined by Aït Ahmed. Rather than a military victory, it looked for "the total weakening of the French army to make victory by arms impossible." In the process, the FLN would establish their bona fides as Algeria's legitimate government and adhere to international law. To that end, the Soummam congress formed a five-man *Comité de Coordination et d'Exécution* (CCE) consisting of Abbane, Ben M'Hidi, Belkacem Krim, Ben Youssef Ben Khedda, and Saad Dahlab—the last two formerly Central Committee members of the MTLD. A larger *Conseil National de la Revolution Algérienne* (CNRA) would serve as the supreme authority. In the meantime, the FLN intended to engineer such social and economic disruption in the metropole and Algeria as to make it impossible for France to continue the war. Equally important, it would work for "the political isolation of France—in Algeria and in the world."[115]

The platform called for a permanent office at the United Nations as well as a delegation in Asia. By October, there would actually be eight different FLN bureaus: in Cairo, Damascus, Tunis, Beirut, Baghdad, Karachi, Djakarta, and New York. The Soummam congress also called for "mobile delegations" to visit other capitals as well as international cultural, student, and trade union meetings. Ferhat Abbas would shortly depart with one such delegation for Latin America. The FLN had already formed a labor affiliate, the *Union Générale des Travailleurs Algériens* (UGTA) and would create a commercial association the following month: the *Union Générale des Commerçants Algériens* (UGCA). While forming links with their counterparts abroad and facilitating contributions, these organizations would also coordinate labor and commercial strikes during the next U.N. General Assembly.[116]

Finally, the platform called for a publicity campaign abroad, including films and photos, along with press offices that would assure their dissemination. They were especially concerned to counter propaganda "describing the Algerian resistance movement as a fanatical religious movement at the service of Pan-Islamism." The platform stressed the "national, political, and social" nature of the revolution, which it depicted as part of the "normal course of the historical evolution of humanity which no longer accepts the existence of captive nations." It was careful to note that the settlers did not constitute an indissoluble and uniformly racist bloc and avowed that Algerian citizenship would be open to all. These positions can be seen as counterpropaganda directed at French liberals and foreign opinion. But Abbane and Mohamed Lebjaoui, the platform's principal authors, were known as secular-minded socialists. Moreover, Ben Bella attacked these planks together with criticism of Islamic leaders as antireligious, though even he may have been appeasing this constituency rather than speaking his conscience.[117] Thus, if the struggle in North Africa was between "Middle Eastern Islamic fanaticism and Western-oriented moderate nationalism," the FLN had decisively opted for the latter while at the same time adopting a more intransigent position toward France.

The Tunisians and Moroccans also refused to fit into the Mollet government's occidental-oriental schema. While Bourguiba was quite willing to help the French to suppress the forces of Ben Youssef, he would not lift a finger against the Algerians. And, just as French officials had feared, he sought freedom of maneuver in defense and foreign policy by pitting Paris against Washington. In July 1956, he declared that, if they could not meet Tunisia's needs, "it is necessary to knock on other doors."[118] But this was hardly the tactics of a rug merchant. Though inspired by the romantic nationalism of Lamartine, Rousseau, and Hugo, this French-educated lawyer was, above all, a pragmatist. Indeed, he expressed disdain toward Egypt and its "extremists" with the same essentialism shown by the French: Their "Oriental mentality," he claimed, "does not allow them to understand that politics is the art of the possible."[119]

The Moroccans were also wary of Nasser and determined to assume command of their own affairs. As the Americans had always feared, in May 1956 they declared that they did not recognize the validity of the U.S.-French base agreements. While the French held out for a comprehensive agreement that might give their own facilities a new lease on life, the Moroccans appeared determined to "plough through" them and deal directly with the United States. In June, they adhered to the Arab League while continuing to talk of joining NATO or the Baghdad pact. They did not feel obliged to choose between "East" and "West." If Islam had anything to do with it, Prince Hassan showed how it could just as easily be invoked to justify keeping both at bay while enjoying the benefits of having "two wives."[120]

With the Tunisians and the Moroccans unwilling to align with France and both already seeking outside aid against the eventuality of retaliation, the American attitude would become even more important. In a September 1956 National Security Council meeting, Eisenhower said that he wanted French influence in North Africa to be maintained as long and as much as possible. He was concerned about the amount of American aid that would be needed if the United States were to take its place. Nevertheless, the president approved budgeting $23 million for North Africa in 1958 and over $50 million in 1959, with John Hollister of the International Cooperation Administration explaining that "we did not believe they could spend our money any faster."[121]

At the same time Eisenhower ordered that the new Spanish bases replace those in Morocco in spite of the Joint Chiefs' insistence that they were indispensable. "The more people we had to deal with in our efforts to secure bases," he complained, "the more blackmail we were exposed to." The new policy also called for American military aid to Morocco and Tunisia "if this becomes necessary to retain the U.S. position." While North Africa was of diminished importance in America's own war plans, the NSC wanted to ensure that the new states would not turn to the Soviets. As the accompanying policy paper warned, "The political and military impact of such a development . . . would be profound."[122]

All of this was antithetical to the French strategy, which relied on a carrot-and-stick combination of aid and—if it came to it—unilateral military action from the remaining bases in Tunisia and Morocco. The possibility of obtaining American assistance would encourage Tunisia to hold out against French demands while a U.S. withdrawal from its bases in Morocco would undermine France's efforts to retain its own. In addition, American arms shipments would deny France control over the defense of both countries and symbolically guarantee their territorial integrity against a possible reoccupation. The new policy was therefore potentially devastating to France's chances of isolating and holding Algeria.

Officials in Mollet's office and the Interior Ministry already felt that time was running out. On September 6 Dillon reported that, while never believing total victory was possible, many of them were now skeptical that they could even improve their negotiating position. They considered November 1 the deadline for action, since psychological and financial factors ruled out another winter campaign. Rather than raise new taxes, the Mollet government was running deficits to finance the war and would be forced to draw on credits from the International Monetary Fund (IMF) that October. Moreover, 90 percent of Muslims were said to be "infected" with Algerian nationalism. Dillon reported that a debate was "raging in Paris [about] whether [a] new statute for Algeria will be negotiated or imposed."[123]

In fact, earlier that week the Socialist Party's acting secretary general, Pierre Commin, met FLN representatives in Belgrade on Mollet's behalf. In two days of talks, he described how new legislative and executive bodies in Algeria would enjoy autonomy, excepting those spheres in which France would share responsibility: public liberties and individual rights, military and foreign affairs, economic planning and government finances. Talks with the new Algerian executive would establish institutional ties to regulate all these areas. If the FLN accepted this framework, official and public negotiations could begin.[124]

At the Soummam conference, the FLN had committed itself to the recognition of Algeria's right to independence as a precondition of any cease-fire and formal negotiations. When Debaghine and Khider conveyed this position to Pierre Herbault in Belgrade on September 22, he protested that no government in Paris could so much as utter the words "independence" and "Algeria" in the same sentence without immediately being thrown out of office. Speaking on his own authority, he proposed that they might agree on the principle of self-determination.[125] It is not clear how Mollet received either the Algerians' demand or Herbault's suggestion. But four days later, Commin told Dillon that the prime minister intended to make an important statement on a statute for Algeria that would "provide the necessary basis for the opening of negotiations" with the FLN.[126]

In light of subsequent events, one might assume that when Dillon's informants had earlier mentioned a November 1 deadline they were referring to the strike at Suez rather than negotiations with the FLN. But at that point the Anglo-French attack was set for October 8, having already been postponed several times.[127] It is hard to believe that the French planned to bring public negotiations with the FLN to a successful conclusion after making war on what they perceived to be its sponsor. Given the apparent seriousness of the prime minister about announcing a new statute for Algeria and the determination of his government to attack Nasser, it seems likely that they envisaged the old combination of reform and repression, albeit at an altogether new level, as the best way to settle the war. Indeed, in view of their concern about Nasser's role in postindependence Morocco and Tunisia they probably deemed it even more vital to eliminate his influence before France began to loosen ties with Algeria.[128]

The debate to which Dillon referred, over negotiating or imposing a new statute, pitted Mollet against the resident minister, who favored more military action and opposed the planned announcement. But Commin noted that "Lacoste had always been very conscious of the necessity of taking dramatic action before the General Assembly debate, and therefore he thought he would eventually agree to support this program."[129] The upcoming General Assembly session was a growing preoccupation as the French decided what position to take in Algeria. Britain's Pierson Dixon was the only one to pledge support while emphasizing that the outlook was "extremely bad."[130]

On October 16, after fifteen Arab and Asian delegations again petitioned for the inscription of the Algerian question, Commin told an

American official that Mollet planned to make his statement before the General Assembly itself and hoped that it would be followed by negotiations. He now denied that there was any difference between Lacoste and Mollet, since the resident minister was also convinced that they had to move quickly in the political field.[131] Indeed, the same day another American official spoke to Lacoste and his advisers and found they had come around to Mollet's view. They now believed that the FLN dominated the nationalist movement and that they would have to negotiate a settlement with its external delegation "as soon as possible."[132]

But that very morning, a French navy cutter had intercepted and boarded a Sudanese flagged vessel, the *Athos*, in international waters off the coast of Morocco. Apparently tipped off by the Israelis, they found 2,300 rifles, 90 mortars, and over one million rounds of ammunition—the biggest Egyptian arms shipment yet and the first incontrovertible proof of Nasser's material support for the rebellion. This was a blow to efforts to establish a cease-fire and begin public negotiations with the FLN, efforts that had gained momentum when Mohammed V and Bourguiba offered their assistance. Now Lacoste denounced both of them in the assembly for aiding the rebellion and attacked those who "risk sabotaging the courageous efforts of those who wish a French solution to the Algerian drama."[133]

All along, officials like Lacoste thought that destroying Nasser would be a suitably French solution.[134] In fact, on the same day the *Athos* was intercepted, the French and the British finally agreed on the main elements of the plan that would culminate in their attack on Suez. Meeting in Mollet's official residence in Paris, Eden assured the French prime minister and Pineau that Britain would intervene in case of an Israeli attack near the canal—an attack that the French lost no time in arranging.[135]

Ben Bella and the rest of the external delegation were then in Morocco to confer with Mohammed V. On October 22, they were to fly to Tunis for a summit with Bourguiba. Abbane had already prepared a communiqué condemning this conference, recognizing that it would provide a platform for Ben Bella to challenge him and the rest of the CCE for leadership. Given Ben Bella's influence in the eastern zones, a public feud would have risked tearing the movement apart. But French intelligence either did not know or did not care. Instead, they were preparing another coup: the interception of the plane carrying Ben Bella together with Khider, Aït Ahmed, and Boudiaf. While Mollet vetoed the plan, Lacoste apparently let them go ahead anyway. In fact, they only needed to persuade the French captain of the Air Maroc DC-3 to lock his passengers in the cabin and land in Algiers. Nevertheless, the fighter escort made a big impression, as did the rows of tanks and troops on the runway of Maison Blanche airport. They introduced their handcuffed captives to the media as "Ben Bella and his associates," reflecting his privileged relationship with the Egyptians and the French view that they all worked for Nasser. The pieds noirs were ecstatic—"At last France has dared!" a radio commentator exclaimed. But President Coty was appalled and urged that they be released. Mollet was also shaken but decided to cover the action rather than see his government fall.[136]

In Morocco rioting mobs killed forty-nine French men, women, and children. Returning from the aborted summit, the sultan made a point of landing his plane at an American air base, as if to suggest that he felt unsafe in French hands—and that he had other options. By November, the American ambassador in Rabat reported that French officials were "being chased from their offices," and with them hopes of their continued influence in the administration.[137] Meanwhile, in Tunisia, the French army had to intervene to protect settlers after a series of violent incidents across the country. The Tunisians attempted to blockade them in their barracks and distributed arms to civilians, which led to further clashes.[138]

Capturing the external leadership did nothing to quell unrest in Algeria. Once sources in Mollet's cabinet read their papers, they admitted that "it is military leaders in Algeria itself who are running [the] affair," not the FLN diplomats, and certainly not Ben Bella (though he benefited enormously from the publicity).[139] The talks broke off, but Mollet would still pay the political price for having conducted them in the first place. The FLN disclosed their contacts over the previous months along with the prime minister's willingness to concede self-government.[140] Whereas French propagandists had long claimed that the rebellion was too faction-ridden to present *interlocuteurs valables*—and would have had a field day if Ben Bella had openly challenged the CCE—now the Fourth Republic itself appeared too divided to negotiate a settlement, much less enforce it. The rebels would never lay down their arms based on nothing more than a minister's promise. They would fight their way through future negotiations.

After Mollet's mobbing in Algiers and this latest debacle, even such normally sympathetic media outlets as *The New York Times* asked whether Paris was still in control of the situation. One of their correspondents, Thomas Brady, was actually on the intercepted plane, so the story was reported under a four-column headline. *Time* magazine called it an aerial kidnapping and the *Economist* also condemned it.[141] At the United Nations, Ambassador Bernard Cornut-Gentille warned that there was no avoiding a debate in which he would be on the defensive from the first day. India, for instance, after having previously helped squelch debate on Algeria, now denounced the French in the most vehement terms. The French delegation therefore faced a choice between humiliation or withdrawal. Four days later, overcome by the stress, Cornut-Gentille had a heart attack in the Security Council chamber.[142]

Thus, the seizing of a foreign-flagged ship in international waters and the interception of the Moroccan plane in international airspace, not to mention the real danger of the war spreading across North Africa, made it obvious that Algeria was no longer an internal affair, if it ever had been. With the Suez expedition, the "Algerian problem" would become "a reality for the entire world," the goal of the FLN from the first day of the revolt.

"The one who ordered this screwup," President Coty declared on hearing of the arrests, "is going to make us lose the Algerian War."[143] In fact, even now no one knows for certain who ordered the arrest, or even who agreed to it, which itself serves as an indictment of the leadership's collective irresponsibility. In any case, France's "losing" Algeria was already overdetermined. But in a way Coty was right. They had now lost the war in the sense that they could no longer control it or contain it. And they could not conclude it without bringing about the collapse of the republic itself.

III

Waging the Algerian War as a
World War, 1956–1958

5

The Battle of Algiers,
the Battle of New York

*The brothers know that our inferiority to the colonialist army in men
and matériel does not permit us to win great and decisive military victories. Is it preferable for our cause to kill ten enemies in some riverbed in
Telergma, which no one will talk about, or rather a single one in Algiers, which the American press will report the next day? Though we are
taking some risks, we must make our struggle known.*

Ramdane Abbane, directive number 9, fall 1956 [1]

*From the beginning France has made the mistake of not appreciat-
ing the full scope of the conflict and of not carrying its defense to the
ground chosen by our adversaries, that of the appeal to passions and the
recourse to international opinion. . . . It is necessary this time that all
means be developed to lead the battle on all fronts: a battle of ideas, as
much as a battle of men, in Algeria, in France, and in all the universe.*

National Defense Subcommittee, *l'Assemblée nationale*, July 1957 [2]

Seldom does one find a statesman so self-conscious in his sense of history
as John Foster Dulles on the morning of November 1, 1956, after listening to his brother Allen brief the National Security Council. The CIA
director had described Hungary's uprising and withdrawal from the War-
saw Pact as "a miracle." Meanwhile, Britain and France were conducting
air strikes in support of an Israeli invasion of the Sinai and their occupation of the Suez Canal appeared imminent. "We had almost reached
the point," the secretary announced, "of deciding today whether we think
the future lies with a policy of reasserting by force colonial control over
the less-developed nations, or whether we will oppose such a course of
action by every appropriate means. . . . [T]his decision," Dulles continued, "must be made in a mere matter of hours—before five o'clock this
afternoon"—when he was scheduled to address the first emergency session of the U.N. General Assembly. [3]

In fact, the president had already decided where the future lay—and
how he might hurry it along. Though more disappointed with the British,

Eisenhower was incensed with the French. From the first intelligence reports, he discerned their ultimate objective:

> Damn it, the French, they're just egging the Israelis on—hoping somehow to get out of their *own* North African troubles. Damn it . . . we tried to tell them they would repeat Indochina all over again in North Africa. And they said, "Oh no! Algeria's part of metropolitan France!"—and all that damn nonsense.[4]

Though publicly opposing the resort to force in both Hungary and Suez, his responses to the two crises were quite different. While refraining from any action that might have worried the Soviets, he employed everything from the General Assembly to the Sixth Fleet to maximize his allies' uncertainty. The ultimate weapon was to withhold monetary and material aid while their economies faltered under an Arab oil embargo, leaving them to "boil in their own oil," as he said even before the NSC meeting.[5]

Eisenhower valued these meetings for ensuring his administration would speak with one voice, and his secretary's opening words, two years to the day after the start of the Algerian War, can be seen as an authoritative statement of their new approach to the problem of decolonization. The "middle of the road" had clearly come to an end. "For many years now," he explained, the United States had been "walking a tightrope" in terms of relations with the British and French on the one hand and their former colonies on the other.

> In view of the overwhelming Asian and African pressure upon us we could not walk this tightrope much longer. Unless we now assert and maintain this leadership, all of these newly independent countries will turn from us to the USSR. . . . In short, the United States would survive or go down on the basis of the fate of colonialism if the United States supports the French and the British on the colonial issue. Win or lose, we will share the fate of Britain and France. . . . [and] the British and French would not win.[6]

America's allies certainly could not win without its support, and the attempt would risk U.N. sanctions, Soviet intervention, the collapse of the sterling trade area and—in the absence of emergency oil shipments—a bone-chilling winter. After the NSC meeting, Dulles flew to New York through stormy weather and rallied a 64:5 majority against the aggressors. In a campaign speech, Vice President Nixon went so far as to describe America's demand for an immediate cease-fire as a "declaration of independence." "For the first time in history," he claimed, "we have shown independence of Anglo-French policies toward Asia and Africa. . . ."[7] This came as a shock to the allies, who thought *they* had been asserting *their* independence from the Americans.

Scores of books have described the Suez drama and its denouement, as American economic pressure abruptly ended the expedition along with the career of Anthony Eden. The French side of the story was thought to conclude when Mollet convinced his cabinet that they could not go it alone, though one could already see how France would eventually find a new vocation in Europe. When Eden telephoned to halt the ground offensive, Mollet happened to be meeting with Adenauer, who was helping to remove the last obstacles to the nascent European Economic Community (EEC). Bonn officially took a reserved position on Suez as it had earlier done on Algeria, viewing both as distractions from the defense of Europe. But then as on subsequent occasions, Adenauer seized the opportunity to cement their relationship, telling Mollet that the European nations had no choice but to unite against an America that might otherwise divide up the world with the Soviets. "We have no time to lose," he warned. "Europe will be your revenge."[8]

In Pineau's telling and those of the historians who cite him, this exchange provides a satisfying coda to the story. But for France, the Suez crisis was just the beginning of a "long crisis." As much as he would have liked to, it was impossible for Mollet to defy the Americans. The Algerian War had made Paris so dependent that Washington had merely to remain silent and do nothing to exert pressure on French policies. Thus, uncertain of the American attitude, the Quai d'Orsay conceded that it could not oppose the inscription of the Algerian issue on the General Assembly's agenda, making inevitable a debate that provoked new FLN military, political, and diplomatic offensives in Algiers and New York.[9] The ALN had already begun to use Tunisia as a sanctuary from which to launch raids into Algeria, killing five French soldiers in one such action on November 5.[10] Later that month, Tunisian Defense Minister Bahi Ladgham said that he hoped for U.S. help in equipping Tunisia's new army.[11] Meanwhile, the capture of the FLN's external delegation had strengthened the most anti-French elements in the Moroccan government, which turned to the Americans for economic aid while the Suez crisis was still unfolding.[12] Granting their requests would "remove the only card which [the] French had left to get negotiations under way again between France and these two countries," as Savary's successor, Maurice Faure, told Ambassador Dillon.[13]

The American embassy urged a supportive policy, going so far as to claim that it could "very largely determine" whether a future French government would remain within the NATO system or become "totally indigestible" to it.[14] U.S. officials believed they possessed this power partly because of the state of France's own finances. The economy was booming, growing by 10 percent a year, but public and private consumption outstripped domestic production. Rather than choose between inflation and austerity, the Mollet government met demand with foreign imports. In the course of 1956, it expended $850 million in credits and hard currency reserves to cover the resulting balance of payments deficits. In October, following a rebuff from Treasury Secretary George Humphrey, it obtained a $262.5 million standby arrangement with the IMF.[15] But on November 16, a Finance Ministry official admitted that they were entering a period of great uncertainty. "1957," he said, will be "a year, I will not say of 'betting,' but at least of anticipation. If, in fact, by the beginning of 1958 things have not improved, the situation will be difficult."[16] Though the official would not say it, in 1957 Paris indeed "bet" that it could avoid a financial crisis that would compel it to submit to American views on outstanding issues, above all the Algerian War. Otherwise, France would not be able to meet the conditions for entry into the EEC, scheduled to get under way at the beginning of 1959. In this way, even Mollet's "revenge" would become contingent on American goodwill.[17]

Yet "the French" and "the Americans" were not drawn up uniformly on opposite sides. The diplomatic historian's shorthand is particularly deceptive in this episode, since even some top French officials encouraged their U.S. counterparts to take the lead in settling the war. The same day the Finance Ministry official spoke of a "bet," the Quai d'Orsay's director of political affairs, Jean-Henri Daridan, told the State Department's William Tyler that " 'everyone' in Paris realized that the Government's program for Algeria would not succeed. . . . [T]he only hope," he continued, "lay in [a] U.S. initiative for a broad settlement of major issues in the Near East, of which Algeria was one." Tyler urged "realistic and statesmanlike" measures that might earn U.S. support, since he "doubted whether it was a very tempting proposition for us to take the initiative and thereby expose ourselves to renewed charges of selling out France. . . ." Indeed, unlike the British, most French politicians had united behind Mollet's government and bitterly criticized the United States over Suez. Nevertheless, Daridan "repeated that he thought the situation would shortly require the leadership of the United States if catastrophe was to be averted in North Africa."[18] Even Lacoste asked for American advice on what France should propose before the General Assembly debate.[19]

From the first weeks of the war, Mendès France invited American advice if not intervention. What had changed in the meantime was that the "internationalization" of the Algerian question was no longer just a matter of individual initiative. The French contributed to it in actions taken against the external delegation, the *Athos*, and Egypt. They had accepted it, without actually admitting it, with their new readiness to debate the issues at the United Nations. And they institutionalized it in the way they organized for war. Though officially the Algerian *départements* were still an integral part of France, the Quai d'Orsay now negotiated with Lacoste on the terms of reform initiatives.[20] Moreover, the Quai established a *Mission de liaison algérien* (MLA) in Algiers under Henri Langlais, who received copies of all pertinent foreign ministry reports while serving as a conduit for distributing material from Lacoste's cabinet to French diplomatic posts around the world. More than facilitating the information flow, these channels provided new means for international pressure—and particularly American pressure—to impinge on the French in Algeria regardless of who ruled in Paris.[21]

Yet, as Tyler's comment indicates, the Americans were still reluctant to proffer their own program for Algeria or even become associated with a French plan. Herbert Hoover Jr., under secretary of state, cautioned that Washington would thereby assume responsibility. But privately he confided to Dillon that nothing short of direct negotiations with the FLN that led to full autonomy would resolve the crisis.[22] The Americans were usually careful not to demand this in return for eventual U.S. aid. Indeed, Vice President Nixon indicated that America might help France just as it would aid Britain. After committing to a prompt and complete withdrawal from Port Said, London secured nearly two billion dollars in credits from the IMF and the U.S. Export Import Bank.[23] Minister of Finance Paul Ramadier urged Pineau to find out whether the Americans would quickly extend them the same assistance.[24] But U.S. aid had been dangled in front of the French only to be yanked away again. When Alphand approached Dulles, the secretary said that they "should not take that [Nixon] speech too literally" and maintained that, while "the Department of State would be glad to help in any way it can and has no objections on political grounds. . . . [s]uch credits . . . must be justified primarily on financial and economic grounds."[25]

The Quai d'Orsay understood that they were not to take *Dulles* too literally. One official explained that "these phrases signify that the American Government . . . wants to make known its opinion on each of the major elements of government expenses, doubtless including those pertaining to Algeria."[26] That opinion was best put by Eisenhower himself. When told that the French had once again asked for more open support in Algeria, he replied that, "having gone so far to try to protect the independence of the Arab nations, he did not want to back a French position which might destroy all the good we had done."[27] So when the French directly requested over $500 million in American military aid, Charles Yost at the embassy in Paris answered, perhaps ironically, that the war in Algeria was a French concern, and the United States had "not considered the financing of such purchases, either directly or indirectly, to be a suitable undertaking. . . ." Yost hoped this attitude would "encourage [the] French to proceed promptly with required drastic economies."[28] But "encouragement" required not foreclosing the possibility of aid altogether. As another State Department official advised Hoover's successor as under secretary, Christian Herter: The "question of U.S. assistance should be kept open. . . . [I]t would be undesirable at this time to agree to forego the use of this incentive to sound [out] French actions."[29]

Some in the French government concluded that they would have to come up with a comprehensive plan of economic recovery and would have more autonomy in formulating it if they did so before the inevitable crisis. Indeed, senior officials used the need for foreign support and the threat of interference to urge austerity and sound money policies on their superiors. As early as December 7, a Finance Ministry official urged Ramadier to take action within two to three months, or at least before France had its "back to the wall." Similarly, one of Bank of France Governor Wilfrid Baumgartner's deputies warned that they were "heading straight for bankruptcy." The bank did not have the institutional autonomy to defend the franc or deny deficit financing, so even Baumgartner resorted to citing the requirements of prospective creditors in pressing Ramadier to adopt a recovery plan.[30] Mollet's advisors also warned of an impending crisis and urged him to talk to the Americans about future aid during a February visit. But this elicited a sharp response from the Quai d'Orsay's deputy director of external finance, Olivier Wormser. "The truth is, the U.S.A. will help us if we present such a recovery plan," he angrily noted in the margins of the offending memorandum, "and such a recovery plan cannot but entail pressure to diminish our Algerian defenses, leading to a settlement in Algeria."[31]

This concern and the sensitivity of the whole issue were confirmed a few days later when the director of the French Treasury, Pierre Schweitzer, gave what he called an "unauthorized" statement to Yost. He said that that very day Ramadier would propose to the cabinet budget cuts totaling 250 billion francs effective almost immediately, with 100 billion coming from the military.

> Schweitzer stated that [the] military cut would not come out of NATO forces, but would be in [the] form [of a] reduction of 100,000 men in Algeria and [the] demobilization [of] such men. . . . Schweitzer maintained that it is imperative that these cuts be announced prior to Mollet's departure for Washington. If they were announced later they would be widely interpreted in France (not only by commies but by others as well) as coming as a result of American pressure. French senior officials recognize [the] necessity [for] France to take such measures before France can expect favorable reaction from [the] US on aid.

Schweitzer "emphatically and repeatedly" asserted that the proposal was not intended to clear the way for aid negotiations during Mollet's visit since the "timing is not appropriate." Indeed, the prime minister never raised the issue. But while Schweitzer was concerned to avoid the appearance that France was winding down the war due to American pressure he made it clear that the Finance Ministry, at least, was prepared to anticipate—and accommodate—what it perceived as U.S. requirements.[32]

Writing in *Le Monde* three days later, Mendès France warned that the balance of payments problem already put France in a difficult position in talks with the United States. But he argued that this made it all the more imperative to negotiate an end to the war directly with the Algerians. "There is still time for it, but only just. Otherwise," he warned, "let us not kid ourselves, we will have to accept a solution imposed from outside which will be much less favorable for France and Algeria."[33]

The French Campaigns and Their Cost

While this confrontation was developing between French and American officials in Paris and Washington, the media were mesmerized by events in Algeria's capital, events which came to be known as the "Battle of Algiers." Contrary to French propaganda depicting Cairo as controlling the Algerian revolution, in January 1957 the *Comité de Coordination et d'Exécution* (CCE) commanded the forces of the FLN from Algiers itself. True, they had to move constantly from one safe house to another. But that, too, attested to the scope of their local network, which included some 1,200 armed militants and 4,500 auxiliaries under the command of Yacef Saadi.[34] That month, they executed over one hundred attacks within the capital and almost four thousand around the country. Even an unsympathetic analyst like Tripier concedes that, with close to twenty thousand ALN regulars and an even greater number of auxiliaries around the country, there was no *arrondissement* in Algeria beyond their reach, no village where their political-administrative network was not active.[35]

But even then, when the FLN was nearing the peak of its strength within Algeria, the leadership directed its efforts toward defeating the French diplomatically. This required attracting international media attention by staging spectacular actions where they would be most visible, even if this made the ALN more vulnerable.[36] For while the Suez crisis had weakened French influence, it had also stolen the spotlight from Algeria. For instance, whereas *The New York Times* had featured eleven editorials and forty-four front-page stories on Algeria in the first six months of 1956, coverage had dropped off to only two editorials and fifteen leading articles in the second half of the year. Action was required to reverse this trend.[37]

So on January 2, the FLN's new representative in New York, M'Hammed Yazid, called for U.N. sponsorship of a new round of negotiations based on a recognition of Algeria's right to independence.[38] That same day Ben M'Hidi told Saadi to prepare for a general strike. Though it would extend to all of Algeria as well as emigrants in the metropole, Algiers would be the focal point. "As the UN session approaches," he explained, "it is necessary to demonstrate that all the people are behind us and obey our orders to the letter." He told the rest of the CCE that this would negate the French government's main argument against negotiating with the FLN. They agreed unanimously, with Abbane predicting that "the international repercussions will be very great and will allow the population to demonstrate its power."[39]

Lacoste's cabinet was panic-stricken by the announced strike, which was scheduled to start January 28, the day the General Assembly debate was expected to begin. His government had already been proved powerless to stop either FLN assassinations and bombings in the city or pied noir reprisals, which were often aided by the police. On January 7 he called in the new general commander of French forces, Raoul Salan, along with the leader of the crack Tenth Paratroop Division, Jacques Massu, and gave them full powers to maintain order.[40]

On the night of January 8, Massu's *paras* marched into the FLN's stronghold, the Casbah, a labyrinth of narrow passages where some 100,000 Muslims lived. They quickly rounded up 950 suspects and set to work torturing them for information. Yet, at the same time, another battle was joined in New York which eventually circled the world, one waged with press releases, public debates, and propaganda films. The day after Massu's men occupied the Casbah, Guy Mollet fired back at Yazid's memorandum in a radio address that rejected what the prime minister characterized as a call for capitulation. While he began by explaining that he would "not attempt to justify France's Algerian policy to the United Nations as this is not a matter which concerns them," he concluded that, after having "described France's Algerian policy in detail and [having] shown it to be liberal and just in intention, I feel fully justified in asking the United Nations not to intervene. . . ." Later that month, the prime minister would continue to justify this policy that needed no justification in a series of meetings with no less than thirty-six ambassadors.[41] The lobbying effort was even more intense in New York, where Pineau personally met with most heads of delegations while agents of the Service de Documentation extérieure et de Contre-Espionnage (SDECE) distributed outright bribes to some representatives.[42]

The French faced stiff competition from capable FLN spokesmen like Yazid, Abdelkadr Chanderli, and Ferhat Abbas, who worked out of offices on East 56th Street when not conducting press campaigns cross-country or abroad. Yazid had been educated in Paris, where he led the Association of Muslim Students in France. He represented the FLN at the Bandung conference and would go on to become the GPRA's first minister of information. Like Yazid, Chanderli was fluent in English and married to a non-Muslim. But he was a comparative latecomer to the cause. Indeed, he was appointed head of the UNESCO press office upon French nomination in 1950 and only joined the FLN in Cairo in 1956. Abbas, as we have seen, had long represented the loyal opposition to France in Algeria before joining the FLN that same year. Though hampered by his lack of English and unfamiliarity with the United Nations, he quickly won the respect of the French delegation. Altogether, the apparent moderation, media-savvy, and cultural sophistication of the FLN team contradicted the picture of Islamic fanaticism portrayed by Paris. They would prove a potent combination in the years to come.[43]

For much of that time, the Algerians were assisted by a remarkable figure—Louise Page Morris, "The American Mata Hari." A former model and OSS agent, Morris worked for the AFL in New York when she was not conducting secret missions abroad for Jay Lovestone and the CIA's James Jesus Angleton. Moreover, she carried on a long-running affair with the American representative to the United Nations, Henry Cabot Lodge.

So in addition to hosting dinner parties for the Algerians and helping them in countless other ways large and small, she was particularly well positioned to influence the American delegation to the U.N.[44]

While Lodge had to vote in consultation with Washington, other delegates were sometimes free to formulate their own positions. Together with the activities of would-be states like the FLN and nonstate actors like the AFL, the United Nations had begun to take on a life of its own. But ultimately this body was the creation of individual states. The Algerians would not even have been admitted had they not been attached to the Iraqi and Syrian delegations. Yet the French and the FLN also appealed to world — as distinct from international — opinion, bypassing official representatives to make their cases before foreign publics, opinion-makers, and the media.[45]

In this competition, the Algerians were heavily outnumbered and outspent. The French U.N. delegation numbered ninety-three and, together with their information center and the embassy in Washington, deployed a "battalion" of secretaries and interpreters.[46] They could also call on reinforcements. The *Grand Rabbin* of France, for instance, was able to obtain a promise from a senior *New York Times* editor to continue faithfully supporting the French line during U.N. debates.[47] They also deployed delegations of pieds noirs and francophile Muslims to tour the States, each one selected to appeal to the targeted region. Thus, a predominantly Muslim group went to Chicago, Boston, Indianapolis, Detroit, Kansas City, and Philadelphia, where they stressed the danger of expanding Soviet influence in Africa. On the other hand, five of six sent to the South were pieds noirs, and the one Muslim, Olympic Marathon champion Alain Mimoun, wore European dress. According to the New Orleans *Times-Picayune*, their spokesman celebrated the virtues of keeping communities separate: "The population of Algeria is divided in two — the Moslems and the European French. The Moslem population has grown from one million in 1830 to eight million today. If they have developed, it is for what we have brought them, namely, hospitals, welfare, work and above all, peace."[48]

Such special projects punctuated an ongoing effort to influence the American media, as evidenced by files in the archives filled with letters to editors. Yet, even when printed, these represented "damage control" in the larger campaign to orient coverage of the war, principally by cultivating correspondents, editors, and publishers. To take just a few representative examples, throughout 1957 Alphand expended "long and patient efforts" to change the attitude of Henry Luce, owner of the Time-Life media empire, whose flagship weekly news magazine had long been critical of French conduct.[49] Meanwhile, the information director at the French mission in New York, Roger Vaurs, worked on Joseph Kraft, a staff writer at *The New York Times*, while Roger Le Tourneau, an orientalist at the University of Algiers, cultivated Gray Cowan, a Columbia University professor. These efforts appeared to pay off when, for instance,

Fortune magazine called for the United States to swing behind the French and Kraft and Cowan argued their case in a March 1957 debate at the New School for Social Research. More concretely, Vaurs's Press and Information Service sought to ensure that *Algérie française* appeared in the best light by distributing 8,000 still photographs to the print media and several film clips to the three major networks before and during the U.N. debate.[50]

The Algerians distributed their own clips, along with some 50,000 copies of various propaganda publications. But the scale of their operation hardly compared. For instance, the French Information Center reprinted a single pamphlet 110,000 times in English, 31,000 in German, and 25,000 in Spanish for circulation around the world. In January and February alone, it produced 1.65 million pages of propaganda—1.28 million just on Algeria—more than in all of 1955. The FLN representatives observed that the 450,000 dollars the French spent on a full-page advertisement in the thirty-one largest newspapers was more than ten times their entire budget.[51]

The French also distributed a new series of U.S.-made propaganda films free of charge to local television stations. In January alone, they were shown 1,579 times to an estimated 60 million viewers. The office later estimated that they had reached the great majority of the American public at least once every week during the U.N. session.[52] Regrettably, few of these films have been preserved in French archives and it is sometimes difficult to determine their date or origin. Still, one can discern the main themes as well as a subtle shift in the overall French propaganda campaign. Early films aimed at French audiences, like *Autour du drame algérien*, included grisly scenes of FLN atrocities. But while *Profile of Algeria* illustrated with images of women being carried away by Moorish types the tyranny and anarchy that supposedly reigned before the French, it stressed that the communities had lived side by side for 130 years.[53] These films portrayed Algeria as an extension of France, made ever closer by modern means of transportation and communication. But, contrary to earlier productions, they no longer spoke of assimilation. Instead, they juxtaposed the church tower and the minaret to present them as part of a common Mediterranean civilization.[54] This theme provided the title for a brochure, "Here live side by side 9,500,000 French citizens," 70,000 copies of which were printed in English, Spanish, and German. The illustrations showed Muslims and Europeans in the same schools, hospitals, and parks, in pointed contrast to the segregation practiced elsewhere.[55]

Since mid-1955, some French propaganda acknowledged that Algeria had problems that predated the insurrection even while insisting that only France could provide the solutions. But now the theme of social, political, and economic integration was beginning not merely to supplement that of civilizational conflict—presenting the war as a choice between one and the other—but to replace it altogether, a trend that would accelerate in the coming years. As an April 1957 memorandum argued, they had to present their cause "in such a way that Algeria not be considered as an isolated domain, lost in a desperate battle between sand and sea."[56] In seeking to influence international opinion, French propaganda had to respond to prevailing ideas about *global* integration on the basis of racial equality, self-determination, and cultural cosmopolitanism.

Of course it would be difficult to demonstrate that this imperative influenced policy, since no contemporary official would have admitted to it. But outside observers like Mendès France argued persuasively that the campaign they waged at the United Nations and around the world, like any campaign, could be costly. For instance, Pineau promised Lodge that elections would follow a cease-fire within three months, a promise that Mendès considered "almost contractual." The French also pledged to invite foreign observers to monitor them, an idea that would have been unthinkable not long before. The former prime minister warned that neutral countries would not participate without FLN consent. "Whether we like it or not they will begin as intermediaries, before long mediators, one day, perhaps, arbitrators."[57] At the very least—and despite Mollet's denials—the French had implicitly conceded to the United Nations a right to monitor their conduct in Algeria. As a Quai d'Orsay report later pointed out, foreign delegations would not have become more sympathetic to them "if we had not opened our dossier with so much frankness and objectivity."[58] In that opening, some items had been taken out and new ones were inserted, even while the dossier itself appeared to remain French.

Even the Algerians had begun to worry about the implications of their international strategy. "Success entails obligations," as Yazid observed. "Alerted as it is, international opinion forces us into objective positions and leads us to play the game." Its object was to appear reasonable enough to win support without settling for less than independence. Yazid favored initially demanding "self-determination" instead, bringing down the criticism of the CCE. But even Abbane Ramdane could see how the process of encouraging internationalization might escape their control: "The UN, meddling in our affairs, may push its intervention too far and impose on us solutions incompatible with our national sovereignty"—perhaps including partition.[59]

As for the French representatives, they finally agreed to prepare a fall-back position: a moderate text that could attract enough votes to defeat the one offered by the Afro-Asian lobby. In the lead-up to the debate, they worked with their American counterparts to come up with a resolution they would hold in reserve. Meanwhile, they engaged in delaying actions to allow the ill will left after Suez to dissipate.[60]

Nevertheless, the FLN command in Algiers decided that the general strike would go ahead as planned. After having stored provisions and taken in the indigent, the Muslim population of Algiers left the streets deserted. Virtually no one went to work, or attended school, or opened a shop. In France, too, the great majority of North African workers honored the strike—82 percent in Paris, according to French estimates. It was "an unquestionable success for the FLN," an internal report admitted. "It has been registered by the administration and recognized by the French and foreign press."[61]

But in Algiers the empty streets were soon filled with French troops, who proceeded to use chains and armored cars to tear the steel shutters off storefronts—sometimes causing the old buildings to collapse. Exposed to looting, the shopkeepers had no choice but to come out and open for business. The *paras* pursued the more recalcitrant into their homes, rousing them from bed and trucking them to work or school. Similar scenes were repeated around the country—in the village of Arba a colonel even ordered a tank to fire point-blank into one storefront. Within a few days, the French could declare that the strike was over.[62]

The FLN had therefore lost momentum by the time the U.N. debate began on February 4. While a majority in the Assembly's Political Commission approved the paragraph in the Afro-Asian resolution that recognized the Algerians' right to self-determination, they rejected by a single vote another calling for France to engage in negotiations under U.N. sponsorship. Japan, the Philippines, and Thailand then broke away to propose a less pointed text, though one that still referred to the U.N. charter and the need for negotiations between France and the "Algerian people." The French delegation hoped that no resolution would obtain the two-thirds vote necessary for adoption, but they feared that this one might at least gain a majority. Italy and a number of Latin American delegations friendly to France therefore proposed the text that Pineau had earlier negotiated with Lodge, and a resolution calling for "a peaceful, democratic, and just solution . . . conforming to the principles of the United Nations charter" was unanimously adopted February 15. The French could claim that it exactly matched Mollet's call for a cease-fire, elections, and negotiations, while the FLN maintained that the reference to the UN charter implied a right to self-determination.[63]

A Pyrrhic Victory

The battle of New York was just beginning, but with the sacrifices being made in Algiers the results of this first engagement could only disappoint the FLN leadership. The same day the resolution was adopted, the dispirited members of the CCE decided to abandon the city and direct the rebellion from abroad. Ben Bella's ally in Tunis, Ali Mahsas, attacked their record. "We have risked the dismantling of the revolutionary Organisation to make a noise at the United Nations," he exclaimed. "It's stupid and ridiculous!"[64] Most disheartening of all, Ben M'Hidi was arrested before he could escape. According to the official account, he was then left alone and hung himself in his cell. Few believed the story, but fewer still suspected how common such incidents had now become.

Since the use of torture was illegal by any standard—the French Penal Code, the Universal Declaration of Human Rights, the 1949 Geneva Conventions—apologists justified the practice as an unavoidable response to rebel crimes. Massu would later write that they "remained well within the boundaries of the Leviticus Law of 'an eye for an eye, a tooth for a tooth.'"[65] Yet the routine use of torture had begun in the first months of the war, before the FLN resorted to indiscriminate terror. In Algiers that did not begin until June 1956, *after* the French began guillotining captured rebels. The FLN retaliated by assassinating European men, but not women or children. This threshold was first crossed by a pied noir vigilante group which, with the connivance of the police, blew up the home of a suspected rebel along with three neighboring houses and all their inhabitants. Needless to say, no one was tortured to discover the culprits. They were well known in Algiers, though never arrested.[66]

On the other hand, in the first eight months of 1957 the French would send 24,000 Muslims from the city to internment centers, where torture was systematically practiced. This was more than four times as many as the entire FLN organization there and almost 10 percent of the city's total Muslim population. The secretary general of the police, Paul Teitgen, found that by the end of the year almost 4,000 had disappeared without a trace.[67] According to French figures, in all of Algeria the rebels had killed only a fourth as many European civilians in the three years since the start of the war, only thirty-four of them in Algiers. The European losses in the Battle of Algiers were fewer even than the number of innocent Muslims killed by vengeful mobs. In just one such incident, the paras machine-gunned nearly eighty in a Turkish bath because it was reputed to be an FLN hideout.[68]

While the authorities allowed these pogroms to proceed unhindered and never punished anyone, dozens of Muslim suspects went from extorted confessions to military tribunals to the guillotine in a matter of weeks—in February there were sometimes three or four executions a day. As Slimane Chikh has observed with reference to the Constantinois massacres of August 1955, far from Leviticus law, "the figures eloquently illustrate this sinister law of retaliation which makes ten Muslims pay for the death of one Frenchman, extend[ing] inequality in life to inequality in death.[69]

It could be said that this inequality extended even to the opponents of torture and summary executions. While there had been some protests from the beginning and increasing interest in the fate of Muslim évolués like Ali Boumendjel, a young FLN lawyer who supposedly leapt to his death during interrogation, such incidents did not create a cause célèbre until there were a few European victims. In June 1957, a young communist lecturer at the University of Algiers, Maurice Audin, disappeared after his arrest. Prominent intellectuals then formed a committee to discover his fate and, more generally, investigate the nature and extent of

French war crimes. Denied access to state radio and television, intellectual opposition was expressed in petitions, pamphlets, articles, and books.[70]

In February 1958, the Comité Audin helped to publish and publicize *La Question*, Henri Alleg's harrowing account of his torture at the hands of French soldiers. It sold 60,000 copies in a few weeks before the censors banned it.[71] This was the first of many such works, though the public who read them often seemed more concerned with how war crimes might corrupt their countrymen than how they maimed and killed Algerians. "The most serious problem is not the atrocities themselves," Robert Delavignette claimed, "but that as a result of them the state is engaged in a process of self-destruction."[72]

Be that as it may, a year after the CCE was driven into exile, the Battle of Algiers began to seem like a Pyrrhic victory because it was impossible to conceal the methods by which it had been won, sapping support for the war at home and abroad. The "special powers" legislation allowed the authorities to ban articles and books like Alleg's, but they applied censorship in an inconsistent and contradictory fashion.[73] It actually lent cachet to forbidden works, which were then circulated in secret and taken up by FLN publicists abroad, who cited them in arguing that France had failed to respect the General Assembly resolution.[74] *La Question* was one of a number of banned texts that appeared in translation and became a bestseller elsewhere in Europe and the United States[75] There would always be an international audience for engagé writers like Simone de Beauvoir and Jean-Paul Sartre, especially when they sparred over Algeria with the likes of Albert Camus, Raymond Aron, André Malraux, and Albert Schweitzer.[76]

Censorship was not only ineffectual, it had "made the worst impression abroad," as the Quai's Director of Information and Press, Pierre Baraduc, pointed out in March 1958.[77] Consequently, FLN atrocities such as the massacre at Melouza in June 1957, where they executed the men of the village because of their loyalty to Messali's rival MNA, did not have as great an effect in the American media as might have been expected. Chet Huntley advised NBC viewers to reserve judgment. "We are trying to get our own men into Algeria to report the fighting," he explained, "but each gives up after a little while because he can't penetrate the wall of regulation and censorship the French build up. This does not mean that the French are lying about the massacre. It does mean the information comes from sources whose primary interest is not to inform."[78]

Even those writers who condemned the FLN, Alphand reported, "observed that the persistence of terrorism implicitly attests to the fact that France cannot take the situation in hand. . . . Little by little," he warned, this "prepares American public opinion for the idea that the Algerian question is on the way to becoming an international problem." Indeed, the FLN cynically used the Melouza massacre as an opportunity to demand a U.N. investigation of each side's conduct.[79] While *The New York*

Times never presented the Algerian point of view in editorials, by 1958 even the paper of record concluded that the war was an international concern and urged a negotiated settlement. Liberal and Christian periodicals like *The New Republic, Commonweal*, and *Christian Century* had always been critical of both French human rights violations and the State Department's unwillingness to condemn them.[80]

The American reaction to atrocities reinforced the preference of French propagandists for themes like development and integration instead of "civilization" versus "savagery." Rather than films with titles like *The Hour of the West* and *Around the Algerian Drama*, they began projecting images of irrigation and social work. As Baraduc argued, "Each time that one can speak of something other than blood in Algeria . . . this is progress for pacification because it represents a return to normal."[81] Yet a "return to normal" did not interest newsmen attracted to a story with strong visuals and plenty of violence. The television and radio formats rewarded the rebels for providing combat footage and creating controversy whereas the French would not even admit they were at war or dignify their adversary with a debate. Thus, the week after the Melouza massacre, Huntley's *Outlook* program showed a 20-minute film including clips taken by *mujahadeen* using a portable camera. Perhaps the FLN staged the scenes of children crying beside their parents' corpses and French soldiers falling in combat, as Paris maintained, but they obviously had more emotional impact than propaganda films like *Water, Crops, and Men*.[82]

Even balanced reports undermined French interests, since the appearance of objectivity required explaining the FLN position. Such was the case with an October 1957 *60 Minutes* segment narrated by Eric Severeid, "Algeria in Flames," which presented each side's arguments in turn. Alphand feared that "the broadcast cannot but inspire in the American viewer a feeling of doubt and perplexity."[83] This was still more true of a CBS radio broadcast a year later, in which the correspondent in Algiers, David Schoenbrun, was surprised to find himself in a transatlantic debate after reporting on a de Gaulle speech. He did not realize that *The World Tonight*'s host, Blair Clark, had invited an FLN spokesman to join him in the studio in New York. Though the form had yet to be perfected, any broadcast news producer would recognize Clark's rationale. He explained that his intention had been "to dramatize the broadcast in a spectacular way by having an American correspondent in Algiers itself respond to the positions taken by the FLN in New York. . . ."[84]

World Opinion—"An Absolute Principle of War"

Thus far, this analysis has concentrated on the United States because both sides considered it to be so important. Yazid called it "the international key to the Algerian problem," while an April 1957 Quai memorandum agreed that "the attitude of the United States is determinant. It is with her that the great majority of countries align themselves."[85] Of course, even close U.S. allies like Britain and West Germany could pursue distinct policies, and there were important differences in media coverage as well. Europeans sympathetic to the French were more likely to use the language of "Western civilization" and "Islamic fanaticism," providing press clippings for a glossy 1957 French propaganda brochure, "World Opinion Judges the Bloody 'Liberators' of Melouza and Wagram." "It is more clear than ever," the *Daily Express* asserted, "that a retreat by France from Algeria would mean the victory of savagery." The Swedish *Stocholms-Tidnongen* predicted that it would be "a preferred field for the forces that use all means to weaken and threaten the Western democratic world." The Swiss *Feuille d'Avis de Neuchatel* hoped that Melouza would make all Europeans "finally understand what face is masked under Algerian nationalism, and what blows are delivered to Western civilization by Islam on the march, the same as were dealt to it in the past by international communism." More than half of the 35,000 copies of this brochure were sent to French Muslims. Similarly, the Arabic service of Radio Algiers would regularly broadcast excerpts from the foreign press favorable to the French in Algeria, providing another example of the interconnections between Algerian and "world" opinion.[86]

Yet notwithstanding a few damning quotes on the very worst FLN atrocity, even sympathetic writers shared American skepticism about France's chance for success. From the very beginning the *Economist* criticized the official view that the rebellion lacked popular support, and by 1958 even the more establishment *Times* of London asked whether the government had lost control. In Germany the mainstream press continually complained that the war distracted France from the task of Western defense and foresaw no solution save independence. As the *Frankfurter Allemeine Zeitung* observed in March 1958, "France is the only European great power that will not recognize the great event of the 20th century, the process of the decline of Europe's hegemony, to which she ought to play her own part." Some shared the view of Algeria as a civilizational conflict but found France's conduct there—and, by association, that of NATO—all the more regrettable for that reason. Thus, a month later, *Die Welt* warned that "France's partners should not in any case be deceived about the fact that they are identified by all people of color with a policy that, according to the Algerians, has cost the lives of 600,000 Muslims in four years." Macmillan and Adenauer were usually able to pursue their own policies of supporting France in Algeria and restraining American efforts to intervene, but both were subject to increasing criticism by the press and opposition parties.[87]

While Italians were initially more favorable, the Battle of Algiers brought a change in popular perceptions. This came about when intrepid reporters from *Il Tempo* and the press agency ANSA developed contacts with the FLN and presented events from its point of view. In Italy as well as Belgium, French tactics aroused opposition not just from the communists but from socialists and Catholics too, who eventually formed committees to campaign for peace in Algeria.[88]

After the Battle of Algiers, German and Italian journalists followed the FLN leadership into exile. As the mujahadeen launched raids back into Algeria, reporters from *Der Stern* and *Il Giorno* endeavored to accompany them and publish eyewitness accounts. The French military complained that the reporters were fooled by the FLN and never crossed the border. But here again it hardly made a difference. By representing the rebels as controlling parts of Algeria, these reports buttressed their claims to international recognition. As one French diplomat later remarked about contacts between the State Department and the FLN, "It's not the reality of what they say or do, but the way it is represented in the radios of Tunis and Cairo and the myth that it gives life to in [Algeria]. . . ." Indeed, this "myth" of a conquering army and diplomats with entrée to every chancellery would gradually transform reality within Algeria itself, making the once unassailable notion of *Algérie française* itself seem illusory.[89]

Of course, there were limits to what FLN propagandists could credibly claim, and over time they chose to concentrate on their successes abroad. Albert Fitte has quantified this trend in an analysis of *El Moudjahid*, the FLN's official paper. It had a clandestine circulation of some 3,000 within Algeria while another 10,000 copies were distributed in Tunis or mailed to sympathizers and journalists abroad. Fitte calculated that the number of articles on the rebel army steadily declined from 1956 through June 1958. Whereas fully 35 percent concerned the ALN in the first period—more than any other category—over time ALN stories declined to 27 percent and then to a mere 16.5 percent. During the same period, coverage of such topics as U.N. debates, FLN participation in international conferences, and foreign opinion on the war increased from 12.5 percent to 30 percent and then 40 percent (see the graph on page 136). If one also counts articles on the French army and France's allies—which often discussed war crimes in terms of international law and criticized NATO support—the FLN's principal propaganda organ was devoting over half of its coverage to the international context of the war by the middle of 1958. This is all the more striking considering that in that same period the intensity of the military struggle attained an all-time high.[90]

This shift was not just the policy of Algerian propagandists, it also reflected the international media's judgment of what was "newsworthy" about their war. For instance, 34 percent of *New York Times* coverage in 1956–1957 originated in Algeria compared to the 24 percent of articles that bore such datelines as Washington, London, Cairo, and other foreign capitals (the balance originated in France). In 1958 and 1959, the relative shares were reversed: 26 percent were reported from Algeria and 34 percent originated abroad. But perhaps the most telling measure of how the war figured on the world stage is the fact that in these two years *The New York Times* printed 197 page-one stories on Algeria—nearly twice as many as before.[91]

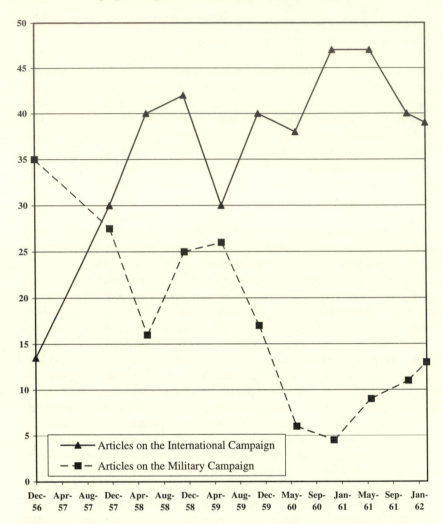

FLN Propaganda: The International versus the Military Campaigns The percentage of *El Moudjahid* articles devoted to the exploits of the ALN within Algeria compared to the percentage describing successes of FLN diplomats abroad shows how rebel propaganda shifted from the military to the international campaigns (adapted from Albert Fitte, *Spectroscopie d'une propagande révolutionnaire*, 74–78).

The French, on the other hand, found that trumpeting their military successes could be counterproductive. In April 1957 a Quai d'Orsay official had already discovered what Jean Lacouture later called the "supreme paradox." After describing to Lacoste's cabinet director how they had lost support abroad because of attacks on the army's methods, he remarked that "this deterioration of our position on the UN front is undeniable even if it is in flagrant contradiction with the improvement that becomes apparent everywhere in Algeria."[92] In fact, the deterioration of the French position at the United Nations was not in contradiction with their improved position in Algeria, it was *conditioned* by it. Thus, French diplomats would often complain that the announcement of figures on FLN losses hurt their image abroad, indicating one of the mechanisms underlying the inverse relationship between France's military and diplomatic strength vis-à-vis Algeria.[93]

That same month, Mollet felt compelled to respond to domestic and international criticism by forming a "Permanent Committee for the Safeguard of Individual Rights and Liberties." But pretending that torture and summary executions were not officially sanctioned practices but military excesses further alienated army commanders, some of whom had been disciplined for protesting what they were led to do in Algeria.[94] As Alistair Horne has observed, "because of the interplay of modern communications with the presence of vast numbers of civilian conscripts on active duty, the Army—try as it might—could no longer see itself as standing aloof, separated and isolated, as it had once done, from *La Nation*."[95] The only way the government might have maintained this separation—and itself—was to take responsibility for what was happening in Algeria. Yet that appeared impossible for any democratic government in terms of both domestic and world opinion as they became increasingly interconnected. Here again, trends toward global integration—especially new communications technologies and international norms on human rights—can be seen undermining local political structures, a connection that is all the more striking when one recalls that Lacoste first ceded power to the army in reaction to an FLN campaign aimed at the United Nations.[96]

Of course, new technologies could be tools in the hands of propagandists working to maintain state power. Thus, the 1959 film *Les trois frontières de l'Algérie* began by showing how "man has become a great traveler." Amid scenes of passenger jets, the narrator describes how one could arrive in a few hours among people who, once far away, now seemed less and less foreign. Diversity and the fluidity of frontiers were to be celebrated and defended against those who would divide communities by inciting hatred and fear—represented by the silhouette of a fez-wearing man speaking into a radio microphone. By modernizing Algeria and opening it to the world, France would bridge the geographical and temporal divide between industrial civilization and "underdeveloped" areas. The French gave a dramatic demonstration of this idea by engineering the first live intercontinental television broadcast between Algeria and France on Bastille day, 1958.[97]

But the import of improved mobility and new means of mass communications was more often ambiguous and even subversive. Traveling to the metropole made many "French Muslims" Algerian nationalists. Moreover, beginning in 1957, the FLN produced its own propaganda films, such as *L'Algérie en flammes*. Using a 16mm camera, the French communist and FLN sympathizer René Vauthier shot scenes of an attack on a French train, Muslim women in the maquis, and FLN aid to Algerian refugees which were eventually shown across the Eastern Bloc and the

Arab world.[98] Though these films could not be screened within Algeria itself, everyone with a transistor radio could vicariously take part in the struggle by listening to FLN broadcasts beamed from abroad, as Fanon had observed.[99] Transistors—and de Gaulle's mastery of the spoken word—would also encourage French conscripts to defy the generals' putsch in 1961, reaffirming the president's authority but only by shattering the chain of command between them.

Globalization disrupted political structures not just vertically—that is, within societies—but also horizontally, across the international system. The French themselves conducted a campaign to influence American policy on Algeria. Following the General Assembly debate, they redoubled their efforts. Between September 1957 and February 1958, for example, they would stage almost 7,500 screenings of their propaganda films before Rotary Clubs, Chambers of Commerce, bankers' associations, student organizations, and others. They even went so far as to hire a public relations firm, Communications Counselors, Inc. (CCI).[100] Yet the advice the consultants provided—that they should show how "France is striving forward into a new era epitomized by Euratom, The Common European Market, Eurafrica"—indicated why holding Algeria had become a Sisyphean task.[101] Mollet had already promised that the European Economic Community would be invited to participate in developing North Africa, predicting that "Eurafrica may become one of the main factors in world politics." In March 1958, this invitation was extended to the United States as well, again signaling the abandonment of a longstanding policy of upholding imperial preferences. This reflected a realization—at least among the technocrats who wrote the 1957 "Modernization and Development Plan"—that "our country cannot choose protectionist and inward-looking policies without running the risk of finding ourselves in a few years an impoverished and isolated country, a historical has-been."[102] The "open door" was accompanied by an "open window," as the Quai described it, in which the Algiers government arranged tours for diplomats, foreign politicians, and organizations like the Socialist International and the International Red Cross.[103]

Yet at a time when writers like Raymond Cartier were demanding cost-benefit analyses for overseas possessions, how could any government justify fighting to keep *Algérie française* if every country would derive the benefits? Indeed, in May 1957, Alphand reported that the theme of "Eurafrica" had been taken up by FLN allies like Morocco, who argued that the prolongation of the conflict was the greatest obstacle to its realization.[104] Even if these plans came to fruition, would Algeria still be part of France if both became "Eurafrican?" Appeals to foreign publics and international organizations as well as a willingness to open Algeria to outside investment and inspection all reflected a sense that "isolated nations cannot hold their own in the world as it is today," as Mollet put it.[105] The erosion of sovereignty was especially apparent in French Algeria only because this was a particularly extreme assertion of a state's prerogatives in the face of social, cultural, political, economic, and even geographical realities.

Yet Americans were also coming to terms with the new limits on national power, as shown by John H. Herz's classic 1957 article, the "Rise and Demise of the Territorial State." Given their dominance of global markets and communications and their heritage of international migration, Herz and Americans generally were more concerned about the security aspects of declining autonomy. Long-range nuclear delivery systems had made it impossible for even the strongest state to guarantee security for their citizens. Yet Herz thought that

> if we add to this the universal interest in the common solution of other great world problems, such as those posed by the population-resources dilemma . . . it is perhaps not entirely utopian to expect the ultimate spread of an attitude of "universalism" through which a rational approach to world problems would at last become possible.[106]

A similar analysis inspired one State Department official, L. W. Fuller, writing on the United States and the United Nations later that year. Fuller began by setting out the "essential dilemma" according to Reinhold Niebuhr's *The World Crisis and American Responsibility*. "Technics have established a rudimentary world community," Niebuhr wrote, "but have not integrated it organically, morally or politically. . . ." Fuller, for his part, specified that

> the Soviet-Western antagonism, the arms impasse and the threat of nuclear war, the obliteration of frontiers by technological advance, the embittered 'North-South' conflict — [have produced] a host of problems that in their very nature are not soluble or even reducible . . . through national policy alone, or even through traditional multilateral diplomacy. More and more problems are "affected with a public interest," and are matters of deep concern to the embryonic world community . . . The U.S. cannot hope to prosper except in a stable and orderly world. We cannot hope to make progress toward such a world unless we develop the rudiments of world order.

"The US is following the trend of history," he concluded, "and serving its own interest in seeking to further the evolution of the inchoate world community inherent in the UN system."[107]

This apparent "trend of history" toward a "world community" in which even the strongest would have to cede part of their sovereignty endangered the whole project of French Algeria. But at first it only appeared to be a problem for French propagandists. In March 1958, Baraduc wrote that they would have to do a better job of showing how "our policy is not behind the times, that we are really [working] in the direction of history." He had recently described French policy to a reporter for *The New York Times*:

> [It was] an effort to bring a population out of the Middle Ages (obscurantism and fanaticism) in order to place it directly in the twentieth century (industrial

development and large economic markets) without going through the eighteenth century (enlightened despotism) and the nineteenth century (nationalism) which appear to be obligatory steps for countries which have recently been given their independence.[108]

While one might criticize his ethnocentrism, Baraduc had tacitly admitted that national self-determination—albeit self-determination within a new set of constraints—was an integral part of progress. But even if one could "skip a step," what was the basis of France's particular vocation in Algeria if *all* peoples would participate in industrial development and international markets? Indeed, the FLN's official paper, *El Moudjahid*, acknowledged in November 1957 that an international contribution would be necessary to develop the Sahara.[109]

Baraduc recognized that the French would have a better claim than the FLN to bringing Algeria into the new age only if they were careful to maintain their reputation as "a civilized nation," "at the forefront of progress and bringing democracy and prosperity to backward populations."[110] That is why censorship and torture, seemingly indispensable to the war effort, were so damaging to the French diplomatic position. And while economic policies did not arouse the same emotional response, France's creditors knew that the war prevented France from removing the exchange controls, tariffs, and export subsidies that made it Western Europe's most protectionist country. Indeed, only six months after Mollet had heralded the coming of "Eurafrica," inflationary and budgetary pressures forced his successors to suspend the trade liberalization measures required by the more modest Organisation for European Economic Cooperation (OEEC).[111]

The most blatant example of how France could not help defying the "direction of history" by fighting to retain control of Algeria was the "Morice line," 300 kilometers of electrified barbed-wire fences, mine fields, and watchtowers the army erected along the Algerian-Tunisian frontier beginning in June 1957. It stood in glaring contradiction to French claims to be opening Algeria to the world and seemed like a throwback to the time when a "hard shell of frontier fortifications," as Herz put it, guarded states against outside interference.[112]

But the Morice line was actually set back from the border some 30–50 kilometers. In between was a no-man's-land, a freefire zone where villages were systematically destroyed. Refugees streamed into Tunisia—some 46,000 by October 1957.[113] The Tunisians appealed to international organizations, and already in July 1957 the project's namesake, Defense Minister André Morice, foresaw how the refugee camps "will be a clever way to draw the attention of the UN to the Algerian conflict and the first step towards the internationalization of the conflict."[114] While the French tried to take responsibility for individuals they still considered French citizens, the International Red Cross and Red Crescent undertook to aid the refugees with contributions from the Americans, the Soviets, and several Arab states. Still more seriously, the FLN used these camps as bases and struck back into Algeria. The French, for their part, claimed a right to pursue rebels across the border, which led to clashes with Tunisia's new army. Thus, France's line in the sand became blurred and indistinct, creating a zone of ambiguity where French soldiers were often uncertain as to whether they fought Algerians or Tunisians, rebels or refugees.

The Morice line did become effective in a narrow military sense, frustrating FLN assaults and inflicting horrendous casualties. But, like the Maginot line, it was outflanked — not by military units, but by the more profound forces that were transforming the international system as a whole, shaking out political structures within and between societies: international groups like the Red Cross and the IMF; transnational phenomena like refugees, the media, and capital markets; and new communications technologies such as transistor radios and portable cameras that helped tell the story, or invent it, for Algerian, French, and world opinion.

"Historians must explore the profound forces," A. J. P. Taylor once conceded, "But I am sometimes tempted to think that they talk so much about these profound forces in order to avoid doing the detailed work."[115] It is hoped that the preceding discussion demonstrated that "profound forces" were not just analytical abstractions imposed after the fact but a conscious part of peoples' experiences. Thus, even something as vague as "world opinion" appeared to the Suez expedition's commander, General Sir Charles Keightley, to be "an absolute principle of war" after it helped defeat his forces.[116] On the other hand, episodes like the Suez crisis and the Battle of Algiers helped to shape world opinion and a general "direction of history" that made *Algérie française* seem like an anachronism. As *El Moudjahid* declared in April 1958: "The Algerian people have experienced concretely the interdependence of historical phenomena. To say that the local destruction of colonialism increases its destruction as a system is no longer to express an abstract principle that only intellectuals can understand."[117]

The most difficult and most necessary task for historians is to do the detailed work necessary to explain how these principles worked in practice — the interaction, in other words, of profound forces and specific events. Having observed how the arguments aimed at winning over world opinion sharpened domestic debates within France and undermined the whole rationale for retaining Algeria, we will now see how in Algeria, as in Suez, the force of world opinion was mediated by American policymakers intent on riding the "trend of history" — and dragging the French with them. But it was Bourguiba and old-fashioned statecraft that finally brought this Franco-American conflict into the open. The next chapter includes some very detailed diplomatic history to demonstrate how that was done.

6

An Anti-American
Revolt

*The implacable judgment of history will . . . not absolve [the army]
for attempting to escape its responsibilities when the fate of our civilization is at stake.*

Général Paul Ely, chef d'Etat-major général, June 1957 [1]

*War requires a war economy. War brings austerity or inflation—
and, in the latter case, it brings defeat.*

Pierre Mendès France, December 1957 [2]

In May 1957, Robert Marjolin, former secretary general of the OEEC,
arrived in Washington on a secret mission to obtain American aid. His
first meeting was with the new deputy under secretary of state for economic affairs, and Marjolin had reason to hope for a sympathetic reception. After all, it was none other than Douglas Dillon, who had succeeded
to the post after serving as U.S. ambassador in Paris. Marjolin did not
waste a minute:

> He explained that while the overt reason for his trip was to discuss the Com-
> mon Market and Euratom, his actual purpose was to approach the United
> States Government at the highest level, at Mr. Ramadier's request, to explain
> what steps France was taking to overcome its financial difficulties, to ascertain
> what the United States' attitude was toward these French measures and,
> frankly, to find out what, if any, help the United States could give France.

Dillon was equally frank. He said that "the French deficit was so huge
that there was nothing the United States could do unless the French took
steps to rectify this situation." Marjolin described plans for new taxes and
spending reductions, but Dillon knew not to take these pledges at face
value. Under his successor, Amory Houghton, the U.S. embassy in Paris
had continued to forward inside information on the faltering economic
reforms. Since Schweitzer's "unauthorized" conversation with Charles
Yost in February, 27 billion francs had been *added* to the special budget
for the war.[3]

Dillon replied that, while "no large sums were available," if France now took the "appropriate steps" the United States might help "in a small way. . . ."[4] He did not specify what he meant by appropriate steps, but Dulles himself was now prepared explicitly to link American aid to ending the war. Three days later, he told Marjolin that there were two obstacles standing in the way of U.S. help. The first was that the Americans thought France could be self-sufficient if its government took the necessary measures.

> The second was the problem posed by the continuation of hostilities in Algeria which seemed like a never-ending drain on French resources. While the US realized the difficulties of the problems involved, it had no suggestions to offer for a solution. Nevertheless, it was difficult to contemplate financial assistance while this drain was continuing.[5]

The very next day, the Mollet government fell on a confidence vote over its economic policies. While the new tax proposals had been too little to satisfy the Americans, they were too much for the conservative Independents. After Pleven and the MRP's Pierre Pflimlin failed to find majorities, Bourgès-Maunoury managed to form a new government with Mollet's backing. It included many of the same ministers, notably Lacoste and Pineau, while excluding dissenters on Algeria like Mitterrand and Defferre. One new face was Félix Gaillard, at 37 the youngest finance minister in sixty years. He managed to push through a slightly more demanding austerity package than that which brought down the preceding government. But the Americans did not budge.[6]

With the possible exception of Dulles' talk with Marjolin, Washington did not demand peace in Algeria as a condition for financial support. Indeed, the secretary publicly rejected the idea when a delegation of ambassadors from eleven Arab states proposed it in June.[7] Yet, that same month, *Le Monde* reported that most U.S. officials privately admitted that any financial recovery required settling the war.[8] In July, Dulles himself told a French diplomat, "as a friendly confidence," that his public assurances that Algeria concerned France alone should not "conceal in the eyes of the French government our profound concern for the consequences of this affair for the military, economic, and financial power of France."[9] From such evidence, French officials concluded that "the settlement of the Algerian question appears, in the eyes of the American authorities, more and more linked to the problem of exceptional and sizeable financial aid."[10]

The only alternative to a bilateral or multilateral bailout—since even an IMF or World Bank package required approval by Washington—was a politically difficult if not impossible austerity program, one even more onerous than what the Americans had in mind. As a Quai d'Orsay memorandum concluded later that same month: "In order to pursue our intended policy in Algeria, we must bring about a financial recovery. The longer we wait to do it, the more we will have need of outsiders and the more they will be in a position to press on our decisions in North Africa."[11]

The most immediate and important decision was how to deal with Tunisia and its deepening involvement in the war. In June 1956, FLN emissaries recognized that their ally Salah Ben Youssef was a spent force and recommended playing "the Bourguiba card." The Tunisian premier was offering logistical and diplomatic support up to and including a break with Paris. But for several months, the constant influx of FLN cadres as well as the continuing dissidence of Ali Mahsas and the bordering regions of Algeria created near anarchy, blocking arms shipments and tempting Bourguiba to meddle.[12] By the spring of 1957, Colonel Omar Ouamrane had finally restored the CCE's authority and evidently arrived at an agreement with Tunis. As long as the ALN avoided clashes with French troops stationed in Tunisia and respected its sovereignty, Bourguiba would help them transport arms from Libya to the Algerian frontier.[13] After Spain started cracking down on the traffic through Morocco as part of a rapprochement with France—in one case seizing 6,000 arms aboard a vessel out of Egypt—the overland Libya-Tunisia route became the lifeline of the ALN. In the summer of 1957, twelve tons of munitions transited every 72 hours—some 2,500 weapons a month, or 70 percent of all ALN arms shipments.[14]

In May 1957—and in one of the last acts of his government—Mollet retaliated by suspending $28 million in aid earlier promised to Bourguiba.[15] Alphand sought assurances that the United States would not substitute for France in aiding Tunisia. American policy was to provide merely complementary aid. Indeed, earlier that month, they accorded only $3 million—leading the Tunisians to joke that they would use the money to build an embassy in Moscow. Nevertheless, while Dulles agreed that France should continue to take the lead, now he warned that, "if circumstances lead France to be driven back, *by its own fault or not*, from playing this role . . . the American government would be obliged, whether it wanted to or not, to give Tunisia and Morocco the economic aid that they solicit."[16]

Bourgès's new government chose to avoid a showdown with Tunisia and instead announced a reduction in the number of French troops in the country from 25,000 to 15,000. But financial aid remained in abeyance and, as French settlers and capital flowed out of Tunisia, the country's economic condition steadily worsened. The U.S. ambassador dealt with the Tunisians' obvious desire for U.S. support by "lying low and avoiding [the] subject," as he later told Dulles.[17]

"Lying low" became more difficult in July when John F. Kennedy launched a blistering attack on U.S. North African policy from the Senate floor. After a briefing by Yazid and Chanderli, he called Algerian independence "the essential first step" if the West were not to lose all influence in North Africa. But Kennedy also urged increased support for Bourguiba lest he turn to the Soviets. All in all, the United States could no longer base its policy on the "myth of French empire."[18] The speech caused an uproar across the Atlantic. French authorities in Algeria warned Americans to keep off the streets, and two days later a bomb exploded outside the U.S. consulate. In the United States it attracted more attention than any other address Kennedy gave as a senator, though much of it was negative—90 of 138 editorials opposed him. As Richard Mahoney later wrote, "Practically no one in the American foreign policy establishment regarded the Algeria speech as anything more than a partisan political blast designed to attract attention."[19]

Yet the speech is no less interesting for being "political," since it shows how Algeria generated debates that spilled over diplomatic channels and national boundaries. Dulles told Alphand that they were "in the same boat" since the senator was targeting the administration as much as the French.[20] Moreover, "the French" were not uniformly hostile. *Le Monde's* correspondent in Washington wrote to the *Times* arguing that he was "more to be commended than blamed for his forthright, frank and provocative speech." *L'Express* reprinted it in full, with Kennedy's picture on the cover.[21] When Alphand complained, the senator was able to point out that the war had little support in France.[22] Dulles, for his part, dressed Kennedy down in public but privately used the opportunity to pressure the ambassador. The secretary "confessed he would himself be at a loss to explain convincingly French policy in Algeria, if he had to do so before the United Nations at this time or later this fall, should there have been no progress by then," even going so far as to warn that "the situation might well blow up."[23]

Perhaps the most interesting exchange on the Kennedy speech occurred between a Quai d'Orsay official and the secretary general of the UGTA, who were meeting in Tunis to discuss the possibility of restarting negotiations. Abdelaziz Rachid insisted that France first recognize their right to independence. "The United States will not abandon us!" he exclaimed. His interlocutor coolly denied that the Kennedy speech had any such significance. But inwardly he recalled the Indochina precedent, worried that Dulles would abandon France once again.[24]

An Event "All out of Proportion to Its Real Significance"

The most likely site of the "blow up" feared by Dulles remained the Algerian-Tunisian frontier. On August 1, Morice announced that French troops would not stop at the border in repelling attacks, questioning whether Bourguiba controlled Tunisian territory.[25] Legally the French were on shaky ground despite Bourguiba's acknowledgement of the arms traffic. As a Quai memorandum pointed out, the "right of pursuit" was intended for an international war, not the "operations for the reestablishment of the civil peace" France claimed to be conducting in Algeria. Practically speaking, even if the Tunisians had been willing to stop the FLN attacks—which seems doubtful—they could, and did, argue that

France deprived them of the means to do so. On August 4, Paris formally suspended further arms shipments to Tunisia—there had been none for more than a year—and subsequently worked behind the scenes to prevent Belgium and Italy from taking its place.[26]

A month later, Tunisian Foreign Secretary Sadok Mokaddem sent for Ambassador G. Lewis Jones to report another border clash. Six Tunisian soldiers had been killed, and the rest had been forced to give up when their ammunition ran out. He finally broached the subject that Jones had for months sought to avoid, officially requesting America's assistance in purchasing arms and ammunition. His government would be forced to go "elsewhere" if it could not get arms from France or another Western supplier.[27]

There was no reply from the State Department for a week, and in the meantime the situation deteriorated—not just between France and Tunisia, but between Bourguiba and the FLN. According to reports by the French ambassador, Georges Gorse, Bourguiba requested that the Algerians halt their attacks and retire 50 kilometers from the border. They refused, explaining that they had orders to commence an all-out offensive to influence the debates at the United Nations. Bourguiba then called on the chiefs of the old Tunisian maquis to mobilize along the frontier to paralyze the movements of the ALN against the French and, conversely, oppose a French invasion.[28]

While it is possible that the Tunisians fabricated these reports to improve their position *vis-à-vis* the French, there is no doubt that they were concerned about the FLN forces. Totaling some 6,500 men by August—3,000 armed and formed into units—they rivaled Tunisia's own tiny army. Moreover, the threat of a French invasion from Algeria was very real. On Morice's orders, the general commanding French forces in Tunisia together with Salan produced a plan for the "Retaking of Temporary Control of Tunisian Territory," including naval and airborne landings around Tunis. According to Salan, on September 8 Chief of Staff Paul Ely ordered him to proceed with preparations.[29]

Bourguiba was certainly in a fighting mood when he met Gorse on August 12, the day after another border clash. He was "visibly exhausted, prey to nervousness," according to the ambassador's account. The president launched into "a long, bitter monologue," asserting that the incursions were not aimed at the FLN:

> These are true aggressions. They are driven by political considerations: you want to inflict insults on Tunisia. . . . [T]he Tunisian government has decided to take responsibility and assure its legitimate defense. Any incursion by French forces would lead to "progressive" reactions on its part: it is ready, if it is necessary, to face "pitched battles" in Tunisia itself.[30]

Later that day, just fifteen minutes before Bourguiba was to record his weekly radio address to the nation, Ambassador Jones "strong-arm[ed]" his way in to see him—a telegram from Washington had arrived "just in time." The State Department assured Bourguiba that it was "giving most urgent attention" to the arms request and pledged to signal to the French "our grave concern at [the] present situation." But it also advised Bourguiba to reconsider his remarks about obtaining arms elsewhere, since "even talk of this kind if publicly known can encourage Soviet intervention."[31]

The president promised "to speak with more serenity," though the speech was still fairly harsh. He alleged that the United States and the countries that had rebuffed his requests for arms bore some responsibility for the attacks along the border, hinting that "such a situation can cause us to knock on other doors, or at least keep our distance." Still, it ended on a hopeful note—in fact, too hopeful from the American point of view. Bourguiba promised his audience that by the end of October Tunisia would receive arms: "If America understands our situation, as I am told, all will be well."[32]

The Americans had not committed to supplying arms, much less given a timetable for doing so. But Bourguiba's public prediction set off two months of frantic diplomacy. All along he set the pace, exploiting the media and the threat to turn to the United Nations, Egypt, or the Eastern Bloc to force American action. Thus, Ambassador Jones had rushed to see Bourguiba based on a reporter's warning that the president would announce that his loyalty to the West was "no more than meaningless sentimental attachment."[33] In fact, it was virtually the only thing protecting him from French forces in Algeria. He realized that an arms deal with the Eastern Bloc would have served as an ideal pretext for an attack.[34] But Bourguiba was one of the few popular, pro-Western leaders of a newly independent country. So when he warned—as he did in a July 1957 article for *Foreign Affairs*—that nationalists "might be tempted to turn, out of sheer despair, to the Communists," the Americans were ready to believe him.[35]

The same day Bourguiba addressed his nation, Dulles sent a personal message to Pineau urging that France supply arms to Tunisia or allow another Western government to do so.[36] After he promised Bourguiba that he might "have to find other means of meeting your requirements," reports began to come out of Cairo indicating that Tunisia had accepted a "gift" of arms from Nasser. One story quoted a Tunisian official predicting that an impending Czechoslovakian trade mission "might also provide for arms."[37] The State Department then authorized Ambassador Mongi Slim to announce that it recognized Tunisia's needs and was disposed to help. Bourguiba obligingly told reporters that the Tunisian negotiators "did not even raise the question of arms" with the Czech mission.[38]

All this publicity was anathema to Bourgès's government. Pineau had already complained that a report leaked to the United Press about the Quai's efforts to arrange an Italian arms delivery to Tunisia infuriated Bourgès and Morice and put Pineau in an "extremely delicate position"—

after all, the Tunisian army had repeatedly clashed with the French and delivered arms to their enemies.[39] The story was all the more unwelcome in that the government was in the midst of a special session of the Assembly called to examine the *loi cadre*, the electoral reform law for Algeria. Though opposed by hard-liners, the *loi cadre* was as "complicated as it was anodyne," as Jean-Pierre Rioux has observed, and it reflected all the contradictions of the French approach to Algeria. Thus, its preamble proclaimed that Algeria remained an integral part of France while the body called for a local parliament and government unlike anything in the metropole—though very like the existing system. In any case, only subsequent decrees would determine the form of these institutions, and nothing whatever was to be done before the end of hostilities.[40] The official government line was that approval was needed before the next U.N. debate. The *loi cadre*'s preamble pandered to international opinion by claiming that the government had been seeking "a peaceful, democratic, and just solution," the very words used in the General Assembly resolution.[41]

On September 30, Bourgès's government lost a vote of confidence on the *loi cadre*. Ambassador Alphand asserted to Assistant Secretary for European Affairs C. Burke Elbrick that the press leaks on Tunisian arms had made the difference in the narrow defeat—Soustelle had actually read *New York Times* articles about it to the Assembly. Bourguiba "was pushing the situation for all the traffic would bear," Elbrick admitted, "and was trying to panic us into action." Alphand warned that any precipitous move by the Americans "would have a profound effect on relations between our two peoples and on the Western alliance which was of much greater importance than [America's] direct relations with Bourguiba."[42]

One can understand Alphand's assumption that choosing between France and Tunisia would not represent a dilemma. But, since the Suez crisis, Dulles conceived of such conflicts as posing a choice not just between two countries but between the past and the future. The very next day he told Defense Minister Bahi Ladgham that Tunisia's prospects were "promising and expanding" whereas "the French future appears to hold diminishing prestige and power."[43] As early as March 1957, he had begun to plan accordingly, as shown by a memorandum he wrote to Christian Herter:

> We may be approaching the time when we shall have to tell the French that in order to keep North Africa out of the Communist camp we must, in the absence of change in French policy, proceed to make our plans for the area. French reaction might entail a large-scale recasting of NATO and of our military defense arrangements in Europe, as well as of our approach to a Summit meeting and the topics there to be discussed. I think we should now be thinking through these implications.
>
> We shall also have to consider the attitudes of the British, German, and Italian Governments and whether, if we have to make a choice, their choice will coincide with ours so that we can count on their support.[44]

At the time, Dulles had just concluded a conference in Bermuda with Harold Macmillan and Foreign Secretary Selwyn Lloyd that renewed the "special relationship," which the prime minister had come to accept as a "junior partnership" for Britain.[45] Now Dulles endeavored to make certain of their backing, telling Lloyd that no other Western country would sell arms to Tunisia and it was "neither practical nor dignified to 'shop around.' " The foreign secretary wanted to keep trying with Belgium and Italy but eventually agreed that unless France supplied arms to Tunisia the United States and Great Britain should do so instead. Eisenhower thought this would reduce the "possibility of France 'lashing out' at either of us."[46]

In fact, Ambassador Alphand was furious. He called the new position an ultimatum and judged that "it would enable [the U.S.] to keep Tunisia but he did not know about France."[47] Similarly, in Paris Pineau warned Sir Gladwyn Jebb that it "might well affect the relations between our two countries."[48] Meeting with Dulles the next day, Alphand pleaded with the secretary not to do anything during the cabinet crisis which could be exploited by the left. Dulles remarked that "France could not expect the whole world to stand still."[49] The secretary was obviously exasperated with the French practice of postponing unpalatable decisions during chronic and seemingly interminable cabinet crises. At thirty-five days, this would be one of the longest of all such crises, with one candidate after another failing to gather sufficient support, and the financial question preoccupied all of them. President Coty first called on Guy Mollet, who consulted with Bank of France Governor Baumgartner even before meeting his fellow Socialists. After presiding over a meeting of top economic officials, Robert Schuman concluded that only a coalition of all the parties could surmount "the serious difficulties of the present hour." The only copy of their report was entrusted to President Coty after all the notes were destroyed. Treasury Director Schweitzer provided a possible explanation for this secrecy to the counselor for economic affairs at the U.S. embassy, John Tuthill, when he revealed that France might actually refuse to pay its external accounts. Amid a wave of strikes and new pressure on the franc, Finance Minister Gaillard began to gather support. France had lost $100 million in foreign currency reserves while awaiting a new government.[50]

On November 1, Alphand came to see Dillon confidentially to discuss a cable from the Quai d'Orsay's secretary general, Louis Joxe, a cable he had shown to no one else in the embassy. Joxe wrote that after the next deficit payment to the European Payments Union (EPU) on November 15 French reserves would be exhausted. He asked if Gaillard could make a lightning visit should he succeed in forming a government. Dillon suggested instead that he first produce an economic stabilization plan and then send a less prominent emissary. Alphand agreed that the proposed visit was "bad politics," but he warned that "the situation was very serious and that if France went bankrupt and could not pay for necessary imports of fuel there might be very drastic changes in her political institutions."[51]

Perhaps because of the evident weakness of the French position, Dulles decided to take action. The next day he wired Tunis setting terms for the U.S. share of a symbolic Anglo-American arms shipment: 500 rifles and 50,000 rounds of ammunition.[52] Lloyd wanted to wait until a new government was formed in Paris but acknowledged that if they were not careful "not only the Egyptians but also the Russians will beat us to it."[53] While the British appeared to have agreed with the Americans on the substance of the issue, their priority in the post-Suez period was, above all, not to disagree.[54] On November 4, the British and American embassies in Paris therefore presented *aides-mémoire* specifying that they would deliver arms on November 12 unless France came to an agreement with the Tunisian government before then.

On November 6, Gaillard presented his cabinet before the National Assembly. Pineau returned as foreign minister and asked for an additional delay so that his new colleagues could consider the matter.[55] Three days later, Gaillard stressed that if the United States pushed ahead it would be considered an "unfriendly act"—strong words in diplomatic parlance. If he still could not deliver the arms after the next cabinet meeting on November 12, the United States would be free to act on its own. Houghton warned that if Washington ignored this warning and supplied arms to Tunisia it would "have effects all out of proportion to its real significance."[56]

Herter had already wired a request for a further delay to Tunis.[57] But now the Tunisians refused, with Foreign Secretary Mokaddem explaining that his government had already given Egypt the go-ahead to deliver its "gift" of arms, which he expected in "several days" (though he could not be sure). "French arms," on the other hand, "would reinforce [the] impression [Tunisia is] still under French tutelage." His country had been negotiating with the United States and Great Britain and did "not particularly welcome [the] addition [of] France as [a] factor [in] these negotiations."[58]

It seems unlikely that Bourguiba ever wanted a deal with Paris. The British ambassador in Tunis judged that he had leaked information about the Egyptian delivery to eliminate the possibility—and put further pressure on France's allies. Indeed, Dulles and Eisenhower felt compelled to proceed without further delay.[59] But Pineau then gave notice that France would cease all aid to Tunisia and "adopt [an] entirely new policy." On the other hand, if the United States did not deliver arms the French would do so themselves that very evening. Speaking unofficially, Pineau said that some ministers had suggested that otherwise France should not participate in the NATO meeting that was to take place in Paris in December. In a personal message, Gaillard warned Eisenhower of "a grave crisis in Western solidarity . . ." and insisted, "in the strongest manner," that the Americans defer to his position. While Houghton doubted the French would actually boycott the NATO conference, he found the threat to adopt a new line *vis-à-vis* Tunisia credible and thought it could hardly be avoided given the probable reaction in Paris.[60]

Connecting the NATO meeting to the Tunisian arms question must have come as a shock to Dulles. The conference had been intended to shore up Western solidarity and self-confidence in the wake of the Sputnik launch. Contrary to the usual practice, it would be a meeting of heads of state rather than foreign ministers. How would it have looked if Eisenhower arrived in Paris in the midst of a new wave of anti-Americanism, if not an actual boycott by the host country? Dulles therefore agreed to allow France to replace the Anglo-American shipment. He sent a sheepish cable to Bourguiba explaining that "the U.S. willingness to deliver defensive arms to Tunisia has now borne fruit in a way which I think provides an important advantage for your Government."[61]

But did the French really want to deliver arms to Tunisia? Recall that this very issue was a precipitant in the fall of Gaillard's predecessor and the new prime minister was already in trouble over his austerity measures.[62] Instead of immediately proceeding with the delivery, Pineau sent Ambassador Gorse back to Tunis to demand that Bourguiba refuse the Egyptian shipment.[63] Gaillard explained to Jebb that the Egyptian arms were an "entirely new element." Jebb responded that, "far from being a new element, all our communications to the French Government had stressed the urgency of getting Western arms in before the Egyptian arms arrived." That same day, the Quai's director of political affairs, Jean-Henri Daridan, told Jebb that he did not know the government's position on the issue—indeed, that "he was 'living in a mad house.'" Perhaps the prime minister had not consulted the Quai before arriving at that position. But if "the matter [was] being handled by the politicians . . . ," as Jebb concluded, then it is all the more likely that domestic political considerations were preeminent.[64]

The secretary called the president at ten o'clock on the morning of November 13 to discuss Gaillard's message. "It gets thicker and thicker," the president remarked. "If the French suddenly dropped out of NATO we are out of Europe." He added that he did "not know what they are capable of doing." But Dulles judged that Gaillard "was using this as a useful domestic political issue to build up internal strength." Proclaiming himself "really fed up with the goddam French," Eisenhower went ahead anyway. He instructed Dulles to fire off a reply warning that without action by that evening the United States would come through the next day.[65]

The French cabinet met late into the night but finally refused to change its position. The American arms did not actually arrive until a day later—though just in time for President Bourguiba to declare a "victory" in his weekly radio address, characterizing the U.S. decision as "a decisive act which reinforces our faith in the free world and confirms the orientation chosen by Tunisia."[66] Meanwhile in France, a "total of fewer than a thousand rifles and machine guns created the effect of an atomic bomb," as *The New York Times* described it.[67] Five hundred riot police were called out to defend the American embassy against the anticipated protests.[68] Gaillard announced that he would use the occasion to demand a new understanding of the Algerian question by the United States and Britain, "knowing that if the desired result cannot be obtained from these efforts to come to an agreement the Alliance to which we are joined will soon fall into dust."[69] The next day, the French delegation walked out of NATO parliamentary talks. The State Department reported that "this hostility to the shipment is overwhelming among every segment of the population, rich and poor, Right and Left."[70]

Macmillan's private secretary, Philip de Zulueta, told him that "there had been nothing like it since Fashoda."[71] Far from mitigating the French reaction, the inclusion of the British only incited charges of a directorate of *les anglo-saxons*. Observing that the French were "bitterly hurt by their feeling of exclusion from the club," Lloyd suggested to Dulles that they do something to "help them over their hurt feelings."[72] Dulles thanked him but told Ambassador Harold Caccia—who had been invited to sit in on a State Department briefing preparatory to a visit by Pineau—that he did not want to give "the impression that France with our two selves was in a different category as one of the three great powers in the Free World."[73] Before concluding bilateral talks with the French later that month, the British passed the joint communiqué by the Americans. The State Department, for its part, gave them a draft position paper on the Tunisian arms for subsequent discussions in Paris. If there was not actually an Anglo-American directorate managing the Atlantic Alliance, there was one managing relations with France. "As a rationalization it amounts to this," Jebb wrote from Paris. "If we have to choose we choose, not Europe, but America."[74]

Yet Britain had broader interests that went beyond the choice between Europe and America, and "a coordinated policy of containment in the Middle East"—as Lloyd described it to Jebb—resulted from competition as much as common thinking. As the foreign secretary would tell Caccia in February, "[I]t is of great importance for our position in the Arab world that the United States Government should not seem to be approaching the problem from a more pro-Arab point of view than our own."[75]

With no such concern, the crisis gave Bonn another opportunity to distinguish its forthright support for the French from that of their other allies. During the NATO meeting, Adenauer deplored the American attitude and called for a common policy on the Middle East and Africa, as Paris had been demanding all along.[76] The crisis helped to convince Gaillard to conclude an agreement with West Germany and Italy to cooperate in nuclear research and development. German scientists were already participating in missile tests in the Sahara.[77] In Moscow, on the other hand, Ambassador Maurice Dejean warned that the crisis would have the opposite effect. The Soviets had calibrated their support for the Arab states at the United Nations to the level of American support for France. Whereas they had previously been reserved in their criticism, in January Khrushchev accused the French of "pretending to believe in God while pursuing a bloody war in Algeria."[78]

As for the Algerians themselves, the episode brought them closer to Bourguiba. Just after the arms crisis, the Tunisian premier and Mohammed V met and offered their "good offices" in negotiating an end to the war, though without endorsing the FLN's demand that France first recognize Algeria's independence. While the FLN had still not attained a "united North African front," as they had hoped for in preparing for the December U.N. debate, they favored the inclusion of this offer in the final General Assembly resolution. FLN officials later explained that they wanted the Tunisians to take part because they were more independent from France than the Moroccans. More important, the FLN moved its military headquarters from Egypt to Tunisia, which gradually became the main base for the exiled leadership—further exasperating the French.[79]

The morning after he had decided to deliver the arms, Eisenhower wrote a long note in his diary on what had happened and why: "For the past three days we have been in a terrible difficulty with France and Tunisia, based partially upon misunderstanding but mostly on what we believe to be French stupidity and refusal to face international facts as they exist." They had threatened "a complete breakup of the Western alliance," but Eisenhower refused to be "blackmailed by French weakness." In contrast to French "stupidity," he characterized Bourguiba as "a true Western friend." As for the Egyptian arms, Bourguiba could not possibly turn down a "gift."[80]

It seems likely that Eisenhower was influenced by his unhappy experience of two years before, when Nasser first turned to the Soviets after Washington refused to deliver new weaponry. That very day he asked Dulles whether they should consider "initiating a drive to attempt to bring back Nasser to our side."[81] The "lesson of history" for the French was different. Joxe complained to Jebb that "the Americans were making the same mistake over Tunisia that they had made over Egypt." Gaillard himself told the ambassador that they would be vulnerable to "perpetual blackmail," sending Bourguiba down the same path as Nasser.[82] In fact, Bourguiba won U.S. support by arguing that it was the only way to *prevent* his public from demanding that he trod the path to "positive neutrality." To this end, Eisenhower noted that Bourguiba "attached the most extraordinary importance to the delivery of some Western arms in Tunisia before the Egyptian shipment could reach there, somewhere between the 15th or 16th of this month."[83]

So when did the Egyptian arms, the catalyst of the crisis, finally arrive? On November 9, Tunisian Foreign Minister Mokaddem told Ambassador Jones that they would arrive "several days" after the 12th.[84] On the 12th, Ambassador Houghton spoke to Pineau of the "imminence" of their arrival.[85] Dulles wrote Selwyn Lloyd on the 13th that they were "now in transit," the same line Bourguiba took with Gorse the next day.[86] It was not until November 25 that confirmation of a sort came from Cairo, when officials there announced that the arms had been delivered to Tunisia overland by way of Libya and that the ship left *four days earlier*.[87] But in an interview with Bourguiba on the 29th it was reported that the Egyptian arms were still "expected."[88] On December 4, a story appeared in *The New York Times* under the headline "A Phantom Ship Puzzles Capital." According to this account, not only had the Egyptian ship not arrived but there was no confirmation that it ever existed.[89]

Bourguiba's Egyptian arms ship may never have been more than a phantom. If so, he had used the ploy to great effect. It gave the French a reason, or an excuse, not to deliver arms, thus showing that Tunisia was no longer under their tutelage. It also ensured that the United States would take their place, both to honor a commitment to Bourguiba and to head off an expansion of Nasserist influence in North Africa. By single-handedly engineering a major international crisis, Bourguiba vindicated his pro-Western policy while at the same time attaining autonomy among the allies.[90]

Yet Eisenhower and Dulles were amenable to Bourguiba's appeals because they knew that, for all their threats, tantrums, and pretensions to membership among the great powers, the French could not pay their dues. Before the crisis broke, Dulles predicted that, "while the situation would be bad for a while, the French would get over it since they needed our help."[91] On the day he decided to defy the French, the president asked whether they would be coming to the United States for economic assistance. Dulles thought they would have to, adding that "we did not do much moneywise during the Suez crisis" (it is not clear whether he meant *to* or *for* France).[92] In fact, Baumgartner and other officials of the Bank of France were already meeting with U.S. representatives to discuss the possibility of a loan package.[93] The franc suffered its greatest ever one-day loss in the Paris gold market while its position in currency exchanges further deteriorated, moving from 476 to 507 against the dollar. Finance Minister Pflimlin concluded that the need for "outside help" was now "obvious."[94] The arms would never have been delivered otherwise, Mendès France concluded, describing their situation as "really humiliating." Indeed, even FLN propaganda tracts in Algeria harped on France's financial straits, warning that an inability to pay for imports would soon lead to runaway inflation and industrial shutdowns.[95]

"Their basic trouble is that they are still trying to act as if they headed a great empire," Eisenhower wrote to his friend, Swede Hazlett. "If they would center their attention mainly on their European problems . . . they could be a happy and prosperous country."[96]

To Put the French in a Corner

The French had lost their "bet." The Americans felt free to disregard protests from Paris as they thwarted efforts to contain the conflict by coercing Tunisia. Moreover, U.S. economic assistance was now indispensable, and to secure it French officials concluded that they would have to scale down the war effort in Algeria itself. As a November 9, 1957, Finance Ministry memorandum argued, the expense of operations in Algeria was "at the heart of the problem," both for "purely economic" reasons and, "on the political level: by risking interference with the conditions [necessary] to obtain outside aid." While the government never publicly admitted that cutting military expenditures was necessary for obtaining American assistance, Gaillard had already told the assembly that he could not secure aid from abroad if it did not approve his overall economic program.[97]

As *l'Express* reported in November,

> The fate of the Algerian War is no longer determined only in the National Assembly. It is determined from now on in the negotiations that have just begun, in secret, between French authorities and two individuals who arrived discretely in Paris last week: the director general of the International Monetary Fund, Per Jacobsen [*sic*], and President . . . [of the European Payments Union Hans Karl von] Mangoldt.[98]

Indeed, while Jacobsson pretended to be on personal business, he took over an office in the Bank of France. Dillon, together with the American representative to the IMF, Frank Southard, soon followed, intending to keep an eye on the negotiations.[99] Gaillard publicly denied that France would accept any political conditions, and Jean Monnet—who would lead the French team—reported hopefully that none likely to "hurt our dignity" would be imposed.[100] But one can debate what is a political condition, as *l'Express* noted before offering this prediction:

> Officially nothing other than a grant of credits will doubtless be announced. Only with time will one know, little by little, what price will have been paid. One will discover what structure our foreign judges will have given to the French economy, that is, to France; what framework they will have fixed for the currency; what solution they will have invited for Algeria.[101]

Indeed, when Monnet finally went to Washington in January 1958 to finalize $655 million in loans from the United States, the IMF, and the EPU, he had to give a confidential written commitment to demobilize 150,000 troops that had been raised for the Algerian War. Paris also agreed not to raise expenditures or renege on plans to cut the deficit by 40 percent—with the military bearing the brunt of the budgetary reductions. In accordance with IMF and American preferences, all of this was in the form of a "sound money" program ostensibly prepared by the French themselves independent of any outside pressure.[102] In form and content, it can be counted among the first of many IMF interventions — with considerable U.S. input — in countries struggling to adjust to the imperatives of international capital markets.[103]

Yet this was not a simple matter of "the French" crumbling before American coercion. The situation was both more complicated and more ambiguous. Until the Sakiet crisis, to be described shortly, the best evidence for an American campaign to use economic leverage to force Paris to wind down the war was produced by French officials and journalists, not the presumed architects of such a campaign. In October, the NSC staff had urged that U.S. military aid to France be reconsidered if it failed to transfer forces from Algeria to Europe. But while Dulles acknowledged that "we might very well indeed follow this course of action," he successfully argued against committing himself to it. "We cannot deal with France on so narrow a basis . . . ," he stressed. "The stakes were just too great." His explanation is still classified, but in preparing for the December NATO summit he told Eisenhower that "we do not wish to create [the] impression we are being tough with [the] French during their financial crisis, to pressure them into giving up Algeria."[104]

It may be that Dulles was only concerned with impressions and did not think that it was even necessary to "connect the dots" — indeed, that it would be counterproductive and risky to do so. An August 1957 National Intelligence Estimate cautioned that, with regard to Algeria, "[i]f the French felt that there had been unwarranted interference by supposedly friendly countries, this would delay any significant change." Moreover, "a crisis over Algeria in some way might become linked in French minds with betrayal by the Western allies; a wave of intense nationalistic feeling might then cause a temporary breakdown of cooperation with France's allies."[105] It was for this reason that Washington negotiated through international agencies and required the French to produce their own recovery plan.[106]

But French officials — many of whom had long been concerned about the costs of empire and the threat to economic liberalization — encouraged their allies to take a tough line and be skeptical about their government's commitments. As early as February 1957, Baumgartner had reportedly said that he hoped the United States "was not going to bail France out of its present difficulties." He also declined to adopt the more extreme arguments for *Algérie française*, merely telling his American counterparts that his government's policy was "probably" the right one.[107] In these discussions, it is clear that U.S. officials had a number of other concerns about French economic policy, including public spending on housing and borrowing from the Bank of France. The U.S. Treasury judged that "[t]he African crisis, though harmful, is not a preponderant influence" in French financial problems.[108] French officials, on the other hand, continually insisted that there would be no solution without first ending the Algerian War. For instance, in December 1957 U.S. embassy official John Tuthill asked one of Baumgartner's advisors, Jean Sadrin, whether his government would honor its agreement to rein in expenditures and cut the over-all budget deficit. "After the usual French shrugging of shoulders . . . ," Sadrin said that the military was the key. They had not implemented Mollet and Bourgès's earlier budget cuts and he was skeptical that Gaillard would have greater success. "He felt, in fact, that if the Algerian war continued that there would be no effective check on military expenditures."[109] Ten days later, Tuthill asked Etienne Hirsch, the director of the Commissariat du Plan, about the prospects for 1958. Hirsch was "very pessimistic, particularly if France were to receive a large foreign credit." He said there was no guarantee the program would be carried out and "pooh-poohed the idea that there might be anything like a 26% cut in military consumption of goods in the next year."

> French Governments are usually unable to control military expenditures—especially when hostilities are continuing. He emphasized, therefore, that the significant decisions regarding where to cut have not been taken. It would apparently, in his view, be almost impossible to obtain such agreements if the Algerian war continues.[110]

The month before, Hirsch had told another U.S. official that Gaillard and his predecessors had deliberately kept the facts from the public. He did not want to " 'go to the country' on the basic issue, which he formulates as a choice between giving up in Algeria and putting into effect the stringent measures . . . which alone would make it possible to support the continuation of the hostilities there."[111] Hirsch's own choice was clear. He told Tuthill that "Mollet and the others were all attacking the wrong issue. . . . Algeria must be settled."[112] Considering the antiwar sentiment of these officials, it is possible that it was they—more than their American counterparts—who had been using France's need for U.S. aid as a way to induce their ministers to wind down the war. Indeed, *The Wall Street Journal* found that "most [French officials] privately concede that American intransigence indirectly helped sell 'austerity' to the parliament."[113]

But considering the antiwar sentiment of *American* officials, why did they not follow their counterparts' advice and take an even harder line, forcing France to confront the choice between settling in Algeria or setting up a war economy? Their initial response to the plan had been to reject it as "quite inadequate and insufficient," a rebuke that made one U.S. official "think of the Marquis de Sade."[114] Why, then, did they not keep turning the screws?

The available evidence does not allow a definitive answer, but one can hazard a few guesses. First, it was not entirely up to the United States, since the EPU could provide at least stopgap aid. Its members had much more to lose if the financial crisis was allowed to become a general economic crisis. The French certainly painted an apocalyptic picture for the board, warning that it would endanger the launch of the EEC and might even cause social unrest. France was "negotiating with the board with a 'knife at its throat,' " the Swiss EPU representative complained. " 'Give us credit or we will cut our imports.' "[115] The British favored a tough line, but they were not in a position to insist because they could not themselves contribute to a bailout.[116] Bonn had the preponderant voice—it would fund fully 80 percent of the EPU loan—and it could hardly be expected to force the French to choose between an aid package or Algeria. While the Germans preferred a stricter austerity plan, political factors were overriding. One official explained that they would "pay for every step the French took" in entering the Common Market "until it was too late for the French to turn back." In 1957, it was still not too late, as the testimony to the EPU made clear.[117]

Consequently, by the end of November, the U.S. representatives to the EPU reported a "progressive and continuous weakening on all sides of [the] earlier resolution to withhold assistance until such time [as an] adequate stabilization program [is] developed."[118] Perhaps Washington could still have blocked assistance, but at what cost? As one official warned, "Are the French likely to come to any other conclusion than that it is the United States that most wants to keep their feet to the fire and this for political reasons. I need not spell this out further."[119] Working through international agencies required the Americans to defend their position before their allies and rally resistance to a rescue package. Rather than reducing the risks of a French backlash, the U.S. strategy had backfired.

One can well understand why Eisenhower and Dulles would shrink from an out-and-out confrontation in which they would have been accused of jeopardizing the future of the European Economic Community and NATO to force France to withdraw from Algeria. The Sputnik launch in October had already shaken Western self-confidence, as shown by the Gaither Committee report completed the following month. It predicted rapid growth in Soviet military and economic strength, and three panel members even recommended a preventative nuclear war. Moreover, after Suez, Dulles had taken criticism for his handling of relations with France and Britain, among other things, and in December he went so far as to offer his resignation.[120] The secretary had always thought that "French North Africa is an awful mess to get into"—as he remarked the last time he considered such an intervention.[121] It was easier to believe Monnet's blandishments or at least postpone the showdown. After all, if the plan failed, the French would need another bailout and Washington would be in an even stronger position. Indeed, when the pessimistic forecasts proved correct and another financial crisis loomed in May 1958, Monnet told Dulles that the earlier loan had been "in the common interest." It had averted a breakdown at a difficult time and "the evolution of thinking in France [since then] had . . . moved French opinion toward a more reasonable position as regards North Africa."[122] Even the FLN came to see a silver lining, as shown by an editorial in *El Moudjahid:*

Although many are now saying that the US, by giving financial aid to France, becomes responsible for the war in Algeria, we would like to point out another aspect of the problem: America is also now in a position to stop this war. America now has the right to interfere with France, France also has a duty to obey America's opinion and direction. It is impossible to imagine that the loan was granted without reference to the Algerian war.[123]

Finally, it was always possible that the French *would* fulfill their commitments. Their representative on the EPU board, Pierre Calvet, had vowed in "a voice choked with emotion and tears" that all his fellow officials were determined to do so, and privately warned that "the word and the honor of France are on the line."[124] If they followed through with the troop cuts, it would have been difficult to continue the war and impossible to win it. When it became known that the military credits included in the loan package could not be used in Algeria, *Le Monde* asked if, from the American perspective, it would have been better "to put the French in a corner? . . . In truth, in their responses American officials have emphasized the French decision to diminish the armed forces and to liberate a part of the forces serving under the flag. In short, in the American view the French government has set out on a path that leads to the end of the conflict."[125]

Defense Minister Jacques Chaban-Delmas appears to have been in earnest when he warned the military chiefs that they had no choice but to adhere to the plan. "In the contrary case," he explained, "the equilibrium of all the budget would be cast into doubt and with it doubtless the external help that France is presently soliciting."[126] Monnet pledged that political instability would not affect the recovery plan. Indeed, in a break with tradition, the prime minister squelched assembly debate that March by making the entire text of the military budget a test of confidence. Gaillard explained that he wanted it adopted "without equivocation and without second thoughts."[127]

But just as Sadrin and Hirsch had warned, in this, the actual budget, the cuts fell on French forces stationed in Europe while appropriations and manpower for the war were maintained at the same levels. Faced with this threat to what little modern fighting power remained to them, the heads of the air force and the Defense Ministry's *Direction technique et industriel* resigned, while Chief of Staff Paul Ely threatened to do so.[128] Rather than compelling the French to shift forces from Algeria, the loan agreement further reduced their strength on the continent and may well have alienated the NATO-oriented officers who might otherwise have defended the regime against those most committed to the war.

Yet the most critical source of tension in civil-military relations — and what would finally impel Washington to use its economic leverage to "put the French in a corner" — remained the conflict with Tunisia. A particularly grave incident occurred on January 11, when an FLN group attacked a French force across the border, killing eleven before returning with five captives. Paris suspended negotiations with Bourguiba and recalled its ambassador, but the clashes continued. Glaring across the frontier, one of the soon-to-be-famous colonels exclaimed to Lacoste, "*Monsieur le ministre*, it can't go on like this!"[129]

The Fall of the Fourth Republic

The very next day, February 8, 1958, ALN forces firing from in and around the Tunisian town of Sakiet Sidi Youssef forced down a French observation plane. Whether the government authorized what happened next has long been a matter of debate. It now appears that Chaban-Delmas had given local commanders the right to retaliate against anti-aircraft fire within three hours of the original attack. But he probably did not expect the local Air Force commander, Edmond Jouhaud—himself a pied noir—to prepare a detailed plan of attack employing 25 B-26 Marauders, Corsairs, and Mistrals that were kept in readiness for just such a contingency.[130]

It was market day when the planes arrived over Sakiet, and the aptly named Marauders made direct hits on the schoolhouse and Red Cross trucks, killing sixty-eight civilians—including many women and children. Like the use of torture in the Battle of Algiers, the Sakiet raid was not a new departure in terms of French tactics; many Algerian villages had suffered the same fate. But in both cases, standard practice stunned the international media when they were able to witness it firsthand. Within hours, Bourguiba arranged to bring foreign correspondents and photographers to the scene, and the resulting articles and images constituted a public relations fiasco for the French. For the first time, demonstrators even protested in front of the French mission in New York.[131]

Eisenhower declared that he had "never been so astounded." Embarrassed by the much-publicized fact that most of the planes were American made, Dulles suspected that the French had deliberately used their equipment in order to involve the United States. Elbrick reminded him that just four days before they had urged Paris to avoid new border incidents and rein in their local commanders.[132] Dulles told Eisenhower that "the French were proving incapable of dealing with the whole North African situation." There was a danger of the West losing the whole northern tier of Africa: "it was a question of trying to save that or trying to save NATO." He warned that they were "liable to lose control of the situation in Congress," noting that "there was criticism of our trying to pull France out of its financial hole without doing anything for North Africa."[133]

Indeed, the next day Senate Minority Leader William Knowland asked Dulles whether the French had gone "moon-crazy"—to which Dulles said "yes"—and warned that there would be "serious repercussions on the Hill in due time."[134] Media heavyweights also began to weigh in against American support for France in Algeria. Walter Lippmann advocated a change "from the policy of neutrality and abstention to a positive policy to promote a settlement."[135] Recalling Kennedy's early and outspoken advocacy for such a position, Eric Severeid observed that the same speech would now elicit an entirely different reaction.[136]

Eisenhower told Dulles that if the French did not disavow the action and offer reparations there would not be congressional support for financial aid to France.[137] The secretary was "abrupt" and "irritated" when he summoned Alphand to his home. He warned that French policy was leading to "a major catastrophe for us all." They had asked for a leading role in the region but had proven incapable of solving its problems, which Dulles predicted would end in "a major war stretching from Morocco to Egypt, with the Soviet Union backing the Moslem states." The secretary even hinted that he might recall the American ambassador from Paris.[138]

Earlier that day, the Dulles brothers had talked about the "large-scale recasting of NATO" that the secretary had foreseen almost a year earlier. The CIA director said that "it was a question of a method of transition, [there] must be a cushioning of it." But his brother was still uncertain: "[H]e did not think that we want to commit ourselves to transition. . . . We are up against an insoluble problem; they are not capable, but to take it out of their hands would have such a bitter reaction in France that it would destroy NATO." The secretary feared that they might be "forced into an anti-Arab position. . . ." But Allen Dulles warned that this "would have tragic repercussions and lose us the oil of the Middle East . . . [139]

Eisenhower was also thinking in these terms and he too was undecided. After making sure that the secretary had passed on his threat about U.S. economic aid, he wondered aloud whether NATO should reduce its dependence on French infrastructure and rely instead on German ports of entry. But like Dulles, he thought that "this would hardly save the situation if a Popular Front government with Communist participation came into power. . . ."[140]

The next day the French cabinet met from 9:30 in the morning until after 8:00 at night, one of the longest sessions of the republic. Lacoste, Chaban-Delmas, and Max Lejeune, minister of the Sahara, wanted to prosecute the war whatever the costs abroad, but Pineau and Faure argued that they could not prevail without their allies.[141] Afterward each went his own way: Gaillard refused to disavow the action in the Assembly but acquiesced in a resolution "regretting the civilian losses." Pineau, for his part, told Joseph Alsop that it was "a sad error" that had never been authorized by the government.[142]

In essence, Gaillard's government was caught between an irresistible force—international and especially American pressure—and an immovable object: the French military in Algeria. The local commander who carried out the Sakiet raid warned Salan that a "disavowal, however nuanced and veiled it may be, would put us in a difficult position. . . . It would signify that we have resolved to allow our adversary to reinforce along the frontier with impunity, to submit to his raids on our frontier posts, his anti-aircraft fire on our planes. And this at a time when our units are making superhuman efforts to stop the wave coming from the East."[143]

Salan himself characterized the operation as an act of legitimate self-defense.[144] He dispatched aides to Paris with dossiers full of documents indicating the government's shared responsibility for the raid, hoping to rally other top commanders and sympathetic civilians. Though some of them were already hostile to the republic, he may have conceived of this as another act of self-defense. The distance between making contact with conspirators and making common cause was only a few steps farther.[145]

Yet even if civilian ministers were evading responsibility for the Sakiet blunder, Salan could hardly blame them for failing to support a winning strategy vis-à-vis Tunisia—he had never articulated one. For all his complaints about Bourguiba's collusion with the FLN, he had actually rejected the idea of invading and destroying the rebel camps. Back in September, he told Morice that overextending their forces would jeopardize the gains already made in Algeria.[146] Withdrawing from the border and perfecting their defenses was a credible alternative, one that his successors would pursue with excellent results. With a similar barrier being erected along the Moroccan frontier, the failure of an FLN attempt to mount a "Saharan offensive" in July 1957, and increasingly effective maritime surveillance, the FLN forces of the interior faced slow strangulation. Just one ship seized off Oran in January 1958, the Yugoslav-flagged *Slovenija*, yielded some 7,000 arms—nearly half of the total estimated ALN complement of modern weapons within Algeria.[147]

Given the slow but steady degradation of the Algerian *maquisards*— who themselves were now losing some 4,500 more weapons a year than they captured from the French—what was the point of the Sakiet raid?[148] It was not only militarily ineffectual without an accompanying ground offensive but politically obtuse as well. It created the impression that French forces were threatening Tunisia, and Tunisian civilians, instead of defending citizens from the FLN. As a result, the French had the worst of both worlds, paying all the political costs of an aggressive strategy without reaping any benefits. Indeed, it gave Bourguiba an excuse to blockade French forces in their bases and begin a "battle of evacuation"— though it was the kind of battle in which diplomats and the media did most of the fighting.

The Americans refused even to relay French protests about the blockade until they made a conciliatory gesture. The cabinet therefore authorized the French Red Cross to evaluate the damage in Sakiet and prepare compensation. They also agreed to consolidate some of their troops in Tunisia. Rather than being "forced to accept a proposal for United States and British 'good offices' "—as Jean-Pierre Rioux and other historians have described it—the French were actually forced to make these conciliatory gestures before their allies would *agree* to represent them.[149] The Quai insisted, however, that the proposed team—Murphy and Harold Beeley, the Foreign Office's assistant under secretary of state—limit their activities to restarting the Franco-Tunisian dialogue and never discuss Algeria. In fact, while nominally just a neutral go-between, Murphy showed his bias from the first day and for the following two months badgered Gaillard to give in to the Tunisians on all the essential issues.[150]

At the same time, Dulles charged Julius Holmes with leading a group to study how they might initiate a broader peace process. "The present

French policy was leading inevitably to a war in which the whole Arab world would be involved with Communist support," the secretary explained to the British ambassador. "France would become exhausted and would collapse, as in Indo-China; and the Russians would be left masters of the field." He wanted London's support to "seize the opportunity" to help reform French relations with all of North Africa, ultimately leading to a commonwealth like Britain's. "There need not be immediate independence for Algeria, but this must be a recognizable goal."[151]

Not surprisingly, the British favored this vision of the future of North Africa, but they were loathe to pressure the French to implement it. As de Zulueta wrote with Macmillan's concurrence that same day: "The French have behaved very foolishly in Tunisia and indeed in Africa as a whole. . . . *At the same time it is surely very much to British interest and to that of the West that France should preserve as much of her position in North Africa as is possible.*" Indeed, he thought it essential that they first reestablish trust with their ally through "patient and careful mediation," helping Paris secure the " 'neutralization' of the Tunisian-Algerian frontier."[152]

Three days later, Bourguiba gave an interview to Agence France Presse that could not have been better calculated to discourage this kind of discreet mediation. "I will never cooperate with France in guarding the frontier," he declared, adding that "I no longer have confidence in a confidential conversation with France." Worst of all, he said that he "trust[ed] in the 'good offices' to find a solution for the Algerian problem."[153] That same day, the French learned that Krim was coming to Tunis to make certain the negotiations did not limit FLN access to Algeria.[154] In the weeks to come, the rebel command would send whole battalions against the border fortifications and the five *parachutiste* regiments now stationed behind them, leading to some of the most intense fighting of the war.[155]

By word and deed, passivity and aggressivity, the Tunisians and Algerians together were forcing foreign powers to weigh in on the future of North Africa. Like the British, virtually all had struggled to avoid a definitive choice—America playing a "double game," Germany conducting a "double strategy," Italy pursuing a "two-track" policy[156]—since none, not even the USSR, wanted to see French influence eradicated in the region. Deputy Foreign Minister Valerian Zorin warned the French ambassador that the Americans would replace them if they did not undertake "an 'audacious' initiative to settle the Algerian problem."[157] Indeed, the only thing now stopping the Americans was uncertainty as to whether NATO could take the strain.

At the February 27 NSC meeting, Dulles repeated his oft-stated concern that the situation was "likely to evolve like Indochina," with a leftist government that would "liquidate the Algerian affair" and "liquidate NATO as well."[158] Dulles asked for advice from the Joint Chiefs, and within a week they advised a hard line, even at the risk of French withdrawal from NATO. All of the members except the army chief of staff judged that "this defense structure would not be unacceptably impaired by the loss of France."[159]

All along, Dulles's memories of Indochina, Mendès France, and the defeat of the EDC had served as the model for his understanding of the interrelationship between French decolonization, domestic politics, and foreign policy. Now it provided the inspiration for what he would do about it: "The time ha[s] come," he told the president that same day, "when we [will] probably have to move in. North Africa makes the European economy viable and is of the utmost importance. This is the same story as Viet-Nam, where we had helped out on condition that the French grant unconditional independence."[160] On March 3, Eisenhower agreed that Algerian independence was the only real solution: "The trick is — how do we get the French to see a little sense?"[161]

Dulles can be faulted for his dubious use of historical analogies — and always the same analogy. Yet the French failure to adhere to a consistent policy on Algeria, even on the issue of outside involvement, invited intervention. For instance, the same day Eisenhower wondered how they might be encouraged to "see a little sense," Joxe described for the British ambassador how Algeria might be settled within the context of a "Mediterranean Pact" between the Maghreb and the southern European states — an idea that France had heretofore opposed. He explained that, "[b]y such means it might . . . be possible for France to accept some 'Algerian personality.' Within such an economic-politico-military framework, France might indeed be induced to accept the emergence of a new Algeria." But Joxe stressed that these were his own ideas, even while submitting that London might sponsor them.[162] Murphy, for his part, concluded that day "that the French government had no clear idea of where they were going in Algeria and . . . they would welcome constructive suggestions from their friends."[163]

On March 5, Dulles offered a few suggestions to the French ambassador. "Speaking personally and as a friend" — as he often did when making threats — the secretary told Alphand that "it is indispensable that you look for a political solution while there is still time." More to the point, he said that "whatever may be the French determination to continue the fight until the total repression of the rebellion, financial conditions could, at some point, stand in their way," adding that certain senators had asked him to go back on the loan decision. "Never . . . has the Secretary of State expressed himself with such force on this subject," Alphand reported to Paris.[164]

The secretary continued to justify his actions based on his old dream of "Eurafrica" and his nightmare of an international race war or Islamic jihad. Thus, he told Pineau during a March 12 meeting in Manila that he "could not overstate the importance of North Africa for Europe." But speaking "as a friend of France more than as a Secretary of State," he said that "the prospect of seeing the hostilities spread beyond North Africa from Algeria to the Persian Gulf — with the communists providing logistical support and armed aid"—was "terrifying" to him. He insisted that France would not find a solution by force alone: "This is the time for statesmanship."[165] It was time, in other words, for Dulles to take charge.

That same day, on the other side of the globe, Murphy described an American peace plan to Beeley, hoping to enlist the British in a joint approach. Eisenhower would send a personal envoy to Paris to demand that France seek a cease-fire and an international conference. The United States and perhaps Britain as well would try to get the FLN to agree. If the French did not go along, the United States would act to preserve the allegiance of Tunisia and Morocco, providing them with political support and economic and military aid. Murphy added that such aid "would be confined in the first instance to those two countries," perhaps indicating that they were even considering support for the Algerians themselves.[166] As we have seen, the CIA was already funneling covert aid to the FLN through the AFL-CIO. French intelligence now reported that the rebels had deferred plans for forming a provisional government in Cairo and placed their faith in Bourguiba. They saw him as the statesman most capable of helping diplomatically, "above all with the American government," and had high hopes for the "good offices" mission.[167] Within the week, the State Department began to upgrade U.S. contacts with the rebels, even flying them to Tunis for clandestine meetings.[168] And by May Yazid's contacts in Washington had raised "delicate questions" that he did not trust to communicate through ordinary channels.[169] It is not clear what they were, but FLN officials in Tunis were so encouraged that they assured Ambassador Jones that they now intended to "win the west" rather than seek Soviet backing.[170] Even without directly aiding the FLN, what Murphy was suggesting would have placed America behind France's adversaries in a public and definitive fashion. As Beeley pointed out, this "would be accepting a commitment the limit of which could not be foreseen."[171]

Macmillan was taken aback upon reading of the American initiative, writing across the top: "This is very serious. What are we doing?" Selwyn Lloyd, for his part, said that "this proposal would come to the French like a bomb." Throughout March, he and the prime minister appealed to the Americans to delay their ultimatum at least until the conclusion of the "good offices" mission.[172] From Bonn, Adenauer also urged patience, prompting Dulles to present once again his nightmare scenario of a France left exhausted by the war and susceptible to the appeal of a popular front government opposing NATO.[173]

Eisenhower encouraged Dulles to press on. Commenting on a letter from Bourguiba that rejected border controls, the president said that he had "a good deal of sympathy with Bourguiba's position" though "the state of France causes him almost more worry than any other problem in the world today." Eisenhower declared that there was "no solution to the North African problem except a political settlement which would give Algeria a chance for independence." Most important, "He indicated that he thought we should accept considerable risks as far as France's role in NATO was concerned in an effort to try to get France to take such a position."[174]

Eisenhower then had a letter drafted for the French prime minister that represented his greatest risk yet. While intended to secure Gaillard's approval for the "good offices" proposals on Tunisia, Eisenhower also urged "comprehension" of Tunisian support for "those in Algeria who seek for the Algerian people an opportunity for self-government and self-determination." He also pointed out that, whereas NATO was intended "to promote stability and well-being . . . [t]here is not, and has not been, such stability and well-being in the Algerian departments of France."[175]

Once again, the British struggled to restrain their ally. Macmillan personally urged Ambassador Caccia to "try to steer the Americans off the most dangerous shoals. . . . If he brings in Algeria the French will react violently" — perhaps wrecking Britain's European Free Trade initiative — leading to "the probable end of NATO and most serious reorientation of British policy."[176] Even Murphy urged that they hold off until he made one last effort to persuade the French to agree to their latest proposals. In their April 9 meeting, Gaillard appeared ready to evacuate all but the largest of the French bases, Bizerte, without securing any Tunisian concessions over the FLN's cross-border attacks. Bourguiba had refused to allow even a neutral investigatory commission with no enforcement powers. But Pineau demanded some assurance of American support if France took the issue to the U.N. Security Council. Gaillard warned that otherwise there would be "a major crisis in the Western Alliance." When Murphy said that he could not give any assurance, Pineau asked "what solution the United States wanted in Algeria." Murphy replied that he was not authorized to speak on the subject, to which Gaillard complained that "France had never received from her Allies in private any friendly advice or suggestions about Algeria."[177]

The exchange underlined the ambivalence, now bordering on confusion, that characterized French attitudes about U.S. involvement in North Africa. They had long sought a "blank check" but now appeared ready to settle for a contract that would force the Americans to state their terms, offer something in return, and limit French losses. Rather than a stark confrontation, this was becoming "decolonization by invitation." But the president's letter, which was presented to Gaillard the next day, did not oblige him. On British urging, Dulles had deleted the sympathetic references to self-determination for Algeria and criticism of French conduct.[178] Instead, Eisenhower merely suggested that accepting the Tunisian terms could provide "an opportunity to deal constructively with the larger aspects of the problem," warned that "time is running out," and asked whether France could continue to enjoy close relations with the region "unless that relationship is freely accepted in North Africa." Pineau complained to Jebb that it was "very vague, and gave no real indication of what the Americans thought the French should actually do as regards North Africa generally, still less what the Americans would do."[179]

The letter was quite enough to enrage those who still opposed any American intervention. In a bitter eleven-hour debate within the Gaillard cabinet, one irate participant proposed reoccupying Tunisia. But Finance Minister Pflimlin warned of the Suez precedent and President Coty rallied reluctant ministers by "underlin[ing] the risks" of rejecting the "good offices" mission. According to Bernard Droz and Evelyne Lever, along with the letter the Americans also drew attention to their earlier loan.[180] There is no evidence for this in the available documents, but after Dulles's earlier warnings it would have been gratuitous. France was on the verge of another balance of payments crisis that jeopardized its ability to adhere to the EEC, now only eight months away. Under these circumstances, America's economic leverage was a 500-pound gorilla. It did not need to announce itself.[181]

Nevertheless, the conservatives in the cabinet insisted that the full Assembly approve their agreement to set aside the issue of Tunisian aid to the FLN and evacuate their bases. On April 15, as the deputies sat in frosty silence, Gaillard insisted that he had made his decision free from outside pressure. But they would have none of it. The ensuing debate was the "apogee" of anti-Americanism, as one historian described it, with everyone from Mitterrand to Jean Marie Le Pen condemning the U.S. "diktat." "What happened," Soustelle asked, "between April 9th, when the good offices mission had practically expired, and the date when the government accepted the good offices? Of course! A single new fact: Eisenhower wrote a letter. . . . [W]hat are we doing here, amusing ourselves with the playthings of a spurious sovereignty?" Many deputies clutched copies of the *Sunday Times*, which had just revealed the contacts between the FLN and the American embassy in Tunis. Gaillard implored the assembly not to bring on another cabinet crisis but could only hint at his reasoning and the risks of rejecting it: "If today . . . the present government assures you that it is in the interests of France," he said, ". . . it has reasons for telling you this. . . . Where will you find a majority for a new government tomorrow? What will happen meanwhile, to the economy, to our finances, and to society? What will happen to Algeria?" But the Independents ignored his pleas and brought down the penultimate government of the Fourth Republic.[182]

Since the beginning of March, a number of prominent politicians including Soustelle, Bidault, Morice, Roger Duchet—leader of the Independents—and the Gaullist Senator Michel Debré had been arguing that only a "government of public safety" could stand up to foreign pressure and save Algeria. That pressure became even more explicit when, on April 17, Murphy told reporters that Paris should negotiate with the FLN. But when Bidault failed to win a majority for a cabinet with Morice and Soustelle on April 22, it became clear that the hard-liners were too few to win over the Assembly.[183] The initiative then passed to politicians willing to pursue a negotiated settlement and plotters in France and Algeria prepared to overthrow them. When Coty next called on René Pleven to begin consultations, Defense Minister Chaban-Delmas's representative in Algiers, Léon Delbecque, helped to organize a massive demonstration against him.[184]

While Chaban-Delmas was working for the return of *le général*, Gaullists were actually a distrusted minority among many factions.[185] The military's role would therefore be crucial not only in deciding any extraparliamentary contest for power but also in providing leadership for these disparate elements. At this point, only a handful of officers were actively plotting against the republic, but the top commanders had already indicated they would not permit any government to abandon Algeria.[186] Following a tour of inspections in Algeria, Ely himself warned Pleven that, "whatever the changes in what you foresee for a solution in Algeria, right now the single word negotiation would have very serious consequences 'on the ground.' "[187]

But Pleven appears to have been undeterred by the danger. On May 1, he told Ambassador Houghton that he "would hope that we would be willing to use our contacts with [the] FLN, if good enough, to try to get it to discuss a cease-fire." Mollet, for his part, said that he would "send a French team to some spot outside France to meet with FLN representatives."[188] Of course, they could say nothing of the kind in public, but Salan was already so perturbed by the general trend that he delivered a virtual ultimatum to Paris. In a May 9 telegram to Coty that referred to rumored plans for a "diplomatic process" to abandon Algeria, he warned that "the French army, in a unanimous fashion, would feel the abandonment of this national patrimony to be an outrage. One cannot foresee how it would react in its despair."[189]

Later that day, the FLN announced that it had executed three French prisoners in retaliation for the execution of three rebels. This "hit overexcited Algiers like a whip across the face," as Horne put it.[190] So when Coty called on Pflimlin, who had indicated that he favored a negotiated settlement, to form a coalition, the die-hards decided to confront the military with the choice of either firing on pied noir insurgents or joining them in revolt. On May 13, as the Assembly debated Pflimlin's investiture, crowds gathered in the center of Algiers for what was to have been a solemn memorial service. Instead it became a raucous demonstration. A mob sacked the American cultural center while the main body stormed the Government House. Meanwhile, Pflimlin pledged to redouble the French war effort and denied that he intended to abandon Algeria.[191] But it was too late. Salan and other top military leaders joined the pieds noirs in a committee of public safety. Two days later, when it appeared that the uprising might fizzle, Salan finally uttered the fateful words to the crowds in Algiers: *Vive de Gaulle!*

It was not an obvious choice. *Le général* had been considered a liberal on colonial questions during World War II, had since made contradictory statements on the future of Algeria, and had most recently gone out of his way to receive and reassure the Tunisian ambassador after the Sakiet bombing. But *le général* had something that no recognized adherent of *Algérie française* could offer. As Soustelle argued that March, "Of all the statesmen in France there is now only one who has the authority abroad to see that our vital interests are respected in North Africa and Black Africa. This is General de Gaulle."[192] Since "a diplomatic Dien Bien Phu" appeared imminent, as Lacoste argued at the time, de Gaulle's international standing was his greatest selling point. Delbecque used these same words in addressing the crowds in Algiers, as did de Gaulle himself in his crucial May 19 press conference.[193]

Ironically, the Americans who were preparing this "diplomatic Dien Bien Phu" actually welcomed de Gaulle's return. They entertained no illusions about his attitude to Atlantic solidarity, but they were better judges than the pieds noirs of his likely policies in North Africa. Yet the main reason that they adopted a "cool and careful noninterventionist pose" as he drove to power, as Irwin Wall writes, was their utter exasperation with the Fourth Republic's chronic instability and inability to unite behind consistent policies.[194] As Eisenhower concluded at the time: "France presents a twelve year history of almost unbroken moral, political and military deterioration. . . . [This] long dismal history," he continued, ". . . almost demanded the presence of a 'strong man'—in the person of de Gaulle."[195] The "double game" had always allowed for the possibility of an entirely new player, and U.S. officials were content merely to prevent the conflict from expanding beyond Algeria. Just in case, the Joint Chiefs drew up contingency plans for a Franco-Egyptian war. In fact, only a last-minute telephone call to de Gaulle by French officials prevented the army from attacking Tunisia.[196]

Historians differ on whether the Fourth Republic was really so decrepit as to have been inevitably doomed. But they usually agree that the Sakiet crisis set off the chain of events that led to its demise.[197] As Michael Harrison has argued, it is only a "slight exaggeration to claim that the events leading up to the '13 May' and the collapse of the Fourth Republic virtually constituted an anti-American revolt on the part of the French."[198] By analyzing these events as an international rather than just a domestic political crisis, one can see what they were revolting *against*.

Yet this was not simply an "Anglo-American intervention" that originated in the mind of John Foster Dulles.[199] Neither he nor any of France's allies would have acted if the North Africans had not put them in the position where they perceived no other choice. Moreover, this was also a *trans*national crisis—not only because capital markets, the media, and refugees played key roles, but also because it created communities of interest that transcended national boundaries. Thus, with the Kennedy speech Dulles found his administration and the French "in the same boat" in confronting criticism of their policies on Algeria.[200] Bourguiba forced a division in the arms crisis, but he could not have done so if Gaillard had not tacitly found that preferable to settling their differences. By agreeing to disagree, Bourguiba strengthened his position vis-à-vis the FLN and Gaillard rallied the support of colonial hard-liners. Some French officials then encouraged their American counterparts to use their economic leverage to help them end the war. In the end, all parties would come to fear an aroused French military in Algeria.

All of this intermixing, of course, was anathema to de Gaulle. He was determined to wield force and diplomacy as instruments of state instead of himself becoming the instrument of his military and the pawn of foreign powers. *Le général* would not be satisfied, however, until he won recognition that France itself was a great power again, with global interests and global influence. Paradoxically, that required regaining the confidence of markets, redoubling efforts to win over world opinion, and repairing relations with allies and especially the United States. All of that implied negotiation and a certain amount of give-and-take. Ultimately it required giving up Algeria.

IV

Waging the Algerian War as a
World War, 1958–1960

7

Decoding de Gaulle

It is time, high time to make ourselves equal to our revolution and to our people.

It is urgent to relieve the efforts and the sacrifices of the interior by a truly revolutionary political and diplomatic action.

It is necessary to stop relying on our martyrs. We must not wait until the blood of our dead alone changes the course of events. . . .

It is time to give the Algerian nation, to independent Algeria fighting the colonial reconquest, the legal status worthy of her, the status of a sovereign state.

Omar Ouamrane, July 1958 [1]

[T]here can be no prestige without mystery, for familiarity breeds contempt. All religions have their holy of holies, and no man is a hero to his valet. In the designs, the demeanor, and the mental operations of a leader there must be always a "something" which others cannot altogether fathom . . .

Charles de Gaulle, 1932 [2]

On June 4, 1958, three days after he had accepted full powers from an assembly that could seemingly deny him nothing, Charles de Gaulle stood before a vast, cheering crowd at the Forum in Algiers. He began his speech with a few simple words: *Je vous ai compris*. "I have understood you." The crowd erupted again as men and women openly cried.[3]

Ever since that day, people have wondered what de Gaulle had understood. The words that followed hardly clarified matters. After characterizing the May 13 movement as one of renewal and fraternity, he declared that, "from this day forward France considers that in all of Algeria there is only one category of inhabitants: there are only Frenchmen in the full sense, Frenchmen in the full sense with the same rights and duties." He even went so far as to include "those who, in despair, have believed it to be their duty to lead on this ground a struggle which I recognize, me, as courageous. . . ." In his memoirs, de Gaulle maintained that, together with an address in Mostaganem two days later, this was "tantamount to saying that the day would come when the majority amongst them could decide the destiny of all."[4] Why, then, did he say, that day in the Forum, that in the upcoming referendum for a new constitution "all of the French including the ten million French of Algeria will have to decide their own destiny"—implying that theirs was a common destiny, to be decided in common? And if it were not then why, in the Mostaganem speech, did he say *"Vive l'Algérie française?"*

These questions are not posed, as they usually are, for the purpose of determining whether de Gaulle betrayed the pieds noirs. Given the hopes raised by his return and his deliberate ambiguity in addressing them, no answer could now convince them otherwise. But if, as Stanley Hoffman has written, the Fifth Republic's foreign policy was "the expression of one man's vision, will, and statecraft," the study of that policy necessarily begins with the nature of his vision, the constancy of his will, and the purposes of his statecraft.[5]

There can be no doubt as to de Gaulle's personal responsibility for policy on Algeria. His strongest criticism of the old regime was reserved for its indecisiveness and general disorganization, which he thought was most egregious in relations with the overseas territories.[6] The June 1958 visit was the first of eight trips he made to Algeria in two and a half years. De Gaulle took charge of the Algerian portfolio as the last prime minister of the Fourth Republic. As president, he was an imposing presence at interministerial meetings on Algeria, which seldom occasioned anything like a debate. From day to day, he directed policy and personnel through his secretary-general, Geoffroy de Courcel, his cabinet director, René Brouillet, and his top aides for Algerian Affairs, Jean-Jacques de Bresson and Bernard Tricot.[7]

According to Tricot, when he once proposed proceeding with some action "if le général de Gaulle agreed," the paper was returned to him. On it de Gaulle had written "[b]adly put: I decide: yes or no; I do not agree." Tricot interpreted this to mean that his seemingly innocent formulation implied "a relationship of a contractual nature with subordinates"—something *le général* would not abide from his political supporters, his cabinet, nor even his prime minister.[8] Thus, when *Algérie française* activists sent a resolution urging him to dissolve political parties he delivered a withering, public rebuke to this "peremptory motion."[9] After Gaullists triumphed in the November 1958 Assembly elections, Brouillet told Alain Peyrefitte, then a young deputy, that "he distrusts them because they believe they have rights over him. In fact, he believes that they owe him everything, which is probably true, and that he owes them nothing, which," Brouillet allowed, "may be inaccurate." De Gaulle retained Michel Debré as prime minister just so long as he served to cover his right flank through the Algerian settlement—a settlement that shattered Debré—and *then* granted his long-standing wish to resign. De Gaulle considered his supporters to be vassals, Brouillet concluded; but in this form of feudalism they had no claim to *his* loyalty.[10]

De Gaulle himself constantly asserted his sovereign power in the Fifth Republic, the constitution of which could be said to have been created by and for him. It is indicative that in his first seven-year term he pronounced the word "I" almost 500 times in 46 radio-television addresses—more even than "France."[11] Never self-effacing, de Gaulle was nevertheless most revealing on this point when he related a conversation with Queen Elizabeth II in his memoirs. She had supposedly asked him "what I thought of her own role. . . . I [de Gaulle] answered:

> In that station to which God has called you, be who you are, Madam; that is to say the person in relation to whom, by virtue of the principle of legitimacy, everything in your kingdom is ordered, in whom your people perceives its own nationhood, and by whose presence and dignity the national unity is upheld.

It was a role, needless to say, not unworthy of de Gaulle.[12] Indeed, during the January 1960 "week of the barricades" in Algiers, de Gaulle called for obedience by virtue of "the national legitimacy that I have incarnated for twenty years. . . ."[13]

Thus, de Gaulle imagined himself as France incarnate and refused to recognize any obligation, even to his loyalists. He could hardly be expected to credit foreigners with any influence in his policies—least of all on Algeria, which had shaken the country to its core and catapulted him back to power. Here again his memoirs are instructive, if not in the way that he intended. Writing some ten years later, he maintained that upon his return to power assimilation was out of the question and that it was also too late to try to bring about "an autonomous Algeria evolving of its own accord into a state attached to France by federal ties. . . ." So, "having decided to accord [Algeria] this right [to self-determination], I would do so only on certain conditions.

> First of all it must be France, eternal France, who alone, from the height of her power, in the name of her principles and in accordance with her interests, granted it to the Algerians. There could be no question of her being compelled to do so by military setbacks, or prevailed upon to do so by foreign intervention, or induced to do so by partisan and parliamentary agitation. We would, therefore, put forth the effort required to make ourselves masters of the battlefield. We would pay no attention to any overtures from any capital, to any offer of "good offices," to any threat of "agonizing reappraisal" in our foreign relations, to any debate in the United Nations.

Only then, almost as an afterthought, does de Gaulle mention guarantees for the safety of the pieds noirs, continued cultural relations, and cooperation in developing Saharan oil.[14] It is as if the way de Gaulle personally reformed France's relationship with Algeria—and the way he was *perceived* doing so—were more important than the relationship itself. Indeed, the idea that de Gaulle "granted" Algeria independence in a kind of victory over die-hard military officers and pieds noirs proved far more enduring than any of the guarantees he obtained in the Evian accords. Almost thirty years later, Xavier Yacono found it necessary to remind readers of his account of the war that it was the FLN, not *le général*, who had actually won.[15]

But de Gaulle's own version does not just obscure the final outcome. It leaves all of his decisions that led up to it remote and inaccessible, as if, after years of wandering in political exile, *le général* went up to the mountain and, "from the height of her power," came down to offer "a solution . . . which would be the most French" (as he put it in January 1960).[16] This elides the problem itself, which was not purely French. That, it would seem, was precisely the problem. His whole approach to Algeria — his insistence, "first of all," that France would act without regard to outsiders — can be read as a reaction to the international character of the war. Thus, he writes that the Algerians "were well aware that if the plight of their fathers had left the world indifferent, there was now a vast wave of sympathy and sometimes active support for their cause abroad." Given their support in the United Nations and the precedents set in Indochina, West Africa, Tunisia, and Morocco, "the Algerians were confident that in the long run, provided they themselves opened the breach, their independence was a foregone conclusion." Conversely, attempting to maintain the status quo "would be to keep France politically, financially and militarily bogged down in a bottomless quagmire when, in fact, she needed her hands free to bring about the domestic transformation necessitated by the twentieth century and to exercise her influence abroad unencumbered."[17]

As we have seen, the "vast wave of sympathy and sometimes active support" did not arise spontaneously; the Algerians had had to earn it. Moreover, self-rule in West Africa, Tunisia, and Morocco was, in part, precipitated by the Algerians' own efforts, which had forced the French to focus on their most prized possession. And if France was then "bogged down" in Algeria and "encumbered" abroad, it was because of the continuing sacrifices by the mujahadeen and the nationalist leadership in exile. To believe de Gaulle's memoirs, with his accession the outcome was already decided — even if French prestige required that the ALN lose a few battles and that the external leadership endure his disdain.

It is hard now to imagine how Algeria's independence ever appeared less than inevitable. Knowing how the end of the war enabled the French under de Gaulle to regain *grandeur*, one wonders why they did not actually welcome it. But at the time most of France's military and political elite assumed that if it suffered yet another defeat it would forever be relegated to the status of a third-rate power. It was hardly obvious, even to de Gaulle, that liquidating the empire would leave France stronger than before — though that process was certain to subject it to the most debilitating domestic strife. One need not doubt his oft-stated admission that, "[f]or a man of my age and upbringing, it was bitterly cruel to become through my own choice the overseer of such a transformation." But his "mind was made up," he writes, "whatever the dreams of the past or the regrets of today, *whatever I myself had undoubtedly hoped for at other times.*"[18]

Historians have had to glean meaning from such musings because de Gaulle's heirs have denied them access to all but a fraction of his papers. But together with the recollections of his contemporaries and the public record, they are sufficient to cast doubt on the idea that in 1958 he was reconciled to Algeria's quickly gaining independence, to suggest that his memoirs present a flat, composite picture of a policy that continually evolved, and to reconstruct a chronology tracing that evolution from the hopes of "other times" to the "regrets of today."

De Gaulle began to gain a reputation as a relative liberal on colonial questions with his opening address to the January 1944 Brazzaville conference of colonial administrators. The conference was called, in part, to consolidate the empire in the face of American anticolonialism. De Gaulle admitted no particular pressure, saying only that "immense events" in the world required that they "establish on a new basis the conditions of the development of our Africa, of the human progress of its inhabitants and of the exercise of French sovereignty." Yet the conference itself concluded that "the civilizing mission accomplished by France in the colonies precludes any idea of autonomy and all possibility of evolution outside the French imperial bloc. Self-government, even in the distant future, is out of the question." Later that year de Gaulle defined France's mission as "to lead each of her peoples to a development which would permit it to administer itself, and, later, to govern itself."[19] These positions are not necessarily contradictory if one keeps in mind a crucial distinction *le général* preferred to leave implicit: the distinction between self-government inside an "imperial bloc"—maintaining the "exercise of French sovereignty" over "her peoples"—and self-government as sovereign independence.

One must also recall the distinction between words and deeds, however powerful de Gaulle's words could be. His provisional government offered only a few relatively insignificant reforms to Tunisia and Morocco. Though it is difficult to assign ultimate responsibility for the repression of the Sétif uprising, de Gaulle's preeminent biographer, Jean Lacouture, judges that he was more "a driving force than an obstacle in the terrible massacre."[20] And while he granted Muslims citizenship in 1944, de Gaulle did not support the 1947 statute for Algeria—contrary to his later assertions—calling instead for "a system in which France will exercise fully the rights and duties of her sovereignty."[21] Here again, French sovereignty was non-negotiable. That same year, his doubts that the Fourth Republic could win the war in Indochina helped convince him to form the *Rassemblement du Peuple Français*.[22] The RPF's failure to take power led him to withdraw from political life from 1952 to 1958, but there was no indication of any loss of interest in the empire. He undertook two lengthy tours of France's overseas possessions and in 1957 inspected the new oil and gas works in the Sahara,[23] encouraging Lacoste to continue his work.

De Gaulle was known for allowing his interlocutors to believe that he shared their views so as to draw them out and maintain their support. Jean Touchard has compiled five solid pages of contradictory quotations showing that "the partisans of *Algérie française* leave General de Gaulle convinced that he is unshakably attached to *Algérie française*. The partisans of a negotiated peace," on the other hand, "leave General de Gaulle convinced that he is a partisan of a negotiated peace."[24]

Two points help us to sort out this mass of conflicting evidence: De Gaulle's occasional predictions that Algeria would be independent need to be read in the context of his unremitting gloom concerning France's prospects under the Fourth Republic. Thus, in the winter of 1957–58, he told the journalist J.-R. Tournoux that the regime "has lost Indochina, Tunisia, Morocco. It will lose Algeria." But he went on to assert that "the system will also lose Alsace, Lorraine, Corsica, Brittany. Nothing will remain to us but the Auvergne because no one will want it."[25] In this case and many more besides, de Gaulle made the prediction of near-term Algerian independence contingent on the continuation of "the system." Thus, he told Louis Terrenoire, the former secretary-general of the RPF, that nothing and no one could any longer stop the Algerian movement, but "a totally different regime, which would rejuvenate France and make it more attractive, could attempt an entirely new experiment of association."[26]

This new experiment appears to have been the French Community— indeed, Charles-Robert Ageron argues that finding a solution to the Algerian problem was the main reason for establishing the community in the first place.[27] De Gaulle presented a stark choice to France's colonies during an August 1958 tour through Africa: they could build on the 1956 *loi cadre* and become self-governing states in this federal system or opt for total independence—and immediate withdrawal of all French aid and advisors. The community had a common Executive Council, consultative Senate, and Court of Arbitration, though each body was subordinate to the presidency, which also retained responsibility for defense and foreign policy.[28] Based on interviews with several of de Gaulle's closest aides and associates, Lacouture concluded that he envisaged the community as a framework for a continuing "close association" between France and Algeria, which would attain independence only later—twenty-five years later, according to his delegate-general, Paul Delouvrier. Even then, "cooperation" would continue.[29] Thus, while some have cited de Gaulle's pre-1958 declarations that Algeria would be independent to argue that he worked for it from the day he returned to power, it appears that, actually, he thought his own return made it possible to postpone Algeria's independence for decades.[30]

If so, this was not the first time that de Gaulle was recalled from political exile when his gloomy prophesies proved correct—nor the first time that he let it go to his head. One of the very few French commanders to win laurels against the Wehrmacht in May 1940, he was also virtually the only one to feel optimistic that France could expel the invader. Lacouture writes that he sometimes "found it difficult to distinguish between what was happening to him and what was felt by the people as a whole."[31] Now that he was president of a renewed republic—rather than a mere brigadier in a retreating army—it must have seemed much easier to turn the tide against the bedraggled *mujahadeen*.

But as early as 1944, de Gaulle had concluded that complete integration was illusory. If the partisans of *Algérie française* were convinced that he was "unshakably attached" to their cause, they appear to have convinced themselves. They can produce little evidence, and even Soustelle noted that de Gaulle voiced reservations.[32] He did not oppose integration because of any liberal ideas about equality and fraternity. As he told Peyrefitte in 1959:

> We have founded our colonization since the beginning on the principle of assimilation. We pretended to make good Frenchmen out of coloreds. We made them recite: "Our ancestors the Gauls"; this was not very bright. That's why decolonization has been so much more difficult for us than for the English.[33]

In another conversation with Peyrefitte that year, de Gaulle described integration as positively dangerous: "The Muslims, have you gone to see them? You've looked at them, with their turbans and their djellabas? You've seen how little they are like Frenchmen?" Comparing the two communities to oil and vinegar, he insisted that

> Arabs are Arabs, Frenchmen are Frenchmen. Do you believe that the French body could absorb ten million Muslims, who tomorrow will be twenty million and the day after that forty? If we pursue integration, if all the Arabs and Berbers of Algeria were considered French, how would we prevent them from coming to settle in the metropole, where the standard of living is so much higher. My village would no longer be called Colombey-les-Deux-Eglises but Colombey-les-Deux-Mosquées![34]

By that point, de Gaulle had also become concerned about the cost of continuing the war, though this cost was not only economic. In public he went out of his way to reject Raymond Cartier's contention that France should withdraw from Africa because colonialism did not pay. This position was "not in agreement with the idea that France has of itself," de Gaulle asserted in 1959, "nor with the idea that the world has of France."[35] Indeed, the previous year he had initiated a five-year plan for developing Algeria that would cost over $400 million (2,043 million new francs). But privately he had already begun to complain that economic integration would require a "ruinous effort" while the war constituted "a grave moral prejudice in the world."[36] Not until an April 1961 press conference did de Gaulle publicly speak of how Algeria "costs us, to say the least, more than it brings us," imposing "military and diplomatic mortgages,"[37] and not just economic ones.

Here, then, is another irony: when de Gaulle eventually conceded Algerians the right to determine their own destiny he was motivated by the most illiberal sentiments. Yet *le général* was "conscious of living his own biography," as Alfred Grosser has argued, "behav[ing] according to what history will say."[38] The 1961 press conference was therefore an exception. "The idea that the world has of France"—and the idea that he wanted the world to have of himself—required that in public de Gaulle present his policy as part of France's "humane and historically generous" tradition, as his memoirs claim.[39] But it is clear that in 1958 he did not intend to be so generous and that he did not think it was too late for "an autonomous Algeria evolving of its own accord into a state attached to France by federal ties." Instead of acknowledging that the Algerians had forced him to abandon this aim, he cultivated the myth that he had intended to offer complete independence all along.

To make this argument, one does not need to rely solely on the accounts of de Gaulle and his associates. One can also compare the records of his wartime foreign ministry with his subsequent statement that France paid "no attention to any overtures from any capital . . . to any debate in the United Nations." Though French diplomats did not decide policy on Algeria, their importance in informing and implementing it is now clear. Moreover, the Quai's archives also contain the files of the *Secrétariat d'Etat aux Affaires algériennes* (SEAA) and the peace negotiations it conducted. These show how much the final settlement differed from de Gaulle's initial design. Most important, we now have access to Algerian documents that reveal the dialogue that continued within and through their war with France. Only by listening to both sides of this argument can we explain how *the Algerians won* and *de Gaulle lost*—and why it took another four years of fighting.[40]

The FLN Prepares its Riposte

However it was viewed in retrospect, in 1958 the FLN considered de Gaulle's return to be a disastrous setback on the path to independence. During the preceding crisis, they had suffered demoralizing losses in assaults on the Morice line, culminating in the battle of Souk-Ahras of April 26–29 when the French captured or killed three-quarters of some 820 *mujahadeen* who attempted to cross the wire.[41] But at the same time, FLN leaders in Tangier achieved another diplomatic coup: the first conference to unite Morocco, Algeria, and Tunisia against France. Though ostensibly organized by the ruling parties rather than governments as such, the Istiqlal delegation included Foreign Minister Ahmed Balafrej while Bourguiba's vice president and defense minister, Bahi Ladgham, headed the one sent by the Neo-Destour. And whereas the meeting of African states in Accra earlier that month and the December 1957 Afro-Asian solidarity conference in Cairo offered little more than moral support, the Tangier resolutions pledged military and financial aid, endorsed the formation of a provisional Algerian government, and even envisioned a North African assembly uniting the three peoples.[42]

The atmosphere was altogether different when Balafrej and Ladgham, this time representing their respective governments, agreed to meet FLN representatives during a conference in Tunis June 17–20, two weeks after de Gaulle obtained full powers. The conference's purpose was for Morocco and Tunisia to sign a cooperation agreement. Not only had they excluded the FLN from the agreement, they even excluded them from the public ceremonies that surrounded it. Nevertheless, in private meetings Ferhat Abbas, Abdelhafid Boussouf, Ahmed Francis, and Belkacem Krim obtained a commitment to designate a common secretariat, though not the promised North African assembly. Nor did they receive any concrete offer of aid, despite repeatedly pressing their interlocutors.[43] But the worst moment came when Ladgham revealed that France and Tunisia had just concluded an agreement that would close within four months all French bases besides Bizerte, the status of which would be determined in subsequent negotiations. The agreement itself was consistent with the Tangier resolutions, which had called for the withdrawal of all French troops from North Africa, but not the secrecy in which it had been concluded. The Algerians must have been all the more unnerved that the Moroccan representatives did not appear surprised. Balafrej, who had become prime minister since the Tangier conference, confirmed that he knew all about the agreement. By contrast, Ladgham refused the Algerians' repeated requests to see a copy of the text.

Toward the end of this contentious meeting, Krim called for a joint communiqué that would demand Algerian independence, which the Tangier conference had described as the only possible solution to the war. Earlier that day Bourguiba had publicly offered to mediate between France and the FLN, which Minister of Economic Affairs Abderrahim Bouabid now endorsed on behalf of Morocco. He urged a formulation that showed a "positive will," stressing that, "[i]f, before de Gaulle, the position of France was very weak on the international plane, since then things have changed." France was moving away from the United States while the Soviets were at the point of sacrificing French Communists in the hope of breaking up NATO. Bouabid even hinted that Egypt might withdraw its support for the FLN.

Mindful of these dangers, the FLN had signaled a willingness to consider "a federal union *implying* the independence of Algeria" on the eve of de Gaulle's trip.[44] But he had answered by shouting "Vive Algérie française," as Abbas reminded his interlocutors:

> In Algeria there is a war, and if we do not face this fact we are doubtless going to come to some absurd conclusions. For us Algerians de Gaulle's position means war, whatever the support de Gaulle could receive from the Americans, the Russians, or even the Egyptians. The word integration means war.

For Abbas, France's revival made it all the more important that North Africans reaffirm their common commitment to a united and independent Maghreb. While Ladgham agreed that it was necessary for the FLN to intensify the war effort, he insisted that they leave de Gaulle room for maneuver. Pointing out that *le général* had paid tribute to the Algerians' courage, which was "noted by all the international press," he called on them to show "political maturity" and "not pronounce certain words."

"De Gaulle has thrown us some flowers," Ahmed Francis retorted, "but we would have preferred that he insulted us if at the same time he spoke of independence." For their part, each word the Algerians pronounced would be weighed and commented upon. "The Algerian people follow events closely and we do not have the right to play with the morale of our people." Boussouf also pointed out that in Algeria people "read all the newspapers and listen to all the radios." The FLN leaders were genuinely worried about how to respond to the hopes raised by de Gaulle's return without undermining the militancy of their supporters. New means of mass communications that could carry their message into Algeria constrained their freedom of maneuver. They realized, with Nasser, that "people in the most remote villages hear what is happening everywhere and form their opinions. Leaders cannot govern as they once did"—or, as in this case, negotiate as they might have liked to.[45]

That same month, the CCE issued guidance to cadres on the message they were to convey to supporters. They vowed that the ALN would never disarm before the flag of independent Algeria flew at the United Nations, but they were not to risk ridicule by predicting that the French army would be driven into the sea. Instead, they were instructed to emphasize that the war was a political rather than a military problem. All their international activities and negotiating initiatives had a single objective: "to weaken the enemy positions in the diplomatic sphere and to hasten our victory." At the same time, they had to emphasize, indeed exaggerate, the strength of their own international positions. Thus, while Algeria at war was hardly oblivious to the feuds dividing her allies, it took no part in them: "[F]or her, the Arab world is one." Above all, and despite Tunisia and Morocco's failings, they had "to maintain against wind and tide the unity of North Africa and the friendship of North African peoples."[46]

The Tunisian army had already begun to impound FLN arms shipments and enforce tighter control over their forces.[47] In July, Bourguiba concluded another agreement with de Gaulle to allow construction of a petroleum pipeline running from the Algerian Sahara through Tunisia to the Mediterranean—thus ignoring an FLN warning that this would be considered "a hostile gesture."[48] He also began to play a subtle, even duplicitous game between the United States, France, and Algeria. On July 25, he told Ambassador Jones that "your Government will have to exert all its energies upon [France] if any progress is to be achieved on [the] Algerian problem; you must never cease pushing and persuading." But just a week later, he assured Joxe that he had "confidence in General de Gaulle, it is necessary to leave him time to work."[49] In the meantime, Bourguiba worked to advance Tunisian interests in an eventual Algerian settlement, claiming a large swath of the Sahara between Tunisia's southern border and the oil fields at Edjelé.[50]

The Moroccans, for their part, had long-standing claims to much of the Western Sahara—not to mention the whole of Mauritania—claims that they had asserted through clashes with local ALN units and harassment of Algerian refugees. Moreover, they had long turned a blind eye to attacks on the Algerians from the remaining French bases in Morocco. But the formation of a mixed Algerian-Moroccan commission in April, the barricading of the French bases in May, and de Gaulle's agreement to a partial withdrawal in June all raised expectations that Morocco might follow through on the pledges of the Tangier conference. Renewed French and Moroccan attacks on the *mujahadeen* and continuing harassment of refugees finally dispelled these hopes. It then became clear that the French had abandoned their isolated posts only because air power could interdict FLN communications no less effectively. Moreover, the Moroccans remained determined to redraw the border with Algeria.[51]

After more than a year in exile—seeing Tunisia rationing its support, Morocco actively hostile, and their Egyptian hosts preoccupied with crises closer to home—the FLN leadership in Cairo viewed an independent Algeria as an increasingly distant prospect. Whereas once they "aroused the admiration of the whole world," the CCE's chief of armaments and logistics, Omar Ouamrane, observed that they were "marking time"—even regressing. Concerned about their support at home and backbiting and bureaucratization abroad, he feared that "disgust and discouragement have taken hold of the best of us." Ouamrane himself was obviously bitter: "We've settled into the war, the world has also gotten used to it. It will continue to turn to the Algerian war as long as it lasts, if necessary until the last Algerian."[52]

Ouamrane observed that the French, on the other hand, had regained self-assurance under de Gaulle. *Le général* could "permanently bar the way to the West and neutralize the Eastern bloc. He has already succeeded in partially cutting us off from our own brothers." The Moroccans and Tunisians now treated the FLN as "a minor and an incompetent," Ouamrane observed. ". . . [W]e have served as a bogeyman, an instrument of blackmail against the French." Wary of becoming another Spain or Korea, the Algerians had neglected potential Communist support and now had nothing to show for their patience with Washington. Yazid was reporting that, "having put a finger in a viper's nest and been bitten," the Americans "were not about to do it again." Indeed, they were unlikely to refuse de Gaulle a loan if he asked for one. Ouamrane concluded that the FLN should no longer act through intermediaries nor rely on any one country. Instead, it should adopt "a policy of balance and blackmail"—not only between the Americans and the Soviets, but also between pro-Western and neutralist Arab states.[53]

While they were delivered with a new sense of urgency, there was nothing original about Ouamrane's recommendations. Hocine Aït Ahmed, imprisoned since 1956 with the rest of the first external delegation, had already called for a balance between the West and the Soviets in his

1948 plan for revolutionary war.[54] In fact, Ouamrane's whole report appears to have been inspired by a study Aït Ahmed had written in his cell in April 1957. But Aït Ahmed had proposed, and Ouamrane now seconded, a "truly revolutionary political and diplomatic action" with which to advance this neutralist policy. Perhaps it was fitting that the plan for proclaiming Algeria's independence while still under French occupation was dreamed up by a prisoner in the Santé.[55]

Here is how Ouamrane summarized Aït Ahmed's critical insight: "Our whole policy consists of requesting, of demanding our independence. We demand it from the enemy. We want that our brothers, our friends, the UN recognize it. We ask it of everyone except ourselves, forgetting that independence proclaims itself and is not given." In fact, independence depended on no one but the Algerians, and Aït Ahmed showed how declaring it would drive the French to the negotiating table.[56] First and most important, reestablishing the *dawla*, or state, was the dream of generations of Algerian Muslims, and would now inspire them to persist in their struggle. Each recognition, beginning with Arab and Asian states pressured by their own publics and mutual competition, would further galvanize their energies. Algeria would then be an integral part rather than merely an outward sign of the Afro-Asian movement, which was increasingly being courted by the superpowers. And if they won recognition from the Communist states, the Americans might be led to end their "complacency and capitulations" to French blackmail. Moreover, a recognized state with all the trappings of a regular government would have a stronger claim to the protection of international conventions that forbade indiscriminate bombardment and mistreatment of prisoners. It would also deprive the French of the excuse that they had no negotiating partner. In any case, once begun, a campaign for recognition could be conducted continuously, confronting the French with an ongoing and seemingly irreversible process rather than the once-a-year test of strength in the General Assembly.[57]

Whatever the hypothetical advantages, Aït Ahmed was conscious of the unreal aspect of proclaiming a government with all its ministries where the mujahadeen could not even count on holding a village during daylight hours. But he insisted on establishing the seat of this government within Algeria—or rather, appearing to—precisely because it would add a "magical" element to the initiative, much like the popular belief that the broadcasting station of 'Fighting Algeria' was in the *maquis*. It hardly mattered whether the French eventually found this headquarters, since the Muslim population would not believe them. Nor would it risk the process of internationalization: "[Q]uite the contrary, the revelations, the denials, the polemic that will not fail to be established on this point, the war of communiqués, the sensational reporting would all contribute to the publicity and the dramatization of the Algerian question."[58]

In reality, of course, most of the government would work abroad in safety. But Aït Ahmed argued that the Algerians should always encourage uncertainty as to its location. Thus, if a minister who was supposed to be in Algeria were spotted abroad, they could claim that he was on a mission. Ferhat Abbas suggested a mobile organization instead in a July 1958 memorandum. But he too emphasized the "magical" aspect. "The members of the CCE would be much more free if they were everywhere and nowhere," Abbas suggested. "When the enemy believes that they are in Cairo, in reality they will be in Rabat, in Tunis, in Madrid, in Belgrade, in Riyadh, in New York, in London and everywhere the interests of Algeria at war call them"—everywhere, it would seem, but Algeria.[59]

One cannot but admire the audacity of these arguments, which show that the Algerians appreciated the importance of cultivating a mystique fully as much as de Gaulle did. But one also detects a note of desperation in their repeated assurances to themselves and each other that forming a government was a logical extension of their war effort.[60] In August 1956, some of these same leaders, including Ouamrane and Krim, had assembled in the heart of Algeria to declare the primacy of the interior over the exterior. A year later, after being forced into exile, the leadership declared that there was no difference between the interior and the exterior.[61] Now they were prepared to institutionalize—and bureaucratize—external direction, even while entertaining the illusion that the government could be "everywhere and nowhere." In fact, they were following in the footsteps of the old external delegation—"in Rabat, in Tunis, in Madrid"—ever farther from their increasingly hard pressed comrades in the maquis. This helps explain the pious, self-conscious tributes to the primary role of "the people," and the many warnings that one could not forever count on their fortitude. The Algerians did not necessarily declare independence and form a government from a conviction that it was a war-winning strategy, but rather because, as Abbas put it, there was little elsethey could do but "give some reasons to hope for those who suffer and die."[62]

In fact, all of the advocates of this course stressed its potential impact on morale, and the CCE's head of liaisons and communications, Abdelhafid Boussouf, claimed that the mujahadeen themselves demanded it. But the leadership's motives may have been personal as well as political. One is struck, for instance, by Abbas's fear that if they lost their base of support in Algeria they would become, "by the force of circumstances, simple charlatans." Ouamrane put it more grandiosely but the sentiment was the same: "Before our dead, before the survivors, before God, our responsibility is very heavy. Let us assume it with honor. Today the destiny of Algeria is in our hands. We will be liberators or assassins."[63] "Charlatans," "assassins"—these were fitting epithets for ambassadors without a country, soldiers without a state. If the war ended in defeat, their responsibility would indeed be heavy. By preparing to proclaim Algerian independence, the leaders of the FLN were reaffirming their faith in themselves and their cause. But in justifying it, they also betrayed their increasing fear of forever remaining rebels unredeemed by victory.

Tous Azimuts Diplomacy

In his original proposal for a provisional Algerian government, Hocine Aït Ahmed cited as precedents everything from America's Declaration of Independence in 1776 to the Polish and Spanish governments in exile. He ignored the differences—the fact, for instance, that all the revolutionary governments he cited had controlled at least part of the claimed territory and that the governments in exile could claim continuity with sovereign, internationally recognized states. The FLN, on the other hand, was hunted down whenever it showed its face in Algeria, where French sovereignty had been unquestioned even by the rebels' closest allies.[64]

The most relevant precedent may have been one Aït Ahmed and the other FLN leaders did not mention, though it could not have escaped their attention: de Gaulle's own wartime *Comité National de la Résistance*. Like the Algerian revolution, de Gaulle's movement was launched against seemingly insurmountable odds. Both confronted the problem of relying on allies without becoming their instruments. Each retained autonomy by playing off stronger powers or by appealing directly to their publics. They also confronted rival organizations, which they co-opted or ruthlessly eradicated. De Gaulle as much as the FLN ultimately relied on the legitimacy conferred by his people's support, with radio playing an important role, even if it required exaggerating the unity and strength of national resistance.[65] Finally, lacking the material fundaments of power, both drew strength from its more abstract and even magical qualities. De Gaulle was already famous for his punctilious observance of diplomatic protocol, but the FLN representatives would impress even the Swiss with their insistence on matters of form.[66] And, as we have seen, the Algerians were quite conscious of the connection between mystery and prestige, a connection de Gaulle demonstrated during his own radio broadcasts from exile. "For four years the words coming from London were to be the night-voice of the imaginary," as Lacouture observes, "—that spiritual rebellion against reality which may also be reality's prefiguration." One need only substitute Cairo and Tunis for London, and the analogy is complete.[67]

De Gaulle may therefore have been genuinely empathetic when he recognized the rebels' courage, thus becoming the first French premier not to dismiss the FLN as a criminal conspiracy of foreign origin. Yet this was part of a strategy to domesticate the Algerian question—to define it as "a French tragedy," as he emphasized in his memoirs, so as to find a French solution.[68] At the time, de Gaulle hardly recognized the FLN as equals. Talking to Ambassador Jebb in March 1958 about eventual negotiations, he asserted that they "knew that they themselves could not possibly govern Algeria: their mental and physical resources were simply not adequate for this purpose. Therefore, in the long run, they would probably be forced to abandon extreme intransigence and something would emerge." In one critical assumption, de Gaulle did not differ from his predecessors. He told Jebb that the "actual length of the physical struggle would probably depend on the extent to which the FLN leaders thought they were supported by outside powers." In other words, the FLN had to be isolated if they were to be brought to terms. For that de Gaulle, no less than the maligned leaders of the Fourth Republic, needed allies.[69]

On June 17, the same day he concluded the base agreement with Bourguiba, de Gaulle told his defense advisors that the French role in NATO would have to be reconsidered. This provided the first inkling of the famous tripartite memorandum he delivered to Eisenhower and Macmillan three months later. "We make a considerable contribution to NATO," he asserted, "Without us, NATO would not exist."[70] On a number of occasions, de Gaulle's predecessors had also been ready to stake participation in NATO against support for the French position in North Africa, and they never stopped demanding tripartite consultations. They also initiated the independent nuclear program that de Gaulle was able to claim as his own—Gaillard approved the first nuclear test in one of the last acts of his government.[71] But *le général*'s personal authority and well-known dissatisfaction with the alliance—especially America's predominant role and advocacy of supranational European integration—would give him more credibility in threatening to withdraw.

And de Gaulle had proved himself "capable of the most extraordinary actions," as Eisenhower reminded his secretary of state. The president recalled how in the midst of the German winter offensive of 1944 de Gaulle had refused orders to withdraw French forces from Strasbourg. Eisenhower replied that the United States and Britain "would win the war anyway" and withhold all logistical support. "De Gaulle . . . would therefore be reduced to impotency." But, as he reflected on it in 1958, the president cautioned against adopting this attitude "in light of De Gaulle's present position of power and influence." He warned Dulles to "watch out for him."[72]

The British were also keeping a close watch on de Gaulle, though Selwyn Lloyd urged that they "act in public as though we had no nervousness at all about French policy in NATO or anywhere else." Ambassador Jebb thought that his ambitions were still limited by his logistics. Writing from Paris, he doubted whether de Gaulle "fully realizes what will happen if the foreigner refuses to go on maintaining Marianne in the position to which she is accustomed. Or possibly he imagines there will always be found a foreigner of some kind who will be prepared to do the right thing."[73]

While pleased with de Gaulle's return, Eisenhower now refused to treat him "like God"—or even like Macmillan.[74] "We must certainly not give up this special relationship," Dulles assured Ambassador Caccia.[75] Even Jebb, who sometimes aroused Macmillan's ire for adopting the

French viewpoint, allowed only that they might "concede even more of the appearance . . . while continuing to withhold the reality" of equality in the alliance.[76]

The appearance and reality of power were key themes in a remarkably candid July 5 discussion in Paris between de Gaulle and Dulles. While suggesting that France be strong in Europe and integrated in NATO against the danger of German nationalism, Dulles described a philosophy of power that also applied to North-South relations:

> I've always felt that in every society since time began, there were a few people who have exercised the controlling force. It all depends on how they do it. We must do it in a manner not to irritate the others. Those of us having greater responsibilities must exercise these powers. France too has great responsibility and must play her role. I feel that any too close association must be avoided in order to avoid offense to smaller nations.

But without America's manifest military and economic power, France could not dispense with appearances, especially since de Gaulle aspired to more than a European role. "France must be a world power," he insisted. "If she ceases to be a world power she ceases to be France." It should therefore control its own nuclear weapons—rather than merely have access to a NATO stockpile in the event of general war—and "participate in a world security control." He also wanted NATO to be extended beyond Algeria's northern *départements* to cover all of North Africa.[77]

The most pressing problem at the time was a nascent civil war in Lebanon. While advising against intervention, de Gaulle insisted that France participate in any joint action. In a private discussion that afternoon, Dulles tried to scale back de Gaulle's expectations:

> [A] world role for France could only come about *pari passu* with the internal strengthening and recovery of France. It was important and a big step forward that General de Gaulle had come to power but until the phase he represented had been consolidated by constitutional amendment, fiscal stability, a settlement of the Algerian problem and the like, there persisted doubts.

When de Gaulle now tried to reassure him "that the foreign exchange situation was in hand for at least this year," Dulles recalled a crack he had made to Monnet—no friend of de Gaulle's—that "the American people were being called on to loan their money to the French government because the French people were too thrifty and too wise to do so."[78]

Ten days later, a revolution in Iraq prompted the Americans and British to proceed with military interventions to prop up pro-Western governments in Lebanon and Jordan. Though de Gaulle was angered that they did not consult him, he had the satisfaction of seeing his prediction that it would be perceived as "an Occidental intervention" come true. "They don't distinguish much between us," he had warned Dulles, "and they are quite right not to."[79]

Indeed, it is difficult to distinguish the Eisenhower administration's position on Egypt in July 1958 from that of Eden and Mollet before Suez. This was the high-water mark of American concern that Nasser, already presiding over Syria and Yemen, might attain "the power to destroy the Western world," as Eisenhower put it.[80] All through the crisis, policymakers used language depicting pan-Arabism as a "wave," a "flood," or a "tide," and by dispatching the Sixth Fleet the president intended to signal that he possessed the appropriate countermeasure. Thus, Nixon insisted that "we could not allow a wave of mob emotionalism to sweep away all our positions in the Near East."[81] Similarly, Dulles had earlier advised that "we must regard Arab nationalism as a flood which is running strongly. We cannot successfully oppose it, but we can put up sandbags around positions we must protect."[82] But the secretary had lost credibility on the issue, admitting that "the Iraqi government fell because Iraq was in an unnatural association . . . in the Baghdad Pact" — an association he himself had advocated. George Allen, Director of the U.S. Information Agency, warned that if they tried to hold their ground "the USSR will beat us to death in public opinion" around the region. "We must adjust to the tide of Arab nationalism," he argued, "and must do so before the hotheads get control in every country. The oil companies should be able to roll with the punches."[83] In an apparent rebuke to Dulles, Eisenhower agreed in the next NSC meeting that, "[s]ince we are about to get thrown out of the area, we might as well believe in Arab nationalism."[84]

The mounting criticism of the operation in Lebanon made Eisenhower all the more determined not to risk another entanglement in Morocco, where nationalist opposition was gathering against the Strategic Air Command bases. In August, he overruled the Joint Chiefs and accepted the principle of evacuation, making it all the more difficult for the French to maintain their own bases. De Gaulle would be incensed but Eisenhower was adamant: "[W]e could not use force to maintain the bases and thus get ourselves into the predicament of the French in Algeria."[85] He withdrew all U.S. troops from Lebanon by October and the next month approved a new policy of "work[ing] more closely with Arab nationalism" and particularly with Nasser.[86] It was not until December that a rapprochement began, as Nasser turned on the Soviets for privileging relations with their new ally in Baghdad and meddling in Egypt's own domestic affairs.[87]

Historians have judged Dulles harshly for not working with Nasser sooner.[88] But Tunisian, Algerian, and Moroccan nationalists also felt threatened by Egyptian ambitions and solicited American aid. In October, Bourguiba went so far as to denounce him before the Arab League and break diplomatic relations because of his involvement with an insurrectionary plot. The following month, the Algerians confirmed the existence of a conspiracy that involved Egyptian agents and high-ranking ALN officers and aimed at overthrowing both the GPRA and Bourguiba and expanding the war to Tunisia. In protest, they shifted all of their ministries except foreign affairs from Cairo to Tunis. "The idea of an ongoing conspiracy against the established regimes in Tunisia and Morocco orchestrated from Cairo is gaining credibility among North African leaders," the French ambassador to Rabat reported.[89]

But whereas Dulles had a "tendency to fret, hover, and meddle," as John Lewis Gaddis has argued, de Gaulle displayed an oriental fatalism. "The Middle East has no solution, it is eternal," he told Dulles in their July meeting. "[I]t is not tragic though, it is there, it must be lived with."[90] In September, de Gaulle approved, in principle, resuming relations with Nasser, though it would prove to be a long and rocky road before normal ties were reestablished.[91] In the meantime, he strove to contain U.S. and Egyptian influence in North Africa and assert France's preeminence in its former protectorates. But while resisting another American arms shipment to Tunisia through most of the fall—at times appearing to threaten another clash on the order of the November 1957 crisis—he could only wage a rearguard action against increased American military and economic aid to the region.[92]

In the meantime, the U.S. confrontation with Cairo had had still more far-flung repercussions that also harmed Franco-American relations. Ever since Chinese Premier Zhou Enlai met Nasser at the Bandung conference, Beijing had viewed Arab nationalism as "the coming force in the Middle East" and urged the Soviets to back it. But during the Lebanon crisis, Khrushchev limited himself to diplomatic support and cautioned Mao against the risks of a nuclear confrontation. Sino-Soviet ties had already become strained because of Moscow's readiness to improve relations with the United States and reluctance to share nuclear weapons technology. Now the U.S. intervention in Lebanon provoked Mao—or provided him with a pretext—to initiate a new crisis over the islands of Quemoy and Matsu, commencing with a withering bombardment on August 23. "We cannot just give moral support," he reportedly said. "We must also support them with real actions."[93] Mao's principal motive was probably to inspire his country for the sacrifices of the "Great Leap Forward," which was intended to erase its inequality with the USSR.[94] But support for "national liberation movements" was a key issue in the Sino-Soviet dispute, one that would soon have a direct impact on Algeria. In the meantime, America's apparent willingness to risk global nuclear war over two small islands in the South China Sea gave de Gaulle another argument in demanding a greater voice in Western councils.

Thus, the international agenda was already crowded in September 1958 when de Gaulle launched a series of new initiatives. First, on September 14 he invited Adenauer to Colombey-les-Deux-Eglises for a "man to man" talk, the first and last time he held such a meeting in his own home. Adenauer, for his part, came alone "as the representative of a vanquished people," as he later told Macmillan.[95] De Gaulle wanted to reassure him that he would not reverse the two countries' rapprochement—indeed, that Germany was France's one possible and desirable partner.

France was hindered by "our responsibilities, our obligations in Africa, in Madagascar, in the Pacific . . ." de Gaulle acknowledged. "[T]here exist centrifugal forces that push us, you toward Prussia, we toward Africa." But he then sketched a startling vision of a new order in Europe. France was no longer menaced, he asserted, "except by the danger that comes from the East."

> [W]e know that the real danger lies in Asia. This is all the more reason to bring Europe together against Asia. We must extend the peace toward the East, toward Poland for example which must not remain within Asian hands. This is also true of Czechoslovakia, of Hungary, and even—why not?—of European Russia.

De Gaulle had long emphasized the national character of the regime in Moscow. Now he urged that Europeans unite to form a broader bloc and resist becoming an instrument of the United States. They had to unify all of Europe, he warned, or there would be no Europe.[96]

Adenauer had already related a conversation with Khrushchev that illustrated the Soviet premier's fear of China, and he, too, had griped about American unreliability. "In these circumstances we must prepare for the worst-case scenario," the chancellor asserted, "and make Europe independent from the United States." But this remained the worst case. After hearing de Gaulle's intentions, he reversed himself. "We have to remain united with the United States," he argued. As long as the Soviets posed a threat, it would be "a terrible thing if the United States disassociate themselves from Europe."[97]

It would prove difficult to woo Adenauer away from the Atlantic Alliance, but de Gaulle did not make it any easier by presenting a very different plan to Eisenhower and Macmillan later that month: the tripartite memorandum. De Gaulle began by arguing that the crises in Lebanon and the Taiwan straits had shown how the "sharing of the risks incurred is not matched by indispensable cooperation on decisions taken." He advanced the broader conclusion that NATO was ill adapted to the global nature of the Soviet challenge and new nuclear delivery systems. What was needed, he argued, was an entirely new organization joining the United States, Britain, and France. On the one hand, it would make joint decisions on international security. On the other, it would establish and—if necessary—implement strategic plans, "notably with regard to the employment of nuclear weapons." He concluded by emphasizing that France would henceforth cooperate in NATO only to the extent that these demands were satisfied, if necessary through a revision of the North Atlantic Treaty.[98]

Though the French requested the strictest secrecy in handling the note, de Gaulle did not wait to receive a reply before giving a copy to NATO Secretary General Paul-Henri Spaak, a committed Europeanist. Considering the nature of his proposal, and the Belgian nationality of his interlocutor, it was all the more puzzling that he told him that one of his principal aims was to create a close link between France, Germany, and Italy, "the only three European countries which mattered." According to the German representative to NATO, who related this conversation to his British counterpart, de Gaulle thought that if these three agreed London would have no choice but to go along.[99] While it is possible that either Spaak or the Germans misrepresented De Gaulle's words, his handling of the memorandum gave them the opportunity and the incentive to do so. He had not even consulted with Adenauer, whose feelings of betrayal "burst out" during a dinner with Macmillan. The chancellor told him that he felt "tricked and deceived."[100]

Still more than the timing and indiscretions of its communication, the greatest puzzle of the tripartite memorandum was what, precisely, was being asked of the allies. Was it to be a global directorate of the big three, a reorganized NATO expanded to include North Africa, or both at the same time? Was it political and diplomatic consultation or military-strategic cooperation that de Gaulle wanted? French diplomats and de Gaulle himself presented countless permutations of his original proposal. One can well understand Adenauer's amazement when, after all this, de Gaulle claimed in December 1959 that "I have always told the Americans that for the time being nothing needs to be changed in the [NATO] organization in Europe, and this is why I am not proposing any changes." The chancellor could hardly contain himself: "But everyone knows that you are dissatisfied with NATO and that this has contributed to the tension between France and America."[101]

Later that month, Eisenhower finally agreed to "tripartite machinery to operate on a clandestine basis"—before then informal talks had been held at the ambassadorial level in Washington. Macmillan quickly approved, and de Gaulle said that he was "very satisfied with this idea." But, as in the past, *le général* never followed up with any specific recommendations.[102] Even before this episode Philip de Zulueta, the prime minister's private secretary, was "tempted to wonder whether the General is not being deliberately obscure":

> He may calculate that by being generally "difficult" he will make people take account of his views, and that his internal position in France will be strengthened if he appears to be in vague but definite opposition to the "Anglo-Saxons." Without pushing matters so far as to disrupt the Alliance he may prefer that his grievances should remain unredressed.[103]

Considering de Gaulle's original discussion with Adenauer at Colombey, his leak to Spaak—who was certain to organize opposition to the tripartite proposal—and his refusal ever to be pinned down on what exactly he wanted, it does seem plausible that *le général* was pursuing a kind of *tous azimuts* diplomacy: one that aimed in every direction, like the nuclear doctrine France adopted in the 1960s. By leaving everyone uncertain as to his ultimate intentions, he gave each of them an incentive to satisfy French demands—especially in issues that they may have thought peripheral but that de Gaulle considered his first priority, that is, issues relating to Algeria.[104]

This is not to say that settling the war on favorable terms was more important to de Gaulle than his other desiderata, only that it was an essential precondition. Obviously, he would have liked the United States to help France manufacture nuclear weapons, but he did not expect it and was reluctant to ask for it.[105] He might have welcomed British and American cooperation in setting up a tripartite directorate, but he was always skeptical that *les anglo-saxons* would willingly give France equal status.[106] Ultimately, he wanted to harness German power to French ambitions and lead an independent Europe, perhaps even Eurafrica, but he first needed the free hand that only an Algerian settlement could give him. Only then could he lead France through "the great turning point," as he described it to his cabinet when at last the settlement came.[107] The tripartite memorandum has been portrayed as a kind of declaration of independence from the Atlantic Alliance, since it subordinated NATO to French national interests, rather than identifying one with the other.[108] But, like the Algerians, de Gaulle had to declare independence as a way to help make independence possible.

8

Tearing the Hand Off

The Algerian people have not waited to be "granted" independence. They take it. They proclaim it. [Now] a new stage begins. Tomorrow our brother countries, the Arab countries of the entire world, will recognize our independence. This recognition will consecrate the support given to us by two thirds of the world. Sooner or later, the "Great" Powers must bow down before the new relation of forces. . . . Tomorrow the enemy will suffer a growing pressure on all fronts. Sooner or later, either in a tête-à-tête or under international pressure, they will have to negotiate with the Algerian government.

El Moudjahid, September 19, 1958 [1]

It's really to our advantage to pass the baton to local leaders before someone tears our hand off to take it from us.

de Gaulle to Alain Peyrefitte, October, 1959 [2]

On August 25, 1958, Algerian militants launched a wave of attacks across the French metropole. They blew up oil tanks, gunned down policemen, attempted to assassinate Soustelle—whom de Gaulle had just named minister of information—and even planted explosives in the Eiffel Tower. While these last two operations failed, the new offensive succeeded in gaining the attention of the foreign press and foreign capitals. "They have remembered that there is a dirty war going on in Algeria capable of contaminating the West," an FLN bulletin explained. "The virus that weakens colonialist France and through her the whole Atlantic Alliance has crossed the Mediterranean."[3]

Having regained the attention of the international community, Ferhat Abbas announced on September 19, 1958 the formation of a *Gouvernement provisoire de la République algérienne* (GPRA) in Cairo. Almost immediately, every Arab state except Lebanon extended diplomatic recognition. Only Morocco and Tunisia risked a rupture with France, as the rest had already broken relations during the Suez crisis. But Paris chose not to retaliate, apparently persuaded that Rabat and Tunis could not afford to appear too deferential and that any new regime would be even more defiant.[4]

194

Paris took a more forceful line with Moscow, warning that a recognition of the GPRA would end normal diplomatic relations.[5] Unbeknownst to the French, the Soviets were preparing for a showdown over Berlin and would not have provoked Paris over what, to them, had always been a secondary issue. China, on the other hand, accorded recognition within the week, followed shortly thereafter by North Vietnam, North Korea, and Indonesia. Altogether, thirteen states recognized the GPRA within ten days of its creation.[6]

While the Algerians would send delegations to China and the other Communist countries, their representatives abroad, accredited or not, were initially concentrated in the Middle East and Europe. The Arab states were particularly important in providing financial assistance. A month after the formation of the GPRA, the Cairo-based Arab League voted $34 million of aid. Whatever their differences on other issues, the member states cooperated in aiding Algeria, though not always to the extent promised. Thus, even while Iraq boycotted Arab League meetings from 1959 to 1962, General Abdel Karim Qassem continued to give Algerian delegations the sums the league had assessed according to a prorata formula. When the rest of the GPRA moved to Tunis, its foreign ministry continued to operate out of Cairo.[7]

Besides its representatives in the states of the Arab League, the GPRA operated offices in West Germany, Spain, Finland, Britain, Italy, Sweden, and Switzerland by October 1958. Along with the United States, Japan, India, and Indonesia—and excluding Morocco and Tunisia—there were some forty-five Algerian representatives in twenty countries.[8] In theory, they reported to the new foreign minister, Dr. Lamine Debaghine, who had also directed external relations for the CCE. But Yazid, now minister of information, was still responsible for the United Nations, while Abdelhamid Mehri held the portfolio for North African Affairs. Debaghine had aspired to the presidency, so he was alienated from the rest of the cabinet right from the start. In March 1959, he left what remained of his diminished fief to Ferhat Abbas, the GPRA's first president.[9]

Yet given the circumstances in which they worked, all of the GPRA ministries had to deal with other governments, or evade them, to carry out their functions. By June 1960, French intelligence counted 177 Algerians affiliated with the GPRA in 38 countries, not counting those based in Tunisia and Morocco. But this figure included, and doubtless excluded, dozens who worked clandestinely as recruiters or money collectors in emigrant communities.[10] While all of this was inimical to rational organization, it would have been impossible for the Foreign Ministry's small staff to oversee the entirety of Algerian activities abroad.[11] With a Ministry of Armaments dealing with everyone from German arms dealers to Communist China and a Ministry of General Liaisons that ran bagmen and agents across Europe and the Middle East, nothing was foreign to the new government. Even the "minister of the interior," Lakhdar Bentobbal, concluded that "each one of our agencies, military, political, diplomatic, social, associational or otherwise should act in its area according to the same objective: *INTERNATIONALIZATION*."[12] That year, the French estimated that GPRA expenditures abroad—for arms purchases, maintenance, support for refugees, and so on—had nearly equaled expenditures in the five Algerian *Wilayat*. If one added the budget of the *Fédération de France*, which was self-supporting, the bulk of the rebels' resources were devoted to maintaining and expanding its activities outside Algeria. The GPRA was like a state turned inside out.[13]

De Gaulle Goes for Victory

If de Gaulle was to domesticate the Algerian question, he had to reverse this process of internationalization. The first step in this strategy was a three-day referendum beginning September 26 on the new constitution in France, Algeria, and all the overseas territories. "The ballot will have certain particularities" in Algeria, the general admitted to his ministers, but he hoped that it would "not embarrass us." In any case, an affirmative vote would mean only that the Muslims "want to settle their affairs with France. That's all for the time being," de Gaulle emphasized, "and there's no use kidding ourselves."[14]

As expected, the FLN called for a boycott and threatened violence at the polls. But when de Gaulle spoke of "particularities" and unrealistic expectations, he was probably thinking of the army rather than the Algerian rebels. "I do not wish that the ballot yield only 'yes' votes," de Gaulle warned Salan, who continued to serve as his representative in Algiers. "It is normal that a consultation such as the one we are organizing will elicit some negative answers." But Salan had other ideas. He had already ordered his men to obtain the maximum number of positive votes.[15] As part of "Operation Referendum," the army trucked peasants to voting places, instructed illiterates in how to cast their ballots, and spread rumors that absentees would be arrested and lose government benefits. In these conditions 80 percent of the population were reported to have voted and 96 percent approved the new constitution, which merely required turning in a white ballot. (So that there could be no confusion, the color chosen for the ballot signifying "no," purple, was considered unlucky.)[16]

However heavy-handed, the referendum merely exaggerated the extent to which many Muslims hoped *le général* could somehow find a solution. Indeed, before the referendum there was talk of a boycott by pied noir activists, who already suspected that de Gaulle was against integration. But on October 3, he pledged a massive development program to bridge the socioeconomic gap between France and its Algerian *départements*. Speaking in Constantine, a city that is itself divided by a 1,000-foot gorge, he promised that in five years 250,000 hectares would be redistributed, 400,000 new jobs would be created, one million Muslims would have new homes, and all youth would be enrolled in schools. A week later, hoping to encourage genuinely representative Muslims to compete in the November legislative elections, he ordered military officers to withdraw from the committees of public safety formed during the May crisis.[17]

Thus, de Gaulle had prepared the ground for his October 23 press conference, the first since his return to power. While deploring the violence in Algeria, he acknowledged once again that the rebels had fought courageously. But he insisted that the solution was not to be found in their increasingly desperate insurgency, nor in "the political dreams and in the eloquence of the propaganda of refugees abroad." Instead, he offered a "peace of the brave," meaning that "those who have opened fire cease [fire] and that they return, without humiliation, to their family and to their work!" If the mujahadeen came forward bearing "the white flag of truce," de Gaulle promised to treat them honorably. Similarly, if the external organization designated representatives to "regulate the end of hostilities," they would be assured safe passage to the metropole. "The political destiny of Algeria" would be decided democratically, though only on the basis of "its close association with the French metropole. . . . [T]his grouping," de Gaulle concluded, "completed by the Sahara, will form a friendship, for common progress, with the free states of Morocco and Tunisia."[18]

De Gaulle's statement was admired for its magnanimity, promising as it did that the only winner of the war would be "fraternal civilization." But he struck an altogether different note the next day in a secret letter to Salan:

> [O]ne could foresee, one day or another, Ferhat Abbas' organization asking to send delegates to the metropole; in such a case, these delegates will not be led to Paris. In some place in France they will only see representatives of the military command. They will not be allowed to speak of anything but a cease-fire and this cease-fire will necessarily include handing over the rebels' arms to the military authority.[19]

The Algerians were therefore absolutely correct in characterizing de Gaulle's offer as a "request for unconditional surrender." They repeated that any negotiations had to treat the whole of the Algerian problem and address their aspirations for independence.[20]

De Gaulle's strategy suffered another setback in November when only "Beni Oui-Ouis," Muslim quislings, could be persuaded to run in the legislative elections. Even liberal pieds noirs found it impossible to campaign in the intimidating atmosphere created by the army and *Algérie française* activists.[21] In one revealing incident, General Massu personally warned one of them not to run, explaining that "the *parachutistes* don't like you." Did Massu really mean, the candidate asked in disbelief, that the army would be against him? "I would use my bayonets against you!"[22] If Muslims had not also received "impulses from on high," the president of the Election Commission judged that they would have "massively abstained."[23] De Gaulle was disappointed, but he was nonplused upon hearing that the GPRA had refused to negotiate: "Things like this cannot be smooth sailing, nor [go] straight ahead," he reportedly said. "But they are wrong. In the eyes of the world they are going to look like bastards."[24]

Of course, de Gaulle's domestication strategy required that his government not betray the least interest in the eyes of the world. It instructed French diplomats not to lobby foreign governments for the upcoming General Assembly debate. And whereas in 1957 Pineau himself took the podium on several occasions to defend French policy, the Quai now prohibited even their permanent representative, Guillaume Georges-Picot, from participating. At the same time, it worked tirelessly to prevent GPRA delegates from taking part, making a strongly worded protest to the State Department over the visas granted to Yazid and Chanderli.[25] Not only did the Americans reject the French argument, but on December 11, in the midst of the debate, five members of the U.S. delegation attended a reception in their honor.[26]

While the State Department apologized for the incident, they could not explain away Lodge's abstention two days later on an Afro-Asian General Assembly resolution that recognized the "right of the Algerian people to independence" and recommended "negotiations between the two parties." The GPRA had insisted on this stronger language rather than settle for another platitudinous text that aroused no opposition. The resolution fell short of a two-thirds majority by only one vote after a number of Scandinavian and Latin American countries also shifted from supporting France to abstention. A paragraph explicitly recognizing the GPRA had actually won a simple majority, which the Quai judged to be even more valuable to the Algerians than the resolution would have been.[27] "If the FLN has lost ground in Algeria," Georges-Picot observed, "there is little doubt that it has gained a good deal on the international level and in all the countries of the world where it has sent missions, especially the United States and the United Nations." Indeed, the U.S. abstention was "incontestably a success" from Ferhat Abbas's standpoint, and encouraged the Algerians' efforts to exploit the escalating "war of nerves" between the putative allies. Debré played into their hands by publicly describing the American decision as "nauseating."[28]

De Gaulle himself was livid. Eisenhower and Dulles had often expressed admiration for his handling of Algeria. He had also charmed the American public—*Time* named him "Man of the Year" for 1958—so there would have been less domestic protest than heretofore had the United States supported him. Moreover, while there were several other areas of contention in Franco-American relations, he had been unfailingly loyal in opposing the Soviets. Indeed, de Gaulle was so intransigent toward Khrushchev's November 10 Berlin ultimatum that it eventually became a new source of tension with Washington.[29]

Paradoxically, it appears that the Americans' respect for de Gaulle and the policy he pursued made them even less inclined to render their support, as Pierre Mélandri has argued. First, the new regime was less fragile than its predecessors and appeared better able to maintain the alliance despite such differences. Moreover, de Gaulle's moves toward a negotiated settlement vindicated those who had been arguing all along that French Algeria was a lost cause. This constituency would only grow now that Congress had created a Bureau of African Affairs in the State Department. Of course, the president and his secretary of state made the ultimate decision on the American position at the United Nations, so to Mélandri's analysis one might add their oft-stated annoyance at having to lobby for the French when they would not speak in their own defense.[30]

But the main reason for the U.S. abstention remained Eisenhower's determination not to alienate Third World opinion. Even Dulles, who had begun to fear that decolonization was proceeding too rapidly and that the General Assembly had grown unmanageable, still preferred risking relations with European allies to confronting the Third World.[31] Thus, what concerned him about the tripartite memorandum, as he told Ambassador Caccia, "was not so much its impact on NATO countries but the disastrous effects it would have on countries in Africa and the Middle East."[32] By 1958, the Eisenhower administration wanted to avoid being associated with colonialism at all costs, and de Gaulle's return had only attracted more attention to Algeria as the anticolonial struggle par excellence.

De Gaulle could not, therefore, domesticate the Algerian problem by demands and decrees, especially since the GPRA's international campaign extended far beyond the United States and the United Nations. While the General Assembly was debating the Algeria resolution, a GPRA delegation arrived in Peking to the kind of reception reserved for the most important statesmen, including a nationwide celebration of "Algeria Day."[33] Abbane and Debaghine had hesitated to take this fateful step, but it did not provoke the violent reaction expected from the West. The GPRA concluded from this experience that appeals to the Communists actually provoked a positive response, as evidenced by the U.S. abstention, and began accepting Chinese military aid. Chairman Mao Tse-Tung's only condition was that they continue fighting until total victory. And while the Algerians' new allies in Africa, like Kwame Nkrumah, could not offer much material support, they too called on them to commit to nothing less than full independence, thus counterbalancing Moroccan and Tunisian pressure to compromise.[34]

In 1959, de Gaulle dropped his feigned indifference to international opinion on the Algerian War. With the powers conferred on the president under the new constitution and a massive Gaullist bloc in the Assembly, *le général* and his government under Michel Debré had all the authority needed to lead a vigorous campaign against the GPRA. The French position was also bolstered by Finance Minister Antoine Pinay's economic program. Together with IMF Director Jacobsson, he had prevailed upon de Gaulle to accept cuts in government spending, accelerate trade liberalization, and adopt a realistic exchange rate. The Fifth Republic and its "heavy" franc—equal to one hundred of the old—thereby avoided inflation without recourse to outside aid. By accepting broader economic integration, de Gaulle would avoid the focused financial pressures the Fourth Republic had endured in defending French Algeria.[35]

In addition, he could be confident in his army and its brilliant new commander, Maurice Challe. Challe's predecessors had limited military and civilian casualties by dividing up the country and garrisoning every sector. But the *quadrillage* system left too few mobile troops to pursue and destroy the elusive enemy. The Challe Plan, on the other hand, left the mujahadeen "neither the mountain nor the night." Through large-scale operations with light pursuit and helicopter-borne units, Challe would attack and continue attacking ALN formations until they were utterly broken. The civilian population would then be treated to the "positive" side of pacification—clinics, schools, and so on—and thus be rendered immune to the rebels' appeals upon their return.[36]

As prime minister, Debré became *le général's* chief lieutenant in defending French Algeria abroad. He had long been an acerbic critic of the Fourth Republic's inability or unwillingness to combat allied and especially American indulgence for the FLN. After assuming office, he quickly established an interministerial committee to coordinate the government's diplomatic, propaganda, and covert campaigns. Compared to "the small, dynamic team of FLN leaders," the briefing paper for the first meeting observed, "the French apparatus fighting subversion is extremely complex and clumsy." Thirteen different government agencies or military commands were charged with receiving or exploiting intelligence on rebel activities, and each acted "according to its own conceptions and methods. *There is no organic link.*"[37] Debré and his new committee would unite efforts by French diplomats, military attachés, and intelligence agents to demonstrate a new and emphatic will to win. The prime minister would speak and act publicly to sway France's allies and foreign opinion while at the same time orchestrating a covert campaign to divide the GPRA and its allies. Just as military intelligence stepped up efforts to sew suspicions among the mujahadeen, French officials abroad employed forged tracts, false radio broadcasts, and fake GPRA directives to subvert its diplomacy. They were especially keen to tarnish the Algerians' image in America and Europe and provoke clashes with their Moroccan and Tunisian hosts. Psychological warfare was delicate and risky, the briefing paper noted. "A player holding all the cards is therefore absolutely necessary." Needless to say, the new "Committee for Psychological and Subversive Action" would report directly to Debré.[38]

The prime minister took a particular interest in the diplomatic contest, personally briefing French ambassadors with his new foreign minister, Maurice Couve de Murville. "A quick and happy solution to the Algerian problem is the first priority of this Government," he declared.

He explained that they had to come to a decisive turning point that year since public opinion and smaller cohorts of draftees could not forever support the war.[39] "It is imperative that the rebellion lose the support and complaisance that it currently benefits from," Debré insisted, "and that it feel abandoned and asphyxiated." The ambassadors' main tasks were to cut off all material aid to the GPRA, to deny it contact with friendly governments, and to use the press, radio, television, and official visits to Algeria to win over foreign opinion. After hearing each ambassador's report—on Swiss banks dealing with the GPRA, on Italian secret services' help against Sicilian arms traders, on Spain's support for French Algeria and "Christian civilization"—Debré concluded by calling on diplomats to show the same spirit of sacrifice demanded of all the French. "Let it be known everywhere," he ordered, "that the French people will judge foreign nations that claim to be its friends and allies on their attitudes toward the Algerian problem."[40] Later that month, embassies were instructed to hint that governments risked retaliation if they did not punish officials found to be aiding the GPRA, block or seize GPRA funds, forbid entry to its representatives, and ban "Free Algeria Committees" and propaganda.[41]

This campaign would be waged around the world, but as before the Americans were the principal objective. "They guide opinion making in a whole part of the world," Couve told the ambassadors, "and their influence at the UN is considerable. We must obtain a change of attitude."[42] The French had already fired a shot across the bow on March 6, when they officially announced the withdrawal of their Mediterranean fleet from the integrated NATO command.[43] While de Gaulle had long been critical of allied force integration, Ambassador Alphand said that "the basic cause of this had been the profound personal shock to General de Gaulle of the US abstention in the UN debate on Algeria."[44]

On April 28, Debré sent a stern message to Ambassador Houghton complaining about Yazid and Chanderli's activities in New York, Washington's failure to cooperate over the Moroccan bases and arms supplies, and American contacts with the GPRA in Tunis. "Will not all this soon separate us one from the other?" This "indulgence towards the rebellion is presently its best trump," Debré asserted, "and I confess that I do not understand this indulgence; it is moreover understood by none of your friends in France."[45] Three days later Debré told Christian Herter—who had succeeded the ailing Dulles as secretary of state—that France would not agree to accept nuclear stockpiles unless it received satisfaction on the tripartite proposal, issues relating to Algeria, and nuclear cooperation. In what participants described as an extremely unpleasant meeting, Herter emphasized the urgency of preparing nuclear warheads for American squadrons based in France in light of the danger of war over Berlin. He pointedly asked what connection there could possibly be between the three issues. "These matters were linked," Debré insisted. "He regretted past practices when France had never clearly expounded her view on the importance of the Mediterranean and Africa to France. . . . Algeria is as vital to France as anything in Europe.[46]

Of course, France's leaders had for years clearly expounded this view. Moreover, the strategy of isolating the Algerians was hardly new, only now it was being pursued with unprecedented urgency. Debré was "highly and continually exercised by the activities of the FLN in New York," his diplomatic advisor confided to one American official. The prime minister, for his part, seemed "to admit that de Gaulle is nearly psychopathic on the subject of Algeria," according to Herter. The Joint Chiefs deemed it prudent to begin planning how to shift U.S. forces out of France. For the moment, Paris's refusal to yield over the nuclear stockpiles forced General Norstad to withdraw nine American squadrons.[47]

Covert operations against FLN activities abroad also dramatically escalated. The struggle was particularly intense in West Germany, where the Algerians worked to raise funds and recruit comrades in the immigrant community, stage operations in the French metropole, and organize arms shipments to North Africa. SDECE, for its part, had arranged attacks on FLN agents and German arms traders as early as the fall of 1956. In September 1958, they even blew up a ship carrying dynamite for the FLN in Hamburg harbor. Two months later, unidentified assailants followed the GPRA's representative to Bonn to the very doorstep of the Tunisian embassy; he barely escaped with a wound to the neck. Both operations were attributed to French secret services. Indeed, the local burgermeister denied French vessels the right to enter the port of Hamburg.[48]

After the assassination attempt in Bonn, German Interior Ministry officials agreed to establish a permanent liaison with the French *Sûreté Nationale*.[49] The domestic security agencies under the *Sûreté* were bitter rivals of SDECE and its *Service Action* wing, which appears to have been responsible for the operations in Germany, so it is possible that the Germans hoped to play them off against each other or perhaps persuade all of the French services to be more discreet. But, six months after the Germans had agreed to exchange names of suspects with their French counterparts, *Service Action* blew up another arms trader in Frankfurt. The local press, and even the local prosecutor, again pointed to the French. But not only did the federal authorities turn a blind eye, they appear to have continued and even expanded their assistance to the French, especially in their surveillance of Algerian immigrants.[50]

Since October 1958, Germany had denied "French Muslims" the right to asylum and required that they pledge not to engage in political activities. Border guards distinguished them from other French citizens by their "name, origin, and physical appearance." In October 1959, the police began to fingerprint and photograph foreigners—"and, in fact, above all the Algerians," as a French official emphasized. Those who were considered particularly suspect were required to report regularly and were placed under surveillance.[51] The Germans undertook these discriminatory measures at the behest of their French counterparts, but at least no more ships were blown up in German harbors. Instead, SDECE now used delayed-action bombs to sink them on the high seas—three more by the end of 1959.[52]

SDECE was less discreet in its continuing attacks on GPRA officials in European capitals. In April 1959, the same month *Service Action* blew up the arms dealer in Frankfurt, it targeted the Algerian representative in Rome, Taïeb Boulahrouf. A stray soccer ball saved his life by prematurely detonating the bomb planted in his Peugeot, though it wounded seven bystanders—one of them losing an arm. The Italian interior minister himself armed Boulahrouf with a Beretta. Meanwhile, the GPRA's man in London was spirited out of his home to spend a week with a Labor MP and only later learned what befell his colleague in Rome.[53] It is impossible to know precisely what led the British to act, much less document French covert operations in every country. But their caution was warranted: one former SDECE official has revealed that in the following year alone *Service Action* destroyed two planes, sank six vessels, and assassinated 135 individuals in France and abroad.[54]

The French and the Algerians engaged in another shadowy struggle over the oil and gas of the Sahara. Ever since the first significant discoveries in 1956, the French feared that the Americans had designs on the area. After the arrest of Ben Bella and the other Algerian leaders, it was widely rumored that their papers included correspondence with U.S. oil companies. There was no truth to these charges, but Debré continued to allude to them more than two years later.[55] By that point, the French *Bureau de Recherches de Pétrole* conservatively estimated Algeria's proven crude oil reserves at about 3.5 billion barrels and American analysts forecast production of 500,000 per day by 1965. If the French retained control, it was hoped the Saharan fields would be enough for national self-sufficiency by 1980, an alluring prospect after the shock of the Suez embargo.[56]

In January 1959, the GPRA decided to warn foreigners against investing in Saharan oil without its consent.[57] According to reports reaching Debré, Yazid even intended to demand subsidies from U.S. oil companies for future concessions. Alphand therefore asked Dillon to relay the message that France would not honor contracts with companies in contact with the GPRA. At first Dillon demurred, but American officials did approach a number of U.S. corporations and chastised Yazid himself for threatening attacks on oil facilities. Ironically, at the same time, the *délégué général's* office in Algiers arranged for French oil and gas companies to pay protection money to the GPRA. Aside from the August 1958 attack *in France* on oil stored for delivery *to Algeria*, the rebels never disrupted the trans-Mediterranean oil trade.[58]

It is difficult to assess the net effect of these actions. Even without the French warnings, it appears unlikely that American companies would have cut deals with the GPRA for options on Saharan oil. Developing these fields required enormous capital outlays at a time when the market was already glutted. Indeed, in 1959 U.S. companies were concealing the extent of the reserves they already controlled in Libya to delay their development. Alphand thought that the Quai's excessive concern might actually have given the GPRA more clout. It had certainly antagonized the State Department and the oil companies, who were still smarting over the spurious accusations arising from the Ben Bella affair.[59]

As for the operations against arms traders, they were largely superfluous since little could be smuggled past the French border defenses. Moreover, "by exporting the struggle, extending the battlefield to other nations," Douglas Porch argues, "*Service Action* operations succeeded in making even France's allies eager to end the war." These operations in themselves did not, as Porch suggests, lead the allies to pressure Paris to settle—indeed, the most severely affected, the Germans, remained their staunchest supporters.[60] But by tolerating and even assisting such actions, Adenauer could compensate the French for their support on Berlin without having to compromise on more vital alliance issues, even if the chancellor was too skilled a statesman to link them explicitly.

Conversely, Algeria's evident importance to France encouraged less friendly states to turn the war to their advantage. Thus, in August 1959, Foreign Minister Andrei Gromyko delivered this warning to Couve during the Geneva conference on Berlin:

> If France continues to lend its support to Bonn's militaristic and vengeful policies, it is quite obvious that the USSR will not be able to maintain the attitude toward France that it has displayed in the past. The USSR's restraint in matters pertaining to Algeria may not have been properly noticed in France. The Soviet government could drop the restraint it has displayed so far.

While Couve rejected this approach, it made clear that the Soviets considered Algeria to be a source of weakness for France, one they would exploit for their own purposes.[61] Similarly, the next month Franco's foreign minister called on de Gaulle to end tolerance toward dissident Spanish emigrés as Madrid had already done vis-à-vis the Algerians. In fact, Debré had already clamped down on their rather harmless activities and authorized intelligence sharing. But now de Gaulle flatly refused. Either he was not informed or, what seems more likely, hated a quid pro quo that equated Spanish republicans with the GPRA.[62]

In this way, de Gaulle and his government were rediscovering all the dilemmas that had bedeviled the Fourth Republic. To ignore the GPRA and concentrate on the war within Algeria would allow it to develop diplomatic, military, and economic resources abroad with which to harry the French on every front. But to engage them in the international arena made the war even more of an international struggle, one in which France would have to deliver and receive blows and risk becoming vulnerable to its adversaries and dependent on its allies.

As Aït Ahmed anticipated, the contest over diplomatic recognition was particularly distracting to French diplomacy. Since September 1958, Lebanon and Mongolia had joined the group of states that recognized the GPRA. French spokespersons privately suggested that a largely Muslim or Arab country like Lebanon could not do otherwise. But, if *le général* was not unduly exercised by anything Ulan Bator said or did, he warned in April 1959 that Paris would sever ties with any "responsible" state that followed suit. Nevertheless, that summer Yugoslavia, Guinea, and Ghana accorded de facto recognition in the form of official visits by GPRA ministers. Paris temporarily recalled the French ambassador from Belgrade, which later denied that it had actually recognized the GPRA. The French had already broken all ties with Guinea after it refused to join the French Community. But nothing was done to Ghana, apparently extending French tolerance from the Arab and Muslim states to all Africa as well. Otherwise, in trying to isolate the GPRA, France risked isolating itself. In this way, the wall de Gaulle's warnings had erected around the Algerians crumbled as more nations were able to accord recognition to the GPRA with impunity. Instead of domesticating the Algerian question, French diplomats had increasingly to rub shoulders with representatives of a provisional Algerian government that appeared less provisional every day.[63]

Self-Determination

Even if de Gaulle would not accept "that Ghana dictates its policy to France," as he told the Australian foreign minister, he could not disregard the importance of diplomatic recognitions and U.N. votes to the Algerians.[64] On Bastille Day 1959, twenty-five Afro-Asian nations petitioned for the inscription of Algeria on the General Assembly's agenda. If it were to approve a resolution favorable to the rebels, this would constitute a "deadly encouragement to continue fighting," warned the new French representative, Armand Bérard. He therefore recommended that de Gaulle speak to Dag Hammarskjöld.[65] Despite his dislike of the secretary general, de Gaulle not only met him on July 31 but also "sketched a plan of action which would put Algeria 'in a state of self-determination,' " according to reports at the time. If so, Hammarskjöld was among the first to be informed of the initiative *le général* would launch in September in his most important address of the war.[66]

Debré had already "lost his self-assurance," as one of his aides reported.[67] If de Gaulle had intimated what he intended to do before the next General Assembly debate, that would help explain the almost desperate character of the diplomatic campaign the prime minister planned with Couve and his advisers on August 7. An earlier interministerial meeting had already determined that France would lobby each and every country with which it maintained relations. Now it was specified that, for instance, Georges Gorse would redouble efforts to win over Cambodia,

Debré would see the Norwegian secretary of state, Soustelle would go to Mexico, and André Malraux would tour South America. France would also warn Greece and Turkey about the implications of their votes for their applications to the EEC, support Austrian and Filipino candidates for U.N. posts, award honorary distinctions to friendly Latin Americans, consider concessions to Ireland over whiskey and lamb imports, and lobby Dublin's ambassador to the Holy See (where Joxe would already be appealing to his friend, the ambassador from Taipei). Virtually nothing was left untried, and even the smallest measures cost France diplomatic capital, depreciating its prestige and influence abroad.[68]

But the only way to ensure a favorable outcome at the United Nations was to address the substance of the issue, as the Americans constantly reminded their French counterparts, and American support would be more important than ever.[69] On August 12, de Gaulle asked each of his ministers to offer recommendations in a special cabinet session to be held two weeks later. According to Soustelle's account, when they reconvened Debré made it immediately apparent that he had altered his *Algérie française* position following discussions with de Gaulle. Thus, he criticized the policy—or knocked down the straw man, in Soustelle's view—positing an "absolute identification" between Algeria and the metropole. One could safeguard France's strategic, economic, and political interests only by "ensuring the democratic expression of Algeria," the prime minister argued, either by unilaterally determining a new status and putting it to a vote or by permitting the Algerian population to choose among different alternatives at a later date. Debré favored the second option, since France would then "have the right to obtain the support of its allies in the free world."[70]

While the ministers in this meeting offered a range of arguments for or against such an initiative, it is striking how the impending General Assembly debate framed the whole discussion. As the information minister, Roger Frey, summarized it: "[T]here was a choice to make between the Algerian policy and the international policy." De Gaulle would not have phrased it this way, since for him everything was related to France's international policy. But the relationship between France's position in Algeria and its position in the world was increasingly a zero-sum equation. De Gaulle did not say on which side he would come down, ending the meeting with this enigmatic statement: "Gentlemen, I thank you. In this category of affairs one must march or die. I choose to march. But this does not exclude [the possibility] that one may also die."[71]

It was thus with a hint of foreboding that *le général* then set off for Algeria to inform his top commanders of his intentions. Challe had made steady gains since beginning his offensive in February 1959. By July 1, the French estimated the number of ALN regulars at 13,300, down from over 23,000 in March 1958. Including auxiliaries, some 38,000 rebels now wielded fewer than 10,000 modern weapons—excluding hunting rifles and pistols—compared to almost 15,000 the year before. The military's renewed optimism under de Gaulle, and his insistence on rapid progress, may have biased these figures. But less easily manipulated statistics confirmed that Algerian morale was suffering: in the same period, the proportion of prisoners to killed rose from 27 percent to 42 percent, and there was a doubling in the monthly rate of rebels who voluntarily rallied to the French, totaling some 2,000 in the first eight months of 1959 (almost half bringing their weapons with them).[72]

No one claimed that Challe's campaign had achieved victory; it had not even begun to reach the eastern zones of the Constantinois and Nementchas Mountains. Even so, officials in Delouvrier's cabinet found that most Europeans and Muslims were pessimistic. They feared "we won't come out of it," according to a July 1959 report, "that the rebellion and the terrorism are hydras with a hundred heads." The rebels were able to reconstitute their political and military formations, and international opinion appeared more and more susceptible to their arguments. The Muslim population had not gone over to them, the authors maintained, but "the blood, plus the tears, plus the FLN (its existence, its dynamism, its organization, its conviction, its exploits) create the consciousness of 'the Algerian nation' and the ideal of independence." Under the circumstances, they concluded, political and economic reforms failed to resonate and military victories were never more than partial.[73]

It is difficult to read such reports without discounting the observation that most Muslims had not rallied to the FLN and crediting only the implication that there was no choice but to accept Algerian independence, the sooner the better. But by reading this history forward rather than backward the question becomes more complex, especially now that we have evidence from both sides. In truth, the GPRA was no less divided and weary than its adversaries. Far from "the small, dynamic team" imagined by Debré's advisors, the Algerian ministers were even less disposed to share information and coordinate their actions. President Ferhat Abbas found himself little more than a figurehead and offered to resign. But he reminded his colleagues that this would not resolve their problems, above all the French border defenses. The GPRA's inability to overcome them demoralized not only supporters within Algeria but also the frontier armies, creating disciplinary problems that culminated in bloody clashes with their Tunisian hosts.[74]

Some ministers suggested it would be necessary to reconsider the GPRA's whole political-military strategy. But it was difficult to imagine alternative arrangements for these troops, now numbering more than 9,000, since Morocco was even less cooperative. The Morice Line was therefore "the key problem of governmental authority and of victory," as Abbas put it, and while there was fanciful talk of submarines and air drops, the Algerians never did crack it. Their president simply urged them to hold on for another year or two in the hopes that France would give up. While he insisted that defeat was "unthinkable," it was no longer unspeakable.[75]

In fact, even the French commanders did not expect the GPRA to acknowledge defeat. The purpose of isolating and eradicating the insurgents was to attain the strongest possible position from which to negotiate a political settlement that would guarantee essential French interests. They were still making steady progress and all of the gains to date depended on the confidence of the Muslim population that the army would remain, especially the more than 100,000 now serving under its command, the harkis. If they came to suspect that the GPRA might prevail after all, it would be a nightmare for the French Army, not to mention the harkis themselves.[76]

So when de Gaulle announced before some one hundred officers at Challe's headquarters high up in the Kabylie that he had decided eventually to hold a referendum that would permit independence, his son-in-law, who held a high-level post at the time, was "a little stunned." The announcement was sure to arouse consternation among the top commanders and the pieds noirs. But de Gaulle was resolute: "The era of administration by Europeans is over," he declared. "All the peoples of the earth are in the process of liberating themselves . . . We must not, therefore, act in Algeria except for Algeria and with Algeria in such a way that the world understands it." Privately, he explained that he hoped "to defuse the debate at the UN at the end of September."[77]

After taking such a risk with his army, de Gaulle felt entitled to his ally's support. His final preparatory step was therefore to inform Eisenhower. In July, *le général* had vowed to Alphand that when the president visited he would say, "in the clearest way," what would happen if Eisenhower did not oblige him on Algeria: "This time it would not be just 200 planes carrying American atomic bombs which would have to leave French soil but General Norstad and the whole Alliance organization." At the end of August, he again vowed that, failing U.S. support at the United Nations, "they should expect to see France disassociate itself from the Alliance. This would then be the end of NATO."[78]

No such threat appears in the record of their September 2 meetings, according to which de Gaulle merely emphasized that, if the United States again abstained, this would be "a very serious matter, especially if it were to occur after the announcement of the new policy." Perhaps he was so confident that this policy would win Eisenhower's endorsement that any more explicit threat seemed unnecessary. Eisenhower pressed him to present this program at the United Nations, but de Gaulle demurred. Even so, he said that he would announce it two weeks later, which happened to coincide with the first day of the new General Assembly session. He also predicted that "it was so in conformity with the U.N. Charter, and with democratic processes, that we would not have difficulty in giving it support." Eisenhower promised only that he "would study it with the greatest of sympathy." In discussing their communiqués, de Gaulle insisted there be no "statement which appeared in principle to internationalize the Algerian situation. [Or make it appear that a later statement by de Gaulle on Algeria might be interpreted as resulting from negotiations carried on in his talks with President Eisenhower (Herter wrote at the bottom of the memorandum)]. This," de Gaulle added, "would make the world draw false conclusions . . . [It] should be clear there was no negotiation."[79]

But it is hardly clear that de Gaulle was unmoved by the constant American requests to offer a liberal political program for Algeria, much as his predecessors had anticipated American requirements in formulating their economic program. Would it be false to conclude that his acceptance of self-determination and the possibility of independence, the single most important policy change of the war, was at least partly the result of such indirect negotiations—not just with Eisenhower, but with the United Nations as a whole? At first, some actually dismissed the speech as intended only for foreign consumption.[80] According to Lacouture, de Gaulle's foremost biographer, Eisenhower's visit reinforced de Gaulle's original inclinations and the impending U.N. debate added a sense of urgency. But "nothing is farther from the spirit of Charles de Gaulle," he insists, "than to take a decision of national interest in order to please the Americans."[81]

This is true, but beside the point. Because if de Gaulle's government still believed that "what kept the FLN going was only the hope of inflicting a political defeat on France outside Algeria," as Debré told Herter that same month, then "pleasing" the Americans—and the United Nations—was *in* the "national interest," as unpleasant as that doubtless was to de Gaulle. It was from such episodes, one can surmise, that *le général* concluded that Algeria "undermines the position of France in the world," as he told Peyrefitte at the time. "As long as we are not relieved of it, we can do nothing in the world. This is a terrible burden. It is necessary to relinquish it."[82]

So on September 16, 1959, de Gaulle declared that, "[t]aking into account all the givens: Algerian, national and international, I consider it necessary that the principle of self-determination be proclaimed from today." No more than four years after the authorities had reestablished security—defined as less than two hundred deaths a year—Muslims would decide their own future in a referendum to which de Gaulle would invite "informants from the whole world." They would choose between 1) "secession"—and partition, as France would protect the pieds noirs, 2) "Francisation," another, less palatable way of saying integration, and 3) "government of the Algerians by the Algerians, supported by aid from France and in close union with it for the economy, education, defense, foreign relations." De Gaulle was obviously stacking the deck in favor of self-government rather than full sovereignty. Moreover, he still refused to negotiate with "ambitious ringleaders resolved to establish by force and by terror their totalitarian dictatorship"— merely renewing, rather incongruously, his offer of an honorable ceasefire. But, by conceding that Muslims had the right to choose independence, his September 1959 address marked the beginning of the end of *Algérie française*.[83]

French officials in Algiers immediately recognized the implications of de Gaulle's statement and the precarious position in which it placed them. "Without spectacular declarations, which would be embarrassing abroad, it is urgent to take a position," one of Delouvrier's adviser's pleaded. They had to let the pieds noirs know that de Gaulle was not unfavorable to "Francisation," however badly chosen the word. Muslims interpreted it as demanding de-islamization, he noted, but they were not his chief concern. "Paris has to understand that in Algiers one cannot go completely against the opinion of the Europeans and the Army without risking the worst chaos." As for the Muslims, "it's the FLN or ourselves who will make their 'self-determination.' "[84]

At the time the GPRA was in no position to take advantage of de Gaulle's offer. It was mired in a complex and protracted power struggle that pitted Krim against Boussouf and Bentobbal in commanding the ALN and these three against the rest of the leadership in directing the GPRA as a whole. It was therefore almost two weeks before Abbas delivered a reply. While recognizing de Gaulle's acceptance of the principle of self-determination, he declared that "free choice cannot be exercised under an army of occupation." Negotiations would therefore have to include the "conditions and guarantees of the application of self-determination."[85]

Nevertheless, in October Couve and Debré renewed the original offer of cease-fire negotiations, the foreign minister specifically naming the FLN.[86] While neither the GPRA nor de Gaulle's own civil and military representatives in Algeria found the self-determination proposal credible, it did put the rebels at a disadvantage in the run-up to the General Assembly vote. "They're leading us in tow," Krim complained.

> We do not have any initiative to influence public opinion. De Gaulle says that he is ready to receive us in France. . . . This will influence the UN. All the more so as we have said we were ready for talks. . . . We have to be united to negotiate. De Gaulle knows that we are not ready. That is why he drives us to the wall.[87]

Pressing his advantage, on November 10 de Gaulle himself invited the external leadership to discuss "the conditions of the end of hostilities. . . . no matter when, either in secret or publicly," with a guarantee that they could freely return. But at the same time he presented a battery of statistics showing how the army was prevailing on the ground.[88] The GPRA finally replied by naming the imprisoned leaders, now designated ministers of state, as its negotiating team. De Gaulle was not amused, but his rebuff did restore some sympathy for the Algerians in the international media—which, perhaps, was the point.[89]

"In the Algerian camp as in the camp of the French," Mohammed Harbi explains, "the internal situation still prevented dispensing with the double talk. Each one advanced by trying to neutralize his opposition"— and no one could afford to be too eager for a compromise peace.[90]

Though Foreign Minister Debaghine was about to be excluded from the leadership and probably had little influence in its deliberations, he offered an astute assessment of de Gaulle's policy from an Algerian perspective. After describing the international pressures playing on de Gaulle, he concluded that "France's position is not less difficult than ours."

> It suffices to make a chart of de Gaulle's statements since the "peace of the brave" offer until the declaration of November 10th, 1959 to realize that these statements are more and more positive, despite certain retreats from time to time intended to appease the colons and the French Army in Algeria. Nevertheless, de Gaulle is not unaware of our difficulties. The conclusion to draw is that de Gaulle is keeping to a certain schedule, that he is perhaps constrained in one way or another to make peace as quickly as possible, and that he is therefore called to make this peace by submitting to certain of our conditions.

Debaghine judged that they would be in a better position to conduct negotiations if they first secured the "diplomatic trump" of a U.N. resolution and persuaded the Arab states to threaten co-belligerence—not so much because of the material contribution they could make, but because it would "provoke a real fear of seeing the conflict spread to the whole Middle East," as in the Suez crisis. This would create "enormous pressure" on the French. The foreign minister recalled that de Gaulle had not spoken of self-determination except "after the pressure of the Western powers desirous of extinguishing the fire of the Algerian war, the persistence of which would of course compromise their interests in the Afro-Asian world."[91]

But despite de Gaulle's acceptance of self-determination, in December 1959 the Americans *still* abstained on a General Assembly resolution calling for negotiations between the two parties. Debaghine was exactly right about the reason for Eisenhower's reluctance. Indeed, it appears that de Gaulle had wasted his breath in trying to win U.S. support. On August 18, two weeks before he went to Paris, the president and his National Security Council discussed a Joint Chiefs of Staff proposal that they "get off the dime" and adopt a pro-French policy. Eisenhower dismissed the very idea: "How could we say that we support the French and still not damage our interests?

> The whole of our history, the President stated, is anti-colonial and the French action in Algeria is interpreted by the rest of the world as militant colonialism. To support the French would be to run counter to everything we have done in the past. . . . To stand up with the colonial powers would be to cut ourselves from our own moorings; it was an adventurous idea.

Lodge pointed out that Algeria "had become a symbol in the Arab countries and in the Muslim world as a whole." If the United States supported France, it would prove unpopular even in Scandinavia. While Eisenhower understood "why military men could take the position that NATO was more important than Algeria," he insisted that "you had to take account of all of the effects of your actions, and on this issue we had to continue to take a somewhat cagey position."[92]

Though the president did not explain this "cagey position," it appears to have precluded giving de Gaulle full and forthright support no matter what policy he proposed, as long as it was not immediately accepted by the Algerians. This was the preeminent anticolonial movement in a profoundly anti-colonial era. Even as the United States and France agreed about the shape of a settlement and the means to achieve it, Eisenhower sought to avoid being identified with the process. Thus, interpreting the proposed policy, he stated that "a solution 'in consonance with U.S. interests' meant that we should avoid the charge that we were one of the colonial powers." The solution itself was apparently secondary; it was avoiding the charge that mattered. And to Eisenhower it mattered a great deal. It was in this meeting that he warned that the "real menace here was the one and a half billion hungry people in the world."[93]

Eisenhower's reasoning shows how, as Bérard wrote in June 1959, "although increasingly well-established, the merits of our case on Algeria are less and less taken into consideration at the UN." It also helps explain why "the evolution of the situation in North Africa and that of our position at the UN are going in exactly opposite directions," as he observed later that summer.[94] Indeed, as the Morice line slowly strangled the insurgency, as the Challe plan drove it to exhaustion, as de Gaulle tried to kill it with kindness, the cause of Algerian independence took on a life of its own at the United Nations and around the world. And this, in turn, helped sustain loyalty to the GPRA within Algeria despite its internal divisions and the reversals suffered by the ALN. As inspectors from the *Institut des Hautes Etudes de Défense Nationale* discovered during a tour of Algeria in January 1960, "the successes, even relative, of the FLN in the international arena seem to have deeply affected Muslim opinion."[95]

The trend Bérard traced was not inexorable. In fact, the General Assembly resolution once again barely missed the required two-thirds majority. But after having achieved virtually the same result as in 1958 despite making a maximum effort and offering a settlement "so in conformity with the UN Charter," it was now clear that de Gaulle could not domesticate the Algerian question in the way that he had hoped. He would continue to fight for a "French solution," but by conceding that Muslims could opt out of the family he had begun a very different process of domestication, the process of dividing France and Algeria into two sovereign states. Now the Algerian question was whether *le général* could pursue the self-determination policy without provoking a military coup or even civil war. As a GPRA minister told a French journalist soon after the September speech: "From now on, his fate is linked to ours."[96]

V

The Domestication of the Algerian Question, 1960–1962

9

A Multicultural Peace?

Why not tell them, then, that it is not with joy in your heart that you have chosen these dramatic solutions, but that they have been imposed on you by implacable circumstances?

Learn that a statesman never says that solutions have been imposed on him. You should never say that you are beaten, because you are beaten if you say so. The solutions, you choose them, you decide them, they are not imposed on you.

de Gaulle interviewed by Pierre Laffont, November 1960 [1]

To envisage the possibility for the Europeans of grouping themselves in a separate union, in separate parties, in separate economic organizations, isn't this to crystallize the position of the communities? To group the minorities in an association, is this not to reinforce their opposition to the majority, to crystallize it?

So as not to crystallize the minorities, are you thinking then of doing away with them?

Exchange between Ahmed Francis and Bernard Tricot, June 1961 [2]

If the Algerian War was, in part, ideological combat, peacemaking required ideological disarmament. Since the Algerians never achieved military victory, a description of how the French cast off their intellectual weapons, like an army in retreat, provides the best measure of who was winning, and by how much. It also shows how the Algerians picked up some of these ideas and wielded them to assert control of the field—above all the principle of undivided and unfettered sovereignty. Others became part of the landscape, half-buried, awaiting another war.

Most of this chapter describes an episodic advance to the negotiating table, as de Gaulle's government and the GPRA fended off internal challenges when they were not fighting each other in Algeria and abroad. Yet it begins with this less familiar story of ideological peacemaking. While now all but forgotten, this period witnessed a flourishing of intellectual and institutional innovation among French officials. It culminated in their proposals for a *multicommunautaire* society at the Evian negotiations, in which both the European community in Algeria and the Algerian community in France would be guaranteed political representation. Perhaps the problem of domesticating the Algerian question, in the sense of dividing France from its former colony, was not amenable to half measures, measures that were patently one-sided when attempted in the eleventh hour. But they do allow us to glimpse how history might have happened differently, and imagine alternative futures for a country that too often seems typecast for tragedy.

French propaganda long portrayed the war as a struggle against pan-Islam and international communism. But as early as 1955, some official films and pamphlets implicitly conceded that Algerian nationalism had Algerian origins. Even so, it was treated as a symptom of social and economic dislocation that would fade as Algeria fully "modernized" and became better integrated with France. With the return of de Gaulle and propaganda films like *The Constantine Plan: Money, Men, Machines*, the FLN all but disappeared from the images France chose to project about Algeria. Instead of fighting Algerians, France was waging "a war against the underdevelopment of their land."[3]

Of course, this war against underdevelopment now appears no less aggressive than the campaigns waged against the ALN, even in these propagandistic portrayals. Thus, in *The Falling Veil*, another film aimed at American audiences, the narrator describes how de Gaulle appealed directly to women during his June 1958 visit to Algeria: "His confidence in the women acted almost as an electric current to many of them, a kind of psychological shock which jolted them out of their old attitude of apathy into a new awareness of themselves." Considering that electricity was the weapon of choice for French torturers, this metaphor could not have been more maladroit. But it reflected the belief that only France could summon Algerians to self-consciousness and endow them with agency—albeit agency guided by a heavy, steadying hand.[4]

If there is a villain in the piece, it is not specifically the FLN, which is not even mentioned, but rather "Many Moslems . . . who insist on total control and total obedience, whose wives are treated little better than chattel." In the scenes that follow, French women take their Algerian counterparts in hand to hat shops and post offices, enacting practices of modernity for their protégés to mimic. Similarly, French-educated children shepherd their parents into an apartment building to marvel at the sight of tap water, radio, and a lightbulb. This was more than a matter of propaganda. In addition to enrolling more girls in school, earlier discussed, de Gaulle's government issued a decree in 1959 prohibiting early or nonconsensual marriages. In this way, women and children were enlisted in the war against "underdevelopment", a war that imposed its own discipline, if not total obedience.[5]

This phase of French propaganda continued to portray Algeria as an extension of France. As the narrator intones in *Visages de l'Algérie*, it was only four hours from Paris and two hours from Marseilles, language that positioned Algeria on the periphery of a metropolitan center. Similarly, pioneers over four generations are credited with giving it the face of

France. But at the same time, they are said to share with the original inhabitants a common Mediterranean civilization, making Algeria "a bridge between Europe and North Africa," even if traffic along this bridge only travels from north to south.[6]

These images recalled some of de Gaulle's earliest public pronouncements about Algeria, like the October 1958 offer of a "peace of the brave," in which he predicted that France and North Africa would form "a friendship, for common progress."[7] Yet they also reflected his later portrayals of decolonization as a component of France's own modernization—and thus as part of its "great national ambition," as he declared in June 1960.[8] When he first described an independent Algerian government six months later, he presented it as part of the inexorable development of world history and French modernization:

> [T]he same conditions that press us to reform ourselves have unleashed, in the entire world, an immense evolution. Being a world power, France does not fail to be concerned with this upheaval, like the lighthouse struck by the wave. Before the passion for emancipation and progress that has seized peoples until now left behind by modern civilization, the liberating genius of France leads her to emancipate peoples who, until then, depended on her.

In this way, de Gaulle set Algeria in the context of "an immense evolution" in which only France retained conscious agency. Colonized peoples could be seized by passions and advance in waves, but only France and her "liberating genius" could give meaning to their movements by making them part of a larger modernization project.[9]

It was not until the final and most sophisticated phase of French propaganda, exemplified by the films of Carlos Vilardebo, that Muslims no longer appeared as fanatics, children, or people trailing behind progress, but rather as subjects of their own history. Thus, the narrator of *One Thousand New Villages* also invokes the idea of a common Mediterranean civilization. But rather than measuring its extent according to proximity to the metropole, he centers it on the sea itself. "All the ports in the Mediterranean resemble each other," he declares, all are open to the world. "The true frontier between the sea and the land is really beyond this coast. Whether in Algeria or Italy or Spain, there comes a place where the noise and the color gives way to aridity and silence. People of the land turn their back on the sea and to change." The film provocatively suggests that nothing might have changed if not for the war. Even when it displays scenes of destruction and the flight of refugees, the FLN is not blamed or even mentioned. And while it depicts some of the resettlement camps as harmonious, where men can go to their fields and "safeguard patriarchal authority," others are admitted to be sites of misery, where "phantoms of men" subsist on handouts.[10]

Finally, we see a new village with features said to be like Camargue and Provence. But like other new villages, dwellings are lined up in rows and meet at 90-degree angles, reflecting the kind of discipline authorities hoped to instill in their inhabitants. Even so, the narrator insists that "there is not one type of village *just as there is not one evolution but a number of evolutions.*" Then, amid scenes of happy children with flocks returning from the fields, we are told that "here is a village like all other Mediterranean villages."[11]

How can these seemingly contradictory ideas be reconciled? Vilardebo allows for "a number of evolutions" along different lines, but these evolutions take place within the same system. All these villages are alike because they are oriented toward a common Mediterranean civilization, which here stands in for modernization. Yet contrary to earlier propaganda, modernization can come about through war and the agency of the unnamed FLN. The film marginalizes only those who would categorically reject change—implicitly including racist colons—or brutally impose it without respecting cultural differences (though patriarchy is apparently the only one worth mentioning). It thus helps viewers imagine a multiethnic society simultaneously pursuing different kinds of progress.

Vilardebo presents this idea of multiple but interrelated evolutions even more subtly in *Bilan d'un Jour* through a series of linked images. The war is never mentioned and, as in earlier films, industrial and irrigation projects are prominently featured. But unlike, for example, *Des Pierres qui lient les hommes*, in which new apartment buildings play the starring role and overshadow their occupants, these images are all interspersed with those of individuals at work and play, segueing from a Coke bottle in a factory to the same bottle in a crowded bar, from neon lights advertising night clubs to the glassworker who crafts them. At a time when such gathering places were often bombed and the sight and sound of broken glass provided the texture of urban combat, Vilardebo's meaning could not have been more clear: these diverse lives are part of an intricate and fragile set of social, cultural, and economic relationships. Each person relies on the others not only for their prosperity and personal safety but for their very identity in a society differentiated by functional occupation rather than by greater or lesser degrees of development. And whereas films like *Visages de l'Algérie* had stridently insisted that diverse communities had to live in harmony, here they are not even mentioned. Instead, the same idea is enacted as a European shares a cigarette with a Muslim coworker:

> Thus all of Algeria is revealed as an immense construction site of iron, concrete, and stone, where each individual is multiplied by those who work . . . five hundred or a thousand kilometers away, and where each is seconded by someone who appears completely different to him. And all that leads, with the cement and the steel made here, to new homes where men on all the roads from Monday to Saturday get up to begin their work again.

Here then we have the official French vision of postwar Algeria, circa 1960. It is apparently independent but self-regulating and securely ensconced within a larger economic and cultural system. In this portrayal of a multiethnic society, war is scarcely imaginable—indeed, politics of any contentious kind apparently has no place. Instead, all that matters is the *bilan*, the bottom line: a balanced equation of production and consumption that is presented as the universal measure of every kind of progress.[12]

De Gaulle's imagery and the propaganda films they helped inspire illustrate the ways in which people were led to imagine an independent Algeria as part of a vision of progress that was above politics. Yet this was hardly an apolitical process, as indicated by de Gaulle's response to the pied noir interviewer quoted at the beginning of this chapter. It reflected a deliberate strategy to cover the retreat from Algeria. Indeed, this glowing vision was like celluloid wrapping around another, classified version of independent Algeria.

In the summer of 1960, the Paris-based Secretariat of State for Algerian Affairs created a "Working Group on the Future Structures of Algeria." Cloaked in secrecy, often declining to sign their work, officials here could be more explicit in repudiating long-standing shibboleths about *Algérie française*. Thus, one of their earliest and most remarkable studies, "Essai d'une discussion historique sur le problème algérien," begins by insisting, against all received wisdom, that "the Algerian problem is not an original problem." According to its author, the "artificiality" of Algerian nationalism, in the sense that it had been consciously created, could not be denied, but the same was true of such countries as Hungary, Croatia, and Greece. True, Algeria had been a French land for 130 years, but each of these countries and many others besides had lost their autonomy for much longer periods—including Bulgaria, Czechoslovakia, and Romania—and sometimes had to recover or even create national languages and myths. And they, too, had large national minorities, as the Europeans would be in an independent Algeria.[13]

Moreover, the author argued, the idea that social, economic, and political "integration" could disarm Algerian nationalism "hardly withstands analysis." Austria-Hungary went much farther than the French in elevating representatives of diverse groups to national office, to no avail. Nor could France create a middle class capable of managing a gradual evolution toward autonomy and multiparty democracy, as liberals hoped. "Without a doubt this is an illusion," the author insisted. "The Algerian state will have a single party. The question is whether this party will be totalitarian or not." Indeed, parliamentary democracy might not even be desirable, since it "is without question the political regime least capable of ensuring order in an Algeria that remains an underdeveloped and primitive country."

But did the GPRA not represent only a small minority? "This claim," the author asserted, "arises from a misunderstanding of the conditions in which revolutions are born." France, Russia, and many more examples were marshaled to show that, once crowned with success, a militant minority would quickly become a majority party. In any case, an election over self-determination would lead to the same result—or worse, since the transition would then be "a blunt fact" rather than organized through direct negotiations.

But would Algerian independence not be "a new step forward for international communism," the official view since the start of the war? Perhaps the French position was the correct one, the author allowed, but it was not shared by other anti-Communist powers. Precedents from the sixteenth through the nineteenth centuries showed that "the parceling out of the intermediate zone" was "the golden rule of European diplomacy," helping to limit the extent and intensity of systemic wars. Moreover, nationalism was not necessarily the precursor of communism, because new states tried to get the maximum from the two powers without depending on either. And experience had shown that countries were less vulnerable to subversion when independence was well planned and executed. By January 1962, the *Délégation Générale* would be reminding French army officers that few newly independent states had become Communist—indeed, no Western country repressed communists as ruthlessly as did Egypt and Iraq.[14]

If the FLN was not simply the stalking horse for international communism, what of the notion that it represented religious fanaticism, Nasser's "empire of Islam," to recall Mollet's phrase? Here again, the Working Group rejected the received wisdom. Their first report insisted that "the main force is a national aspiration and not religious faith. The key word which rouses the masses is not holy war, but rather independence." Similarly, a September 1961 report by the *Délégation Générale* denied that the rebellion represented a *jihad*. Indeed, it predicted that, given its "high degree of spirituality, its humanism," Islam would play "a stabilizing role and preserve this country from the dangers of atheistic materialism and from communism."[15]

But how could independence be real or lasting, the ghosts of French propagandists past might have asked, if Algeria did not continue to develop, and how could that occur if it did not remain integrated with the metropolitan economy? According to the Working Group, integration made stagnation more likely. "A local power emanating directly from the Algerian people," on the other hand, "would naturally be armed [with full powers] to decide the best development policy to follow," if necessary including "the most effective authoritarian methods."[16]

Yet no argument against retaining Algeria, no matter how clever or far-sighted, would make the slightest difference unless and until the French army could be brought to agree or at least acquiesce. Indeed, "Essai d'une discussion historique" frankly acknowledged fears that the return of the army and a sizable portion of the settler population would provoke a fatal crisis of the parliamentary republic. But the war itself, it countered, was what created the conditions for a coup. Algeria gave the army the confidence that it could govern, younger officers were increasingly isolated from society, and 1958 had given voice to *La Grande Muette*. Moreover, the integration policy would continue to provoke internal crises that created opportunities for intervention. The only solution, then, was to act boldly, the author concluded, since the dangers of delaying Algerian independence would only increase with time.[17]

From the Barricades to the Negotiating Table

As French officials had feared, the pieds noirs turned on de Gaulle and his government once he accepted the Algerians' right to independence. They responded with mounting fury to his peace overtures to the GPRA, which coincided with a resurgence of rebel attacks in Algiers. One of their representatives in the National Assembly, Pierre Lagaillarde, who had led the storming of the Government General building in May 1958, vowed that de Gaulle would face trial for his deeds. *Le général* himself belittled these *ultras* as hotheads. But they now had access to thousands of weapons, even armored vehicles, as members of the *Unités territoriales* (UT). While ultimately under army command, the settler militia were really controlled by the demagogue Jo Ortiz and his quasi-fascist *Front National Français*.[18]

Mindful of the earlier crisis, Delouvrier and his advisers were most concerned about the position the army would take in any showdown. They knew that Ortiz met frequently with Colonel Antoine Argoud, chief of staff for Massu's *corps d'Alger*, and Colonel Jean Gardes, who directed psychological warfare. Delouvrier hoped that they would dissuade him from any rash action. Instead, Argoud and Gardes, along with many other officers, openly sympathized with the pieds noirs' determination to oppose independence. When Delouvrier tried to explain to Argoud the importance of accepting self-determination in the fight for world opinion, the colonel derided these "history professor, intellectual" arguments. Argoud and Gardes considered *Algérie française* to be a front line in the defense of "the Christian West."[19]

General Massu, victor of the Battle of Algiers, was supposed to control the colonels and, by extension, the *ultras*.[20] But he had grown disaffected over the direction of de Gaulle's policy and, in particular, his unwillingness to defend the army. On January 5, *Le Monde* published excerpts from a secret Red Cross report that confirmed that many soldiers acted "in flagrant contradiction with elementary humanitarian principles" in their treatment of prisoners.[21] A week later, a judge in Rennes summoned one of Massu's officers to testify about the fate of Maurice Audin, and many more were thought to be implicated in his suspected death under torture. De Gaulle secretly issued strict new directives against torture to army commanders. But like Mollet before him, de Gaulle only succeeded in antagonizing them.[22]

Massu finally gave vent to his frustration in an interview for a West German magazine later that month. *"L'armée a la force,"* he boasted.

> It has not shown it until now because the opportunity has not presented itself, but it will intervene if the situation demands it. We no longer under-

stand the policy of President de Gaulle. The Army had not been able to foresee that he would pursue such a policy. Our greatest disappointment was to see General de Gaulle become a man of the left. . . . Perhaps the Army made a mistake.

On January 18, the interview was published in Munich and immediately picked up by international wire services.[23]

That same day, de Gaulle confirmed Massu's suspicions in a series of conversations with three deputies from Algeria. He confided his belief that, if a referendum was truly free and fair, only the areas around Oran and Algiers would choose to remain attached to France. It would then be necessary to regroup the population and partition Algeria. A Muslim deputy pointed out that the FLN had already struck at thirty of his relatives, exclaiming "We will suffer!" "Yes, you will suffer," De Gaulle coldly replied. As reports of this interview circulated in Algiers, word came that de Gaulle had relieved Massu of his command.[24]

Ortiz had been waiting for just such an opportunity to test the army's loyalty. He called a general strike for Sunday, January 24, and prepared to gather his forces near the war memorial, the traditional launching pad for pied noir insurrections. Lagaillarde, for his part, led a rival group to occupy the University of Algiers. Delouvrier and Challe counted on cordons of *parachutistes* to further divide and isolate the protesters. They did not realize that Gardes and Argoud had actually encouraged Ortiz to demonstrate in support of Massu. So when the UT began to rally to the Ortiz command post on rue Charles-Péguy, the paras simply stood aside and let them pass. Allowed to gather en masse and erect barricades, Ortiz's 1,500 heavily armed followers were ready when the gendarmes were finally sent in—but not before their officers, determined to avoid a bloodbath, ensured their weapons were unloaded. Consequently, the insurgents were able to aim volley after volley at their advancing ranks before the gendarmes could return fire. Altogether, 14 were killed and 123 wounded. The UT, for its part, counted 6 dead and 26 injured. All the while, the paras stood back from the battle, intervening only to stop the incensed crowds from finishing off even more wounded policemen.[25]

The pieds noirs' gamble had paid off: confronted with a pro-*Algérie française* uprising and direct orders to oppose it, the army refused to fire. Lacouture well describes the mood of that moment. After "the battle of 1957, the exuberance of 1958, the anguish of 1959 . . . [t]oo many things had been lived, suffered, and overcome together." The state was "distant, and cold, and negative" and could not command loyalty from soldiers who had become married to the passions of the pieds noirs—in some cases literally.[26] The commander of the Tenth Airborne Division made it clear that his men would not use force against the protesters—indeed, they openly fraternized with them. It was "a bad blow to France," de Gaulle declared. "A bad blow to France in Algeria. A bad blow to France in the world." When Debré himself flew to Algiers, Argoud demanded that de Gaulle repudiate the self-determination policy. If not, he warned that the president would be replaced by Challe or perhaps even a junta of like-minded colonels. Debré quickly returned to a capital rife with rumors of a military coup.[27]

Yet while this state of affairs was maddening to de Gaulle and his advisers, open insubordination did not spread beyond Algiers. As the days passed, the standoff there remained all the protesters had to show for their efforts. And, unlike May of 1958, they could not even pretend that the Muslims were with them—one miserable truckload of aged veterans hardly stayed long enough to have their pictures taken. Finally, on January 29, Delouvrier together with Challe and his staff withdrew from their Algiers command post to an air force base 30 kilometers away, concerned that their presence—and impotence—created the impression that they acquiesced in the insurrection. Before Delouvrier left, he made an emotional appeal to the protesters, calling directly on Ortiz and Lagaillarde to leave the barricades and join him at the war memorial to grieve Sunday's losses. After their fifth day on the street, Delouvrier's appeal—together with a cold, driving rain—sapped much of the insurgents' remaining enthusiasm. Moreover, now that the dissident colonels faced the choice of either following their superiors out of the city or remaining as renegades, they began to counsel the *ultras* to stand down.

De Gaulle himself delivered the coup de grace. "French of Algeria," he declared in a radio-television address, "how can you listen to the liars and conspirators who tell you that in according free choice to Algerians France and de Gaulle want to abandon you, to withdraw from Algeria and deliver it to the rebellion?" He brushed aside the "details" of "this or that French solution" until after the war, signaling that he had not foreordained independence. While mollifying the pieds noirs, de Gaulle, dressed in uniform, issued the army an uncompromising call to order:

> What would the French Army become if not an anarchic and ludicrous mess of military fiefdoms if some elements put conditions on their loyalty?. . . . To cede on this point [of self-determination] and in these conditions would burn the assets we still have in Algeria. This would also abase the state before this outrage and threat. From this blow France would become no more than a poor toy broken up on an ocean of adventures.[28]

After Challe allowed the insurgents to leave the barricades with military honors, the crisis finally ended. The Fifth Republic was shaken but intact. Those who had attacked it were driven from Algeria—Ortiz fleeing to exile in the Balearics, Lagaillarde and Gardes imprisoned—while those who were judged irresolute resigned or were removed from office, including Soustelle and, after a decent interval, Challe himself.

While injuring the cause of *Algérie française,* the crisis also delayed peace negotiations. Its timing was particularly unfortunate: Massu's interview appeared on the very day that the meeting of the CNRA ended and a new cabinet emerged. Abbas remained as president—actually little more than a spokesman—and Krim, Boussouf, and Bentobbal retained formal control of the ALN through an interministerial committee. Power had begun to shift to the army's chief of staff, Houari Boumedienne, but the new team still had ample authority to negotiate. Indeed, in the course of the crisis, Krim told a U.S. diplomat that if de Gaulle needed support the GPRA would mobilize against their "common enemy."[29]

After the denouement, Abbas addressed a letter to de Gaulle offering to dispatch negotiators to Paris.[30] De Gaulle did not respond directly. In effect, he gave his answer to his troops during another tour of Algeria, urging them to crush the Algerian *maquis*. If at one point he apparently spoke of "an Algerian Algeria linked to France," he also predicted that outright independence would bring only misery and necessitate partition. Most important, he indicated no inclination to negotiate the matter with the GPRA. De Gaulle had always been determined to establish dominance on the battlefield, but now it appeared all the more vital if he was to hold the army together. And if he was unready to consider political negotiations with the GPRA even before he confronted the threat of military revolt, every reaffirmation of this position made it more difficult to reverse course. The Algerians were only confirmed in their suspicion that the army and the settlers would not allow de Gaulle to negotiate independence, even if he wished to.[31]

The GPRA responded by implementing a dangerous new strategy, one that Debaghine began to devise in his last days as foreign minister. Noting that U.S. support for France weakened the moment it was rumored China might back the Algerians, he had proposed that they continue to escalate. De Gaulle's difficulties increasingly affected the West, and "the process is going to intensify."

> The Arab states will commit themselves further, and so too will the Afro-Asian countries. On the French side it will be necessary to involve the West even more. The radicalization of the war, with the co-belligerence of the Arab countries and the participation of Chinese volunteers, will lead in the end to a confrontation between the West and the East. . . . This will lead the West to put a stop to the war in Algeria. If not this would be world war.[32]

But Debaghine did not possess sufficient authority to attempt anything of the kind. Instead, Krim took charge of the Foreign Ministry and embarked on this bold new course. He began by establishing a political secretariat staffed with brilliant advisors like Mabrouk Belhocine and Mohamed Harbi, the latter heading up a section charged with obtaining support from socialist countries. At the same time, Krim disciplined representatives abroad for extravagance or pretending to the title of ambassador. Those he judged "useless and notoriously incompetent" were summarily dismissed and replaced with young intellectual militants.[33]

Krim confirmed the new strategy in one of the first documents he signed as foreign minister, "Our Foreign Policy and the Cold War." The Algerians would no longer present themselves as potential allies of the United States or limit themselves to threats to turn to "the East." While the goal remained the same—to exacerbate divisions in the West and thereby exert indirect pressure on Paris—they would pursue it through a policy of brinkmanship, confronting France's allies with actual and increasing Communist support.[34] Outside aid might help the military situation, but for Krim the main purpose was political. Thus, when he called for foreign volunteers, initially limited to the Arab and African states, there was no discussion of how they might actually be used. "The modalities of putting this into practice will be discussed and debated later," Krim explained in an internal note. "Right now what matters is to conduct a vigorous propaganda [campaign] around the principle of volunteering and above all to demonstrate, if the war continues, that de Gaulle alone will be responsible and world peace will be directly threatened." For Krim, African and Arab support were alike a "means of pressuring the East and the West."[35]

This propaganda campaign was aimed at arousing both Cold War and race war fears, as indicated by Debaghine's suggestion that Chinese intervention would incite an immediate response. Similarly, while Krim assured the American ambassador in Tunis that he "did not want to suggest that volunteers would be trained for race warfare in black Africa," it seems likely that he hoped to play on just this kind of concern. Westerners were particularly susceptible at a time when Belgian settlers were suffering attacks in the Congo.[36] Of course, the GPRA had to wield this threat with care, since it could not afford to alienate liberal opinion in France and abroad. So while Krim visited Peking and leaked rumors about enlisting Chinese volunteers, Abbas confided to a French reporter that this would be a "disaster for the whole world" and publicly pledged that the pieds noirs would not encounter discrimination in the new Algeria.[37]

This did not stop the French from exploiting Congolese atrocities and the "Yellow Peril" in their propaganda.[38] But those who were sympathetic to the Algerians' cause could be quite understanding about the need to threaten escalation. Even John F. Kennedy, that consummate cold warrior, privately suggested that Chinese intervention would serve "to force either a revision of the State Department's overall policy or an 'international' settlement of this war." His Algerian interlocutor concluded that the senator meant to encourage "the positive introduction of the communist factor"—as Kennedy had phrased it—by repeatedly emphasizing that it would force Washington to act.[39]

The GPRA's position on prisoners of war provides another example of the "flexible, multiform" nature of its diplomacy and propaganda, as an internal note put it, always using "the argument that seizes and holds the attention of the audience." At a conference of African peoples in Tunis in January 1960, Ahmed Boumendjel had aroused delegates by announcing that France, after a year and a half of reprieves, had just resumed guillotining Algerian prisoners. Boumendjel ominously warned of retaliation.[40] But rather than immediately executing French prisoners, as in 1958, the GPRA sent the Swiss government a formal instrument of accession to the Geneva Conventions. This move began to pay off when the Swiss circulated it to other parties to the conventions, albeit with the reservation that it did not recognize the GPRA.[41]

Thus, while the Algerians' international campaign appeared increasingly militant and focused on the armed struggle, its multiple and diverse elements remained interdependent and essentially political in purpose. Obtaining support from African and Arab states sought after by the superpowers was meant to impel the Communists to provide more active assistance. The threat of a wider war, in turn, would drive France and its allies to seek a way out. All the while, the GPRA availed itself of every opportunity to receive international recognition, profess sweet reason, and demonstrate an unwavering readiness to negotiate.

For their policy of brinkmanship to succeed, the Algerians had to show that continued fighting could indeed spark an international crisis, even a world war. Yet with the exception of China, the Communist states still showed scant interest. For instance, East Germany and Czechoslovakia provided arms for cash, but both refused to allow the opening of FLN offices.[42] The Soviet Union, of course, was the main objective; even the first trip to Beijing seemed most important to Ferhat Abbas for having "made free and open the road which leads to Moscow."

> In this regard let's not forget, let's never forget, that the [existence of the] USSR is the great good fortune of the colonized peoples in their fight for independence. Without her the United States would have lined up, as in 1918, on the side of the colonialist nations and would have abandoned the principles of the San Francisco Charter with the same ease as it abandoned Wilson's 14 points in 1918.[43]

But Abbas had to issue this reminder to his colleagues because the Soviets had so often disappointed them. During the trip to China, the GPRA delegation passed through Moscow without so much as a mention in the local press. Soviet ministers would only meet unofficially and withheld military aid or even de facto recognition.[44] Khrushchev had actually endorsed the French offer of self-determination, explaining to de Gaulle that "he hoped the French would remain in some form in Algeria because if they left the Americans would move in and that would be worse."[45]

In response, Krim sought to play the China card. During another visit to Peking in May 1960, he said that he "would have loved to see . . . the Soviet Union adopt very firm positions like those of the government of the People's Republic of China."[46] But Mao defended his ally, explaining that "the Soviet Union does not want France to fall completely into the American orbit. . . . The USSR exploits the contradictions existing between the Americans, the French, and the British."[47] While Krim failed in this attempt to exploit contradictions among the Communist powers, events had obviated the need. The day before, Khrushchev had given up on de Gaulle for supporting Eisenhower during the failed Paris summit—his host had professed to see no difference between U.S. U-2 overflights and Soviet satellites. Khrushchev condemned his "war against the Algerian people that has lasted five years and for which France needs American support." While Khrushchev, for his part, still hesitated to deliver military support to the GPRA, this marked the end of his efforts to encourage French independence by displaying moderation on Algeria.[48]

That same month, Chanderli privately warned an Agence France-Presse correspondent in New York that the ALN's need for arms and money could lead to new alliances, hinting at the danger of more direct East Bloc involvement. While acknowledging de Gaulle's difficulties with the army, he claimed that the GPRA could not go farther in their peace overtures "because we have our own difficulties." Certain of their units would not surrender their arms if they did not first discuss how self-determination was to be implemented. "Even if we are ready to return to the ranks after the end of hostilities," Chanderli insisted, "it's with us that you will have to talk." If they were included, "there is room in Algeria for everyone." They therefore waited "anxiously" for de Gaulle's next statement.[49]

If the GPRA was anxious—and Chanderli's suggestion that it might compete as just another party after a cease-fire was particularly significant—the reason was perhaps that the Algerians knew that some ALN commanders were actually eager to accept *le général*'s standing offer of a cease-fire and self-determination. Since March, his top aide for Algerian affairs, Bernard Tricot, had been engaged in secret talks with one of the six *wilaya* commanders in Algeria, Si Salah. French operations had decimated his forces operating around Algiers—not only in battle, but also through the skillful use of disinformation. Si Salah had tried and executed 386 of his own men, deluded into thinking they were disloyal.[50] Demoralized and desperately short of matériel, he and his top lieutenants now refused to follow a leadership in Tunis that could neither supply his men for war nor negotiate a compromise peace. They told Tricot that they were willing not only to turn in their weapons but also to persuade their comrades in other *Wilayat* to do the same.[51]

De Gaulle took their offer seriously, even agreeing personally to meet with them. In their surreal June 10 encounter in the Elysée Palace, Si Salah and his fellow mujahadeen repeated their long-standing request for a pause in the fighting in which to go to Kabylia and win over other commanders. All along they had been concerned to avoid accusations that they had betrayed their comrades—at one point they even wanted safe passage to consult with the imprisoned ministers and the GPRA itself. De Gaulle had ruled out these initiatives and now said that he wanted to make one last attempt to start cease-fire negotiations with the GPRA. If it rejected his offer, he would accept Si Salah's plan and together they would try for the broadest possible truce. But soon after de Gaulle ended their meeting with a salute, Si Salah began to have doubts. He feared that the GPRA would accept the offer only to buy time in which to reassert its authority.[52]

Four days later, de Gaulle delivered another radio-television address. While his tone was more conciliatory than ever before, he did not make any concrete concessions. His offer to negotiate "an honorable end to the fighting" was only a slight variation on his earlier assurance that cease-fire "conditions . . . would be honorable." And if his first public use of the words *Algérie algérienne* to describe the ultimate outcome implicitly ruled out "Francisation," in September 1959 few listeners had doubted that he favored a "government of the Algerians by the Algerians."[53]

Despite an uncertain welcome, the GPRA consented to send Boumendjel and Mohammed Benyahia to France on June 25, 1960, to prepare for negotiations. They met Secretary General for Algerian Affairs Roger Moris at the prefecture of Melun, a town outside of Paris. Moris was struck that his counterparts were most interested in an eventual meeting between Abbas and de Gaulle "as implicit recognition of the 'GPRA' that it could exploit on the diplomatic level."

> The goal in fact is political discussion at the highest level possible, and in conditions more favorable to the "GPRA" propaganda, in view of solving the problem as a whole. This explains [Boumendjel's] insistence on obtaining for the delegates the right to meet the press, ambassadors, and their friends in the metropole.[54]

De Gaulle was determined to deny the GPRA this recognition, so Moris refused their delegates contact with the press or anyone else. For five days, they were confined to the grounds of the prefecture, littered as it was with listening devices, until he peremptorily announced that the preparatory talks were over. If the main Algerian delegation arrived, this would mean they had accepted these working conditions and were ready to negotiate a cease-fire *tout court*.[55]

That same day, Delouvrier's director of political affairs, François Coulet, told the *Comité Central de l'Information* that officials in Paris anticipated a GPRA surrender. The *comité* handled the press and propaganda in Algiers, so Coulet counseled them not to brag that "they are beaten," though they could say it discreetly, but rather "they have understood." "The end of the Algerian conflict is the ineluctable result of current international events," Coulet asserted, "and more than any other sentiment it is this aspect of the question which has led to the response of the GPRA." They were to explain that the GPRA's Arab allies were divided and self-serving, China's support only discredited them, and the Western powers now backed France without reservations. "It is more and more apparent," he concluded, "that the President of the French Republic is the leader of the Free World."[56]

But before Delouvrier's public relations team could set to work "spinning" the GPRA's submission and crowning de Gaulle with laurels, the Algerians flatly rejected the French conditions. The negotiations were off, leading a disappointed press to blame Debré for sabotaging what they assumed was de Gaulle's plan to conclude a compromise peace. But, as Rédha Malek points out, *le général* had never promised to negotiate anything more than an end to the fighting. It was journalists like Jean Daniel and Jean-Jacques Servan-Schreiber who created the expectation that he would go much farther, pressuring the GPRA, which was already in a weak position, to accept his invitation. Yet de Gaulle and his prime minister paid the price for their misplaced optimism.[57] The French learned that they would have to better manage the media next time or else, as one official put it, be "blamed for the failure of the negotiations in the eyes of the Muslims, of French in the metropole and, *above all*, foreigners."[58]

"The Algerian Republic Will Exist One Day"

In the aftermath of the aborted talks at Melun, the ALN restored discipline in its ranks by executing Si Salah's lieutenants (Si Salah himself died in a firefight with the French on his way to face trial in Tunis). At the same time, Krim escalated his campaign to mobilize the anticolonial movement and win East Bloc backing. In August, he urged the GPRA to provide military aid to opposition parties in Cameroon and Senegal—independent but still allied with France—reasoning that insurgencies there would distract their adversaries.[59] In September, the GPRA pledged solidarity with Fidel Castro's revolution, declaring that Latin Americans were engaged in the same anti-imperialist struggle.[60] That same month, they also denounced the North Atlantic Treaty Organization as a "colonialist coalition," vowing that any further aid to France would be considered an act of aggression.[61]

Ironically, three days after the GPRA condemned NATO, France came under withering criticism at the North Atlantic Council. Algeria was not the main issue at the time. The British and the Germans were preoccupied with the possibility that de Gaulle's opposition to American leadership might lead to a U.S. withdrawal from Europe. Adenauer's closest adviser, Herbert Blankenhorn, went so far as to predict that French policy would eventually result in a deal between a newly nationalist Germany and the Soviets. But in the meeting itself, mounting opposition to de Gaulle's diplomacy was expressed through near-unanimous disapproval of his tripartite proposals and, in particular, his seeming hypocrisy over Algeria. When the French representative called for support at the United Nations, several delegates pointed out that Paris had never consulted the council over Algeria or even allowed it to be discussed.[62]

The increasing acrimony among France's allies did not bode well for the upcoming General Assembly session, especially since Khrushchev was about to embrace, quite literally, the Algerian cause in the person of Belkacem Krim. During the chairman's famous, shoe-pounding visit to New York, they held cordial conversations and a photo session at the Soviet estate in Glen Cove, Long Island. Khrushchev later confirmed that this constituted de facto recognition of the GPRA and pledged all possible aid.[63]

By this point, the Algerian office in New York had become a formidable operation, "making the best use of American public relations technology," as their French counterparts observed. In 1960, it distributed forty-six different brochures, most of them designed locally for targeted audiences. Chanderli appeared regularly on network radio and television programs while the French estimated that he and his colleagues had spoken to at least 150 different organizations. Ferhat Abbas, in particular, became "a star" after visits to Beijing and Moscow. *The New York Times* put him on the front page while CBS sent cameramen to Tunis for an hour-long television interview. Moreover, Arab and African delegations—especially those of Morocco, Tunisia, Ghana, and Guinea—seconded the Algerians. Thus, it was Accra's representative to the United Nations who rebutted Jacques Soustelle on NBC.[64]

Soustelle himself was acting independently to augment the considerable efforts of the French mission. That same year officials gave seventy-seven talks—compared to just ten in 1956—to audiences as large as 1500 people, including groups ranging from the Quakers to the American Jewish Congress as well as elite gatherings at the Council on Foreign Relations and Columbia University. Yet audiences now reacted with "polite incredulity" and sometimes open hostility to the argument that Algeria was an integral part of France. About half invited the Algerians to present the opposing view. Even more unnerving than the Algerians' habit of shadowing French propagandists when not striking out on their own was their collective élan:

> the [GPRA's] representatives, solidly implanted in the United Nations, received by three quarters of the delegations, displaying an absolute confidence in the future, present from now on an aspect of respectability which opens new doors for them and facilitates their action. Still expanding their contacts, multiplying the invitations, presenting themselves in every way as moderates.

Altogether, their efforts "had contributed in great part to counterbalance, on the overall political level, the weakening of the military capability and of the arsenal of the rebellion in Algeria itself."[65]

There was no chance that de Gaulle would actually allow the United Nations to play any direct role in Algeria. His contempt for the organization had only been reinforced by the Congo crisis. As in the past, the French opposed such a resolution for fear that a success at the United Nations would encourage the FLN to continue fighting in the hope of an international intervention.[66] Ironically, by this point the GPRA itself would have opposed such an intervention, since it too thought the Congo operation had discredited the United Nations. But as a GPRA delegation to Belgrade explained to Marshal Tito, "[W]e also knew, on the one hand, that General de Gaulle was frightened by the idea of an internationalization of the Algerian problem and that, on the other hand, our proposition would deepen the divisions that reign among France's allies." Similarly, Interior Minister Bentobbal judged that this kind of internationalization "does not exclude bilateral negotiation and may even provoke it." Thus, both Paris and the GPRA approached the debate as a chance to gain negotiating leverage and neither considered the United Nations capable of halting hostilities.[67]

Within Algeria itself, on the other hand, the international struggle impassioned both the pied noir and Muslim communities. In September, the delegate general's office found that it incited settlers against voices of moderation.[68] The threat posed by the United Nations was a key theme in the propaganda of the Union pour le Salut et le Renouveau de l'Algérie française and the new *Front d'Algérie française*, which claimed one million supporters by the fall of 1960. In one particularly striking poster, the USRAF represented the United Nations as a pair of massive hands ripping France from Algeria. "Foiled by Khrushchev, ridiculed by Nasser, the UN wants to take revenge on France," according to the legend, and "France says no."[69]

Conversely, broad segments of Muslim society now placed their hopes in the United Nations. In August 1960, a meeting of top French officials in Algiers determined that public opinion increasingly thought that only the United Nations could put an end to the conflict. The delegate general's monthly report for September agreed, observing "that the Muslims of Algeria today turn toward the UN as they recently still turned toward General de Gaulle." Similarly, on a visit to Algiers in October, Tricot found that Muslims were showing increasing interest in the activities of the GPRA abroad and the upcoming General Assembly debate. Indeed, Bentobbal urged them "not to place too much hope in the decisions of the UN so as not to be disappointed." But Muslims appeared not to listen. Indeed, they even placed hopes in the outcome of the American presidential election because of its potential impact in Algeria. Thus, a correspondent who visited an ALN camp high in the Atlas Mountains at the time was astonished to find grizzled mujahadeen asking what Kennedy's chances were against Nixon, doubtless recalling his 1957 speech calling for Algerian independence. On the night of the election, they huddled around campfires and listened to transistor radios as the returns came in, cheering whenever Kennedy pulled ahead, cursing when Nixon threatened to overtake him.[70]

So despite their bitterness over the previous year's debate, the French felt compelled to work with the Americans in coming up with a moderate text while continuing to pretend that they opposed any resolution.[71] The Algerians, for their part, seized on the opportunity to use the United States and Great Britain to exert pressure on de Gaulle. On October 24, Ferhat Abbas made the GPRA's first formal request for Chinese "volunteers," specifically ninety military instructors and advisors. At the same time Morocco's Crown Prince Hassan, before departing for an official visit to London, told the British ambassador that the Algerians had delivered a written request to admit them.[72]

Bourguiba despaired that "soon 'Chinese hordes' would trample across Tunisian soil," even while assuring Paris that he would stand in their way.[73] Hassan, on the other hand, warned Macmillan that he could delay their entry for two months, but no more. He urged progress toward peace talks before the U.N. General Assembly debated the question. Macmillan called it "a very dangerous" proposal and urged Hassan not to force the Western powers to choose between Paris and the GPRA.[74] Eisenhower asked his National Security Council "whether such intervention would not mean war." The council agreed that if Communist regulars managed to infiltrate Algeria the United States would be bound by the terms of the North Atlantic Treaty.[75]

In fact, Hassan and Krim cooked up this request for the express purpose of "putting pressure on Macmillan," as Krim noted at the time. "Result: Macmillan felt the pressure." He was equally pleased with Hassan's self-imposed deadline, "[w]hich leaves the Anglo-Americans two months to make their move and avoid letting Algeria become a theater of the Cold War."[76] They decided not to wait. While Hassan was still in London, the Foreign Office pressed de Gaulle to declare his peaceful intentions or risk defeat in the General Assembly debate.[77] Similarly, on November 3 Alphand conveyed a warning by Herter that the United States would not defend the French position without a declaration by de Gaulle reaffirming his readiness to negotiate.[78]

The very next day, de Gaulle made another radio-television address on Algeria—and took another big step toward accepting its independence. As in his June 1960 statement, he mentioned no particular pressure, only the inexorable development of world history and French modernization. While praising the "magnificent pacification effort," he acknowledged that it did "not resolve the fundamental problem." De Gaulle had therefore decided to follow a new path:

> This way leads, no longer to Algeria governed by the French metropole, but to an Algerian Algeria. This is to say an emancipated Algeria, an Algeria in which the Algerians themselves will decide their destiny, an Algeria where the responsibilities will be in the hands of the Algerians, an Algeria which, if the Algerians want it—and I think this is the case—will have its own government, its institutions, and its laws.

While he still refused to privilege the GPRA over other potential negotiating partners, he now specified that, provided it agreed to a cease-fire, it could participate in organizing the eventual referendum. Moreover, even while denigrating their claim to represent the Algerian republic, *le général* conceded that such a republic "will exist one day."[79]

In replying to Herter's letter three days later, Couve was at pains to show that his requests were coincidental with de Gaulle's statement and had not been the cause of it. Thus, while the original draft explained that "we have always said that no new initiative would be taken on the French side concerning Algeria before the end of the Assembly debate," he now struck out this sentence—it drew attention to how they appeared to have succumbed to American and British pressure. Instead, he wrote simply that "General de Gaulle thought, indeed, that the moment had come to define his position, not so much for the sake of the United Nations, as for French public opinion. What he has just said appears to me to be, to a great extent, in line with your concern."[80]

Perhaps it was a mere coincidence, though it was a particularly uncanny one. The same could be said for Herter's next communication, on November 15. The secretary welcomed de Gaulle's statement and Couve's elaboration on it. The foreign minister had described a four-step process: first a cease-fire, then negotiations with different constituencies in Algeria on a referendum, followed by the referendum itself, and finally the establishment of "new institutions." But Herter pointed out that "there was no reference to any early initiative for the execution of this program in the speech," and that "a more precise declaration of French intentions, particularly as to timing," would make it easier to ensure a moderate General Assembly resolution. After a cabinet meeting the very next day, it was announced that there would be a nationwide referendum on self-determination for Algeria.[81] A week later, it was specified that the referendum would take place in January. While it is impossible to prove that the Americans had driven de Gaulle to do it, the next day he lashed out at their "bad faith and the stupidity of their attitude towards us in the Maghreb. This is what [we] should have made them understand. But we're not doing that."[82]

Whether or not de Gaulle's hand had been forced, it was now obvious that he intended to let go of Algeria. This intention was reflected not only in his rhetoric but also in a reorganization of the lines of authority. When Delouvrier resigned in November 1960—having long since forfeited de Gaulle's confidence—his responsibilities were divided between a downgraded "Government-Delegate" in Algiers, Jean Morin, and a Paris-based secretary of state for Algerian affairs, Louis Joxe. It was Joxe who would oversee peace talks and postwar planning while reporting directly to the president.

As Joxe's office prepared for negotiations with the GPRA, the *ultras* began plotting in earnest—not just in Algeria and the metropole, but also in Spain. It had become their favored exile, harboring Ortiz, Lagaillarde, and Salan. Given the unhappy experience of French settlers in Tunisia and Morocco, which de Gaulle himself had implied were precedents, the idea of continued cooperation reassured no one. When Chaban-Delmas asked *le général* to calm the pieds noirs—"who suffer, mon Général"—de Gaulle rose from his chair and, in a "holy rage," shot back: ". . . and de Gaulle? Do you believe that he has been created and put in this world to let go of Algeria? You believe that he does not suffer, de Gaulle?"[83]

Nevertheless, in the weeks before the referendum, *le général* decided to go to Algeria one last time—Lacouture suspects partly out of a "suicidal temptation."[84] Indeed, in five days he faced four separate assassination plots and innumerable mobs of angry pieds noirs. But while this was fully expected, no one was prepared for the Muslims of Algiers and Oran to mount massive counterprotests—marching in their thousands down from the Casbah, waving homemade Algerian flags, chanting "long live the GPRA!" Though FLN cadres had been working quietly to reestablish their organization within the capital and hoped to demonstrate their support during the U.N. debate, the GPRA itself was surprised by the popular response. It was all the more shocking for rioting *Algérie française* activists, who were forced to wheel around and close ranks with the police. *Para* officers, for their part, scrapped plans for a coup under air force general Edmond Jouhaud and instead rushed to meet the onslaught. De Gaulle cut short his visit and returned to Paris. All told 112 Muslims and 8 Europeans were killed in the fighting.

Meanwhile, the demonstrations in Algiers led France's supporters in New York to waver. Once-moderate delegations like India's attacked de Gaulle's policies—Nehru claimed that the French had killed thousands of protesters. Even normally friendly representatives from Francophone African states like Mali and Togo defected.[85] While the paragraph calling for an internationally supervised referendum failed by a single vote, a majority of 63 to 8 demanded effective guarantees for the application of self-determination on the basis of Algeria's territorial integrity, thereby denouncing the French threat of partition, and insisted on the responsibility of the United Nations to contribute to its success. As a French army report noted, "Nearly all of the nations of the world have thus proved their will to see an end to the Algerian conflict, if need be through a foreign intervention."[86] Once again, Algerians had paid a heavy price for a diplomatic victory. Yet perhaps the most significant casualties of this second Battle of Algiers were three political myths, as *The New Yorker's* Paris correspondent, Janet Flanner, wrote at the time: the myth that Algeria was French, that only a handful of rebels wanted independence, and that de Gaulle alone could impose peace.[87]

On January 8, 1961, three-quarters of voters in the metropole approved a referendum on self-determination that gave de Gaulle a mandate to end the war on the best terms obtainable. In Algeria, 42 percent honored a GPRA boycott, 39 percent voted "yes," and 18 percent "no." The results showed that even when the pro-independence Communists were included only a small minority in the metropole opposed de Gaulle's Algeria policy. And even with the inevitable army vote-rigging, at least a plurality of Algerians were either openly obeying the FLN or had sunk into passivity. Later that month, de Gaulle confided to Macmillan that the purpose of the referendum had been "to make a national decision to abandon Algeria. This he has achieved."[88]

The Putsch

Even if de Gaulle and most of his compatriots had resigned themselves to abandoning Algeria, the officials charged with preparing for political negotiations with the GPRA could not admit, even to themselves, that they were ready to abandon the pieds noirs. Indeed, de Gaulle himself had described them as "children of France" in a December 20 speech, promising that all the communities of Algeria would have "appropriate guarantees." Even so, we have already seen how the Working Group was skeptical about prospects for liberal democracy in postwar Algeria. "There is little doubt," their second report stated in January 1961, "that Algeria of the future, like most young African states, will be socialist in its economic structure and totalitarian in its political structure." It was only in a footnote, and seemingly as an afterthought, that the authors suggested that these structures might be subject "to corrections linked to an organization based on the statutory coexistence of communities."[89]

These officials could not even begin to secure real protections for the pied noir community until they confronted the contradictions and trade-offs in their own position. Thus, they had long refused to negotiate with any single, unelected group. Yet, if they allowed a referendum that endorsed independence, they would lose much of their leverage without having obtained any guarantees for the settlers and other French interests, such as the Sahara and military bases. As one Algerian negotiator, Rédha Malek, later exclaimed: "France's concern is to obtain these guarantees from the future leaders of Algeria, in other words from the GPRA, even while denying its existence!"[90]

Once de Gaulle had consented to negotiate with the GPRA, his officials had to determine what guarantees would be most effective. It seemed obvious that the pieds noirs should be full and equal citizens of the new state—indeed, more than equal, since they would expect special judiciary procedures, separate schools, and guaranteed representation in government. Yet, at the same time, de Gaulle's negotiators would insist on their retaining French citizenship, fearing that its prospective loss would start a panic. As one of these officials admitted: "The natural tendency is to pile up the guarantees in the hope of doing good. This is partly an illusion, because certain factors can cancel each other out."[91] After all, how could Algerians be expected to accept the pieds noirs as compatriots if they demanded a privileged status while keeping one foot in France?

The last major dilemma for French negotiators, one that would haunt them long after the Evian settlement, was in deciding what priority to accord the welfare of their fellow citizens versus other national interests. These included massive investments in the Sahara in hydrocarbons and nuclear testing facilities—France's first atomic bomb was detonated in Reggane in February 1960. There were also scores of military installations, including the huge naval base at Mers el-Kebir. In addition, there were the more intangible but no less valued aspects of *grandeur*, like influence in Algeria's educational system. Some of these interests were interdependent. The continued presence of French troops and teachers, for instance, would serve to reassure the pieds noirs. But negotiators could not avoid wrenching choices, since concessions in some areas—such as economic cooperation, where the GPRA had long signaled flexibility—might only be secured at the expense of the pieds noirs.

French officials' straightforward if unrealistic answer to these zero-sum equations was to resolve them all at the expense of Algerian sovereignty. According to the early planning of the Working Group, the sovereignty of the new state would be limited in its constitutional structures—to secure permanent guarantees for the pieds noirs—and in its territorial extent, as the new state would include only the coastal *départements*. Many officials, and de Gaulle himself, realized that the GPRA might be either unwilling or unable to make such far-reaching concessions. The leader of the Working Group, Gilles Warnier de Wailly, even suggested that Paris pursue such a settlement through international rather than bilateral negotiations, involving members of the European Economic Community as well as Francophone African states.[92] Many more hoped that the newly independent states that bordered the Sahara would support French plans for international cooperation rather than see all of it go to the Algerians. Tunisia, for instance, favored joint exploration and development of the oil-rich region below its southern border. Yet de Wailly was the only one who went on record in favor of inviting outsiders into the negotiations. The habit of regarding Algeria as an internal affair was too ingrained and, after six years of war and countless peace initiatives, it was obvious that only bilateral talks stood any chance of quickly ending the fighting.[93]

In February 1961, the two sides finally renewed direct contacts through the good offices of a discrete Swiss diplomat, Olivier Long. Georges Pompidou, de Gaulle's former cabinet director and future prime minister, would be assisted by a top official from the Algeria ministry, Bruno de Leusse. They easily agreed with Boumendjel and Boulahrouf, the GPRA's representatives, that they needed no other intermediary—the press had been speculating that Bourguiba might play this role after he met with de Gaulle that month. But on virtually every other point, their exploratory talks revealed profound differences. At the first meeting in the Hotel Schweitzer in Lucerne, Pompidou set the tone by insisting that France had the situation in hand and that Algeria was no Indochina. He particularly emphasized the strength of their international position: Paris had loyal allies, aid promised to the FLN was "either verbal or too dangerous," and the USSR was not about to go to war for Algeria. "De Gaulle is not afraid of Khrushchev's threats or anyone else's," Pompidou declared. "In no case will he cede to the UN." While he assured his interlocutors that France did not fear Algerian independence, it required a halt to the fighting before talks with all tendencies—not just the GPRA—about the conditions of self-determination.[94]

"If you have the situation in hand," Boumendjel countered, "why did you not conclude this on the ground? In fact, your methods have not succeeded. The proof is that we are here, the both of us, forced to negotiate." The Algerians refused to budge on the question of a cease-fire, because they feared that they would be unable to restart the insurgency if the exhausted mujahadeen laid down their arms.[95] Meeting on March 1 in Rabat with Bourguiba and Hassan II, who had just succeeded his father, they threatened once again to turn to the Soviets and Chinese if the talks failed. Indeed, within a month, a GPRA mission would return from Eastern Europe with the promise of massive aid, including 200,000 grenades, 8,000 rifles, and over 100 artillery pieces from Czechoslovakia.[96]

Finally, on March 8, de Leusse read a communiqué from de Gaulle in which *le général* insisted that talks start without either side imposing preconditions. Dropping the demand for a truce appeared to clear the way for the first public, high-level negotiations between Paris and the GPRA. It also revealed de Gaulle's modus operandi: while continually forced to concede substantive points, he would never stop striving to shape perceptions—in this case, by pretending his concession was a command from on high.[97]

Nevertheless, there would be one precondition to which France would be forced to accede. On March 30, a week before negotiations were to begin in Evian, Louis Joxe declared that he would consult with both the FLN and Messali's MNA. The Algerians had agreed that the French could talk with whomever they wished—they could hardly do otherwise—but they would not accept even the hint of a roundtable negotiation, least of all with the moribund MNA. They answered by immediately calling off the talks.[98]

The mere announcement of political negotiations with the GPRA, something de Gaulle had long deemed unthinkable, had already tipped the political balance within the French military to the point of insurrection. Salan, Jouhaud, and Marie-André Zeller, former chief of staff of ground forces, had long been ready, perhaps even overripe, and their civilian counterparts in Paris had gone so far as to designate a shadow cabinet in the event of de Gaulle's "unexpected" departure. But Jouhaud's abortive plot in December had shown that they needed a leader who commanded respect throughout the ranks.[99]

Challe was the obvious choice. Already deeply disaffected after the Si Salah affair, he was now outraged to learn that de Gaulle intended to call a unilateral halt to offensive military operations at the outset of peace negotiations, squandering his hard-fought gains on the ground. It also betrayed Challe's personal commitment to those Muslims who had placed their faith in France.[100] Yet before committing himself to a coup, Challe wanted to hear de Gaulle's reaction to the GPRA's rebuff. In a press conference on April 11, *le général* reacted not with outrage, but disdain, asserting that ". . . Algeria costs us, to say the least, more than it brings us." De Gaulle therefore contemplated its independence, sovereign within and without, "with the greatest sangfroid." But would not an independent Algeria become a cockpit of the United States and U.S.S.R.? one reporter asked. "I wish them lots of luck." De Gaulle's quip was funny but unforgivable to all the officers haunted by the specter of a Soviet base at Mers el-Kebir. It was what finally convinced Challe to cast his lot with the conspirators.[101]

Near midnight on April 20, a military transport slipped below air defense radar and landed safely in Algiers. With the clandestine arrival of Generals Challe and Zeller, joining Jouhaud, the long-awaited uprising to save *Algérie française* had begun. Directed by a network of loyal officers and spearheaded by elite troops like the First Airborne Foreign Legion regiment, the putsch rapidly succeeded in seizing key points around the capital and detaining Morin and Fernand Gambiez, de Gaulle's top civil and military representatives. With the broadcast of Challe's proclamation and his vow "to hold Algeria, so that our dead will not have died for nothing," pieds noirs spilled into the streets to cheer the army and, it seemed, their salvation.

But even before he made this promise, Challe knew his coup was unraveling. One after another, key participants were found to be absent or hesitant. Even the top commanders had difficulty maintaining their cohesion, much less presenting a compelling vision of how they could keep Algeria French. Salan did not even arrive until April 23, though his Spanish keepers presented scant obstacle. Lagaillard remained in Madrid, symptomatic of how pieds noirs were left on the sidelines. This is all the more remarkable considering that Challe's whole plan was predicated on mobilizing local reserves for an all-out, three-month campaign to crush the ALN and present Paris with a pacified Algeria. It was not until the first day of the coup that Zeller discovered that there were only enough supplies on hand to last a fortnight. Even if they had been better provisioned how, one might ask, could they have accomplished in one campaigning season what all the force of France had failed to do in six and one-half years?[102]

Most coup participants, especially the less cautious colonels and captains, recognized that they could do nothing without first removing de Gaulle. In fact, co-conspirators in the metropole had prepared a move on Paris. But the quick-thinking interior minister, Roger Frey, arrested the general who was to command them. Nevertheless, on the morning of April 23, Parisians were presented with the alarming spectacle of armored vehicles in front of the National Assembly—alarming as much because they were deemed necessary as because the government could muster nothing more than World War II–vintage Sherman tanks. Later that evening, volunteers were issued uniforms and helmets in anticipation of an attack on the capital. If the coup could never have succeeded as originally planned, it could easily have plunged France into civil war.

De Gaulle would again have to act as the shield of the republic. Appearing once more in uniform, he rallied support in another brilliant radio-television address. Recalling the work of the previous three years "to remake the state, to maintain our national unity, to reconstitute our power, to restore our rank abroad," he bemoaned the fact that all of it had been jeopardized by an "odious and stupid adventure." Belittling the retired generals who appeared to command, de Gaulle instead blamed "fanatical" officers like Argoud—fanatics who, it was rumored, were supported from abroad.[103]

Some of the insurgents had indeed sought foreign backing. Considering the state of their supplies and the navy's staunch loyalty to de Gaulle, they could not hope to survive otherwise. But according to Yves Courrière, even South Africa told them they had first to hold for at least a week.[104] If there was any chance of more immediate assistance, it would have to come from the United States or Spain, which were also the subjects of the most persistent rumors. It was thought that Washington would welcome a change of leadership in Paris while Franco would support anyone who would prevent the GPRA from offering the Soviets a base in the Western Mediterranean. Ironically, the two countries who were thought to be scheming against *Algérie française* for the first half of the war were now, in its final year, regarded as its natural allies.[105]

While it is always possible that rogue CIA operatives and Falangists encouraged the plotters, who were only too ready to be encouraged, even the slightest familiarity with American and Spanish foreign policy should have dispelled any illusions that either state would actually supply an uprising against de Gaulle. The Kennedy administration viewed him as the only French leader who might survive Algeria's independence and avert a civil war, something that was all the more worrisome when another showdown over Berlin loomed. As for Madrid, de Gaulle had lately supported its bid for NATO membership and cracked down on republican exiles. Franco's tolerance for asylum seekers like Salan constituted leverage to extract even tighter controls on the loyalists in France, nothing more. In both countries, official spokespersons, the press, and public opinion gave de Gaulle their unequivocal support.[106] The real significance of these rumors of outside backing was the way they served to discredit partisans of *Algérie française* and cast them out of the nation, much as the FLN had been marginalized years before.

But the most effective line in de Gaulle's speech was his call on draftees, many of whom were listening on the ubiquitous transistor radios, to disobey the orders of the insurgents. Minister of Public Works Robert Buron, trapped in Algiers during the coup, later remarked that "the transistor decided the outcome of the conflict. The man in the street in France and the young draftee in Algeria reacted in unison."[107] Indeed, as the metropole showed its defiance through massive demonstrations, signs began to sprout across Algeria proclaiming the solidarity of regular army units. Challe had already shown himself unwilling to risk any real combat between French soldiers. By Tuesday, April 24, virtually every transport plane had slipped out of Algeria, and with them any chance of striking at Paris. That morning Challe decided to join them, flying back to Paris and what he assumed would be a firing squad. Ten days later, Zeller also gave himself up. Jouhaud and Salan, on the other hand, changed out of their uniforms and resolved to continue the fight by other means. They would assume command of the last hope of the pied noir *ultras*, the *Organization Armée Secrète* (OAS).

"The Integrity of the National Territory and the Unity of the Algerian People . . ."

Among the Algerians were a few harried officials who actually welcomed the flap over the MNA and the putsch that followed—it gave them more time to prepare for the negotiations. Whereas the French had been assembling their dossier for many months, the Algerians did not begin to plan their positions until eight days before the first meeting was to have taken place at Evian. The much smaller corps of qualified officials already had its hands full directing a global struggle without preparing for negotiations that might never take place—especially if the GPRA did not keep up the pressure. In particular, Boumedienne's frontier army had launched a series of artillery strikes and almost suicidal attacks on the Morice line. With little hope of breaking through, they intended to inflict casualties on French forces and divert them from operations in the interior. Acting as if peace were imminent might discourage troops from undertaking such sacrifices. Indeed, Boumedienne argued that the GPRA should not even begin to negotiate until it could present a more united front.[108]

With internecine infighting continuing to plague the Algerian leadership, no high-ranking official wanted to risk an accusation of complacency. So it is not surprising that the commission preparing for negotiations under Ahmed Francis—GPRA finance minister and a reputed liberal—advocated a hard line on all key issues, beginning with an outright rejection of French demands for a cease-fire. And while suggesting that negotiators might be flexible over economic cooperation in the Sahara, its report argued for remaining "intractable" over the principle of political sovereignty. Similarly, the commission recommended rejecting any territorial enclave at Mers el-Kebir and the very idea of a common defense, instead demanding a timetable for troop withdrawals. As for the pieds noirs, it opposed any measures that might "bring about the crystallization of any minority whatsoever." Yet it would also deny settlers the right to participate in the referendum on independence, at least as a negotiating tactic, which might indeed have frozen their status as a minority. Like their French counterparts, the Algerians sought "to pile up the guarantees" even when they appeared to cancel each other out. And they were no more inclined to see the referendum as the source of their independence and sovereignty. Instead, it was "a permanent weapon" that they would use "each time that the substantive discussion risks turning against us."[109]

Armed with these instructions, the Algerian delegation left Tunis on May 18 and took up residence at the Bois d'Avault, a Swiss château belonging to the emir of Qatar. While more luxurious than the French quarters at the Hôtel du Parc in Evian, both sides were prisoners of their own security. Indeed, journalists found the electrified barbed wire fences and trigger-happy Swiss machine gunners so intimidating that they took to approaching the château under a white flag of truce.[110] Yet with the OAS murdering Muslims daily in Algeria, hoping to touch off an all-out civil war that might obviate negotiations, everyone had to take precautions. The GPRA representatives had the added worry of protecting themselves against French espionage. Just as at Melun, SDECE planned to infiltrate the delegation in every imaginable way, from electronic eavesdropping devices to agents acting as chauffeurs and maîtres d'hôtel.[111]

Two days later, when they arrived by helicopter in Evian and finally came face to face with the French delegation, the Algerians had even more cause for concern. Arrayed before them was a phalanx of veteran diplomats and technical experts who had been preparing many months for this moment. Their leader, Louis Joxe, might have been preparing all his life. Trained as a historian, Joxe chose to make his career as a diplomat, serving as ambassador to Bonn and Moscow before becoming secretary-general at the Quai d'Orsay. A seasoned negotiator, Joxe was also a man of some courage. As secretary-general of the *Comité de la Libération Nationale*, he had led missions into occupied France and only the month before had flown to Algeria to rally resistance against the generals' putsch. Krim's education, by contrast, came in the Italian campaign, a decade leading insurgents in the Kabylie, and four years of infighting and diplomacy in exile. His hard-won political skills would be well tested at Evian and back in Tunis, where he would have to defend any agreement against the inevitable criticisms of Boumedienne, his arch-rival.

After they were introduced, performing slight bows instead of the handshakes that neither side was yet willing to make, Joxe seized the opportunity to set the agenda. "The page must be turned," he began. The talks had two objectives: to establish the peace and to study the principles upon which a new Algeria could be founded. The government had decided to discuss these questions with all tendencies and, "from today, in particular, with those whom we fight." They would present the population with three choices, though Joxe quickly set aside the now irrelevant idea of "Francisation." France would have no problem with an Algerian state "sovereign within and without," but it could come about in only one of two ways, secession or association. "France would accept that the two states have no special relationship," he asserted. "She would devote to her own development resources in men and money that she presently gives to Algeria." Immigrants would receive no preferential treatment and the state would carry out a partition to protect those who wished to remain French along with all its other national interests.[112]

"France would accept this solution," Joxe emphasized, "but does not wish it." Indeed, it asked for nothing. But if the Algerians themselves so desired it, they might instead negotiate a continuing association in the economy, culture, and defense, contingent on popular approval. Such an association would have to include an "organic statute" that safeguarded the different communities and a delimitation of the military bases where France would remain sovereign. Joxe then announced that the government was suspending offensive military operations and freeing 6,000 detainees. While Ben Bella and his cellmates would remain in custody, they would be moved to more comfortable lodgings where they could receive visitors and communicate with the GPRA.[113]

Krim's statement would be even briefer and simpler and would have surprised no one who had read the FLN's proclamation more than six years before. The problem they confronted, Krim began, was "total decolonization," the "disappearance of an outmoded system and the accession of our people to independence." They had agreed to proceed through self-determination but only if it came with real guarantees and without "unrealistic" clauses that would rob Algerian sovereignty of its substance. Rather than offering the French any choice, Krim insisted on two principles: "the integrity of the national territory and the unity of the Algerian people." If they were respected, then "all men of good will, without any distinction based on race or religion, will have their place" in an independent Algeria.[114]

Krim offered no concession in answer to Joxe's announcement of a unilateral cease-fire. Indeed, he demanded that the five Algerian captives be allowed to participate in the negotiations. Joxe refused, and it soon became apparent that they would remain in custody as long as the ALN continued to pursue military operations. With the introductory meeting at an end, the Algerians rushed through lunch and waited impatiently to board the helicopters back to Switzerland. In Geneva, some three hundred and fifty journalists awaited their spokesman, Rédha Malek, and the GPRA's reaction. After describing the day's discussion, he read a communiqué from Tunis denouncing the French cease-fire as "pure propaganda."[115]

Propaganda or not, the cease-fire initiative along with Joxe's "take it or leave it" opening position were difficult to answer. So in their very next meeting on May 23, Krim resorted to the ultimate "weapon" recommended by the Francis commission. Since both sides accepted the principle of self determination, he began, they had only to decide the territory and the population to which it would apply. The GPRA had "a fundamental position": it must apply to all of Algeria, the Sahara included. Moreover, "[s]elf determination ought to apply to a single entity: the Algerian people, who decide by majority, the minority having to accept the verdict of the Algerian people. . . . [T]here cannot be," Krim insisted, "any grouping there which creates artificial and non-viable entities." Any such arrangement would assume that "the new Algerian state could not defend the rights of French nationals." There was but one question to put to the Algerian people: "Does Algeria want to constitute an independent state, sovereign both internally and externally? Yes or no."[116]

Taking this position so early in their discussions indicated that the Algerians already felt themselves to be on the defensive. But it was a position that was certainly easy to defend, perhaps impregnable. After all, Krim was expressing one of the cardinal principles of France's own political tradition, one that is explicitly affirmed in the Rights of Man: "The source of all sovereignty resides essentially in the nation; no group, no individual may exercise authority not emanating expressly therefrom." It was up to the sovereign and independent Algerian state, he concluded, to negotiate relations with France, just as Tunisia and Morocco had done before.

That afternoon, the French delegation struggled valiantly to refute Krim's arguments. Bernard Tricot contended that the Algerian case was sui generis because of the size of the pied noir minority. Yet in 1956 there had been nearly 600,000 non-Muslims in the two protectorates and as recently as 1931 they made up more than 10 percent of Tunisia's population, the same percentage as the pieds noirs in Algeria. Moreover, a slew of French studies, and de Gaulle himself, had suggested that the settlements with Tunis and Rabat provided precedents. This analogy cut both ways, of course, which may be why Krim did not pursue it. The settler communities in Tunisia and Morocco had been dwindling ever since independence, subject as they were to property seizures and sporadic violence. What could the pieds noirs expect after a far more acrimonious struggle for independence?[117]

Perhaps mindful of this history, Joxe argued that since self-determination would take place without the protection of pre-established civil liberties, guarantees for the pieds noirs' safety were essential. Yet how could the GPRA negotiate these guarantees if, as Joxe once again insisted, it represented only a part of the population and the people would have the final word? And if these were natural rights that trumped even the popular will, how could they apply only to the Europeans? It was absurd to pretend, as Joxe did, that "this was a question of the organic status of Algeria which did not in any way limit its eventual sovereignty or its coming independence." As we have seen, French officials had formulated the proposals Joxe was now presenting with the express purpose of creating an "organic structure" to limit the sovereignty of the new state.[118]

Upon their return to the Bois d'Avault, the Algerian delegation began to prepare to meet the press and argue their case. That evening, the new technology of teleconferencing would transmit Krim's voice and image live to a throng of journalists in Geneva. But the medium proved to be more novel than the message: Krim dismissed the French cease-fire as yet another attempt to disarm the Algerians before they had definitively secured their independence. Krim, for his part, offered another vague assurance that independence would ensure "fruitful relations" between the communities, an assurance that was all the more unconvincing while attacks continued on civilians in both France and Algeria. The delegation did nothing to discourage them—indeed, they had requested that ALN headquarters increase the number of military communiqués and thus boost their bargaining position at Evian. That very day, French intelligence discovered that the ALN in Morocco had been ordered to expand operations. As might have been expected, rebel cadres claimed that France was on the brink of defeat and the harkis began to desert in droves.[119]

Since the Algerians refused to be drawn out, recognizing that time was on their side, the French had no choice but to detail their own proposals and demonstrate their merit. At the next meeting on May 26, Joxe spent an hour and a quarter describing how they envisioned the new state. Krim's thesis that "the minority ought to submit to the verdict of the majority . . . inspires some very keen anxieties," Joxe began. "We cannot, as you ask us, trust you blindly." Instead, "[i]t's a question of determining the fate of a portion of the Algerian population, and its way of living inside a *'multicommunautaire'* Algeria." Joxe proposed that the Europeans remain French and, at the same time, automatically acquire Algerian citizenship. While he demanded that "no discrimination de facto or de jure distinguish them from other Algerian citizens," he went on to claim a panoply of special privileges and guarantees, including proportional representation in political and economic institutions as well as their own judicial and educational systems. Europeans would also be organized into a "community." It would not be "a political organ," he insisted, "but a group which will participate in the representation of Europeans and the defense of their interests."[120]

The French presented a convoluted defense of this position in a memorandum delivered to the Algerians the next morning, asserting that it was consistent with traditional conceptions of individual rights. But the essence of their case rested on an idea entirely contrary to the Rights of Man, above all Article 6: "the law ought to be the same for all, whether it protects or punishes." Instead, they held that special laws for the minority were essential in "a *'multicommunautaire'* society such as Algeria." This minority was defined by its ethnic origin, civil status, religions, language, and way of life. "These outlines are clear," the authors declared. "They result in certain particularisms. These cannot be guaranteed solely by the adoption of general principles which would be meaningless if applied without taking these particularisms into account." As an example, they cited the right to education, which would be pointless if it were provided in anything but the students' own language.[121]

This must have seemed bitterly ironic to the Algerian negotiators, men who had often struggled and sometimes failed in French schools. One of them, Ahmed Boumendjel, had earlier vowed never to forgive France for preventing him from practicing his mother tongue.[122] It would be easy to dismiss this and the rest of the French argument as a cynical exercise. It contradicted not only the French constitution but also the ideal of integration they had for years preached in Algeria. In 1958, Jean-Marie Le Pen himself argued that "nothing in the Muslim religion is opposed, from the moral point of view, to making the believer or the practicing Muslim a full French citizen. Quite the contrary . . . Besides, I do not believe that there exists an Algerian race any more than there exists a French race."[123]

Of course, the defenders of *Algérie française* had for decades shouted down even the most modest proposals for a more equal status for Muslims. They embraced the cause of full integration simply because it represented the last chance to head off independence. Similarly, Joxe was assuredly a late convert to the idea of a *multicommunautaire* society. This seemed the only way to end the war without appearing to abandon the Europeans.

Yet the government's proposals were not all self-serving and one-sided. To secure a special status for the Europeans in Algeria, Joxe declared that "we are prepared to plan for the Algerians in France a system of representation and of defense of their special interests." For instance, in exchange for guaranteed European representation in the Algerian administration, Muslims in France would be guaranteed participation in the administration of the areas in which they lived. The French position at Evian may have been a last-ditch effort to defend European privilege in Algeria, but it also provided a glimpse of a new, *multicommunautaire* vision of France itself.[124]

Indeed, the implications of these ideas went beyond Algeria and France to touch on the very structure of the international system, as Joxe himself suggested in his report to de Gaulle. "I did not hide from my counterparts that the thought which dominated my presentation is—they had realized it themselves—the idea of an association inside of the country."[125] This analogy between their proposal for shared sovereignty between the two states and their vision of multicommunautaire societies in France and Algeria became more clear in the next session, which was devoted to the French proposal for an international association to develop the Sahara. Like good lawyers, they marshaled all available arguments against the Algerians' exclusive claim to this vast region and its untold petroleum riches: it was peopled by tribes with no particular connection to the north, it had been charted by French explorers, its borders delineated according to the convenience of French administrators. But they also detailed plans to develop its resources in cooperation with all the bordering states through the *Organisation Commune des Régions Sahariennes* (OCRS). "Contemporary life proves to us," Joxe declared, "that in certain cases order has been established by means other than those of the state."[126]

To be sure, this could be seen as a non-state defense of narrow state interests, and one suspects this was de Gaulle's own view. "The petroleum," he privately insisted to Joxe, "that's France and uniquely France."[127] Yet there was an important idea here, if only in fragile and embryonic form: just as unlimited state sovereignty and individual rights could not ensure order and equity within diverse *multicommunautaire* societies, unlimited state sovereignty and exclusive claims to territory and resources could not ensure order and equity in international society, populated as it was by vastly unequal states and peoples living in ever closer contact.

For sovereign states to undertake such non-state solutions required a "double renunciation," as the French argued in their memorandum on a *multicommunautaire* society: a political renunciation by the state to which the minority was linked, renouncing the territory in which they lived, and a "psychological renunciation" on the part of the new state: "it renounces considering them as representatives of a foreign power and admits them as nationals." This double renunciation could only happen in a climate of peace and cooperation — that is, the context created by the association between the states.[128] Conversely, the French proposals for the Sahara could also be seen as requiring a double renunciation: Algeria's renunciation of the territory and a renunciation by France of its full sovereignty such that it would regard the resources contained therein as belonging to all the bordering states. Such an economic association between states also required that the association between communities in both countries remain amicable.

Considering the Algerians' reluctance to make detailed proposals of their own, it was a good negotiating tactic for the French to present all of theirs in a neat package — they wanted their "renunciations" to be reciprocated. Yet if the proposals were not necessarily interdependent, taken as a whole they reflected a radically new view of international relations: by linking relations within the two states and between them, requiring that both renounce a measure of their sovereignty, and presenting diasporic communities as legitimate actors in their own right, the French design for associated *multicommunautaire* societies suggested the outlines of a *trans*national system. At the very least, the "double renunciation" described by the French would create an autonomous space in which the Algerians of France and the French of Algeria would constitute a community of fate and begin to push back the bounds of state sovereignty.

While curious about the French proposals, the Algerians quickly decided that they did not want to have anything to do with them. On June 3, Saad Dahlab, himself a native of the Sahara, forcefully declared that "the maintenance of the present situation would be contrary to our war aims. After seven years of struggle," he continued, "we cannot allow, to restore peace, the amputation of 4/5 of our territory." To end French rule only in the north would make inevitable another conflict in the south. "If, in the colonial era, France penetrated the Sahara, this was to establish order in Africa," he acknowledged. "Now we are in an era which demands, to reestablish order, the liberation of the Sahara." Otherwise, he warned his French counterparts, "all of your work in Africa will be null and void." In this way, Dahlab associated the work of the GPRA with that of France before them, thus establishing a common basis for their cooperating in future. "We are prepared to make a distinction between the integrity of the territory and the exploitation of its riches. There can be no question for us of opposing ourselves to this exploitation which concerns Algeria, France, Africa and Europe."[129]

Boulahrouf joined in assuring Joxe that they were ready to "go beyond Algeria's frontiers in the economic sphere," but not in terms of population or territory. Indeed, his words were heavy with menace:

> [T]he Sahara problem is "the problem" which can only have an Algerian solution. We are telling you "look out.". . . . You have before you the Algerian delegation with which you must solve the problem. [You should] fear that if we must prolong the war we will not be the only ones with whom you will be led to deal.[130]

That afternoon, the verbal sparring shifted to the French proposals for a *multicommunautaire* society. Tricot suggested that the European minority would otherwise be eliminated—and that perhaps that was what the Algerians intended.[131] Yet if the real issue underlying their disagreement was whether the European community might survive without identifying itself against the new nation, nothing on the table compared with the effect of the killings the OAS now carried out daily in Algiers. After all, what did it matter if the Europeans were guaranteed proportional representation in an independent Algeria if the vast majority voted with their feet, convinced as they were that they had no real choice but "the suitcase or the coffin"—the OAS slogan of the time?[132]

On June 6, Krim gave a definitive answer, reading a long and solemn statement. The Algerian people, he declared, were not about to be born through the reconstitution of their state. They were already a historical, sociological, and political reality, composed of those commonly called "natives." This was a telling rejoinder to the argument that France had created Algeria: "natives," the term settlers used to distinguish themselves from those who came before, would now mark them apart from those with a right to remain afterward. But the Algerian people were not defined only by what they were not: they were characterized by a common language, religion, and mores, Krim continued, a shared history and destiny. Their suffering and struggle had only made them more conscious of their unity. As for the European community, "far from assimilating into the Algerian people, it has opposed it, taken its place, and consigned it to servitude. Rejecting any spirit of vengeance, the Algerian people want that their accession to independence allow them 'to invite the Europeans to integrate themselves.' " Krim assured Joxe that "all the assurances compatible with internal law could be given them" with respect to their "rights as men and as citizens, as well as their personal status in matters of religion and teaching." But this excluded any "privileges crystallizing a community."[133]

Though the talks sputtered on for another week, it was already clear that they had reached an impasse. The two sides were no closer on the disposition of French bases and issues associated with the referendum—

for example, whether and how the French army and administration might be "neutralized" to ensure a free and fair consultation. But these matters paled in comparison to their fundamental, zero-sum disagreement over the Sahara and the settlers. Finally, on June 13, Joxe announced that France had decided to suspend the discussions. The Algerians disagreed— indeed, Boumendjel suggested that they should continue talking "even if they have nothing very serious to say." This only added to French suspicions that their counterparts were more concerned with the publicity they gained from negotiations than in cutting the deals that might actually result in an agreement.[134]

While privately angry, Krim tried to avoid any public polemic. Speaking once more through the Swiss teleconferencing system, he told the assembled reporters that "he did not want to say anything to insult the future."[135] It was an interesting choice of words, the very ones de Gaulle had used in February 1958 after French forces had bombed the border village of Sakiet, the crisis that propelled him to power. "Between you and we," de Gaulle had told the Tunisian ambassador, "there is always geography; we agree then we disagree, we fit together again and we remain linked because the law of geography wants it and nothing can resist geography. So whatever happens, let's not insult the future!"[136] Alas, geography would soon divide France and Tunisia—and Tunisia and Algeria—as the unfinished business of the Sakiet affair and the portentous question of the Sahara occasioned the last international crisis of the Algerian War.

10

Drawing the Line

But sir, it's not about the French minority. It's about the majority of Algerians and the destiny of Algeria. We have not taken up arms to resolve the problem of the French minority, which is just one problem among many others.

Saad Dahlab to Louis Joxe, March 1962 [1]

The truth is, it is miraculous that we have gotten to these accords. Because, think of it, for a hundred and thirty years [the Algerians] have not ceased to be dominated, skinned, humiliated.

de Gaulle to Michel Debré, March 1962 [2]

Even after it became obvious to all but a few holdouts that Algeria was not France, there remained many more lines to draw or redraw across the Maghreb if Algerians were to have peace as well as independence. First, there were the contested boundaries of the new state. Would it be allowed to come into being only at the price of permanent territorial enclaves—such as the base at Mers el-Kebir—or even partition? And would Algeria make good its claim to so great a share of the Sahara? It was also necessary to parcel out the various competencies that came with statehood. In particular, Algerian negotiators would have to clarify the distinction they drew between French *multicommunautaire* proposals and what they considered to be more acceptable forms of economic and cultural association within and between states. Finally, they had to draw a line in time indicating when and how they would accept these responsibilities—either from France or some transitional authority. Organizing the transfer of power first appeared as a pressing, practical matter. But that was merely a premonition of a larger problem that continues to trouble the postcolonial world: what was the real nature and extent of decolonization?

Outside France and Algeria, no one had so much at stake in the answers to these questions as the people of Tunisia. The decolonization of the two countries had always been linked in a complex dynamic of shared and conflicting interests. Without the Algerian War, Tunisia would not have won full independence so soon, yet without Tunisia's subsequent support the Algerians might not have lasted so long. Each felt the other was in its debt, and neither could tolerate, or avoid, the demands the other felt justified in making.

If the Tunisians and the Algerians often differed about the means to employ in their strategies toward France, on most issues they could at least agree on the ends: complete and unfettered independence, including the closure of bases like Bizerte and Mers el-Kebir. But in one vast area, the Sahara, their interests were completely opposed. The GPRA insisted that the settlement of territorial disputes be put off until after independence, a position that Morocco accepted. The smallest state in North Africa could not afford to wait. "We pose the problem now," Tunisian Defense Minister Bahi Ladgham admitted to the Algerians, "while you have a knife at your throat. Because you are a difficult people, and tomorrow it will be much too late."³

On June 12, 1961, while the French and the Algerians were still engaged in the first round of negotiations at Evian, Bourguiba issued a joint statement with the president of Mali, Modibo Keita, asserting that the Sahara was an "integral part of the African territory." But no other country would take Bourguiba's side against the GPRA, which rallied support behind its position that much of the Sahara was an integral part of Algeria. Indeed, even Keita backed off.⁴

Bourguiba therefore seized on the issue of Bizerte. Its French commander provided a pretext when, on June 30, he began to lengthen its runway.⁵ On July 6, the Tunisian premier sent a personal message to de Gaulle reminding him of repeated requests for a French withdrawal—not only from Bizerte, but also from "our territories in the South." Bourguiba was vague because he was not prepared to say how far Tunisia's territory should extend. During the ensuing crisis, he indicated "with broad curving gestures" across a map "that the unsurveyed western border might bulge deep into the Sahara." If it included the oil fields around Edjelé, he suggested, "so much the better for us." In his message, Bourguiba told de Gaulle that he had made a "firm and irrevocable decision" to settle these issues, demanding that Paris accept the principle of evacuation and begin implementation talks. By this point, trenches had already begun to appear around Bizerte and public demonstrations started two days later.⁶

Bourguiba planned a reprise of the strategy that had served him so well in previous confrontations, mobilizing international support and relying on the United States as an intermediary. He had reason to believe that Kennedy would be even more supportive than Eisenhower. Pro-Western and socially progressive, Bourguiba had been favored with the first formal head-of-state reception at Kennedy's White House and his country had received more U.S. aid per capita than any other. All through the opening stages of the crisis, he was careful to give advanced notice of each new initiative to the American ambassador, Walter Walmsley.⁷

Yet unlike the crisis over the French bombing of Sakiet, when Tunisians had blockaded their bases amid international outrage, Bourguiba would need to provoke an incident over Bizerte. Moreover, the world media were preoccupied with the far more dangerous situation in Berlin. On July 12, de Gaulle announced he was withdrawing a division from Algeria to make a greater contribution to European defenses and signal that the war was winding down. This was a particularly inauspicious time to ask Washington to pressure *le général*, an ally who was as obstinate as he was irreplaceable.[8]

For almost a week, de Gaulle did not even deign to answer Bourguiba's letter. He had understood from their February meeting in Rambouillet that the Tunisian premier would postpone the Bizerte issue until the war in Algeria was settled. *Le général* now declared that he could not settle the matter—or even address it—"in an atmosphere of passion, nor under threat of mass demonstration."[9] According to a friend, de Gaulle's "contemptuous silence" humiliated Bourguiba. "If I had given in," he later explained, "my attitude would have been considered a definitive renunciation and my demands would no longer have been taken seriously."[10]

In an address to the National Assembly on July 17, Bourguiba threatened to blockade Bizerte and send troops into the Sahara to stake Tunisia's claim if he did not receive a satisfactory response from France within 24 hours. At the same time, he mocked Algerians for claiming all of the Saharan hinterland. While he was still "crouching in French jails," they "were asking themselves if Algeria was part of Africa or part of Europe"—a stinging reference to President Abbas. That same day, a GPRA delegation departed Tunis for a new round of negotiations near Evian. No one from the Tunisian government bothered to see them off.[11]

Despite Paris's warning that force would be met with force, on the morning of July 19 Tunisian troops, backed by crowds of unemployed, student, and women volunteers, blockaded the base and the smaller installations that surrounded it.[12] Unlike the small arms clashes after the Sakiet bombing, the Tunisians now wielded anti-aircraft guns and 105mm artillery. Consequently, they shot down a helicopter that was attempting to supply an isolated post and even managed to hit the headquarters of the base commander. At the same time, they dispatched a contingent from Fort Saint to stake Tunisia's claim in the Sahara.

The French riposte was swift and devastating: three warships forced the harbor, while sorties from the carrier *Arromanches* helped silence the Tunisian guns. Reinforced by the arrival of 7,000 paratroops, an armored column plowed through the barricades around the base and began to pulverize the heavily populated Arab quarter of Bizerte. "There were pockets of resistance high up in other buildings and now and then men could be seen scampering across rooftops," *The New York Times* correspondent reported. "Invariably, an explosion would follow. A great cloud of dust would hide the man and the roof. When it cleared nothing more moved across that particular rooftop."[13]

Unbeknownst to the men on the rooftops of Bizerte, Bourguiba's "battle for evacuation" had already shifted to New York—where his representative requested an emergency meeting of the U.N. Security Council—

and to Washington, where Walmsley's cables conveyed increasingly urgent demands for intervention.[14] Since Bourguiba had recalled his ambassador from Paris and sent the French chargé packing, he depended on the United States to reinforce his demands to de Gaulle, if necessary under threat of seeing Tunisia ally with the non aligned or Communist powers.

Yet when Secretary of State Dean Rusk met with the Tunisian ambassador, Bourguiba's own son, he tried to persuade him to call off the Security Council request. The Tunisian premier found the U.S. response "disconcerting." "If they think this is not like Bourguiba," he declared, "they don't know the real Bourguiba.[15] He then praised the USSR and Egypt for supporting him and vowed to accept foreign help from any quarter.[16] Meanwhile, protestors marched on the U.S. economic mission in Tunis. "Down with America. Down with Colonialism," they chanted. "These are your cannons, these are your shells that slaughter us."[17]

Ladgham finally called on Walmsley "in extreme agitation . . . to beg our immediate intervention with the French."[18] But the United States and Britain instead helped to kill a Security Council resolution that demanded negotiations for the evacuation of Bizerte. Almost all of the fighting had already stopped both there and in the Sahara, where the Tunisian probe had quickly been repulsed. Altogether at least a thousand Tunisians had been killed—perhaps four times as many—most of them civilians.[19]

That same day Bourguiba wrote directly to Kennedy. Invoking their personal friendship, he declared that Tunisia was counting on the United States.[20] Kennedy promised to urge France to negotiate, but he also criticized Bourguiba.[21] He was angry with the Tunisian premier for putting him in this position with de Gaulle, who had proved himself steadfast in the Berlin crisis and now faced "an explosive disciplinary situation," according to the CIA, even without making further concessions in North Africa.[22] Yet Kennedy did not want to alienate a valued new ally over an unwanted foreign base, which reminded everyone of Guantanamo Bay, and thereby present Moscow with a perfect opportunity to rally the Third World against the West. He sought to escape this dilemma by adopting the same "middle-of-the-road" policy he had ridiculed in his 1957 Senate speech on North Africa: "tepid encouragement and moralizations to both sides, cautious neutrality on all real issues."[23]

Meanwhile, the Algerians broke off negotiations with the French. Krim had begun to offer more explicit assurances about the safety of the pieds noirs but he would not even discuss proposals for joint development of Saharan oil until the French accepted Algeria's sovereignty over the region.[24] The Algerians received a warm welcome upon their return to Tunis, Bourguiba's Saharan claims having been set aside amid the bloodshed at Bizerte. Indeed, the GPRA offered to help him against the French. Though Bourguiba wisely declined, on July 31 American observers in Libya spotted Egyptian military vehicles heading for Tunisia, the first concrete assistance after numerous offers.[25] On August 4, the Soviet Union announced that it would extend a $27 million credit while Khrushchev pledged "all possible help."[26]

The United States, for its part, continued to refrain from taking any position either in public or private on the substance of the dispute. Instead, Rusk pressed Couve de Murville to reestablish contact with the Tunisians. Even apart from the danger of foreign intervention, or at least increased Soviet influence in North Africa, some forty-eight states were now clamoring for a special General Assembly session to discuss Bizerte. Kennedy worried that this would distract attention from the Soviet threat to Berlin.[27] But when Rusk urged de Gaulle to renew talks with Tunis, *le général* became "icily furious" and abruptly broke off the meeting. Weeks later, Rusk was still talking about the dressing down he had endured.[28]

When the special General Assembly session finally forced the United States to take a stand, Kennedy found the decision relatively easy. "Everyone forgets how shaky de Gaulle's position is," he told Arthur Schlesinger. "With all his defects, de Gaulle represents the only hope of gaining a solution in Algeria. Our sympathy continues to be with the nations throwing off the bond of colonialism; but the cause of anti-colonialism will not be helped by the overthrow of de Gaulle."[29] Adlai Stevenson therefore "worked on" the Tunisian delegation to produce a milder resolution and finally joined twenty-nine other representatives in abstaining. But sixty-six countries endorsed Tunisia's sovereign right to demand that French forces withdraw, including NATO allies like Denmark and Norway and normally friendly Francophone states like Senegal. In the whole assembly, only the Ivory Coast and Niger stood with France in boycotting the vote.[30]

When compared to the Sakiet crisis, the Bizerte affair illustrates important elements of continuity and change in North Africa and international relations generally since 1958. Bourguiba's strategy was virtually the same during the two episodes, seeking to exploit the media, the United Nations, and American fears of Communist advances to redress the imbalance of power between France and Tunisia. But even if Kennedy and Rusk had been so inclined—and Rusk "always looked upon the U.S. as the junior partner in Africa," as he later wrote—they could not reprise Eisenhower and Dulles's role in coercing Paris behind the scenes.[31] This was not only because of Bourguiba's bad timing and de Gaulle's formidable personality. The whole material basis for Franco-American relations had changed. As one indication, the French were about to pay off in advance the last of the debt they had incurred in the mid-1950s. Indeed, they had begun to complain that the mounting American balance of payments deficit served to export inflation. By 1963, the tables had turned completely, as France threatened to use its economic leverage against the United States. According to Walt Rostow, "the image of de Gaulle sitting there sassing him from his little pile of gold" became Kennedy's obsession.[32] It was already apparent that the days when Washington could dictate to Paris were over.

Moreover, while the French government was still internally besieged, it now spoke with a single voice abroad. De Gaulle made this perfectly clear to Stevenson when he visited Paris. "You realize," he said, "that the

Atlantic Alliance is now at stake; if we abandon Germany over Berlin the West will lose Germany, and if the Atlantic Alliance abandons France in its efforts to resolve colonial problems the Alliance will lose France."[33] Yet if France had achieved a measure of independence within the alliance, the General Assembly debate demonstrated that, in the wider world, it remained in less-than-splendid isolation. This gave little satisfaction to Bourguiba, but his loss was not France's gain. Indeed, de Gaulle believed that Bourguiba would not have even dared to mount such a challenge if he did not assume, along with the rest of the world, that, "assailed from all sides," de Gaulle would be "unable to stand firm."[34] *Le général* had not only stood firm but had reacted with ruthlessness — providing a punching bag for his frustrated army and a show of force for the GPRA. He had shown that France could crush small countries in conventional combat while ignoring the rest of the world. But after three years in office, and in his seventieth year, he still found it necessary to prove his resolve, still found himself "assailed from all sides," and still had before him the ever more daunting task of restoring France's prestige abroad.

The Box of Sorrows

De Gaulle was deeply depressed even before the Bizerte affair and the breakdown of negotiations with the GPRA. With Bourguiba now hostile, there was no chance of launching the multilateral Saharan development scheme. What was unusual about de Gaulle's pessimism both for himself and his country was his admission that he might not be able to do anything about it.[35] That may explain why, beginning in July, he had Alain Peyrefitte publicize the idea of partition, something that the Working Group — and de Gaulle himself — had always considered "a solution of despair."[36] "The FLN," he explained, ". . . is afraid of making peace. It is afraid of assuming its responsibilities. It only knows how to do two things: train troops in Tunisia and Morocco and, for its propaganda, line up as many countries as possible against us."[37]

The threat of partition only provided ammunition for Boumedienne and all those hostile to a negotiated peace. The top commanders of the frontier army had threatened to resign when they were compelled to turn over a captured French pilot. They seized on the incident to criticize Krim's diplomacy, signalling the opening move in Boumedienne's drive for power. During an August meeting of the CNRA, he blocked Krim's attempt to replace Ferhat Abbas. Forced to cede the diplomatic portfolio to his deputy, Saad Dahlab, Krim had to content himself with the Interior Ministry while Ben Youssef Ben Khedda became president. Rather than a shift in the GPRA to radical Marxism, as outsiders assumed, the choice of Ben Khedda owed more to the fact that, by sitting out the second cabinet, he had managed to remain neutral in its Byzantine faction fights. While ultimately disastrous for the Algerian people, the deepening divisions among their leaders doomed any French attempt to obtain fundamental concessions on the Sahara. By 1961, it was impossible to create a consensus in the CNRA for any significant policy shift, much less a radical revision of the war aims that had been declared in November 1954 and constantly reaffirmed ever since.[38]

De Gaulle abruptly conceded the point in a September 5 press conference. He now recognized what he called "the realities."

> I know there is not a single Algerian who does not think that the Sahara ought to be part of Algeria and any Algerian government, no matter what its relations with France, would unceasingly assert Algerian sovereignty over the Sahara. . . . If an Algerian state is established and if it associates itself with France the great majority of the Saharan populations will tend to link themselves to it.

These peoples would have to be consulted, of course, but according to de Gaulle, France's only concern was to safeguard its interests in the area: oil, airfields, and communications with the rest of Francophone Africa.[39]

As if to minimize the concession, de Gaulle characterized the population of nearly half a million in the two Saharan *départements* as "infinitesimal and extremely rare." Debré insisted that the consultation of the Sahara's inhabitants "reflect their nature and their diversity," while privately admitting bitter disappointment—even offering to resign. Joxe only regretted that *le général* had not tried to secure any compensation, and he tried to exploit the continuing ambiguity over the Saharan peoples in subsequent negotiations. But de Gaulle himself was now determined not to be long delayed by what he considered comparatively minor details, shouting at Joxe that they had to finish with "this box of sorrows." Using the same expression with Alphand, he explained that, unburdened of Algeria, France could consecrate all its resources to "world problems."[40]

De Gaulle was also nearing the end of his patience with the pieds noirs, especially since they appeared determined to sabotage efforts made on their behalf. Indeed, the quarrel became personal. Three days after de Gaulle conceded the Sahara, he narrowly escaped an OAS bombing along the road to Colombey-les-Deux-Eglises. Under the nominal leadership of Salan since May, the OAS had more success in killing random Muslims, liberal Europeans, and loyal officials. The fact that so many pieds noirs appeared complicit dispelled the already faint hope that they might unite with pro-French Muslims to form a "third force." The polarization left no one for the French to negotiate with but the GPRA, while OAS violence discredited their assertions that the pieds noirs would be irreplaceable in building the new state.

By December de Gaulle was criticizing Peyrefitte for succeeding only too well in publicizing the idea of partition. "We are not," de Gaulle exclaimed, "going to defer our national destiny according to the moods of the pieds noirs! . . . If we follow your solution we will set the whole world against us. The Third World is going to join together with the Arabs. We will have created a new Israel. Every heart in the Arab world, in Asia, in Latin America, will beat as one with the Algerians."[41] Indeed, the GPRA was picking up new allies with each passing month. Over the preceding year, Mali, Czechoslovakia, Bulgaria, Cuba, Pakistan, Yugoslavia, Afghanistan, Cambodia, and Ghana had all recognized it as Algeria's legitimate government. The United States, for its part, upgraded contacts to unprecedented levels, including an unofficial but prearranged meeting with Dean Rusk at the Saudi embassy and a much publicized rendez-vous in Tunis between Yazid, Dahlab, and the assistant secretary of state for Africa, G. Mennen Williams. The increasingly fruitless campaign to deny this recognition to the GPRA was all the more distracting to French diplomacy at a time when nuclear war was threatened over Berlin. De Gaulle's refusal to renegotiate allied rights in the beleaguered city left him increasingly isolated in NATO while inciting Moscow to step up military aid for the Algerians. In September, a Soviet freighter off-loaded some 1,500 tons of arms and ammunition in Morocco. Most if not all of it was thought to be destined for ALN bases.[42] In light of all these pressures, it is understandable that de Gaulle responded with "controlled vehemence" to Peyrefitte's argument that France had no right to abandon its own: "And me, do you believe this is with joy in my heart? I who was raised in the religion of the flag, of French Algeria and French Africa, of the army as the guarantor of the Empire? Do you think that this isn't an ordeal?"[43]

What made de Gaulle's ordeal all the more trying was that the GPRA did not even appear to want to negotiate seriously. Since his shift on the Sahara, lower-ranking French and Algerian officials had had a number of informal, and inconclusive, meetings in Switzerland. The GPRA's representatives felt free only to record the French proposals and reiterate their opposition to anything that impugned the new state's sovereignty. They might have felt constrained not only by the known hostility of Boumedienne and the general staff but also by the great unknown: the views of the five imprisoned ministers, who began a hunger strike on November 1 to protest their isolation. After three weeks, de Gaulle gave ground on that issue, too. While remaining in France, the ministers would henceforth be entrusted to the custody of Moroccan diplomats and enjoy virtually unlimited visitation rights. That same month, Boumedienne dropped his opposition to renewed peace talks. "Go ahead," he told Ben Khedda, "we're not children!"[44]

While Boumedienne was only too happy to have the GPRA assume the burden of negotiations and the compromises they would inevitably entail, he quickly dispatched one of his officers, Abdelaziz Bouteflika, to make contact with the imprisoned ministers. To the sound of running water and a blaring radio—the better to foil French listening devices—the young emissary told his eminent but out-of-touch hosts about the feud raging between the general staff and the GPRA. Aït Ahmed hesitated and Boudiaf remained distrustful, but Ben Bella quickly chose sides. He entrusted Bouteflika with a handwritten letter for Boumedienne along with his personal phone number. Ironically, by making martyrs of their captives and then allowing them to receive emissaries, the French had facilitated the rise of Ben Bella, his alliance with Boumedienne, and thus the eventual triumph of those within the FLN who were the most hostile to them.[45]

Putting It in Writing

On December 9, 1961, the day after de Gaulle told Peyrefitte that France had to unburden itself of Algeria, Joxe met secretly with Saad Dahlab. Considered one of the most brilliant and least compromising of the Algerian negotiators, the GPRA foreign minister was determined to bring the talks to a rapid and successful conclusion. "The time has come," he declared, "to set aside clever negotiating tactics." He asked Joxe straight out: "Does France agree, yes or no, that self-determination extends to the Sahara in the same conditions as in Algeria? If the response is positive, then everything becomes possible."[46]

Joxe demurred, insisting that the different populations would decide their fate through "a special breakdown of the voting." Dahlab was incredulous: "Why treat them differently than the Kabyles, the inhabitants of the Aurès and, above all, the Europeans?" Why indeed, if not to raise the possibility that the Saharans might opt out of Algeria? In fact, many of the nomadic tribes of the south had remained loyal to France, and their fate raised a fundamental question: what would be the constitutive principle of the new nation?[47] In applying self-determination, the GPRA insisted on territorial integrity, even if it meant defending borders drawn by colonial powers for colonial purposes. Yet in according citizenship, being born and raised on Algerian soil was not deemed sufficient. Those of European origin also had to declare their allegiance to the new state.[48] Joxe pointed out that the pieds noirs would hesitate to risk such an affirmation, and few would therefore be permitted to participate in its construction. The natural distrust toward this minority would only grow until the Europeans left Algeria in bitterness and despair. "You mustn't take back with one hand what you give with the other," he insisted, "giving guarantees to the Europeans on condition that there not be any Europeans."[49]

Joxe would not clarify France's position on the Sahara or make other concessions until he was confident that he had specific commitments not just from Dahlab but all of the Algerian leaders. Moreover, a bewildering array of other questions still divided the two sides, many requiring technical expertise and precise answers. Who would compensate property owners for land redistribution, grant permits for oil exploration, or assure order during the transition period? How long could France base troops in Algeria, or have access to Mers el-Kebir, or conduct nuclear tests in the Sahara? At their next meeting on December 23, Joxe began to present written proposals to resolve these issues and demanded that Dahlab do the same.[50]

The much smaller Algerian team struggled to respond, realizing full well that Paris was setting the agenda. Feeling "submerged by documents," as Rédha Malek later recalled, "sometimes of a discouraging complexity," the Algerians sought out advice from sympathetic British, Italian, German, and Saudi experts, especially concerning oil concessions.[51] Like Boumedienne before them, they also took care to consult the imprisoned Algerian ministers. While the negotiators intended primarily to associate the captives with their work, Mohammed Khider noticed that they had neglected to demand compensation for refugees, many of whom had been bombed out of their homes. Important issues, and potential bargaining chips, could easily be elided in the French proposals and go unnoticed by the Algerians.[52]

The GPRA transmitted its first written proposals on January 9 and the two sides found themselves in agreement on a number of important principles. The ideas of cultural and scientific cooperation and economic aid elicited no objection from either side. Though the Algerians did not obtain compensation for refugees, eventually they were promised a minimum of three years of assistance at the same level as in 1961. From Paris's standpoint, this aid not only created an incentive to honor the rest of the agreement, it also provided a means to resolve the thorny question of land redistribution. In effect, and with their counterparts' consent, the French planned to deduct payments for the Europeans' losses from aid to Algeria, in that way indirectly subsidizing land reform.[53]

It proved more difficult to fix the terms for economic cooperation in the Sahara. While the Algerians agreed to accord France a "privileged position" in developing oil resources, they assigned the Franco-Algerian organization established for that purpose a strictly advisory role. They also refused to commit to assuring French companies preference in new contracts or the right to pay in francs. At the same time, they insisted that existing concessions would require renewal after three years, raising the possibility that France's "privileged position" would prove precarious.[54]

While differences over military issues were quantitative rather than qualitative, they were so great as to provoke an altercation. The Algerians were appalled when the French military representative, Général Philippe de Camas, peremptorily announced at a January 28 meeting that French troops might not withdraw for a decade. Even then, they would continue to operate Mers el-Kebir for an additional twenty years, with a renewable lease. The base would sprawl across no fewer than 550 square kilometers, where the French would have total autonomy in civil administration and justice. France would also ensure security at Colomb-Béchar and Reggane, and nuclear and missile tests could continue for another decade. Dahlab expressed shock at the general's demands and the attitude they implied. Joxe tried to dismiss the clash as a simple misunderstanding, which in a sense it was: the military still did not understand that France had lost the war.[55]

For the rest of the country, the two sides agreed on a four-to-six month transition period after the cease-fire as well as a jointly appointed Provisional Executive. But they diverged on who would actually maintain order during the interregnum. In general terms, the Algerians wished to dissolve municipal governments, minimize the powers of the French high commissioner, and accelerate the "Algerianization" of the bureaucracy. They feared that otherwise OAS sympathizers in the administration would undermine the Provisional Executive at every level. The French agreed to consider strengthening the forces at its disposal, transferring riot police from the metropole, and training levees of Algerian Muslims. But they envisioned a much less sweeping reform of the existing administration to ensure continuity in government and encourage reconciliation.[56]

Looking beyond the transition period, the GPRA readily agreed that there should not be any reprisals for actions committed before the cease-fire and that basic human rights should be respected. They also guaranteed Europeans representation in political assemblies and respect for cultural differences. When disputes arose, a court of guarantees could arbitrate. Yet the structure of the court and the guarantees themselves continued to raise doubts and questions—concerning the specific right to circulate to and from the metropole, for instance, and the use of French in schools. There was also no specific provision for pied noir participation in the municipal government of Algiers, Oran, and Bône, where most of them lived. And while the GPRA agreed that they could form an association so long as it was not a party or political grouping, they said nothing about what other role it could play. The disagreement over how Europeans could become Algerian citizens, on the other hand, was explicit and seemingly intractable.[57]

Over time, a series of proposals and counterproposals, nineteen in total, narrowed the margin of difference over the future of the pieds noirs. While the French continued to oppose the idea that Europeans had to choose to become Algerians, by early February the GPRA had begun to suggest the outlines of a compromise that appeared to meet their objections: for three years pieds noirs could exercise all the rights of citizenship, and thus participate in the construction of the new state, without having to declare their loyalties. Even if they then opted to become Algerians, Paris could continue to consider them—and their children—French citizens. The rest could remain in Algeria as resident aliens with the same right to repatriate.[58]

Race to the Finish

The "drafts, written commentaries, additions, revisions" about which Malek first complained permitted the negotiations to become ever more precise and comprehensive.[59] But this increasingly legalistic exercise began to seem surreal amid the daily bombings and assassinations on both sides of the Mediterranean. The closer the French officials came to conceding sovereignty, the more sovereignty seemed to slip through their fingers. Indeed, one of the participants in the last round of negotiations likened it to a race between de Gaulle and Salan. While *le général* sought an honorable way out by securing safeguards for the pieds noirs, Salan tried to head him off by destroying his authority in Algeria, and with it any basis for a negotiated peace. De Gaulle himself feared that he had already lost, concluding that "there is nothing real in Algeria except the FLN and the OAS."[60]

In February alone, OAS bombs or bullets killed 553 people. Most were random victims of racial violence, but others were targets of assassination or had the misfortune to live near one—such as André Malraux's four-year-old neighbor, Delphine Renard, whose horribly disfigured face would forever haunt OAS apologists. But the worst single incident, from the standpoint of the French state, occurred the next day, February 8, when more than ten thousand Parisians turned out to protest its inability or unwillingness to stop the attacks. In fact, the government had gone so far as to hire free-lance assassins to regain control of Algiers, but the OAS had quickly wiped them out with the complicity of local officials. Now OAS sympathizers among the riot police launched a merciless assault on the demonstrators, continuing to bludgeon even those who sought refuge in a Metro entrance that had no exit. In the largest demonstration since the liberation, half a million marched in silence to mourn the dead: four men, three women, and a boy of sixteen.[61]

With state authority dissolving even in the capital, de Gaulle was determined to disengage France from Algeria "one way or another," as he had put it in his New Year's address. The day after the police riot, he summoned Joxe and two other members of his government to begin secret and, he hoped, decisive negotiations with a high-level GPRA delegation. Robert Buron, minister of public works, and Jean de Broglie, secretary of state for Saharan affairs, would assist the hard-pressed Joxe and also associate their parties, the MRP and the Independents, with whatever agreement they reached. "Succeed or fail," Buron recorded de Gaulle as telling them, "but just don't let the negotiations go on indefinitely. And don't get mired in details. Some things are possible and others are not."[62]

Joxe and his compatriots set off for the ski station of Rousses on the Swiss border, the secret location of the talks. It was only 45 kilometers from Geneva, like Evian, but it was worlds away from both in terms of the comfort of its accommodations. The French delegation would work in a small lodge located over a garage for road maintenance vehicles. They had to sleep in the same cramped, smoky rooms where they met their Algerian counterparts. A different minister might have taken his cues from the dismal surroundings and de Gaulle's impatience and rapidly liquidated the bankrupt estate of French Algeria, but Joxe was a dedicated public servant who found it difficult to sell cheaply interests that had been held for so long and at such cost. Though de Gaulle continued to urge him by telephone each day to extricate France from Algeria, he stubbornly defended the French positions on military questions, the transition, and the status of the pieds noirs.[63]

By all accounts, Joxe's negotiating skills earned the respect of the men across the table—Dahlab, Krim, Bentobbal, Yazid, Malek, Benyahia, and Seghir Mostefai. Initially they did little more than critique his proposals, wary of falling into a trap that would make them vulnerable to Boumedienne's attacks. The Algerians' material circumstances were no less trying. Each night, their Swiss hosts arranged a different place for them to sleep. Each morning, they spent hours shaking off reporters and snaking their way along snow-blown mountain roads, all the while fearing ambush by OAS assassins. On the third day, they asked to rest before the meeting and immediately collapsed into a deep sleep.[64]

By that point, the close quarters and shared hardships had begun to break down barriers between the two groups. Paradoxically, it led the French to forget the pretense of not recognizing their counterparts' rank—even General de Camas found himself addressing Bentobbal as *Monsieur le Ministre*. There was also a practical reason: the four members of the GPRA appeared to be less rigid than the rest of the Algerian delegation. So, after they had awoken, Joxe proposed that *les politiques* should hold plenary meetings to proceed more rapidly. The ministers finally began to make progress on the crucial issue of citizenship along the lines of the compromise Algerian proposal. But four days later they had still not settled the matter and many other serious differences remained: pied noir participation in municipal administration, the length of the lease to Mers el-Kebir and the Saharan installations, and the form of the cease-fire. This last item was simple in itself, but the French did not want the Algerians to sign it in the name of a government they still did not recognize.[65]

Finally, on February 18, Joxe spoke with de Gaulle by telephone and described the impasse. Listening in on an extension, Buron strained to hear de Gaulle's barely audible response:

> What's essential is to reach an agreement composed of a cease-fire followed by self-determination, as long as this agreement does not lead to sudden disruptions in the present conditions relating to the material and political interests of the Europeans, the French military presence in Algeria, the practical conditions in which the exploitation of oil and gas takes place, and finally the economic, technical, and cultural relations between Algeria and the metropole. It is this result, I repeat, this result that must be achieved today.[66]

As de Gaulle himself well knew, agreement on a simple cease-fire and vote on self-determination could have been reached nine months earlier, at the very beginning of the Evian negotiations. Joxe had not then taken up Krim's offer, and challenge, because de Gaulle had always insisted on guarantees regarding the pieds noirs, military bases, and the Sahara. By directing Joxe to arrive at an agreement that day and remaining vague about what it should include, de Gaulle obviously wanted him to settle for the best terms possible. As was typical of *le général*, he then downplayed the significance of the inevitable concessions, despite—or perhaps because of—the fact that he had resisted them for nearly four years: "Let's not exaggerate too much the importance of the declarations we will end with. Who knows what is going to happen in ten or twenty years." They represented a "secondary interest," de Gaulle concluded, and could not be allowed to stand in the way of the "essential interest": ending the war.[67]

After a marathon negotiating session lasting until five AM, the two exhausted delegations finally arrived at an agreement. They sealed it with their first handshake, promising to meet again the following month and sign a formal text, which would also settle the few remaining issues. But on most matters Joxe had managed to split the difference: France would have a lease to Mers el-Kebir for fifteen years and could operate the Saharan bases and experimental centers for five. Outside these areas, it would withdraw all but 80,000 troops within twelve months and the last would be gone within three years. But the Algerians had insisted, and the French finally had to agree, that the pieds noirs would also face a deadline. Within three years, they would need to "confirm" their status as citizens of the new state or else be considered resident aliens.[68]

Even at the time they negotiated this agreement, the French delegates wondered whether it would make any difference for the pieds noirs. Buron anticipated an exodus of "2 or 300,000 Europeans, maybe more." If it was any more, then the agreement would offer little protection to those who remained—after all, proportional representation would be pointless if they only represented a few percent of the population.[69] The OAS had always insisted they wanted all or nothing, and now that a settlement was in sight Salan announced a "generalized offensive." The OAS would fire at will on police, rain Molotov cocktails on their vehicles, and "destroy the best Muslim elements in the liberal professions." In fact, it was not only doctors, pharmacists, and government workers who were gunned down or strung up, but hairdressers, flower vendors, and any other Muslim who fell into the hands of enraged pied noir mobs.[70]

The ALN, for its part, occasionally retaliated but mostly bided its time. While the OAS attacks weakened the French bargaining position, they also bolstered the Algerian hard-liners. At a special meeting of the CNRA called to consider the outline agreement, Boumedienne criticized the negotiators for having guaranteed European representation in the assembly and preference for French oil companies, thereby opening Algeria to neocolonial exploitation. But Krim would have none of it: "And you who are at the head of the army," he responded, sarcasm dripping from every syllable, "explain to us how you will expel the French? By arms?"[71]

How indeed? Even with French security forces under constant attack by their own civilian population, the Algerians were well aware that they could not impose their will. Boumedienne's own ally, Ben Bella, recognized along with the rest of the imprisoned ministers that "our situation in the interior" required that "negotiations be pursued until their completion." Although France was obviously eager to get out, it had to accept the terms of its defeat. Moreover, de Gaulle had made it known that he would publish the draft agreement if the Algerians tried to change the terms. "International opinion will be for us," he predicted, ". . . and we will resume fighting." To the very end, the Algerians had to be mindful of their international standing and content themselves with a diplomatic rather than a military victory. The CNRA therefore voted 45 to 4 to authorize the GPRA to sign a cease-fire.[72]

Yet, if the GPRA could not impose its will in Algeria, neither could the French—a fact that its negotiators used to their advantage in the last round of talks at Evian beginning on March 7. How, Dahlab asked, could they hold their forces in place if they were not confident that French commanders would combat the OAS? Joxe reacted angrily every time the Algerians made such insinuations, but Buron himself wondered whether they, for their part, were as confident as they pretended.[73] More than just an embarrassment to French representatives, the state's loss of control in Algeria had practical implications for the peace agreement they were trying to conclude. If Paris could not protect the civilian population, then some of its responsibilities would naturally devolve to the Provisional Executive and through it to the GPRA, which would help name its members. Thus, if the police were "largely in the hands of the OAS," as Dahlab insisted, "the first to throw bombs," then the Provisional Executive should be empowered to remove suspect officials. It could also regulate the return of the refugees, since for "psychological reasons" the GPRA did not want them to confront the French army at the border. Paris had equally compelling psychological reasons for not appearing to disown its already demoralized army. On March 11, after Dahlab repeatedly called for expanding the Provisional Executive's forces and "Algerianizing" the police, Joxe finally snapped. "I'm asking you, be serious. If there is a difficult and even distressing job to do you know very well it's not a more or less Algerianized police nor a local force, whatever the number of its personnel, who will be in a position to act, but only the army."[74]

Though there are no records available for the last week of negotiations, it apparently included the bitterest exchanges. Saad Dahlab later recalled that the talks were often on the verge of breaking down, indicating that his team was ready to walk away. Tricot denied any such risk, suggesting that he and his colleagues were not. "There was one day," he allowed, "when le général de Gaulle perhaps said that he had had enough." Most likely, Tricot was referring to March 17, when Buron described a "less serene, less sovereign" de Gaulle "muttering" at his ministers' insistence that to threaten partition yet again would serve no purpose. While he admonished his negotiators for not making a better deal, de Gaulle did not overrule them, and they therefore agreed to increase the size of the Provisional Executive's security force, promise the "Alger-

ianization" of the police, and allow the ALN greater freedom to maneuver. Compared to earlier concessions, these were minor points, but they
demonstrated that the French wanted an agreement more than the GPRA
did, which weakened their position in the inevitable disputes over its
application. Finally, rather than simply signing the minutes of the final
meeting and issuing a joint statement, consistent with Paris's claim that
these were merely consultations with one political tendency among many,
the two sides would put their signatures to a formal document. If France
would still not recognize the GPRA, it had at last recognized that its
representatives were the only ones capable of engaging the future government of Algeria.[75]

The next day, March 18, 1961, the French delegation sat down with
relief and resignation to sign the massive document required to end 130
years of colonial rule. But Krim had one last demand: They had to read
it aloud, all ninety-eight pages. So while the world press and de Gaulle
himself waited, the French delegates took turns reading article after article,
declaration after declaration, as the ever-vigilant Algerians followed their
every word. Finally, Joxe declared that it was time to sign. Krim had been
practicing for this moment for many days, often testing his gold pen to
ensure it would not fail him. But he was surprised to see not only Joxe
but also Buron and de Broglie attach their signatures to the agreement.
Hesitating for an awkward moment, Dahlab explained that only the leader
of the Algerian delegation would sign for the FLN. So when the moment
passed, Krim's colleagues looked on with emotion as this veteran *ma-
quisard*, now vice president of the provisional Algerian government, sealed
their victory.[76]

The End of the Line

"The battles are over," Joxe declared. "Our first thought ought to be for
those who have fallen in these years of struggle." It was also, a fortiori,
the first thought of the Algerian delegates. Lakhdar Bentobbal and Mostefa Benaouda, among the twenty-two who had first decided to break
away from the MTLD and launch the war for independence, might have
considered the fate of their comrades. Nine had been tortured to death
or killed in combat, while another seven still languished in prison. Krim
was part of an even more select group. Among the *neuf historiques* who
first led the FLN, he alone remained alive and at liberty.[77]

In more ways than one, the Algerian leaders represented a nation that,
by its own account, had lost a million people in the course of the war,
literally decimating its prewar population. While most historians are suspicious of such a large, round number, it is unseemly to quibble over
whether it was more like 227,000—the army's figure, which attributed
66,000 civilian deaths to the FLN but not one to themselves, or
500,000—an estimate of those "missing" based on prewar demographic
patterns, albeit one that includes wartime emigration and other causes.

Even the army's estimate is an order of magnitude more than the number of Europeans killed in action or unaccounted for at the time of the cease-fire: 11,200 soldiers and 3,663 civilians. One might accept the average of the two figures and compare it to Algeria's prewar Muslim population of 8.8 million. Based on this middle-range estimate, the war was proportionally far more devastating than America's Civil War, more even than France's losses in World War I.[78]

Well over two million Algerians had been uprooted—most "re-grouped" behind barbed wire, 250,000 exiled to Tunisia or Morocco, still more eking out an existence in urban shanty towns. Nor did the metro-pole provide any refuge: more than 44,000 Algerians had been arrested there, and one cannot even venture a guess as to how many were killed. In just one night, October 17, 1961, Paris police killed more than 200 Algerians protesting a curfew. They dumped too many bodies in the Seine to allow an exact accounting.[79]

Yet even if we knew the precise number of killed, wounded, exiled, and imprisoned, and then somehow found the words to make them more than statistics, they would still not convey all that the Algerians had endured. Who among them could have escaped unscathed after more than seven years of civil war? How many were terrorized, tortured, raped, or otherwise humiliated through the everyday indignities of insurgency and counterinsurgency warfare? Anecdotal evidence suggest an appalling toll—and that it was sometimes exacted by the mujahadeen who meant to defend them. Whether through the ill discipline of irregular troops or the sometimes inhuman discipline of their leaders, the FLN imposed upon the Algerian people a price for independence that was bearable only in comparison to the costs of colonial rule.[80]

Indeed, it was only because Algerians had already suffered trials with-out number before 1954 that some among them had the courage to un-dertake this terrible war and that most kept faith with such flawed, squab-bling leaders. *Le général* himself recognized this in admitting that the Algerians were remarkably magnanimous considering what the French had done to them over 130 years.[81] Indeed, while insisting on their sov-ereignty, the Algerians consented to cooperate in a host of common en-deavors. According to the Evian agreement, they would create an orga-nization with France to continue the development of the Sahara. They not only recognized the rights of French companies, but also promised them preference in future contracts. They agreed to accept payment in francs for oil and gas and to remain in the French monetary zone. They allowed France to retain test centers and airfields in the Sahara for five years and Mers el-Kebir for fifteen. Finally, teachers, technicians, and ad-visors of every kind would help preserve French influence.[82] Indeed, when the Evian agreement became known, the British Foreign Office consid-ered it a "triumph" for de Gaulle. Harold Macmillan himself expressed envy, complaining that it "contrasted strongly with what we got out of our colonies when we turned them into independent countries."[83]

But the enormous efforts expended to defend the French position in Algeria inevitably radicalized people on both sides of the Mediterranean. The magnanimity that de Gaulle found "miraculous" was based on a calculation that colonialism could not be undone in a day. The Evian agreement was "a starting point to arrive ultimately at a complete liberation of our economy and our territory," as a contemporary GPRA memorandum explained, because it recognized Algeria's sovereignty. This is what would enable Ben Bella to legalize the seizure of pied noir property in 1963, and Boumedienne to nationalize the oil and gas industry in 1971, even though they scorned the accords as a base betrayal.[84]

Indeed, one wonders whether some of the agreement's own authors acted in good faith. In September 1958, when the Algerians first began to contemplate negotiating peace with de Gaulle, Mabrouk Belhocine suggested that they not refrain from offering "beautiful promises" and "tempting guarantees," including dual nationality for the pieds noirs.

> [Let's] dispense with the idea that the engagements we make today bind us indefinitely. For all governments declarations, even written treaties, are valid "until further notice"; tomorrow, unburdened by the colonial straitjacket, our soil evacuated, who will prevent us from revising our decisions?

As secretary general of Saad Dahlab's foreign ministry, Belhocine would help formulate the GPRA negotiating proposals. As a deputy in Algeria's National Assembly, he also helped write the legislation that made Muslim ancestry the criterion for citizenship, betraying the promises made at Evian.[85]

Some have argued that French negotiators were either naive in accepting the Algerians' assurances or deliberately betrayed the pieds noirs to secure the concessions to state interests Macmillan found so enviable.[86] The American consul in Algiers observed that Paris was careful to protect even the statues of colonial leaders, packing them for transport back to France, while many thousands of desperate pieds noirs waited on the docks.[87] At the very least, one can fault the French state for doing so little to prepare for their return. As early as January 1961, de Gaulle confided to Macmillan that he thought entrepreneurs, technicians, and others with the skills to benefit from economic development would remain while "small" colonists would eventually fade out. Yet when his advisors warned of a massive exodus, he professed surprise and insisted that only one in ten would leave.[88] In March 1961, fully a year before the Evian agreement, Joxe was urged to begin preparations for their repatriation. He was told that under the best-case scenario, a "climate of association," 375,000 Muslims and Europeans would want to return; in the worst case, a "climate of hostility" would induce one million to flee. Even so, a *Secrétariat d'Etat aux Rapatriés* was not set up until August. Joxe would later claim that they never thought that the pieds noirs would flee en masse, that the possibility never even came up in the course of the negotiations.[89]

If Joxe was negligent in not preparing for a pied noir exodus, it is probably because he did not want to do anything to encourage it. He and his advisors certainly did all they could to prevent it, making a secure position for the pieds noirs the top priority throughout the negotiations. As Tricot put it during the Lugrin talks, the interests of the European minority were "primordial." "This problem is the counterpart for France that the Sahara is for the FLN," a French planning paper insisted. "We cannot compromise beyond a minimum which satisfies the normal demands of the Europeans and the engagements the government has made in their regard." In the secret one-on-one talks that ensued, Joxe observed that he did not risk a "rupture" with Dahlab over French bases or the Sahara, but rather over the nationality question. Buron, for his part, felt that this part of the negotiations at Rousses was a question of conscience—they would all be judged on the guarantees to the pieds noirs.[90]

While it is possible that Buron was self-consciously writing for history, the Algerians themselves considered the French delegation tenacious in its defense of the pieds noirs from the first to the last round at Evian. A decade later, Dahlab's most vivid memory was Joxe's solicitude for their safety. He finally obtained much more than the Algerians initially intended to concede, though they, for their part, negotiated long and hard until the very end over seemingly minor differences in language. If the GPRA delegates did not take these commitments seriously, it is difficult to see why they would have bothered, or why Boumedienne would criticize them so bitterly for the concessions they did make.[91]

In the end, of all the contentious issues settled by the Evian accords, the provisions relating to the pieds noirs most nearly met Joxe's opening demands. Aside from exercising all the rights of Algerian citizens, without actually having to declare themselves as such for the first three years, the pieds noirs were promised proportional representation in legislative assemblies as well as public enterprises and administration. For four years, they would also preside over the municipal councils of Algiers and Oran and all the city districts in which they were a majority. Even those who chose not to become Algerian citizens would enjoy the same civil liberties and guarantees against discrimination, the same freedom to circulate and transfer property to and from the metropole, the same terms of access to schools and courts. They could choose to be educated in French, which would also be used at least part of the time in radio and television programming as well as all official documents. Europeans would always be represented among the judges and jurors in any case involving non-Muslims. Moreover, a court of guarantees including two European judges (out of four) would decide disputes over the application of these provisions. And if all else failed, if all these proved to be "beautiful promises," the Europeans would always be French citizens with the right to repatriate and claim compensation.

When some 800,000 Europeans left Algeria in the first year, they made almost all the other guarantees meaningless. Considering that while these were being negotiated thirty to forty people were being killed every day in Algiers alone, the decision to flee was entirely understandable. Yet in determining who was *ultimately* responsible, it must not be forgotten that this climate of violence was overwhelmingly the work of the OAS. In the last six months of the war, it killed or wounded three times as many people in the Algiers zone as had the FLN over the six preceding years.[92] The day after the cease-fire, for instance, it lobbed mortar rounds into the happy crowds milling about the Place du Gouvernement, killing twenty-four. In keeping with Salan's instructions, OAS militants also killed those struggling to keep the peace between the two communities — eighteen gendarmes in a single attack two days later.[93] So, in judging the good faith of the negotiators at Evian, one must also consider what the pieds noirs did to demonstrate *their* good faith. At the very least, by passively if not actively supporting efforts to provoke a fight to the death, they ensured that neither they nor anyone else would ever know if they could have lived in peace in the land of their birth.

In the end, events bore out Joxe's prediction: it was not the police or even the ALN who performed the "difficult and even distressing job" of smashing the ultra's resistance, it was the long-suffering army. After the OAS mowed down seven young conscripts on March 23, General Charles Ailleret finally ordered an assault on their Algiers stronghold, Bab-el-Oued. Some 20,000 troops sealed off the area and slowly reduced resistance block by block. On the fourth day, the OAS called a general strike and rallied supporters near the Place du Gouvernement. As they marched on Bab-el-Oued, Muslim draftees fresh from the field blocked their way at the Rue d'Isly. The crowd jeered and jostled the nervous and outnumbered troops until shots suddenly rang out from one of the rooftops. The soldiers began to fire into the crowd and, in the several long minutes before their officers restored order, forty-six people were killed, and with them the pieds noirs' last hopes that they could somehow prevent independence.[94]

Desperate, even disoriented, the OAS took its revenge on still more hapless Muslims, sparing not even patients lying in hospital beds. Never very disciplined, they would soon lose all direction. French forces had already captured their commander in Oran, General Jouhaud, the day before the Rue d'Isly massacre. Over the following month, they picked up the leader of the death squads, Lieutenant Roger Degueldre, along with Salan himself. Even so, the killing continued. On May 2, for instance, a single car bomb felled sixty-two dock workers. A particularly odious operation nearly succeeded in rolling a 30,000-gallon gas tank down from the heights over Algiers, which would have set the whole Casbah ablaze. The ALN, which had been showing "remarkable discipline and restraint," as Alistair Horne writes, finally began to bomb OAS hangouts on May 14. But by then, the European exodus had already begun: 100,000 by the middle of May, half a million by July. That month 92 percent of the remaining population participated in a referendum in which 99 percent affirmed independence. In one last nihilistic spasm, the *ultras* launched a scorched earth campaign, setting fire to schools and hospitals, the oil storage tanks in Oran, the university library in Algiers.[95]

Is it any wonder that some Algerians sought vengeance? On July 3, two days after the referendum, enraged mobs in Oran massacred twenty-one Europeans after someone fired on a victory celebration (around a hundred Algerians were also killed). It is perhaps more surprising that this was the only such incident, and that in the following days the ALN executed dozens of Muslim rioters while ruthlessly restoring order. Kidnappings were more common, nearly three thousand in total. These often targeted OAS operatives, but not always. By 1964, about a third had been released, the rest presumed dead in circumstances their kin could only imagine.[96]

Without minimizing the tragedy of the pieds noirs—especially those who had accepted Algerian independence and wanted only to be left alone—it must be placed in the context of other calamities. While the settlers were the focus of contemporary concerns and occupy center stage in most historical accounts, the Algerian War concerned Algerians above all, as Dahlab had to remind Joxe.[97] The hardships faced by the European minority paled in comparison not only to what Muslims had long endured at the hands of the French, but also to what those who had collaborated now suffered at the hands of their compatriots. The ordeal of the *harkis* was greater not just in degree—at least 10,000 were killed, with credible estimates ranging as high as 100,000—but also in kind: old men made to swallow their medals, others burned alive, some literally fed to dogs. Those who had for years avoided taking sides often took the lead in inflicting these torments, only too eager to prove their newfound patriotism.[98]

All of this, of course, constituted a gross violation of the Evian agreement. Yet the French were actually the first to betray their commitments. Because while pieds noirs suffered delays and discomfort during their exodus, the harkis were actually prevented from escaping despite explicit assurances. This was not the result of negligence or poor planning, but a policy decision made long before. As early as February 1961, a report produced by Joxe's *Secrétariat d'Etat aux Affaires Algériennes* acknowledged that the fate of a "small number" of loyalists would be "very precarious, even tragic," when the GPRA came to power. In principle, the door should remain open to them, but "the essential point," the author insisted, was that "the permanent settlement in France of large numbers of Muslims is not indeed to be anticipated nor to be desired."[99] Some Algerian families had already started to flee until, in November, the Ministry of the Interior barred the way. The *Secrétariat d'Etat aux Rapatriés*, for its part, showed no interest in their fate, setting aside the now inconvenient fiction that Muslims were French.[100]

Finally, on February 19, 1962, the same day the French and Algerians agreed on the outline of an agreement, Joxe's ministry created a committee on the *harkis* under Michel Massenet. Two months later, as harkis across Algeria were being disarmed and left to their fate, he was instructed to continue studying the problem. Warning that the prospects for the harkis were "extremely dark," Massenet instead urged Joxe to take immediate action, or at least take a position.[101] In May, army officers forced Joxe's hand by secretly organizing the escape of harkis under their command. He then ordered the new high commissioner, Christian Fouchet, to unmask and punish those responsible. Consequently, out of some 300,000 Algerian Muslims who had fought for France, fewer than one in ten found asylum in the metropole by November 1962. That month, the general commanding the remaining French troops ordered them to turn away any Muslims who were still seeking refuge.[102]

History: The Never-Ending Battle

Perhaps more than the Evian Accords and cease-fire, which were quickly overwhelmed by OAS atrocities, more even than the referendum on independence—which merely touched off the worst reprisals—this last ignominious order marked the definitive end of the Algerian War. By repudiating the *harkis*, France consigned Muslims as a class to another country. Quite literally, no one would be permitted to stand between the two states.

By then, Ben Bella and, behind him, Boumedienne and the frontier armies of the ALN had established uncontested power in Algiers. Their rivals in the GPRA were imprisoned, exiled, or driven underground. Three quarters of the pieds noirs had departed, Algerians quickly occupying their homes. This obviated one of the reasons for Franco-Algerian cooperation, which had supposedly constituted "the guarantee of guarantees" for European lives and property. But France would not abandon the policy: "this rests on another foundation," one official explained. "For reasons of neighborliness, along with ancient affinities between our two countries, France has an interest in seeing that the Algerian state does not descend into misery or anarchy."[103]

Here again, the matter had been decided months earlier, even before the Evian agreement was signed. In a February 21 cabinet meeting that considered its outlines, de Gaulle cut short the protests of Secretary of State for Social Affairs Nafissa Sid Cara, the only Muslim member of his government, who had tearfully lamented the fate of all those who had kept faith with France. "Do you really believe, Mademoiselle, that aside from a few exceptions who we have a duty to take care of today, who we must be worried about tomorrow, the great majority of Muslims do not favor independence . . . ?" Yet de Gaulle did not, even then, display much concern for these "exceptions." "It is necessary to take into account the realities of the world," he explained:

> This is an honorable outcome. It is not necessary to hold forth on what has been done or not done a short time ago. People are people and can make mistakes. But it was indispensable to extricate France from a situation that only brought it misfortunes.

> That the accords [will] be capricious in their application, that's certain.
> We will have to make things easier for this Algeria that is going to appear.
> But one can't prevent it from being born and it's necessary to give it a chance.
> It will not be said that France does not help Algeria.
>
> As for France, she has to interest herself in something else now. We
> must take care of ourselves.[104]

The "something else" was de Gaulle's dream of seeing France become
a great power again, and taking care of themselves paradoxically meant,
in part, taking care of the Algerians. Malraux went so far as to say that
"the texts have no importance; the question," he asserted, "is whether we
may change the struggle; the new one will be harder perhaps but it will
finally mark in its way a kind of 'liberation of France.' " Debré could not
share his enthusiasm, blaming France's inability to arrive at a better solution on "the division of the communities, the revolt of the Muslim
world, the external support." His long ordeal almost at an end, the prime
minister would soon be allowed to resign. But he somehow found better
words to express an idea he could never quite bring himself to believe:
"André Malraux has used the word 'victory.' The term surprised me. But
I understand it in this way: this is above all a victory over ourselves."
Explaining *le général's* thoughts, he repeated that "it's about France, and
France first of all."[105]

Once again, as he did after World War II, de Gaulle would convince
his countrymen that they had not been defeated, that they had liberated
themselves—in this case by liberating Algeria. The former colony, "dominated, skinned, humiliated" for 130 years, would now be made a symbol
of the magnanimity of France, a great power that could once again afford
to be generous. Indeed, at the start of 1963, there were over 100,000
French advisers, teachers, and technicians working in Algeria, and France
accorded Algeria fully 35 percent of its foreign aid budget. Even after Ben
Bella ordered the nationalization of European-owned property, French
aid continued. The following year, for instance, French teachers filled 80
percent of all secondary school posts.[106]

Uncharacteristically, de Gaulle would ignore these and many more
offenses. It was not only because shrugging them off increased France's
stature—"because you are beaten if you say so"—but also because it
served his all-important foreign policy goals. Jean de Broglie, a signatory
of the Evian accords who became the ambassador to Algiers, was forthright about the self-interest motivating this indulgence. Algeria is "above
all the 'narrow door' by which we penetrate the third-world," he explained
in a November 1964 press conference. "A quarrel between France and
another North African state is just simple bilateral tension. A quarrel with
Algeria goes beyond the limits of Franco-Algerian relations and risks undermining our diplomatic efforts in the entire world."[107] The Algerians
had succeeded, de Broglie seemed to be admitting, in internationalizing
not only their war for liberation but also the peace that replaced it.

Of course, while de Gaulle's postwar strategy could not ignore the conflict's international nature, and actually exploited it, the French would remain victorious only so long as they were convinced that the only decisive battles were the ones they waged among themselves. As René Gallissot has written, de Gaulle was the "conjurer" who pulled off this sleight of hand:

> How to make believe that one accords independence, when one has tried everything to slow down if not avoid this conclusion? How to conceal the blow and the loss to French nationalism, contributing to a decline in national glory, if not by integrating this abandonment to the benefit and the cult of a certain idea of France?

In essence, the French needed to remember the war as a successful fight *by Frenchmen* to redeem the true, generous France by *giving* Algerians their independence. This helps explain why de Gaulle fought so long and so hard against anything that appeared to internationalize the conflict, even after concluding the Evian agreement. For instance, when the Soviet Union accorded official recognition to the GPRA, de Gaulle recalled his ambassador from Moscow the next day. It was only by remaining within France's *domaine réservé* that Algeria could be "given" its independence—not just at the official ceremony, which happened to fall on the 4th of July, but again and again, whenever the war was taught or talked about.[108]

Indeed, while the FLN took possession of the field, the traditional test of victory, de Gaulle has prevailed in the larger field of history—at least in France, where Gallissot's insight is all too rare. Long afterward, most French remembered the war as a domestic political crisis. In a 1990 poll, only 11 percent of respondents characterized it as an international conflict. That year, the historian Jacques Julliard went even farther, asserting "without the least irony" that one "can do a history of the Algerian War completely without speaking of Algerians." Writing in the same volume, Charles-Robert Ageron, the dean of French North Africanists, showed still less interest in investigating the role of France's allies and adversaries abroad. In summarizing some of the handful of articles on this subject, he accepted de Gaulle's claim to have been unaffected by the attitudes of other governments "barring new revelations." But, one might ask, how could there not have been "new revelations," since Ageron rendered this verdict when almost all of the relevant French archives were still closed?[109]

Thus, the annual contests at the United Nations, the clashes with the allies, the diplomatic campaigns without end are all but forgotten. By contrast, the use of torture, the abandonment of the harkis, and the bitterness of the pieds noirs have become the most open of secrets. Indeed, they form part of a collective memory that allows even the bitterest pied noir, even the most marginalized harki—perhaps especially them—to express their Frenchness through the quarrels they share with their countrymen.[110]

Benedict Anderson captured the essence of this phenomenon in his exegesis of Renan's famous essay, *Qu'est-ce qu'une nation?* "The essence of a nation," Renan wrote, "is that all the individuals have a lot of things in common and also that they have forgotten a lot of things. . . . Every French citizen ought to have forgotten the Saint Bartholomew [massacre], the massacres in the Midi in the 13th century." As Anderson points out, who but the French could possibly understand these allusions? In fact, " 'already having forgotten' ancient tragedies" is actually "a prime contemporary civic duty." Albigensians and their persecutors, Huguenots and Catholics are thereby reconciled as equal participants in *national* dramas — even though they would hardly have recognized themselves as such. "The effect of this tropology," Anderson concludes, "is to figure episodes in the colossal religious conflicts of medieval and early modern Europe as reassuringly fratricidal wars between — who else? — fellow Frenchmen."[111]

Yet contrary to Anderson, it is doubtful that even with reminding, enough Frenchmen and women will remember the Saint Bartholomew and Albigensian massacres sufficiently well for the collective act of "forgetting" to have its intended, incantatory effect. This is the case not only for the secular-minded but still more for Muslims, now the second largest religious community in France, who are even less likely to be impassioned over centuries-old sectarian strife among Christians. The Algerian War, by contrast, is a tragedy with more resonance because its protagonists more nearly resemble contemporary French society. What many at the time conceived of as an international, religious, even civilizational conflict is now reassuringly rendered as a contest between competing nationalisms, or even competing ideas of these two nations.

In Algeria, too, one can observe a phenomenon of supposedly forgetting that which is constantly recalled. It might seem impossible for Algerians to even pretend to forget the war — not only because the losses were so great and the legacies are so obvious, but also because for decades FLN governments consciously promoted it as the wellspring of their legitimacy. Yet the history they taught glossed over the violence between Algerians — not just the reprisals against collaborators, but also the fratricidal struggles among the mujahadeen. And rather than raise awkward questions about those who lost out in Algerian nationalism's innumerable internal struggles, like Messali Hadj, Abbane Ramdane, or Belkacem Krim, the official version elevated "a single hero: the people."[112] Perhaps it is not impossible then, as is often asserted, that some younger Algerians did not respect the FLN because they did not witness its wartime exploits and were uninspired by the sanitized history they were made to memorize from textbooks.

Yet most Algerians appear keenly aware of this history, as a rich oral tradition nourishes new generations.[113] Moreover, they could hardly be unaware of the conflicts within the wartime FLN. After all, Algerian politics was long populated by the protagonists, including Ben Bella, Boumedienne, Aït Ahmed, Boudiaf, and Bouteflika, some of whom pursued feuds for decades afterward. Indeed, politicians must still account for, and compete over, their national service during the war for independence.[114] If young Algerians did not honor the sacrifices of the wartime generation, it would be difficult to explain why the *Front Islamique du Salut* (FIS), which finally ended the FLN's reign, constantly strove to present itself as its rightful heir. As Hugh Roberts explains, the FIS developed a discourse contrasting the "good" FLN that won independence by exemplifying and expounding Islamic ideals with the "bad" FLN that betrayed the faith upon taking power.[115]

Of course, the Islamists' claims were not uncontested, as diverse groups struggled to control historical memory.[116] Whereas the FIS viewed France's enduring influence as evidence of continuing servitude, members of the secular elite can argue that the French language is one of the spoils of a long war finally won in 1962. Like the Islamists, President Bouteflika harked back to a golden age, though for him the era of "the good FLN" extended through the 1970s.[117] At the same time, others accused the Islamists of being children of harkis intent on revenge. Women, for their part, cited their participation in the war for independence in struggles for gender equality. Conversely, the government has invoked the contribution of Berbers to invite them to identify more closely with the official version of Algerian nationalism.[118]

Thus, far from Algerians having an unconflicted understanding of their independence struggle — or no understanding at all — it remained a central theme in their political and cultural contestation for decades afterward. Indeed, these contests can be seen to extend beyond France and Algeria. For instance, in Roy Mottahedeh's fictional account of the life of an Iranian mullah, *The Mantle of the Prophet*, he depicts his protagonist as reaching a turning point in his life while learning of one particularly atrocious episode in the Algerians' fight for independence, as he resolves to combine Islam and anti-imperialism.[119] On the other hand, what Robert Malley has called Algeria's ideology of "Third Worldism" had a profound influence on the European left, as a generation disenchanted with Stalinism placed their hopes in national liberation movements. Communist China, for its part, considered the Algerian revolution to be "a brilliant example" for the rest of Africa.[120] More recently, some postcolonial theorists credit the experience of the Algerian War with helping to inspire postmodernist approaches to political and cultural analysis.[121] Thus, people far beyond Algeria have long staked claims to its history to make sense of their own.

Memories of Algeria's war for independence serve multiple political projects because they contain multiple valences — many more, alas, than any one book can reveal. This can be a source of conflict, as different groups will continue to discredit one another by laying claim to the one, true version. But it can also indicate opportunities, since a richer historical understanding reveals that, just as the sources of this history are many and diverse, it can lead in many different directions. By following a few of them we will see how the Algerian War was not just an episode in international history but was emblematic of an emerging transnational system.

Conclusion

The Sense of History

This work has been sustained by a sense that the Cold War and its denouement obscured subtler but no less significant changes in the nature of international relations. These developments were a long time in the making, and the Algerian War did not cause them or even mark their beginning. But it can serve to illustrate how one can recover continuities in contemporary history and discover some of the origins of the post–Cold War era. This era is still named for what it is not, because we lack the distance to define it precisely. But it may one day be deemed most significant for having witnessed the emergence of a new, transnational system.[1]

Much of modern history can be described in terms of international systems, as Gordon Craig and Alexander George demonstrated in their classic text, *Force and Statecraft*. They identified three features essential to any viable system: the principal states must share aims and objectives that reflect the values the system is meant to advance; the system's structure must be appropriate to the power and position of participating states; and the states must agree on procedures—that is, "norms, rules, practices, and institutions"—to achieve those aims.[2]

According to this definition, even the Cold War could be considered a viable international system, albeit a "primitive" one. While during the earlier part of the period covered in this study some Soviet and American leaders were willing to risk nuclear war to "roll back" their adversary's dominion, by the end one can speak of a shared determination to avoid even conventional clashes and to respect spheres of influence. And while

France had finally obtained nuclear weapons and financial independence, de Gaulle would discover that a yawning gap remained between the superpowers and other states. After Moscow and Washington's tight management of the Cuban Missile Crisis and the Nuclear Test Ban Treaty, he was right to suspect that they sought to stabilize and even institutionalize this system.[3]

Yet at the same time it was already apparent that the Cold War had created dynamics that would combine to subvert these efforts. As North African nationalists quickly realized, it presented opportunities not just to play off the two superpowers but also to exploit differences over Cold War strategy in each alliance. Even seemingly straightforward instruments of power projection like military bases could be turned to their advantage—like the American installations in Morocco, or the French posts in Tunisia—or even taken hostage. Over the longer run, overseas bases could also undermine the fundaments of power, as Washington discovered with the mounting balance of payments problem in the 1960s, contributing to their occupiers' vulnerability to economic coercion. Bases could be closed or subsidized, of course, but the Cold War created countless other occasions for states and nonstate actors to harness it to their own agendas, sapping the strength of the superpowers and straining their alliances.

Moreover, Moscow and Washington's efforts to stabilize the Cold War could undermine their coalitions. At the start of the Algerian War, France and China were at opposite poles of an unmistakably bipolar system. Yet they came to share a grievance against their respective allies for not trusting them with nuclear technology and for shirking responsibility in the struggle for the Third World. While the Algerian War was only one case among many for Moscow and Beijing, it was a major reason for the schism between Washington and Paris. Ironically, it is now apparent that, rather than "freeing" Algeria, the Algerians' victory enabled the French to become free—free from their colonial charges, and free from the United States. After Algerian independence, de Gaulle was able to maintain considerable authority over former African colonies and reestablish France's prestige in the Middle East and Southeast Asia. In a sense, having failed to beat the nonaligned movement, he joined it—fighting undue U.S. influence, expelling military bases, and pursuing a course independent of either superpower. Barely a year after concluding peace in Algeria, de Gaulle had the satisfaction of chastising Americans for their own war in Vietnam. In time, there was even a rapprochement with the "yellow masses of China," as he once called them. Thus, France and China began to oppose their allies by arguing for more belligerent policies—whether in Africa or Berlin—but their independent paths eventually led to closer relations both with the opposing superpower and with each other. Circumstances came full circle, and the Algerians provided part of the impetus and momentum in this turn of events.[4]

Yet what occurred during the Algerian War and its aftermath went beyond a mere redistribution of power or even a reordering of the international system. The implications for the nature of state power and state systems went beyond the Cold War itself. Part of this phenomenon was produced by the U.S.-Soviet confrontation. The development of long-range nuclear weapons, for instance, made citizens of the mightiest states the most likely to suffer utter annihilation, reversing the traditional relationship between power and security. But contemporaries also cited population growth, environmental scarcities, and North-South conflict as rendering obsolete the very idea of absolute sovereignty. As State Department official L. W. Fuller argued in 1957, the United States would be "following the trend of history" if it instead developed "the rudiments of world order."[5] These were not just idle musings of isolated visionaries. The following year, Dulles actually proposed that the United Nations have its own army.[6] The very power of the United States in this period led U.S. officials to recognize the limits of state power.

The French, on the other hand, inferred from their inability to conduct an independent foreign policy that France had become too small in a world dominated by superpowers—or civilizations. That helps explain why they were so desperate to retain Algeria as the keystone of "Eurafrica." But ironically, French Algeria was one of sovereignty's most vulnerable redoubts. While the French were able to exercise awesome power over its population—"regrouping" over two million people and subjecting them to psychological warfare and constant surveillance—their efforts nearly rendered both ungovernable. By comparison, even the "rudiments of world order" like the U.N. General Assembly appeared to the pieds noirs like massive hands ripping their country apart.[7] They credited the United Nations with this power because it was the most visible manifestation of a phenomenon that was difficult to grasp. It was better illustrated by the quiet cooperation between technocrats in Paris, Washington, and international financial institutions in imposing economic constraints on Paris's ability to protect them. The loan agreement Jean Monnet concluded in January 1958 was a precursor and a precedent for many more economic liberalization programs with unmistakably political "conditionality" undertaken under duress and at the behest of the International Monetary Fund.

Subject to pressure from international organizations, NGOs, the international media, and other governments, French officials quickly discovered that asserting "Algeria is France" was no defense. Instead, they had to justify French rule in terms of human rights, women's liberation, economic development, and so on, thus accepting that states were answerable for their actions—that international norms, in other words, could trump national sovereignty. There was no other way of showing how "our policy is not behind the times," as one official explained, "that we are really in *le sens de l'histoire*." *Sens* can be translated as either "sense" or "direction," but when it refers to history it carries both connotations. History cannot, after all, have a direction if it does not appear to have some definite meaning, making nonsense of ideas and actions heading in the "wrong" direction.[8]

The problem for the French was that their adversaries already appeared to be leading the new direction of history—indeed, that they represented a kind of *natural* history. Whereas in 1948 George Kennan felt certain that the "older cultural centers of Europe . . . are the meteorological centers in which much of the climate of international life is produced," just eight years later Eisenhower warned of what he called "winds of change . . . from the deserts of North Africa to the islands of the South Pacific." In his famous 1960 address to the South African Parliament, Harold Macmillan spoke of this same "wind of change" as compelling decolonization. Later that year, de Gaulle put it a little differently, describing the "spirit of the century" as bringing the end of empires. "It is altogether natural," he admitted, "that one misses the softness of oil lamps, the splendor of ships under sail. . . . But really, no worthwhile policy ignores the realities."[9]

What were these realities, these "winds of change" blowing across the world, strong enough to compel even a leader as indomitable as de Gaulle to trim sails and shift course? They are really another way of expressing what Braudel called *waves* of structural change—not only in norms on human rights and self-determination, but also in population growth and movement, communications technologies, and market integration. This was the metaphor de Gaulle himself favored, as when he described how the "immense evolution" in the world had hit France like a wave, and how the Algerians had been buoyed by "a vast wave of sympathy and sometimes active support." Images of a "wave," a "flood," or a "tide" also imbued American discussions of anticolonial nationalism. Together they appeared to create a "climate of international life" that was increasingly hostile to colonialism while nurturing national liberation movements like Algeria's.[10]

Thus, whereas international law had drawn a sharp distinction between international and internal conflicts before, now any movement that called itself anticolonial could expect a sympathetic reception at the United Nations. Where such movements previously had to meet stringent requirements to expect recognition, now the principle of self-determination was accepted by all but a handful of international pariahs.[11] By winning rights and recognition traditionally reserved only for sovereign states, the Algerians had set precedents that would show the way and smooth the path before many more such movements. When the ALN marched in a victory parade through their main base in Morocco, Nelson Mandela was there to see them, having come to learn revolutionary strategy and tactics. In his autobiography, he recorded that the mujahadeen appeared to him like an apparition of the future African National Congress forces. And when they finally entered Algiers in triumph, Yasser Arafat was in the crowd cheering. He would consciously model Fatah after the FLN. Soon Algiers became known as the "Mecca of the revolutionaries."[12]

Even without the Algerian example, revolutionaries would probably have realized the power of the international media and the potential of a United Nations increasingly dominated by states that were themselves sometimes sovereign in name only. But the Algerian War exemplified a crisis in the colonial world that created a demand for new strategies and tactics with which peoples lacking the means of exercising control over a claimed territory could proclaim their independence and even obtain aid to make their claims effective. Just as individuals who lived in colonial territories came to view full citizenship and social benefits as their due, so too did the leaders of colonized peoples demand statehood and foreign aid as entitlements.[13]

While most observers celebrated decolonization as a progressive development, the manner in which it was achieved raised nagging questions. "The problem arises today for Algeria," Guy Mollet observed in 1957, "but do not many other countries have their own 'Algeria'? . . . They too have to contend with serious domestic difficulties caused by the conflict between the inhabitants of a particular territory or racial minorities and the rest of the nation. It would be easy to mention names and to quote examples. They occur readily to everyone."[14] The examples occur even more readily now—indeed, even Algeria could be said to have its own "Algeria" in the recurring tension in Kabylia. The fight against France temporarily obscured this latent division, but it heightened the consciousness of other minorities in the very heart of the colonial metropoles while helping to nurture transnational identity formations among Africans and Muslims. In a world in which time and space had seemingly collapsed, white westerners who insisted on their separateness appeared as neither more nor less than its most privileged and conspicuous minority.[15]

Of course, nascent nationalisms differ in degree and kind. The FLN sympathizer who returned to his native Vaucluse and joined the Occitan movement, concluding that it too had been colonized by the French, was surely atypical. Similarly, the pan-Arabism that terrified French and U.S. leaders appeared to be a spent force by 1967.[16] But as long as national identities can be constructed and deconstructed, no state can be absolutely secure from challenge. By the end of the Algerian War, French officials themselves came to realize that this had been happening for more than a century. Economic change had not only failed to reduce the salience of territorial and cultural distinctions, it had created conditions and incentives that encouraged a host of new and competing claims to aid and autonomy. And rather than strengthening élites' ability to guide the process of *re*imagining communities—and making some communities *uni*-maginable—new means of mass communication actually expanded it to include illiterate peoples. They also empowered relatively small but determined groups prepared to use violence to seize the international spotlight.

Indeed, the media became actors and even arbiters in their own right. This was most vividly illustrated in the last phase of the Algerian War, when packs of journalists hounded negotiators, interposed themselves as mediators, and finally led the Algerian spokesman to conclude that "what matters is not what the statesman says, but what the media want to make him say."[17]

If the Cold War system unleashed dynamics that led to its own destruction, this underlying erosion of state sovereignty made it difficult to imagine how any other international system could take its place. Let us recall that the "principal states" must agree on a system's objectives, structure, and procedures. But what if even the most powerful states conclude that, whether acting alone or in concert, they cannot provide security for their citizens? Conversely, what if the institution of sovereignty means so little that even self-proclaimed governments that cannot control their own territory are accorded diplomatic recognition? And what if states can be made or broken according to norms like "self-determination" and procedures like U.N. or IMF intervention? Without even speaking of the other actors in the international arena—NGOs, diasporas, multinationals, and so on, all of which will have a say in any new system's objectives, structure, and procedures—the nature and claims of states had become so contested by the end of the Algerian War as to render them incapable of constituting a "system" worthy of the name.

What, then, were the alternatives? This account has emphasized two opposing approaches to the apparent erosion of sovereignty, each of which could be seen as potentially constituting a new, *transnational* system. The first, the idea of development, was premised on the notion of inevitable progress, defining the "direction of history" as the path between tradition and modernity. Adherents agreed on a shared goal, modernization, as well as procedures to achieve it, including integrating markets, international aid, and centralized, top-down planning. The structure of this system reflected and reinforced a status hierarchy not only between developed and underdeveloped peoples but also between more and less modern kinds of knowledge and cultural practices.

In April 1961, the month the Evian negotiations were to begin, a special supplement to *Le Monde Diplomatique* sought to instruct readers on how to think and talk about countries like Algeria in terms of development. Whereas fifteen years before, one would have described individual Algerians with words like "poverty," "misery," and "destitution" with a certain amount of commiseration and "without looking for an explanation," the authors stressed that "today the vocabulary has changed, the term 'under-development' has replaced the others." This change of vocabulary reflected a change of attitude: one no longer referred to individuals (and their shortcomings) but rather to their collective situation as a people with "the will to understand and explain." The countries of the Third World were not monolithic, the authors emphasized, so the same solutions would not work everywhere. But since the problems of underdevelopment transcended borders, no country could remain indifferent to the fate of others and all would have to cooperate in addressing them.[18]

The ability to imagine oneself in the place of another, what development theorists like Daniel Lerner had considered a benchmark for modernizing peoples, was therefore also essential for modernizers. It allowed them to imagine a transnational community that permitted diversity but was disciplined by the market and accountable to universal norms. This provided the moral justification for crossing borders on behalf of others and *in their own interest*.[19]

Even if one did not subscribe to the neocolonialist interpretation of the development agenda, it was enormously helpful to the leaders of industrialized countries. It allowed them to channel an international movement against imperialism into a common project in which they would continue to define and direct progress. Moreover, it gave them a new mission and a new identity with which to maintain internal cohesion. For instance, replacing the *mission civilisatrice* with a "modernizing mission" helped the French to appropriate and internalize a set of ideas and practices that had sometimes seemed like an American import—and imposition—as France itself underwent rapid socioeconomic change. Rather than confront the trade-offs between new conveniences and treasured customs—Americanization against traditional French culture—it was easier to contrast "Western"-led modernization with the archaism that countries like Algeria were made to represent.[20]

Indeed, by 1961 Paris could once again claim to be leading the forces of modernization by presenting French Algeria as a "a small-scale model of the relationship between the underdeveloped countries and the industrialized nations of the world." In an English-language brochure, "The Constantine Plan for Algeria: Opening New Frontiers in Development," the authors offered it as "a formula for human and material progress" that could address both "overabundant population" and anti-Western antagonism, though only if other countries followed Algeria's example in "throwing her doors wide open to Western influences."[21]

While this development project could be destructive to agrarian societies and deadly to "overabundant populations," it also offered them possible advantages—particularly the élites who would take charge of its local management. "Backwardness" was no longer determined by race or religion. With sufficient capital, training, and technology, any society could catch up with the former colonial powers and join the modern world. In the meantime, the Algerians and others could use these norms to claim aid and negotiate the terms of their integration in the development system, beginning with their own political independence.

For the Algerians and most of the international audience to which they appealed, each nation needed to be formally independent if only to obtain the mandate to participate in the development project. The French, on the other hand, argued for a time that independence was illusory and even counterproductive since every nation was becoming "interdependent." But by portraying economic integration as an inexorable, universal trend, they undermined their particular claim to Algeria. After all, if formal independence was unimportant, why deny it to the Algerians—especially when they themselves accepted the need for international trade and investment?[22] Indeed, the officials who planned the Evian agreements calculated that a politically independent Algeria could better manage development by using "the most effective authoritarian methods."[23] Why, then, should France continue to bear that burden, especially if it had to attend to its own transformation or else lose ground to economic competitors? Eventually de Gaulle himself articulated this view, describing decolonization as part of France's own modernization project. Thus, the Algerian War illustrated how new and old states could overcome internal opposition and claim expanded powers by presenting themselves as agents of an apolitical development project.

The Evian accords were based on an agreement between Paris and the GPRA to draw a line between national political independence on the one hand and transnational economic development on the other. The French pledge to provide teachers and technicians as well as to maintain funding for the Constantine Plan provided striking examples of the continuity between the colonial and postcolonial periods. Though Ben Bella would criticize the Evian accords for inviting neocolonial exploitation, his own policy statement, the Tripoli Platform, called for a "national, revolutionary, and scientific" state. And while his new regime favored nationalist and revolutionary rhetoric, it continued to implement projects first drawn up under the old regime. Whether in water allocation or investment, independent Algeria favored industry over agriculture, just like the French before them.[24] And years later, many Algerians still lived in the resettlement camps and villages built during the war. Indeed, the "Thousand Socialist Villages" plan of 1973 bore astonishing similarities to the thousand new villages projected by the Constantine Plan. Both aimed at integrating the rural population into a larger economy and encouraging a more modern lifestyle. Both plans were highly standardized, centralized, and seemingly "scientific."[25] The aim of Algeria's development policies was not just to reduce poverty, as Deborah Harrold has shown, but to promote a certain version of modernity. "We shall become clean, instructed, modern," the novelist al-Tahir Wattar has one of his mujahadeen say, "like the French."[26]

Of course, there were revolutionary experiments in the tumultuous history of postwar Algeria, above all Ben Bella's sponsorship of local "self-management" and Boumedienne's call for a "New International Economic Order." But as Robert Malley has argued, Ben Bella was really making a virtue of necessity. Economic policy became far more top-down once the government had the personnel to administer it.[27] Similarly, Boumedienne's campaign was an attempt to renegotiate the terms of "development," not question its essential premises. "We have constantly insisted in Algiers," he declared in 1973, "that if politics can divide us, economics can only unite us." "Development" appeared to transcend politics, even if regimes differed on how North and South would cooperate, or compete, to achieve it.[28]

Yet the Algerian War made it clear that the development project would not go unchallenged. There were many alternatives, but one held a particular fascination for contemporaries: the idea of decline. As a system, it can be described more by what participants opposed—crass materialism, cultural promiscuity, a naïve faith in progress—than what they were for. But they all imagined history as unremitting struggle. Rather than providing an example to the world, much less empathizing with it, they sought to preserve essential differences. As for accepted procedures, real or imagined violence was the preferred instrument for reifying or reinforcing racial and religious divisions.

In the same year *Le Monde Diplomatique* instructed readers in how to think about development, Sartre illustrated the idea of decline in his preface to Fanon's *The Wretched of the Earth*. Instead of seeing Algeria as a backward but developing country, Sartre argued that it was at the vanguard of historical change and Fanon was its prophet. While the Eastern and Western blocs were deadlocked, Algeria was leading "an invasion into universality." Nothing could happen in the Bled or Bizerte that the whole world did not hear about. Europe, on the other hand, was now revealed as a "fat, pale continent," "neither more nor less than a minority." "It's our turn," Sartre declared, "to tread the path, step by step, which leads down to the native level." Natives, on the other hand, would ascend on the backs of their oppressors, recreating themselves through violence against any and all Europeans—settlers, liberals, and leftists alike.[29]

Sartre's statement shows how a fascination with decline could extend even to those who saw themselves as its deserving victims. However implausible, volunteering to be victims of a race war at least offered his disciples the possibility of a new identity free of embarrassing ideological baggage left over from Stalinist times. For their more numerous opponents, on the other hand, defending the West against both emancipatory movements and this enemy within allowed them to claim to be part of the beleaguered vanguard of civilization. Thus, while Fanon's views were atypical, they did help the FLN to provoke disarray in the opposing camp. Moreover, some among the Algerians sincerely believed the war was a defense of Arab and Islamic civilization, especially when the French army or the OAS indiscriminately targeted Arabs and Muslims.

But while elements on both sides shared this view of the war as civilizational conflict, on balance it was of far greater help to those fighting against French Algeria. If its defense would indeed require unceasing struggle, proponents had to issue increasingly hyperbolic warnings against "abandonment." It "would signify Europe besieged, flanked from the South and in danger of death," the *Colloque de Vincennes*—an elite organization that included the likes of Jacques Soustelle and Georges Bidault—claimed in November 1960. "There would not be peace but generalized subversive war on the European continent."[30] But de Gaulle and many other conservatives concluded that integration and the immigration it entailed were far more immediate threats. This "anticolonialism of the right" called for a strategic withdrawal to more favorable terrain from which to defend a race-based *European* identity. Thus, like development, the idea of decline ultimately militated against denying Algeria independence.[31]

If the text of the Evian accords was based on developmentalist assumptions, its application revealed a subtext distinguishing between transnational economic and technological integration on the one hand and narrower communal and cultural cohesion on the other. For instance, France continued *cooperation* even after the pied noir exodus while blocking the escape of their erstwhile Muslim allies. The relatively few harkis who found sanctuary were segregated from French society in barbed-wire camps for years afterward. Like all stateless peoples they were treated as if they carried "the germs of a deadly sickness," as Hannah Arendt put it, because their very existence subverted the authority of nation-states.[32] Algerian nationals who chose to emigrate, on the other hand, could with a clearer conscience be instructed to leave their cultures and communities behind and integrate themselves as individual citizens. The prevailing attitude was captured in a poll taken forty years after the start of the Algerian War, when more than half of French respondents agreed that, "[t]he more one is integrated in French society, the less one is Muslim."[33] Immigrants had to adhere to an ostensibly secular faith in which Muslim schoolgirls were forbidden to wear the *chador* but obliged to observe Christian holidays. In effect, Algeria would continue to be aided in developing, but at arm's length, while Muslims would become French by ceasing to be Muslim.

Obviously, the subtext of the Evian accords was no more capable than the agreement itself of providing the basis for a lasting settlement in relations between the two countries and among their diverse communities. Thus, whereas Algerians are the least likely of all immigrants to petition for French citizenship, the vast majority of second-generation North Africans affirm their desire for integration. Less than a third of their countrymen, on the other hand, consider them to be French, and the pieds noirs are disproportionately represented among those who regularly vote to send them "home."[34] Meanwhile in Algeria, some Islamists see themselves as completing the unfinished business of the war by attacking foreigners and the Francophone elite. The Algerian War and its legacies show how a world of civilizational conflict can operate as a system, with extremists justifying each other's excesses while jointly silencing dissident voices.

While this account has contrasted two transnational systems, it seems unlikely that either can defeat, or even survive without, the other. Policymakers can easily entertain ideas of "development" and "decline" simultaneously, usually conceiving of them as either-or choices, as when they proposed "Eurafrica" or "North-South development" as the only way to avert international race war or *jihad*. Boumedienne offered an Algerian version of this argument in his call for a New International Economic Order in 1974. It was imperative, he argued, "to search together for a new way of life that would permit the subsistence of the eight thousand million human beings expected to populate the planet in the year 2000. . . . If not, there would not be enough atomic bombs to dam the tidal wave made up of the billions of human beings who will leave one day from the southern and poor part of the world to invade the relatively open spaces of the wealthy northern hemisphere in a quest for survival." More recently, one-sided proposals for economic "partnership" between the European Union and the countries of the Southern Mediterranean have been interpreted—and perhaps intended—as an effort to avert mass migration.[35]

But as the Algerian War amply demonstrated, "development" is the antithesis of international race or class war, not its antidote. Economic integration can cause political and cultural particularisms and even separatism to flourish. This can be seen not only in the way that urbanization, say, or new communications technologies can exacerbate communal conflicts; it is also revealed by the implausibility of portraying opposing sides as "for" or "against" modernization (rather than as participants in contests over what modernity means.)

Thus, while many take comfort in categorizing xenophobic movements like the FIS or the *Front National* as history's losers, frightened of the future, Islamists organize through the internet and favor economic liberalization as much or more than their adversaries. The FN, for its part, cultivates a radical chic and ridicules its opponents as leftovers of the 1960s. In both countries, more mainstream parties have co-opted their cultural policies, with an ostensibly anti-Islamist regime in Algiers condemning secularism and feminism while center-right politicians in Paris court the FN's anti-immigrant supporters. Indeed, the relationship between the apparent means and extremes in both countries are symbiotic rather than parasitic. While groups like the FIS and FN serve as bogeymen for those who package and market themselves as moderate alternatives, the scare-mongering that often accompanies their calls for accelerating development in Algeria and ending *exclusion* in France lend credibility to those who would instead enforce the borders between "us" and "them" at home and abroad. It is revealing, in this regard, that Boumedienne's warning about "eight thousand million human beings" was used by Jean Raspail as the epigraph for his racist novel about an immigrant invasion of Europe.[36]

There *is* a transnational system emerging from events like the Algerian War and the underlying trends they represent. But it is driven by processes of integration *and* disintegration, discourses of development *and* decline, operating together in a complex dialectic. In their origin, both are based on "either-or" choices and "us-them" dichotomies; in their effects, they both transcend and undermine state borders. But rather than gracefully withdrawing from the scene, states both cooperate and compete with one another and a host of other actors to control or at least profit from the expanding array of international and transnational transactions. Indeed, what de Gaulle called the "box of sorrows" that first opened in Algeria during its war for independence, revealing the potential for internecine communal strife uncontained by sovereign states, appears to have burst open once again. And once again the origins of the crisis can be found in development projects and populist opposition that are intimately, indeed causally related.[37]

A survey of what has been called "the Second Algerian War" would show many more parallels between the two periods. But such a snapshot would quickly fade and perhaps leave the wrong impression. Beginning with one war and ending with another would imply that communal conflict is primordial and perhaps inevitable, whereas the point of this book is to show how violence and the conditions from which it arises are the work and will of human beings. Indeed, this history reminds us that even during the worst of times—perhaps especially then—people across the Mediterranean have exchanged ideas and even traded places. Occasionally, as in the vision of interdependent, *multicommunautaire* societies, their meetings help us to imagine how people might share the same space, and much else besides, without any one community imagining that its language, its history, and its faith define all the rest. History can thus have a third "sense"—not as meaning, nor direction, but *purpose:* providing glimpses of how things might have transpired differently and helping us to imagine alternatives for a future that surely needs them. Perhaps it is only a myth. But after all the plagues and horrors have escaped from the Pandora's box of sovereignty, we are still left with hope.

Appendix: The Rise and Fall of the Armée de Libération Nationale

The three graphs that follow illustrate various aspects of the strength of the Armée de Libération Nationale during the Algerian War: numbers and types of combatants, numbers and types of weaponry, and numbers of rebel actions. Figures are compiled from intelligence reports in SHAT, Algérie 1H 1682/1, 1683/1–2, 1689/1–4, 1692/1–3; Triper, *Autopsie de la guerre*, annexe 22; and Shrader, *The First Helicopter War*, tables 5.1 and 6.5.

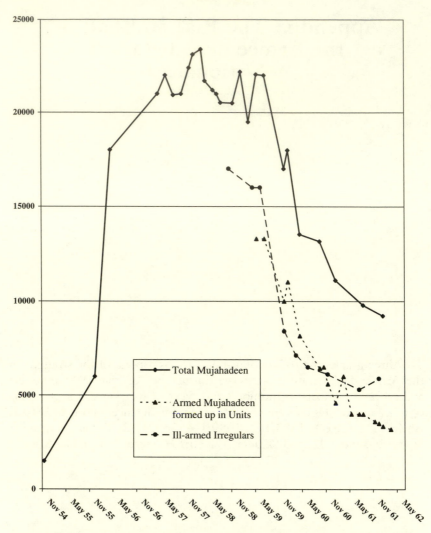

Rebel Forces, 1954–1962   In the spring of 1957 French intelligence began to issue regular estimates of the number of rebel combatants within Algeria. As the counterinsurgency campaign intensified, they were able to distinguish between mujahadeen with modern weapons operating in and out of regular units and a reserve force partially armed with pistols and hunting rifles. While fluctuations can reflect the varying quality of intelligence, changes in methodology, and perhaps political biases too, the overall trend is clear. The number of Algerian combatants of every sort peaked in 1958 and was steadily falling by the end of 1959.

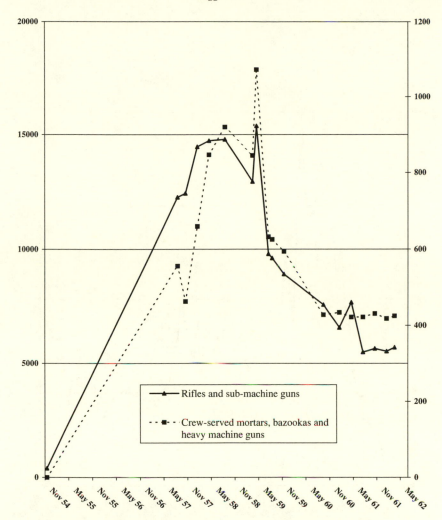

Rebel Armament French staff officers privately admitted that a large pool of volunteers was ready to join the ALN if it could find a way to arm them. The numbers of individual and team-serviced weapons—measured here along the left and right axes respectively—were therefore key determinants of rebel strength. By carefully tabulating arms lost and captured each month French intelligence was able to track the decline in the rebels' armament within Algeria, especially after border fortifications effectively sealed them off from resupply.

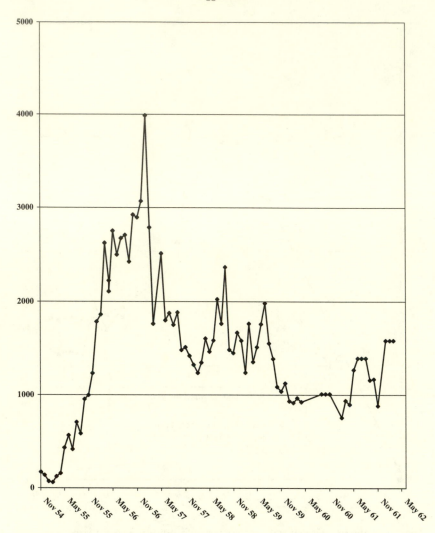

Monthly Tally of Rebel Activity   The number of rebel actions provides the
most objective measure of the military strength of the insurgency. Here too the
data is incomplete, and for 1960 and 1961 quarterly totals have been
disaggregated when monthly tallies were unavailable. It should also be noted
that these figures combine actions of every kind—ranging from a single shot
fired at a passing jeep to a battalion-sized assault. Yet once again it is clear that
the rebels peaked militarily long before formal negotiations began and never
fully recovered.

Notes

Preface

1. *That Noble Dream*, 220.

2. McMahon, "Study of American Foreign Relations," 556–558; Immerman, "The History of U.S. Foreign Policy: A Plea for Pluralism," 578. For a critical view, see Marks, "World According to Washington," 281–282.

3. The scholars who have been the most diligent in comparing U.S. with foreign perspectives tend to be the most critical of claims about U.S. influence based only on U.S. archives; see, e.g., Lundestad, "Moralism, Presentism"; Marks, "World According to Washington"; Milward, "Was the Marshall Plan Necessary"; Thorne, "After the Europeans"; Watt, "Britain and the Historiography." On the two-way flow of influence between big and small states, see Gaddis, "New Conceptual Approaches," 411–414.

4. Robinson and Gallagher, *Africa and the Victorians*.

5. Immerman, "History of U.S. Foreign Policy," 580–581.

6. See, for instance, Thelen, "Of Audiences, Borderlands, and Comparisons," and the rest of the special issue of the *Journal of American History* devoted to the subject.

7. Thorne, "After the Europeans," 201–208; Iriye, "Internationalization of History," 1–10.

8. See, for instance, Hunt, "Long Crisis," 138; Immerman, "History of U.S. Foreign Policy," 575–576.

9. Immerman, "History of U.S. Foreign Policy," 577 (my emphasis).

10. May, "Decline of Diplomatic History," 399–430; Kolko, *Limits of Power*, 7. See also McCormick, "State of Diplomatic History," 114–119.

11. Labaree, *Patriots and Partisans*, viii–ix. Labaree's was among the first works of American history influenced by *Annalistes* like Pierre Goubert and Em-

manuel Le Roy Ladurie. For recent accounts of the evolution of the *Annales* school, see Chartier, "Intellectual History and the History of *Mentalités*," 1–52, and introduction to the same volume, as well as Burke, *The French Historical Revolution*.

12. Braudel writes that a "bad conscience" only came twenty years later, in "Personal Testimony," 450–452. In her new biography, *Fernand Braudel*, Giuliana Gemelli suggests that *The Mediterranean* can be seen as a response to decolonization and the apparent decline of Europe.

13. McDonald, *Historic Turn*.

14. The title of one of the most widely read examples of this work—Germain Tillion's *Algeria: The Realities*—reveals the authority with which they typically offered this conclusion.

15. "Notions Essentielles sur l'Algérie," undated but circa 1956, AOM, 12/CAB/161; Peyrefitte, *C'était de Gaulle*, 52; Arthur Conte, "Rapport d'Information sur l'Aide aux Pays sous-développés," June 26, 1959, AN, Georges Bidault papers, 457AP, dossier 180, Notes Politiques reçus et divers, 1958–1961.

16. Solinas, *Gillo Pontecorvo's The Battle of Algiers*, 165–166, 174. See also Sartre's preface to Fanon's *The Wretched of the Earth*, 20.

17. Guha, "Prose of Counterinsurgency," 45–47. I discuss these issues at greater length in "Taking off the Cold War Lens."

18. Immerman, "The History of U.S. Foreign Policy," 583; Kennedy, "Imperial History and Post-Colonial Theory," 346. Kennedy advocates a dialogue between the fields, though he used the imperial metaphor knowing that it "resonated with readers," 359.

19. Hunt, "Long Crisis."

Introduction

1. This description is based on accounts in "La Délégation française se montrait sereine et assurée," *Le Monde*, May 21–22, 1961, 2; "Algeria Talks On," *The New York Times*, May 21, 1961, 1,4; and Horne, *A Savage War of Peace*, 467–468. The rest of this introduction raises issues and themes that will be more thoroughly discussed and documented in subsequent chapters. Citations are provided for direct quotations.

2. Jean Lacouture, *Algérie, La Guerre est finie*, 11.

3. The reader will note that "the Algerians" is shorthand for the *Front de Libération Nationale* or the GPRA, which is not to deny that their bona fides was in dispute. "The Muslims" will refer to the entire non-European population.

4. See, for instance, Connelly, "The Algerian War for Independence"; Thomas, *The French North African Crisis;* and Wall, *France, the United States, and the Algerian War*, as well as their various articles. The bibliography includes a number of other works which draw on archives on either side of the Atlantic, though rarely both.

5. Memoirs by former FLN officials are also invaluable, though Malek's *L'Algérie à Evian* is apparently the only publication to use these archives. This work also owes much to the efforts of Algerian scholars to publish primary materials on the FLN, especially Mohammed Harbi and Daho Djerbal.

6. *Islam and the Modern World*, 213–214.

7. "Modernization theory" will be critiqued in chapter 1—without the scare quotes.

8. Chevalier, *Le Problème démographique*, 148. Chevalier compared the Al-

gerians to nineteenth-century workers from the provinces arriving in Paris, and it seems likely that this study influenced his seminal work, *Classes laborieuses et classes dangereuses.*

9. "Une révolution démocratique," *El Moudjahid*, November 15, 1957.

10. For introductions to the globalization literature that share this book's emphasis on the changing significance of territory, contests over sovereignty, and the transformation of state power, see Geyer and Bright, "World History in a Global Age"; Held et al., *Global Transformations;* and Maier, "Consigning the Twentieth Century to History."

11. Mitterrand, quoted in Giesbert, *François Mitterrand*, 131; Bourdieu, *The Algerians*, 187.

1. The Failure of Progress

1. Quoted in Lerner, *The Passing of Traditional Society*, 214.

2. "Perspectives Géopolitiques: Destin de l'Europe," undated but circa 1952, AN, René Mayer papers, 363 AP32, dossier 4, correspondence.

3. "L'Algérie du demi siècle vue par les autorités," undated, AOM, 10/CAB/28.

4. Ruedy, *Modern Algeria*, 119–120; Ageron, *Modern Algeria*, 82, 86–87.

5. Breil, "Etude de Démographie Quantitative," vol. 2, 110.

6. "L'Algérie du demi siècle," 49, 53–55.

7. Quoted in Headrick, *Tools of Empire*, 66–67. See also Curtin, "Medical Knowledge," 594–613.

8. "L'Algérie du demi siècle," 243.

9. Ibid., 65–66.

10. Bourdieu, *The Algerians*, 120–122; Wolf, *Peasant Wars*, 211–216.

11. Ageron, *Modern Algeria*, 83–84; Bourdieu, *The Algerians*, 128.

12. Ageron, *Modern Algeria*, 84, 87; Ruedy, *Modern Algeria*, 120–121, 123.

13. "L'Algérie du demi siècle," 27, 72–73.

14. Wolf, *Peasant Wars*, 231; Bourdieu, *The Algerians*, 138.

15. "L'Algérie du demi siècle," 242.

16. Ruedy, *Modern Algeria*, 100–102; Stora, *Sources du Nationalisme*, 83–84.

17. "L'Algérie du demi siècle," 125–126.

18. Johnson, "Algeria: Some Problems," 237–239.

19. Ageron, *Histoire de l'Algérie*, 326–329. For opposing views on the 'ulama, see Harbi, *La Guerre Commence*, 115, 118–119, 122–124, and Stora, *Sources du Nationalisme*, 50–51, 83–86.

20. Quoted in Ageron, "Naissance d'une nation," in Ageron, *L'Algérie des Français*, 191.

21. "L'Algérie du demi siècle," 44.

22. Ibid., 261.

23. Ageron, "Français, juifs et musulmans," in Ageron, *L'Algérie des Français*, 113; Ruedy, *Modern Algeria*, 121; Alleg, *La guerre d'Algérie*, vol. 1, 146.

24. Preface to Descloitres and Reverdy, *L'Algérie des bidonvilles*, 7.

25. Ruedy, *Modern Algeria*, 125; Bourdieu, "The Algerian Subproletariat," 86–87.

26. "L'Algérie du demi siècle," 61.

27. Ageron, *Histoire de l'Algérie*, 524–526; Alleg, *La guerre d'Algérie*, vol. 1, 144–146.

28. Ruedy, *Modern Algeria*, 105, 126; Ageron, *Histoire de l'Algérie*, 534.

29. "L'Algérie du demi siècle," 125

30. Ruedy, *Modern Algeria*, 126; Gordon, *Women of Algeria*, 44–45.

31. On the importance of family influences on the *évolués*, see Quandt, *Revolution and Political Leadership*, 26–29. Regarding French policies toward Algerian women, see Lazreg, *The Eloquence of Silence*; Guernine, "Femmes Musulmanes en Algérie."

32. Even so, this was more than twice as many compared to 1950 (Ageron, *Histoire de l'Algérie*, 518, 536–537 and *Modern Algeria*, 91). See also Nouschi, "Culture et Décolonisation," 38–39.

33. Pervillé, *Les étudiants algériens*; Charnay, *La Vie Musulmane*.

34. Julien, *L'Afrique du Nord en Marche*, 113–123, 343–345.

35. Laroui, *The History of the Maghrib*, 346–347. Julien, *L'Afrique du Nord en Marche*, is the classic statement of the liberal thesis. For a more recent, nuanced restatement, see Ageron, *Modern Algeria*, 127–128.

36. Ageron, *Histoire de l'Algérie*, 526–529. Regarding the origins of Algerian nationalism through contact with the metropole, see Lyotard, *La Guerre des Algériens*, 149–150. On discrimination against Algerian immigrants, see Manceron and Remaoun, *D'une rive à l'autre*, 161–165.

37. Schoen, "Note sur l'Exode de la Main-Oeuvre Algérienne dans la metropole," undated but circa March 1949, AOM, 12/CAB/158; Jean-Jacques Rager, "L'émigration en France des Musulmans d'Algérie," undated, idem, 12/CAB/210; Ruedy, *Modern Algeria*, 125.

38. Bourdieu, *The Algerians*, 126–128.

39. "L'Algérie du demi siècle," 74–75.

40. R. J. Vincent, "Racial Equality," in Bull and Watson, *The Expansion of International Society*, 244. See also Anderson, *Imagined Communities*, 116–119.

41. Pervillé, "La Révolution Algérienne," 59–60; Julien, *L'Afrique du Nord en Marche*, 106–111; Le Tourneau, *Evolution Politique*, 312–313, 326–328; Ruedy, *Modern Algeria*, 136–138.

42. Julien, *L'Afrique du Nord en Marche*, 240–258; Le Tourneau, *Evolution Politique*, 335–345.

43. Ageron, *Modern Algeria*, 98–102; Ruedy, *Modern Algeria*, 147–150.

44. Le Commissaire Principal Bergé, Chef du Service Judiciaire à la Direction de la Securité Générale, to M. le Directeur de la Securité Générale, Bringard, June 17, 1945, AOM, MA, dossier 586.

45. Ibid.

46. Barrat, "Additif à mon Rapport sur les événements de Guelma," AOM, MA, dossier 586; "Résumé de l'entretien . . ." with Tixier, Chataigneau, et al., June 25, 1945, in *La Guerre d'Algérie par les Documents*, ed. Jauffret, vol. 1, 416–417.

47. "Répression des Emeutes de Guelma: Rapport du Commissaire Divisionnaire Bergé," January 20, 1946, AOM, MA, dossier 586.

48. Quandt, *Revolution and Political Leadership*, 52.

49. Moch to Schuman, January 31, 1948, AOM, MA, dossier 18.

50. Julien, *L'Afrique du Nord en Marche*, 284–288; Abbas quoted in Ageron, *Modern Algeria*, 106. See also Elgey, *République des tourmentes*, vol. 2, 448–449.

51. Harbi, *Le FLN*, 69–77.

52. Harbi, *Le FLN*, 60–65; Quandt, *Revolution and Political Leadership*, 61–62; Wolf, *Peasant Wars*, 232–235.

53. Harbi, *Le FLN*, 109–113.

54. Harbi, *La Guerre Commence*, 154; and see also Stora, *Sources du Nationalisme*, 22.

55. *Le FLN*, 131–137.

56. "L'Algérie du demi siècle," 112–113, 125–126, 243.

57. Headrick, *Invisible Weapon*, 127–129.

58. Courrière, *La Guerre d'Algérie*, vol. 1, 92–96; Ageron, *Modern Algeria*, 107.

59. "L'Algérie du demi siècle," 49, 53–57, 61, 69, 118–119; Schoen, "Note sur l'Exode" (see note 37).

60. Frederick Cooper makes a similar argument in the case of the Mau Mau insurgency, where a discourse opposing civilization to savagery and rationality to irrationality led to a reaction that was itself savage and even schizophrenic (*Decolonization and African Society*, 348, 359–360).

61. Vincent, "Racial Equality," 252 (see note 40); Bancel and Mathy, "La propagande économique," 221–222.

62. On this point, see Cooper, *Decolonization and African Society*, 468.

63. Quoted in Zoubir, "Decolonization of the Maghreb," 83, and see also 59.

64. Shriver, *Point of the Lance*, 8–9, quoted in Cobbs, "Foreign Policy of the Peace Corps," 79.

65. Shafer, *Deadly Paradigms*, 138–165.

66. For the following critique of development and modernization theory, I am indebted to Shafer, *Deadly Paradigms*, 66–77, Frederick Cooper, "Africa and the World Economy," in Cooper et al., *Confronting Historical Paradigms*, 87–90; Cooper and Randall Packard, Introduction to *International Development and the Social Sciences*, 1–41; and Gendzier, *Managing Political Change*, 1–13.

67. Frank, "The Underdevelopment of Development," 23.

68. Lerner, *The Passing of Traditional Society*, 232, 235, 254. That same month, November 1954, marked the introduction of the first commercially available transistor radio.

69. Fanon, *Studies in a Dying Colonialism*, 83; Charles-Robert Ageron, "Un aspect de la guerre d'Algérie: la propagande radiophonique du FLN et des Etats arabes," in Ageron, *La Guerre d'Algérie et les Algériens*, 245–250.

70. Boulanger, *Le Cinéma colonial*, 272.

71. Coup de Frejac, "Note à l'attention de M. le Délégué Général," February 11, 1961, and Figière, "Note au sujet des films égyptiens," April 25, 1960, AOM, 15/CAB/119.

72. Youssef Chahine, dir., *Djamila Bouhired*, Magda Films, circa 1959. While the film is highly embellished, this conception of Western education as a weapon was shared by Zohra Drif, one of Bouhired's comrades. See Quandt, *Revolution and Political Leadership*, 117–119.

73. Roche to Couve de Murville, December 20, 1959, and preceding telegrams, MAE, MLA, Propagande, dossier 7.

74. Guy Hennebelle, preface to Boulanger, *Le cinéma colonial*, 6.

75. Harrison, "Government and Press," 276, 280.

76. Le Tourneau, *Evolution politique*, 233; Horne, *A Savage War of Peace*, 79, 133; Bourdieu, *The Algerians*, 157, 162. On rumor more generally, see Scott, *Domination and the Arts of Resistance*. Of course, older technologies could also be effective. For instance, in 1956 an American diplomat in Amman complained that "[e]very report of Algerians killed prompts a telegram of protest from someone

or somebody to all and sundry. . . . One wonders what the Arabs did before the invention of the telegraph," Richard B. Parker to State, April 17, 1956, USNA, RG59, Central Decimal Files, 751S.00. For examples, see *Maḍābiṭ jalēt daur al-ijtimā' al-'ādī, Al-Majlis Jāmi'a Al-Dūl Al-'arabiah* (minutes of the meetings of the regular session of the Council of the Arab League), 25th session, March 29, 1956, Archives of the Arab League, Cairo, no. 9973.

77. Lerner, *The Passing of Traditional Society*, 255–257. By the 1970s, many social scientists began to view ethnic conflict as a by-product of modernization, and especially the proliferation of cross-cultural contacts through new media and migration (Horowitz, *Ethnic Groups in Conflict*, 3, 99–100). See especially Connor, *Ethnonationalism*, chapter 2, and Rothschild, *Ethnopolitics*, chapter 2.

78. Gendzier, *Managing Political Change*, 132.

79. Wolf, *Peasant Wars*, 280–281.

80. Skocpol, "What Makes Peasants Revolutionary?" 175–176; Adas, "Market Demand Versus Imperial Control," 106–108.

81. Wolf, *Peasant Wars*, 223–224; Marseille, "L'Algérie était-elle rentable?" in Ageron, *L'Algérie des Français*, 153; Marseille, "L'Algérie dans l'économie," 169–176; Fitzgerald, "Did France's Colonial Empire Make Economic Sense?" 378.

82. Bourdieu, cited in Ageron, *Histoire de l'Algérie*, 526; Marseille, "L'Algérie dans l'économie," 173.

83. Hargreaves, *Decolonization in Africa*, 23, 100–112; Frederick Cooper, "Modernizing Bureaucrats, Backward Africans, and the Development Concept," in Cooper and Packard, *International Development and the Social Sciences*, 76–81.

84. Albertini, *Decolonization*, 439–442.

85. Strachey, *The End of Empire*, 190; Fitzgerald, "Did France's Colonial Empire Make Economic Sense?"

86. Cooper, "Africa and the Development Idea," Conference on "Population and Security," Centre for History and Economics, Cambridge, UK, February 17–19, 1995.

87. Connelly and Kennedy, "Must It Be the Rest," 72 (the latter is responsible for this point).

88. Szreter, "The Idea of Demographic Transition," 661–663.

89. Coale and Hoover, *Population Growth*, 13–16.

90. "World Population Trends and Problems," July 23, 1959, State Department Intelligence Report no. 8057, USNA, RG59. Of course, dividing world population into racial categories presupposes that they have political significance, and producing the intended effect requires a foreshortened historical perspective. See Sen, "Population: Delusion and Reality," 63.

91. "Rapport d'Information sur l'Aide aux Pays sous-développés," June 26, 1959, AN, Georges Bidault papers, 457AP, dossier 180, Notes Politiques reçus et divers, 1958–1961. The author, Arthur Conte, later wielded immense influence as the director of the French radio and television broadcasting authority (ORTF). See also Strachey, *The End of Empire*, 312.

92. On the ideological confusion provoked by the war, see Lindenberg, "Guerres de mémoire," 91–94, and Rioux, "La Guerre d'Algérie dans l'histoire des intellectuels français," in Rioux and Sirinelli, *La Guerre d'Algérie et les intellectuels français*, 46–47.

93. Fanon, *The Wretched of the Earth*, 50; Camus, *Essais*, 1882.

94. Mitchell Stephens, "Deconstructing Jacques Derrida," *Los Angeles Times*

Magazine, July 21, 1991, 14, and see also Wood and Bernasconi, *Derrida and Différence*, 74–75.

95. Lucas and Vatin, *L'Algérie des anthropologues*, 72–75. See also Bourdieu, "Les Conditions sociales," 416–427.

96. Forest, *Histoire de Tel Quel*, 94–102.

97. Fischer, "Is Islam the Odd-Civilization Out?" 54–55. "If so called 'so-called poststructuralism' is the product of a single historical moment," Robert Young tentatively suggests, "then that moment is probably not May 1968 but rather the Algerian War for Independence—no doubt itself both a symptom and a product." He adds Sartre, Althusser, and Lyotard to the who's who list of those "either born in Algeria or personally involved with the events of the war" (*White Mythologies*, 1). Unfortunately, Young mythologizes the Algerian "moment" rather than considering how the war's complex and protracted history might have given rise to new critiques of Western philosophy—a question ripe for further research.

98. Schofield, *The Falling Veil*, AOM.

99. The histories of imperialism and environmentalism have long been intertwined; see MacKenzie, *The Empire of Nature*, and Grove, *Ecology, Climate, and Empire*. *Guardian* article quoted in Sangmuah, "The United States and the French Empire," 221.

100. See, for instance, "L'Algérienne dans la révolution," *El Moudjahid* no 3; Amrane, *Les femmes algériennes*; Benallègue, "Algerian Women," 703–715; Gordon, *Women of Algeria*, 53–56.

101. Quoted in Shafer, *Deadly Paradigms*, 66. On secular nationalism, see Juergensmeyer, *The New Cold War?* 11–13.

102. Shafer, *Deadly Paradigms*, 49–50.

103. For a survey and analysis see Herman, *The Idea of Decline*.

104. Wu, *Yellow Peril*, 30–46. The standard work on the subject in the late nineteenth and early twentieth century is Gollwitzer, *Die Gelbe Gefahr*. See also Thorne, *The Issue of War*, 27–32, and Dower, *War without Mercy*, 156–64, which survey the same theme through the onset of World War II.

105. Spengler, *The Hour of Decision*, 227.

106. Valéry, "The Crisis of the Mind," vol. 10, 31 (emphasis in the original). See also Albertini, *Decolonization*, 11–12.

107. Quoted in Pruessen, *John Foster Dulles*, 425.

108. Alphand to Pineau, April 25, 1958, MAE, Série MLA, Dossier 24. See also NSC 5614/1, October 3, 1956, FRUS, 1956–58, XVIII, 139–141; Rountree memo to Dulles, August 28, 1957, ibid., 276.

109. Girard de Charbonnière to Pineau, November 13, 1957, MAE, Série MLA, Vol. 23 bis (provisional number), Action extérieure, Etats-Unis, déc. 1956–déc 1957, Cote EU.

110. Charles-Robert Ageron, " 'L'Algérie dernière chance,' " 134.

111. Debré, "Programme du gouvernement," January 15, 1959, *Journal Officiel*, 1959, n° 12, 27–28.

112. "Conférence prononcée le 26 février 1955 à All Souls College Oxford par le Général de l'armée A. Guillaume," AN, Georges Bidault papers, 457AP, Documents défense nationale 1954–55.

113. "L'Action du Communisme en Afrique," September 1, 1959, MAE, Série MLA, Propagande, dossier 2; Raoul-Duval to Couve de Murville, December 30, 1959, MAE, Série MLA, Action Extérieure, dossier 19, Chine Populaire, avril '57–janvier 1962.

114. Memcon Lodge-Mollet, March 13, 1956, FRUS, 1955–57, XVIII, 119; Bouffanais to Parodi, November 26, 1959, MAE, Série MLA, Action Extérieure, dossier 19, Chine Populaire, avril '57–janvier 1962.

115. October 10, 1956 circular, MAE, Série ONU, dossier 550.

116. "Algérie," 1956, MAE, Série ONU, dossier 549.

117. On the FLN's use of Islamic names and symbols, see Mūrū, *Al-Jazā'ir ta'ūdu*, 101–102. See also Ageron, "Une guerre religieuse?" 27–29; Frémeaux, *La France et l'Islam*, 248–250. The Indonesian independence movement also used the symbols of earlier religious resistance, see Bernhard Dahm, *Sukarno and the Indonesian Struggle*.

118. Mohammed Harbi, "Le Complot Lamouri," and Charles-Robert Ageron, "La 'Guerre psychologique' de l'Armée de libération nationale algérienne," both in Ageron, *La Guerre d'Algérie et les Algériens*, 153–154, 208–210.

119. Even Fanon appeared to recognize the danger of provoking a backlash when he insisted that "the capitalist regime must not try to enlist the aid of the socialist regime over 'the fate of Europe' in face of the starving multitudes of colored peoples"; see *The Wretched of the Earth*, 45–46, 50, 53, 93, 104–106.

120. Picot to Pineau, February 1, 1957, MAE, Série ONU, dossier 550; Rédha Malek interview with author, Algiers, December 1999.

121. As early as 1945, Pierre Leprohon noted that a generation of films like *Beau Geste* had implied that "the Frenchman has nothing else to do in Africa except fight the infidel," observing astutely that this constituted a kind of "counter-propaganda" to French colonialism (*L'Exotisme et le cinéma*, 208–209).

122. Editorial Note, June 14, 1957, FRUS, 1955–57, XIX, 527. Similarly, the U.S. Information Agency under Kennedy sought to "subdue the racial aspect and also to disassociate Americans from disorders involving Europeans" by avoiding the term "white." Tubby memo for Edward R. Murrow, circa August 1961, USNA, RG59, PPS, Lot 67D548, box 120, Information Policy.

123. Memcon Dulles-Lloyd-Pineau, March 12, 1958, DDF, 1958, I, No. 179. Regarding U.S. skepticism toward French claims about Communist influence among North African nationalists, see chapter 3.

124. Brands, *Specter of Neutralism*, 266–267, 276, 294. In fact, the Arab League later considered an embargo against France over Algeria but was deterred by the French role in Iraqi oil production (Majāhid, *Al-Jazā'ir 'abr Al-Ijyāl*, 515–516).

125. Quoted in Brands, *Specter of Neutralism*, 274.

126. See Connelly, "Taking off the Cold War Lens," 759–760.

127. Eisenhower, 417th NSC, August 18, 1959, DDEL, AWF, NSC Series, and see also idem, the 408th Meeting of the NSC, May 28, 1959.

128. Quoted in Shafer, *Deadly Paradigms*, 100.

129. Memcon de Gaulle-Adenauer, September 14, 1958, DDF, 1958, II, no. 155.

130. La Tournelle to MAE, May 19, 1956, MAE, Série ONU, dossier 548.

131. Lorillot to MAE, April 17, 1959, DDF, 1959, I, no. 230.

132. Seydoux to MAE, October 8, 1958, December 9, 1958, and October 28, 1959, MAE, Série MLA, Action Extérieure, R.F.A., dossiers 2 and 4.

133. Quoted in Yacono, *De Gaulle et le F.L.N.*, 20–21.

134. "L'Algérie du demi siècle," 261.

135. De Gaulle, Radio-television address, June 14, 1960, *Discours et Messages*, 225–228.

2. The Ambivalence of Power

1. "Rapport d'Aït Ahmed, membre du Bureau Politique du PPA, au Comité Central élargi," December 1948, in Harbi, *Les Archives*, 41.

2. Juin to Henri Queuille, July 10, 1952, MAE, Schuman Papers, vol. 6, Maroc.

3. This account is based on the official army history: Howe, *Northwest Africa*, vol. 1, 202–204, 241–244, 249–250, 679. Roosevelt quoted in "Appeals and Proclamation to French People," *The New York Times*, November 8, 1942, 8.

4. Quotes are from Howe, *Northwest Africa*, 104, 108.

5. Pierre Mélandri and Maurice Vaïsse, "La 'boîte à chagrin,' " in Rioux, *La Guerre d'Algérie et les Français*, 439.

6. Ageron, *Modern Algeria*, 99. Sultan Mohammed V also appealed to Roosevelt, who may have suggested that he would help Morocco regain independence (Sangmuah, "Sultan Mohammed ben Youssef's American Strategy," 131–132).

7. Kettle, *De Gaulle and Algeria*, 31.

8. For an analysis of American wartime policy in North Africa, see Hoisington, "The American Presence in Morocco," 153–168, and Bills, *Empire and Cold War*, 27–36.

9. M'Hammed Yazid report to the CNRA, July 1957, reprinted in Harbi, *Les Archives*, 172–173.

10. On the Soviets, see Zoubir, "Decolonization of the Maghreb," 59–60. For Britain, see Louis, "Libyan Independence," 168–170, and Thomas, *The French North African Crisis*, 19–21.

11. The great powers, which in this period still included France and the UK, will be discussed in greater detail anon, but for Germany see Klaus Jürgen Müller, "Le Réalisme de la République fédérale d'Allemagne," in Rioux, *La Guerre d'Algérie et les Français*, 409–410.

12. Regarding Algerian oil, see Yergin, *The Prize*, 526–527; Furniss, *France, Troubled Ally*, 199–202.

13. 406th Meeting of the NSC, May 13, 1959, FRUS, 1958–60, XIII, 729–730.

14. Yergin, *Shattered Peace*, 143; Louis, *The British Empire in the Middle East*, 271.

15. Leffler, *A Preponderance of Power*, 75–77.

16. Pelt, *Libyan Independence and the United Nations*, 139–141; Louis, "Libyan Independence," 166.

17. Pelt, *Libyan Independence and the United Nations*, 74–84.

18. This is Louis's argument in "Libyan Independence"; see especially 165–166, 176, 182–184.

19. "Maroc et Tunisie," *La Nef*, March 1, 1953, 7–9. See also Julien, *L'Afrique du Nord en marche*, 60–62, and Bonnet, *Quai d'Orsay*, 375–376.

20. El Méchat, *Tunisie, Les Chemins vers l'indépendance*, 35–51, 91–96; Khider memo to Political Commission of Arab League, September 3, 1953, in Harbi, *Les Archives*, 50–51.

21. Blair, "The Impact of Franco-American Military Agreements," 65.

22. The British and the Soviets shared this view, see Louis, "Libyan Independence," 168–169, and Hadhri, *L'URSS et la Magrheb*, 101–103.

23. Marshall to Caffery, June 10, 1947, FRUS, 1947, V, 686–689.

Notes to Pages 45–49

24. "Note: Déclaration faite à M. Chauvel par M. Jefferson Caffery," July 15, 1947, AOM, MA, dossier 30.

25. Ibid. See also Marshall to Caffery, July 25, 1947, in which Dean Acheson repeated these urgings, FRUS, 1947, V, 700–701.

26. "Recommendations in Report of North African Conference in Paris," June 20, 1947, FRUS, 1947, V, 691–698. For an analysis, see Sangmuah, "The United States and the French Empire," 152–169.

27. Hogan, "The Search for a 'Creative Peace,' " 279.

28. Kennan quoted in Harper, *American Visions of Europe*, 218–222.

29. Young, *France, the Cold War and the Western Alliance*, 166–167.

30. Bidault to Depreux, undated but circa August 1947, AOM, MA, dossier 30.

31. André Nouschi, "France, the Empire and Power (1945–1949)," in Becker and Knipping, *Power in Europe*, 478–482.

32. Sangmuah, "Sultan Mohammed ben Youssef's American Strategy," 131–134.

33. Bourguiba to Abbas, July 29, 1946, reprinted in El Méchat, *Tunisie, Les Chemins vers l'indépendance*, 259–263.

34. This and subsequent citations are from "Rapport d'Aït Ahmed," 15–49 (see note 1). One could quibble with Aït Ahmed's assessment. The Irish faced these same obstacles to their independence, but their experience would hardly have encouraged the Algerians. For a comparative study, see Lustick, *Unsettled Lands*.

35. See Aït Ahmed's account in *Mémoires d'un combattant*, 156–158. The Moroccans placed a similar emphasis on the international aspect of their independence movement, and they, too, sought to exert pressure on the allies by pointing to the danger of Communist expansion in North Africa. See Istiqlal leader Allal al-Fassi's *The Independence Movements in Arab North Africa*, 381–394.

36. Naimark provides a harrowing account in *The Russians in Germany*, 69–140.

37. Memcon MacArthur-Bidault et. al., January 29, 1948, FRUS, 1948, III, 618–620.

38. Ibid., 618. "Little Bidault" quoted in Wall, *The United States and the Making of Postwar France*, 46. On war scare, see 133–134.

39. Trachtenberg, *History and Strategy*, 119–120; Borowski, *A Hollow Threat*, 121.

40. Poole, HJCS, IV, 162, 164.

41. Leach memo to Finletter, December 26, 1950, DDEL, Norstad Papers, box 21, Misc. 1950 (4).

42. Wall, *The United States and the Making of Postwar France*, 171. For striking examples of the weakness French policymakers felt vis-à-vis the United States, see René Girault, "The French Decision-Makers and their Perception of French Power in 1948," in Becker and Knipping, *Power in Europe*, 47–48.

43. Robert Frank, "The French Dilemma: Modernization with Dependence or Independence and Decline," in Becker and Knipping, *Power in Europe*, 263–280; Bossuat, *La France, l'aide américaine*, vol. 1, 260–268, 273.

44. Schelling first spelled out the general principles of what are now known as "two-level games" in *The Strategy of Conflict*, 19–28.

45. Young, *France, the Cold War and the Western Alliance*, 218–219; Lundestad, *America, Scandinavia, and the Cold War*, 195–196.

46. Trachtenberg, *History and Strategy*, 166. In his impressive study, *France*

Restored, William I. Hitchcock shows how Paris played a weak hand masterfully from 1945 to 1954. But by following the story through the end of the Algerian War, we shall see that this recovery was quite provisional, even precarious, in terms of both financial and political independence.

47. "Suggested Approach by Department Representatives during Informal Talks with Representatives of National Military Establishment," June 9, 1949, and "Views of the JCS on Military Rights in Foreign Territories," following May 19, 1949, letter from Johnson to Acheson, FRUS, 1949, I, 304–305, 327; Poole, HJCS, IV, 169–170.

48. See, for instance, "Views of the JCS," and PPS/56, "Progress Report on the Department's Study of 'Views of the JCS . . . '," August 4, 1949, FRUS, 1949, I, 309, 370–371; Lovett to Forrestal, January 17, 1949, FRUS, 1949, IV, 38–39.

49. "Suggested Approach," FRUS, 1949, I, 327. See also "Notes on the JCS Paper," idem, 321–323.

50. Kaplan, *The Wizards of Armageddon*, 93.

51. On Korean invasion, Leffler, *A Preponderance of Power*, 361–374. On Attlee summit, Trachtenberg, *History and Strategy*, 120. The Moroccan bases were conceived of as an alternative to those in the U.K. (Poole, HJCS, IV, 169). For the text of the base agreements, see Bruce to Acheson, December 17, 1950, FRUS, 1950, V, 1764–70.

52. Direction d'Amérique, "La Politique Américaine des Bases," April 5, 1948, MAE, Série B, Amérique, 1944–1952, Etats-Unis, VoP 62.

53. Bonnet to Schuman, July 18 and July 20, 1950, MAE, B-Amérique, Etats-Unis, 1944–52, vol. 106. On the shift in American policy, see also Lacroix-Riz, *Les Protectorats*, 79–86.

54. Malone quoted in Hamburger, "Franco-American Relations, 1940–1962," 46–50. On Marshall plan, Bossuat, *La France, l'aide américaine*, I, 545–546.

55. Bonnet to Schuman, July 18, 1950, MAE, B-Amérique, Etats-Unis, 1944–52, vol. 106.

56. Naegelen quoted in Sangmuah, "The United States," 263.

57. For Juin's threat, see memcon Juin-Sultan, January 26, 1951, MAE, Schuman Papers, Maroc, vol. 6.

58. Memcon McGhee-Juin, January 31, 1951, USNA, RG59, lot file 53D468, box 16, "Morocco 1948 Memoranda." Earlier that month, the Americans were reported to be urging the Arab League to end propaganda against the French in North Africa, Duparc to Schuman, January 5, 1951, MAE, B-Amérique, Etats-Unis, 1944–52, vol. 125.

59. McGhee summary of conclusions of Tangier conference, October 24, 1950, FRUS, 1950, V, 1571–1573.

60. Louis and Robinson make this argument for Britain in "The Imperialism of Decolonization," which applies Robinson and Gallagher's earlier approach to the Cold War period. Regarding South Africa, see Noer, *Cold War and Black Liberation*, 27–30.

61. Memcon McGhee-Juin, January 31, 1951, USNA, RG59, lot file 53D468, box 16, "Morocco 1948 Memoranda."

62. Memcon Pendar-Richey, February 2, 1951, USNA, RG59, Central Decimal Files, 711.56371. Pendar had been an OSS agent in North Africa. Ironically, French Communists had pointed to him as exemplifying how espionage could be

Coca-Cola's secret ingredient (Wall, *The United States and the Making of Postwar France*, 123).

63. Elbrick to Dulles, May 31, 1956, FRUS, 1955–57, XVIII, 531–533.

64. Pendar to Finletter, October 28, 1951, USNA, RG59, Central Decimal Files, 711.56371. On reminding Americans, see French Embassy Aide Mémoire to the State Department, October 17, 1951, MAE, B-Amérique, Etats-Unis, 1944–52, vol. 126. To Bonnet, the rise of anti-Western nationalism in Egypt and Iran comprised "unquestionable trump cards which we ought to use to the best possible advantage" (Bonnet to Schuman, October 19, 1951, idem).

65. Juin's successor, Augustin Guillaume, told one American consul that, when Moroccan nationalists came to his office, he should tell them "get out pigs, you are enemies of France which is our friend" (Sangmuah, "The United States," 313–314). The base agreement made Muslim neighborhoods off limits to American personnel and gave the French the right to manage the local labor force (Zartman, *Morocco: Problems of New Power*, 23–24; Blair, "The Impact of Franco-American Military Agreements," 65–66). On Tunisia, see Périllier to Schuman, September 20, 1951, MAE, B-Amérique, Etats-Unis, 1944–52, vol. 125. On Vietnam, see Laurent Césari, "The French Military and U.S. Participation in the Indochina War," in Kaplan, Artaud, and Rubin, *Dien Bien Phu*, 50–51. On Marshall Plan aid, see Bossuat, *La France, l'aide américaine*, vol. 1, 548–549.

66. U.S. policy toward British-Egyptian relations followed a similar pattern, as nationalists used their strategic position to play off the great powers and end European colonialism (Brands, *Specter of Neutralism*, 234, 243; Hahn, *The United States*, 102–107).

67. On U.S. warning, see Acheson to Delegation in Tangier, February 2, 1951, FRUS, 1951, V, 1371–1373. On Schuman's caution, see "Principes de Politique Marocaine," February 7, 1951, MAE, Schuman Papers, Maroc, vol. 6.

68. Juin to Schuman, February 26, 1951, MAE, Schuman Papers, Maroc, vol. 6.

69. On Juin, see McBride to State Department, September 26, 1950, USNA, RG59, Central Decimal Files, 711.56371. On troop limit, see Bruce to Acheson, March 1, 1951, USNA, RG59, Lot File 52–19, Bray Records, box 24, Base Facilities, 8.04. On strategic command, see Juin to Koenig, March 1, 1951, SHAT, Maroc 3H, Carton 684. On (unsuccessful) resignation threat, see Doise and Vaïsse, *Diplomatie et outil militaire*, 555.

70. For supporting evidence, see "Le 'Strategic Air Command,'" SHAA, Château de Vincennes, Série E 0/2, Cabinet Militaire, 19v, Carton 2911; Note for Secrétaire Général Permanent de la Défense Nationale from le Présidence du Conseil, June 13, 1952, SHAA, Série E 0/2, 29e, Carton 2977; Ministre de la Défense—Affaires Générales to Secrétaire d'Etat de l'Armée de l'Air, March 4, 1953, idem. In these plans, the French were doubtless mindful of the death and destruction they endured from Allied bombing during World War II.

71. Schuman to Juin, April 26, 1951, MAE, Schuman Papers, Maroc, vol. 6. On economic negotiations, see Wall, *The United States and the Making of Postwar France*, 207–210. On Germany, see Hitchcock, *France Restored*, 152–156.

72. Juin to Henri Queuille, July 10, 1952, MAE, Schuman Papers, Maroc, vol. 6. Lacroix-Riz maintains that American criticism cost Juin his job (*Les Protectorats*, 103). The Americans were at least considering linking the removal of Juin to support for the French position at the United Nations, Bourgerie memo

to McGhee, April 23, 1951, USNA, RG59, Lot 53D468, box 16, Morocco 1948 Memoranda (1948).

73. For early discussions of the "blank check," see the September 21, 1951, memo by Bourgerie and October 8, 1951, memo by Perkins and Jones, USNA, RG59, lot file 53D468, box 16, "Morocco 1948 Memoranda"; Acheson, *Present at the Creation*, 561.

74. HJCS, V (1953–54), 169.

75. "United States Policy in Morocco," November 21, 1951, FRUS, 1951, V, 1392–1394.

76. Wainstein et al., *The Evolution of U.S. Strategic Command and Control*. I am grateful to Marc Trachtenberg for providing me with this document.

77. The following discussion is based on Bossuat, *La France, l'aide américaine*, vol. 1, 553–558; Sangmuah, "The United States," 460–487; and Rivlin, "The United States and Moroccan International Status," 72–73.

78. Sangmuah, "The United States," 213.

79. Sangmuah, "Sultan Mohammed ben Youssef's American Strategy," 133.

80. Quoted in Rivlin, "The United States and Moroccan International Status," 73.

81. For a contemporary account of the U.N. debates, see Day, *Les Affaires de la Tunisie et du Maroc*.

82. Quoted in Sangmuah, "The United States," 304; Kaufman, *The Korean War*, 297–298.

83. "Reception de M. Binoche par le Bey," August 11, 1952, MAE, Schuman Papers, vol. 8, Tunisie.

84. See, for instance, Auriol, *Mon septennat*, 465–472 and, more generally, Smouts, *La France à L'ONU*, 146–155.

85. El Méchat, *Tunisie, Les Chemins vers l'Indépendance*, 178–179.

86. Juin to Schuman, May 3, 1951, MAE, Schuman Papers, vol. 6, Maroc. For an account of the Indonesia case, see McMahon, *Colonialism and Cold War*, 251–303.

87. "Note pour le Ministre," April 18, 1952, MAE, Schuman Papers, vol. 7; de Hautecloque to Bidault, January 13, 1953, AN, Bidault Papers, 457AP, 113/1952–1954, lettres de M. de Hauteclocque.

88. Memcon Pinay-Acheson, May 28, 1952, FRUS, 1952–54, XI, 768–771.

89. Bonnet to Diplomatie, April 13, 1951, MAE, B-Amérique, Etats-Unis, 1944–52, vol. 125; Acheson, *Present at the Creation*, 638–639.

90. Bonnet to Schuman, February 2, 1952, MAE, B-Amérique, Etats-Unis, 1944–52, vol. 126.

91. Schuman does not explicitly name McCarthy. Instead, he refers to "a parliamentary representative who is eager to criticize the men as well as the action of American diplomacy." Guillaume singled out the China expert John Carter Vincent, already a victim of McCarthyism, who was serving in bureaucratic exile as Minister in Tangier, Schuman to Guillaume, November 24, 1951, MAE, B-Amérique, Etats-Unis, 1944–52, vol. 126.

92. Schuman (Service d'Information et de Presse) to Guillaume, November 30, 1951, MAE, B-Amérique, Etats-Unis, 1944–52, vol. 126—"eventually" because for some time they squabbled over who would pay for it. See, for instance, Bonnet to Schuman, August 8, 1952, MAE, Amérique, Etats-Unis, 347, AFN, Maroc—1952–1956.

93. Sangmuah, "The United States," 268.

94. See note 113.

95. Le Tourneau, *Evolution politique*, 233–234.

96. One is tempted to tag de Gaulle with the original sin, but of course the army never lived up to its reputation as *la grande muette* in the empire; see Andrew and Kanya-Forstner, *France Overseas*, 10, and more generally, Porch, *The Conquest of Morocco* and *The Conquest of the Sahara*.

97. Poidevin, *Robert Schuman*, 358.

98. Auriol, *Mon septennat*, 438.

99. Dillon to Dulles, August 12, 1953, and Dorman to Dulles, August 17, 1953, FRUS, 1952–54, XI, 615, 617.

100. "Note pour le Ministre," AN, René Mayer Papers, 363 AP24, dossier 9: Notes de Léon Marchal sur le Maroc, Mai 1953–Janvier 1955.

101. Williams, *Politics in Post-War France*, 23–25.

102. Bossuat, *La France, l'aide américaine*, vol. 2, 840–842; Wall, *The United States and the Making of Postwar France*, 229–231.

103. Bossuat, *La France, l'aide américaine*, vol. 2, 856; Kaplan, "NATO and French Indochina," in Kaplan, Artaud, and Rubin, *Dien Bien Phu*, 233–234, 236–237.

104. Quoted in Rolf Steininger, "John Foster Dulles, the European Defense Community, and the German Question," in Immerman, *John Foster Dulles*, 88.

105. Bonnet to Schuman, MAE, Amérique 1952–1963, Etats-Unis-AFN, 30, 1952–55.

106. France, "AFL-CIO Foreign Policy," 96, 104, 153–155; Morris, *CIA and American Labor*, 69–100.

107. Wayne G. Jackson and the Historical Staff, Central Intelligence Agency, *Allen Welsh Dulles as Director of Central Intelligence 26 February 1953–29 November 1961, Volume III: Covert Activities*, USNA, RG263, 190-24-34, 104–105.

108. Morgan, *A Covert Life*, 214–217, 254–256; Costigliola, *France and the United States*, 66–67; Lacroix-Rix, *Les Protectorats*, 83–86.

109. Quoted in Lacroix-Riz, *Les Protectorats*, 221.

110. Bonnet to Schuman, January 2, 1953, MAE, Amérique 1952–1963, Etats-Unis-AFN, 30, 1952–55. See also Bonnet to Bidault, March 5, 1953, idem.

111. NSC 114/2, October 12, 1951, FRUS, 1951, I, 186. On evolution of defense plans, see Watson, HJCS, V, 190–191, 307–308; Poole, HJCS, IV, 163.

112. Al Dib, *Abdel Nasser et la Révolution Algérienne*, 11–13.

113. Dorman to Dulles, August 17, 1953, FRUS, 1952–54, XI, 617; National Intelligence Estimate 71–89, "Probable Developments in North Africa," August 31, 1954, idem, 154, 167; Norris, Arkin, and Burr, "Where They Were," 26–35.

114. Memcon DDE-Dulles, October 14, 1953, MTC, Dulles-Herter, UPA microfilm publication (1980), reel 8, frame 812.

115. Smith quoted in 144th Meeting of the NSC, May 13, 1953, FRUS, 1952–54, VI, 1944.

116. Kaplan, *Wizards of Armageddon*, 100–107; Rosenberg, " 'A Smoking Radiating Ruin," 25; Trachtenberg, *History and Strategy*, 134, 162.

117. Trachtenberg, *History and Strategy*, 163–164.

118. Quoted in Pruessen, "John Foster Dulles and the Predicaments of Power," in Immerman, *John Foster Dulles*, 35.

119. Trachtenberg, *History and Strategy*, 166.

120. For an account of Franco-Spanish relations over North Africa based on archives in both countries, see Otero's excellent memoire, "L'Algérie dans les relations franco-espagnoles 1954–1964."

121. Bidault to Guillaume, January 17, 1954; Bonnet to Bidault, January 21, 1954; and unsigned memorandum "A[u] S[ujet] du rassemblement de Tétouan," all in AN, Bidault Papers, 457AP, 119/Maroc, 1954; Meyrier to Bidault, January 19, 1954, and Bonnet to Bidault, January 21, 1954, both in MAE, Europe 1949–1955, Espagne, No. 188, January 5–January 30, 1954. See also Sangmuah, "The United States," 373–375.

122. Quoted in Pierre Mélandri, "La France et le 'Jeu Double' des Etats-Unis," in Rioux, *La Guerre d'Algérie et les Français*, 433.

123. Sangmuah, "Eisenhower and Containment," 78; Pruessen, "John Foster Dulles and the Predicaments of Power," in Immerman, *John Foster Dulles*, 23; 269th Meeting of the NSC, December 8, 1955, FRUS, 1955–57, X, 54.

124. Quoted in Sangmuah, "The United States," 349.

125. Ferrell, *The Eisenhower Diaries*, 223.

126. Hough, *The Struggle for the Third World*, 147–149; Rodman, *More Precious than Peace*, 48–54.

127. Ferrell, *The Eisenhower Diaries*, 245.

128. Paret, *French Revolutionary Warfare*, 15–17, 22.

129. "Note pour le Ministre," April 18, 1952, MAE, Schuman Papers, vol. 7. On Eurafrica's earlier history, see Ageron, "L'idée d'Eurafrique," 446–475. On the revival of the idea, see René Girault, "Les Indépendances des pays d'Afrique noire dans les relations internationales," in Ageron and Michel, *l'Afrique noire française*, 470–472.

130. Girardet, *L'idée coloniale en France*, 323–326.

131. De Hautecloque to Bidault, August 11, 1953, AN, Bidault Papers, 457AP, 113/1952–1954, lettres de M. de Hauteclocque.

132. "Exposé présenté devant M. Foster Dulles," February 2, 1953, AN, Bidault Papers, 457AP, 44/2-Relations Franco-Américains. See also Juin to Moch, March 27, 1951, AN, F60, Cote 3054.

133. "Exposé présenté devant M. Foster Dulles."

134. Eisenhower to Gruenther, June 8, 1954, EOF, Part 1: Eisenhower Administration Series, UPA (1991), reel 13, frames 926–27.

135. Lodge to Dulles, June 11, 1954, DDEL, JFDP, General Correspondence and Memoranda Series, box 2, Strictly Confidential (2).

136. 151st Meeting of the NSC, June 25, 1953, DDEL, AWF, NSC Series.

137. Lodge to Juin, June 14, 1954, DDEL, JFDP, General Correspondence and Memoranda Series, box 2, Strictly Confidential (2).

138. Ibid.

139. 215th Meeting of the NSC, September 24, 1954, DDEL, AWF, NSC Series.

140. Denise Artaud, "France between the Indochina War and the European Defense Community," in Kaplan, Artaud, Rubin, *Dien Bien Phu*, 262–263; Trachtenberg, *A Constructed Peace*, 123–125. In February 1958, Dulles judged that Algeria was "likely to evolve like Indochina. Eventually we may see a leftist government in Paris which will liquidate the Algerian affair. But unfortunately such a leftist government was likely to liquidate NATO as well," 356th Meeting of the

NSC, February 27, 1958, DDEL, AWF, NSC Series. See also Costigliola, *France and the United States*, 116–117, where Dulles is quoted making the same prediction two months later.

141. Jernegan memo to Merchant, September 5, 1954, USNA, Lot 58D48, Subject Files of the Officer in Charge of Northern African Affairs 1945–1956, box 3.

142. 215th Meeting of the NSC, September 24, 1954, DDEL, AWF, NSC Series; 267th Meeting of the NSC, November 21, 1955, FRUS, 1955–57, XIX, 150–151. On hopes for European integration, see Ambrose, *Eisenhower*, vol. 2, 404–405; Trachtenberg, *History and Strategy*, 163–164; Ninkovich, "The End of Diplomatic History?" 443–444.

143. George C. Herring, Gary R. Hess, and Richard H. Immerman, "Passage of Empire: The United States, France, and South Vietnam, 1954–55," in Kaplan, Artaud, and Rubin, *Dien Bien Phu*, 177–178. See also George C. Herring, " 'A Good Stout Effort': John Foster Dulles and the Indochina Crisis, 1954–1955," in Immerman, *John Foster Dulles*, 213–233.

144. NSC 5436/1, October 18, 1954, FRUS, 1952–54, XI, 173.

145. Figures on FLN strength are from Al Dib, *Abdel Nasser et la Révolution Algérienne*, 23. Harbi calculates that there were even less than twenty-five hundred mujahadeen, with fewer than a thousand all told, *Le FLN*, 127.

146. Ferrell, *The Eisenhower Diaries*, 73–74.

3. From Conspiracy to Total War

1. Reprinted in Harbi, *Les Archives*, 101–103.

2. Memcon, November 20, 1954, FRUS, 1952–54, VI, 1504.

3. Harbi, *Le FLN*, 121–122; Tripier, *Autopsie de la guerre*, 11, 69, 568.

4. Maquin, *Le Parti socialiste et la guerre d'Algérie*, 29. The following discussion of French reactions to the outbreak of the war is indebted to this perceptive study. See also Alleg, *La guerre d'Algérie*, vol. 1, 437–446 and, for briefer treatments of *la main de l'étranger* theme in French rhetoric, Pervillé, "Guerre étrangère et guerre civile," 175–177; Manceron and Remaoun, *D'une rive à l'autre*, 26–27.

5. Christopher M. Andrew, "France: Adjustment to Change," in Bull and Watson, *The Expansion of International Society*, 339.

6. "Conférence prononcée le 26 février 1955 à All Souls College Oxford par le Général de l'armée A. Guillaume," AN, Bidault Papers, 457AP, Documents Défense Nationale 1954–55. On the Socialists, see Maquin, *Le Parti socialiste et la guerre d'Algérie*, 27–30.

7. The British Colonial Office was unreceptive. One official described the idea of a colonialist alliance as "repugnant." The Foreign Office tried to be conciliatory but did not differ on the substance (Bourdillon minute, April 21, 1954, Goldsworthy, *The Conservative Government and the End of Empire*, Series A, vol. 3, part I: International Relations, no. 119).

8. Paret, *French Revolutionary Warfare*, 3–4; Horne, *A Savage War of Peace*, 445–446; *L'Année Politique, 1961* (Paris: Presses Universitaires de France, 1962), 435.

9. Quoted in Maquin, *Le Parti socialiste et la guerre d'Algérie*, 28.

10. F. Lagrot and J. Greco, "Les Mutilations Faciales au Cours du terrorisme en Algérie et leur réparation," *La Presse Médicale* 51 (June 27, 1956): 1193–1198; A. Fourrier, P. Michaux, and Jacques Thiodet, "Aspects particuliers à la criminalité

algérienne," *Algérie Médicale* 61 (1957): 5–39. Copies of both articles are in the AOM, 12/CAB/161.

11. "Le Drame Algérien," *Revue militaire d'information* no. 269 (March 1956). This was more than rhetoric, as important as that was in patterning the way people thought about the war. The notion that Islam provided the organizing framework for anticolonial resistance was literally institutionalized. For instance, after the beginning of the uprising in Algeria, the Conseil Supérieur du Renseignement formed a "Commission on Muslim Information" to track Islamic issues through regular information exchanges and meetings between police agencies, the Service de Documentation extérieure et de Contre-Espionnage (SDECE), the military, and several ministries. Similarly, the prime minister's office soon established its own Bureau Central de Documentation et d'Information specifically charged with gathering information "concerning North African problems in particular and Islam in general" (unsigned memorandum to Seydoux, Ministre Plénipotentiaire attached to the Résidence Générale, February 2, 1955, MAE, Tunisie, 1944–1955, dossier 377; "Les Relations publiques de la France," May 12, 1957, AOM, 12/CAB/184).

12. Quoted in Alleg, *La guerre d'Algérie*, vol. 1, 442.

13. Quoted in Paret, *French Revolutionary Warfare*, 15.

14. Maquin, *Le Parti socialiste et la guerre d'Algérie*, 32–33.

15. Chauvel to Massigli, March 30, 1955, MAE, René Massigli Papers, vol. 95.

16. Quoted in Lacouture, *Pierre Mendès France*, 306.

17. Quoted in Stora, *La gangrène*, 15. On this theme, see also Ageron, " 'L'Algérie dernière chance de la puissance française.' "

18. Stora, *La gangrène*, 15–16.

19. Ibid., 13, and see also Pervillé, "Guerre étrangère et guerre civile," 171–172; Manceron and Remaoun, *D'une rive à l'autre*, 26–27.

20. Proclamation, *Front de Libération Nationale*, November 1, 1954, in Harbi, *Les Archives*, 101–102; Harbi, *Le FLN*, 122.

21. See their entries in Stora's *Dictionnaire Biographique*.

22. Al Dib, *Abdel Nasser et la Révolution Algérienne*, 13–19.

23. El Méchat, *Tunisie, les chemins vers l'Indépendance*, 223–225.

24. Al Dib, *Abdel Nasser et la Révolution Algérienne*, 39.

25. M'Hammed Yazid recounts the incident in his July 1957 report to the CNRA, reprinted in Harbi, *Les Archives*, 172–173.

26. Khider to Djouad Zakari, December 14, 1954, CNAA, GPRA, dossier one; Hoppenot to Mendès France, January 5, 1955, MAE, ONU, dossier 546; Mendès France to Mitterrand, Service de l'Algérie, January 13, 1955, idem.

27. Mendès France to Mitterrand, January 13, 1955, No. 237, MAE, ONU, dossier 546; Gillet to Mendès France, December 11, 1954, idem.

28. Lacouture, *Pierre Mendès France*, 309.

29. Memcon Dulles-Mendès France, November 20, 1954, FRUS, 1952–54, VI, 1502–1503.

30. Ibid., 1503–1505.

31. Ibid., 1504.

32. 225th Meeting of the NSC, November 24, 1954, FRUS, 1952–54, II, 789–796.

33. Ibid., 792. Radford was doubtless influenced by the Chiefs' consensus at the time that the United States ought to opt for Germany over France if it

would not acquiesce in German rearmament. On the continuing strategic importance of North Africa, see 160th Meeting of the NSC, August 27, 1953, ibid., 454, and NSC 5436/1 staff study, October 18, 1954, FRUS, 1952–54, XI, 175.

34. Jean-Charles Jauffret, "L'Armée et l'Algérie en 1954," 23.

35. Grisard to Mendès France, January 1, 1955, MAE, Série ONU, dossier 546; Dillon to Dulles, June 21, 1955, USNA, College Park, MD, RG59, Central Decimal Files, 751S.00.

36. Dulles to Lodge, December 11, 1954, FRUS, 1952–54, XI, 662; Dulles to Dillon, December 14, 1954, Dulles-Herter Papers, Chronological Correspondence Series, UPA, microfilm publication (1986), reel 7, frames 223–224.

37. Léon Marchal, "Note pour Monsieur le Ministre des Affaires Marocaines et Tunisiennes," January 17, 1955, AN, René Mayer papers, 363 AP24, dossier 9: Notes de Léon Marchal sur le Maroc Mai 1953–Janvier 1955. Leaks were so common at the Quai d'Orsay that Secretary General René Massigli advised one ambassador not to use cables for truly confidential information (Massigli to Chauvel, March 31, 1955, MEA, René Massigli Papers, vol. 95).

38. Mayer, quoted in Bernard, *The Franco-Moroccan Conflict*, 236. Of course, and as Bernard argues, Mayer was also casting doubt on Mendès' intentions in foreign policy and may have used the North Africa debate as a pretext. Fourth Republic governments rarely rose or fell over a single issue, and it would be two years before the Algerian War became the most important among them.

39. Jauffret, "L'Armée et l'Algérie en 1954," 24–25; Tripier, *Autopsie de la guerre*, 73–75; Hamon, "Chronique du Conflit Algérien," 36–37.

40. Quoted in Lacouture, *Pierre Mendès France*, 333. On French repression as an aid to FLN recruitment, see Horne, *A Savage War of Peace*, 113–115.

41. Ambler, *The French Army in Politics*, 222; Andreopoulos, "The Age of National Liberation Movements," 205–206.

42. Courrière, *La Guerre d'Algérie*, vol. 2, 112.

43. Droz and Lever, *Histoire de la Guerre d'Algérie*, 110–111, 134; Tripier, *Autopsie de la guerre*, 81–110.

44. Stora, *La gangrène*, 182.

45. Al Dib, *Abdel Nasser et la Révolution Algérienne*, 40–41.

46. Ibid. While it is often parochial and self-serving in its description of North Africans' debt to Egypt, Dib's information on meetings and arms deliveries is very precise, is often corroborated by contemporary French intelligence reports, and has been found credible by otherwise critical reviewers. See, for instance, the unsigned "Note" on Ben Bella's comings and goings between Egypt, Spain, and Morocco, August 19, 1955, MAE, Tunisie, 1944–1955, dossier 378, which parallels Dib's account, 57–59, 75, and see also Meynier, "Les Algériens vus par le pouvoir égyptien," 89–127. This rarely used work compels a sharp upward revision of earlier estimates of Egyptian aid to the FLN; cf. Horne, *A Savage War of Peace*, 85, 158.

47. Jernegan to Dulles, December 31, 1954, FRUS, 1952–54, IX, 2323 and Alpha memorandum, January 14, 1955, FRUS, 1955, XIV, 10–17. On the *Ouragans*, see Kyle, *Suez*, 112.

48. Quoted in Burns, *Economic Aid and American Policy*, 24.

49. Al Dib, *Abdel Nasser et la Révolution Algérienne*, 48–49.

50. Ibid., 56–59, 68–69.

51. Tripier, *Autopsie de la guerre*, 76. French naval forces were also stretched thin, see Kessler, "La Surveillance des frontières maritimes," 95–98.

52. Clark to Dulles, March 28, 1955, USNA, RG59, Central Decimal Files, 751S.00.

53. *L'Année Politique, 1955* (Paris: Presses Universitaires de France, 1956), 205–210, 226–227. On censorship, see Harrison, "Government and Press."

54. Courrière, *La Guerre d'Algérie*, vol. 2, 46–49; Tillion, *Algeria: The Realities*, 16–22.

55. Courrière, *La Guerre d'Algérie*, vol. 2, 9–20; Horne, *A Savage War of Peace*, 105–109, 115–118.

56. Stora, *La gangrène*, 16; Horne, *A Savage War of Peace*, 110–111.

57. Courrière, *La Guerre d'Algérie*, vol. 2, 108–109, 113.

58. El Méchat, *Tunisie, Les Chemins vers l'Indépendance*, 222–228.

59. Boyer de la Tour to Contrôleurs Civils et Chefs des Bureau des Affaires Indigènes, July 23, 1955, MAE, Tunisie, 1944–1955, dossier 378.

60. M'Hammed Yazid, "Rapport," July 1957, in Harbi, *Les Archives*, 173; Aït Ahmed, "Bandoeng Trente Ans Après," *Jeune Afrique*, no. 1272 (May 22, 1985): 18–19; El Méchat, *Tunisie, Les Chemins vers l'Indépendance*, 231–233; *L'Année Politique, 1955*, vi, 383–386. "The spirit of Bandung" would become an important theme in FLN propaganda (Gadant, *Islam et Nationalisme en Algérie*, 149–150; Malley, *The Call from Algeria*, 124).

61. Commandant Rousset, "Note sur la Première Conférence Afro-Asiatique," April 6, 1955, AOM, MA, dossier 28.

62. Tripier, *Autopsie de la guerre*, 211; Talbott, *War without a Name*, 53.

63. Quoted in Ageron, " 'L'Algérie dernière chance," 125.

64. Tripier, *Autopsie de la guerre*, 210–212; Langlais to Algiers, September 4, 1958, MAE, Série ONU, dossier 557. Slimane Chikh, an ALN veteran who offers sharply different interpretations on almost everything else, agrees with Tripier about how "the distinction between 'interior' and 'exterior' became meaningless," *L'Algérie en Armes*, 421.

65. "Documentation Destinée à la délégation française aux Nations Unis," July 23, 1955, MAE, Série ONU, dossier 547.

66. Clark to Dulles, September 19, 1955, USNA, RG59, Central Decimal Files, 751S.00.

67. Dillon to Dulles, July 25, 1956, USNA, RG59, Central Decimal Files, 751S.00. See also Dillon to Dulles, November 16, 1956, idem, in which Lacoste asserted that, absent a U.N. debate, he could "break [the] back of rebellion in [the] next weeks."

68. Lodge to Dulles, November 1, 1955, FRUS, 1955–57, XVIII, 230.

69. Dillon to Dulles, June 3, 1955, USNA, RG59, Central Decimal Files, 751S.00. On the importance of helicopters in Algeria, see Shrader, *The First Helicopter War*.

70. Dulles to Dillon, May 25, 1955, USNA, RG59, Central Decimal Files, 751S.00. For examples of their démarches, see USNA, RG59, Lot 58D48, Subject Files of the Officer in Charge of Northern African Affairs 1945–1956, box 2.

71. Dulles to Dillon, May 27, 1955, FRUS, 1955–57, XVIII, 219–220.

72. Clark to Dulles, June 15, 1955, USNA, RG59, Central Decimal Files, 751S.00.

73. Clark to Dulles, June 23, 1955 and July 1, 1955, ibid.

74. *L'Année Politique, 1955*, 244–245.

75. Dillon to Dulles, June 16, 1955, DDEL, JFDP, Subject Series, box 6, North African Survey-1955, Julius Holmes.

76. Dillon to Dulles, July 2, 1955, USNA, RG59, Central Decimal Files, 751S.00. Clark to Dulles, July 5, 1955, idem. On the other hand, Algerians were bitter about U.S. military assistance to France; see Horne, *A Savage War of Peace*, 243–244.

77. Dillon to Dulles, June 16, 1955.

78. Couve de Murville to Pinay, August 26, 1955, MAE, Amérique 1952–1963, Etats-Unis-AFN, 30, 1952–55. On Reuther, see France, "AFL-CIO Foreign Policy," 104.

79. Tyler memo for Merchant, June 28, 1955, USNA, RG59, Central Decimal Files, 751S.00; Merchant memo for Dulles, July 2, 1955, idem.

80. Merchant memo for Dulles, July 2, 1955, ibid.

81. Harrison, *The Reluctant Ally*, 33–35; Doise and Vaïsse, *Diplomatie et outil militaire*, 571.

82. For insightful analyses see Paret, *French Revolutionary Warfare* and Perville, "La Revolution Algérienne."

83. Soustelle, "France Looks at Her Alliances," 116, 126. See also Grosser, *Affaires Extérieures*, 139, which quotes Mitterrand saying much the same thing.

84. Tyler memo for Jones, June 16, 1955, FRUS, 1955–57, XVIII, 98–99.

85. Allen memo for Dulles, July 8, 1955, USNA, RG59, Central Decimal Files, 751S.00, and see also May 25, 1956, Moorman memo to Furnas, USNA, RG59, Central Decimal Files, 751S.001. In fact, in June 1955 the Algerian Communist Party began to stage its own operations, though the FLN treated them with suspicion. Perhaps still bitter over the Indochina experience, the Americans would judge French claims that the FLN was dominated by communists to be an "obvious and somewhat clumsy attempt [to] play on US antipathies," Cootes to Dulles, October 18, 1956, USNA, RG59, Central Decimal Files, 751S.00. This attempt became all the more clumsy as cabinet ministers contradicted one another. When asked about Pineau's concern regarding Communist infiltration, Prime Minister Guy Mollet replied that "Pineau was often given to exaggeration and over simplification and he would not himself say that communism was an important danger in Algeria as of the present moment," Dillon to Dulles, December 11, 1956, USNA, RG59, Central Decimal Files, 751S.001.

86. "Trouble Ahead with Paris," *The New York Times*, June 15, 1955.

87. Quoted in Pruessen, "Beyond the Cold War," 73.

88. Dulles to Holmes, July 12, 1955, DDEL, JFDP, Subject Series, box 6, North African Survey-1955, Julius Holmes.

89. Dulles to Holmes, July 13, 1955, DDEL, JFDP, Subject Series, box 6, North African Survey—1955.

90. Quoted in Sangmuah, "The United States and the French Empire in North Africa," 349.

91. Julius Holmes, "Report on French North Africa," July 29, 1955, USNA, RG59, Central Decimal Files, 751S.00; Holmes to State, July 29, 1955, idem.

92. Joyce to Dillon, "British Thinking on Tunisia and Algeria," July 28, 1955, USNA, RG59, Central Decimal Files, 751S.00. See also Jebb, *Memoirs*, 280–282. For a good discussion of British attitudes toward the Algerian War, see Thomas, "The Dilemmas of an Ally."

93. Joyce to Dillon, "British Thinking on Tunisia and Algeria."

94. Dulles to Makins, August 17, 1955, DDEL, JFDP, John Foster Dulles Chronological Series, box 12.

95. Grandval, "Situation Politique au Maroc," August 2, 1955, MAE, Tunisie 1944–1955, dossier 378; Bernard, *The Franco-Moroccan Conflict*, 264–283.

96. Bernard, *The Franco-Moroccan Conflict*, 283–288.

97. Courrière, *La Guerre d'Algérie*, vol. 2, 208–211.

98. Horne, *A Savage War of Peace*, 120. Official figures varied widely, but these were the highest. For the best documented account, see Ageron, "L'insurrection du 20 août 1955 dans le Nord-Constantinois. De la résistance armée à la guerre du peuple," in Ageron, *La Guerre d'Algérie et les Algériens*, 27–50.

99. Horne, *A Savage War of Peace*, 121–122; Courrière, *La Guerre d'Algérie*, vol. 2, 211–212.

100. Boyd to Murphy, September 22, 1955, USNA, RG59, Central Decimal Files, 751S.00.

101. Talbott, *War without a Name*, 53; Tripier, *Autopsie de la guerre*, 78.

102. Harbi, *Le FLN*, 127–128; Ageron, "L'insurrection du 20 août 1955," 30–33.

103. *L'Année Politique, 1955*, 278.

104. *La Guerre d'Algérie*, vol. 2, 203–204. See also Horne, *A Savage War of Peace*, 118–119.

105. Boyd to Murphy, September 22, 1955; Monteil quoted in Talbott, *War without a Name*, 50.

106. Clark to State, September 15, 1955, USNA, RG59, Central Decimal Files, 751S.00.

107. "Documentation Destinée à la délégation française aux Nations Unis," July 23, 1955, MAE, Série ONU, dossier 547.

108. "Notions Essentielles sur l'Algérie," undated but circa 1956, AOM, 12/CAB/161.

109. "Algérie," 1956, MAE, Série ONU, dossier 549.

110. "L'Algérie du demi siècle vue par les autorités," undated, pp. 58, 243, AOM, 10/CAB/28.

111. "Les Missions de l'Armée française dans la Guerre révolutionnaire d'Algérie," November 15, 1957, MAE, ONU, dossier 544.

112. Unsigned introduction to *Algérie surpeuplée*.

113. Sanson, "Caractères du Surpeuplement," *Algérie surpeuplée*, 76–88.

114. Pierre Boyer, "Historique du Surpeuplement," 28–29 (emphasis in original); "Deuxième Partie, Politique Malthusienne et Surpeuplement Algérien," (unsigned) 198–199, both in *Algérie surpeuplée*.

115. Arrus, *L'eau en Algérie*, 21–23. The situation was much the same in Morocco; see Swearingen, *Moroccan Images*, 133–141, 148–149.

116. Arrus, *L'eau en Algérie*, 269.

117. Quoted in Horne, *A Savage War of Peace*, 55. During World War II authorities paid Muslim recruits 38 percent as much as Europeans and officially allotted their families a bread ration of 250 grams—in fact, usually 100–150—compared to 300g for pieds noirs, Elgey, *La République des tourmentes*, vol. 2, 405, 414.

118. Of course, dominion over nature through science had long been part of imperialist projects. Yet instead of leading by example—which required, for instance, that scientists living in nature lead a civilized life—a whole society would be made to serve as an example of the transformative power of science to transcend cultural differences. For studies of the earlier tradition see Pyenson, *Civilizing Mission*, and Osborne, *Nature, the Exotic, and the Science of French Colonialism*.

119. Quoted in Kelly, *Lost Soldiers*, 138, and see also 188–189. On FLN

propaganda, see Charles-Robert Ageron, "La 'guerre psychologique' de l'Armée de libération nationale algérienne," in Ageron, *La Guerre d'Algérie et les Algériens*, 218, 225, 227.

120. Alleg, *La Guerre d'Algérie*, vol. 3, 208–213; Andreopoulos, "The Age of National Liberation Movements," 208–209.

121. *The Constantine Plan: Money, Men, Machines*, Tangent films, undated, AOM.

122. Breil, "Etude de Démographie Quantitative," in *La Population en Algérie*, vol. 2, 114.

123. "Les problèmes d'Afrique du Nord," Académie des Sciences Coloniales, Séances des 6 et 20 Janvier, 3 et 24 Février 1956, Tome XVI, AOM.

124. Mass rape may seem like a counterintuitive response, but it has long been used by soldiers seeking to "pollute" and subvert enemy populations (Seifert, "The Second Front," 39–40).

125. Bernard, *The Franco-Moroccan Conflict*, 620.

126. Khider to Aït Ahmed, April 9, 1956, CNAA, GPRA, dossier 1.

4. Confronting the Empire of Islam

1. Memcon Mollet-Eden, March 11, 1956, DDF, 1956, I, no. 161.

2. *L'Année Politique, 1956* (Paris: Presses Universitaires de France, 1957), 207.

3. Quoted in Olson, "Eisenhower and the Indochina Problem," 98.

4. Holmes memo for Dulles, September 29, 1955, FRUS, 1955–57, XVIII, 105, 108–109. Holmes made the same argument about the "tide" of "Islamic nationalism" to Macmillan, memcon Macmillan-Holmes, October 6, 1955, PRO, PREM 11/951. Another State Department official proposed that, if the French continued to attempt to prevail by force alone, the United States should assume a mediating role, come up with an "American program," and "stand ready to push these objectives actively, even impose them, on both sides," Bovey to Cyr, September 6, 1955, USNA, RG59, Lot 58D48, Subject Files of the Officer in Charge of Northern African Affairs 1945–1956, box 2.

5. Elbrick, Jernegan memo to Murphy, September 15, 1955, USNA, RG59, Central Decimal Files, 751S.00. July may have been telling them what he thought they wanted to hear, but Faure was among the most ardent advocates of peaceful decolonization in North Africa; see Elgey, *La République des tourmentes*, vol. 1, 473–474.

6. Bernard, *The Franco-Moroccan Conflict*, 317–318.

7. Alwan, *Algeria before the United Nations*, 27–28.

8. Thomas, *The French North African Crisis*, 100–101. French authorities were forced to withdraw claims that the cameraman had paid him to do it ("France Retracts on Atrocity Film," *The New York Times*, December 31, 1955).

9. Clark to Dulles, September 23, 1955, USNA, RG59, Central Decimal Files, 751S.00; Chikh, *L'Algérie en Armes*, 421.

10. Séance du Conseil du Gouvernement, September 27, 1955, AOM, GGA 3F 353.

11. Aït Ahmed to Margaret Pope, October 15, 1955, Aït Ahmed personal archive.

12. Guiringaud to Pinay, October 4, 1955, MAE, Série ONU, 546.

13. Dixon to Macmillan, October 1, 1955, PRO, PREM 11/902.

14. Scholars have not yet explored Soviet archives to explicate Khrushchev's Third World strategy, but for an analysis based on public sources, see Zoubir, "U.S. and Soviet Policies," 445–450.

15. Dillon to Dulles, October 4, 1955, FRUS, 1955–57, XVIII, 222–224. Quai d'Orsay Secretary General Massigli privately admitted that Alphand had performed poorly and he was soon shifted to Washington (Massigli to Chauvel, November 7, 1955, MAE, René Massigli Papers, vol. 95).

16. Chauvel to Massigli, November 7, 1955, MAE, René Massigli Papers, vol. 95.

17. Al Dib, *Abdel Nasser et la Révolution Algérienne*, 78–84; Bernard, *The Franco-Moroccan Conflict*, 319–320; Seydoux to Pinay, October 4, 1955, MAE, Tunisie 1944–1955, dossier 378.

18. Dillon to Dulles, October 4, 1955, FRUS, 1955–57, XVIII, 222–224.

19. Memcon Dulles, Merchant, Holmes, October 3, 1955, FRUS, 1955–57, XVIII, 515–518.

20. Ambrose, *Eisenhower*, vol. 2, 272–273.

21. *L'Année Politique, 1955* (Paris: Presses Universitaires de France, 1956), 73.

22. Reilly to Macmillan, October 2, 1955, PRO, PREM 11/902.

23. *L'Année Politique, 1955*, 73–74; Bernard, *The Franco-Moroccan Conflict*, 328, 358–369.

24. *L'Année Politique, 1955*, 75–76.

25. Dillon to Dulles, February 25, 1956, USNA, RG59, Central Decimal Files, 751S.00; Dillon to Dulles, February 17, 1956, idem; Dillon to Dulles, March 2, 1956, USNA, RG59, Central Decimal Files, 651.71. For yet another example, see the "Note: Réflexions préliminaires sur le problème marocain," (unsigned) February 1956, FNSP, Alain Savary Papers, SV9, Dr2. Said's *Orientalism* is the classic study of how these dichotomies are constructed and maintained, constraining the way people imagine themselves and others.

26. Note sur la Situation de la Tunisie," (unsigned) February 9, 1956, MAE, René Massigli Papers, vol. 88, Afrique du Nord; "Note pour le President," October 31, 1955, MAE, Cabinet du Ministre, dossier 213, Maroc.

27. Khider to Madrid, October 19, 1955, CNAA, GPRA, dossier 1.

28. Fauvet, *La IVᵉ République*, 300.

29. Alphand to Pinay, November 5, 9, and 22, 1955, MAE, ONU, 547. On Nehru, see Khider to Ben Yahia and Brahimi, October 10, 1956, CNAA, GPRA, dossier 1.

30. *L'Année Politique, 1955*, 300–304. On Bourguiba and "Bourguibism," as it was called, see Moore, *Tunisia Since Independence*, 41–48; Ruf, "The Bizerte Crisis," 201–211.

31. This was apparent even during the talks; see "Negotiations Franco-Tunisiennes," March 12, 1956, FNSP, Alain Savary Papers, SV13, Dr4.

32. Barker, "The Politics of Decolonization in Tunisia," 140. See also idem 115–17 and 135–36 for a similar critique.

33. 267th Meeting of the NSC, November 21, 1955, DDEL, AWF, NSC Series.

34. DDE memcon with Wilson, Radford, March 13, 1956, FRUS, 1955–57, XIX, 238–241.

35. Medvedev, *Khrushchev*, 43–44; McDougall, *Heavens and the Earth*, 239–241, 245–248.

36. MacFarlane, *Superpower Rivalry*, 142; Rubinstein, *Moscow's Third World Strategy*, 39–40.

37. Shultz and Godson, *Dezinformatsia*, 24, 28, 153. See also Zubok, "Spy vs. Spy," 29–31, on the later period.

38. Porter, *The USSR in Third World Conflicts*, 37–40; Wolfe, *Soviet Power and Europe*, 139.

39. 277th Meeting of the NSC, February 27, 1956, DDEL, AWF, NSC Series. On supporting neutralism and economic aid, see DDE memcon with Wilson, Radford, March 13, 1956, FRUS, 1955–57, XIX, 238–241; Kaufman, *Trade and Aid*, 65–68.

40. 267th Meeting of the NSC, November 21, 1955, DDEL, AWF, NSC Series. See also Stivers, "Eisenhower and the Middle East," 194–195, 198.

41. Quoted in Cohen, *Dean Rusk*, 82–83.

42. Memcon Root, Bovey, Looram, and Aït Ahmed, December 5, 1955, USNA, RG59, Central Decimal Files, 751S.00; memcon Aït Ahmed-Bovey, May 16, 1956, idem.

43. Memcon Nes, Allen, Ben Bella, Ali Hawazi, December 6, 1955, ibid.

44. Mollet quoted in Elgey, *La République des tourmentes*, vol. 1, 400.

45. Algeria, however, was only one of a number of issues in the election, and perhaps not even the most important one. In December 1955, only a quarter of survey respondents thought it should be the government's top priority, though this figure rose to 65 percent by April 1956 (Ageron, "L'Opinion française à travers les sondages," in Rioux, *La Guerre d'Algérie et les Français*, 32).

46. Bidault, *Algérie: l'oiseau aux ailes coupées*.

47. Wall, *France, The United States, and the Algerian War*, 26.

48. Courrière, *La Guerre d'Algérie*, vol. 2, 271–277; Lacouture, *Pierre Mendès France*, 360–363.

49. Quoted in Julliard, *"Naissance et mort . . . ,"* 201, which also critiques Mollet's policy.

50. Horne, *A Savage War of Peace*, 151, 154–157, 181.

51. Dillon to Dulles, February 25, 1956, USNA, RG59, Central Decimal Files, 751S.00.

52. *Revue Militaire d'Information* no. 269 (March 1956).

53. Stora, *La gangrène*, 30.

54. Ely, *Mémoires*, vol. 2, 85–86.

55. Tripier, *Autopsie de la guerre*, 79.

56. Michel de Lombares, "Note sur les Moyens des Forces Armées en Algérie," February 24, 1956, AOM, 12/CAB/211.

57. Quoted in Zoubir, "Decolonization of the Maghreb," 70–71.

58. Dillon to State, March 2, 1956, USNA, RG59, Central Decimal Files, 751S.00.

59. Champeix to Ministre Résident en Algérie, Cabinet, February 16, 1956, AOM, MA, dossier 30.

60. Dillon to Dulles, March 2, 1956, FRUS, 1955–57, XVIII, 115–116. See also Wall, "The United States, Algeria," 498.

61. When Lodge met with Mollet to discuss the incident, the prime minister agreed that it was unwarranted. He explained that "[a]ll of the French intelligence services have been unable to uncover a single particular instance which would support the charge of anti-French American actions"—which would suggest that

they were indeed looking (Lodge-Mollet memcon, March 13, 1956, FRUS, 1955–57, XVIII, 117–120).

62. Moorman to Gaither, March 3, 1956, and Moorman to JCS, March 12, 1956, EOF, 1953–1961, Part 2: International Series, UPA microfilm publication (1991), reel 7, frames 910, 912, 922, 927. See also Gruenther to Radford, March 12, 1956, FRUS, 1955–57, XVIII, 238–239.

63. Valluy memo for Collins, March 12, 1956, EOF, 1953–1961, Part 2: International Series, UPA microfilm publication (1991), reel 7, frames 903–907.

64. Hoover to Eisenhower, March 27, 1956 (referring to the earlier decision), idem, 900.

65. Ferrell, *The Eisenhower Diaries*, 318–319.

66. Dickson to Monckton, April 3, 1956, PRO, PREM 11/1937. I am grateful to Salim Yaqub for providing me with a copy of this document.

67. Ferrell, *The Eisenhower Diaries*, 319.

68. On the "machiavellian plan," see Dickson to Monckton, April 3, 1956. On backing Saud, see Gerges, *The Superpowers*, 51–52. On his financial contributions, see Al Dib, *Abdel Nasser et la Révolution Algérienne*, 75, 115.

69. March 21 presidential news conference, *The New York Times*, March 22, 1956, 20.

70. "Text of Address by Ambassador Dillon on North Africa," *The New York Times*, March 21, 1956, 4.

71. Dillon to Dulles, March 20, 1956, USNA, RG59, Central Decimal Files, 751S.00.

72. Dillon to Dulles, July 26, 1956, USNA, RG59, Central Decimal Files, 651.71.

73. Couve de Murville to Pineau, March 21, 1956, Direction Amérique 1952–63, Etats-Unis–Afrique du Nord, Dossier 31.

74. Subestre to Risterucci, April 6, 1956, SHAA, Série E 0/2, Cabinet Militaire, 19v, carton 2911.

75. "Note pour le Directeur Général Politique," December 27, 1956, MAE, MLA, vol. 23 bis (provisional number), Action extérieure, Etats-Unis, déc. 1956–déc. 1957, Cote EU, which described the earlier conversation to explain America's post-Suez policy.

76. Aït Ahmed to Khider, March 26 and April 7, 1956, CNAA, GPRA, dossier 1.

77. Grimal, *Decolonization*, 352, 363–366; Cooper, *Decolonization and African Society*, 408, 413, 415–416, 424–431. See also Albertini, *Decolonization*, 431–433.

78. Dillon to Dulles, February 4, 1956, USNA, RG59, Central Decimal Files, 751S.00.

79. "Conversation du President avec l'Ambassadeur d'Egypte," February 5, 1956, FNSP, Alain Savary papers, SV9, Dr5.

80. Yazid to Khider, April 18, 1956, CNAA, GPRA, dossier 2; Khider to Madrid, October 19, 1955, idem, dossier 1.

81. Pineau to Mollet, March 14, 1956, MAE, Secrétariat Général, dossier 56; Kyle, *Suez*, 116; *L'Année Politique, 1956*, 279–280. For the "empire of Islam" quote and the reference to the memorandum of conversation, see note 1.

82. Al Dib, *Abdel Nasser et la Révolution Algérienne*, 120–121.

83. This was one of the reasons why Ben M'Hidi opposed Ben Bella at the upcoming Soummam congress (Harbi, *Le FLN*, 174).

84. Khider to Aït Ahmed and Yazid, May 9, 1956, CNAA, GPRA, dossier 2.

85. Al Dib, *Abdel Nasser et la Révolution Algérienne*, 123–132.

86. Kyle, *Suez*, 116, and see also Chauvel to Massigli, March 15, 1956, MAE, René Massigli Papers, vol. 95.

87. Khider to Aït Ahmed, Yazid, and Lahouel, March 26, 1956, CNAA, GPRA, dossier 1; Malek, *L'Algérie à Evian*, 22–23.

88. Al Dib, *Abdel Nasser et la Révolution Algérienne*, 133–137; Droz and Lever, *Histoire de la Guerre d'Algérie*, 99–100.

89. Charles G. Cogan, "The Suez Crisis: Part I, The View from Paris," and Zachary Karabell, "The View from Israel," Conference on "The Suez Crisis and Its Teachings," the American Academy of Arts & Sciences, Cambridge, MA, February 15–16, 1997.

90. Quoted in Golan, *Shimon Peres*, 36.

91. Cohen, *Israel and the Bomb*, 52–53. See, for instance, the unsigned "Note" by Sous-Direction de Tunisie, March 5, 1956, MAE, Cabinet du Ministre, dossier 157, Tunisie, and "Note sur les ingérences égyptiennes en Afrique du Nord," October 20, 1956, MAE, Cabinet du Ministre, dossier 155, Algérie, Loi Cadre.

92. Cogan, "The View from Paris," 17–18; Kyle, *Suez*, 117–118.

93. Al Dib, *Abdel Nasser et la Révolution Algérienne*, 146–149.

94. Malek, *L'Algérie à Evian*, 23; "La France refuse d'intervention d'un intermédiaire pour régler le problème algérien," *Le Monde*, September 15, 1956.

95. Cohen, *Israel and the Bomb*, 53–60.

96. Horne, *A Savage War of Peace*, 152–153.

97. Emphasis in original. This and subsequent quotes are taken from the resident minister's "Directive Générale," May 19, 1956, AOM, DOC.SAS 1.

98. The brochure accompanies McBride to Dulles, June 11, 1956, USNA, RG59, Central Decimal Files, 751S.00.

99. "Il s'agit, davantage encore du choc de conceptions politiques différentes, de celui de deux civilizations," October 10, 1956 circular, MAE, Série ONU, dossier 550.

100. *L'Année Politique, 1955*, vii–x.

101. Memcon Lodge-Mollet, March 13, 1956, FRUS, 1955–57, XVIII, 117–119. This was the meeting in which Mollet asserted that the Algerians looked to Mao Tse-Tung as their leader, see chapter 1.

102. Harbi, *Les Archives*, 111–112.

103. Dejean to Pineau, July 7, 1956, MAE, Europe 1944–1960, URSS, dossier 271; memcon de la Grandville-Crawford, July 11, 1956, USNA, RG59, Central Decimal Files, 751S.00; Carol R. Saivetz, "The Suez Crisis: Part I, The View from Moscow," Conference on "The Suez Crisis and Its Teachings," 19, see note 89.

104. Dillon to Dulles, July 31, 1956, FRUS, XVI, 1955–57, 74–77.

105. Memcon Eisenhower, Dulles, et al. with congressional leadership, August 12, 1956, FRUS, 1955–57, XVI, 189–192; memcon Eisenhower, Dulles, et al. July 31, 1956, idem, 63–64.

106. Cogan, "The View from Paris," 3 (see note 89).

107. See notes 1, 25, 78, 97. Couve de Murville was actually transferred from Washington to Bonn largely because he did not share this view (Couve de Murville oral history, MAE).

108. Droz and Lever, *Histoire de la Guerre d'Algérie*, 103.

109. Malek, *L'Algérie à Evian*, 278.

110. See, for instance, Horne, *A Savage War of Peace*, 143–146.

111. Khider to Aït Ahmed, Yazid, Lahouel, March 26, 1956, CNAA, GPRA, dossier 1; Daho Djerbal, "Alliances et mesalliances tunisiennes, ou les relations algéro-tunisiennes vues par le FLN 1954–1958," Actes du IXᵉ Colloque International sur Processus et enjeux de la décolonisation en Tunisie (1952–1964), 8–10 mai, 1998 (Tunis: 1999); Malek, *L'Algérie à Evian*, 27.

112. Khider letter, October 19, 1955, CNAA, GPRA, dossier 1; Khider to Aït Ahmed, August 17, 1956, idem; Khider letter, September 17, 1956, idem. The platform was released after the external delegation was captured and is reprinted in Tripier, *Autopsie de la guerre*, 571–601.

113. Tripier, *Autopsie de la guerre*, 599–600. Ben Bella later argued that most of the shipments had gone to border zones like Souk Ahras and the Aurès-Nementchas, which were unrepresented at the Congress (Al Dib, *Abdel Nasser et la Révolution Algérienne*, 172). Ben M'Hidi's western zone of Oranie, which was represented, counted more modern weapons than all of the others put together. Yet even he had suffered from the vicissitudes of Egyptian diplomacy; see note 83.

114. Tripier, *Autopsie de la guerre*, 578–579, 598.

115. Ibid., 583.

116. Ibid., 600; Pervillé, "L'insertion internationale," 374, 377.

117. This was Abbane's view, and it was shared by Aït Ahmed and Mabrouk Belhocine in interviews with the author (Abbane, "Rapport du CCE au CNRA," c. April 1957, 195, and see also Laremont, "Islam and the Politics of Resistance in Algeria," 156–161; Tripier, *Autopsie de la guerre*, 593–595, 599–600).

118. Habib Bourguiba with Mohammed Sayah, "Ma Vie, Mon Oeuvre, 1956–1958," unpublished manuscript, Centre d'Etudes Maghrébines à Tunis, vol. 2, 56–58. See also Barker, "The Politics of Decolonization," 240–241.

119. Quoted in Moore, *Tunisia Since Independence*, 43.

120. Lamont to Dulles, April 10, 1956, FRUS, 1955–57, XVIII, 524; El-brick memo for Dulles, May 31, 1956, idem, 531–533; Phleger memo for Dulles, May 31, 1956, idem, 534; Zartman, *Morocco: Problems of New Power*, 27, 32–33. For the Hassan quote, see note 2.

121. 298th NSC Meeting, September 27, 1956, FRUS, 1955–57, XVIII, 130–137. Aid projections are in the NSC 5614/1 Staff Study, October 3, 1956, DDEL, White House Office, Office of the Special Assistant for National Security Affairs, NSC Series, Policy Papers Subseries, box 18. Note, however, that the NSC staff did not yet favor independence for Algeria, fearing that it "would put power in the hands of a grossly unprepared people," idem.

122. 298th NSC Meeting, September 27, 1956. On the Chiefs and bases, see 301st meeting of the NSC, October 26, 1956, DDEL, AWF, NSC Series. On loss of region to Soviets, see NSC 5614/1 Staff Study. On military aid, see NSC 5614/1, FRUS, 1955–57, XVIII, 143.

123. Dillon to Dulles, September 6, 1956, USNA, RG59, Central Decimal Files, 751S.00. For an example of the pessimistic reports that were reaching ministers, see "Note, a/s de la situation en Algérie," unsigned, October 19, 1956, MAE, Cabinet du Ministre, dossier 155, Algérie, Loi Cadre. The authors traveled to Algeria and found that none of Lacoste's advisers any longer claimed that the rebels represented a minority. All insisted on the profound influence of the ALN on the whole of the population. Regarding the French financial situation, see chapter 5.

124. Differing accounts of these talks can be found in Harbi, *Le FLN*, 196–197, Alleg, *La guerre d'Algérie*, vol. 2, 273–275, and Droz and Lever, *Histoire de la Guerre d'Algérie*, 99–100. Malek's is the most specific and credible, see *L'Algérie à Evian*, 24–26.

125. Malek, *L'Algérie à Evian*, 26.

126. Dillon to Dulles, September 26, 1956, USNA, RG59, Central Decimal Files, 751S.00. On independence as a precondition, see Al Dib, *Abdel Nasser et la Révolution Algérienne*, 158, as well as the Soummam platform, in Tripier, *Autopsie de la guerre*, 583–584.

127. Cogan, "The View from Paris," 29–30, see note 89.

128. Alleg offers a somewhat different interpretation, arguing that they hoped Nasser's downfall would compel the FLN to come to terms (*La guerre d'Algérie*, vol. 2, 275).

129. Dillon to Dulles, September 26, 1956.

130. Cornut-Gentille to Pineau, September 22, 1956, MAE, ONU, dossier 550.

131. Dillon to Dulles, October 16, 1956, USNA, RG59, Central Decimal Files, 751S.00.

132. Ibid.

133. Quoted in Alleg, *La guerre d'Algérie*, vol. 2, 276–278; Horne, *A Savage War of Peace*, 157–158. On the Israeli connection, see Porch, *The French Secret Services*, 369–370, 581, though he notes that some authors credit SDECE.

134. Clark to Dulles, August 27, 1956, USNA, RG59, Central Decimal Files, 751S.00. See also Jacques Fauvet, "Il y a désormais un préalable égyptien à la solution du problème algérien," *Le Monde*, August 22, 1956.

135. Shlaim, "The Protocol of Sèvres," 512–513.

136. Alleg, *La guerre d'Algérie*, vol. 2, 278–285; Horne, *A Savage War of Peace*, 159–161. The Americans learned that Mollet's order had been defied; see Wall, "The United States, Algeria," 493–494.

137. Cannon to Dillon, October 26, 1956, USNA, RG59, Central Decimal Files, 651.71; Zartman, *Morocco: Problems of New Power*, 25.

138. Roger Seydoux, "Compte Rendu de Fin de Mission (29 octobre 1956–21 décembre 1956)," MAE, Cabinet du Ministre, cabinet de Pineau, dossier 157.

139. Dillon to Dulles, October 31, 1956, USNA, RG59, Central Decimal Files, 651.71.

140. See reports in *Le Populaire*, October 27, 1956, and *Le Monde*, October 29, 1956.

141. Barkaoui, "The New York Times and the Algerian Revolution," 92.

142. Cornut-Gentille to Pineau, October 27, 1956, DDF, 1956, III, No. 35; Ostrorog to Pineau, October 25, 1956, MAE, ONU, dossier 551; Boyd, *Fifteen Men on a Powder Keg*, 28.

143. Quoted in Alleg, *La guerre d'Algérie*, vol. 2, 282 ("screwup" is a polite translation of *connerie*).

5. The Battle of Algiers, the Battle of New York

1. Quoted in Duchemin, *Histoire du FLN*, 263–264.

2. Rapport d'Information, no. 5383, July 5, 1957, reprinted as an annex to the *procès-verbale* of the same day, MAE, Série ONU, dossier 553.

3. 302nd Meeting of the NSC, November 1, 1956, DDEL, Abilene, Kansas, AWF, NSC Series.

4. Quoted in Ambrose, *Eisenhower*, vol. 2, 356.

5. Quoted in Kyle, *Suez*, 386, and see Kunz, *The Economic Diplomacy of the Suez Crisis*, chapters 6–7.

6. 302nd Meeting of the NSC. On Ike and NSC meetings, see Greenstein, *The Hidden-Hand Presidency*, 133.

7. William M. Blair, "Nixon Hails Break with Allies' Policies," *The New York Times*, November 3, 1956, 1, 19.

8. Quoted in Pineau, *1956/Suez*, 191. For the official *compte rendu*, see DDF, 1956, III, no. 138. See also Vaïsse, "Post-Suez France," in Louis and Owen, *Suez 1956*, 336–337 and, for German policy, Klaus-Jürgen Müller, "Le réalisme de la République fédérale d'Allemagne," in Rioux, *La Guerre d'Algérie et les Français*, 421–428.

9. Dillon to Dulles, November 16, 1956, USNA, College Park, MD, RG59, Central Decimal Files, 751S.00.

10. Bourgès-Maunoury to Pineau, November 5, 1956, MAE, Cabinet du Ministre, Cabinet de Pineau, dossier 157.

11. Palmer to Jones, December 18, 1956, FRUS, 1955–57, XVIII, 658–659.

12. Hoover to Cannon, November 19, 1956, FRUS, 1955–57, XVIII, 546–547.

13. Dillon to Dulles, November 10, 1956, USNA, RG59, Central Decimal Files, 651.71.

14. Quoted in Wall, *France, the United States, and the Algerian War*, 73.

15. Kaplan and Schleiminger, *The European Payments Union*, 270–272; Pitman, "The French Crisis," 220–221; Feiertag, "Wilfred Baumgartner," 531–533.

16. "L'évolution de la balance des paiements en 1956 et les perspectives pour 1957," November 16, 1956, MAE, DE-CE, vol. 362, Union Européenne de Paiements. Finance Minister Paul Ramadier made the same prediction two months later, once again setting 1958 as the deadline, C.-J. Gignoux, "Quand les réserves seront épuisées," January 18, 1957, *Journal des Finances*.

17. Economic historians such as Kaplan and Schleiminger, *The European Payments Union*, Pitman, "The French Crisis," and Feiertag, "Wilfred Baumgartner," all mention the Algerian War as a factor in France's financial difficulties, but none give it any particular emphasis. Political historians, on the other hand, neglect Franco-American economic diplomacy in their explanations of the May 1958 uprising and the fall of the Fourth Republic. This chapter and the next emphasize the interconnection between the economic and political aspects of the crisis, expanding on an argument first presented in Connelly, "The French-American Conflict over North Africa."

18. Memcon Tyler, Daridan, et al., November 16, 1956, USNA, RG59, Central Decimal Files, 751S.00.

19. Clark to State, November 27, 1956, ibid.

20. For an example, see Gazier to Pineau, November 21, 1956, MAE, Cabinet du Ministre, Cabinet de Pineau, dossier 155, Algérie, Loi Cadre.

21. The establishment of the MLA is described in its *inventaire*, MAE.

22. Hoover to Dillon, November 27, 1956, USNA, RG59, Central Decimal Files, 751S.00.

23. On Nixon, see "Note Pour le Ministre," December 27, 1956, MAE, DE-CE, vol. 331, Aide Américaine, 1954–1957. Eisenhower's request for $200 million in aid for the Middle East, intended to underwrite the new Eisenhower Doctrine of supporting states threatened by communism or its unwitting allies, provided further proof of U.S. largesse, see Kunz, *The Economic Diplomacy of the Suez Crisis*, 153–160.

24. Ramadier to Pineau, January 5, 1957, FNSP, Wilfred Baumgartner Papers, 2BA31, Dr1.

25. Memcon Dulles-Alphand, January 22, 1957, FRUS, 1955–57, XXVII, 96–98.

26. "Note pour Monsieur Gazier," January 30, 1957, MAE, DE-CE, vol. 331, Aide Américaine, 1954–1957.

27. Memcon DDE-Dulles, January 11, 1957, DDEL, JFDP, White House Memoranda Series, box 6, Meetings with the President 1957 (8).

28. Yost to Dulles, February 11 and February 13, 1957, FRUS, 1955–57, XXVII, 100–101, 115–118.

29. Kalijarvi memo to Herter, February 19, 1957, USNA, RG59, Central Decimal Files, 851.00

30. "Note pour le Ministre," December 7, 1956, MAE, DE-CE, vol. 470, OTAN, 1952–1960; Feiertag, "Wilfrid Baumgartner," 537–545; Kaplan and Schleiminger, *The European Payments Union*, 266–268.

31. See his marginal comments in "l'Eventualité d'une Aide Américaine," February 16, 1957, MAE, DE-CE, vol. 331, Aide Américaine, 1954–1957.

32. Yost to Dulles, February 20, 1957, USNA, RG59, Central Decimal Files, 851.10.

33. "Après le vote de l'O.N.U. sur l'Algérie," February 23, 1957, *Oeuvres Complètes*, vol. 4, 289.

34. Alleg, *La guerre d'Algérie*, vol. 2, 440. On the CCE in Algiers see Quandt, *Revolution and Political Leadership*, 103–106.

35. *Autopsie de la guerre*, 78–79.

36. See note 1.

37. Barkaoui, "The New York Times and the Algerian Revolution," 282–283. This quantitative study is both a useful gauge of general media interest and a critique of bias in some of the leading outlets, as subsequent citations will indicate.

38. Yazid, "Rapport d'activité au cours de la onzième session de l'Assemblée Générale des Nations Unies," CNAA, GPRA, dossier 4; the memorandum is reprinted as an annex to Georges-Picot's report to Pineau, January 4, 1957, DDF, 1957, I, no. 17.

39. Courrière, *La Guerre d'Algérie*, vol. 2, 448–450.

40. Ibid., vol. 2, 451–452; Horne, *A Savage War of Peace*, 187–188.

41. "Statement by Guy Mollet, Premier on French Policy in Algeria," January 9, 1957, MAE, Série ONU, dossier 550; "Minute" from the Secrétariat des conférences to Georges-Picot, January 23, 1957, MAE, Série ONU, dossier 549.

42. Porch, *The French Secret Services*, 366.

43. Horne, *A Savage War of Peace*, 244–246; Georges-Picot to Menthon, March 9, 1957, MAE, Série ONU, dossier 551; "Note sur M. Chanderli," June 19, 1959, MAE, MLA, vol. 24 (provisional number), Action extérieure, Etats-Unis, janvier 1958–juin 1959, Cote ML 4.

44. Morgan, *A Covert Life*, 289–294.

45. On this distinction, see Hill, "World Opinion," 117ff.

46. Yazid, "Bureau de New York: Rapport d'Activité—Propagande et Documentation octobre 1956–février 1957," February 18, 1957, CNAA, GPRA, dossier 4.5.

47. Lagarde to Alphand, October 19, 1956, MAE, ONU, dossier 550.

48. Alphand to Pineau, January 31, 1957, MAE, MLA, vol. 23 bis (provisional number), Action extérieure, Etats-Unis, décembre 1956–décembre 1957, Cote EU.

49. Alphand to Pineau, January 28, 1958, MAE, MLA, vol. 24 (provisional number), Action extérieure, Etats-Unis, Janvier 58–Juin 59, Cote ML 4; Barkaoui, "The New York Times and the Algerian Revolution," 43, 77–78, 92.

50. Vaurs to Alphand, March 18, 1957, MAE, MLA, vol. 23 bis (provisional number), Action extérieure, Etats-Unis, déc. 1956–déc. 1957, Cote EU; "Le Cabinet du Ministre Résident & les titres d'ouvrages et de brochures qu'il a diffusés depuis 15 mois," undated, but circa early 1957, AN, Bidault Papers, 457AP, box 110; Vaurs to Pineau, April 26, 1957, MAE, MLA, propagande, dossier 1.

51. Copies of "Notions Essentielles sur l'Algérie" can be found in the AOM, 12/CAB/161; Vaurs to Langlais, March 15, 1958, MAE, MLA, propagande, dossier 1; Yazid, "Bureau de New York: Rapport d'Activité" (see note 46).

52. Vaurs to Langlais, March 15, 1958; "Le Cabinet du Ministre Résident & les titres d'ouvrages et de brochures" (see note 50).

53. *Autour du drame algérien* and *Profile of Algeria*, numbers 56 and 91 in the AOM *inventaire*, are otherwise unidentified.

54. Bonnot, "Les Représentations de l'Algérie française," 70–76.

55. MAE, Série ONU, dossier 554.

56. "Note: Thèmes provisoires avant les débats sur l'Algérie," April 31, 1957 [*sic*], MAE, Cabinet du Ministre, Cabinet de Pineau, dossier 155, Algérie, Loi Cadre.

57. February 23, 1957 article for *Le Monde, Oeuvres Complètes*, vol. 4, 285–286.

58. "Note: La Question Algérienne à la XIme Session de l'Assemblée Générale," March 9, 1957, MAE, Série ONU, dossier 551.

59. Yazid, "Après le vote de la resolution à l'ONU," undated but circa March 1957, CNAA, GPRA, dossier 4; Abbane, "Rapport du CCE au CNRA," c. April 1957, 208.

60. "Note: La Question Algérienne à la XIme Session de l'Assemblée Générale"; Memcon Dulles-Pineau, January 12, 1957, DDF, 1957, I, no. 35.

61. "Note pour Monsieur le Directeur de Cabinet" from the Service de Défense Nationale, February 1, 1957, MAE, Série ONU, dossier 548.

62. Alleg, *La guerre d'Algérie*, vol. 2, 428–439.

63. Ibid., 438; "Note: La Question Algérienne à la XIme Session de l'Assemblée Générale," March 9, 1957, MAE, Série ONU, dossier 551; "Note: Retrospective Annuelle de Politique Etrangère: Le problème algérien aux Nations Unies," December 19, 1957, idem.

64. Horne, *A Savage War of Peace*, 224.

65. Andreopoulos, "The Age of National Liberation Movements," 206–208, 277.

66. Horne, *A Savage War of Peace*, 183–184.

67. Courrière, *La Guerre d'Algérie*, vol. 2, 516–517; Alleg, *La guerre d'Algérie*, vol. 2, 466–469; Manceron and Remaoun, *D'une rive à l'autre*, 177–178.

68. Horne, *A Savage War*, 208–209; Tripier, *Autopsie de la guerre*, 135; Alleg, *La guerre d'Algérie*, vol. 2, 444. Civilian casualty figures are included in *Aspects véritables de la rébellion algérienne*, reprinted in Eveno and Planchais, *La Guerre d'Algérie*, 150.

69. Chikh, *L'Algérie en Armes*, 95. For an account of the executions see the "Temoignage de Djamila Bouhired," *Majallat et-Tarikh* 17 (1984): 109–112.

70. Jean-Pierre Rioux, "La Guerre d'Algérie dans l'histoire des intellectuels français," in Rioux and Sirinelli, *La Guerre d'Algérie et les intellectuels français*, 37.

71. Stora, *La gangrène*, 28–31.

72. Quoted in Horne, *A Savage War of Peace*, 234.

73. Harrison, "Government and Press," 277–280.

74. De Guiringaud to Pineau, April 3, 1957, DDF, I, no. 290; Pineau circular, April 13, 1957, idem, no. 312.

75. See, for instance, the favorable reviews in the June 8, 1958 *Herald Tribune*, *Washington Post*, and *New York Times*.

76. For a good introduction, see Rioux and Sirinelli, *La Guerre d'Algérie et les intellectuels*.

77. Baraduc to Gorlin, March 22, 1958, AOM, 12/CAB/234.

78. Vaurs to Baraduc, June 5, 1957, MAE, MLA, vol. 23 bis (provisional number), Action extérieure, Etats-Unis, déc. 1956–déc. 1957, Cote EU.

79. Alphand to Pineau, June 14, 1957, MAE, MLA, vol. 23 bis. (provisional number), Action extérieure, Etats-Unis, déc. 1956–déc. 1957, Cote EU; Georges-Picot to Pineau, June 3, 1957, idem. See also Henri Pierre, "Une tendance croissante se dessine à Washington pour tenter de mettre un terme à l'affaire algérienne," *Le Monde*, June 4, 1957.

80. Ruedy, "La Réaction de la presse," is an excellent overview of American press coverage. On *The New York Times*, see also Barkaoui, "The New York Times and the Algerian Revolution," 105–109, 285.

81. Baraduc to Gorlin, March 22, 1958.

82. Alphand to Baraduc, June 14, 1957, MAE, Direction Amérique 1952–63, Etats-Unis–Afrique du Nord, dossier 32. While the authorities avoided images of combat in official films, French journalists sometimes faked action footage, see Stora, *La gangrène*, 42–45.

83. Alphand to Pineau, October 15, 1957, MAE, MLA vol. 23 bis (provisional number), Action extérieure, Etats-Unis, déc. 1956–déc. 1957, Cote EU.

84. Vaurs to Pineau, October 6, 1958, MAE, Série ONU, dossier 559. The 1957 Overseas Press Club awards for best book, radio/television reporting, and broadcast interpretation all went to works that dealt in whole or in part with the war.

85. Yazid, "Préparation de la douzième Assemblée Générale des Nations Unies," June 19, 1957, CNAA, GPRA, dossier 4; "Action de propagande dans le monde en faveur de la cause française en Algérie," April 1957, MAE, MLA, propagande, dossier 1.

86. "L'Opinion Mondiale Juge les Sanglants 'Libérateurs' de Melouza et de Wagram," August 1957, AOM 12/CAB/161; copies of the "Synthèse Bi-Mensuelle de l'activité des Emissions arabes de Radio Alger" are in AOM, 14/CAB/31.

87. Barkaoui, "The New York Times and the Algerian Revolution," 41–45, 63–69, 115–120; Müller, "La guerre d'Algérie vue par la presse," 177–185. Struck by the strength and persistence of concerns about Algeria, Roland Delcour wrote that "one would be tempted to conclude that in Federal Germany as in France all political discussions, whatever the subject, always finish with the participants confronting the *tragédie du jour*" ("L'Opinion publique allemande condamne la politique française en Algérie," *Le Monde*, May 9, 1958).

88. Rainero, "L'Italie entre amitié française et solidarité algérienne," in Rioux, *La Guerre d'Algérie et les Français*, 392; Masset, *La Belgique et la guerre d'Algérie*.

89. "Note sur le rôle réservé par le F.L.N. à la Presse, au profit de sa propagande," May 11, 1957, MAE, Série ONU, dossier 544; "Exploitation de la Presse par la Propagande du FLN," undated, MAE, MLA, propagande, dossier 2; Lebel letter to Langlais, June 16, 1959, MAE, MLA vol. 24 (provisional number), Action extérieure, Etats-Unis, Janvier 58–Juin 59, Cote ML 4. On the importance of diplomatic successes in boosting morale, see also Teguia, *L'Algérie en guerre*, 352.

90. Fitte, *Spectroscopie d'une propagande*, 6–7, 15, 20–22, 74–78.

91. Barkaoui, "The New York Times and the Algerian Revolution," 285, 299.

92. Unsigned letter to Maisonneuve, April 15, 1957, MAE, MLA, propagande, dossier 1.

93. Cornut-Gentille to Pineau, September 21, 1956, MAE, Série ONU, dossier 550; "Note: préparation du débat," August 22, 1959, MAE, Série ONU, dossier 557. Eventually the French discontinued the release of figures on Algerian casualties (Lyon to Herter, March 3, 1960, USNA, RG59, Central Decimal Files, 751S.00).

94. Ambler, *The French Army in Politics*, 138.

95. Horne, *The French Army and Politics*, 85.

96. On the establishment of international standards for human rights in this period see Menand, "Human Rights as Global Imperative," 181.

97. Maxime Damain, *Les trois frontières de l'Algérie*, AOM, number 131 in the *inventaire*. The broadcast from Algiers was relayed by a plane flying over the Balearics, "Des Champs-Elysées au Forum d'Alger," *Le Figaro*, July 15, 1958, 10. The French more commonly used radio hookups between the metropole and Algeria to send the same message. See, for instance, "Compte-rendu de la réunion du Comité 'Information-Algérie,' " October 27, 1959, AOM, 14/CAB/238.

98. Alleg, *La guerre d'Algérie*, vol. 2, 571–573. In the course of the war, nine FLN film workers would be killed in action (Megherbi, *Les Algériens au miroir*, 64–67).

99. See chapter 1, note 69.

100. J. Y. Goëau-Brissonnière, "Note: Réunion interministérielle en date du 19 Mai 1957," May 24, 1957, MAE, Série ONU, dossier 155; Vaurs to Baraduc, Langlais, February 20, 1958, MAE, Direction Amérique 1952–63, dossier 345.

101. The CCI report is attached to the "Note concernant les problèmes d'information sur l'Algérie," circa March 1957, MAE, MLA, propagande, dossier 1.

102. "Statement by Guy Mollet"; (see note 41) "Modernization and Development Plan" quoted in Gauron, *Histoire économique et sociale*, 60. On this point, see also Feiertag, "Wilfrid Baumgartner," 539–540, and Kaplan and Schleiminger,

The European Payments Union, 266–267, who show how the same spirit animated officials at the Bank of France and the Ministry of Finance.

103. Etienne de Crouy Chanel circular, July 15, 1957, MAE, MLA, propagande, dossier 1. For a typical example of these tours, see "Note de Service," Cabinet Militaire du Ministre de l'Algérie, October 16, 1957, AOM, 12/CAB/170. They also enabled the French to obtain information on visitors' opinions—not always by overt means, judging from the reports.

104. Alphand to Pineau, May 10, 1957, MAE, Série ONU, dossier 552.

105. "Statement by Guy Mollet" (see note 41).

106. Herz, "Rise and Demise of the Territorial State," 492–493.

107. L. W. Fuller, "The United States and the United Nations," December 10, 1957, USNA, RG59, PPS, Lot 67D548, United Nations 1957–1960.

108. Baraduc to Gorlin, March 22, 1958, AOM, 12/CAB/234.

109. Mandouze, *La révolution algérienne*, 74–79.

110. Baraduc to Gorlin, March 22, 1958.

111. Kaplan and Schleiminger, *The European Payments Union*, 267–276.

112. Horne, *A Savage War of Peace*, 263; Herz, "Rise and Demise of the Territorial State," 477.

113. Bénard to Couve de Murville, November 18, 1958, MAE, Série ONU, dossier 566.

114. Morice to Pineau, July 15, 1957, MAE, Cabinet du Ministre, Cabinet de Pineau, dossier 157. Indeed, the FLN began developing relations with the Red Cross for precisely this reason, see Khider to Taieb, March 18, 1956, CNAA, GPRA, dossier 1.

115. A. J. P Taylor, "War Origins Again," 113.

116. Quoted in Kyle, *Suez*, 392.

117. "Décolonisation et indépendance," April 16, 1958, *El Moudjahid*.

6. An Anti-American Revolt

1. "Le Chef et l'évolution de la guerre," *Revue militaire d'information* No. 284 (June 1957): 17.

2. *Oeuvres Complètes*, vol. 4, 374.

3. Memcon Marjolin-Dillon, May 17, 1957, FRUS, 1955–57, XXVII, 124–126; Houghton to Dulles, May 18, 1957, USNA, RG59, Central Decimal Files, 851.10.

4. Memcon Marjolin-Dillon, May 17, 1957.

5. Memcon Dulles-Marjolin, May 20, 1957, USNA, RG59, Central Decimal Files, 851.10.

6. Le Douarec, *Félix Gaillard*, 85–92.

7. Alphand to Pineau, June 11, 1957, MAE, MLA, vol. 23 bis (provisional number), Action extérieure, Etats-Unis, déc. 1956–déc. 1957, Cote EU.

8. Henri Pierre, "La France aura de grandes difficultés à obtenir une aide financière des Etats-Unis," *Le Monde*, June 26, 1957, 1, 6.

9. Memcon Dulles-Vimont, July 11, 1957, MAE, MLA vol. 23 bis. (provisional number), Action extérieure, Etats-Unis, déc. 1956–déc. 1957, Cote EU.

10. Cottier to Sadrin, July 15, 1957, MAE, DE-CE, vol. 331, Aide Américaine, 1954–1957.

11. "Note pour le President," July 20, 1957, MAE, DE-CE, sous série OECE, vol. 362.

12. Mokhtar and Aït Ahcene to Khider, June 6, 1956, CNAA, GPRA, dossier 1; Gaid Mouloud to Khider, June 5, 1956, idem; Dahmani Mohamed to Khider, July 12, 1956, idem.

13. Abbane, "Rapport du CCE au CNRA," c. April 1957, 194–196, 200–201; Djerbal, "Alliances et mésalliances tunisiennes, ou les relations algéro-tunisiennes vues par le FLN 1954–1958," Actes du IXe Colloque International sur Processus et enjeux de la décolonisation en Tunisie (1952–1964), 8–10 mai, 1998 (Tunis: 1999); Tripier, *Autopsie de la guerre*, 170–171; Barker, "The Politics of Decolonization in Tunisia," 149–150.

14. Arar Khemissi (a.k.a. Mohamed El-Hadi), "Rapport Moral aux Frères Responsables du CCE," July 30, 1957, CNAA, GPRA, dossier 4; "Aide extérieure à la rébellion algérienne," August 1957, MAE, Série ONU, dossier 569; Ruyssen, "Fiche de Renseignements: Sources extérieures de l'armement rebelle," September 19, 1958, idem.

15. *L'Année Politique, 1957* (Paris: Presses Universitaires de France, 1958), 220–21, 249; Barker, "The Politics of Decolonization in Tunisia," 236–237.

16. Thomas F. Brady, "Tunisian Rebukes U.S. on Aid Policy," *The New York Times*, May 11, 1957, 1, 6; Alphand to Pineau, May 24, 1957, DDF, 1957, I, no. 424 (emphasis added).

17. *L'Année Politique, 1957*, 242–243; Jones to Dulles, September 4, 1957, FRUS, 1955–57, XVIII, 681; Furniss, *France, Troubled Ally*, 221.

18. The text is reprinted in Kennedy, *The Strategy of Peace*, 65–81.

19. Malek, *L'Algérie à Evian*, 33; Mahoney, *JFK*, 21–22; Nurse, "Critic of Colonialism."

20. Alphand to Pineau, July 1, 1957, MAE, Direction Amérique 1952–63, Etats-Unis–Afrique du Nord, Dossier 32.

21. Henri Pierre letter, *The New York Times*, July 10, 1957, 26; *L'Express*, July 5, 1957, 1, 15–18; For a similarly favorable reaction, see Jean Masson, "Les opinions amicales valent mieux que les attaques malveillantes," *Combat*, July 13, 1957.

22. Schlesinger, *A Thousand Days*, 553–54; David Halberstam, *The Best and the Brightest*, 95.

23. Memcon Dulles-Alphand, July 1, 1957, FRUS, 1955–57, XVIII, 270–71.

24. Goëau-Brissonnière, *Mission Secrète*, 113; Wall, *France, the United States, and the Algerian War*, 86.

25. *L'Année Politique, 1957*, 248–249 (see note 15).

26. Emile Giraud, "Du 'droit de suite' . . . L'inexistence et l'inutilité de ce droit," September 12, 1957, MAE, Série ONU, dossier 567–568; memcon Dulles-Ladgham, October 2, 1957, FRUS, 1955–57, XVIII, 707–714; Habib Bourguiba with Mohammed Sayah, "Ma Vie, Mon Oeuvre, 1956–1958," unpublished manuscript, Centre d'Etudes Maghrébines à Tunis, vol. 2, 108–109.

27. Jones to Dulles, September 4, 1957, FRUS, 1955–57, XVIII, 679–80.

28. Gorse to Pineau, September 14, 1957, MAE, Série ONU, dossier 567–568.

29. Morice to Gambiez, "Instruction personnelle et secrete," August 22, 1957, SHAT, Série 0/2, Carton 2977, 29f, Tunisie; Morice to Gambiez, September 2, 1957, SHAT, Algérie 1H 1969/3; "Etude de l'hypothèse No. 2: Reprise du contrôle temporaire du territoire tunisien," September 6, 1957, idem; Salan, *Mémoires*, vol. 3, 245–247.

30. Gorse to Faure, September 12, 1957, MAE, Série ONU, dossier 111.

31. Dulles to Jones, September 11, 1957, FRUS, 1955–57, XVIII, 683–84; Jones to Dulles, September 12, 1957, idem, 685–687.

32. Bourguiba, *Discours*, 1957, vol. 3, 236–44.

33. Jones to Dulles, September 12, 1957, FRUS, 1955–57, XVIII, 685–687; Brady, "Tunisia Says Need for Arms Is Vital," *The New York Times*, September 12, 1957, 1, 8.

34. Bourguiba and Sayah, "Ma Vie, Mon Oeuvre, 1956–1958," 119 (see note 26).

35. Bourguiba, "Nationalism: Antidote to Communism," 646–653.

36. Dulles to Pineau, September 12, 1957, FRUS, 1955–57, XVIII, 688–689.

37. Dulles to Jones, September 22, 1957, ibid., 695; Osgood Caruthers, "Tunisia Accepts Cairo Arms Gift," *The New York Times*, September 24, 1957, 1, 6; "Czech Accord Due Today," idem, 6.

38. Memcon Palmer-Slim, September 26, 1957, FRUS, 1955–57, XVIII, 697–701; Thomas F. Brady, "Tunisia Pledges Loyalty to West," *The New York Times*, September 27, 1957, 3.

39. Houghton to Dulles, September 21, 1957, FRUS, 1955–57, XVIII, 693–694.

40. Rioux, *The Fourth Republic*, 294.

41. Heggoy, *Insurgency and Counterinsurgency*, 256–257.

42. Memcon Alphand-Elbrick, October 1, 1957, FRUS, 1955–57, XVIII, 704–707; "U.S. Tunisia Stand Factor in Paris," *The New York Times*, October 1, 1957, 1, 7.

43. Memcon Dulles-Ladgham, October 2, 1957, FRUS, 1955–57, XVIII, 712.

44. Dulles memo for Herter, March 25, 1957, USNA, RG59, PPS, Lot 67D548, box 124.

45. Louis and Robinson, "The Imperialism of Decolonization," 481.

46. Memcon Dulles-Caccia, October 9, 1957, FRUS: 1955–57, XVIII, 716–717; Memcon Dulles-Lloyd, October 15, 1957, idem; Memcon Eisenhower-Spaak, October 25, 1957, FRUS, 1955–57, IV, 182.

47. Memcon Alphand-Elbrick, October 17, 1957, FRUS: 1955–57, XVIII, 723–726.

48. Jebb to Lloyd, October 17, 1957, PRO, PREM 11/2560.

49. Memcon Alphand-Dulles, October 18, 1957, FRUS, 1955–57, XVIII, 726–729; Dulles to Jones, November 2, 1957, idem, 729.

50. "Le leader socialiste va s'entretenir avec M. Baumgartner de la situation financière," *L'Information*, October 5, 1957; "Situation financière et Algérie étudiées par M. Pleven," *France-Soir*, October 9, 1957; Memcon Tuthill-Schweitzer, October 24, 1957, USNA, RG59, Central Decimal Files, 851.00; Le Douarec, *Félix Gaillard*, 107–109.

51. Memcon Alphand-Dillon, November 1, 1957, USNA, RG59, Central Decimal Files, 851.10.

52. Dulles to Jones, November 2, 1957, FRUS, 1955–57, XVIII, 729–730.

53. Lloyd to Caccia, November 2, 1957, PRO, PREM 11/2560.

54. De Zulueta to Macmillan, "Arms for Tunisia," October 29, 1957, PRO, PREM 11/2560; Lloyd to Caccia, November 12, 1957, idem.

55. Jebb to Lloyd, November 6, 1957, ibid.

56. Houghton to Dulles, November 9, 1957, FRUS, 1955–57, XVIII, 737–740.

57. Herter to Jones, November 9, 1957, ibid., 736.

58. Jones to Dulles, November 11, 1957, ibid., 739–740.

59. Malcolm to Lloyd, October 26 and November 9, 1957, PRO, PREM 11/2560; Dulles to Houghton, November 11, 1957, FRUS, 1955–57, XVIII, 744–745.

60. Houghton to Dulles, November 12, 1957, ibid., 746–748. The message is attached to the Houghton-Dulles memcon, November 13, 1957, DDEL, JFDP, Telephone Calls Series, box 7, Memoranda of Telephone Conversations, General, November 1, 1957–December 27, 1957 (3).

61. Dulles to Jones, November 12, 1957, FRUS, 1955–57, XVIII, 748.

62. Le Douarec, *Felix Gaillard*, 125.

63. Pineau to Alphand, Chauvel, Bénard, November 12, 1957, DDF, 1957, II, no. 328; Gorse to Pineau, November 14, 1957, idem, No. 333.

64. Jebb to Lloyd, November 13, 1957 (numbers 294 and 298), PRO, PREM 11/2560.

65. Memcon DDE-Dulles, November 13, 1957, MTC, Dulles-Herter, UPA, microfilm publication (1980), reel 10, frames 145–150; Larson, *Eisenhower*, 101; Dulles to Houghton, November 13, 1957, FRUS, 1955–57, XVIII, 750–752.

66. Bourguiba, *Discours*, 1957, vol. 3, 312–324.

67. Henry Giniger, "France Is Angered by Decision to Send Arms Aid to Tunisians," *The New York Times*, November 15, 1957, 2.

68. Pierre Mélandri, "La France et le 'jeu double' des Etats-Unis," in Rioux, *La Guerre d'Algérie et les Français*, 429.

69. *L'Année Politique, 1957*, 117 (see note 15).

70. "Public Opinion in France: The Tunisian Arms Issue," Research Report PA-25, January 7, 1958, USNA, RG59, Lot 61D30, Records of the Office of Western European Affairs, Subject File Relating to France, 1944–60, Alpha-Numeric, box 2, Public Opinion.

71. De Zulueta to Macmillan, November 18, 1957, PRO, PREM 11/2560.

72. Lloyd to Caccia, November 18, 1957, PRO, PREM 11/2560.

73. Caccia to Lloyd, November 18, 1957, ibid.

74. Caccia to Lloyd, November 18, 1957; Lloyd letter to Dulles, November 25, 1957; Jebb to Lloyd, December 4, 1957; Hood to Lloyd, December 9, 1957, all in PRO, PREM 11/2560.

75. Lloyd to Jebb, January 15, 1958, ibid.; Lloyd to Caccia, February 12, 1958, PRO, PREM 11/2561.

76. Müller, "Le réalisme de la République fédérale d'Allemagne," in Rioux, La Guerre d'Algérie et les Français, 423. German support was more than rhetorical. Adenauer gave instructions to all the ministerial departments to help the French. For instance, they prevented the screening of pro-FLN films and turned over Algerian refugees (Couve de Murville to Pineau, December 11, 1957, MAE, MLA, Action Extérieure, R.F.A. [West Germany], dossier 2; Langlais to Lacoste, December 18, 1957, idem.

77. Elbrick memo for Dulles, February 5, 1958, USNA, RG59, PPS, Lot 67D548, box 151, Europe 1958; Soutou, "Les Accords de 1957 et 1958," 131–140.

78. Dejean to Pineau, February 4, 1957, DDF, 1957, I, 106; Khrushchev quoted in "Note: Le bloc soviétique et l'affaire algérienne," April 30, 1958, MAE,

MLA, Action Extérieure, URSS, dossier 86. Dejean may not have been altogether sincere in analyses such as this one, which shifted the onus of Soviet support for the FLN to the Americans. The ambassador was reportedly the target of sexual blackmail by the KGB in 1958, though some argue that he was working for the Soviets even before arriving in Moscow (Porch, *The French Secret Services*, 292, 415, 586). Andrew and Gordievsky contend that the operation was blown before Dejean could do any real damage (*KGB: The Inside Story*, 376).

79. Gorse to Pineau, September 17, 1957, MAE, Série ONU, dossier 567–68; Alphand to Pineau, January 7, 1958, MAE, Série ONU, dossier 557.

80. Diary entry, November 14, 1957, FRUS, 1955–57, XVIII, 758–761.

81. Eisenhower to Dulles, November 13, 1957, FRUS, 1955–57, XVII, 795.

82. Jebb to Lloyd, November 12, 1957, PRO, PREM 11/2560; Jebb to Lloyd, November 14, 1957, idem.

83. Diary entry, November 14, 1957, FRUS, 1955–57, XVIII, 760.

84. Jones to Dulles, November 11, 1957, ibid., 739.

85. Houghton to Dulles, November 12, 1957, ibid., 748.

86. Dulles to Lloyd, November 13, 1957, ibid., 756; Gorse to Pineau, November 14, 1957, DDF, 1957, II, no. 333.

87. "Egypt Ships Cargo of Rifles to Tunisia," *The New York Times*, November 26, 1957, 3.

88. "Tunis Petitions France," *The New York Times*, November 29, 1957, 10.

89. Dana Adams Schmidt, "Egyptian Arms Ship to Tunis a Phantom," *The New York Times*, December 4, 1957, 1 ("A Phantom Ship" headline appears over the continuation of the story, 24).

90. For a different analysis of the arms crisis, see Sangmuah, "Eisenhower and Containment," 81–86.

91. Memcon Dulles-Eisenhower, November 11, 1957, FRUS, 1955–57, XVIII, 741.

92. Memcon DDE-Dulles, November 13, 1957 (6:00 P.M.), MTC, Dulles-Herter, UPA, reel 10, frames 145–150.

93. Memcon Baumgartner-Burgess et al., November 12, 1957, FNSP, Wilfred Baumgartner Papers, 2BA38, Dr3.

94. Jebb to Lloyd, November 16, 1957, PRO, PREM 11/4248; Henry Giniger, "France Is Angered by Decision to Send Arms to Tunisians," *The New York Times*, November 15, 1957, 2.

95. Henry Giniger, "France Will Call for Satisfaction on Tunisian Arms," *The New York Times*, November 16, 1957, 1, 4; Daniel Lefeuvre, "Les Réactions algériennes à la propagande économique pendant la guerre d'Algérie," in Ageron, *La Guerre d'Algérie et les Algériens*, 239–240.

96. Griffith, *Ike's Letters to a Friend*, 192.

97. "Note pour le Ministre," November 9, 1957, Archives Economiques et Financières, Paris, B2206; Le Douarec, *Félix Gaillard*, 127–130. On the importance of Algeria in these negotiations, see also Feiertag, "Wilfred Baumgartner," 548–549.

98. "Mm. von Mangoldt et Jacobsen [sic] à Paris," *L'Express*, November 28, 1957, 4.

99. James, *International Monetary Cooperation*, 104–105. The French director of the fund's European department, Gabriel Ferras, reported Southard's and Dillon's plans to Baumgartner, and he would continue to inform him discretely about

IMF and U.S. views during the ensuing negotiations, Ferras to Baumgartner, December 9, 1957, FNSP, Wilfred Baumgartner Papers, 2BA38, Dr5.

100. Monnet to Gaillard, November 30, 1957, FNSP, Wilfred Baumgartner Papers, 2BA38, Dr3.

101. "M. Jacobsen [sic] ausculte la France," *L'Express*, December 12, 1957, 1, 3.

102. Robert Anderson to DDE, January 25, 1958, EOF, 1953–1961, part 2: International Series, UPA, reel 7, frames 793–798, which presented to Eisenhower a summary version of the January 11, 1958, memorandum that the French gave the lending agencies (MAE, DE-CE, vol. 331, Aide Américaine, 1958–60). On the importance of appearing to formulate the plan independently, see Monnet to Gaillard, December 10, 1957, FNSP, Wilfred Baumgartner Papers, 2BA38, Dr5, and see also Feiertag, "Wilfred Baumgartner," 556–557.

103. Harold James suggests that the 1959 stabilization program in Spain provided the "model for imitation" in non-European countries (*International Monetary Cooperation*, 103–108, 110). But since the Monnet program also required that the government take responsibility for a program based on trade liberalization, sound money, and shrinking the public sector, France deserves that dubious distinction.

104. 340th Meeting of the NSC, October 17, 1957, Declassified Documents Reference System, document number 1987030101003; Dulles to DDE, undated, EOF, Part 1: Eisenhower Administration Series, UPA, reel 22, frames 821–822.

105. NIE 22–57, August 13, 1957, FRUS, 1955–57, XXVII, 147, 160.

106. Dulles to Houghton, November 21, 1957, ibid., 206–207; Feiertag, "Wilfred Baumgartner, 550.

107. On Baumgartner, see memcon Dulles-Houghton, April 1, 1957, FRUS, 1955–57, XXVII, 118–120, and Feiertag, "Wilfrid Baumgartner," 550. On officials' growing skepticism about the value of France's overseas empire, see Fitzgerald, "Did France's Colonial Empire Make Economic Sense?" 382–384.

108. Burgess memo to Humphrey, February 25, 1957, EOF, Part 1: Eisenhower Administration Series, UPA, reel 17, frame 892.

109. Memcon Sadrin-Tuthill, December 16, 1957, USNA, RG59, Central Decimal Files, 851.00.

110. Memcon Tuthill-Hirsch, December 27, 1957, ibid.

111. Isenbergh to Dulles, November 27, 1957, ibid.

112. Memcon Hirsch-Tuthill, October 23, 1957, ibid., 851.00.

113. "Will New $655 Million Loan Bring Needed Fiscal Reforms or Just Buy a Breather?" *The Wall Street Journal*, February 5, 1958.

114. Dulles to Houghton, November 21, 1957, FRUS, 1955–57, XXVII: 205–209; Kaplan to Cleveland, November 23, 1957, USNA, RG59, Bureau of European Affairs, Office of European Regional Affairs, Political-Economic Numeric Files 1957–1960, box 2, file 9.6. While they were apparently overruled, embassy officials like Yost and Tuthill probably opposed the loan judging from the aforementioned reports. See also their skeptical review of "The French Economic and Financial Program for 1958; Its Contents and Prospects," attached to Yost to State, December 31, 1957, USNA, RG59, Central Decimal Files, 851.00.

115. Kaplan to Timmons, November 16, 1957, USNA, RG59, Bureau of European Affairs, Office of European Regional Affairs, Political-Economic Numeric Files 1957–1960, box 2, file 9.6.

116. Lloyd to Caccia, November 7, 1957, PRO, PREM 11/4248.

117. Steel to Lloyd, November 21, 1957, ibid.

118. Nolting to Dulles, November 30, 1957, USNA, RG59, Central Decimal Files, 851.10.

119. Kaplan to Cleveland, November 23, 1957, USNA, RG59, Bureau of European Affairs, Office of European Regional Affairs, Political-Economic Numeric Files 1957–1960, box 2, file 9.6.

120. Ambrose, *Eisenhower*, vol. 2, 434–35, 443.

121. Memcon Dulles, Merchant, Holmes, October 3, 1955, FRUS, 1955–57, XVIII, 515–519.

122. Memcon Dulles-Monnet, May 10, 1958, DDEL, JFDP, Chronological Series, box 16, 5/58 (3).

123. *El Moudjahid*, February 12, 1958.

124. Kaplan and Schleiminger, *The European Payments Union*, 280; Feiertag, "Wilfrid Baumgartner," 562.

125. Henri Pierre, "L'experience montrera si notre confiance est justifiée estiment les Américains," *Le Monde*, February 1, 1958.

126. Chaban-Delmas to Secrétaires d'Etat aux Forces Armées, January 10, 1958, SHAA, E17149. The army was also worried about the cuts in manpower; see Etienne Antherieu, "Grave problème pour l'Algérie: La crise des effectifs," *Le Figaro*, February 1, 1958.

127. Monnet to Gaillard, January 16, 1958, MAE, DE-CE, vol. 331, Aide Américaine, 1958–60; Didier Maus, "La guerre et les institutions de la République," in Rioux, *La Guerre d'Algérie et les Français*, 166.

128. Planchais, *Une Histoire Politique de l'Armée*, vol. 2, 295–296; Patrick Facon, "Le général Bailly, chef d'état-major de l'armée de l'Air, ou l'impossible équilibre," a paper kindly provided by the author; Jean Planchais, "Des effectifs pour l'Algérie vont être prélevés en Allemagne et en metropole," *Le Monde*, February 20, 1958.

129. *L'Année Politique, 1958* (Paris: Presses Universitaires de France, 1959), 245–246; "Monsieur" quoted in Horne, *A Savage War of Peace*, 267.

130. The relevant documents are in SHAT, Algérie, 1H 1965/1. See especially Salan's proposal—and Ely's acceptance—of a "riposte systematique" within three hours, February 1 and February 2, 1958, Jouhaud to Salan, February 13, 1958, and Salan, "Action Aérienne de légitime défense à Sakiet," February 13, 1958. Of course, since much of this documentation is concerned with exculpating the military and some of it was for external consumption, one might well be skeptical about any of the claims therein. For a discussion of the question of responsibility, see Wall, "The United States, Algeria," 494–495.

131. Mélandri, "La France et le 'jeu double' des Etats-Unis," in Rioux, *La Guerre d'Algérie et les Français*, 429.

132. Diary entry, February 10, 1958, AWF, Diary Series, box 9; Memcon Elbrick-Dulles, February 9, 1958, DDEL, AWF, Diary Series, box 30, Toner Notes, February 1958; Dulles-Knowland memcon, February 10, 1958, idem. For the U.S. warning, see Francfort to Alphand, February 4, 1958, MAE, Direction Amérique 1952–63, Etats-Unis–Algérie, Dossier 33.

133. Memcon DDE-Dulles, February 9, 1958, FRUS, 1958–60, XIII, 821–822.

134. Dulles-Knowland memcon, February 10, 1958.

135. "Turning Point in North Africa," *The New York Herald Tribune*, February 11, 1958, 22.

136. Mahoney, *JFK*, 22–23.
137. Memcon DDE-Dulles, February 9, 1958, FRUS, 1958–60, XIII, 821–822.
138. Alphand to Pineau, February 9, 1958, DDF, 1958, I, no. 81; Memcon Alphand-Dulles, February 9, 1958, USNA, RG59, PPS, Lot 67D548, box 144. On threat to recall the ambassador, Bozo and Mélandri, "La France devant l'opinion américaine," 196. London's reaction was much more restrained, merely expressing the "hope the French Government will bear in mind the embarrassing situation in which these developments are putting France's friends and allies" ("Aide Mémoire," February 12, 1958, MAE, Série ONU, dossier 111).
139. Memcon, February 9, 1958, DDEL, JFDP, Telephone Calls Series, box 8.
140. Memcon DDE-Dulles, February 10, 1958, DDEL, JFDP, Special Assistant Chronological Series, box 12, Greene-Peacock Chronological 2/58 (3).
141. Le Douarec, *Félix Gaillard*, 166.
142. "Pineau Calls Tunisia Bombing 'Sad Error,' " *The New York Herald Tribune*, February 11, 1958, 1, 6.
143. Loth to Salan, February 11, 1958, SHAT, Algérie, 1H 1965/1.
144. Salan to Chaban-Delmas, February 13, 1958, ibid.
145. Copies of these dossiers along with distribution lists are in SHAT, Algérie, 1H 1965/1. See also Williams, *Wars, Plots and Scandals*, 144, and Merry and Serge Bromberger, *Les 13 Complots du 13 Mai*, 120–122.
146. Salan to Morice, September 27, 1957, SHAT, Algérie 1H 1969/3.
147. Ruyssen, "Fiche de Renseignements: Sources extérieures de l'armement rebelle," September 19, 1958, MAE, Série ONU, dossier 569; Mohammed Harbi, *Le FLN*, 227, 417; Kessler, "La Surveillance des frontières maritimes," 99–101.
148. Ruyssen, "Fiche de Renseignements." See also appendix.
149. "Note: Affaire de Sakiet devant les Nations Unies," February 19, 1958, MAE, ONU, Dossier 112; Rioux, *The Fourth Republic*, 297.
150. Murphy was a bête noire to many French because of his dealings with Vichy, see Pierre Mélandri and Maurice Vaïsse, "La 'boîte à chagrin,' " in Rioux, *La Guerre d'Algérie et les Français*, 439; Le Douarec, *Félix Gaillard*, 166. For examples of U.S. pressure on the French, see Dulles to Tunis, February 19, 1958, FRUS, 1958–60, XIII, 829; memcon Gaillard-Murphy-Beeley et al., March 11, 1958, PRO, FO 371, 131590; memcon Gaillard-Murphy-Beeley et al., March 19, 1958, idem; memcon Dulles, Rountree, et al., April 2, 1958, FRUS, XIII, 1958–60, 838–840.
151. Caccia to Lloyd, February 19, 1958, PRO, PREM 11, 2561. Regarding Holmes, see chapter 3. On preparations for the diplomatic offensive, see Greene memo, February 12, 1958, DDEL, JFDP, Special Assistant Chronological Series, box 12, Greene-Peacock, 2/58 (3); Herter-Holmes telephone call, February 26, 1958, DDEL, Herter Papers, Telephone Calls August 15, 1957-December 31, 1957, box 11.
152. Emphasis is Macmillan's, who also wrote "yes" in the margin (de Zulueta to Macmillan, February 19, 1958, PRO, PREM 11/2561).
153. *L'Année Politique, 1958*, 248 (see note 129).
154. Bénard to Pineau, February 23, 1958, MAE, Série ONU, dossier 112.
155. Tripier, *Autopsie de la guerre*, 163–166; *L'Année Politique, 1958*, 249–250 (see note 129).

156. Müller, "Le réalisme de la République fédérale," 418–421; Rainero, "L'Italie entre amitié française et solidarité algérienne," 394–395; Mélandri, "La France et le 'Jeu Double' des Etats-Unis," 429–433, all in Rioux, *La Guerre d'Algérie et les Français.*

157. Dejean to Pineau, March 17, 1958, MAE, Europe 1944–1960, URSS, Dossier 271. See also Zoubir, "U.S. and Soviet Policies."

158. 356th Meeting of the NSC, February 27, 1958, DDEL, AWF, NSC series.

159. Twining to McElroy, March 1, 1958, USNA, RG 218, CCS 092 Africa (4-20-50), sec 7. For the other reasons for this advice, see Sangmuah, "Eisenhower and Containment," 87.

160. Memcon DDE-Dulles, March 1, 1958, DDEL, AWF, Diary Series, box 31, Toner Notes, March 1958. Regarding the Indochina precedent, see George C. Herring, " 'A Good Stout Effort': John Foster Dulles and the Indochina Crisis, 1954–1955," in Immerman, *John Foster Dulles*, 213–33.

161. DDE Dictation, March 3, 1958, DDEL, AWF, Diary Series.

162. Jebb to Lloyd, March 3, 1958, PRO, PREM 11, 2561.

163. Lloyd to Jebb, March 4, 1958, ibid. See also Murphy's memoirs, *Diplomat among Warriors*, 396.

164. Alphand to MAE, March 5, 1958, Direction Amérique 1952–63, Etats-Unis–Algérie, dossier 33 (provisional number).

165. Memcon Pineau-Dulles-Lloyd, March 12, 1958, DDF, 1958, I, no. 179.

166. Beeley to Lloyd, March 12, 1958, PRO, PREM 11, 2561.

167. Directeur général de la Sûreté Nationale, Direction de la Surveillance du Territoire, to Pineau, March 12, 1958, MAE, Cabinet du Ministre, cabinet de Pineau, dossier 155.

168. Herter to Houghton, Murphy, Jones, March 17, 1958, FRUS, 1958–60, XIII, 629–630, and see also Wall, "The United States, Algeria," 508–509.

169. Yazid to Khider, May 15, 1958, CNAA, GPRA, dossier 3.

170. Wall, *France, the United States, and the Algerian War*, 148.

171. Beeley to Lloyd, March 12, 1958. For Eisenhower's discussion—and approval—of this initiative see memcon with Herter, March 8, 1958, Dulles-Herter Papers, Chronological Correspondence Series, UPA microfilm publication (1986), reel 24, frame 1126. According to Barnet, senior FLN members and labor officials acknowledged the CIA involvement in subsequent interviews (*Intervention and Revolution*, 316–317). The George Meany Memorial Archives in Silver Spring, MD, contain copious documentation on AFL-CIO efforts to aid the North African nationalists but the author found nothing that sheds light on the CIA role.

172. Beeley to Lloyd, March 12, 1958, PRO, PREM 11, 2561; Lloyd to Caccia, March 22, 1958, PRO, FO 371, 131588; Lloyd to Beeley, March 13, 1958, PRO, PREM 11, 2561; Ganiage, *Histoire Contemporaine du Maghreb*, 601. On March 25, they apparently agreed, in principle, to proposing a conference after the conclusion of the good offices mission (Jebb to Lloyd, March 25, 1958, PRO, PREM 11, 2562; Beeley to Ross, March 31, 1958, PRO, FO 371, 131588).

173. Dulles to Bruce, April 2, 1958, FRUS, 1958–60, VII, Part 2, 4–5.

174. Memcon DDE-Dulles, April 3, 1958, FRUS, 1958–60, XIII, 841.

175. The text is in Caccia to Lloyd, April 5, 1958, PRO, FO 371, 131589.
176. Macmillan to Caccia, April 7, 1958, ibid.
177. Caccia to Lloyd, April 7, 1958, ibid.; Jebb to Lloyd, April 9, 1958, idem.
178. Caccia to Lloyd, April 5, 1958, ibid., and the accompanying correspondence. "Decolonization by invitation" alludes to Lundestad's "Empire by Invitation?" thesis.
179. DDE to Gaillard, April 10, 1958, EOF 1953–1961, Part 2: International Series, UPA, reel 7, frames 782–784; Jebb to Lloyd, April 11, 1958, PRO, FO 371, 131590.
180. Droz and Lever, *Histoire de la guerre d'Algérie*, 168.
181. On the cabinet meeting, see Pflimlin, *Mémoires d'un Européen*, 103–104. When he succeeded Gaillard Pflimlin deemed economic and financial problems even more critical than Algeria (idem, 115). See also Raymond Aron, "Où en est l'économie française?" April 11, 1958. *Le Figaro*; "Status of French Stabilization Program as of the end of April 1958," May 16, 1958, USNA, RG59, Central Decimal Files, 851.10; and Rueff, *Combats pour l'Ordre financier*, 154.
182. "Apogee," in both Mélandri, "La France et le 'Jeu Double' des Etats-Unis," in Rioux, *La Guerre d'Algérie et les Français*, 439–440, and Harrison, "French Anti-Americanism," 173–174. See also Rémond, *Le Retour de de Gaulle*, 44–48. For the *Sunday Times*, see Alleg, *La guerre d'Algérie*, vol. 2, 586. For Soustelle and Gaillard, see Le Douarec, *Félix Gaillard*, 179, and Maier and White, *The Thirteenth of May*, 186, a useful collection of documents and articles on the crisis.
183. Wall, *France, the United States, and the Algerian War*, 131, 136–137; *L'Année Politique, 1958*, 26, 45–46 (see note 129).
184. Ambler, *The French Army in Politics*, 241.
185. The Brombergers' very title, *Les 13 Complots du 13 Mai*, captures the diversity of these groups.
186. Williams, *Wars, Plots and Scandals*, 135.
187. "Note," undated but circa early May 1958, AN, Pleven Papers, AP560, dossier 53.
188. Houghton to State, May 1, 1958, USNA, RG59, Central Decimal Files, 751.00.
189. The telegram is reprinted in *L'Année Politique, 1958*, 529–530.
190. Horne, *A Savage War of Peace*, 281.
191. "M. Pflimlin sollicite l'investiture de l'Assemblée," *Le Monde*, May 14, 1958.
192. *L'Année Politique, 1958*, 26.
193. Rémond, *Le Retour de de Gaulle*, 61–62; Maier and White, *The Thirteenth of May*, 276–279; *L'Année Politique, 1958*, 535.
194. "The United States, Algeria," 510, and see also 491–492, 511.
195. DDE to Paul Hoffman, June 23, 1958, EOF, Part 1: Eisenhower Administration Series, UPA, reel 16, frame 206. See also Wells, "Charles de Gaulle and the French Withdrawal," 92.
196. Alphand to Pleven, May 26, 1958, MAE, MLA vol. 24 (provisional number), Action extérieure, Etats-Unis, Janvier 58-Juin 59, Cote ML 4. Regarding the contingency planning, see Thomas, "France Accused," forthcoming. On the planned attack against Tunisia, see Gorse, "La Nuit de Mai," 304–306.

197. Grosser, *Affaires extérieures*, 141; Horne, *A Savage War of Peace*, 250; Mélandri and Vaïsse, "La 'boîte à chagrin,' " in Rioux, *La Guerre d'Algérie et les Français*, 375.

198. "French Anti-Americanism," 173–174.

199. Wall, *France, the United States, and the Algerian War*, chapter 4.

200. Alphand to Pineau, July 1, 1957, MAE, Direction Amérique 1952–63, Etats-Unis–Afrique du Nord, Dossier 32.

7. Decoding de Gaulle

1. "Rapport au CCE," July 8, 1958, reprinted in Harbi, *Les Archives*, 192.

2. De Gaulle, *The Edge of the Sword*, 58.

3. De Gaulle, *Discours*, 15.

4. Ibid., 16; *Memoirs of Hope*, 48.

5. Foreword of Grosser, *French Foreign Policy*, vii. This analysis of de Gaulle's policies expands on material first presented in Connelly, "The Algerian War for Independence."

6. *Memoirs of Hope*, 11.

7. Lacouture, *De Gaulle*, vol. 3, 18–21.

8. Tricot, *Mémoires*, 88–89.

9. Terrenoire, *De Gaulle et l'Algérie*, 86.

10. Peyrefitte, *C'était de Gaulle*, 48; Lacouture, *De Gaulle*, vol. 3, 23–25, 247–248.

11. Cotteret and Moreau, *Le Vocabulaire du Général*, 181, 190.

12. *Memoirs of Hope*, 235.

13. *Discours*, 166.

14. *Memoirs of Hope*, 45–46.

15. Yacono, *De Gaulle et le F.L.N.*, 5–6.

16. *Discours*, 165.

17. *Memoirs of Hope*, 43, 45. See also 15, where he writes that, "[I]n terms of our credit abroad it was expensive too, because the world as a whole deplored this endless tragedy."

18. Ibid., 37, 45–46, emphasis added.

19. Ageron, "De Gaulle et la Conférence de Brazzaville," 246, 249–251; Rioux, *The Fourth Republic*, 86.

20. Albertini, *Decolonization*, 372. Lacouture, *De Gaulle*, vol. 3, 181–182.

21. Alleg, *La guerre d'Algérie*, vol. 1, 272; de Gaulle, *Discours*, 289.

22. Touchard, *Le gaullisme*, 97.

23. Lacouture, *De Gaulle*, vol. 2, 414.

24. Touchard, *Le gaullisme*, 147–152.

25. Ferniot, *De Gaulle et le 13 mai*, 117–118.

26. Terrenoire, *De Gaulle et l'Algérie*, 48.

27. "Les Etats africains de la Communauté et la guerre d'Algérie (1958–1960)," in Ageron and Michel, *l'Afrique noire française*, 229–231.

28. Grosser, *French Foreign Policy*, 52–55.

29. Lacouture, *De Gaulle*, vol. 2, 512; Horne, *A Savage War of Peace*, 310. See also Tricot, *Mémoires*, 102.

30. Yacono, *De Gaulle et le F.L.N.*, 5–6.

31. Lacouture, *De Gaulle: The Rebel*, 184.

32. Lacouture, *De Gaulle*, vol. 2, 512–513; Jacques Soustelle, *L'Espérance*

trahie, 3. See also Ageron, "De Gaulle et l'Algérie algérienne," in Ageron, *l'Algérie algérienne*.

33. Peyrefitte, *C'était de Gaulle*, 54–55. "Coloreds" is an approximate translation of *nègres*.

34. Ibid., 52. De Gaulle is quoted saying much the same thing on a number of other occasions, see Yacono, *De Gaulle et le F.L.N.*, 20–21.

35. De Gaulle, *Discours*, 140–141. See also Touchard, *Le gaullisme*, 149.

36. Peyrefitte, *C'était de Gaulle*, 57. On the Constantine Plan, see Lefeuvre, "Les Réactions patronales."

37. De Gaulle, *Discours*, 288.

38. *French Foreign Policy*, 26.

39. *Memoirs of Hope*, 43.

40. Ibid., 45–46

41. Horne, *A Savage War of Peace*, 265–266.

42. "Compte Rendu de la Conférence de Tanger," CNAA, GPRA, dossier 8.2; "Note de la Direction générale des Affaires marocaines et tunisiennes," May 12, 1958, DDF, 1958, I, no. 312.

43. "La conférence maghrébine de Tunis se poursuit dans une atmosphère pesant," *Le Monde*, June 19, 1958; Ahmed Boumendjel, "Le Gouvernement provisoire de la République algérienne face à la France," August 1959, reprinted in Harbi, *Les Archives*, 260–261. The following account of the meetings and quotations are from the *procès-verbaux*, June 17, 1958-June 20, 1958, reprinted in Harbi, *Les Archives*, 414–426.

44. *L'Année Politique, 1958* (Paris: Presses Universitaires de France, 1959), 271 (emphasis added).

45. See chapter 1.

46. Département d'information et de presse, "Instructions aux chefs responsables de la presse, de la radio, de l'information et de la propagande en Algérie et à l'étranger," June 1958, CNAA, GPRA, dossier 17.

47. Harbi, *Le FLN*, 212–213.

48. CCE to Bourguiba, July 10, 1958, Harbi, *Les Archives*, 427–428.

49. Jones to Dulles, July 25, 1958, USNA, RG59, Central Decimal Files, 651.51S; Joxe to Couve de Murville, August 2, 1958, MAE, Série ONU, dossier 112.

50. "Note de la Direction générale des Affaires marocaines et tunisiennes," February 5, 1959, MAE, Série ONU, dossier 113.

51. Harbi, *Le FLN*, 212–213; Boussouf to GPRA, October 1, 1958, Harbi, *Les Archives*, 429–445.

52. Ouamrane to CCE, July 8, 1958, Harbi, *Les Archives*, 189–190.

53. Ibid., 190–193; Yazid, "Rapport sur l'Attitude américaine," June 1, 1958, CNAA, GPRA, dossier 4.4.

54. See chapter 2.

55. The study is reprinted in Aït Ahmed, *La Guerre et l'Après-guerre*, 9–57. In his introduction, Aït Ahmed doubts that his study ever reached the CCE, but Ouamrane attached it to his report, and its influence is also evident in the "Rapport de la Commission gouvernementale sur la Formation d'un Gouvernement provisoire de l'Algérie libre," September 6, 1958, reprinted in Harbi, *Les Archives*, 210–214.

56. Ouamrane to CCE, July 8, 1958, 191–192; Aït Ahmed, *La Guerre et l'Après-guerre*, 25–26.

57. Aït Ahmed, *La Guerre et l'Après-guerre*, 25, 27–29, 33–36, 55

58. Ibid., 38–39.

59. Ibid. 39–43; Abbas to CCE, July 29, 1958, Harbi, *Les Archives*, 196–197.

60. "Rapport de la Commission," 210.

61. Harbi, *Le FLN*, 175–176.

62. Abbas to CCE, July 29, 1958, 195–196.

63. Ibid., 196; Ouamrane to CCE, July 8, 1958, 193.

64. Abdelmadjid Belkherroubi holds that the rebels controlled some remote and inaccessible areas, but he does not deny the unprecedented nature of their claims to constitute a legitimate government (*La Naissance et la reconnaissance*, 69–70, 85–95).

65. Ibid., 83.

66. Long, *Le Dossier Secret*, 29.

67. *De Gaulle: The Rebel*, 216.

68. De Gaulle, *Memoirs of Hope*, 40.

69. Jebb, "Record of conversation with General De Gaulle," March 20, 1958, PRO, PREM 11/2339.

70. Vaïsse, "Aux origines," 266.

71. Soutou, "Les Accords de 1957 et 1958," 155.

72. Memcon Eisenhower-Dulles, December 12, 1958, FRUS, 1958–60, VII, part 2, 145. See also memcon Eisenhower-Herter, June 2, 1959, idem, 203–207.

73. Jebb to Lloyd, June 2, 1958, PRO, PREM 11/2339.

74. Quoted in Costigliola, *France and the United States*, 121

75. Caccia to Lloyd, June 3, 1958, PRO, PREM 11/2339.

76. Jebb to Lloyd, June 3, 1958, ibid.

77. Memcon Dulles-de Gaulle et al., July 5, 1958, USNA, RG59, Central Decimal Files, 611.51. There is another, shorter version reprinted in FRUS, 1958–60, VII, Part 2, 53–64.

78. Memcon Dulles-de Gaulle, July 5, 1958, DDEL, AWF, International Series, box 11, de Gaulle June 1958–October 30, 1959 (4).

79. Memcon Dulles-de Gaulle et al., July 5, 1958. Dulles had actually shared this concern, worried that intervention "would lead to solidification of opposition throughout [the] Moslem world not only to Christians in Lebanon but to the West in general," quoted in Gendzier, *Notes from the Minefield*, 278.

80. Memcon with Vice President, July 15, 1958, FRUS, 1958–60, XI, 244. See also chapter 1 and Louis and Robinson, "The Imperialism of Decolonization," 482–483.

81. 373rd Meeting of the NSC, July 25, 1958, DDEL, AWF, NSC series. Nixon spoke as an authority on mobs, having almost been killed by one in Caracas two months earlier.

82. Quoted in Ambrose, *Eisenhower*, vol. 2, 474.

83. 373rd Meeting of the NSC, July 25, 1958.

84. Gaddis, *We Now Know*, 175.

85. 378th Meeting of the NSC, August 27, 1958, FRUS, 1958–60, XIII, 767–770. Eisenhower's repeated assertions to this effect suggest that some indeed wanted to fight for the bases; see Connelly, "The Algerian War for Independence," 377.

86. Gaddis, *We Now Know*, 175.

87. Laqueur, *The Struggle for the Middle East*, 84–86.

88. Gaddis, *We Now Know*, 176; McMahon, "Eisenhower and Third World Nationalism," 465–466; Rabe, "Eisenhower Revisionism," 108–109.

89. Regarding Tunisia, see Gorse to Couve, October 9, 1958, MAE, Série ONU, dossier 113; Bénard to Couve, October 17, 1958, idem. On the conspiracy see Mohammed Harbi, "Le Complot Lamouri," in Ageron, *La Guerre d'Algérie et les Algériens*, 161–163, and Abbas, *Autopsie d'une Guerre*, 246–250, 260. "The idea," Parodi to Couve, December 1, 1958, MAE, MLA, Action Extérieure, Maroc, Novembre-Décembre 1958, dossier 49, and see also Parodi to Couve, November 20, 1958, idem.

90. Gaddis, *We Now Know*, 176; Memcon Dulles-de Gaulle et al., July 5, 1958 (see note 78).

91. "Relevé des decisions du Conseil de Cabinet," September 11, 1958, AN, F60, Cote 2774. The decision is in a *très secret* attachment.

92. The sequel to the arms crisis can be followed in MAE, Série ONU, dossier 113, "livraison d'armes à la Tunisie Sept. 57—Nov. 58"; FRUS, 1958–60, XIII; and PRO, PREM 11/2339.

93. Gaddis, *We Now Know*, 170, 250–253. Mao quoted in Christensen, *Useful Adversaries*, 238.

94. Christensen, *Useful Adversaries*, 203–213, 221–223, 237–241.

95. Lacouture, *De Gaulle*, vol. 2, 636; memcon Macmillan-Adenauer et al., October 8, 1958, PRO, PREM 11/3002.

96. Memcon de Gaulle-Adenauer, September 14, 1958, DDF, 1958, II, no. 155.

97. Ibid.

98. De Gaulle to Eisenhower, September 17, 1958, FRUS, 1958–60, VII, part 2, 81–83.

99. Jebb to Lloyd, October 2, 1958, PRO, PREM 11/3002; Roberts to Lloyd, October 3, 1958, idem.

100. Macmillan to Caccia, October 8, 1958, PRO, PREM 11/3002.

101. Memcon de Gaulle-Adenauer, December 2, 1959, MAE, Secrétariat Général, dossier 60, "entretiens et messages juin—décembre 1959." Caccia and Samuel Hood's reports on the tripartite meetings provide a good account of the ever-changing French position, see PRO, PREM 11/3002.

102. Harrison, *The Reluctant Ally*, 91. Marc Trachtenberg has shown that Herter undermined the president's initiative by downgrading the original offer and claiming that it was de Gaulle's, not Eisenhower's, idea (Trachtenberg, *A Constructed Peace*, 242–244, and see also Alphand to Couve de Murville, December 31, 1959, and February 4, 1960, FNSP, Couve de Murville Papers, CM7). But if de Gaulle had been intent on the tripartite idea, one would expect that, after working to obtain U.S. assent for more than a year, he would have tried to hold Eisenhower to his commitment, especially if he suspected that Herter had been insubordinate, as Trachtenberg suggests.

103. Memorandum for Macmillan (though it was not actually shown to him), August 4, 1959, PRO, PREM 11/3002.

104. The chronology of the tripartite proposal is consistent with this interpretation, see Connelly, "The Algerian War," 371–372, 385, and see also Wall, "Les Relations Franco-Américaines," 79–80. In contrast, Trachtenberg portrays

de Gaulle as seriously pursuing the tripartite idea, "a centerpiece of his policy," though it contradicted his desire for national autonomy and even top French diplomats thought he was posturing (*A Constructed Peace*, 225–227, 242).

105. Vaïsse, "Un dialogue de sourdes," 415, 423; Alphand, *L'Etonnement d'Etre*, 311.

106. Lacouture, De Gaulle, vol. 2, 641; Doise and Vaïsse, *Diplomatie et outil militaire*, 603.

107. Peyrefitte, *C'était de Gaulle*, 125.

108. See, for instance, Vaïsse, "Aux origines," 268.

8. Tearing the Hand Off

1. *L'Année Politique, 1958* (Paris: Presses Universitaires de France, 1959), 434.

2. *C'était de Gaulle*, 54.

3. "La Nouvelle Forme de la Lutte Inaugurée le 25 Août 1958 — ses effets," September–October 1958, reprinted in Harbi, *Les Archives*, 228–229.

4. Parodi to MAE, September 18, 1958, MAE, MLA, Action Extérieure, Maroc, dossier 48.

5. Joxe to Dejean, September 22, 1958, MAE, Europe 1944–1960, URSS, dossier 271.

6. A "Liste des Etats Ayant Reconnu le G.P.R.A.," November 22, 1961, is attached to the "Note: Reconnaissance du 'G.P.R.A.'" SDECE, November 24, 1961, MAE, SEAA, dossier 6.

7. MacDonald, *The League of Arab States*, 94–96.

8. "Les Animateurs de la Rébellion Algérienne," October 16, 1958, MAE, Série ONU, dossier 560.

9. Debaghine to GPRA, October 2, 1959, CNAA, GPRA, dossier 5.8; "Fiche: Epurations au sein du FLN depuis juillet 1958," Division Renseignement, EMGDN, undated but circa September 1959, MAE, Série ONU, dossier 544, and see also Harbi, *Le FLN*, 245–246.

10. See SDECE note number 23754/A in MAE, SEAA, dossier 6, and the "Condense des Renseignements" for Debré, Division Renseignement, EMGDN, November 10, 1959, MAE, MLA, Action Extérieure, R.F.A. (West Germany), dossier 4. Numerous studies of the GPRA's external organization can also be found in SHAT, Château de Vincennes, Série 1H, dossier 1743, and see also Connelly, "The Algerian War for Independence," 389–390.

11. Pervillé, "L'insertion internationale," 375–377. See also Chikh, *L'Algérie en Armes*, 418–419.

12. Lakhdar Bentobbal, "Directives générales: Plan d'organisation pour l'Organisation politique," November 12, 1960, CNAA, GPRA, dossier 8.2 (emphasis in original).

13. "Les Dépenses du FLN a l'Extérieur de l'Algérie," Delegation Générale du Gouvernement en Algérie, Bureau d'Etudes, May 2, 1960, AOM, 14/CAB/193. GPRA expenditures abroad for 1959 were estimated at 8.3 billion (old) francs. Compare this with "Les Dépenses du FLN à l'Intérieur de l'Algérie," idem, April 16, 1960, 14/CAB/48, which estimated total expenses inside Algeria at 9.4 billion, with a margin of error of plus or minus 10 percent. Unfortunately, budget documents were not accessible in the Algerian archives.

14. "Indications donnés par le Président du Conseil sur le Référendum en Algérie," August 14, 1958, AOM, MA, dossier 564.

15. De Gaulle to Salan, August 13, 1958, AOM, MA, dossier 564; Salan, "Directive Particulière," July 12, 1958, idem.

16. Droz and Lever, *Histoire de la Guerre d'Algérie*, 194–196.

17. Ibid., 197–199. In fact, the Constantine Plan fell far short of these goals. See Lefeuvre, "Les réactions patronales au Plan de Constantine," 182–183.

18. De Gaulle, *Discours*, 55–56.

19. Salan, *Mémoires*, 4, 155.

20. "Algerian Rebels Reject Paris Bid for Peace Talks," *The New York Times*, October 26, 1958, 1, 2.

21. Lacouture, *De Gaulle*, vol. 2, 616–619.

22. Hoppenot (Président de la Commission Centrale) to de Gaulle, November 4, 1958, AOM, MA, 564.

23. Hoppenot to de Gaulle, December 1, 1958, ibid.

24. Lacouture, *De Gaulle*, vol. 2, 616.

25. Couve to Georges-Picot, December 6, 1958, MAE, Série ONU, dossier 557. Regarding visas, see Alphand to Couve, September 26, 1958, MAE, MLA, vol. 24 (provisional number), Action extérieure, Etats-Unis, Janvier 58–Juin 59, Cote ML 4 and, more generally, Série ONU, dossier 566, "Situation juridique à New York des représentants du F.L.N.," which contains copious documentation.

26. Alphand to Couve, October 25, November 26, and December 12, 1958, MAE, MLA, vol. 24 (provisional number), Action extérieure, Etats-Unis, Janvier 58–Juin 59, Cote ML 4.

27. "La Question algérienne à la session 1958 de l'O.N.U.," August 28, 1958, CNAA, GPRA, dossier 8.2; "Question Algérienne," undated but circa January 1959, MAE, Série ONU, dossier 557.

28. Georges-Picot to Couve, December 16, 1958, MAE, Série ONU, dossier 557; Abbas, "Rapport de Politique Générale," June 20, 1959, CNAA, GPRA, dossier 5.3; "L'Algérie et l'Actualité internationale," circa January 1959, idem, dossier 8.2; Thomas, "France Accused," forthcoming.

29. On de Gaulle's reaction, see Hervé Alphand, *L'Etonnement d'Etre*, 301. For a particularly effusive example of Dulles' praise for de Gaulle's Algerian policy, see Alphand to Couve, October 17, 1958, MAE, MLA, vol. 24 (provisional number), Action extérieure, Etats-Unis, Janvier 58–Juin 59, Cote ML 4. Regarding U.S. public opinion, Alphand to Couve, October 29, 1958, idem, and Bozo and Mélandri, "La France devant l'opinion américaine," 205–209.

30. Pierre Mélandri, "La France et le 'Jeu Double' des Etats-Unis," in Rioux, *La Guerre d'Algérie et les Français*, 440–442.

31. Jebb to Lloyd, October 2, 1958, PRO, PREM 11/3002; Alphand, *L'Etonnement d'Etre*, 291.

32. Caccia to Lloyd, October 25, 1958, PRO, PREM 11/3002. On this point see also Caccia to Lloyd, October 17, 1958, and memcon Dulles-Lloyd, October 19, 1958, idem.

33. "Note: Le FLN et la Chine Communiste," January 8, 1959, MAE, MLA, Action extérieure, dossier 19, Chine Populaire, avril 57–janvier 1962. The delegation also visited Ho Chi Minh in Vietnam and Kim Il Sung in North Korea, Raoul-Duval to Couve, March 15, 1959, idem.

34. Abbane, "Rapport du CCE au CNRA," 208; Mostefai, "Quelques idées

sur les tâches actuelles," December 23, 1958, CNAA, GPRA, dossier 5.3; "Rapport du GPRA sur les activités internationales," January 1959, Harbi, *Les Archives*, 381. For confirmation of military aid in 1959, see memcon Benyoucef Ben Khedda and Foreign Minister Chen-Yi, October 4, 1959, idem, 521. On Mao and Nkrumah, see Azzedine, *On nous appelait fellaghas*, 428–435, and Ben Khedda, "Entrevue avec le President Nkrumah au Caire le 17 Juin 1958," CNAA, GPRA, dossier 4.1.

35. James, *International Monetary Cooperation*, 106–108; Kaplan and Schleiminger, *The European Payments Union*, 282–286; Jacques Rueff, *Combats pour l'Ordre financier*.

36. Alistair Horne, *A Savage War of Peace*, 330–340.

37. "Note: Sur la coordination de l'action gouvernementale dans les domaines politiques, diplomatiques et de l'information, contre la rebellion en Algérie et ses aides extérieures," February 19, 1959, attached to Debré note of February 16, 1959, AOM, MA, dossier 1397 (emphasis in original).

38. Ibid.

39. Nor would it allow the loss of Algeria, Debré maintained in contradictory fashion. In fact, by February 1959, 51 percent of those polled thought it would be necessary sooner or later to accord independence and 52 percent were favorable to negotiations leading to a cease-fire—the remainder either disagreed or expressed no opinion. Interestingly, only 40 percent of respondents belonging to the professional and managerial class favored independence (Charles-Robert Ageron, "L'Opinion française à travers les sondages," in Rioux, *La Guerre d'Algérie et les Français*, 34).

40. Memcon Debré-Couve et al., March 14, 1959, MAE, Cabinet du Ministre, Cabinet de Couve de Murville, dossier 212 bis, Algérie confidentiel. In one measure of the escalation of the diplomatic campaign, in 1959 the French organized eight trips to Algeria by groups of foreign and French diplomats with even more the following year; see AOM, 14/CAB/119.

41. "Instruction: Lutte contre les activités du F.L.N. à l'étranger," April 2, 1959, AOM, 14/CAB/177.

42. Memcon Debré-Couve et al., March 14, 1959. Moreover, as Debré told Houghton later that year, whenever Paris protested to allies like Canada and Italy about FLN activities, they always excused themselves by pointing to what the Americans did (memcon Debré-Houghton, June 16, 1959, MAE, MLA, vol. 24 [provisional number], Action extérieure, Etats-Unis, janvier 58–juin 59, Cote ML 4).

43. Herter to Paris, March 6, 1959, FRUS, 1958–60, XIII, 650.

44. Memcon Herter-Alphand, March 3, 1959, USNA, RG59, Records of the Policy Planning Staff 1957–1961, Lot 67D548, box 136, France, and see also Lyon to Herter, March 6, 1959, FRUS, 1958–60, VII, part 2, 185–186, and Wall, "Les Relations Franco-Américaines," 64, 85.

45. Debré to Houghton, April 28, 1959, FRUS, 1958–60, XIII, 652–654.

46. Memcon Debré-Herter et al., May 1, 1959, FRUS, 1958–60, VII, Part 2, 195–203.

47. Cameron to Merchant, May 6, 1959, USNA, RG59, Central Decimal Files, 611.51; Memcon Herter-Eisenhower, May 2, 1959, Declassified Documents Reference System, document number 1997110103475; editorial note, FRUS, 1958–60, VII, Part 2, 234–235. Gaillard had also withheld permission for the nuclear stockpiles, but unlike de Gaulle he had resisted suggestions to link

this issue to Algeria (Roux to Alphand, January 21, 1958, MAE, MLA, vol. 24 [provisional number], Action extérieure, Etats-Unis, janvier 1958–juin 1959, Cote ML 4).

48. Porch, *The French Secret Services*, 371–372; Malek, *L'Algérie à Evian*, 74.

49. Memcon Verdier-Ritter von Lex et al., November 18, 1958, MAE, MLA, Action Extérieure, R.F.A., dossier 2.

50. Seydoux to Couve, April 16 and April 22, 1959, MAE, MLA, Action Extérieure, R.F.A., dossier 3.

51. Seydoux to Couve, October 8, 1958, December 9, 1958, and October 28, 1959, MAE, MLA, Action Extérieure, R.F.A., dossiers 2 and 4. Seydoux to Couve, December 15, 1959, MAE, Europe 1944–1960, Allemagne, dossier 1273.

52. Melnik, *La mort était leur mission*, 13.

53. Malek, *L'Algérie à Evian*, 74–75.

54. Constantin Melnik, *La mort était leur mission*, 11–13.

55. Alphand to Couve, February 20, 1959, MAE, Cabinet du Ministre, Cabinet de Couve de Murville, dossier 212 bis. On the original controversy, see McBride to Looram, February 25, 1957, USNA, RG59, Lot 61D30, Records of the Office of Western European Affairs, Subject File Relating to France, 1944–60, Alpha-Numeric, box 2, Algeria-Aramco file.

56. "Economic and Political Significance of North African Oil Discoveries," August 27, 1958, USNA, RG59, State Department Intelligence Reports, no. 8091; Horne, *A Savage War of Peace*, 241.

57. *Rapport* of cabinet decisions, January 18, 1959, Harbi, *Les Archives*, 382.

58. Roux to Alphand, February 4, 1959, MAE, MLA, vol. 24 (provisional number), Action extérieure, Etats-Unis; Alphand to Couve, February 4, 1959, idem; Alphand to Couve, February 13, 1959, idem; Alphand to Couve, February 6, 1959, DDF, 1959, I, no 70; Lefeuvre, "Les réactions patronales au Plan de Constantine," 173. In 1961, French intelligence claimed that the Italian oil magnate Enrico Mattei had offered the GPRA 100 million francs if it held out against French demands in the Sahara. Whether his ensuing death in a plane crash was engineered by SDECE is still a matter of debate (unsigned June 2 report, MAE, SEAA, dossier 114-Affaires Politiques, Evian Accords; Porch, *The French Secret Services*, 372–373, 581).

59. 406th meeting of the NSC, May 13, 1959, FRUS, 1958–60, XIII, 729–730; Alphand to Couve, February 20 and March 9, 1959, MAE, MLA, vol. 24 (provisional number), Action extérieure, Etats-Unis.

60. Porch, *The French Secret Services*, 372.

61. "Note," August 5, 1959, MAE, Secrétariat Général, dossier 60.

62. Memcon de Gaulle-Castiella, September 5, 1959, MAE, Secrétariat Général, dossier 60; Otero, "L'Algérie dans les relations franco-espagnoles," 90–98.

63. Bedjaoui, *La Révolution algérienne et le droit*, 124–127. Regarding Yugoslavia, "Des 'représentants' yougoslaves signent avec M. Ferhat Abbas un communiqué conjoint soutenant le point de vue du F.L.N.," *Le Monde*, June 15, 1959, and Harbi to Krim, November 28, 1960, *Les Archives*, 503–505.

64. Memcon de Gaulle-Casey, August 21, 1959, MAE, Secrétariat Général, dossier 60.

65. This note is undated and untitled but it is attached to Bérard's July 25, 1959, letter to Couve, MAE, Série ONU, dossier 561.

66. Lacouture, *De Gaulle*, vol. 3, 65.

67. Ibid., 63.

68. "Note pour le ministre," August 7, 1959, MAE, Série ONU, dossier 561.

69. Bérard to Couve, September 3, 1959, MAE, Série ONU, dossier 560.

70. Soustelle, *L'Espérence trahie*, 108, 112–114.

71. Ibid., 114.

72. See appendix along with Tripier, *Autopsie de la guerre*, 331–338.

73. Délégation générale du gouvernement en Algérie, cabinet, "Note: Le Problème psycho-politique actuel," July 15, 1959, AOM, 14/CAB/48.

74. Abbas, "Rapport de Politique Générale," June 20, 1959, CNAA, GPRA, dossier 5.3; Harbi, *Le FLN*, 244–250.

75. Abbas, "Rapport de Politique Générale"; Yazid, "La Politique Nord-Africaine," September 6, 1959, CNAA, GPRA, dossier 17.2.

76. The term *harki*—from *harka*, or "movement"—once referred to a specific type of unit but is now taken to mean all those who served under French command. It is difficult to say how many did so out of loyalty to France. Some undoubtedly did, others were coerced. But for many harkis and rebels alike, the independence struggle sometimes served as an opportunity to settle clan feuds. In other cases, individual families would "cover their bets" by placing members on both sides. Not surprisingly, the harkis were notoriously unreliable and French officers were often reluctant to arm them (Saliha Abdellatif, "Algérie 62: 'Cessez-le-feu' et devenir des supplétifs musulmans," in Gallissot, *Les Accords d'Evian*, 128; Manceron and Remaoun, *D'une rive à l'autre*, 204–207).

77. Lacouture, *De Gaulle*, vol. 3, 69–71.

78. Alphand, *L'Etonnement d'Etre*, 304, 309. That same month, Debré publicly condemned France's "enslavement to foreign powers" and declared that the Algerian problem resulted, in part, from "a sort of global greediness" that sought to exploit North Africa's strategic and economic value. Though the prime minister did not name the United States, no one could mistake his target (*L'Année politique, 1959* [Paris: Presses Universitaires de France, 1960], 479–480).

79. Memcon Eisenhower-de Gaulle, September 2, 1959, FRUS, 1958–60, VII, Part 2, 258; memcon Eisenhower-de Gaulle et al., idem, 262–266.

80. Jean Touchard, *Le gaullisme*, 179.

81. Lacouture, *De Gaulle*, vol. 3, 32–33, 57.

82. Memcon Debré-Herter et al., September 3, 1959, USNA, RG59, PPS, Lot 67D548, box 136; Peyrefitte, *C'était de Gaulle*, 59.

83. De Gaulle, *Discours*, 117–123.

84. Service d'Etudes Générales, "Note pour Monsieur le délégué général," September 23, 1959, AOM, 14/CAB/48.

85. Harbi, *Le FLN*, 243–250, 258–259. Abbas's response is reprinted in Planchais, *L'Empire embrasé*, 426–427.

86. *L'Année Politique*, 1959, 284.

87. Malek, *L'Algérie à Evian*, 50.

88. De Gaulle, *Discours*, 135–139.

89. Malek, *L'Algérie à Evian*, 53.

90. Harbi, *Le FLN*, 259.

91. Debaghine to CCE, November 17, 1959, Harbi, *Les Archives*, 272–274.

92. 417th Meeting of the NSC, August 18, 1959, DDEL, AWF, NSC series.

93. Regarding the "real menace," see chapter 1. Of course, de Gaulle had given Eisenhower grief over a number of other issues, but it does not appear that Eisenhower used the U.N. vote to retaliate. The president was sympathetic to *le*

général's position on NATO and nuclear sharing, telling Spaak and the Dutch foreign minister that "these difficulties can be ironed out. Algeria is the main problem" (memcon Eisenhower–Luns–Spaak, September 3, 1959, FRUS, 1958–60, VII, 480–484). But he interpreted de Gaulle's withdrawal of the Mediterranean fleet and refusal to admit nuclear stockpiles as an attempt to extort U.S. support in North Africa, even going so far as to compare it to Khrushchev's Berlin ultimatum. He was "not going to be blackmailed," he vowed, "by de Gaulle or anyone else," (417th Meeting of the NSC).

94. "Scéma d'un plan d'action," June 5, 1959, MAE, Série ONU, dossier 561; "Note: la question à la XIVème session . . . ," July 23, 1959, idem; Commandement en Chef des Forces en Algérie, "Evolution de la situation militaire en Algérie," July 1959, SHAT, 1H, 1751, dossier 2.

95. Essig to Delouvrier, January 13, 1960, MAE, 14/CAB/142.

96. Lacouture, *De Gaulle*, vol. 3, 76.

9. A Multicultural Peace?

1. Jean Lacouture, *De Gaulle*, vol. 3, 137.

2. Uncorrected procès-verbaux, June 3, 1961, AOM, MA, dossier 542.

3. *The Constantine Plan: Money, Men, Machines*, Tangent films, circa 1959, AOM, and see also *Les trois frontiers de l'Algérie*, Max Demain, undated but circa 1959, AOM.

4. Robert W. Schofield, dir., *The Falling Veil*, Tangent films, circa 1960, AOM.

5. For an analysis of this policy's limitations and the debates it touched off, see Lazreg, *The Eloquence of Silence*, 90–97.

6. *Visages de l'Algérie*, Films du matin, circa 1959, AOM; Bonnot, "Les Représentations de l'Algérie française," 70–87.

7. De Gaulle, *Discours*, 55–56.

8. Ibid., 227–228.

9. Ibid., 256–257.

10. Vilardebo, dir., *One Thousand New Villages*, Cinétest, 1960, AOM. Braudel shared a similar vision in *The Mediterranean and the Mediterranean World in the Age of Philip II*, which he was then re-editing.

11. Vilardebo, dir., *One Thousand New Villages*, emphasis added.

12. Vilardebo, dir., *Bilan d'un jour*, Cinétest, circa 1960, AOM; J. Ch. Carlus, dir., *Des Pierres qui lient les hommes*, AOM. Another of Vilardebo's films would win the Palme d'Or at Cannes in 1961.

13. Groupe d'Etude des Structures Futures de l'Algérie, "Essai d'une discussion historique sur le problème algérien," September 28, 1960, MAE, SEAA, dossier 5, Affaires Politiques, Evian Accords.

14. Délégation Générale en Algérie, direction générale des affaires politiques et de l'information, to SAS officers, January 5, 1962, AOM, 15/CAB/75.

15. Groupe d'Etude des Structures Futures de l'Algérie, "Premier Rapport: Note de Présentation," July 1960, MAE, SEAA, dossier 5; Commandant Carret, "L'Evolution du Sentiment Religieux chez les Musulmans d'Algérie," September 16, 1961, AOM, 15/CAB/75.

16. Groupe d'Etude des Structures Futures de l'Algérie, "Premier Rapport."

17. "Essai d'une discussion historique sur le problème algérien."

18. On de Gaulle's attitude, see Lacouture, *De Gaulle*, vol. 3, 86. The fol-

lowing account of "The Week of the Barricades" is based on Lacouture along with Courrière, *La Guerre d'Algérie*, vol. 3, 545–616, and Horne, *A Savage War of Peace*, 349–372.

19. Courrière, *La Guerre d'Algérie*, vol. 3, 553–554, 559–563. On Argoud's determination to maintain Algeria as a "Christian land"—and Debré's judgement that it was impossible without allied support—see also Debré, *Mémoires*, vol. 3, 236–237.

20. Courrière, *La Guerre d'Algérie*, vol. 3, 559–563.

21. "Le Rapport de la Croix-Rouge Internationale sur les camps d'internement d'Algérie," *Le Monde*, January 5, 1960.

22. Johnson to State, January 22, 1960, USNA, RG59, Central Decimal Files, 751S.00.

23. Lacouture, *De Gaulle*, vol. 3, 88.

24. Ibid., 88–91.

25. Courrière, *La Guerre d'Algérie*, vol. 3, 568–591.

26. Lacouture, *De Gaulle*, vol. 3, 86–87; de la Gorce, *The French Army*, 458.

27. Courrière, *La Guerre d'Algérie*, vol. 3, 592; De Gaulle, *Discours*, 160; Lacouture, *De Gaulle*, vol. 3, 96–97.

28. De Gaulle, *Discours*, 162–166.

29. Walmsley to Herter, January 30, 1960, USNA, RG59, Central Decimal Files, 751S.00.

30. Walmsley to State, March 5, 1960, ibid.

31. Lacouture, *De Gaulle*, vol. 3, 106–112; Terrenoire, *De Gaulle et l'Algérie*, 177–180.

32. Debaghine to GPRA, October 27, 1959, CNAA, GPRA, dossier 5.3; Debaghine to GPRA, November 17, 1959, Harbi, *Les Archives*, 272–274.

33. Krim, "Rapport d'Activité du Ministère, Periode février-mars 1960," April 2, 1960, CNAA, GPRA, dossier 8.2 and, more generally, dossier 37.7; Pervillé, "L'insertion internationale," 376–377; and Chikh, *L'Algérie en Armes*, 418.

34. Krim, "Notre Politique extérieure et la Guerre froide," March 13, 1960, CNAA, GPRA, dossier 5.3.

35. Krim, "Note sur Notre Politique Actuelle," "Notre Politique à Moyen Orient," "Note sur Notre Politique dans le bloc Afro-Asiatique," all dated March 13, 1960, CNAA, GPRA, dossier 5.10. While recruiting offices were established in several Arab capitals, none made any serious effort to send volunteers to the ALN; see the SDECE notes in MAE, SEAA, dossier 9, Affaires Politiques, Algérie Généralités.

36. Walmsley to Herter, January 30, 1960, USNA, RG59, Central Decimal Files, 751S.00; Malek, *L'Algérie à Evian*, 59–60; EMGDN, Division Renseignement, "Note d'Information: Volontaires étrangères pour l'ALN," May 6, 1960, MAE, SEAA, dossier 9, Affaires Politiques, Algérie Généralités.

37. *L'Année Politique, 1960* (Paris: Presses Universitaires de France, 1961), 284; Waverly Root, "Offer of Massive Chinese Aid Hangs over Algerian Talks," *The Washington Post*, July 20, 1960, section A, 8.

38. See the *Procès-Verbaux* of the Comité Central de l'Information, July 18 and 29, 1960, AOM, 14/CAB/177, and Coup de Frejac, "Note pour Monsieur le délégué général," October 17, 1960, AOM, 15/CAB/118. Delouvrier himself suggested making the "Yellow Peril" a propaganda theme.

39. "Aide mémoire sur un entretien avec le Senateur John Kennedy," CNAA,

GPRA, dossier 5.3. Unfortunately, the author and date are not specified in this remarkable document, but the context indicates that he was speaking to Chanderli in the summer of 1960.

40. "Instructions aux Chefs Responsables de la Presse, de la Radio, de l'Information et de la Propagande en Algérie et à l'Etranger," circa July 1958, CNAA, GPRA, dossier 17.21; Malek, *L'Algérie à Evian*, 59.

41. The Algerians had long claimed to accord their captives the status and protections of POWs, see FLN New York Delegation, "The Treatment of Prisoners of War by the Algerian Army of National Liberation," circa 1957, SHAT 1H, 1751, dossier 1. Fraleigh, "The Algerian Revolution as a Case Study," 194–199; Wilson, *International Law and the Use of Force*, 152–154.

42. Aït Challal Messaoud, "Rapport de Mission en DDR," June 1960, in Harbi, *Les Archives*, 499.

43. "Rapport de Politique Générale," July 20, 1959, CNAA, GPRA, dossier 5.8.

44. Dejean to Couve, January 7, 1959, MAE, MLA, Action Extérieure, URSS, dossier 86; memcon Gromyko-Ben Khedda et al., October 13, 1959, Harbi, *Les Archives*, 517–519.

45. At least that is how de Gaulle described the conversation to Eisenhower, memcon, April 22, 1960, FRUS, 1958–60, VII, 344–345.

46. Memcon Krim, Boussouf, Francis and Ho Long, May 1, 1960, CNAA, GPRA, dossier 5.12.

47. Memcon Krim, Boussouf, Francis and Mao Tse Tung, May 17, 1960, CNAA, GPRA, dossier 5.12. In December 1958, a Polish diplomat had offered the same explanation, stating that the Communist states had jointly agreed to this position (M'hamad Yala, "Entretien avec le premier Secrétaire de l'ambassade de Pologne," December 24, 1958, ibid., dossier 7.2).

48. Dejean to Couve, May 28, 1960, MAE, MLA, Action Extérieure, URSS, dossier 87, de Avril 1960–September 1960.

49. Bérard to Couve, May 11, 1960, FNSP, Couve de Murville Papers, CM7.

50. Horne, *A Savage War of Peace*, 324–325.

51. Tricot, *Les Sentiers de la Paix*, 166–172.

52. Ibid., 173–176; Lacouture, *de Gaulle*, vol. 3, 116–119; Horne, *A Savage War of Peace*, 387–392.

53. De Gaulle, *Discours*, 121, 136, 229.

54. "Discussions avec l'émissaire des dirigeants de l'organisation extérieure de la rebellion: Conclusion sur les entretiens de Melun," July 5, 1960, MAE, SEAA, dossier 92.

55. See Moris's instructions dated June 20, 25, and 28, 1960, along with the "Discussions avec l'émissaire des dirigeants de l'organisation extérieure de la rébellion," June 25, 26, 27, 29, 1960, MAE, SEAA, dossier 92. Regarding the listening devices, see Constantin Melnik, "Note" to Joxe, March 21, 1961, MAE, SEAA, dossier 100, Affaires Politiques, Evian Accords.

56. "Procès-Verbal," June 29, 1960, AOM, 14/CAB/177.

57. Malek, *L'Algérie à Evian*, 83–84, 387–389.

58. "Note pour le Ministre," January 12, 1961, MAE, SEAA, dossier 92 (emphasis added).

59. Krim to the cabinet, August 10, 1960, CNAA, GPRA, dossier 3.3.

60. Mandouze, *La révolution algérienne par les textes*, 68.

61. A copy of the GPRA's "Memorandum sur la dénonciation du traité de l'Atlantique Nord," September 19, 1960, is in the PRO, FO 371, 147358; Alphand to Couve, October 11, 1960, MAE, Amérique, 1952–63, Etats-Unis, dossier 414, Algérie.

62. Roberts to Foreign Office, September 14, 1960, PRO, PREM 11, 3334; Roberts to Foreign Office, September 22, 1960, idem. This was not entirely true, since the council had passed a supportive resolution on Algeria in March 1956.

63. "Note," October 5, 1960, MAE, Europe 1944–1960, URSS, dossier 271; La Grandville to Couve, October 7, 1960, MAE, MLA, Action Extérieure, URSS, dossier 88.

64. J. F. Roux, "Rapport A.s. de l'affaire algérienne aux Nations Unies sous l'angle des relations publiques," February 25, 1961, AOM, MA, dossier 25; Jean Daniel, "Entre Mao et de Gaulle," *L'Express*, October 27, 1960.

65. Roux, "Rapport."

66. Lacouture, *De Gaulle*, vol. 3, 136; Carbonnel to Bérard, October 6, 1960, MAE, Cabinet du Ministre, Cabinet de Couve de Murville, dossier 212 bis, Algérie 1959–1962.

67. Memcon Tito-Abbas et al., April 12, 1961, Harbi, *Les Archives*, 509; Lakhdar Bentobbal, "Directives Générales: Plan d'organisation pour l'Organisation politique," November 12, 1960, CNAA, GPRA, dossier 8.2.

68. Délégation Générale du Gouvernement en Algérie, Affaires Politiques, "Rapport Mensuel sur l'évolution de la situation générale," September 23, 1960, AOM, 15/CAB/74.

69. AOM, Iconothèque, Affiches, 9F.79.

70. Comité Central de l'Information, "Procès-Verbal," August 19, 1960, AOM, 14/CAB/177; Délégation Générale du Gouvernement en Algérie, Affaires Politiques, "Rapport Mensuel sur l'évolution de la situation générale," September 13, 1960, AOM, 15/CAB/74; Tricot, *Les Sentiers*, 194; Bentobbal, "Directives Générales"; Mahoney, *JFK: Ordeal in Africa*, 22.

71. Carbonnel to Bérard, October 6, 1960, MAE, Cabinet du Ministre, Cabinet de Couve de Murville, dossier 212 bis, Algérie 1959–1962; Bérard to Couve, October 17, 1960, idem. Note that all cable traffic concerning the French lobbying effort at the United Nations was treated with the greatest secrecy—marked "no distribution," and so on—which suggests that de Gaulle did not want it to be known even within the Quai.

72. Abbas to Zhou Enlai, October 24, 1960, Harbi, *Les Archives*, 527–528; Chauvel to Couve, October 27, 1960, DDF, 1960, II, no. 186.

73. Raoul Duval to Couve, November 17, 1960, Asie-Oceanie 1956–1967, Chine, dossier 523.

74. Macmillan to Lloyd, October 28, 1960, PRO, FO 371, 147351; memcon Macmillan-Home-Hassan, October 28, 1960, PREM 11/3200.

75. "Note," October 5, 1960, MAE, Europe 1944–1960, URSS, dossier 271; La Grandville to Couve de Murville, October 7, 1960, MAE, MLA, Action Extérieure, URSS, dossier 88; Abbas to Zhou Enlai, October 24, 1960, Harbi, *Les Archives*, 527–528; 446th meeting of the National Security Council, FRUS, 1958–60, XIII, 706.

76. "Entrevue avec Moulay El Hassan," October 21, 1960, CNAA, GPRA, dossier 8.4; "Rapport du Ministre des Affaires extérieures sur son Séjour au Maroc," undated but circa October 1960, idem.

77. "Note pour le Ministre," October 26, 1960, MAE, Cabinet du Ministre, Cabinet de Couve de Murville, dossier 212 bis, Algérie 1959–1962.

78. Bérard to Couve, November 1, 1960, ibid.; Alphand to Couve, November 3, 1960, idem.

79. De Gaulle, *Discours*, 257–262.

80. Couve was careful to note that Herter's letter had arrived at the same time as de Gaulle's speech. But even if this were the case, Bérard had relayed Wadsworth's suggestion of a presidential statement on November 1 while Alphand reported that Herter required it as a condition for U.S. support the day before de Gaulle spoke. De Gaulle looked at diplomatic cables each morning and almost certainly would have seen these (Couve to Herter, November 7, 1960, MAE, Cabinet du Ministre, Cabinet de Couve de Murville, dossier 212 bis, Algérie 1959–1962; Lacouture, *De Gaulle*, vol. 3, 21).

81. Herter to Couve, November 15, 1960, FRUS, 1958–60, XIII, 709–710; Couve to Herter, November 7, 1960. If de Gaulle felt compelled to act in haste, that might explain why he failed to inform a mediating mission led by the presidents of Senegal, Cameroon, and Niger. They were then in Tunis attempting to persuade the GPRA to accept a cease-fire and could not conceal their surprise and anger when the Algerians passed on the news, "Compte rendu des Entretiens," November 16, 1960, CNAA, GPRA, dossier 8.11.

82. *L'Année Politique, 1960*, 316–317 (see note 37); De Gaulle to Couve, November 24, 1960, FNSP, Couve de Murville, CM7.

83. Lacouture, *De Gaulle*, vol. 3, 51. Regarding Spain, the best source is Otero's "L'Algérie dans les relations franco-espagnoles."

84. Lacouture, *De Gaulle*, vol. 3, 137.

85. "Note: a/s l'Inde et la question algérienne," March 10, 1961, MAE, Asie 1944 . . . , Inde 1956–1967, dossier 248; Bérard to Couve, December 21, 1960, AOM, 15/CAB/149.

86. Lt.-Col. Thozet, "La Politique du GPRA de la 15e session de l'Assemblée Générale des Nations Unies à l'ouverture des pourparlers d'Evian," June 14, 1961, SHAT, Château de Vincennes, 1H, 1111/3.

87. Flanner, *Paris Journal*, 162.

88. Memcon de Gaulle-Macmillan, January 28, 1961, PRO, PREM 11/3200.

89. De Gaulle, *Discours*, 264; "Mission d'Etudes: Groupe d'Etude des Structures Futures de l'Algérie: Deuxième Rapport (Janvier 1961)," in annexe, "L'Algérie indépendante devant le choix de systèmes de solidarité extérieure," MAE, SEAA, dossier 100.

90. Malek, *L'Algérie à Evian*, 97.

91. "Note Sur les Garanties des Communautés en Algérie," December 12, 1960, MAE, SEAA, dossier 100.

92. De Wailly, "Note pour le Ministre d'Etat," December 29, 1960, MAE, SEAA, dossier 103. On de Gaulle's skepticism, see Malek, *L'Algérie à Evian*, 79.

93. Ruf, "The Bizerte Crisis," 205–207.

94. Malek, *L'Algérie à Evian*, 90–92, 95. The archives of the Secrétariat d'Etat aux Affaires Algériennes do not contain any *compte-rendus* of these talks, so the following account relies on Malek.

95. Ibid., 92.

96. Seydoux to Couve, March 9, 1961, MAE, Cabinet du Ministre, Cabinet

de Couve de Murville, dossier 212 bis, Algérie 1959–1962; "Mission du Docteur Francis dans les Pays de l'Est," March 23, 1961, CNAA, GPRA, dossier 5.3. De Gaulle sought assurances that the Algerians had not already become tools of the Communists (Lacouture, *De Gaulle*, vol. 3, 149).

97. Malek, *L'Algérie à Evian*, 92–101; Long, *Le Dossier Secret*, 41–42.

98. Malek, *L'Algérie à Evian*, 103–106; Long, *Le Dossier Secret*, 50–54.

99. Vaïsse, *Alger: Le Putsch*, 83–88; Courrière, *La Guerre d'Algérie*, vol. 4, 783.

100. Courrière, *La Guerre d'Algérie*, vol. 4, 775–776.

101. *Discours*, 288; Lacouture, *De Gaulle*, vol. 3, 155–158.

102. For good accounts of the putsch, see Fauvet and Planchais, *La Fronde des généraux;* Vaïsse, *Alger, Le Putsch;* Courrière, *La Guerre d'Algérie*, vol. 4, 773–870.

103. *Discours*, 306–308.

104. Courrière, *La Guerre d'Algérie*, vol. 4, 782.

105. Horne, *A Savage War of Peace*, 445–446.

106. Otero, "L'Algérie dans les relations franco-espagnoles," 135–136; Alphand to Couve, April 28, 1961, MAE, Amérique, 1952–63, Etats-Unis, dossier 414, Algérie. Rhodri Jeffreys-Jones points up the absurdity of the idea that the CIA would have backed the coup. Instead, the agency had long been charged with securing America's "option" on Algerian independence (*The CIA and American Democracy*, 124). See also Malek, *L'Algérie à Evian*, 115–116. Kennedy repeatedly asked de Gaulle for information on CIA involvement and was "shocked" when he did not deign to reply (Alphand to Couve, April 29, 30, and May 2, 1961, FNSP, Couve de Murville Papers, CM7).

107. Vaïsse, *Alger: Le Putsch*, 106–107.

108. Malek, *L'Algérie à Evian*, 108–110.

109. Ibid., 111–113.

110. Ibid., 118–119;

111. Constantin Melnik, "Note" to Joxe, March 21, 1961, MAE, SEAA, dossier 100, Affaires Politiques, Evian Accords.

112. Courrière, *La Guerre d'Algérie*, vol. 4, 885–886; Joxe to Présidence de la République, May 20, 1961, MAE, SEAA, dossier 114, Affaires Politiques, Evian Accords.

113. Joxe to Présidence de la République, May 20, 1961, MAE, SEAA, dossier 114, Affaires Politiques, Evian Accords; Malek, *L'Algérie à Evian*, 130–131.

114. Joxe to Présidence de la République, May 20, 1961; Malek, *L'Algérie à Evian*, 126–127.

115. Malek, *L'Algérie à Evian*, 127–129.

116. Memcon, Joxe to de Gaulle, May 23, 1961, MAE, Cabinet du Ministre, Cabinet de Couve de Murville, dossier 212 bis., Algérie 1959–1962.

117. For examples of French studies of Tunisia and Morocco as precedents, see Groupe d'Etude des Structures Futures de l'Algérie, "Premier Rapport: Note de Présentation," July 1960, SEAA, dossier 5.

118. Memcon, Joxe to de Gaulle, May 23, 1961. On limiting sovereignty, see G. de Wailly, "Note pour le Ministre d'Etat," December 29, 1960, MAE, SEAA, dossier 103.

119. Malek, *L'Algérie à Evian*, 133–134, 157; Massignac, antenne EMGDN

to Evian, May 23, 1961, MAE, SEAA, dossier 114, Affaires Politiques, Evian Accords; Horne, *A Savage War of Peace*, 470.

120. Joxe to de Gaulle, May 26, 1961, MAE, Cabinet du Ministre, Cabinet de Couve de Murville, dossier 212 bis., Algérie 1959–1962.

121. Untitled memorandum, May 26, 1961, MAE, SEAA, dossier 92.

122. Malek, *L'Algérie à Evian*, 92.

123. Intervention, January 29, 1958, *Journal Officiel de la République Française*, 1958, numéro 28, 309–311.

124. Joxe to de Gaulle, May 26, 1961, MAE, Cabinet du Ministre, Cabinet de Couve de Murville, dossier 212 bis., Algérie 1959–1962. Here again, Joxe's proposal departed from the Rights of Man, which holds that, "[a]ll citizens, being equal in the eyes of the law, are equally admissible to all dignities, positions, and public employment according to their capacity, and with no distinction other than their own virtues and talents."

125. Ibid.

126. Joxe to de Gaulle, June 3, 1961, MAE, Cabinet du Ministre, Cabinet de Couve de Murville, dossier 212 bis., Algérie 1959–1962; Malek, *L'Algérie à Evian*, 137.

127. Courrière, *La Guerre d'Algérie*, vol. 3, 887.

128. Untitled memorandum, May 26, 1961 (see note 121).

129. Joxe to de Gaulle, June 3, 1961.

130. Ibid.

131. See note 2.

132. Malek, *L'Algérie à Evian*, 138–139.

133. Joxe to de Gaulle, June 6 and June 10, 1961, MAE, Cabinet du Ministre, Cabinet de Couve de Murville, dossier 212 bis., Algérie 1959–1962; Malek, *L'Algérie à Evian*, 140–142.

134. Joxe to Présidence, June 13, 1961, MAE, SEAA, dossier 114, Affaires Politiques, Evian Accords.

135. Malek, *L'Algérie à Evian*, 144–145.

136. Vaïsse, *La Grandeur*, 79–80.

10. Drawing the Line

1. Lacouture, *De Gaulle*, vol. 3, 236.

2. Louis Terrenoire, "Le Conseil Historique du 19 mars 1962," *Le Monde*, March 16, 1982, 22.

3. Malek, *L'Algérie à Evian*, 152–153.

4. Ruf, "The Bizerte Crisis," 207; Malek, *L'Algérie à Evian*, 152–154, 301–304.

5. Barker, "The Politics of Decolonization in Tunisia," 210–211.

6. Bourguiba to de Gaulle, July 6, 1961, DDF, 1961, II, annex to document no. 17; Ruf, "The Bizerte Crisis," 205–206; Brady, "Tunis Gives Paris 24 Hours to Agree to Leave Bizerte," *The New York Times*, July 18, 1961, 1,6.

7. Barker, "The Politics of Decolonization," 211, 214. On U.S. policy, see "Outlines of United States Policy Towards Tunisia," July 12, 1961, JFKL, National Security Files (NSF), box 166, Tunisia, July 1961–December 1961; Ibezim, "The New Frontier and Africa," 166–169, 179–180.

8. Robert C. Doty, "De Gaulle Asserts West Won't Yield to Russia in Berlin," *The New York Times*, July 13, 1961, 1,3.

9. Guiringaud to Raoul-Duval, July 7, 1961, DDF, 1961, II, no. 17; de Gaulle to Raoul-Duval, July 12, 1961, idem, no. 25; Raoul-Duval to Couve, July 13, 1961, idem, no. 28.

10. Rous, *Habib Bourguiba*, 61.

11. Brady, "Tunis Gives Paris 24 Hours"; Malek, *L'Algérie à Evian*, 153–154.

12. Raoul-Duval to Couve de Murville, July 18, 1961, DDF, 1961, II, no. 35.

13. Robert Daley, "Battle of Bizerte, Gunfire and Death," *The New York Times*, July 23, 1961, 1,4. Accounts of the fighting can also be found in Barker, "The Politics of Decolonization in Tunisia"; Ruf, "The Bizerta Crisis"; and Moore, " 'Bourguibism' in Tunisia."

14. Walmsley to Rusk, July 20, 1961, JFKL, NSF, box no. 166, Tunisia, Bizerte Crisis, June 28, 1961–July 22, 1961.

15. Tasca to Rusk, July 20, 1961, FRUS, 1961–63, XXI, 250–251; Walmsley to Rusk, July 20, 1961, JFKL, NSF, box no. 166, Tunisia, Bizerte Crisis, June 28, 1961–July 22, 1961; Brady, "French Air-Land Attack Breaks Siege of Bizerte," *The New York Times*, July 21, 1961, 1.

16. "French Occupy Bizerte; Tunis Asks Foreign Help," *The New York Times*, July 22, 1961, 1,3.

17. "Cette semaine à Tunis," *L'Afrique Action*, July 24, 1961, 17.

18. Walmsley to Rusk, July 21, 1961, JFKL, NSF, box no. 166, Tunisia, Bizerte Crisis, June 28, 1961–July 22, 1961.

19. Moore, "Bourguibism in Tunisia," 35; Ruf, "The Bizerte Crisis," 209.

20. Bourguiba to Kennedy, July 22, 1961, JFKL, Presidential Office Files (POF), box no. 125, Tunisia General, May 1961–November 1963.

21. Kennedy to Bourguiba, July 23, 1961, JFKL, POF, box no. 125, Tunisia General, May 1961–November 1963.

22. Bahi Ladgham interview, La Marsa, August 1992; memo for John McCone, "France-Tunisia," July 22, 1961, Declassified Documents Series—CIA, 1988, document number 1984010100763. See also Gavin to Rusk, August 9, 1961, JFKL, NSF, box no. 70, France General, July 1, 1961–August 20, 1961.

23. Reprinted in Kennedy, *Strategy of Peace*, 65–81.

24. The records of the Lugrin negotiations can be found in MAE, Cabinet du Ministre, Cabinet de Couve de Murville, dossier 212 bis, Algérie 1959–1962, and idem, SEAA, dossier 114, Affaires Politiques, Evian Accords.

25. Dorman to Rusk, July 31, 1961, JFKL, NSF, box no. 166, Tunisia, Bizerte Crisis, July 23, 1961–July 31, 1961.

26. Theodore Shabad, "Moscow Assures Tunisia of Help," *The New York Times*, August 6, 1961, 1,16.

27. Memcon Rusk-Couve de Murville, August 4, 1961, MAE, Secrétariat Général, dossier 62, entretiens et messages 1961.

28. "Random Notes in Washington: Rusk Is Ruffled by a Brush-Off," *The New York Times*, August 28, 1961, 14. It is possible that Rusk exaggerated de Gaulle's annoyance to discourage those in the administration like Adlai Stevenson, G. Mennen Williams, and Chester Bowles who might have favored more active lobbying on behalf of the Tunisians (cf. Memcon Rusk-de Gaulle, August 8, 1961, MAE, Secrétariat Général, dossier 62, entretiens et messages 1961, and Rusk to

State, August 8, 1961, *Foreign Relations of the United States*, 1961–63, XXI, 259–260; Rusk, *As I Saw It*, 241).

29. Schlesinger to Stevenson, August 23, 1961, FRUS, 1961–63, XXI, 260–261.

30. Stevenson to Mrs. Ronald Tree, August 18, 1961, in Johnson, *The Papers of Adlai Stevenson*, vol. 8, 110; Bérard to Couve de Murville, August 27, 1961, DDF, 1961, II, no. 87.

31. Rusk, *As I Saw It*, 245.

32. Quoted in William Borden, "Defending Hegemony: American Foreign Economic Policy," in Paterson, *Kennedy's Quest for Victory*, 63–64. See also Frank Costigliola, "The Pursuit of Atlantic Community," idem, 30, and Gavin, "The Gold Battles."

33. Memcon de Gaulle-Stevenson, July 28, 1961, MAE, Secrétariat Général, dossier 62, entretiens et messages 1961. See also Martin, *Adlai Stevenson and the World*, 651.

34. De Gaulle, *Memoirs of Hope*, 117.

35. Wahl to Gavin, August 6, 1961, JFKL, NSF, box 70, France General, August 21–August 31, 1961; Lacouture, *De Gaulle*, vol. 3, 189–190; Horne, *A Savage War of Peace*, 473.

36. Peyrefitte, *C'était de Gaulle*, 76–83, 92; Groupe d'Etude des Structures Futures de l'Algérie, "Premier Rapport: Note de Présentation," July 1960, AOM, SEAA, dossier 5.

37. Peyrefitte, *C'était de Gaulle*, 76.

38. Ibid., 79; Malek, *L'Algérie à Evian*, 166–171; "Mémoire de l'Etat-Major Général de l'ALN à Monsieur le Président," July 15, 1961, reprinted in Harbi, *Les Archives*, 322–332. See also Terrenoire, *De Gaulle et l'Algérie*, 236–237.

39. Malek, *L'Algérie à Evian*, 171–174; de Gaulle, *Discours et Messages*, 340–341; Tricot, *Mémoires*, 161–162.

40. "Directives," December 7, 1961, SEAA, dossier 111; Terrenoire, *De Gaulle et l'Algérie*, 237; Lacouture, *De Gaulle*, vol. 3, 190, 203; Alphand, *L'Etonnement d'Etre*, 365.

41. Peyrefitte, *C'était de Gaulle*, 88–89.

42. Morin to Joxe, September 21, 1961, DDF, 1961, II, no. 450; "Note de la Direction des Affaires politiques [MLA], Reconnaissance du 'G.P.R.A.,' " November 24, 1961, DDF, 1961, II, no. 190; M. Ghany, "Note d'Activités," April 19, 1961, CNAA, GPRA, dossier 6.1. On the Williams meeting and the bureaucratic struggles that surrounded it, see Lefebvre, "Kennedy's Algerian Dilemma." The Soviets later claimed to have provided the FLN with 25 thousand rifles, 21 thousand machine guns and submachine guns, and 1,300 howitzers, cannons, and mortars between 1960 and 1962. Yet these figures should be treated with caution, since they were offered during a bitter debate with Deng Xiaoping over who had done more to support national liberation movements ("Stenogram: Meeting of the Delegations of the Communist Party of the Soviet Union and the Chinese Communist Party, Moscow, 5–20 July 1963," reprinted in the Cold War International History Project *Bulletin*, no. 10 [March 1998]: 180).

43. Peyrefitte, *C'était de Gaulle*, 89.

44. "Note au sujet de l'entrevue des 28 et 29 octobre," AOM, MA, dossier 563; Malek, *L'Algérie à Evian*, 157, 180–190, 195.

45. Malek, *L'Algérie à Evian*, 190–193; Harbi, *Le FLN*, 295–297; Hélie, *Les Accords d'Evian*, 165–169.

46. Memcon Dahlab-Joxe, December 9, 1961, MAE, SEAA, dossier 111; Tricot, *Mémoires*, 136.

47. Memcon Dahlab-Joxe, December 9, 1961; Jacques Frémeaux, "La Guerre d'Algérie et le Sahara," in Ageron, *La Guerre d'Algérie et les Algériens*, 107–108.

48. Memcon, Joxe to de Gaulle, June 6, 1961, MAE, Cabinet du Ministre, Cabinet de Couve de Murville, dossier 212 bis., Algérie 1959–1962.

49. Memcon Dahlab-Joxe, December 9 and 31, 1961, MAE, SEAA, dossier 111.

50. Ibid., December 23, 1961.

51. Tricot, *Mémoires*, 139–140; Malek, *L'Algérie à Evian*, 195–196.

52. Ben Khedda, *Les Accords d'Evian*, 33.

53. "Examen critique des deux textes, January 12, 1962, MAE, SEAA, dossier 111; Tricot, *Mémoires*, 147–148; Malek, *L'Algérie à Evian*, 200.

54. "Examen critique des deux textes."

55. Malek, *L'Algérie à Evian*, 204–206, 212.

56. Ibid., 202–204; Tricot, *Mémoires*, 145–146.

57. "Examen critique des deux textes."

58. Malek, *L'Algérie à Evian*, 207–208.

59. Ibid., 195–196.

60. Buron, *Carnets Politiques de la guerre d'Algérie*, 234; Terrenoire, *De Gaulle et l'Algérie*, 239.

61. Courrière, *La Guerre d'Algérie*, vol. 4, 1026–1028.

62. De Gaulle, *Discours*, 375; Lacouture, *De Gaulle*, vol. 3, 221–222; Buron, *Carnets Politiques de la guerre d'Algérie*, 183, 187.

63. Tricot, *Mémoires*, 136; Lacouture, *De Gaulle*, vol. 3, 222. There are no records available of the Rousses negotiations. The following account largely relies on Buron, who took notes, and Malek, who draws on contemporary FLN documents.

64. Tricot, *Mémoires*, 136; Buron, *Carnets Politiques de la guerre d'Algérie*, 194–195, 208.

65. Malek, *L'Algérie à Evian*, 213; Buron, *Carnets Politiques de la guerre d'Algérie*, 207–208, 220–222.

66. Buron, *Carnets Politiques de la guerre d'Algérie*, 220–222, 228–229.

67. Tricot, *Les Sentiers de la Paix*, 286, and see also Lacouture, *De Gaulle*, vol. 3, 227–228.

68. "Exposé des résultats de la négociation," MAE, SEAA, dossier 107; Buron, *Carnets Politiques de la guerre d'Algérie*, 227–235.

69. Buron, *Carnets Politiques de la guerre d'Algérie*, 225, 233–234.

70. Horne, *A Savage War of Peace*, 516; Courrière, *La Guerre d'Algérie*, vol. 4, 1037–1041.

71. Courrière, *La Guerre d'Algérie*, vol. 4, 1043.

72. Malek, *L'Algérie à Evian*, 222–224; Buron, *Carnets Politiques de la guerre d'Algérie*, 236–237.

73. "Deuxième séance," March 7, 1962, MAE, SEAA, dossier 113; Buron, *Carnets Politiques de la guerre d'Algérie*, 248–252.

74. "Troisième séance" and "Cinquième séance," March 8 and 9, 1962, MAE, SEAA, dossier 113; Buron, *Carnets Politiques de la guerre d'Algérie*, 254.

75. Buron, *Carnets Politiques de la guerre d'Algérie*, 255–256, 260, 263; Ma-

lek, *L'Algérie à Evian*, 238, 240–241; Lacouture, *De Gaulle*, vol. 3, 235–236; Tricot, *Mémoires*, 144. Though *comptes-rendus* numbered one through nine can be found in both DDF and the archives of the Sécrétariat d'Etat aux Affaires Algériennes, there is a gap between eight and nine corresponding to the period March 11–18. Malek's account may provide part of the answer. While the French had categorically refused to extend the amnesty to non-Muslim *porteurs de valises*, so-called because they transported funds for the FLN, he reports that they finally assented to a "gentlemen's agreement" in which the prisoners would not suffer further prosecution and would eventually be released (236–237). If so, it is understandable that the French negotiators would not want this committed to paper.

76. "Neuvième séance," March 18, 1962, MAE, SEAA, dossier 113; Malek, *L'Algérie à Evian*, 241–244.

77. "Neuvième séance," Regarding the fate of the CRUA and the *neufs historiques*, see Stora, *Dictionnaire biographique*.

78. Stora, *La gangrène*, 180–184, and Manceron and Remaoun, *D'Une Rive à l'autre*, 154–157.

79. Malek, *L'Algérie à Evian*, 233; Manceron and Remaoun, *D'Une Rive à l'autre*, 161–172; Alleg, *La guerre d'Algérie*, vol. 3, 208–213; Benjamin Stora, "La Politique des camps d'internement," in Ageron, *L'Algérie des Français*, 295; Lacouture, *De Gaulle*, vol. 3, 207; Stora, *La gangrène*, 93–105.

80. One of the best firsthand accounts is the *Journal* of Mouloud Feraoun, who managed to be critical of all sides until he was felled by the OAS in the last days of the war.

81. See note 2. On the contrast between the weakness of the FLN leadership and the strength of popular support, see Harbi, *Le FLN*, 276–279.

82. Malek provides the complete texts in *L'Algérie à Evian*.

83. Horne, "The Evian Agreement," April 3, 1962, PRO, CAB 129 1962, 58; "Note for the record," March 19, 1962, PRO, PREM 11, 4094.

84. Malek, *L'Algérie à Evian*, 224, and "Base et contenu de l'accord intervenu avec la France," reprinted in idem, 312. Buron recognized that the Algerians did not consider the accords to be definitive (Buron, *Carnets Politiques de la guerre d'Algérie*, 264–265). Tricot stresses that flexibility in their application was also in France's interest, as it too was undergoing revolutionary changes (Tricot, *Les Sentiers de la Paix*, 300–302).

85. Belhocine, "Quelques suggestions pour la formation d'un gouvernement," September 11, 1958, reprinted in Harbi, *Les Archives*, 228; Malek, *L'Algérie à Evian*, 198; Jean-Louis Planche, "Français d'Algérie, Français en Algérie (1962–1965)," in Gallissot, ed., *Les Accords d'Evian*, 105; El Hadi Chalabi, "Nationalité, citoyenneté: entre l'Etat, l'individu et le citoyen le droit en question," idem, 206–207.

86. See, for instance, Soustelle, *Vint-huit ans de gaullisme*.

87. Porter to Rusk, July 13, 1962, USNA, RG59, Central Decimal Files, 651.51s.

88. Memcon de Gaulle-Macmillan, January 28, 1961, PRO, PREM 11, 3200; Peyrefitte, *C'était de Gaulle*, 88; Tricot, *Les Sentiers de la Paix*, 303–304.

89. De Wailly, "Note sur le rapatriement éventuel des Français—européens et musulmans—d'Algérie," March 28, 1961, MAE, SEAA, dossier 100, Affaires Politiques, Evian Accords; Lacouture, *De Gaulle*, vol. 3, 235.

90. "Perspectives d'une reprise des négociations franco-FLN," September 26,

1961, AOM, MA, dossier 535; "Cinquième séance," July 27, 1961, DDF, 1961, II, no. 54; Memcon Dahlab-Joxe, December 23, 1961, MAE, SEAA, dossier 111; Buron, *Carnets Politiques de la guerre d'Algérie*, 193.

91. Malek, *L'Algérie à Evian*, 161, 209–210; Lacouture, *De Gaulle*, vol. 3, 235–236; Lacouture, *Algérie, La Guerre est finie*, 147–148; Lakhdar Bentobbal, "Souvenirs du 'Chinois,' " in Gallissot, *Les Accords d'Evian*, 22.

92. Horne, *A Savage War of Peace*, 516; Cros, *Le Temps de Violence*, 205.

93. Courrière, *La Guerre d'Algérie*, vol. 4, 1047–1048.

94. Ibid., 1050–1064

95. Planche, "Français d'Algérie," 98–99 (see note 85); Horne, *A Savage War of Peace*, 526–530.

96. Patrick Eveno, "Mourir à Oran," in Eveno and Planchais, *La Guerre d'Algérie*, 333–334; Planche, "Français d'Algérie," 93–101; Stora, *La gangrène*, 193–194.

97. See note 1.

98. Stora, *La gangrène*, 175–176, 200–202; Horne, *A Savage War of Peace*, 537–538.

99. "La protection des musulmans fidèles à la France," February 8, 1961, MAE, SEAA, dossier 103, Affaires Politiques, Evian Accords.

100. "Note concernant l'émigration de familles musulmanes algériennes en metropole," November 9, 1961, AOM, 15/CAB/40; Massenet to Joxe, May 2, 1962, AOM, MA, dossier 563.

101. Delaballe to Massenet, April 19, 1962, AOM, MA, dossier 563; Massenet to Joxe, May 2, 1962; Joxe to Massenet, May 10, 1962, idem.

102. Saliha Abdellatif, "Algérie 62: 'Cessez-le-feu' et devenir des supplétifs musulmans," in Gallissot, *Les Accords*, 129–130; "Le problème des Anciens Supplétifs Algériens . . . ," November 22, 1962, AOM, MA, dossier 540; Manceron and Remaoun, *D'une rive à l'autre*, 205.

103. "Politique de la France à l'égard de l'Algérie," November 28, 1962, AOM, MA, dossier 540. On economic cooperation as the "guarantee of guarantees," see "L'Algérie à l'heure de la Paix," a pamphlet given to the European population after the conclusion of the Evian accords, Centre de Documentation Historique sur l'Algérie, Aix-en-Provence, 7417/965–5 MIN.

104. Buron, *Carnets Politiques de la guerre d'Algérie*, 244; J.-R. Tournoux, *La Tragédie du Général*, 401–402.

105. Buron, *Carnets Politiques de la guerre d'Algérie*, 244; Tournoux, *La Tragédie du Général*, 400–401. The slogan "victory over ourselves" quickly caught on: Fouchet would later tell Horne that this was his thought when the French flag was finally lowered on July 4, 1962, and Horne would use it to end his last chapter on the war (*A Savage War of Peace*, 533–534). It also serves as the title of Lacouture's chapter on the settlement, *De Gaulle*, vol. 3, 219.

106. Maurice Vaïsse, *La Grandeur*, 460–463.

107. Quoted in ibid., 462–463.

108. Gallissot, "Les Accords d'Evian dans la longue durée: signification et limites d'une libération nationale," in Gallissot, *Les Accords d'Evian*, 243; Couve de Murville circular, March 26, 1962, DDF, 1962, I, no. 104.

109. Stora, *La gangrène*, 284; Julliard, "Le mépris et la modernité," 153, and Ageron, "Conclusion," 622, both in Rioux, *La Guerre d'Algérie et les Français*.

110. Consider, for instance, that by 1989 more than 1,000 books had been published about the Algerian War, but not one focused on its international his-

tory. The one partial exception, Elsenhans's *Frankreichs Algerienkrieg*, was written by a German, and not one of the five scholars who began working on diplomatic histories of the war when the archives opened was French. On the other hand, this "forgotten war" has inspired many French authors to write about how it is remembered, and many more to insist it is still forgotten: Stora, *La gangrène et l'oubli;* Roux, *Les Harkis, ou, les oubliés de l'histoire;* Muller, *Le Silence des Harkis;* Manceron and Remaoun, *D'une rive à l'autre: de la mémoire à l'histoire;* Jordi and Hamoumou, *Les harkis, une mémoire enfouie* (the list goes on).

111. Anderson *Imagined Communities*, 199–201.

112. Stora, *La Gangrène*, 151–177; Fouad Soufi, "La Fabrication d'une mémoire: les médias algériens (1963–1995)," and Hassan Remaoun, "Pratiques historiographiques et mythes de fondation: le cas de la Guerre de libération à travers les institutions algériennes d'éducation et de recherche," both in Ageron, *La Guerre d'Algérie et les Algériens*, 289–321.

113. Roberts, "From Radical Mission to Equivocal Ambition," 457–458; Deborah Harrold, "The Political Economy of the Algerian Crisis," talk given at the University of Michigan, Ann Arbor, February 15, 1999. This observation is also based on my conversations with Algerians of all ages.

114. This was most vividly illustrated in the controversy over the candidacy of the most prominent Islamist-oriented leader, Sheikh Mahfouz Nahnah, in the 1999 presidential election. The Constitutional Council barred him from participating on the grounds that he had not fought in the war, a requirement for candidates born before 1942, which touched off a debate among veteran mujahadeen (Hisham Fahim, "Algerian Army Plays with Fire," *Al-Ahram Weekly*, March 18–24, 1999).

115. Roberts, "From Radical Mission to Equivocal Ambition," 454–455, 458; Martinez, *La Guerre Civile*, 15. On the connections and parallels between the FLN and FIS, see also Quandt, *Between Ballots and Bullets*, 19, 99.

116. Martinez, *La Guerre Civile*, 15.

117. See, for instance, his 1999 election *Programme*, which links the independence struggle with postwar development programs. [Online] Available:http://abdelaziz-bouteflika.org/franc/home.html. [March 17, 2001].

118. Guy Pervillé, "Histoire de l'Algérie et mythes politiques algériens: du 'parti de la France' aux 'anciens et nouveaux harkis,'" in Ageron, *La Guerre d'Algérie et les Algériens*, 323–326; Lazreg, "Gender and Politics in Algeria," 769–770; Entelis, *The Revolution Institutionalized*, 95.

119. New York: Simon and Schuster, 1985.

120. *The Call from Algeria*; Peter Van Ness, *Revolution and Chinese Foreign Policy*, 141.

121. Fischer, "Is Islam the Odd-Civilization Out?" 54–55; Young, *White Mythologies*, 1.

Conclusion

1. Others have debated the still more obscure connections between the present and earlier times. See, for instance, Wolfowitz, "Bridging Centuries"; Rothschild, "Globalization and the Return of History"; and especially Held et al., *Global Transformations*, which provides a masterly synthesis.

2. *Force and Statecraft*, x.

3. Ibid., 105–106. In an important new study, *A Constructed Peace: The Mak-*

ing of the European Settlement, Marc Trachtenberg describes the consolidation and elaboration of this system at what he considers to be its core. But as the author acknowledges, whether areas not covered were "of secondary or even tertiary importance" is a question of perspective (352). More than four-fifths of the world's population might disagree. Moreover, and as this study has sought to demonstrate, key policymakers on both sides of the Atlantic believed that even Europe's security could not be assured without amicable relations between North and South.

4. Irwin Wall offers a very different assessment in a provocative new book. He argues that Algerian independence marked the collapse of de Gaulle's efforts to obtain an American guarantee of French interests in Africa in exchange for its assuming a subordinate position within the alliance. While U.S. support was indeed essential for de Gaulle's preferred solution to the war, this account has stressed that he viewed both as means to his ultimate end: national independence and international prestige. Despite setbacks such as the forced concession of Algerian sovereignty and, still more, West Germany's refusal the following year to join him in defying the United States, his success can be measured by the stridency with which Americans have felt compelled to deny it (Wall, *France, The United States, and the Algerian War*, chapter 7 and conclusion). Regarding his criticism of U.S. Vietnam policy, see Logevall, "De Gaulle, Neutralization." On the failure of his German policy, see Trachtenberg, *A Constructed Peace*, 371–377.

5. L. W. Fuller, "The United States and the United Nations," December 10, 1957, USNA, RG59, PPS, Lot 67D548, United Nations 1957–1960, and see also Herz, "Rise and Demise of the Territorial State," 492–493.

6. Brian Urquhart describes the episode in a February 16, 1995, editorial, "Peace-Keeping Saves Lives," *The Washington Post*, A, 23.

7. AOM, Iconothèque, Affiches, 9F.79.

8. Baraduc to Gorlin, March 22, 1958, AOM, 12/CAB/234.

9. Stephanson, *Kennan and the Art of Foreign Policy*, 157; Ambrose, *Eisenhower*, vol. 2, 376; Macmillan, *Pointing the Way*, 475; de Gaulle, *Discours et Messages*, 228.

10. De Gaulle, *Memoirs of Hope*, 43, 45.

11. On Algeria's importance in international law, see Higgins, *The Development of International Law*, 95–97; Fraleigh, "The Algerian Revolution as a Case Study," 179–183, 224–231; Wilson, *International Law and the Use of Force*, 65–67, 108–111; Andreopoulos, "The Age of National Liberation Movements," 191–213.

12. On Mandela, see his autobiography, *Long Walk to Freedom*, 259–260, and his testimony at the Rivonia Trial, 1963–1964, 11.1 on the CD-ROM *Apartheid & the History of the Struggle for Freedom*. Arafat's deputy and first representative in Algiers, Abu Jihad, later recalled that the "fact that we were seen to have Algeria as our friend gave us a revolutionary credibility that was worth more than gold and guns at the time" (Hart, *Arafat*, 102–104, 112–113, and Rubin, *Revolution until Victory*, 7, 10). On Algiers as a Mecca, see Entelis, *Algeria: The Revolution Institutionalized*, 189. Note, however, that their adversaries could also learn from Algeria. South Africa sent officers to learn French methods and developed a strategy based on *guerre révolutionnaire* doctrine (Cawthra, *Brutal Force*, 28–29).

13. For an early, and unsympathetic, survey of other revolutionary movements that challenged the sovereignty regime, see Bell, "Contemporary Revolutionary Organizations," and see also Robert Jackson's insightful analysis, *Quasi-*

States. On Muslims' new, more demanding attitude toward social benefits, see Bourdieu, *The Algerians*, 160.

14. "Statement by Guy Mollet, Premier on French Policy in Algeria," January 9, 1957, MAE, ONU, dossier 550.

15. The observations of French diplomats posted to the United States are particularly revealing in this regard. They nervously reported on the rise of the Nation of Islam and rallies that joined representatives of the NAACP with Algerian and other African nationalists. See "Bulletin de synthèse et de dépêches de la sous-direction d'afrique, Juin 1959," MAE, MLA vol. 24 (provisional number), Action extérieure, Etats-Unis, Janvier 1958 à Juin 1959, Cote ML 4; Alphand to Couve, March 17, 1960, MAE, MLA vol. 25 (provisional number), Action extérieure, Etats-Unis, Juillet 1959 à Mars 1960, Cote ML 4.

16. Evans, *The Memory of Resistance*, 113, and see also Silverstein, who argues that the Algerian War helped inspire other minority movements in France ("French Alterity," 24–25).

17. Malek, *L'Algérie à Evian*, 84. "Reimagining communities" is a reference to Anderson's *Imagined Communities*, which has been criticized for its emphasis on print to the neglect of other media. Robert Hayden discusses how communities become unimaginable in "Imagined Communities and Real Victims."

18. "Le 'Tiers Monde' n'est pas monolithique," *Le Monde Diplomatique*, April 1961.

19. Lerner, *The Passing of Traditional Society*. In this regard, it is interesting to note that the French have led the way in founding organizations like *Médecins Sans Frontières, Reporters Sans Frontières, Pharmaciens Sans Frontières, Marins Sans Frontières*, even *Clowns Sans Frontières*.

20. For the controversies occasioned by American cultural influence in France, see Kuisel, *Seducing the French*. The subject of "Americanization" has inspired an outpouring of new historical studies, yet aside from Kristin Ross's intriguing but ultimately unsatisfying *Fast Cars, Clean Bodies*, little attention has been paid to its relationship to decolonization and development projects. For an overview, see Reinhold Wagnleitner's "The Empire of the Fun, or Talkin' Soviet Union Blues: The Sound of Freedom and U.S. Cultural Hegemony in Europe," *Diplomatic History* 23.3 (summer 1999): 499–524.

21. "The Constantine Plan for Algeria: Opening New Frontiers in Development," undated but circa May 1961, The British Library, London, SE.47/23.

22. In Sub-Saharan Africa, too, both Britain and France were "trapped by the logical and political consequences of their universalism," as Cooper has argued, *Decolonization and African Society*, 468–470.

23. Groupe d'Etude des Structures Futures de l'Algérie, "Premier Rapport: Note de Presentation," July 1960, AOM, SEAA dossier 5.

24. Brandell, *Les Rapports franco-algériens*, 16–22; Arrus, *L'eau en Algérie*, 27. The French délégué général, Paul Delouvrier, characterized the small portion of the Constantine Plan's budget devoted to agriculture as "charity"; see the compte rendu of the "Conseil Supérieur du Plan de l'Algérie," June 22, 1959, AOM, 14/CAB/239. On the investment priorities prescribed by development theory, see Worsley, *The Three Worlds*, 17–21.

25. Lesbet, *Les 1000 villages socialistes*, 324–334.

26. *Al-Laz* [The Ace] (Algiers, 1974), quoted in Harrold, "The Menace and Appeal of Algeria's Parallel Economy," 20. As Harrold demonstrates, this has created an almost *irrational* concern about Algeria's large informal economy.

27. Malley, *The Call from Algeria*, 140.

28. Quoted in Grimaud, *La Politique extérieure de l'Algérie*, 294.

29. Preface, *The Wretched of the Earth*, 12–13, 20–21, 25–26, 29.

30. Ageron, " 'L'Algérie dernière chance de la puissance française,' " 133–134.

31. Anne-Marie Duranton-Crabol, "Du combat pour l'Algérie française au combat pour la culture européenne: Les origines du Groupement de Recherche et d'Etudes pour la Civilisation Européenne (GRECE)," in Rioux, *La Guerre d'Algérie et les intellectuels français*, 67–76.

32. *The Origins of Totalitarianism*, 290. Arendt's discussion of "The Decline of the Nation-State and the End of the Rights of Man" remains compelling half a century after it first appeared.

33. "La France et l'Islam: si proche et si loin," *Le Monde*, October 20, 1994.

34. Hargreaves and McKinney, *Post-colonial Cultures in France*, 18–19.

35. Boumedienne quoted in Raspail, *Le Camp des Saints;* "Building a Mediterranean Economy: An Unequal Proposition," *The North Africa Journal Paper Series—Weekly Service*, August 7, 1998.

36. Raspail, *Le Camp des Saints*, and see also Connelly and Kennedy, "Must It Be the Rest." I am indebted to Ann Stoler for the point regarding the FN.

37. On this last point, see Roberts, "From Radical Mission to Equivocal Ambition," 462–465.

Bibliography

A Note on Sources:

In the course of my research, archivists were kind enough to allow me to use collections that they were still organizing. I returned to some after this process was completed, so references to the Quai d'Orsay's *Direction Amérique 1952–63* and *Mission de liaison algérien* will sometimes provide provisional file numbers that have since been changed. In other cases, it was too early to tell whether and how collections would be organized, or even whether some of the documents that I was permitted to see would make it through the declassification process—especially those concerning intelligence matters. These include the Quai's *Sécrétariat d'Etat aux Affaires Algériennes*, the Archives d'Outre-mer's *Série MA (Affaires Algériennes)*, and the papers of the *Gouvernement Provisoire de la République Algérienne* in the Algerian national archives. The citations referring to these collections should all be considered provisional.

Unless otherwise noted, all translations are my own.

I—Archives and Interviews

Algeria

Centre National des Archives Algériennes, Algiers (CNAA) Le Fond du Gouvernement provisoire de la République algérienne (GPRA)
Interviews:
Hocine Aït Ahmed

Mabrouk Belhocine
Rédha Malek

Egypt

Arab League Documentation and Information Center, Cairo (AL)

France

Archives Nationales, Paris (AN):
    F60, President du Conseil
    Groupe Socialiste Parlementaire (GS)
    Mouvement Républicain Populaire (MRP)
    Archives Privées:
        Vincent Auriol Papers
        Georges Bidault Papers
        René Mayer Papers
        René Pleven Papers
Archives d'Outre-Mer, Aix-en-Provence (AOM):
    Affaires Algériennes, Echelons de liaison Sections
        Administratives Specialisées, 1955–1962 (SAS)
        Fonds du Cabinet Civil du Gouverneur Général de l'Algérie (CAB)
        Gouvernement Général de l'Algérie (GGA)
        Iconothèque
        Ministre de la France d'Outre-Mer, Cabinet Ministériel
        Série MA, Affaires Algériennes (MA)
Centre de Documentation Historique sur l'Algérie, Aix-en-Provence
Fondation Nationale des Sciences Politiques, Paris (FNSP):
    Archives d'histoire contemporaine
        Wilfred Baumgartner Papers
        Cletta and Daniel Mayer Papers
        Couve de Murville Papers
        Alain Savary Papers
Ministère des Affaires Etrangères, Paris (MAE):
    Amérique, 1952–1963
    Archives Oraux
    Archives Privées
        Maurice Dejean
        Henri Hoppenot
        René Massigli
        Robert Schuman
    Asie-Oceanie 1944–1955
    Asie-Oceanie, 1956–1967
    Cabinet du Ministre
    Direction des Affaires Economiques/Service de Coopération Economique (DE-CE)
    Europe, 1949–1960
    Mission de liaison algérien (MLA)
    Nations-Unies (ONU)
    Secrétariat d'Etat aux Affaires Algériennes

Secrétariat Général
Tunisie, 1944–1955
Ministère de l'Economie, des Finances, et de l'Industrie, Paris:
Archives Economiques et Financières
Série 1A
Série B
Service historique de l'Armée de l'Air, Château de Vincennes (SHAA):
Série E, Cabinet Militaire
Service historique de l'Armée de Terre, Château de Vincennes (SHAT):
Série 0/2
Sous-Série 1H, Algérie

Great Britain

The British Library, London
Public Record Office, Kew (PRO):
CAB 128 and 129, Cabinet minutes and memoranda
CAB 159, Meetings of the Chiefs of Staff Committee
DEFE 4–5, Chiefs of Staff Meetings and Memoranda
FO 371, Foreign Office correspondence
FO 800, Foreign Office personal papers
Anthony Eden
Selwyn Lloyd
PREM 11, Prime Ministers' office files

Tunisia

Centre d'Etudes Maghrébines à Tunis
Centre de Documentation Internationale, Tunis
Interviews:
Habib Bourguiba, Jr.
Rachid Driss
Slaheddine El Golli
Ali Hedda
Bahi Ladgham
Mahmoud Mestiri
Mohamed Sayah

United States

Dwight D. Eisenhower Library, Abilene Kansas (DDEL):
John Foster Dulles Papers
Dwight D. Eisenhower Papers
Al Gruenther Papers
James C. Hagerty Diary
Christian A. Herter Papers
C. D. Jackson Papers
Lauris Norstad Papers
Oral History Interviews:
John Eisenhower

Andrew Goodpaster
Mary Lord
Vernon Walters
U.S. Council on Foreign Economic Policy
U.S. President's Commission on Foreign Economic Policy
White House Central Files
White House Office Files
John F. Kennedy Library, Boston, MA (JFKL):
John F. Kennedy Papers
National Security Files
President's Office Files
Oral History Interviews
Mongi Slim
Habib Bourguiba, Jr.
George Meany Memorial Archives, Silver Spring, MD:
RG1–027, AFL, CIO, AFL-CIO Office of the President's Files:
George Meany, 1944–1960
RG 18, International Affairs Department:
Jay Lovestone Files, 1944–1973
Irving Brown Files, 1943–1989
Country Files, 1945–1971
United Nations Archives, New York, NY:
Office of Legal Affairs
Office of the Secretary General
Dag Hammarskjöld
U Thant
United States National Archives, College Park, MD (USNA):
Record Group 59, General Records of the Department of State
Decimal Files
Lot Files:
Assistant Secretary of State for African Affairs
Bray Records
Bureau of African Affairs
Bureau of European Affairs
Office of Western European Affairs
Policy Planning Staff
Subject Files of the Officer in Charge of Northern African Affairs 1945–
1956
Record Group 218, Records of the Joint Chiefs of Staff Central Files
Record Group 263, Records of the Central Intelligence Agency National
Intelligence Estimates Concerning Soviet Military Power

Published Sources, Primary and Secondary

Official Publications

France

French propaganda publications and films are cited in the archives where they are
to be most easily found.

Ministère des Affaires Etrangères. Commission de Publication des Documents Diplomatiques Français. *Documents Diplomatiques Français* (DDF):
1954 (July 21–December 31). Paris: Imprimerie Nationale, 1987.
1955 (two volumes). Paris: Imprimerie Nationale, 1987–1988.
1956 (three volumes). Paris: Imprimerie Nationale, 1988–1990.
1957 (two volumes). Paris: Imprimerie Nationale, 1990–1991.
1958 (two volumes). Paris: Imprimerie Nationale, 1992–1993.
1959 (two volumes). Paris: Imprimerie Nationale, 1994–1995.
1960 (two volumes). Paris: Imprimerie Nationale, 1996.
1961 (two volumes). Paris: Imprimerie Nationale, 1997.
1962 (volume one). Paris: Imprimerie Nationale, 1998.
Jauffret, Jean-Charles, ed. *La Guerre d'Algérie par les Documents, I: L'Avertissement 1943–1946*. Vincennes: Service historique de l'Armée de Terre, 1990.
Journal Officiel de la République Française. Paris: Imprimerie des Journaux Officiels, 1954–1962

Great Britain

Goldsworthy, David, ed. *The Conservative Government and the End of Empire, 1951–1957*. Part I: International Relations. London: HMSO, 1994.

Tunisia

Bourguiba, Habib. *Discours*. Vols. 3–9. Tunis: Secrétariat d'Etat à l'Information, 1975–1976.

United States

Department of State, Office of the Historian. *Foreign Relations of the United States* (FRUS) (only volumes cited are listed here):
 1947: Vol. 5: The Near East and Africa
 1948: Vol. 3: Western Europe
 1949: Vol. 1: National Security Affairs, Foreign Economic Policy
 1950: Vol. 5: The Near East, South Asia, and Africa
 1951: Vol. 5: The Near East and Africa
1952–1954: Vol. 2: National Security Affairs
 Vol. 6: Western Europe and Canada
 Vol. 9: The Near and Middle East
 Vol. 11: Africa and South Asia
 1955: Vol. 14: Arab-Israeli-Dispute
1955–1957: Vol. 4: Western European Security and Integration
 Vol. 10: Foreign Aid and Economic Defense Policy
 Vol. 17: Arab-Israeli-Dispute
 Vol. 18: Africa
 Vol. 19: National Security Policy
 Vol. 27: Western Europe and Canada
1958–1960: Vol. 7: Western European Integration and Security, Canada
 Vol. 11: Lebanon and Jordan

Vol. 13: Arab-Israeli Dispute; United Arab Republic; North Africa

1961–1963: Vol. 13: West Europe and Canada

Vol. 21: Africa

Howe, George F. *Northwest Africa: Seizing the Initiative in the West. United States Army in World War II: The Mediterranean Theater of Operations.* Department of the Army Office of the Chief of Military History. Washington, DC: U.S. Government Printing Office, 1957.

Jackson, Wayne G., and the Central Intelligence Agency Historical Staff. *Allen Welsh Dulles as Director of Central Intelligence 26 February 1953–29 November 1961, Volume 3: Covert Activities.* Available in the USNA, RG 263, 190-24-34.

Joint Chiefs of Staff, Historical Office. *History of the Joint Chiefs of Staff:*

Vol. 4: Poole, Walter. *The Joint Chiefs of Staff and National Policy, 1950–1952.* Wilmington, DE: Michael Glazier, 1980.

Vol. 5: Watson, Robert J. *The Joint Chiefs of Staff and National Policy, 1953–1954.* Washington: GPO, 1986.

Wainstein, L., et al. "The Evolution of U.S. Strategic Command and Control and Warning, 1945–1972." Institute for Defense Analyses, June 1975. Available from Department of Defense Freedom of Information Office.

Internet, Microform, and CD-ROM Sources

Apartheid & the History of the Struggle for Freedom in South Africa (CD-ROM). Bellville, South Africa: Mayibuye Center, University of the Western Cape, 1993.

Declassified Documents Reference System. Online. Available: http://www.ddrs.psmedia.com. March 17, 2001.

"Dulles-Herter Papers, Chronological Correspondence Series." University Publications of America (UPA), 1986.

"Eisenhower Office Files, 1953–61 (EOF), Part 1: Eisenhower Administration Series." UPA, 1991.

"Eisenhower Office Files, 1953–61, Part 2: International Series," UPA. 1991.

"Executive Sessions of the Senate Foreign Relations Committee," Vols. 1–10. Congressional Information Service. (1979–1980).

La Guerre d'Algérie (CD-ROM). Paris: La Découverte, 1996.

"Minutes of Telephone Conversations of John Foster Dulles and Christian Herter (1953–1961)" (MTC, Dulles-Herter), UPA, 1980.

Trachtenberg, Marc. "A Constructed Peace: Appendices." Online. Available: http://www.history.upenn.edu/trachtenberg/appendices/annexlist.html. March 17, 2001.

Other Printed Primary Materials, including Memoirs

Abbane, Ramdane. "Rapport du CCE au CNRA." *Naqd* 12 (summer 1999): 191–211.

Abbas, Ferhat. *Autopsie d'une Guerre.* Paris: Garnier, 1980.

Acheson, Dean. *Present at the Creation: My Years in the State Department.* New York: Norton, 1969.

Aït Ahmed, Hocine. *La Guerre et l'Après-guerre*. Paris: Minuit, 1964.

———. *Mémoires d'un combattant: L'esprit de l'indépendance, 1942–1952* (Paris: Sylvie Messinger, 1983).

Al Dib, Mohamad Fathi. *Abdel Nasser et la Révolution Algérienne*. Paris: L'Harmattan, 1985.

Alphand, Hervé. *L'Etonnement d'Etre: Journal, 1933–1973*. Paris: Fayard, 1977.

Auriol, Vincent. *Mon septennat: 1947–1954*. Paris: Gallimard, 1970.

Azzedine, Rabah Zerari. *On nous appelait fellaghas*. Paris: Stock, 1976.

Ben Khedda, Benyoucef. *Les Accords d'Evian*. Alger: O.P.U., 1986.

Bouhired, Djamila. "Temoignage de Djamila Bouhired." *Majallat et-Tarikh* 17 (1984): 109–112.

Buron, Robert. *Carnets politiques de la guerre d'Algérie*. Paris: Plon, 1965.

Debré, Michel. *Trois Républiques pour une France: Mémoires*. 5 vols. Paris: Albin Michel, 1984–94.

de Gaulle, Charles. *Discours et Messages, Avec le Renouveau, Mai 1958–Juillet 1962*. Paris: Plon, 1970.

———. *Lettres, Notes et Carnets: Juin 1951–Mai 1958*. Paris: Plon, 1985.

———. *Lettres, Notes et Carnets: Juin 1958–Décembre 1960*. Paris: Plon, 1985.

———. *Lettres, Notes et Carnets: Janvier 1961–Décembre 1963*. Paris: Plon, 1986.

———. *Memoirs of Hope: Renewal 1958–1962, Endeavor 1962–*. Trans. Terence Kilmartin. London: Wiedenfeld and Nicolson, 1971.

Eisenhower, Dwight D. *The White House Years*. 2 vols. Garden City, NY: Doubleday, 1963–65.

Ely, Paul. *Mémoires*. 2 vols. Paris: Plon, 1964–69.

Feraoun, Mouloud. *Journal 1955–1962*. Paris: Le Seuil, 1962.

Ferrell, Robert H., ed. *The Diary of James C. Hagerty: Eisenhower in Mid-Course, 1954–1955*. Bloomington: Indiana University Press, 1983.

———. *The Eisenhower Diaries*. New York, W.W. Norton, 1981.

Flanner, Janet. *Paris Journal*. Ed. William Shawn. Vol. 2, 1956–1965. New York: Harcourt Brace Jovanovich, 1988.

Griffith, Robert, ed. *Ike's Letters to a Friend, 1941–1958*. Lawrence, KS: University Press of Kansas, 1984.

Harbi, Mohammed, ed. *Les Archives de la Révolution algérienne*. Paris: Jeune Afrique, 1981.

Jebb, Gladwyn. *The Memoirs of Lord Gladwyn*. New York: Weybright and Talley, 1972.

Johnson, Walter, ed. *The Papers of Adlai E. Stevenson, Vol. VIII: Ambassador to the United Nations*. Boston: Little Brown, 1979.

Khrushchev, Nikita. *Khrushchev Remembers*. Trans. Strobe Talbott. Boston: Little, Brown, 1970.

Long, Olivier. *Le dossier secret des Accords d'Evian: Une mission suisse pour la paix en Algérie*. Lausanne: 24 heures, 1988.

Macmillan, Harold. *Pointing the Way, 1959–1961*. London: Macmillan, 1972.

Melnik, Constantin. *La mort était leur mission: Le Service Action pendant la guerre d'Algérie*. Paris: Plon, 1996.

Mendès France, Pierre. *Oeuvres Complètes*. 6 vols. Paris: Gallimard, 1984–90.

Murphy, Robert. *Diplomat among Warriors*. New York: Doubleday, 1964.

Peyrefitte, Alain. *C'était de Gaulle*. Paris: Fayard, 1994.

Pflimlin, Pierre. *Mémoires d'un Européen de la IVᵉ à la Vᵉ République*. Paris: Fayard, 1991.

Pineau, Christian. *1956/Suez*. Paris: Robert Laffont, 1976.

Rueff, Jacques. *Combats pour l'Ordre financier*. Paris: Plon, 1972.

Rusk, Dean. *As I Saw It*. London: I. B. Tauris, 1991.

Salan, Raoul. *Mémoires*. 4 vols. Paris: La Cité, 1972.

Shriver, Sargent. *Point of the Lance*. New York: Harper & Row, 1964.

Soustelle, Jacques. *L'Espérance trahie: 1958–1961*. Paris: l'Alma, 1962.

———. *Vint-huit ans de gaullisme*. Paris: La Table Ronde, 1968.

Terrenoire, Louis. *De Gaulle et l'Algérie. Temoignage pour l'histoire*. Paris: Fayard, 1964.

———. *Les Sentiers de la Paix: Algérie 1958/1962*. Paris: Plon, 1972.

Tricot, Bernard. *Mémoires*. Paris: Quai Voltaire, 1994.

Books, Articles, and Dissertations

Adas, Michael. "Market Demand versus Imperial Control: Colonial Contradictions and the Origins of Agrarian Protest in South and Southeast Asia." *Global Crises and Social Movements: Artisans, Peasants, Populists, and the World Economy*. Ed. Edmund Burke III. Boulder, CO: Westview Press, 1988. 89–116.

Ageron, Charles-Robert. "Les accords d'Evian (1962)." *Vingtième Siècle* 35 (July–September 1992): 3–15.

———, ed. *l'Algérie algérienne de Napoléon III à de Gaulle*. Paris: Sinbad, 1980.

———. " 'L'Algérie dernière chance de la puissance française,' Etude d'un mythe politique (1954–1962)." *Relations internationales* 57 (Spring 1989): 113–139.

——— ed. *L'Algérie des Français*. Saint-Quentin: Seuil, 1993.

———. "De Gaulle et la Conférence de Brazzaville." *"L'Entourage" et Général de Gaulle: ouvrage collectif*. Ed. Gilbert Pilleul et al. Paris: Plon, 1979. 243–251.

———, ed. *La Guerre d'Algérie et les Algériens*. Paris: Armand Colin, 1997.

———. *Histoire de l'Algérie Contemporaine (1830–1964)*. Paris: Presses universitaires de France, 1964.

———. "L'idée d'Eurafrique et le débat colonial franco-allemand de l'entre-deux-guerres." *Revue d'Histoire Moderne et Contemporaine* 22 (July–September 1975): 446–475.

———. *Modern Algeria: A History from 1830 to the Present*. Trans. Michael Brett. London: Hurst, 1991.

———. "Une guerre religieuse?" *Les Cahiers de L'IHTP* 9 (October 1988): 27–29.

Ageron, Charles-Robert, and Marc Michel, ed. *L'Afrique noire française: L'heure des Indépendances*. Paris: CNRS, 1992.

Albertini, Rudolph von. *Decolonization: The Administration and Future of the Colonies, 1919–1960*. Garden City, NY: Doubleday, 1971.

Algérie surpeuplée. Algiers: Secrétariat Social, 1958.

Alleg, Henri. *La guerre d'Algérie*. 3 vols. Paris: Temps actuels, 1981.

Alwan, Mohamed. *Algeria before the United Nations*. New York: Robert Speller, 1959.

Ambler, J. S. *The French Army in Politics, 1945–1962*. Columbus: Ohio University Press, 1966.

Ambrose, Stephen E. *Eisenhower*. 2 vols. New York: Simon and Schuster, 1983–1984.

Amrane, Djamila. *Les femmes algériennes dans la guerre*. Paris: Plon, 1991.

Anderson, Benedict. *Imagined Communities: Reflections on the Origin and Spread of Nationalism*. Rev. ed. London: Verso, 1991.

Andreopoulos, George J. "The Age of National Liberation Movements." *The Laws of War: Constraints on Warfare in the Western World*. Ed. Michael Howard, George J. Andreopoulos, and Mark R. Shulman. New Haven: Yale University Press, 1994. 191–213.

Andrew, Christopher M., and Oleg Gordievsky. *KGB: The Inside Story*. London: Hodder & Stoughton, 1990.

Andrew, Christopher M., and A. S. Kanya-Forstner. *France Overseas: The Great War and the Climax of French Imperial Expansion: 1914–1924*. Stanford, CA: Stanford University Press, 1981.

Arendt, Hannah. *The Origins of Totalitarianism*. 1951. New York: Harcourt, Brace, 1973.

Aron, Raymond. *L'Algérie et la République*. Paris: Plon, 1958.

———. *La tragédie algérienne*. Paris: Plon, 1957.

Aron, Raymond, et al. *Les origines de la guerre d'Algérie*. Paris: Fayard, 1962.

Arrus, René. *L'Eau en Algérie: De l'impérialisme au développement (1830–1962)*. Grenoble: Presses Universitaires de Grenoble, 1985.

Bancel, Nicolas, and Ghislaine Mathy, "La Propagande économique." *Images et Colonies: Iconographie et propagande coloniale sur l'Afrique française de 1880 à 1962*. Ed. Nicolas Bancel, Pascal Blanchard, and Laurent Gervereau. Paris: Bibliothèque de documentation internationale contemporaine, 1993.

Barkaoui, Miloud. "The New York Times and the Algerian Revolution, 1956–1962: An Analysis of a Major Newspaper's Reporting of Events." Ph.D. dissertation. University of Keele, 1988.

Barker, Carol Mae. "The Politics of Decolonization in Tunisia: The Foreign Policy of a New State." Ph.D. dissertation. Columbia University, 1971.

Barnet, Richard J. *Intervention and Revolution: The United States in the Third World*. Rev. ed. New York: Mentor, New American Library, 1972.

Barraclough, Geoffrey. *An Introduction to Contemporary History*. New York: Basic Books, 1964.

Becker, Josef, and Franz Knipping, eds. *Power in Europe? Great Britain, France, Italy and Germany in a Postwar World, 1945–1950*. New York: de Gruyter, 1986.

Bedjaoui, Mohamed. *La Révolution algérienne et le droit*. Brussels: International Association of Democratic Lawyers, 1961.

Belkherroubi, Abdelmadjid. *La Naissance et la reconnaissance de la république algérienne*. Brussels: Bruylant, 1972.

Bell, J. Bowyer. "Contemporary Revolutionary Organizations." *International Organization* 25 (Summer 1971): 503–518.

Benallègue, Nora. "Algerian Women in the Struggle for Independence and Reconstruction." *International Social Science Journal* 35.4 (1983): 703–715.

Bernard, Stéphane. *The Franco-Moroccan Conflict, 1943–1956*. Trans. Marianna Oliver, Alexander Baden Harrison, Jr., and Bernard Phillips. New Haven: Yale University Press, 1968.

Bidault, Georges. *Algérie: l'Oiseau aux ailes coupées*. Paris: La Table Ronde, 1958.

Bills, Scott L. *Empire and Cold War: The Roots of US-Third World Antagonism, 1945–47*. New York: St. Martin's Press, 1990.

Blair, Leon B. "The Impact of Franco-American Military Agreements on Moroccan Nationalism, 1940–1956." *Rocky Mountain Social Science Journal* 9.1 (1972): 61–68.

Bonnet, Georges. *Quai d'Orsay*. Isle of Man: Times Press, 1965.

Bonnot, Xavier Marie. "Les Représentations de l'Algérie française à travers les courts métrages du Gouvernement Général (1945–1961), Une étude de cas: La représentation de l'espace." Maîtrise.Université d'Aix-en-Provence, 1991.

Borowski, Harry R. *A Hollow Threat: Strategic Airpower and Containment before Korea*. Westport, CT: Greenwood Press, 1982.

Bossuat, Gérard. *La France, l'aide américaine et la construction européenne, 1944–1954*. 2 vols. Paris: Imprimerie Nationale, 1992.

Boulanger, Pierre. *Le Cinéma colonial: De "l'atlantide" à "lawrence d'arabie."* Paris: Seghers, 1975.

Bourdieu, Pierre. *The Algerians*. Trans. Alan C. M. Ross. Boston: Beacon Press, 1961.

——. "The Algerian Subproletariat." *Man, State, and Society in the Contemporary Maghrib*. Ed. I. William Zartman. New York: Praeger, 1973. 83–92.

——. "Les Conditions sociales de la production sociologique: Sociologie coloniale et décolonisation de la sociologie." *Le Mal de voir: ethnologie et orientalisme: politique et épistémologie, critique et autocritique*. Paris: Union Générale d'Editions, 1976. 416–427.

Bourguiba, Habib. "Nationalism: Antidote to Communism." *Foreign Affairs* 35 (July 1957): 646–653.

Boyd, Andrew. *Fifteen Men on a Powder Keg: A History of the UN Security Council*. London: Methuen, 1971.

Bozo, Frédéric, and Pierre Mélandri. "La France devant l'opinion américaine: Le retour de de Gaulle début 1958–printemps 1959." *Relations internationales* 58 (Summer 1989): 195–215.

Brandell, Inga. *Les Rapports franco-algériens depuis 1962: Du pétrole et des hommes*. Paris: L'Harmattan, 1981.

Brands, H. W. *The Specter of Neutralism: The United States and the Emergence of the Third World, 1947–1960*. New York: Columbia University Press, 1989.

Braudel, Fernand. *The Mediterranean and the Mediterranean World in the Age of Philip II*. Trans. Siân Reynolds. 2 vols. London: Collins, 1972.

——. "Personal Testimony." *Journal of Modern History* 44 (December 1972): 448–467.

Breil, M. Jacques. "Etude de Démographie Quantitative." In *La Population en Algérie: Rapport du Haut Comité Consultatif de la Population et de la Famille*. 2 vols. Paris: La Documentation Française, 1957.

Bromberger, Merry, and Serge Bromberger. *Les 13 Complots du 13 Mai*. Paris: Fayard, 1959.

Bull, Hedley, and Adam Watson. *The Expansion of International Society*. New York: Oxford, 1984.

Burke, Peter. *The French Historical Revolution: The Annales School, 1929–89*. Cambridge, UK: Polity Press, 1990.

Burns, William. *Economic Aid and American Policy toward Egypt, 1955–1981*. Albany: State University of New York Press, 1985.

Camus, Albert. *Essais*. Paris: Gallimard, 1965.

Cawthra, Gavin. *Brutal Force: The Apartheid War Machine*. London: IDAF, 1986.

Charnay, Jean-Paul. *La Vie Musulmane en Algérie d'après La Jurisprudence de la Première Moitié du XXᵉ Siècle*. Paris: Presses Universitaires de France, 1965.

Chartier, Roger. "Intellectual History and the History of *Mentalités*, A Dual Re-evaluation." *Cultural History: Between Practices and Representations*. Trans. Lydia G. Cochrane. Ithaca: Cornell University Press, 1988. 1–52.

Chevalier, Jacques. *Le Problème Démographique Nord-Africain. Institut National d'Etudes Démographiques: Travaux et Documents*. Paris: Presses Universitaires de France, 1947. Cahier n° 6.

———. *Classes laborieuses et classes dangereuses à Paris pendant la première moitié du XIXᵉ siècle*. Paris: Plon, 1958.

Chikh, Slimane. *L'Algérie en Armes, ou, Le Temps des Certitudes*. Alger: Office des Publications Universitaires, 1981.

Christensen, Thomas J. *Useful Adversaries: Grand Strategy, Domestic Mobilization, and Sino-American Conflict, 1947–1958*. Princeton: Princeton University Press, 1996.

Coale, Ansley J., and Edgar M. Hoover. *Population Growth and Economic Development in Low-Income Countries: A Case Study of India's Prospects*. Princeton: Princeton University Press, 1958.

Cobbs, Elizabeth A. "Decolonization, the Cold War, and the Foreign Policy of the Peace Corps." *Diplomatic History* 20.1 (Winter 1996): 79–105.

Cohen, Avner. *Israel and the Bomb*. New York: Columbia University Press, 1998.

Cohen, Warren I. *Dean Rusk*. Totowa, NJ: Cooper Square Publishers, 1980.

Connelly, Matthew. "The Algerian War for Independence: An International History." Ph.D. dissertation. Yale University, 1997.

———. "America, France, and the Algerian War: The Forgotten Conflict over a 'Clash of Civilizations.'" *Sea among Lands: Policy and Strategy in the Mediterranean Sea Past, Present, and Future*. Ed. John B. Hattendorf. Portland, OR: Frank Cass, 1999. 329–343.

———. "Déjà Vu All Over Again: Algeria, France, and Us." *The National Interest* 42 (Winter 1995/96): 27–37.

———. "The French-American Conflict over North Africa and the Fall of the Fourth Republic." *Revue française d'histoire d'outre-mer* 84 (June 1997): 9–27.

———. "Rethinking the Cold War and Decolonization: The Grand Strategy of the Algerian War for Independence." *The International Journal of Middle East Studies* 33.2 (May 2001): 221–245.

———. "Taking Off the Cold War Lens: Visions of North-South Conflict during the Algerian War for Independence." *The American Historical Review* 105 (June 2000): 739–769.

Connelly, Matthew, and Paul Kennedy. "Must It Be the Rest against the West?" *The Atlantic Monthly* (December 1994): 61–84.

Connor, Walker. *Ethnonationalism: The Quest for Understanding*. Princeton, NJ: Princeton University Press, 1994.

Cooper, Frederick. *Decolonization and African Society: The Labor Question in French and British Africa*. New York: Cambridge University Press, 1996.

Cooper, Frederick, et al., eds. *Confronting Historical Paradigms: Peasants, Labor, and the Capitalist World System in Africa and Latin America*. Madison: University of Wisconsin Press, 1993.

Cooper, Frederick, and Randall Packard, eds. *International Development and the Social Sciences: Essays on the History and Politics of Knowledge*. Berkeley: University of California Press, 1997.

Costigliola, Frank. *France and the United States: The Cold Alliance since World War II*. New York: Twayne, 1992.

Cotteret, Jean-Marie, and René Moreau. *Le Vocabulaire du Général de Gaulle.* Paris: Armand Colin, 1969.

Courrière, Yves. *La Guerre d'Algérie.* 4 vols. Paris: Fayard, 1968–74.

Craig, Gordon, and Alexander George. *Force and Statecraft: Diplomatic Problems of Our Time.* 3rd ed. New York: Oxford University Press, 1995.

Cros, Vitalis. *Le Temps de Violence.* Paris: Presses de la Cité, 1971.

Curtin, Philip D. "Medical Knowledge and Urban Planning in Tropical Africa." *The American Historical Review* 90 (June 1985): 594–613.

Dahm, Bernhard. *Sukarno and the Indonesian Struggle for Independence.* Ithaca, NY: Cornell University Press, 1969.

Daniel, Jean. *De Gaulle et l'Algérie.* Paris: Seuil, 1986.

Day, Georges. *Les Affaires de la Tunisie et du Maroc devant les nations unies.* Paris: Pédone, 1953.

de Gaulle, Charles. *The Edge of the Sword.* 1932. Trans. Gerard Hopkins. New York: Criterion, 1960.

de la Gorce, Paul-Marie. *The French Army: A Military-Political History.* New York: G. Braziller, 1963.

Descloitres, Claudine, Robert Reverdy, and Jean-Paul Reverdy. *L'Algérie des bidonvilles. Le tiers monde dans la cité.* Paris and Le Haye: Mouton, 1969.

Dine, Philip. *Images of the Algerian War: French Fiction and Film, 1954–1962.* Oxford: Clarendon Press, 1994.

Doise, Jean, and Maurice Vaïsse. *Diplomatie et outil militaire, 1871–1969.* Paris: Imprimerie nationale, 1987.

Dower, John. *War without Mercy: Race and Power in the Pacific War.* New York: Pantheon, 1986.

Droz, Bernard, and Evelyne Lever. *Histoire de la guerre d'Algérie (1954–1962).* Paris: Seuil, 1982.

Duchemin, Jacques. *Histoire du FLN.* Paris: La Table Ronde, 1962.

El Machat, Samya. *Les Etats-Unis et l'Algérie: De la méconnaissance à la reconnaissance, 1945–1962.* Paris: L'Harmattan, 1996. (Contains lengthy excerpts from earlier accounts, including Bernard Droz and Evelyne Lever, *Histoire de la guerre d'Algérie [1954–1962]* [Paris: Seuil, 1982], and articles by Pierre Guillen, Pierre Mélandri, and Maurice Vaïsse in Jean-Pierre Rioux, *La Guerre d'Algérie et les Français* [Paris: Fayard, 1990]; only original sources are cited here.)

El Méchat, Samya (variant spelling). *Tunisie, les chemins vers l'Indépendance,1945–1956.* Paris: L'Harmattan, 1992.

Elgey, Georgette. *La République des tourmentes, 1954–1959.* 2 vols. to date. Paris: Fayard, 1992–.

Elsenhans, Hartmut. *Frankreichs Algerienkrieg, 1954–1962.* Munich: C. Hanser, 1974.

Ely, Paul. "Le Chef et l'évolution de la guerre." *Revue militaire d'information* no. 284 (June 1957): 13–17.

Entelis, John P. *Algeria: The Revolution Institutionalized.* Boulder, CO: Westview Press, 1986.

Evans, Martin. *The Memory of Resistance: French Opposition to the Algerian War (1954–1962).* Oxford, UK: Berg, 1997.

Eveno, Patrick, and Jean Planchais, eds. *La Guerre d'Algérie.* Paris: La Découverte et *Le Monde*, 1989.

Fanon, Frantz. *Studies in a Dying Colonialism*. Trans. Haakon Chevalier. London: Earthscan, 1989.

——. *The Wretched of the Earth*. Trans. Constance Farrington. New York: Grove, 1968.

al-Fassi, Allal. *The Independence Movements in Arab North Africa*. Trans. Hazem Zaki Nuseibeh. Washington: American Council of Learned Societies, 1954; New York: Octagon Books, 1970.

Fauvet, Jacques. *La IVᵉ République*. Paris: Fayard, 1959.

Fauvet, Jacques, and Jean Planchais. *La Fronde des généraux*. Grenoble: Arthaud, 1961.

Feiertag, Olivier. "Wilfred Baumgartner: Les finances de l'Etat et l'économie de la Nation (1902–1978), Un grand commis à la croisée des pouvoirs." Mémoire. Université de Paris-X-Nanterre, 1995.

Ferniot, Jean. *De Gaulle et le 13 mai*. Paris: Plon, 1965.

Fischer, Michael M. J. "Is Islam the Odd Civilization Out?" *New Perspectives Quarterly* 9.2 (1992): 54–59.

Fitte, Albert. *Spectroscopie d'une propagande révolutionnaire, El Moudjahid des temps de guerre*. Montpellier: Comité Internationale des Sciences Historiques, Commission Française d'Histoire Militaire, 1973.

Fitzgerald, Edward Peter. "Did France's Colonial Empire Make Economic Sense? A Perspective from the Postwar Decade, 1946–1956." *Journal of Economic History* 48 (1988): 373–385.

Forest, Philippe. *Histoire de Tel Quel, 1960–1982*. Paris: Seuil, 1995.

Fraleigh, Arnold. "The Algerian Revolution as a Case Study in International Law." *The International Law of Civil War*. Ed. Richard A. Falk. Baltimore, MD: Johns Hopkins University Press, 1971. 179–243.

France, Judith. "AFL-CIO Foreign Policy: An Algerian Example, 1954–1962." Ph.D. dissertation. Ball State University, 1981.

Frank, Andre Gunder. "The Underdevelopment of Development." *The Underdevelopment of Development: Essays in Honor of Andre Gunder Frank*. Ed. Sing C. Chew and Robert A. Denemark. London, 1996. 17–56.

Frémeaux, Jacques. *La France et l'Islam depuis 1789*. Paris: Presses Universitaires de France, 1991.

Furniss, Edgar S. *France: Troubled Ally: De Gaulle's Heritage and Prospects*. New York: Harper/Council on Foreign Relations, 1960.

Gadant, Monique. *Islam et Nationalisme en Algérie*. Paris: L'Harmattan, 1988.

Gaddis, John Lewis. "New Conceptual Approaches to the Study of American Foreign Relations." *Diplomatic History* 14.3 (summer 1990): 405–423.

——. *We Now Know: Rethinking Cold War History*. Oxford: Clarendon Press, 1997.

Gallissot, René, ed., *Les Accords d'Evian: En conjoncture et en longue durée*. Paris: Karthala, 1997.

Ganiage, Jean. *Histoire Contemporaine du Maghreb de 1830 à nos jours*. Paris: Fayard, 1994.

Gauron, André. *Histoire économique et sociale de la Cinquième République*. 2 vols. Paris: La Découverte, 1983–88.

Gavin, Francis J. "The Gold Battles within the Cold War: American Monetary Policy and the Defense of Europe, 1960–1963." *Diplomatic History*, forthcoming in Winter 2002.

Gemelli, Giuliana. *Fernand Braudel*. Trans. Brigitte Pasquett and Béatriz Propetto Marzi. Paris: Odile Jacob, 1995.

Gendzier, Irene L. *Managing Political Change: Social Scientists and the Third World. Westview Special Studies in Social, Political, and Economic Development*. Boulder, CO: Westview Press, 1985.

———. *Notes from the Minefield: United States Interventions in Lebanon and the Middle East, 1945–1958*. New York: Columbia University Press, 1997.

Gerges, Fawaz. *The Superpowers and the Middle East*. Boulder, CO: Westview, 1994.

Geyer, Michael, and Charles Bright, "World History in a Global Age." *American Historical Review* 100 (October 1995): 1034–1060.

Giesbert, Franz-Olivier. *François Mitterrand, ou la tentation de l'histoire*. Paris: Seuil, 1977.

Girardet, Raoul. *L'idée coloniale en France de 1871 à 1962*. Paris: La Table Ronde, 1972.

Goëau-Brissonnière, Jean-Yves. *Mission secrète pour la paix en Algérie*. Paris: Lieu Commun, 1992.

Golan, Matti. *Shimon Peres*. Trans. Ina Friedman. London: Wiedenfeld and Nicolson, 1982.

Gollwitzer, Heinz. *Die Gelbe Gefahr*. Göttingen: Vandenhoeck & Ruprecht, 1962.

Gordon, David C. *Women of Algeria: An Essay on Change*. Cambridge: Harvard University Press, 1968.

Gorse, Georges. "La Nuit de Mai." *Revue des Deux Mondes* (November 1984): 299–309.

Greenstein, Fred I. *The Hidden-Hand Presidency*. New York: Basic Books, 1982.

Grimal, Henri. *Decolonization: The British, French, Dutch and Belgian Empires 1919–1963*. Trans. Stephan de Vos. London: Routledge & Kegan Paul, 1965.

Grimaud, Nicole. *La Politique extérieure de l'Algérie (1962–1978)*. Paris: Karthala, 1984.

Grosser, Alfred. *Affaires extérieures: La Politique de la France, 1944–1984*. Paris: Flammarion, 1984.

———. *French Foreign Policy under de Gaulle*. Trans. Lois Ames Pattison. Boston: Little, Brown, 1967.

Grove, Richard H. *Ecology, Climate and Empire: Colonialism and Global Environmental History, 1400–1940*. Cambridge, UK: White Horse Press, 1997.

Guernine, Tassadit. "Femmes Musulmanes en Algérie: Statut Juridique et promotion Sociale? 1930–1960." Maîtrise. Université de Provence, 1988.

Guha, Ranajit. "The Prose of Counter-Insurgency." *Selected Subaltern Studies*. Ed. Ranajit Guha and Gayatri Chakravorty Spivak. New York: Oxford University Press, 1988. 45–84.

Hadhri, Mohieddine. *L'URSS et la Magrheb: De la Révolution d'Octobre à l'indépendance de L'Algérie, 1917–1962*. Paris: L'Harmattan, 1985.

Hahn, Peter. *The United States, Great Britain, and Egypt, 1945–1956: Strategy and Diplomacy in the Early Cold War*. Chapel Hill: University of North Carolina Press, 1991.

Halberstam, David. *The Best and the Brightest*. New York: Random House, 1972.

Hamburger, Robert Lee. "Franco-American Relations, 1940–1962: The Role of United States Anticolonialism and Anti-Communism in the Formulation of

United States Policy on the Algerian Question." Ph.D. dissertation. University of Notre Dame, 1970.

Hamon, Olivier. "Chronique du Conflit Algérien, 1954–1962." *Revue Historique des Armées* 187 (June 1992): 33–42.

Harbi, Mohammed, ed. *Les Archives de la révolution algérienne*. Paris: Jeune Afrique, 1981.

——. *Le FLN: Mirage et Réalité*. Paris: Jeune Afrique, 1980.

——. *La Guerre Commence en Algérie: 1954*. Bruxelles: Editions Complexe, 1984.

Hargreaves, Alec G., and Mark McKinney, eds. *Post-colonial Cultures in France*. New York: Routledge, 1997.

Hargreaves, John D. *Decolonization in Africa*. New York: Longman, 1988.

Harper, John Lamberton. *American Visions of Europe: Franklin D. Roosevelt, George F. Kennan, and Dean G. Acheson*. New York: Cambridge University Press, 1994.

Harrison, Martin. "Government and Press in France during the Algerian War." *The American Political Science Review* 58.2 (June 1964): 273–295.

Harrison, Michael. "French Anti-Americanism under the Fourth Republic and the Gaullist Solution." *The Rise and Fall of Anti-Americanism: A Century of French Perception*. Ed. Denis Lacorne, Jacques Rupnik, and Marie-France Toinet. London: Macmillan, 1990. 169–178.

——. *The Reluctant Ally: France and Atlantic Security*. Baltimore: Johns Hopkins University Press, 1981.

Harrold, Deborah. "The Menace and Appeal of Algeria's Parallel Economy." *Middle East Report* (January–February 1995): 18–22.

Hart, Alan. *Arafat: A Political Biography*. London: Sidgwick & Jackson, 1994.

Hayden, Robert M. "Imagined Communities and Real Victims: Self-Determination and Ethnic Cleansing in Yugoslavia." *American Ethnologist* 23 (November 1996): 783–801.

Headrick, Daniel R. *The Invisible Weapon: Telecommunications and International Politics 1851–1945*. New York: Oxford University Press, 1991.

——. *Tools of Empire: Technology and European Imperialism in the Nineteenth Century*. New York: Oxford University Press, 1981.

Heggoy, Alf Andrew. *Insurgency and Counterinsurgency in Algeria*. Bloomington: Indiana University Press, 1972.

Held, David, et al. *Global Transformations: Politics, Economics and Culture*. Stanford, CA: Stanford University Press, 1999.

Hélie, Jérome. *Les accords d'Evian: Histoire de la paix ratée en Algérie*. Paris: Olivier Orban, 1992.

Herman, Arthur. *The Idea of Decline in Western History*. New York: Free Press, 1997.

Herz, John H. "Rise and Demise of the Territorial State." *World Politics* 9.4 (July 1957): 473–493.

Higgins, Rosalyn. *The Development of International Law through the Political Organs of the United Nations*. New York: Oxford University Press, 1963.

Hill, Christopher. "World Opinion and the Empire of Circumstance." *International Affairs* 72 (1996): 109–131.

Hitchcock, William I. *France Restored: Cold War Diplomacy and the Quest for Leadership in Europe, 1944–1954*. Chapel Hill: University of North Carolina Press, 1998.

Hogan, Michael. "The Search for a 'Creative Peace': The United States, European Unity, and the Origins of the Marshall Plan." *Diplomatic History* 6.3 (Summer 1982): 267–285.

Hoisington, William A., Jr. "The American Presence in Morocco during the Second World War." *The Atlantic Connection: 200 Years of Moroccan-American Relations, 1786–1986.* Ed. Jerome B. Bookin-Weiner and Mohamed El Mansour. Morocco: Edino, 1990. 153–168.

Horne, Alistair. *The French Army and Politics, 1870–1970.* London: Macmillan Press, 1984.

———. *A Savage War of Peace: Algeria, 1954–1962.* Rev. ed. New York: Penguin, 1987.

Horowitz, Donald L. *Ethnic Groups in Conflict.* Berkeley: University of California Press, 1985.

Hough, Jerry F. *The Struggle for the Third World: Soviet Debates and American Options.* Washington: Brookings Institution, 1986.

Hunt, Michael. "The Long Crisis in U.S. Diplomatic History: Coming to Closure." *Diplomatic History* 16.1 (Winter 1992): 115–141.

Ibezim, Chukwamerije. "The New Frontier and Africa, 1961–1963." Ph.D. dissertation. State University of New York, Stony Brook, 1976.

Immerman, Richard. "The History of U.S. Foreign Policy: A Plea for Pluralism." *Diplomatic History* 14.4 (Fall 1990): 574–583.

———, ed. *John Foster Dulles and the Diplomacy of the Cold War.* Princeton: Princeton University Press, 1990.

Iriye, Akira. "The Internationalization of History." *The American Historical Review* 94 (February 1989): 1–10.

Jackson, Robert. *Quasi-States: Sovereignty, International Relations, and the Third World.* New York: Cambridge University Press, 1990.

James, Harold. *International Monetary Cooperation since Bretton Woods.* New York: Oxford University Press, 1996.

Jauffret, Jean-Charles. "L'Armée et l'Algérie en 1954." *Revue Historique des Armées* 187 (June 1992): 15–25.

Jeffreys-Jones, Rhodri. *The CIA and American Democracy.* New Haven: Yale University Press, 1989.

Johnson, Douglas. "Algeria: Some Problems of Modern History." *Journal of African History* 5 (1964): 221–242.

Jordi, Jean-Jacques, and Mohand Hamoumou. *Les Harkis, une mémoire enfouie.* Paris: Autrement, 1999.

Juergensmeyer, Mark. *The New Cold War? Religious Nationalism Confronts the Secular State.* Berkeley: University of California Press, 1993.

Julien, Charles-André. *L'Afrique du Nord en Marche: Nationalismes Musulmans et Souveraineté française.* 3rd ed. Paris: Julliard, 1972.

Julien, Charles-André, and Charles-Robert Ageron. *Histoire de l'Algérie contemporaine.* Paris: P.U.F., 1964 and 1969.

Julliard, Jacques. *"Naissance et mort . . ." La IVe République (1947–1958).* Rev. ed. Paris: Calmann-Lévy, 1968.

Kaplan, Fred. *The Wizards of Armageddon.* New York: Simon and Schuster, 1983.

Kaplan, Jacob Julius, and Günther Schleiminger. *The European Payments Union: Financial Diplomacy in the 1950s.* Oxford: Clarendon Press, 1989.

Kaplan, Lawrence S., Denise Artaud, and Mark Rubin, eds. *Dien Bien Phu and* the Crisis of Franco-American Relations, 1954–1955*. Wilmington, DE: Scholarly Resources, 1990.

Kaufman, Burton I. *The Korean War: Challenges in Crisis, Credibility, and Command*. Philadelphia: Temple University Press, 1986.

———. *Trade and Aid: Eisenhower's Foreign Economic Policy 1953–1961*. Baltimore: Johns Hopkins University Press, 1982.

Kedourie, Elie. *Islam and the Modern World*. New York: Holt, Rinehart and Winston, 1980.

Kelly, George Armstrong. *Lost Soldiers: The French Army and Empire in Crisis, 1947–1962*. Cambridge: MIT Press, 1965.

Kennedy, Dane. "Imperial History and Post-Colonial Theory." *The Journal of Imperial and Commonwealth History* 24 (September 1996): 345–363.

Kennedy, John F. *The Strategy of Peace*. New York: Harper, 1960.

Kessler, Jean. "La Surveillance des frontières maritimes de l'Algérie 1954–1962." *Revue Historique des Armées* 187 (June 1992): 94–101.

Kettle, Michael. *De Gaulle and Algeria, 1940–1960: From Mers El-Kebir to the Algiers Barricades*. London: Quartet, 1993.

Kolko, Gabriel. *The Limits of Power*. New York: Harper & Row, 1972.

Kuisel, Richard. *Seducing the French: The Dilemma of Americanization*. Berkeley: University of California Press, 1993.

Kunz, Diane. *The Economic Diplomacy of the Suez Crisis*. Chapel Hill: University of North Carolina, 1991.

Kyle, Keith. *Suez*. London: Weidenfeld and Nicolson, 1991.

Labaree, Benjamin. *Patriots and Partisans: The Merchants of Newburyport, 1764–1815*. Cambridge: Harvard University Press, 1962.

Lacouture, Jean. *Algérie, La Guerre est finie. La Mémoire du siècle*. Brussels: Editions Complexe, 1985.

———. *De Gaulle*. 3 vols. Paris: Seuil, 1984–1986.

———. *De Gaulle: The Rebel, 1890–1944*. Trans. Patrick O'Brian. New York: Norton, 1990.

———. *Pierre Mendès France*. Trans. George Holoch. New York: Holmes and Meier, 1984.

Lacroix-Riz, Annie. *Les Protectorats d'Afrique du Nord entre la France et Washington*. Paris: L'Harmattan, 1988.

LaFeber, Walter. *America, Russia, and the Cold War, 1945–1992*. 7th ed. New York: McGraw-Hill, 1993.

Laqueur, Walter. *The Struggle for the Middle East: The Soviet Union and the Middle East 1958–70*. Baltimore: Penguin, 1972.

Laremont, Ricardo René. "Islam and the Politics of Resistance in Algeria." Ph.D. dissertation. Yale University, 1995.

Laroui, Abdallah. *The History of the Maghrib: An Interpretive Essay*. Princeton: Princeton University Press, 1977.

Larson, Arthur. *Eisenhower: The President Nobody Knew*. New York: Scribner's, 1968.

Lazreg, Marnia. *The Eloquence of Silence: Algerian Women in Question*. New York: Routledge, 1994.

———. "Gender and Politics in Algeria: Unraveling the Religious Paradigm." *Signs* 15 (1990): 755–780.

Le Douarec, François. *Félix Gaillard, 1919–1970: Un Destin inachevé*. Paris: Economica, 1991.

Le Tourneau, Roger. *Evolution politique de l'Afrique du Nord Musulmane, 1920–1961*. Paris: Armand Colin, 1962.

Lefebvre, Jeffrey. "Kennedy's Algerian Dilemma: Containment, Alliance Politics and the 'Rebel Dialogue.'" *Middle Eastern Affairs* 35 (April 1999): 61–82.

Lefeuvre, Daniel. "Les Réactions patronales au Plan de Constantine." *Revue Historique* 276.1 (1986): 167–189.

Leffler, Melvyn P. *A Preponderance of Power: National Security, The Truman Administration, and the Cold War*. Stanford: Stanford University Press, 1992.

Leprohon, Pierre. *L'Exotisme et le cinéma*. Paris: J. Susse, 1945.

Lerner, Daniel. *The Passing of Traditional Society*. Glencoe, IL: Free Press, 1958.

Lesbet, Djaffar. *Les 1000 villages socialistes en Algérie*. Paris: Syros, 1984.

Lindenberg, Daniel. "Guerres de mémoire en France." *Vingtième Siècle* 42 (April–June 1994): 77–95.

Logevall, Fredrik. "De Gaulle, Neutralization, and American Involvement in Vietnam, 1963–1964." *Pacific Historical Review* 41 (February 1992): 69–102

Louis, Wm. Roger. *The British Empire in the Middle East, 1945–1951: Arab Nationalism, the United States, and Postwar Imperialism*. Oxford: Clarendon Press, 1984.

———. "Libyan Independence, 1951: The Creation of a Client State." *Decolonization and African Independence: The Transfers of Power, 1960–1980*. Ed. Prosser Gifford and Wm. Roger Louis. New Haven: Yale University Press, 1988. 159–184.

Louis, Wm. Roger, and Roger Owen, eds. *Suez 1956: The Crisis and its Consequences*. Oxford: Clarendon Press, 1989.

Louis, Wm. Roger, and Ronald Robinson. "The Imperialism of Decolonization." *Journal of Imperial and Commonwealth History* 22.3 (September 1994): 462–511.

Lucas, Philippe, and Jean-Claude Vatin. *L'Algérie des anthropologues*. Paris: Maspero, 1975.

Lundestad, Geir. *America, Scandinavia, and the Cold War*. New York: Columbia University Press, 1980.

———. "Empire by Invitation? The United States and Western Europe, 1945–1952." *Society for the History of American Foreign Relations Newsletter* 15 (September 1984): 1–21.

———. "Moralism, Presentism, Exceptionalism, Provincialism, and Other Extravagances in American Writings on the Early Cold War." *Diplomatic History* 13 (Fall 1989): 527–545.

Lustick, Ian. *Unsettled Lands: Britain and Ireland, France and Algeria, Israel and the West Bank-Gaza*. Ithaca: Cornell University Press, 1993.

Lyotard, Jean-François. *La Guerre des Algériens. Ecrits, 1956–1963*. Paris: Galilée, 1989.

MacDonald, Robert W. *The League of Arab States: A Study in the Dynamics of Regional Organization*. Princeton: Princeton University Press, 1965.

MacFarlane, S. Neil. *Superpower Rivalry & 3rd World Radicalism*. Baltimore: Johns Hopkins, 1985.

Machula, David. "Alain Savary et la décolonisation du Maroc et de la Tunisie." Mémoire. Institut d'Etudes Politiques de Paris, 1992.

MacKenzie, John M. *The Empire of Nature: Hunting, Conservation, and British Imperialism*. New York: St. Martin's Press, 1988.

Mahoney, Richard. *JFK: Ordeal in Africa*. New York: Oxford University Press, 1983.

Maier, Charles S. "Consigning the Twentieth Century to History: Alternative Narratives for the Modern Era." *The American Historical Review* 105 (June 2000): 807–831.

Maier, Charles S., and Dan White, eds. *The Thirteenth of May: The Advent of De Gaulle's Republic.* New York: Oxford University Press, 1968.

Majāhid, Mas'ūd. *Al-Jazā'ir 'abr Al-Ijyāl.* Algiers: n.p., n.d.

Malek, Rédha. *L'Algérie à Evian: Histoire des négotiations secrètes, 1956–1962.* Paris: Seuil: 1995.

Malley, Robert. *The Call from Algeria: Third Worldism, Revolution, and the Turn to Islam.* Berkeley: University of California Press, 1996.

Manceron, Gilles, and Hassan Remaoun. *D'une rive à l'autre: La Guerre d'Algérie de la mémoire à l'histoire.* Paris: Syros, 1993.

Mandela, Nelson. *Long Walk to Freedom.* New York: Little, Brown, 1995.

Mandouze, André, ed. *La révolution algérienne par les textes: documents du F.L.N.* Paris: Aujourd'hui, 1975.

Maquin, Etienne. *Le Parti socialiste et la guerre d'Algérie: La fin de la vieille maison (1954–1958).* Paris: L'Harmattan, 1990.

Marks, Sally. "The World according to Washington." *Diplomatic History* 11.3 (Summer 1987): 265–282.

Marseille, Jacques. "L'Algérie dans l'économie française (1954–1962)." *Relations Internationales* 58 (Summer 1989): 169–176.

Martin, John Bartlow. *Adlai Stevenson and the World.* Garden City, NY: Doubleday, 1977.

Martinez, Luis. *La Guerre Civile en Algérie 1990–1998.* Paris: Karthala, 1998.

Masset, Dominique. *La Belgique et la guerre d'Algérie.* Brussels: CIACO, 1988.

May, Ernest. "The Decline of Diplomatic History." *American History: Retrospect and Prospect.* Ed. George Billias and Gerald Grob. New York: Free Press, 1971. 399–430.

McCormick, Thomas J. "The State of Diplomatic History." *The State of American History.* Ed. Herbert Bass. Chicago: Quadrangle Books, 1970. 114–119.

McDonald, Terrence J., ed. *The Historic Turn in the Human Sciences.* Ann Arbor, MI: University of Michigan Press, 1996.

McDougall, Walter A. . . . *the Heavens and the Earth: A Political History of the Space Age.* New York: Basic Books, 1985.

McMahon, Robert. *Colonialism and Cold War: The United States and the Struggle for Indonesian Independence, 1945–49.* Ithaca, NY: Cornell University Press, 1981.

——. "Eisenhower and Third World Nationalism: A Critique of the Revisionists." *Political Science Quarterly* 101.3 (1986): 453–473.

——. "The Study of American Foreign Relations: National History or International History?" *Diplomatic History* 14.4 (Fall 1990). 554–564.

Medvedev, Roy, and Zhores Medvedev. *Khrushchev: The Years in Power.* New York: Columbia, 1976.

Megherbi, Abdelghani. *Les Algériens au miroir du cinéma colonial.* Algiers: SNED, 1982.

Menand, Louis. "Human Rights as Global Imperative." *Conceptualizing Global History.* Ed. Bruce Mazlish and Ralph Buultjens. Boulder, CO: Westview, 1993. 173–204.

Meynier, Gilbert. "Les Algériens vus par le pouvoir égyptien pendant la guerre d'Algérie d'après les mémoires de Fathi al Dib." *Cahiers de la Méditerranée* 41 (December 1990): 89–127.

Milward, Alan S. "Was the Marshall Plan Necessary?" *Diplomatic History* 13 (Spring 1989). 231–253.

Moore, Clement Henry. " 'Bourguibism' in Tunisia." *Current History* 44 (January 1963): 34–40.

——. *Tunisia Since Independence: The Dynamics of One Party Government.* Berkeley: University of California Press, 1965.

Morgan, Ted. *A Covert Life: Jay Lovestone: Communist, Anti-Communist, and Spymaster.* New York: Random House, 1999.

Morris, George. *CIA and American Labor: The Subversion of the AFL-CIO's Foreign Policy.* New York: International Publishers, 1967.

Mottahedeh, Roy. *The Mantle of the Prophet.* New York: Simon and Schuster, 1985.

Müller, Klaus-Jürgen. "La guerre d'Algérie vue par la presse ouest-allemande." *Relations internationales* 58 (Summer 1989): 177–185.

Muller, Laurent. *Le Silence des Harkis.* Paris: L'Harmattan, 1999.

Mūrū, Muhamad. *Al-Jazā'ir taʿūdu.* Cairo: Al-Mukhtar Al-Islami, 1992.

Naimark, Norman A. *The Russians in Germany: A History of the Soviet Zone of Occupation, 1945–1949.* Cambridge, MA: Belknap Press, 1995.

Ninkovich, Frank A. "The End of Diplomatic History?" *Diplomatic History* 15 (Summer 1991): 439–448.

Noer, Thomas J. *Cold War and Black Liberation: The United States and White Rule in Africa, 1948–1968.* Columbia, MO: University of Missouri Press, 1985.

Norris, Robert S., William M. Arkin, and William Burr. "Where They Were." *Bulletin of the Atomic Scientists* 55.6 (November/December): 26–35.

Nouschi, André. "Culture et décolonisation au Maghreb." *The Maghreb Review* 19.1–2 (1994): 34–48.

Novick, Peter. *That Noble Dream: The "Objectivity Question" and the American Historical Profession.* New York: Cambridge University Press, 1988.

Nurse, Ronald J. "Critic of Colonialism: JFK and Algerian Independence." *Historian* 39.2 (February 1977): 307–326.

Olson, Gregory A. "Eisenhower and the Indochina Problem." *Eisenhower's War of Words: Rhetoric and Leadership.* Ed. Martin J. Medhurst. East Lansing, MI: Michigan State University, 1994. 97–135.

Osborne, Michael A. *Nature, the Exotic, and the Science of French Colonialism.* Bloomington: Indiana University Press, 1994.

Otero, Maruja. "L'Algérie dans les relations franco-espagnoles 1954–1964." Mémoire. Institut d'Etudes Politiques de Paris, 1996.

Paret, Peter. *French Revolutionary Warfare from Indochina to Algeria: The Analysis of a Political and Military Doctrine.* New York: Praeger, 1964.

Paterson, Thomas G., ed. *Kennedy's Quest for Victory: American Foreign Policy, 1961–1963.* New York: Oxford University Press, 1989.

Pelt, Adrian. *Libyan Independence and the United Nations: A Case of Planned Decolonization.* New Haven: Yale University Press, 1970.

Pervillé, Guy. *Les Étudiants algériens de l'université française (1880–1962).* Paris: CNRS, 1984.

——. "Guerre étrangère et guerre civile en Algérie, 1954–1962." *Relations Internationales* 14 (1978): 171–196.

——. "L'insertion internationale du F.L.N. algérien." *Relations Internationales* 31 (Autumn 1982): 373–386.

———. "La Révolution Algérienne et la Guerre Froide 1954–1962." *Etudes Internationales* 16.1 (March 1985): 55–66.

Pitman, Paul M. "The French Crisis and the Dissolution of the European Payments Union, 1956–1958." *Explorations in OEEC History*. Ed. Richard T. Griffiths. Paris: Organisation for Economic Co-operation and Development, 1997. 219–227.

Planchais, Jean. *L'Empire embrasé: 1946–1962*. Paris: Denoël, 1990.

———. *La Guerre d'Algérie*. Paris: la Découverte, 1990.

———. *Une Histoire Politique de l'Armée: De de Gaulle à de Gaulle, 1940–1967*. 2 vols. Paris: Seuil, 1967.

Poidevin, Raymond. *Robert Schuman: Homme d'Etat, 1886–1963*. Paris: Imprimerie Nationale, 1986.

Porch, Douglas. *The Conquest of Morocco*. New York: Alfred A. Knopf, 1983.

———. *The Conquest of the Sahara*. New York: Fromm International, 1986.

———. *The French Secret Services: From the Dreyfus Affair to the Gulf War*. New York: Farrar, Straus and Giroux, 1995.

Porter, Bruce. *The USSR in Third World Conflicts*. Cambridge: Cambridge University Press, 1984.

Pruessen, Ronald W. "Beyond the Cold War—Again: 1955 and the 1990s." *Political Science Quarterly* 108.1 (Spring 1993): 59–80.

———. *John Foster Dulles: The Road to Power*. New York: Free Press, 1982.

Pyenson, Lewis. *Civilizing Mission: Exact Sciences and French Overseas Expansion, 1830–1940*. Baltimore: Johns Hopkins University Press, 1993.

Quandt, William B. *Between Ballots and Bullets: Algeria's Transition from Authoritarianism*. Washington, DC: Brookings Institution Press, 1998.

———. *Revolution and Political Leadership: Algeria, 1954–1968*. Cambridge, MA: M.I.T. Press, 1969.

Rabe, Stephen G. "Eisenhower Revisionism: A Decade of Scholarship." *Diplomatic History* 17 (1993): 97–115.

Raspail, Jean. *Le Camp des Saints*. 1973. Reprint, Paris: Robert Laffont, 1978.

Rémond, René. *Le Retour de De Gaulle*. Bruxelles: Editions Complexe, 1983.

Rioux, Jean-Pierre. *The Fourth Republic, 1944–1958*. Cambridge: Cambridge University Press, 1987.

———, ed. *La Guerre d'Algérie et les Français*. Paris: Fayard, 1990.

Rioux, Jean-Pierre, and Jean-François Sirinelli, eds. *La Guerre d'Algérie et les intellectuels français*. Paris: Editions Complexe, 1991.

Rivlin, Benjamin. "The United States and Moroccan International Status 1943–1956: A Contributory Factor in Morocco's Reassertion of Independence from France." *International Journal of African Historical Studies* 15.1 (1982): 64–82.

Roberts, Hugh. "From Radical Mission to Equivocal Ambition: The Expansion and Manipulation of Algerian Islamism, 1979–1992." *The Fundamentalism Project; Volume Four: Accounting for Fundamentalisms: The Dynamic Character of Movements*. Ed. Martin E. Marty and R. Scott Appleby. Chicago: University of Chicago Press, 1994. 428–489.

Robinson, Ronald, and John Gallagher. *Africa and the Victorians: The Official Mind of Imperialism*. New York: St. Martin's Press, 1961.

Rodman, Peter W. *More Precious than Peace: The Cold War and the Struggle for the Third World*. New York: C. Scribner's Sons, 1994.

Rosenberg, David Alan. " 'A Smoking Radiating Ruin at the End of Two Hours':

Documents on American Plans for Nuclear War with the Soviet Union, 1954–1955." *International Security* 6.3 (1981): 3–38.

Ross, Kristin. *Fast Cars, Clean Bodies: Decolonization and the Reordering of French Culture.* Cambridge, MA: MIT Press, 1995.

Rothschild, Emma. "Globalization and the Return of History." *Foreign Policy* 115 (Summer 1999): 106–116.

Rothschild, Joseph. *Ethnopolitics: A Conceptual Framework.* New York: Columbia University Press, 1981.

Rous, Jean. *Habib Bourguiba.* Paris: Martinsart, 1984.

Roux, Michel. *Les harkis, ou, les oubliés de l'histoire.* Paris: La Découverte, 1991.

Rubin, Barry. *Revolution until Victory? The Politics and History of the PLO.* Cambridge: Harvard University Press, 1994.

Rubinstein, Alvin. *Moscow's Third World Strategy.* Princeton: Princeton University Press, 1988.

Ruedy, John. *Modern Algeria: The Origins and Development of a Nation.* Bloomington, IN: Indiana University Press, 1992.

———. "La Réaction de la presse et de l'opinion publique américaine à la politique du gouvernement Eisenhower envers la revolution algérienne." *Revue d'Histoire Maghrebine* 31 (June 1986): 116–137.

Ruf, Werner Klaus. "The Bizerte Crisis: A Bourguibist Attempt to Resolve Tunisia's Border Problems." *Middle East Journal* 25.2 (Spring 1971): 201–211.

Said, Edward. *Orientalism.* New York: Pantheon Books, 1978.

Sangmuah, Egya. "Eisenhower and Containment in North Africa, 1956–1960." *Middle East Journal* 44 (1990): 76–91.

———. "Sultan Mohammed ben Youssef's American Strategy and the Diplomacy of North African Liberation, 1943–61." *Journal of Contemporary History* 27 (1992): 129–148.

———. "The United States and the French Empire in North Africa, 1946–1956: Decolonization in the Age of Containment." Ph.D. dissertation. University of Toronto, 1989.

Schelling, Thomas C. *The Strategy of Conflict.* Cambridge, MA: Harvard University Press, 1960.

Schlesinger, Arthur. *A Thousand Days: John F. Kennedy in the White House.* Boston: Houghton Mifflin, 1965.

Scott, James. *Domination and the Arts of Resistance: Hidden Transcripts.* New Haven, CT: Yale University Press, 1990.

Seifert, Ruth. "The Second Front: The Logic of Sexual Violence in Wars." *Women's Studies International Forum* 19 (1996): 35–43.

Sen, Amartya. "Population: Delusion and Reality." *The New York Review of Books* 41 (September 22, 1994): 62–71.

Shafer, D. Michael. *Deadly Paradigms: The Failure of U.S. Counterinsurgency Policy.* Princeton, NJ: Princeton University Press, 1988.

Shlaim, Avi. "The Protocol of Sèvres, 1956: Anatomy of a War Plot." *International Affairs* 73 (July 1997): 509–530.

Shrader, Charles R. *The First Helicopter War: Logistics and Mobility in Algeria, 1954–1962.* Westport, CT: Praeger, 1999.

Shultz, Richard, and Roy Godson. *Dezinformatsia: Active Measures in Soviet Strategy.* McLean, VA: Pergamon, 1984.

Silverstein, Paul. "French Alterity: Articulating Intra-National Difference in the New Europe." *Replika* 2 (1997): 13–35.

Skocpol, Theda. "What Makes Peasants Revolutionary?" *Power and Protest in the Countryside: Studies of Rural Unrest in Asia, Europe, and Latin America*. Ed. Robert P. Weller and Scott E. Guggenheim. Durham, NC: Duke University Press, 1982. 157–179.

Smouts, Marie-Claude. *La France à L'ONU: Premiers Rôles & Second Rang*. Paris: Fondation Nationale des Sciences Politiques, 1979.

Solinas, Franco. *Gillo Pontecorvo's The Battle of Algiers*. New York: Scribner, 1973.

Soustelle, Jacques. "France Looks at Her Alliances." *Foreign Affairs* 35 (1956): 116–130.

Soutou, Georges-Henri. "Les Accords de 1957 et 1958: Vers une communauté stratégique et nucléaire entre la France, l'Allemagne et l'Italie?" *La France et l'Atome: Etudes d'Histoire nucléaire*. Ed. Maurice Vaïsse et al. Brussels: Bruylant, 123–162.

Spengler, Oswald. *The Hour of Decision, Part One: Germany and World-Historical Evolution*. Trans. Charles Francis Atkinson. New York: Knopf: 1934.

Stephanson, Anders. *George Kennan and the Art of Foreign Policy*. Cambridge, MA: Harvard University Press, 1989.

Stivers, William A. "Eisenhower and the Middle East." *Reevaluating Eisenhower: American Foreign Policy in the Fifties*. Ed. Richard A. Melanson and David Mayers. Urbana, IL: University of Illinois Press, 1987. 192–219.

Stora, Benjamin, ed. *Dictionnaire Biographique de Militants Nationalists Algériens, 1926–1954 (ENA-PPA-MTLD)*. Paris: L'Harmattan, 1985.

———. *La gangrène et l'oubli: La mémoire de la guerre d'Algérie*. Paris: La Découverte, 1992.

———. *Les Sources du Nationalisme Algérien*. Paris: L'Harmattan, 1989.

Strachey, John. *The End of Empire*. New York: Frederick A. Praeger, 1959.

Swearingen, Will D. *Moroccan Images: Agrarian Dreams and Deceptions, 1912–1986. Society and Culture in the Modern Middle East*. Ed. Michael Gilsenan. London: I. B. Tauris, 1988.

Szreter, Simon. "The Idea of Demographic Transition and the Study of Fertility Change: A Critical Intellectual History." *Population and Development Review* 19.4 (December 1993): 659–701

Talbott, John. *The War Without a Name: France in Algeria, 1954–1962*. New York: Knopf, 1980.

Taylor, A. J. P. "War Origins Again." *Past and Present* 30 (1965): 110–113.

Teguia, Mohamed. *L'Algérie en guerre*. Algiers: Office des Publications Universitaires, 1988.

Thelen, David. "Of Audiences, Borderlands, and Comparisons: Toward the Internationalization of American History." *Journal of American History* 79 (September 1992): 432–462.

Thomas, Martin. "The Dilemmas of an Ally of France: Britain's Policy towards the Algerian Rebellion, 1954–1962." *Journal of Imperial and Commonwealth History* 23 (January 1995): 129–154.

———. "France Accused: French North Africa Before the United Nations, 1952–1962." *Contemporary European History*, forthcoming.

———. *The French North African Crisis: Colonial Breakdown and Anglo-French Relations, 1945–62*. New York: St. Martin's Press, 2000.

———. "Policing Algeria's Borders, 1956–1960: Arms Supplies, Frontier Defenses and the Sakiet Affair." *War and Society* 13.1 (May 1995): 81–99.

Thorne, Christopher. "After the Europeans: American Designs for the Remaking of Southeast Asia." *Diplomatic History* 12.2 (Spring 1988): 201–208.

——. *Allies of a Kind: The United States, Britain and the War Against Japan, 1941–1945*. New York: Oxford University Press, 1978.

——. *The Issue of War: States, Societies, and the Far Eastern Conflict of 1941–1945*. London: Hamish Hamilton, 1985.

Tillion, Germaine. *Algeria: The Realities*. Trans. Ronald Matthews. New York: Knopf, 1958.

Touchard, Jean. *Le gaullisme 1940–1969*. Tours: Seuil, 1978.

Tournoux, Jean Raymond. *La Tragédie du Général*. Paris: Plon, 1967.

Trachtenberg, Marc. *A Constructed Peace: The Making of the European Settlement, 1945–1963*. Princeton, NJ: Princeton University Press, 1999.

——. *History and Strategy*. Princeton: Princeton University Press, 1991.

Tripier, Philippe. *Autopsie de la guerre d'Algérie*. Paris: France-Empire, 1972.

Vaïsse, Maurice. "Aux origines du mémorandum de septembre 1958." *Relations internationales* 58.2 (Summer 1989): 253–268.

——. *La Grandeur: Politique étrangère du général de Gaulle, 1958–1969*. Paris: Fayard, 1998.

——. *1961, Alger, Le Putsch*. Paris: Complexe, 1983.

——. "Un dialogue de sourdes: Les relations nucléaires franco-américaines 1957–1960." *Relations Internationales* 68 (1991): 407–423.

Valéry, Paul. "The Crisis of the Mind." *The Collected Works of Paul Valéry*. Trans. Denise Folliot and Jackson Mathews. Vol. 10: *History and Politics*. New York: Pantheon, 1962.

Van Ness, Peter. *Revolution and Chinese Foreign Policy: Peking's Support for Wars of National Liberation*. Berkeley, CA: University of California Press, 1970.

Wagnleitner, Reinhold. "The Empire of the Fun, or Talkin' Soviet Union Blues: The Sound of Freedom and U.S. Cultural Hegemony in Europe." *Diplomatic History* 23 (Summer 1999): 499–524.

Wall, Irwin. *France, the United States, and the Algerian War*. Forthcoming from the University of California Press, 2001.

——. "Les Relations Franco-Américaines et la Guerre d'Algérie 1956–1960." *Revue d'Histoire diplomatique* 110 (1996): 63–89.

——. "The United States, Algeria, and the Fall of the Fourth French Republic." *Diplomatic History* 18 (Winter 1994): 489–511.

——. *The United States and the Making of Postwar France, 1945–1954*. New York: Cambridge University Press, 1991.

Watt, Donald Cameron. "Britain and the Historiography of the Yalta Conference and the Cold War." *Diplomatic History* 13 (Winter 1989): 67–98.

Wells, Samuel F. "Charles de Gaulle and the French Withdrawal from NATO's Integrated Command." *American Historians and the Atlantic Alliance*. Ed. Lawrence S. Kaplan. Kent, OH: Kent State University Press, 1991. 81–94.

Williams, Philip M. *Politics in Post-War France: Parties and the Constitution in the Fourth Republic*. 2nd ed. New York: Longmans, Green, 1958.

——. *Wars, Plots and Scandals in Post-War France*. Cambridge: Cambridge University Press, 1970.

Wilson, Heather A. *International Law and the Use of Force by National Liberation Movements*. Oxford: Clarendon Press, 1988.

Wolf, Eric R. *Peasant Wars of the Twentieth Century*. New York: Harper and Row, 1969.

Wolfe, Thomas. *Soviet Power and Europe*. Baltimore: Johns Hopkins, 1970.

Wolfowitz, Paul. "Bridging Centuries: Fin de Siecle All Over Again." *The National Interest* 47 (Spring 1997): 3–8.

Wood, David, and Robert Bernasconi, ed. *Derrida and Différence*. Warwick, UK: Northwestern University Press, 1985.

Worsley, Peter. *The Three Worlds: Culture and World Development*. London: University of Chicago Press, 1984.

Wu, William F. *The Yellow Peril: Chinese Americans in American Fiction, 1850–1940*. Hamden, CT: Archon Books, 1982.

Yacono, Xavier. *De Gaulle et le F.L.N. 1958–1962: L'échec d'une politique et ses prolongements*. Versailles: l'Atlanthrope, 1989.

Yergin, Daniel. *The Prize: The Epic Quest for Oil, Money, and Power*. New York: Simon & Schuster 1991.

——. *Shattered Peace: The Origins of the Cold War and the National Security State*. Boston: Houghton Mifflin, 1977.

Young, John W. *France, the Cold War and the Western Alliance, 1944–49: French Foreign Policy and Post-War Europe*. London: Leicester University Press, 1990.

Young, Robert. *White Mythologies: Writing History and the West*. London: Routledge, 1990.

Zartman, William. *Morocco: Problems of New Power*. New York: Atherton, 1964.

Zoubir, Yahia H. "U.S. and Soviet Policies towards France's Struggle with Anticolonial Nationalism in North Africa." *Canadian Journal of History* 30 (December 1995): 439–66.

——. "The United States, the Soviet Union and Decolonization of the Maghreb, 1945–62." *Middle Eastern Studies* 31.1 (January 1995): 58–84.

Zubok, Vladislav M., and Constantine Pleshakov. *Inside the Kremlin's Cold War: From Stalin to Khrushchev*. Cambridge: Harvard University Press, 1996.

——. "Spy vs. Spy: The KGB vs. the CIA, 1960–1962." *Bulletin* of the Cold War International History Project 4 (fall 1994): 22–33.

Index